In the Shadow
of the Gallows

IN THE SHADOW OF THE GALLOWS

Race, Crime,
and American Civic Identity

Jeannine Marie DeLombard

PENN

UNIVERSITY OF PENNSYLVANIA PRESS

PHILADELPHIA

Published by
University of Pennsylvania Press
Philadelphia, Pennsylvania 19104-4112
www.upenn.edu/pennpress

Printed in the United States of America
on acid-free paper
2 4 6 8 10 9 7 5 3 1

Library of Congress Cataloging-in-Publication Data
DeLombard, Jeannine Marie.
In the shadow of the gallows : race, crime, and American civic
identity / Jeannine Marie DeLombard. — 1st ed.
    p. cm.
Includes bibliographical references and index.
ISBN 978-0-8122-4422-9 (hardcover : alk. paper)
1. African Americans in literature—History and criticism.
2. American literature—African American authors—History
and criticism. 3. African Americans—Race identity—History.
4. African Americans—Legal status, laws, etc.—History.
5. Crime and race—United States—History. 6. Citizenship—
United States. I. Title.
PS173.N4D44 2012
810.9'896073—dc23   2012007874

For my mother, Jacquelyn DeLombard

Master. NOW, villain! what have you to say . . . ?
    —"Dialogue Between a Master and a Slave," *Columbian*
                                           Orator (1797)

Who ever supposes himself guilty, because Congress does not pass a law
abolishing slavery in the United States?
        —Francis Wayland, *The Limitations of Human*
                                    Responsibility (1838)

I feel no consciousness of guilt in the matter, nor even mortification on
account of my imprisonment and irons.
        —John Brown, "Letter to His Wife and Children" (1859)

Contents

Introduction: How a Slave Was Made a Man

You have seen how a man was made a slave; you shall see
how a slave was made a man.

 —Frederick Douglass, *Narrative of the Life of Frederick
 Douglass, an American Slave, Written by Himself* (1845)

Writing was an indispensable tool for the public assertion of black humanity in the eighteenth and nineteenth centuries, when millions of Africans
and their descendants were being bought and sold as objects of property
throughout the Atlantic world. Following the slave trade's inaugural
violence, a man was made a slave in early America through the scriptive
technologies that enabled the recording, circulation, and preservation of
colonial and then state statutes, state and federal constitutions, and judicial
decisions, as well as passes, bills of sale, wills, and mortgages.[1] In such a
world, writes Henry Louis Gates, Jr., "the recording of an authentic black
voice—a voice of deliverance from the deafening discursive silence which
an enlightened Europe cited to prove the absence of the African's humanity—was the millennial instrument of transformation through which . . . the
slave [would] become the ex-slave, brute animal become the human being."[2]
Collectively as well as individually, African Americans challenged both enslavement and racial exclusion through their insistent participation in a rapidly industrializing transnational print culture—most notably, by publishing
slave narratives, their eyewitness accounts of bound servitude.[3] Displaying a
"command of written English" that decisively distinguished "titled property
from fledgling human being," Frederick Douglass stands as the paragon of
the black subject whom Anglo-American culture "demanded to write himself . . . into the human community."[4]

 This twice-told literary historical tale has helped to institutionalize and
popularize African American literature and history in the decades since the
Civil Rights, Black Power, and Black Studies movements. But this creation

story gives only a partial account of how a slave was made a man in the eyes of the American reading public.[5] If, as some have suggested, the dramatic tale of the canon's formative racial agon neglects the collectivist civic impulses of early African American publicists and audiences, it also understates the individual black subject's definitively anti-civic and uncivil role *within* early American law and print culture.[6]

Consider three advertisements from the May 28, 1787, issue of Philadelphia's *Independent Gazetteer; or the Chronicle of Freedom*, printed just days after the opening of what would become the Constitutional Convention (see Figure 1). "This Day is Published," announces the first, "A VOLUME of MISCELLANEOUS POEMS . . . By PETER MARKOE."[7] Seldom remembered now, Markoe is the Philadelphia poet and playwright believed to have written *The Algerine Spy in Pennsylvania: or, Letters Written by a Native of Algiers on the Affairs of the United States in America* (1787). Published later that year and circulating among the Convention's delegates, the novel is credited with having influenced the adoption of the new Constitution.[8] One column over from the book notice, in the lower right corner, appears a smaller advertisement for "A Negro Man Slave," available "on easy terms" upon "inquir[ing] of the Printer."[9] Together, the two ads seem to illustrate how, during the Enlightenment, "mastery of the arts and letters" demarcated a "solid line of division between human being and thing."[10] Markoe, a Euro-American author, could contribute to the civic "affairs of the United States" by actively participating in the republic of letters, while the anonymous slave circulated in that republic much as the poet's published volume does, as an object to be bought and sold—by a printer, no less.[11]

Read alone, these artifacts would appear to confirm that "the creation of formal literature could be no mean matter in the life of a slave, since . . . writing was the very commodity that separated animal from human being, slave from citizen, object from subject."[12] But this transformation—in effect, from property to person—involved more than relocation from a newspaper slave advertisement to a book's title page, monumental feat though that was. Positioned in the eye-catching upper-right verso corner and set in a large font relieved by ample white space, a third *Gazetteer* ad urges us to reassess the priority traditionally assigned to authentically black-authored "formal literature," even as it affirms the importance of "creating a public, historical self" in print.[13] "JUST PUBLISHED, and to be Sold, at the several Book Stores in this city" the notice proclaims, "the remainder of the Tryals at the late Court of Oyer and Terminer; among others that of Alice Clifton for the MURDER

THE INDEPENDENT GAZETTEER, &c.

JUST PUBLISHED,
And to be Sold
At the several Book Stores in this city,
The remainder of the Tryals at the late Court of Oyer and Terminer; among others that of Alice Clifton for the
MURDER
of her bastard Child. price 1s.
May 25, 1787.

The Subscriber has removed
his OFFICE from the fourth to the north side of Chesnut-street, three doors below the corner of Third-street,
Where he continues to perform
ALL THE DUTIES OF AN
Attorney at Law, Notary Public,
CONVEYANCER and BROKER,
With accuracy and dispatch——And Draws, at a moderate charge,
Deeds, Bonds, Mortgages, Letters of Attorney, Charter Parties, Bills of Bottomry, Memorials, Petitions, and other Instruments in Writing.
He buys and sells on Commission,
Bank Stock, Bills of Exchange on England, Holland, France, Spain, &c.
Also, Houses, Lots and Lands,
Either in Town or Country; and
procures Money on Loan,
Upon approved security.
Asheton Humphreys.
Philadelphia, May 15.

To the Reverend Doctor E——g.

For the INDEPENDENT GAZETTEER.

This Day is Published,
PRINTED BY
PRICHARD and HALL,
A VOLUME OF
MISCELLANEOUS POEMS,
PRICE FIVE SHILLINGS,
By PETER MARKOE.
Philadelphia, May 28, 1787.

Now LANDING at Hamilton's Wharf,
and for SALE by
Andrew Clow, and Co.
A choice CARGO OF
SHERRY WINE,
May 25.

To be Sold,
For want of Employment,
A Negro Man Slave,

of her bastard Child."[14] "A mulatto girl" and "slave of John Bartholomew" of Philadelphia, convicted infanticide Alice Clifton originally "received [the] sentence of DEATH" but had been "respited by the Honorable Supreme Executive Council" before the pamphlet went to press.[15]

Emerging from the same print and legal milieu as the U.S. Constitution, these advertisements for an unidentified bondman, a volume of poetry by one of the nation's first authors, and a pamphlet featuring an African American criminal, have all the makings of a reconceived American literary history. In order to understand how the "Negro . . . Slave" advertised as chattel might lay claim to the civic authority of a published author such as Peter Markoe (or, for that matter, Frederick Douglass), we need to take into account the intermediate role played by a figure such as the enslaved felon Alice Clifton. Like the other African American convicts who so intrigued American readers, Clifton appeared in the newspaper and in the advertised trial pamphlet not as civilly dead property but as a responsible legal person.[16] No writer, Clifton stood as a public, historical black individual whose personhood and racial representativeness lay neither in her literary skill, nor in her civic virtue, but in her criminality. Held accountable to the social compact through the legal prosecution that affirmed her membership in the polity, Clifton entered the public sphere of print as an individualized black subject.

It is this more complete, if also more troubling, version of the story of the black persona's rise that this book seeks to tell. From the colonial period through the Civil War, when enslaved people (especially men) of African descent spoke in print as individuals, their first-person narratives were often occasioned by or responsive to their encounters with law.[17] Prior to abolitionists' mass publishing campaign of the 1830s, blacks appeared most frequently in newspapers, broadsheets, and legal records as property to be purchased, sold, rented, or recovered. On those rare occasions when they entered print as persons, it was more likely to be in sensationalized crime accounts or in the criminal code than in the belletristic works or exemplary accounts of piety, adventure, and enterprise that today form the early African American canon. Next to the human chattel, it was the black malefactor—not the African picaro, the "pious Negro," or the sable entrepreneur—who would have been most familiar to colonial and early national audiences.[18]

"He that exasperates them, soon espies / Mischief and Murder in their very eyes," Boston judge and poet John Saffin cautioned of "Blacks" upon entering America's first pamphlet debate over slavery in 1701.[19] Two years earlier, Cotton Mather's *Pillars of Salt* (1699) had presented "a Picture of *Hell* . . . in a *Negro* then *Burnt* to *Death* at the Stake, for *Burning* her Masters House, with some that were in it."[20] In 1721, the prolific Mather appended a jailhouse interview with emancipated Boston slave and condemned wife-murderer Joseph Hanno to the sermon he published as *Tremenda. The Dreadful Sound with which the Wicked Are To Be Thunderstruck*. In early national Philadelphia, the hanging of another former bondman led to the *Address of Abraham Johnstone, a Black Man* (1797)—and the opportunity to criticize the republic's unredressed history of slavery, racism, and genocide from a distinctly African American perspective.

Clifton, Hanno, and Johnstone were among the roughly sixty condemned black criminals who figured prominently in early America's thriving gallows literature tradition.[21] Published in conjunction with Execution Day rituals, the biographical portion of this crime literature was gradually superseded by more politicized forms of personal narrative. As the scaffold tradition's confessing malefactor gave way to the antebellum slave narrative's testifying "eye-witness to the cruelty," new models of black selfhood arose to accommodate more critical African American print engagements with law.[22] Still appearing as the product of penality, the black persona now exposed the brutality of so-called plantation justice in order to criticize a legal order that, in Douglass's words, "form[ed] bulwarks around the system of slavery."[23] Nearly a tenth of the London edition of the *Narrative of William W. Brown, Written by Himself* (1849) is taken up with "EXTRACTS FROM THE AMERICAN SLAVE CODE."[24] Extensive references to court cases and statutes provide ballast to sensational accounts like the *Narrative of the Life of Henry Box Brown* (1851) and William Craft's *Running a Thousand Miles for Freedom* (1860). The title page of James Watkins's *Struggles for Freedom* (1860) promises readers both "a Graphic Account of His Extraordinary Escape from Slavery" and "Notices of the Fugitive Slave Law."[25]

Gallows literature did not end with the advent of organized abolitionism, of course, but it was in the 1830s that the baton of African American life-writing can be said to have passed from the criminal confession to the slave narrative.[26] On New Year's Day 1831 William Lloyd Garrison marked the beginning of a new print-based, grassroots mass abolitionist movement when he published the first issue of the *Liberator*, but the year closed with the printing of Thomas R. Gray's *Confessions of Nat Turner*, which the Virginia lawyer-turned-pamphleteer presented as integral to the notorious slave insurgent's conviction and execution.[27] Seven years later, James Williams, the subject of the first slave narrative published under the auspices of the

American Anti-Slavery Society (AASS), was accused of being not only a fraud, but a scape-gallows poisoner.[28] And one of the last slave narratives to be recorded before Emancipation, the *Story of the Life of John Anderson* (1863), centered on a Missouri fugitive who narrowly escaped being extradited from Canada to the United States to face murder charges.[29] From Puritan New England to the Civil War, crime shaped evocations of black personhood in American print culture.

Mixed Character

Personhood, not humanity. Tracing the impress of American law on the African American self for well over a century, this black life-writing reminds us that the metamorphosis of property into person—or, in Douglass's words, from "slave" into "man"—did not entail the transformation of a thing into a human being.[30] The tendency, then as now, to use the words "human," "man," and "person" interchangeably makes it easy to lose sight of this fact—and thereby to miss an important development in American literary history.[31] Less poetic but more precise than the apophasis that structures Douglass's *Narrative* is the definition of "the legal and social relation of master and slave" that the former bondman offered in his December 1850 speech, "The Nature of Slavery." "A master is one . . . who claims and exercises a right of property in the person of a fellow-man," Douglass told his Rochester, New York, audience; the slave, for his part, "is a human being, divested of all rights—reduced to the level of a brute—a mere 'chattel' in the eye of the law. . . . In law, the slave has no wife, no children, no country, and no home. He can own nothing, possess nothing, acquire nothing."[32] Denied the self-possession and other forms of proprietorship that constitute liberalism's rights-bearing (and normatively male) person, the enslaved "human being" finds himself in the same legal position as other civilly dead forms of property, notably nonhuman animals.

Douglass's usage in his explanation of what it means for the slaveholder to claim "human" property in the "person" of his "fellow-man" is consistent with John Bouvier's *Law Dictionary: Adapted to the Constitution and Laws of the United States of America and of the Several States of the American Union* (1839). The first edition's entry for "person" opens by distinguishing "natural persons," such as "men, women, and children," from an "artificial person," namely, "a corporation."[33] The entry goes on to divide natural persons first by gender (with women having only limited civil capacity), and then by condition, into "free persons and slaves." Because they belong to a master, enslaved natural persons "are sometimes ranked not with persons but with things." Seeking to avoid such confusing redundancy, the entry in the revised 1856 edition clarifies that "in law, man and person are not exactly synonymous terms."[34] Whereas "any human being is a man, whether he be a member of society or not, whatever may be the rank he holds, or whatever may be his age, sex, &c.," legally, "a person is a man considered according to the rank he holds in society, with all the rights to which the place he holds entitles him, and the duties which it imposes." All men may have been created equal, but not all were recognized as persons.

Forming as much as describing a body of legal thought, Bouvier's *Law Dictionary* contributed to the broader publishing endeavor that legal historian Laura F. Edwards sees as instrumental in the attempt to transform an often messy, patriarchal, local, colloquial, discretionary, process-based "law" into "the law," a rights-based, state-centered, standardized, outcomes-oriented knowledge system.[35] While these changes curtailed the everyday participation in legal proceedings by subordinates such as women, the poor, and people of color, professionalizing reformers still had to contend with an exuberant, confident popular legal consciousness that likewise expressed itself in print.[36] As the *Law Dictionary*'s very existence suggests, such comprehensive publishing initiatives also made legal terminology and logic accessible to a lay public, enabling "an unlearned fugitive slave" like Douglass to "talk 'lawyer like' about law."[37] Acquainted with the doctrinal and practical dilemmas that first slavery and then the corporation posed to the common law tradition, Americans had little difficulty distinguishing—in thought, if not always in words—those flesh-and-blood beings who were endowed with reason and souls (humans) from those artificial or natural bodies that incorporated a bundle of legally defined rights and responsibilities (persons).

The point is borne out when we note, with critic Markman Ellis, that on both sides of the Atlantic "the late-eighteenth-century slave narrative" was "considered a form of biography or life writing, and not an it-narrative."[38] (A popular fiction genre of the period, the it-narrative told the history and experiences of a nonhuman protagonist such as a coat, a hackney-coach, a rupee, or—more aptly—a guinea, as those inanimate objects circulated through society.) A passage from the *Narrative of the Life and Adventures of Venture, A Native of Africa* (1798) illustrates how, under the legal-literary logic of slavery, the enslaved protagonist's property status did not belie his humanness. Smith recalls how he and others "kept for market" were told by their master "to appear to the best possible advantage for sale" prior to his being "bought . . . by one Robertson Mumford, steward . . . , for four gallons of rum, and a piece of calico, and called VENTURE, on account of his having purchased me with his own private venture."[39] As his new name suggests, the commoditization of the youth born as Broteer, son of "Saungm Furro, Prince of the Tribe of Dukandarra," is complete when he is exchanged for a quantity of cloth and alcohol and stripped of his personal, familial, cultural, and political identities (5). In the very act of depriving the newly enslaved youth and his fellow Africans of their personhood, however, the slaveholder enlists their human self-consciousness in his efforts to enhance their property value. If Karl Marx's famous prosopopoeia ("Could commodities themselves speak, they would say . . .") betrays his own susceptibility to the fictive ascription of human qualities to these particular objects of property, Smith's account of being instructed "to appear to the best possible advantage for sale" confirms the commensurability of slaves' humanity with their commodity status.[40]

Circulating in a print culture suffused with Romanticism's humanitarian reform impulses, abolitionist slave narratives played up indifference to black humanity so as to politicize sympathetic or horrified readers.[41] But as Cotton Mather's vivid "Picture of *Hell*" documents, Americans had, since the seventeenth century, been arresting, trying, preaching to, hanging, and praying for slaves and others of African descent precisely because whites recognized, on the one hand, blacks' capacity for reason (with *mens rea* swiftly becoming the main legal ingredient of criminal culpability) and, on the other, their candidacy for heaven.[42] Throughout this period, slaveholders purchased, mortgaged, willed, and speculated on women and men, girls and boys, cooks and carpenters, field hands and fancy girls—not an assortment of dehumanized "its." Far from dismissing blacks' affective ties on purely ideological grounds, masters and mistresses manipulated these human relationships so as to maximize slaves' tractability and profitability.[43] What the Rev. James W. C. Pennington deplored in *The Fugitive Blacksmith* (1849) as "the chattel principle, the property principle, the bill of sale principle" worked best, in fact, when slaveholders' exploitation of blacks' humanity was coordinated with legal authorities' occasional recognition of slaves' culpable personhood.[44] To assign slaves "the mixed character of persons and of property" in this way was inhuman, but the designation had no bearing on blacks' status *as* humans.[45]

Noting once again that "slaves are sometimes ranked not with persons but things," the revised 1856 edition of Bouvier's *Law Dictionary* continues with the proviso: "But sometimes they are considered as persons; for example, a negro is in contemplation of law a person, so as to be capable of committing a riot in conjunction with white men."[46] It was no accident that slave personhood was inscribed in the nation's leading law dictionary in terms of criminality. Once discretionary and situational, the slave's mixed character had hardened into doctrine under an increasingly authoritative, integrated state and federal system of law. Given the colonial legal regime's tendency to treat individual bondpeople as part of a larger web of local circumstances and relationships, Edwards finds, slaves' status had been determined literally on a "case-by-case basis."[47] With the trend away from viewing all community members as subjects of a shared social order, and toward seeing some as rights-bearing citizens, however, legal scrutiny moved "away from individual lives to individual rights" (238). Perhaps as important as the historical turn from a legal culture where "slaves occupied a place as subjects of the peace" to one where they "appeared primarily as property" is the corresponding shift in their characterization on those occasions when they did appear as persons—as civil nonentities capable of only criminal agency (237).

One of the more explicit efforts to popularize this legal definition of black personhood occurred during debate over ratification of the U.S. Constitution, when James Madison took up his pen to address the question of slave character. Published in three New York newspapers in early 1788, Madison's lengthy defense of Article I, Section 2's already notorious three-fifths clause appeared in book form that May as *Federalist* 54—one year after the *Independent Gazetteer* had run the ad for the "Negro Man Slave" alongside the notice for the Alice Clifton trial pamphlet.[48] The Virginian, writing as "Publius" in collaboration with Alexander Hamilton and John Jay, cannily ventriloquized his own sectional voice to offer a rebuttal to the "objection" that, "considered as property, not as persons," slaves ought to count only for taxation, not representation.[49] Publius, adopting the perspective of "one of our Southern brethren," insisted, "we must deny the fact, that slaves are considered merely as property, and in no respect whatever as persons. The true state of the case is that they partake of both these qualities" (332). In "being compelled to labor, not for himself, but for a master; in being vendible by one master to another master; and in being subject at all times to be restrained in his liberty and chastised in his body, by the capricious will of another," Publius admitted, "the slave may appear to be degraded from the human rank, and classed with those irrational animals which fall under the legal denomination of property." But, he continued, "in being protected . . . against the violence of all others, even the master of his labor and his liberty; and in being punishable himself for all

violence committed against others—the slave is no less evidently regarded by
the law as a member of the society, not as a part of the irrational creation; as
a moral person, not as a mere article of property."[50] Clearly, then, "the federal
Constitution . . . decides with great propriety on the case of our slaves, when it
views them in the mixed character of persons and of property." After all, Publius concluded, "this is in fact their true character. It is the character bestowed
on them by the laws under which they live; and it will not be denied that these
are the proper criterion."

For early national legal publicists whose first priority was to enhance the
uniformity and thus predictability of an already highly professionalized, cosmopolitan property law, the slave's "retractable personhood" enabled the new
legal machine to operate smoothly.[51] Local discretion over criminal matters
would not receive serious challenge from state authorities until well into the
antebellum period.[52] But the very impulse, at the Founding, to establish not
only the property status but the criminal liability of the enslaved highlights
how important it would be to mark out civil from criminal areas of law under
the emerging rights regime. No longer seen in a continuum, private and
public wrongs became separable as some colonial subjects became American citizens—and could, as self-possessed, autonomous individuals, assert
rights that were denied to their nonwhite and non-male counterparts.[53] In
this changing legal climate, citizenship was increasingly predicated upon
recognized personhood, limiting the civil standing and civic participation
of women, the disabled, and people of color.[54] As Publius noted, "it is only
under the pretext that the laws have transformed the Negroes into subjects
of property that a place is disputed them in the computation of numbers;
and it is admitted that if the laws were to restore the rights which have been
taken away, the Negroes could no longer be refused an equal share of representation with the other inhabitants."[55] This legal fiction singled "Negroes"
out from other incapacitated subordinates in a particularly devastating way:
slaves alone were credited with a legal agency that was legible only as criminality. The definitively uncivil and anti-civic personhood reserved exclusively
for blacks was uniquely, foundationally antithetical to the citizenship that so
many would continue to claim over the coming century.

Liberation from property status no more ensured freedpeople's citizenship than designation as chattel nullified slaves' humanity. In roughly
ascending order, acknowledgment as a human being in eighteenth- and
nineteenth-century America did *not* guarantee access to: legal personhood
(as a criminal defendant, for instance); civic presence (as a participant in the

public sphere); civil standing (as a signatory to a deed or contract); citizenship (as a formal member of the polity); or the franchise (as an eligible voter or office-holder).[56] After the First Emancipation in the early national North, the gender and racial "borders of belonging" became increasingly apparent as, in state after state, legislatures expanded voting rights for white men while disenfranchising their black counterparts—often on the basis of African Americans' civil disabilities.[57] Consistently recognized as persons for the purposes of criminal law, blacks were often legally as well as figuratively denied what Immanuel Kant called "civil personality"—the capacity that underwrote active participation in the polity.[58] If, by law, slaves were considered civilly dead, nominally free blacks routinely experienced civil mortification. ("What is the use of living, when in fact I am dead," wondered radical free black pamphleteer David Walker in 1829.)[59] Asserting black political qualification could not, then, be simply a matter of displaying the humanity of commoditized involuntary laborers whom centuries of racial thought and the exigencies of a capitalist slaveholding society threatened to render indistinct from "the brute creation."[60] Those who would transform slaves into Jacksonian men through print had to do more than "inscribe their selves . . . in language" through authentic literary production.[61] They had to detach black personhood from the criminality in which it had become firmly rooted and graft it onto a civil personality that might, then, flower into full-blown citizenship.

Cast Away on the Black Atlantic

We cannot understand this process without reassessing gallows literature's importance to early black life-writing. Documenting the Puritan origins of the Afro-Protestant self, classic studies of the slave narrative place criminal confessions alongside spiritual autobiographies in the prehistory of the genre and thus of the larger African American literary tradition.[62] In 1979 Frances Smith Foster identified crime ephemera with "the emergence of the black narrator," observing that "before the nineteenth century, it was rare that a writing was primarily concerned with relating the experiences of a particular black person. . . . When the black person as . . . subject gave way to the black person as narrator, the most common protagonist was the social degenerate," the criminal in particular.[63] The following decade, the genre's foremost scholar, William Andrews, acknowledged that "the largest group of slave narratives published during this time" were "the confessions of condemned black felons."[64] Although these findings comport with the broader critical consensus regarding confessional crime literature's integral role in the development of the responsible, interiorized, individualist modern self posited by both autobiography and the novel, a number of critical blind spots have obscured the black criminal's significance to early articulations of African American subjectivity.[65]

Just as a habit of identifying race slavery with the antebellum South has concealed its formative importance in the early national North, the ongoing tendency to treat the civil death of the slave and that of the (normatively white) convict as occurring in "parallel sites" before the Civil War and thus sequentially in American history has rendered the black convict under slavery all but unimaginable.[66] The well-trodden—and comparatively recent— path "from plantation to prison" can divert us from other, earlier routes hewn by race and crime in a slaveholding nation.[67] As African Americans' disproportionate representation on the pages of early American gallows literature and in the cells of the nation's first prisons attests, slavery and criminality coexisted prior to Reconstruction and the convict-lease system. Much as places like Mississippi's Parchman Farm reveal the postbellum prison as a palimpsest of plantation slavery, the birth of the new nation literally alongside Philadelphia-based abolitionist and penal reform movements suggests the foundational nexus of citizenship, race, and crime in the United States. The criminalization of a growing free black community as a threat to local and national security in a gradually abolitionizing North meant that disciplinary as well as biopolitical control of African Americans coincided with slavery in the early republic, rather than supplanting it in the century between the Civil War and the Civil Rights Movement.[68] "Criminality was racialized and race was criminalized" well before the Thirteenth Amendment, and certainly by the First Emancipation.[69]

The ongoing reorientation from national "roots" to crisscrossed Atlantic "routes" has enriched our knowledge of that earlier period by directing critical and editorial attention to such peripatetic figures as Olaudah Equiano, Ottobah Cuguano, Ignatious Sancho, John Marrant, Phillis Wheatley, and Venture Smith.[70] "The black writing that appeared during the eighteenth and early nineteenth centuries," Vincent Carretta and Philip Gould note in their introduction to *Genius in Bondage: Literature of the Early Black Atlantic* (2001), "included the genres of spiritual autobiography, captivity narrative, travel narrative, public epistle, sea adventure, and economic success story"—virtually all written from a first-person perspective.[71] Yet even as this scholarship has entrenched the Afro-diasporic canon's foundations ever more deeply in masculinist life-writing, it has ignored arguably the most widely circulated, influential form of early black personal narrative, the criminal confession.[72] Thus, whereas both *The Life and Confession of Johnson Green* (1786) and *The Confession of John Joyce* (1808) appear in Dorothy Porter's slender *Early Negro Writing 1760–1837* (1971), such black malefactors have been cast away from the recent flotilla of early Black Atlantic anthologies and monographs.[73]

As the recent critical consternation over "gangsta lit" and its Murder, Inc. soundtrack suggests, however, this studious disregard of black crime ephemera's literary historical importance may well be a case of benign neglect.[74] During the same thirty-year period in which the broader American canon grew to accommodate a new cohort of black texts, the criminal justice system underwent a parallel expansion, incorporating unprecedented numbers of nonwhite offenders into carceral and supervised populations.[75] "For the first time, more than one in every 100 adults is now confined in an American jail or prison," the Pew Center on the States reported well into the twenty-first century—with African American men aged twenty through thirty-four holding the peak one-in-nine incarceration rate.[76] Due to felony disenfranchisement laws, "1.4 million African American men, or 13% of black men, are disenfranchised, a rate seven times the national average"; on the basis of these trends, "three in ten of the next generation of black men can expect to be disenfranchised at some point in their lifetime," with "as many as 40% of black men . . . permanently los[ing] their right to vote" in states that disenfranchise ex-offenders.[77]

In an era when, in the words of prison activist and philosopher Angela Y. Davis, "the racial imbalance in jails and prisons is treated . . . as proof of an assumed black monopoly on criminality," canon-building has offered symbolic redress.[78] In contrast to the perceived "implication of almost all black criminal narratives . . . that the slave youth was at home in bondage," literary performances of civic and moral virtue by "black Ben Franklin[s]" like Equiano, Marrant, and Smith or "Black Founders" such as Wheatley, Jupiter Hammon, Richard Allen, and Absalom Jones righteously challenged the legitimacy of racial oppression.[79] Presenting an incisive critique of Anglo-American culture, these recovered accounts of exemplary blackness simultaneously ground a reassuring literary historical narrative of transcendent value, unassailable authority, and cultural authenticity—to say nothing of moral superiority.[80] And why wouldn't those making the transition from slavery to freedom in a Christian republic seek to gain political inclusion through such respectable self-fashioning?[81] Since Aristotle, the figure of the

virtuous bondman had threatened to expose slavery's injustice. (Expediently
concluding that slaves require only enough virtue to fulfill their instrumental
role in society, the *Politics* leaves open the possibility that slaves exhibiting
more than the requisite quantum would call into question the difference between them and the freemen whose own unstable virtue required strength-
ening by a system of laws.)[82] In the eighteenth and early nineteenth centuries,
convincing "parable[s] of capability," it was hoped, would demonstrate
blacks' eligibility to participate in the new American republic.[83]

Affirming black eligibility for salvation in tones of divinely sanctioned
authority, the spiritual autobiography in particular seemed to prepare African American personal narrative to participate in the antebellum slavery
debate's lively "Bible politics."[84] In the 1980s, conversion narratives' inclusion
in the canon was eased by the joint recovery efforts of African American and
women's studies.[85] "The priority of the spiritual autobiography to the slave
narrative holds true," Andrews notes, "whether we speak of the history of
black women's or black men's writing in the United States."[86] Not so criminal
confessions, "the majority of which concern slave-born men."[87] With other
forms of personal narrative serving as stepping stones on the long journey to
an African American literature, crime ephemera have been more of a stum-
bling block. If, for Foster, confessions introduced a first-person perspective
that asserted black individuality, the repressive conditions under which they
were produced finally "limit their importance in the history of the slave narratives."[88] Written "in the shadow of the gallows," these texts, Andrews suggests, "teach many of the same moral lessons that the spiritual autobiography
urges, but by negative object lesson."[89] The "obvious literary ancestor" to the
slave narrative, the criminal confession has served primarily to throw into
relief its progeny's "rhetorical achievements."[90]

Yet however much "conversion," along with other displays of virtuous
blackness, may have "provided an avenue for admission into subjecthood,"
sociologist Jon Cruz contends, it was "irrelevant to the legal force of slavery.
Converted or not, slaves by civil law were property; they were objects, not
subjects."[91] The criminal law was an entirely different matter. Thanks to the
legal fiction of mixed character, the criminous slave was assigned a degree
of legal personhood routinely denied to even free blacks. In this important
sense, criminal confessions provided a more viable route to autonomous
liberal subjectivity than the path of virtue charted by spiritual autobiographies, adventure narratives, and other genres of eighteenth-century Afro-
diasporic life-writing. Equally concerned with salvation, the divine order,

and exemplary conduct, gallows literature differed in its public attribution of individual responsibility to an ever more personal self in a world increasingly seen to be governed by human rather than providential agency.[92] The criminal confession's innovation was to introduce, in rhetorician Michael Mascuch's formulation, "the person as his own author, cultivating and nurturing the development of his unique 'character,' or self-identity, and who is therefore perceived in his social relations as being individually responsible for his life."[93] Viewed in light of today's rising incarceration and disenfranchisement rates, early black crime ephemera seem to present, in order to discipline, "an excessively uncompromising self" that "needed to be restrained and punished by the world."[94] But the American gallows tradition developed alongside such liberal notions of individuality.[95] Criminal confessions do not so much curb a preexisting, transgressive black self as imagine an unprecedentedly autonomous one.

Scaffold literature's surprisingly aspirational (as opposed to simply repressive) evocation of black subjectivity is, indeed, a central discovery of this book. In an epoch when the majority of African Americans were consigned by American law and print to the civil death described by the *Federalist*, presentation of a slave's *Life* as plausibly "Written by Himself," in the experiential as much as the textual sense, stood as a persuasive public counterassertion of autonomous black personhood. With the new individualist self posited by modern autobiography as his corollary, the legally accountable black felon of early American crime narratives displayed not merely a "yearning for autonomy," but its realization.[96] In this respect, gallows ephemera offer much more than an uncomfortable way station en route to the more politically and aesthetically satisfying antebellum slave narrative.

Last and Dying Words

In British North America, public executions ritualistically reminded the assembled spectators of the simultaneously punitive and redemptive power of God in the life of the individual and the community even as the day's carefully orchestrated exercises vividly displayed the terrifying power of local authorities.[97] People of both genders, all classes, and every hue traveled from great distances to attend executions, with crowds eventually reaching into the tens of thousands.[98] On both sides of the Atlantic, print extended the spatio-temporal effects of the spectacle.[99] English gallows literature was dominated by the *The Ordinary of Newgate's Account of the Behaviour,*

Confession and Dying Words of the Condemned Criminals . . . Executed at Ty-burn (1679–1772), with its over 400 editions containing biographies of some 2,500 executed criminals.[100] In colonial New England, the scaffold ritual's theatrical and oratorical components were supplemented by the publication of execution sermons, which sometimes featured appendices containing confessions by or interviews with the condemned.[101] In 1717, notes historian Daniel A. Cohen, "[Cotton] Mather claimed that a local bookseller had sold off nearly one thousand copies of his newest execution sermon in just five days. Later that same year, at a time when published sermons typically appeared in editions of one to five hundred, a printer in Boston reportedly produced no fewer than twelve hundred copies of yet another of Mather's" more than a dozen "scaffold orations"—"approximately one for every ten inhabitants of the town, or about one for every two households" (6).[102] The sermons' wide circulation resulted from their affordability (costing "only a small fraction of a single day's wages" for a typical unskilled worker), but also, like the executions on which they centered, from their comparatively wide geographic reach and broad demographic appeal (4).

Over the course of the eighteenth century, gallows literature became more popular and secular. As commercial printers replaced ministers and magistrates in transcribing, editing, and circulating these texts, the increasingly sensational confessions began to be published separately from the execution sermons to which they had been appended.[103] "Before the sun closes upon us this evening," execution sermons conventionally admonished the condemned, "you will launch into an awful eternity, and go to appear at the tremendous bar of God, to give up an account of your conduct in the body."[104] En route to the divine tribunal, many appeared to pause and account for themselves to the reading public.

On Execution Day, the condemned person stood not merely as a negative exemplar whose gruesome end expiated collective guilt and offered a warning to the surrounding community. Ideally he or she stood as a "dramatic embodiment of the fundamental Christian paradigm of the penitent sinner confronting death."[105] In the words of Ipswich minister John Rogers, execution spectators (or readers of publications like his) could "*behold a Tragick Scene, strangely changed into a Theater of Mercy, a Pillar of Salt Transformed into a Monument of Free Grace.*"[106] In this particular case a white woman named Esther Rodgers, having entered "*into Prison a Bloody Malefactor, her Conscience laden with Sins of a Scarlet Die,*" after "*the Space of Eight Months . . . came forth, Sprinkled, Cleansed, Comforted, a Candidate of*

Heaven."[107] The execution sermon, like the requirement of individual public confession for church membership, was an important Puritan innovation.[108] The latter, recounting each believer's progress through a common conversion process, simultaneously delineated an individual self and joined it to the surrounding community. In similar fashion, criminal confessions symbolically reincorporated the penitent condemned into the communities from which their crimes had expelled them.[109] During the revolutionary period, crime narratives joined a broader "ideological insurgency" as marginal figures like Esther Rodgers gained public presence and textual authority through their ever more critical contributions to the proceedings.[110]

Potent as such resistance may have been, the execution ritual yielded not only insurgent texts but dead bodies. Given that a disproportionate number of the condemned were of African heritage, gallows texts might be seen as a grim realization of the "trope of the dying Negro" as, in Phillip Gould's words, "the ultimate erasure of the African voice engaging in cultural critique."[111] Ministers often turned the black condemned to political account in the final, application section of the tripartite Puritan execution sermon by specifically addressing others of the malefactor's race or condition. Cotton Mather saw just such an "Opportunit[y]" in his May 1721 sermon for Joseph Hanno who, having "been in the Country about 44 years, and about 14 Years free for himself," would soon be hanged for "Barbarously Murdering his Wife," Nanney.[112] Among the "Great Assembly" who flocked to Boston's Old North Church, Mather singled out bound people of color, who were perceived to harbor an inappropriate "*Fondness* for *Freedom.*"[113] "The *Ethiopian*, and Other *Slaves* among us," observed Mather pointedly, "may hear a *Dreadful Sound* in the Fate of their Unhappy Brother here before them; and they are to take warning from it" (27).[114] (As exemplar, Hanno did double duty: along with "*Ethiopian* Slaves," Mather noted in his diary, "wicked and froward Husbands" would "have this Day, their Portion with a due Pungency given to them.")[115] If, as Hal Gladfelder has found, in early eighteenth-century Britain "the racializing of deviance" had become commonplace in a crime literature that routinely opposed the "tribe" of Sodomites to Britons or traced cant back to Egyptian or Gypsy languages (predictably, via Ireland), the established literary "conflation of criminality and racial difference" only intensified under race slavery in colonial and early national America.[116]

Like the early American Execution Day rituals from which it arose, gallows literature is disproportionately devoted to criminals of African descent, who appear in approximately one-third of the well over 160 works published from 1674 to 1800.[117] Our first glimpse of the black condemned in colonial North America is the "Black Fellow-Sufferer" who "for the very same Crime, stands"—mutely—"in the same Condemnation" with "Elizabeth," the confessing, presumptively white, infanticide who dominates Cotton Mather's *Warnings from the Dead* (1693).[118] Although she would be followed in six years by the silent female arsonist of Mather's *Pillars of Salt* and almost a century later by the equally taciturn Alice Clifton, the vast majority of these texts depict men who, as the decades pass, prove much more loquacious.[119] For over a century, from Mather's *Tremenda* to Gray's *Confessions of Nat Turner*, crime publications were one of the primary means by which the American public apprehended the individual black self from a putatively first-person perspective.[120]

The ubiquity of the black condemned on the early American scaffold and in its accompanying ephemera speaks to more than racial injustice and literature's hegemonic function. Undoubtedly, the growing legal and cultural association of blackness with criminality complicated the execution ritual's ability "to induce a strong sense of moral and spiritual identification with the condemned criminal, then urge the listener/reader to look beyond the bloody crime to the triumphant conversion of the [criminal] and follow his spiritual example."[121] Nevertheless, it is a matter of no small importance that black individuals made their most prominent print appearance in a genre whose office was to insist on its (auto)biographical subject's oneness with an audience understood to encompass all of society, precisely on the basis of a shared (however flawed and sinful) humanity. Nor is it insignificant, as Chapter 1 argues, that such legal and print recognition, punitive as it was, formally marked even the slave's membership in the polity.

These cheap publications' ephemerality attests to their relative lack of investment in memorialization.[122] Neither elegies nor epitaphs, gallows texts do not participate in the mournful rites of cultural memory, much less the "mortuary politics" of Anglo-American abolitionism.[123] The condemned first-person subject is very much alive, speaking in the fleeting present, rather than from beyond the grave or, indeed, "from inside it."[124] Prompted and authorized by the execution ritual, criminal confessions are far more concerned with the life lived than with the death to come. Recounting the offenses that catalyze recognition of the felon's legal personhood, these works stress the untimeliness of his or her immanent death. Their intended spiritual and political effects turn on their subjects' conspicuous, albeit abbreviated, presence in the community of the living.

Despite its high body count and the rhetorical temptation to identify the criminal's "black" sin with his dark skin, gallows literature has surprisingly little to say about "the body" per se.[125] Notwithstanding the branding and mutilation that routinely inscribed the early American criminal's record into his or her flesh and in contrast to the "scalpings, decapitations, eviscerations, and burnings" that feature so prominently in the period's captivity narratives (not to mention the abolitionist slave narrative's whippings, brandings, and beatings), colonial and early national crime literature devoted very little space to the violence inflicted upon the bodies of either the victim or the condemned.[126] Bordered with skulls and emblazoned with illustrations of scaffolds and coffins, gallows ephemera featured an iconography as stylized as its verbal imagery was restrained (at least where bodies were concerned)[127] (see Figures 2, 3, and 4). When, in the antebellum period, advances in print technology furthered the new sensationalist aesthetic, gallows ephemera featured more detailed illustrations. With one or two notable exceptions (see Figure 5), these images are surprisingly static and antiseptic. Even the most dramatic typically are set just before or just after the murders or hangings in question, when the bodies of victim and criminal alike appear intact (see Figures 6, 7, 8, and 9). This lack of attention to the corporeal is doubtless due to the fact that historically the gallows tradition concerned itself with souls, in contradistinction to bodies, and that, later, the rise of the novel, *mens rea*, and Romanticism made the workings of the criminal mind more compelling than the resulting physical actions.[128] (Contrast Gray's gothic portrayal of Nat Turner as "a gloomy fanatic . . . revolving . . . schemes of indiscriminate massacre to the whites" with the *Confessions'* dispassionate account of the actual killings.)[129]

Just as, in early broadsides and pamphlets, the racial identity of the black condemned features far more prominently in the titles than the content of the confessions attributed to them, few of the (possibly recycled) woodcuts accompanying these accounts delineate phenotype.[130] When circumstances invited such differentiation, as in the simultaneous hangings of interracial pirate duo Charles Gibbs and Thomas Wansley (discussed in Chapter 2), compositional symmetry and contrapuntal shading could produce the same visual equivalence as the paired coffins that embellished some of the fifteen or so pamphlets devoted to their case (see Figures 4 and 6).[131] Indispensable as race had been to musings on the nation since the Founding, efforts to racialize political belonging in print—as with other articulations of citizenship in the early republic—initially tended toward abstraction rather than

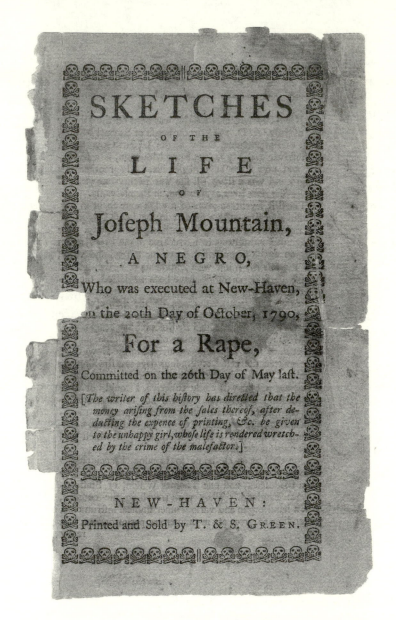

Figure 2. David Daggett, *Sketches of the Life of Joseph Mountain, a Negro, Who Was Executed at New-Haven, on the 20th Day of October, 1790, for a Rape, Committed on the 26th Day of May Last. (The writer of this history has directed that the money arising from the sales thereof, after deducting the expence of printing, &c. be given to the unhappy girl, whose life is rendered wretched by the crime of the malefactor.)* (New Haven, Connecticut, 1790). Beinecke Rare Book and Manuscript Library, Yale University.

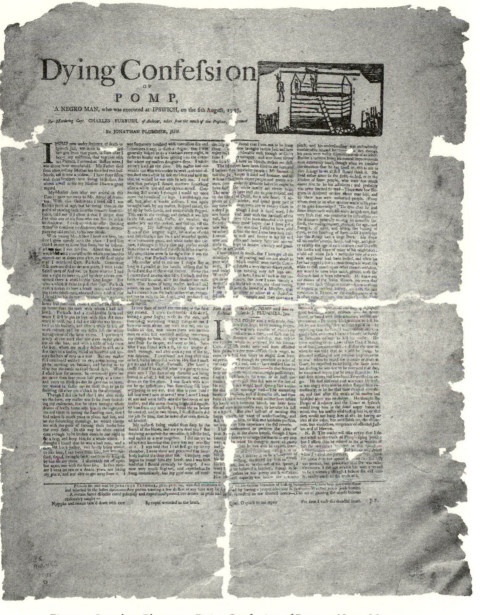

Figure 3. Jonathan Plummer, *Dying Confession of Pomp, a Negro Man, Who Was Executed at Ipswich, on the 6th August, 1795, for Murdering Capt. Charles Furbush, of Andover, Taken from the Mouth of the Prisoner, and Penned by Jonathan Plummer, Jun.* (Newburyport, Massachusetts, 1795). Courtesy Phillips Library at Peabody Essex Museum, Salem, Massachusetts. Access/Negative Number BR910.42.

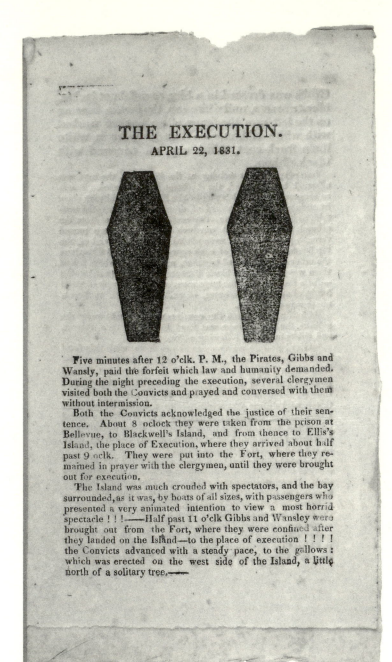

THE EXECUTION.
APRIL 22, 1831.

Five minutes after 12 o'clk. P. M., the Pirates, Gibbs and Wansly, paid the forfeit which law and humanity demanded. During the night preceding the execution, several clergymen visited both the Convicts and prayed and conversed with them without intermission.

Both the Convicts acknowledged the justice of their sentence. About 8 oclock they were taken from the prison at Bellevue, to Blackwell's Island, and from thence to Ellis's Island, the place of Execution, where they arrived about half past 9 oclk. They were put into the Fort, where they remained in prayer with the clergymen, until they were brought out for execution.

The Island was much crouded with spectators, and the bay surrounded, as it was, by boats of all sizes, with passengers who presented a very animated intention to view a most horrid spectacle ! ! !——Half past 11 o'clk Gibbs and Wansley were brought out from the Fort, where they were confined after they landed on the Island—to the place of execution ! ! ! ! the Convicts advanced with a steady pace, to the gallows : which was erected on the west side of the Island, a little north of a solitary tree.——

Figure 4. Charles Gibbs, *Confession of Charles Gibbs the Pirate: Who Was Executed on the 22d of April, 1831* (New York, 1831). Courtesy American Antiquarian Society.

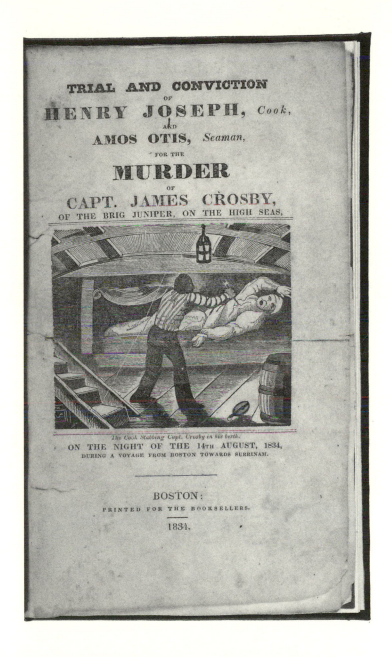

Figure 5. Henry Joseph, *Trial and Conviction of Henry Joseph, Cook, and Amos Otis, Seaman, for the Murder of Capt. James Crosby, of the Brig Juniper, on the High Seas, on the Night of the 14th August, 1834, during a Voyage from Boston towards Surrinam* (Boston, 1834). Courtesy American Antiquarian Society.

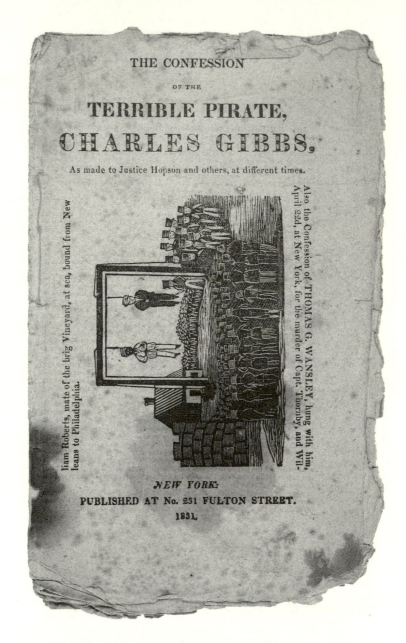

Figure 6. Charles Gibbs, *The Confession of the Terrible Pirate, Charles Gibbs, as Made to Justice Hopson and Others, at Different Times. Also the Confession of Thomas G. Wansley, Hung with Him, April 22d, at New York, for the Murder of Capt. Thornby, and William Roberts, Mate of the Brig Vineyard, at Sea, Bound from New [Or]leans to Philadelphia.* (New York: 1831). Courtesy American Antiquarian Society.

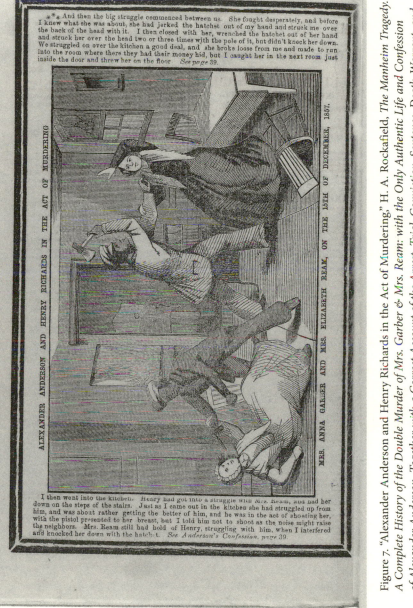

***And then the big struggle commenced between us. She fought desperately, and before I knew what she was about, she had jerked the hatchet out of my hand and struck me over the back of the head with it. I then closed with her, wrenched the hatchet out of her hand and struck her over the head two or three times with the pole of it, but didn't knock her down. We struggled on over the kitchen a good deal, and she broke loose from me and made to run into the room where there they had their money hid, but I caught her in the next room just inside the door and threw her on the floor. *See page 39.*

ALEXANDER ANDERSON AND HENRY RICHARDS IN THE ACT OF MURDERING

MRS. ANNA GARBER AND MRS. ELIZABETH REAM, ON THE 15TH OF DECEMBER, 1857.

I then went into the kitchen. Henry had got into a struggle with Mrs. Ream, and had her down on the steps of the stairs. Just as I came out in the kitchen she had struggled up from him, and was about rather getting the better of him, and he was in the act of shooting her, with the pistol presented to her breast, but I told him not to shoot as the noise might raise the neighbors. Mrs. Ream still had hold of Henry, struggling with him, when I interfered and knocked her down with the hatchet. *See Anderson's Confession, page 39.*

Figure 7. "Alexander Anderson and Henry Richards in the Act of Murdering," H. A. Rockafield, *The Manheim Tragedy. A Complete History of the Double Murder of Mrs. Garber & Mrs. Ream: with the Only Authentic Life and Confession of Alexander Anderson. Together with a Correct Account of the Arrest, Trial, Conviction, Sentence, Death-Warrant, and Execution of Anderson and Henry Richards, His Accomplice; To Which Is Appended Some Brief Reflections on the Causes and Consequences of Crime* (Lancaster, Pennsylvania, 1858). The Library Company of Philadelphia.

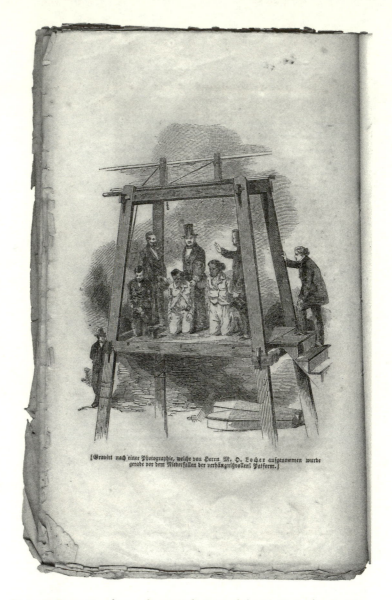

[Gravirt nach einer Photographie, welche von Herrn M. H. Locher aufgenommen wurde gerade vor dem Niederfallen der verhängnißvollen! Patform.]

Figure 8. Engraving from salt-print photograph by M. H. Locher, in H. A. Rockafield, *Das Manheimer Trauerspiel. Eine vollständige Geschichte von dem Doppel-Morde der Frau Gerber und Frau Riem; mit dem allein wahrhaften Leben und Bekenntniss des Alexander Anderson. Nebst einem richtigen Bericht von der Verhaftung, dem Verhör, der Ueberführung, der Verurtheilung, dem Todesbefehl, und der Hinrichtung von Anderson und Henry Richards, seinem Mitschuldigen; welchem hinzugefügt sind einige kurze Betrachtungen über die Ursachen und Folgen von Verbrechen* (Lancaster, Pennsylvania, 1858). The Library Company of Philadelphia. The original caption reads, "Gravirt nach einer Photographie, welche von Herrn M. H. Locher aufgenommen wurde gerade vor dem Nieberfallen der verhängnissvollen! Patform [*sic.*]."

THE
Life and Confession
OF
THOS. J. WANSLEY,
ONE OF THE PIRATES,
CONCERNED WITH
CHARLES GIBBS, *alias* JAMES JEFFERS,
IN THE MURDER AND PIRACY
COMMITTED
ON BOARD THE BRIG VINEYARD.
[WRITTEN BY HIMSELF.]

TO WHICH IS ADDDED,
Several interesting Letters ; together with the Trial, Sentence, and Execution of GIBBS and WANSLEY ; the latter of which took place on the 22d day of April, 1831.

New=York :
PRINTED, PUBLISHED, AND SOLD, WHOLESALE AND RETAIL, BY
CHARLES N. BALDWIN,
BOOKSELLER AND STATIONER,
NO. 19 CHATHAM STREET.

1831.

Figure 9. Thomas J. Wansley, *The Life and Confession of Thos. J. Wansley, One of the Pirates, Concerned with Charles Gibbs, alias James Jeffers, in the Murder and Piracy Committed On Board the Brig Vineyard. Written by Himself. To which Is Added, Several Interesting Letters; Together with the Trial, Sentence, and Execution of Gibbs and Wansley; the Latter of Which Took Place on the 22d Day of April, 1831* (New-York: 1831). Courtesy American Antiquarian Society.

corporeal specificity.[132] In its narrative content, the gallows tradition thus offered an unexpectedly suitable medium for the first-person black subject to
display the qualities associated with a citizenship that, however normatively
gendered and raced as male and white, was definitively disembodied and
unencumbered.[133] Less concerned with physical or symbolic dissolution than
the legal procedures that, by authorizing state-administered execution, give
the lie to the slave's civil death, these works perversely animate black personhood and enliven African American civic existence.

Puffed Up

Even the best-known exemplars of black righteousness fashioned public
selves in a late eighteenth-century Anglo-American culture where, as legal
scholar Steven Wilf notes, an "abundance of execution iconography" made
"criminal law the lingua franca of popular politics."[134] A year before publishing her breakout elegy for the Rev. George Whitefield, nineteen-year-
old Phillis Wheatley included "On The Death of Mr. Snider Murder'd By
Richardson" (1770) in the prospectus for the volume of poetry she hoped
to publish in Boston.[135] Anglo-African activist Olaudah Equiano closed his
Interesting Narrative (1789) by protesting his innocence of the "crimes he is
accused" of having committed as "Commissary to the black Poor."[136] The following year, evangelist minister John Marrant offered his *Journal* (1790) as
a rebuttal to similar charges of financial "impropriety."[137] Back in America,
ministers Absalom Jones and Richard Allen published their *Narrative of the
Proceedings of the Black People, during the Late Awful Calamity* (1794) to refute allegations that African American nurses cheated and robbed their white
patients during Philadelphia's recent yellow fever epidemic. Allen, founder of
the African Methodist Episcopal Church, went on to publish the *Confession
of John Joyce* "for the benefit of Bethel Church." Whether defending themselves or censuring others, these virtuous black writers found incrimination
closely correlated to print publicity. A full two centuries before Huddie Let-
better recorded "Angola Blues" (1933), Martin Luther King, Jr., published his
"Letter from a Birmingham Jail" (1963), Angela Davis gave the Black Power
salute in a San Rafael courtroom (1970), or Henry Louis Gates, Jr., sat down
to the White House Beer Summit (2009), public imputations of criminality
occasioned individual black civic assertion on behalf of the collective.[138] If,
as Davis suggests, "crime is . . . one of the masquerades behind which 'race,'
with all its menacing ideological complexity, mobilizes old public fears and

creates new ones," criminality was nevertheless the guise under which the black persona routinely entered the public sphere of print in early America.[139]

To appreciate this point is radically to reconfigure the relations among African Americans, law, and publicity in the century leading up to Emancipation and the Reconstruction Amendments. Influenced by Jürgen Habermas's controversial account of the eighteenth-century emergence of the public sphere, many of us share historian John L. Brooke's image of a liberal state where the deliberations of executive, legislative, and judicial officials at the governmental core are informed not only by the direct participation of enfranchised citizens (through jury duty, elections, and the like) but also by the indirect contributions of a much larger, more diverse population whose intersubjective communications form the public sphere.[140] In Brooke's schema, "civil outlaws" like slaves, insurgents, and criminals occupy a peripheral "arena of force," where their only "political voice is violence, and in turn they are met with state-sanctioned force," whereas other subordinates contribute not only to culture but to politics in its more limited, conventional sense through their persuasive interventions in the deliberative process.[141] Closed out of *both* the public sphere and the liberal state through their enslaved or outlaw status, how could the black majority ever achieve political membership in the form of citizenship?

Whether we picture eighteenth-century African American activists and writers creating a "black print counterpublic" through institution-building and publishing efforts directed primarily toward constituencies of color, or we see these black publicists as "invad[ing] the public sphere and persuad[ing] Americans that they were equal citizens of the Republic in theory if not in reality," we tend to think of publicity as the avenue by which marginalized or excluded subordinates gained access to the polity.[142] Indeed, the enduring appeal of the fugitive slave narrative lies in the way it spatializes and materializes the slave's escape from the marginal zone of force into the public sphere: fleeing from the repressive South to the cultural centers of the North, the fugitive demonstrates African Americans' civic and political qualifications by publishing his or her personal narrative of bound servitude as a critique of the slaveholding legal regime. As Edlie Wong reminds us, however, movement was seldom so liberating for those facing "the predicament of territorialized freedom" in an Atlantic world structured by localized race slavery.[143] The lithographic and narrative "Resurrection of Henry Box Brown" notwithstanding, publicized geopolitical relocation alone could not bring the civilly dead to political life.[144]

Under the legal fiction of the slave's mixed character, however, criminality could do just that. The slave's offenses activated his personhood,
removing him from the extralegal zone of force and ushering him, through
his arrest and prosecution, into the nucleus of state power. Having been
transformed from human property into legal person, he is then transmuted
from flesh-and-blood human being into print persona. Through published
trial transcripts, press accounts, scaffold orations, gallows broadsides, or
pamphlet confessions, the criminous slave participates in the public sphere,
thereby contributing to the popular opinion that cycles back into deliberative governmental processes.[145] Passage through the criminal justice system
punitively affirmed the black individual's political membership, making it
possible to envision him in alternative public, civic roles. Activist former
slaves like Douglass could "talk 'lawyer like' about law" in their antebellum
narratives because for well over a century the American reading public had
become accustomed to seeing enslaved and other felons of African descent
talk defendant-like about law in popular crime ephemera. Rather than approaching the state from a position of legal outsidership, African American
publicists speaking on behalf of the collective sought *reentry* into the polity
on more equitable, civil terms.[146]

It is in this sense that the black persona developed in tandem with modernity's individualist self. Habermas finds the "growing autobiographical
literature of confessions and self-examinations" crucial to the process in
which, from the eighteenth century onward, "exemplary instructions in the
virtuous life and recommended models of the good life" were supplanted by
"an increasingly pronounced, abstract demand for a conscious, self-critical
appropriation, the demand that one responsibly take possession of one's own
individual, irreplaceable, and contingent life history."[147] It is through just
such public, printed acceptance of "liability for one's own existence" in the
form of the criminal confession, we might say, adapting Habermas's phrasing, that those punitively addressed by law are transformed into identifiable
"bearers of the political public sphere," if not yet fully recognized "members
of society" (96, 365).[148] State-administered apprehension, conviction, and
punishment authorized criminous slaves as "consociates in an abstract community . . . produced by legal norms," providing the occasion for printed
first-person confessional narratives to depict these legal persons "both as
members of a concrete community and as irreplaceable individuals . . . individuated through their life histories" (112). Portraying their putative black
authors as possessors of both "the free (and authentic) will of a morally (and

ethically) accountable person" and "the free choice of a legal subject oriented toward her own preferences," gallows texts commence the *augmentation* (what for other civil subjects is the "reduction") of that responsible, autonomous selfhood into eligibility for full political membership through participation in the public sphere (112).[149]

Confession did not, of course, connote this sort of possessive individualism for the vast majority of African Americans routinely subjected to extrajudicial or even paralegal interrogations and punishment.[150] Extracted to resolve disputes, restore the peace, or furnish information, the informal, usually coerced, confessions that were regularly elicited outside the courtroom from blacks and other subordinates served very different purposes than the public attribution of personal accountability.[151] Whether demanded by slaveholders, citizen patrols, or municipal authorities, these confessions, the slave narrative's frequent interrogation scenes remind us, occurred in the extralegal zone where plantation justice, summary police powers, and vigilantism thrived.[152] Rather than embracing the privilege against self-incrimination as a timeless, immutable inheritance from English common law or as an innovation of revolutionary American legal reform, authorities in British North America increasingly depended upon incriminating statements gained through summary pretrial examinations, usually conducted by the justice of the peace or magistrate, that preceded and often supplanted the trial by jury.[153] Even as reforms in criminal legal procedure gradually limited use of unsworn confessions extracted from whites, the widespread statutory restriction of the admissible courtroom speech of enslaved and often free blacks to confession or incriminating testimony against nonwhites continued to place a distinctive burden of guilt on legally admissible African American speech.[154] Slaveholding societies' need to "limit black access to the legal process," historian Christopher Waldrep observes, racialized the "layering . . . characteristic of all criminal justice systems": "at the bottom, petty cases received the roughest and most informal handling," whereas in "well-publicized cases . . . lawmen carefully observed all the elements of due process."[155]

It is in the context of the largely invisible summary proceedings that, in Waldrep's words, "detached [slavery] from the public sphere," that we must view the era's crime literature.[156] Read against this legal historical backdrop, the published confessions attributed to condemned black criminals are noteworthy less for their authenticity or their dissent than for the way in which they formalized, publicized, and thus politicized individual black speech (incriminating though it may have been). That the voice attributed to the convict was rarely a critical one on par with that of David Walker or Frederick Douglass does not eliminate its political significance. For by expressing the consent that at least initially served as their raison d'être, even the most formulaic gallows broadsheets and criminal confessions credited the black felon with a political voice that, authorized by its passage through the legal system, was articulated in the persuasive realm of print culture, and resonated—if only in tones of affirmation—in the deliberative realm of the state. (Moreover, as we shall soon see illustrated in statements attributed to condemned African Americans as diverse as farmer Abraham Johnstone and sailor Thomas J. Wansley, gallows literature's specifically juridical impetus was all the more likely to prompt commentary, however neutral or laudatory, on law and its procedures.)[157] Print, and especially popular crime literature, converted the theoretical, retroactive, punitive political membership of the enslaved or free black convict into a more positive form of civic belonging. It did so by ascribing to him a political voice that, however supportive of the white supremacist status quo, nevertheless held the potential for alternative forms of expression (including dissent) that could also shape the polity, albeit in a muffled, indirect manner. Through the formulaic confessions attributed to them, the black condemned entered the public sphere that engaged and influenced the more narrowly political deliberations of those directly involved in governance. Regardless of its specific political effects, such published speech was, nevertheless, political. And, as such, it endowed its putative enunciator, the black persona, with an undeniable civic presence.

We can glimpse that process at work in one of the earliest first-person portrayals of a black criminal. The transcribed "Conference between a MINISTER and the Prisoner, on the Day before his Execution" appears as an appendix to *Tremenda*, Cotton Mather's "Sermon Delivered unto a Great Assembly, in which Was Present, a Miserable African, Just Going to be Executed for a most Inhumane and Uncommon Murder."[158] Without a doubt, the admission attributed to the condemned Joseph Hanno—"*I am a Sinner. And I deserve to Dy*"—buttresses state authority.[159] But in such routine first-person endorsements of the death penalty, the criminal confession also depicted its speaker signing on to the social contract through his individual, reciprocal, express consent to this constitutive act of political power by the state.[160] Hanno's admission of guilt thus confirms rather than compromises his assertion, elsewhere in the text, of a radically individual and, above all, *civic* identity. When asked how he spent his "many Months in the Prison," Hanno answers, predictably, "*In Reading and Praying, Sir.*"[161] His rote catechistic reply is complicated, however, by the minister's outraged response: "In *Reading*! Of what, I pray? . . . you had no *Bible* with you. . . . You lived many Months without Reading a word in that most Necessary Book, *The Bible*. . . . it looks very strangely, very oddly, how you could Live quietly so long, and have no *Bible* with you" (32). Although Hanno's nonscriptural reading is lost to us, its civic possibilities become evident later in the interview. Exhorted to attain "Righteousness" through repentance and asked, "Do you understand what I say to you?" Hanno retorts, "*Yes, Sir, I have a Great deal of Knowledge. No body of my Colour, in Old* England *or New, has so much*"—prompting the curt ministerial rejoinder, "I wish you were less *Puffed up* with it" (38).[162] Implicitly refuting allegations of black intellectual inferiority, Hanno also differentiates himself from the larger transatlantic Afro-British population.[163] He does so by alluding to a black self expanded (or "Puffed up") by its participation in the public sphere. Provoking clerical consternation by his avid prison reading, Hanno belies Mather's portrayal of him in the sermon as a "*Black Thing . . .* in Irons" (26).

"As One within a Few Hours of an awful Eternity," Hanno was expected to turn to the Bible as a guide toward "*a Sincere and Serious Repentance*," in keeping with the Calvinist doctrine of *sola scriptura* (33, 32). No respecter of persons, the "Glorious CHRIST" held out to Hanno "is a SAVIOUR, whom *Negro's* themselves, yea, the *worst of Sinners* among those poor *Black Outcasts*, may be welcome to," thereby "fulfilling that word; *He shall Sprinkle many Nations*" (31). But the Hanno portrayed here seeks civic rather than spiritual transcendence, preferring membership in a cosmopolitan public sphere to fellowship with a global community of saints.[164] Instead of leading to inward contemplation, Hanno's reading projects him beyond the confines of Boston's Queen Street jail, into the new republic of letters that, comprising "*Old* England" and "*New*," could also accommodate the "Knowledge" contained in a "body of [his] Colour."[165] Through its publication Mather's *Tremenda* ensured the continued, posthumous participation of "Joseph Hanno" in the public sphere of print culture. Far from killing that nascent civic persona, the condemned man's execution, at once expiating his criminal act and occasioning the pamphlet, marked its birth.

The Death of the Condemned Black Author

Convicted felons' relationship to those who sought to capture their "lives" in print was characterized by a remarkable diversity of motives as well as varying degrees of participation.[166] The black condemned must have taken careful measure of the value of their published personal narratives—as a carefully considered step on the road to salvation, maybe, or as a calculated effort to improve the likelihood of pardon. Some clearly sought to exchange their stories for notoriety, a decent burial, or material support for families left behind. Others may have had nothing whatsoever to do with the process of writing and publication. Did it matter?[167]

Intriguing though it may be to the field's new cadre of Book History scholars, the slippage between author and writer has troubled African American studies since its inception.[168] Historians repeatedly find themselves defending the documentary integrity of specific black-authored texts.[169] But for literary scholars whose institutional authority has traditionally rested, as Susan Stewart notes, in "the legislation of originality, authenticity, and authorship," the black canon itself is at stake.[170] Committed to both the disciplinary "science of attribution" and the post–Civil Rights rhetoric of Black Firsts, critics have long struggled to establish the legitimate origins of a distinctive Afro-diasporic literary tradition.[171]

It has proven difficult to ascertain exactly where the current of black culture flowed into the main stream of American literature. In his survey of the "forms and conventions that seemed to provide . . . for a distinctively black intervention into the public sphere," Dickson Bruce discovers throughout eighteenth-century Anglo-American letters traces of "black authority— . . . an authoritative literary persona and a distinctive black perspective," that may or may not have been inscribed by an African American "hand"—or, for that matter, uttered by an African American tongue. [172] A generation later, in the nation's founding romances, Toni Morrison finds an elusive but pervasive "Africanist presence" to have been instrumental in "the self-conscious but highly problematic construction of the American as a new white man."[173] The "unassailable, integral, black self" with which the antebellum slave narrative countered this "fabricated, mythological" presence only appeared to give voice to a pure black experience; in fact, this, like other vernacular genres, bespoke complex processes of racial, cultural, and class transmission and exchange.[174] As the field's boundaries have expanded and contracted over the past several decades, it has become clear that, however much African American literature presupposes the existence of writers of African heritage, black authorship has long existed without them.[175]

To appreciate this point, one need only look to the strongest contender for the title of first freestanding slave narrative, *A Narrative of the Uncom-*

mon Suffering and Surprising Deliverance of Briton Hammon (1760). In both typographical form and narrative content, the work bears an uncanny resemblance to another, white-authored, account of Indian captivity. *A Plain Narrative of the Uncommon Suffering and Remarkable Deliverance of Thomas Brown* (1760) was published earlier that year, also in Boston, by printers with business and family connections to the firm that brought out Hammon's *Narrative*. This pioneering slave narrative, John Sekora has demonstrated, resulted from neither an eruption of black consciousness nor a burst of abolitionist fervor, but to the timely convergence of political events and market forces. "If the story of a black man or woman was to be told at all" in colonial America, concludes Sekora, "that story would necessarily be shaped into a popular form."[176] Sekora's research offers nothing new about Briton Hammon as historical person or early black writer, but it speaks volumes about how the racially indeterminate, formulaic Indian captivity narrative attributed to him "create[d] the terms of possibility for the slave narrative" (103). Examining how the Execution Day ritual provided one set of conditions from which canonical forms of black life-writing emerged, the present study joins more recent efforts to reconceptualize literary historical change over time.[177] As an alternative to models of direct literary influence, we might imagine the criminal confession and the abolitionist slave narrative as successive iterations of black subjectivity—in effect, feedback loops where the cultural output generated by the interplay of law and popular culture became input for new articulations of African American selfhood.[178]

For insight into this process, it helps to revisit Marxist theorist Louis Althusser's well-known account of subject formation. Imagining someone on the street turning around in response to "the most commonplace everyday police (or other) hailing: 'Hey, you there!'" Althusser maintains that "by this mere one-hundred-and-eighty-degree physical conversion, he becomes a *subject*."[179] It is in such simultaneously physical and mental actions that we "constantly practice the rituals of ideological recognition, which guarantee for us that we are indeed concrete, individual, distinguishable and (naturally) irreplaceable subjects" (117). As Althusser admits, his famous "*[m]ise-en-scene* of interpellation" relies upon a bit of stagecraft (120). Acknowledging how his tableau artificially splits a continuously constituted subject into a before and after, Althusser insists that "concrete subjects only exist insofar as they are supported by a concrete individual" (118). But an earlier passage in the essay complicates this claim. Right after alluding to the friendly social rituals that confirm our uniqueness as subjects, Althusser points out that, in fact, "the writing I am currently executing and the reading you are currently performing are also in this respect rituals of ideological recognition"—with the footnoted proviso that "these two 'currentlys' are separated by an indefinite interval; I am writing these lines on 6 April 1969, you may read them at any subsequent time" (117). Here temporality once again splits subjectivity, although not in this case under the narrative exigencies of a thought experiment. Due to the time lag and physical distance enabled by scriptive technologies, the subject represented in the text is not only detached from the concrete individual "writing these lines" but takes on a new material form, "supported by" ink and paper rather than flesh and blood. Writing, and especially the printed page as manuscript's decorporealizing successor, concretizes subjectivity in the absence of a body.

Doubtless, real-life individuals like Hanno and Clifton were hailed as subjects by legal rituals of arrest, trial, and execution as well as by the cultural rituals that generated gallows texts.[180] Less obviously, however, print representations of the black condemned also entailed their recognition as "concrete, individual, distinguishable and (naturally) irreplaceable subjects"—rather than as fungible commodities or amorphous subhuman security threats.[181] However artificial, depictions of African American felons were unquestionably premised on a documentary facticity. Even if readers didn't think Nat Turner told his story the way Thomas Gray said he did, few questioned that the *Confessions of Nat Turner* represented an actual individual situated in historical time.[182] And it is the recognition of the black subject as a unique, self-authored person *within* ideology that alters its ongoing formation in law, politics, communications, and culture.[183]

Breaking from earlier efforts to detect "when we are hearing an authentic black voice instead of witnessing an act of literary ventriloquism," this study recalls that prosopopoeia is in fact the parlor trick performed by *all* autobiography.[184] Much as the printed first-person narrative figures forth the absent human subject as if he were speaking, the (usually) posthumously published confessions of condemned criminals present the deceased felon as if he were alive and speaking in the present. In his well-known theory of autobiography, Paul de Man elaborates how "it is the figure of prosopopeia, the fiction of an apostrophe to an absent, deceased or voiceless entity, which posits the possibility of the latter's reply and confers upon it the power of speech."[185] This fiction is literalized in the interplay between the execution sermon and the criminal confession—especially when we understand apostrophe both as a form of address that animates its object *and* as a sudden turning aside to address a new audience.[186] Convoking the very civic and religious communities that it addresses, the execution sermon turns in its application section to address the condemned, as well as the groups he represents (froward husbands, "Ethiopian" slaves); when the confessing condemned person responds, the apostrophic sermon has accomplished its animating mission. The textual object reenters print as a self-articulating subject: Mather's *"Black Thing . . . in Irons"* gives way to informed cosmopolite Joseph Hanno.[187]

The challenge facing Afro-diasporic life-writing was, as we have seen, to display black personhood, rather than humanity; the resulting print subject should not, then, be confused with its fleshly counterpart. A back formation of portrayals of individuals of African descent, the black persona predated (and maybe even provoked or required) more explicitly political and artistic representations of a shared racial experience by actual black writers from the late eighteenth century onward.[188] Telling us a great deal about the origins of African American authorship—and almost nothing about early black writing—gallows literature inserts the theoretical death of the author into literary history.[189] Given the practical futility of any critical pursuit of authenticity, literary value, or political integrity in early American gallows literature, we may be excused from attempting to reconstruct strategic negotiations over the production of gallows texts or gauge their resistance to enslavement and incarceration.[190]

Neither political intentions nor literary pretensions can explain crime ephemera's significance to the rise of the black print subject. The value of confessions attributed to the black condemned lies in the way even fictive first-person participation in print culture filled out the partial, culpable personhood recognized and publicized by criminal proceedings.[191] Print parlayed legal liability into civic presence. Emphasizing figuration over fact, this study finds print performance of black authorship far more important than the historical authenticity of that authorship.[192] Our interpretive energies will therefore be directed toward the individualized black persona and not its historical referent. That that individual was often highly conventional, perhaps entirely fictional, does not diminish its significance in a print culture that abetted black political exclusion through the persistent identification of African Americans collectively as objects of property, agents of social disorder, or both. Rather than merely reinforcing the legal "designation of [enslaved] subjectivity [that] utterly negated the possibility of a nonpunitive, inviolate, or pleasurable embodiment," gallows literature unexpectedly thwarted the process by which "the black captive vanished in the chasm between object,

criminal, pained body, and mortified flesh."[193] Detached from the body of
the condemned and materialized in print, the black persona gained new life
in early American print culture. For by hailing that subject, crime literature,
regardless of who composed specific texts and under what conditions, helped
to create the terms of possibility for the civic presence assumed by a later
generation of black autobiographers.[194] Attending to the dynamic convergence of law and print culture in the figures of the slave and the convict—
and especially the enslaved felon—we can see how the first-person black
subjectivity publicized through eighteenth- and nineteenth-century crime
literature patterned subsequent print attempts to model African American
citizenship, as well as literary efforts to fashion a distinctly American identity
in a nation increasingly perceived to be tainted by the crime of slavery.

Our Permanent Literature

Foregrounding black crime ephemera to complicate African American literature's creation story, this study calls not for a revised canon but a shift
in critical focus. What if, rather than viewing black criminality (real or
imagined) through the lens of pathology or persecution, we instead considered it from the vantage of African American civic presence? Temporarily
redirecting our gaze toward crime and punishment, and away from artistry,
piety, industry, and activism, we can concentrate our attention on the rise
of the black persona. With the gallows tradition as a point of departure, we
can observe that persona's metamorphosis from the *Federalist*'s impossible
amalgam of civilly dead property and criminally liable person to the protocitizen conjured in the nineteenth-century polemics of David Walker and
Maria Stewart, personal narratives of Frederick Douglass and Harriet Jacobs,
and fiction of William Wells Brown, Frank Webb, and Martin Delany. Such
a reassessment of criminal responsibility's importance to political membership sheds light not only on the emergence of the black persona and African
American authorship, but on that of American literature more broadly. For,
while white writers like Edgar Allan Poe, Herman Melville, George Lippard,
and Edward Everett Hale were asserting their cultural independence from
England by developing and promoting a sovereign national literature with
themselves as its most prominent (if critical) citizens, black reformers such
as Douglass, Wells Brown, and Jacobs sought to authorize (or perhaps, more
ambitiously, to *author*) African American citizenship through their critical
engagements with American print culture.[195] As they wrote black civic pres-

ence into existence, these and other African American activists helped create a distinctive American literary tradition.

This fact did not go unnoticed. In the mounting clamor for a national literature, the antebellum slave narrative provided an unexpected (if awkward) answer to the perennial question of when America's "long apprenticeship to the learning of other lands," would finally "draw . . . to a close."[196] In July 1849, the Rev. Ephraim Peabody commenced his omnibus review essay of narratives by Douglass, Wells Brown, Henry Watson, and Josiah Henson by announcing that "America has the mournful honor of adding a new department to the literature of civilization—the autobiographies of fugitive slaves."[197] Unitarian minister and reformer Theodore Parker concurred in a speech he gave at Colby College the following month, singling out "the Lives of Fugitive Slaves" as the "one portion of our permanent literature, if literature it may be called, which is wholly indigenous and original," having indisputably been "written by none but Americans."[198] In a period when there is little evidence for a self-consciously African American—or, more fluently, "negro"—literature, some commentators found the long-deferred promise of an authentic national literature fulfilled through first-person black authorship.[199] For the antebellum slave narrative, as for modern blues, jazz, R&B, and rap, authenticity resided in a blackness that betokened not so much bona fide Afro-diasporic expressivity as genuine *Americanness.*[200]

Of course, the introduction of the alternative, historical black self of the slave narrative neither extinguished the nineteenth-century romance's Africanist presence nor halted its construction of a normatively white, male American self. Quite the contrary, because fictions of black subjectivity were so indispensable to, among other things, literary "meditations on . . . accountability," crime ephemera's evocation of an actual, individual, and, above all, legally *responsible* black self necessarily questioned the integrity of a white, male, American personhood constituted by but stubbornly unanswerable for what was with ever greater urgency being figured as the crime of slavery.[201] Otherwise placed in mutually definitive opposition, slaves and citizens shared an accountability to the polity. "Punishment" was "annexed to personality" for John Locke, whose influential *Essay Concerning Human Understanding* (1689), defined "person" as a continuously conscious, legally responsible "self."[202] Surely this state of affairs held true not just for those "other Persons" of the Constitution's three-fifths clause but its "free Persons" as well? If slaves' political membership lay in their everyday culpability as legal persons, did Americans' citizenship rest upon their quotidian complicity in slavery?[203]

Legal and other fictions of slave character may have resonated so deeply in early national and antebellum America because their uneasy mixture of civil incapacity and criminal accountability presented a starker version of the discrepant legal standards to which the (normatively white, male) subject was held. At a time of growing, and often quite sensational, capacity litigation, legal historian Susanna L. Blumenthal finds, "responsibility talk was at least as common as rights talk."[204] By no means confined to the courtroom or to a particular segment of U.S. society, the question of answerability suffused conversations about humanity, personhood, and citizenship as Americans meditated on the forms, meanings, and implications of subjectivity in a slaveholding nation at once united and divided by a robust print culture. Silhouetted against both the slavery controversy and the rise of market capitalism, the Jacksonian common man in print displayed remarkable anxiety about both civil capacity and civic participation. Whether characterized by its "infantile citizenship," "necro citizenship," "eager . . . incompetence," or "*esprit de corpse*," the normatively white, male citizen limned in legal and literary portrayals of the time is characterized by naïveté, passivity, inarticulateness, and withdrawal, if not downright silence and absence.[205]

In antebellum literature, this citizen's evacuated civil standing and shrinking civic presence contrasted sharply with the black persona's advance up from slavery. Thus, even as this study tracks the burgeoning personality of the black subject in eighteenth- and nineteenth-century print culture, it also considers its white counterpart's corresponding civil mortification. For if African American authorship can be traced to the recognized legal personhood, retroactive political membership, and print-derived civic presence that publicized culpability conferred on the black subject, the era's (implicitly white) national literature registers broader disquietude about the meaning of citizenship in a slaveholding polity. In a reversal of the punitive logic that maintained black civic exclusion by holding the enslaved criminally accountable yet civilly incompetent, this literature suggests that the collective national failure to take responsibility for the crime of slavery threatened to deprive individual Americans of legal personhood by consigning them to the civil death African Americans were striving to escape.[206] Voiced in pamphlets, newspapers, magazines, books, and professional journals, this ongoing political reassessment of how criminal responsibility inflected the civil capacity and civic participation of normatively white, male citizens inspired short fiction by (among others) Poe, Melville, Lippard, and Hale. The overall effect is that of transverse trajectories of racialized subjectivity, in which the white print subject's declension originates in the very criminal accountability that authorizes his black counterpart's ascent.

Such a history of the black print persona in its formative years, from the eve of the Revolution to the eve of the Civil War, thus entails broader analysis of the centrality of the question of criminality to political belonging for not only African Americans but all American citizens in a nation that encountered remarkable difficulty, in print as in law, disentangling persons from property, criminal responsibility from civil capacity, and civic activity from crime. For African Americans, what was the legacy of a citizenship underwritten by legal culpability? For white Americans, was membership in a slaveholding (colloquially, "manstealing") nation always premised on criminality? How must acknowledgment of black civility or white culpability necessarily reconfigure a nation literally constituted by their opposites, the paired myths of race-based chattel slavery and Anglo-American civic virtue?

Chapter 1 begins to answer these questions by examining how, within the founding American myth of the social contract, the legal fiction of slave character mandated retroactive, albeit purely formal and punitive, recognition of the criminous slave's prior political membership. Chapter 2 considers how contractarianism's tacit acknowledgment of the black felon's political belonging was expanded by this individualized subject's participation—fictive or otherwise—in the public sphere of early American print culture through its popular gallows literature. Part Two builds on this conceptual framework to present readings of a range of early national and antebellum texts. Situating the unusually exculpatory *Address of Abraham Johnstone* in the Philadelphia of the First Reconstruction and the yellow fever epidemic, Chapter 3 demonstrates the illegibility of textual performances of black virtue in an early national North that persistently misapprehended black civility as criminality. Chapter 4 reads the only canonical black gallows narrative, *The Confessions of Nat Turner*, alongside the first testimonial slave narrative, *Narrative of James Williams, An American Slave* (1838), and what is often heralded as the first detective story, Edgar Allan Poe's "Murders in the Rue Morgue" (1841). (Poe's tale was inspired in part by newspaper coverage of the trial and execution of African American wife-murderer Edward Coleman.)[207] Distinguishing criminal motives from violent acts, these three early antebellum works, along with Samuel A. Cartwright's "Report on the Diseases and Physical Peculiarities of the Negro Race" (1851), reveal the fraught racial implications of locating personhood in criminal responsibility under a slaveholding legal regime. Chapters 4 and 5 probe the rhetorical and political underside of reformers' efforts to hold white American citizens rather than victimized blacks responsible for slavery and its attendant crimes. Stripped of the intent and accountability that had, since Locke, tied responsible personhood to human consciousness, abolitionism's newly decriminalized black subject risked becoming a dehumanized tool in slavery's deadly labors. That free African Americans were not immune from the increasing tendency to link personhood to humanity at midcentury is evident, Chapter 5 finds, in print coverage of the trial of William Freeman. In 1846, the black former inmate of New York's Auburn State Prison attracted public attention as much for the insanity defense mounted by his famous abolitionist attorney, William H. Seward, as for his senseless slaughter of a local white family. Occurring a year after the publication of Douglass's *Narrative* and in the aftermath of the Sixth Census controversy (which culminated in the State Department's authoritative correlation of black insanity to a racialized criminality), the Freeman case illustrates the continued indispensability of culpability to legal and popular understandings of black legal competence, political membership, and civic belonging. In its survey of literary, reportorial, and courtroom "slaver narratives," including short fiction by Melville and Lippard, Chapter 6 finds that it was precisely the refusal of American mariners and merchants to acknowledge such criminal accountability that threatened figuratively to consign these nineteenth-century pirates to the civil death they imposed on their black "cargo." Less concerned with the act of trafficking in human commodities than with the national identity of the men, ships, and officials involved, anti-slave trade legislation and litigation supplied a punitive working definition of U.S. citizenship in the absence of a formal, constitutional one. The book concludes by following the transverse arcs of the black and white print subjects to their antebellum endpoints, reading a late gallows pamphlet from Lancaster, Pennsylvania, alongside Edward Everett Hale's widely reprinted Civil War story, "The Man Without a Country" (1863). By identifying the importance of culpable selfhood to the black persona's transition from chattel to protocitizen in American print culture, this study seeks to chart the conditions under which one version of African American subjectivity emerged, as well as to delineate some of their enduring cultural and political effects, particularly the ongoing misapprehension of black civility as racialized criminality and the heightened awareness of guilty white citizenship.[208]

The Pathway of Insult and Mortification

We can see the literary uptake of the gallows tradition into canonical African American autobiography in Chapter 19 of Frederick Douglass's second personal narrative, *My Bondage and My Freedom* (1855). With "The Run-Away Plot," that most revised of antebellum slave narratives complicates the familiar critical account of liberation through life-writing by suggesting that African American authorship must be disassociated from both incriminating scriptive technologies and inculpatory personal narrative before it can emerge as a form of civic assertion capable of bridging the two subject positions designated by the title.

Douglass recounts how he and his fellow slaves were caught in the act of conspiring to escape from the benevolent Mr. Freeland, to whom young Frederick has been rented by his master, Thomas Auld. Betrayed, Frederick and his co-conspirators are taken by constables to be interrogated by Auld in nearby St. Michael's before being temporarily lodged in Easton jail. From the outset, the investigation centers on "*those protections' which Frederick was said to have written for his companions.*"[209] Despite having earlier designated book learning as the "direct pathway from slavery to freedom" (218), Douglass now recounts how his contraband literacy has instead diverted the enslaved men onto a "pathway . . . of insult and mortification" (321). "Could the kind reader have been quietly riding along the main road to or from Easton, that morning," Douglass reflects, "his eye would have met a painful sight. He would have seen five young men, guilty of no crime, save that of preferring *liberty* to a life of *bondage*, drawn along the public highway— firmly bound together— . . . fastened to three strong horses, whose riders were armed to the teeth, with pistols and daggers—on their way to prison, like felons, and suffering every possible insult from the crowds of idle, vulgar people, who clustered around, and heartlessly made their failure the occasion for all manner of ribaldry and sport" (319). He goes on to recall that, "while the constables were looking forward, Henry and I, being fastened together, could occasionally exchange a word, without being observed by the kidnappers who had us in charge" (320). Asked by Henry what to do with his pass, Frederick urges, "Eat it with your biscuit . . . it won't do to tear it up," and as the procession nears St. Michael's, "the direction concerning the passes was passed around, and executed" as the injunction "'*Own nothing*' . . . '*Own nothing!*' was passed around and enjoined, and assented to" (320).

Drafted as tickets to freedom, the passes become the only direct "evi-

dence" against the enslaved conspirators (321). Rather than liberating the
men, Frederick's insurgent act of authorship threatens to reinscribe them in
the same technology that, from plantation records and slave passes to the
statute book and the Constitution, instituted, enforced, and maintained race
slavery in America. Nor was the discursive threat limited to the written page.
As the men's furtive pact of silence reveals, under the legal regime of slavery
black personal narrative could pose the greatest hazard of all. If, due to one's
enslaved status, one could "own nothing"—and particularly not the bundle
of civil rights and privileges that had constituted legal personhood under
Anglo-American law—verbally owning, or admitting, nothing is far more
expedient than owning up to the one thing a slave *could* own: guilt.[210] Denied
a property right in himself and his story, the slave is well advised to eschew
incriminating narrative, the form of first-person utterance most commonly
available to the bondman caught in the crosshairs of law and narrative in
early America.[211]

The account of the captives' journey first to the St. Michael's examination and then to Easton jail evokes that other journey along the pathway of
insult and mortification, the gallows procession.[212] Douglass's depiction of the
"crowds of idle, vulgar people, who clustered around, and heartlessly" seized
"the occasion for all manner of ribaldry and sport" by flinging taunts that "*I
ought to be hanged, . . . I ought to be burnt*," accords with revisionist antebellum portrayals of scaffold processions (319–20). In keeping with the trend
toward privatizing executions, midcentury Americans no longer viewed the
rites of state-sanctioned public death as parts of a solemn communal ritual.[213]
Because "the gallows blunts all the better feelings of human nature, and
stimulates all the bad," Douglass would explain at an 1858 rally to protest the
execution of white forger-turned-murderer Ira Stout, "the hanging day is the
high day for gamblers, thieves, robbers and murderers."[214] As Douglass suggests, Execution Day was now seen as itself a catalyst for criminal disorder,
uniting an uncouth mob in an orgiastic spectacle of violent entertainment.[215]

But it is not enough for Douglass in "The Run-Away Plot" to portray
Southerners as participating in an outmoded ritual widely held to be at odds
with the progressive, reformist values of his Northern readers: he must demonstrate that the enslaved actors appear under false pretenses. The South's
backwardness is evident, that is, not only in its enthusiasm for the degrad-
ing, corrupting spectacle, but in its misapprehension of that spectacle's black
subjects. This misapprehension lies in a fundamental confusion of civic for
criminal agency. "Such," Douglass reflects on the scene, "is the power of

public opinion, that it is hard, even for the innocent, to feel the happy consolations of innocence, when they fall under the maledictions of this power. How could we regard ourselves as in the right, when all about us denounced us as criminals, and had the power and the disposition to treat us as such[?]" (321–22). Here Douglass displays a striking confidence in his Northern audience's ability to cut the Gordian knot of criminal and civic motivations that bedevil white Southerners. Cued by Douglass's rhetoric to view the young men as sable Patrick Henrys, preferring liberty to the civil death of bondage, "the kind reader" will recognize the true criminals to be "the kidnappers" who masquerade as "constables."[216] Cleansing Frederick and his fellow slaves of the taint of criminality so as to present them as would-be citizens, Douglass calls on the reader to interpret black subjectivity in ways that run counter to American law. The reader must read civic agency where law can only see criminal acts.

Urging his audience to read against the legal grain, marshalling higher law principles to rescript incipient slave insurgency as black civic virtue, and deploying juridical rhetoric to highlight the denial of even summary due process to this black "band of brothers," Douglass in Chapter 19 carries out in narrative form the exculpatory print strategy that in the "Editor's Preface" to *My Bondage and My Freedom* he identifies as the impetus for the work as a whole—and, indeed, the slave narrative as a genre (301). For Douglass, abolitionist literature's duty to provide a corrective to slaveholding law at once requires and authorizes first-person black literary participation in the public sphere. To explain why he is publishing the autobiography merely a decade after his bestselling *Narrative*, Douglass offers the time-honored abolitionist justification for entering into the print fray over slavery: "this system is now at the bar of public opinion . . . for judgment. Its friends have made for it the usual plea—'not guilty;' the case must, therefore, proceed. Any facts, either from slaves, slaveholders, or by-standers, calculated to enlighten the public mind, by revealing the true nature, character, and tendency of the slave system, are in order, and can scarcely be innocently withheld" (106). With these prefatory remarks Douglass calls attention to the intertwined legal and literary histories that complicated any effort to authorize antebellum black speech through such juridical tropes. "I see, too," he continues, "that there are special reasons why I should write my own biography, in preference to employing another to do it. Not only is slavery on trial, but . . . the enslaved people are also on trial. It is alleged, that they are, naturally, inferior; that they are *so low* in the scale of humanity, and so utterly stupid, that they are unconscious of their wrongs, and do not apprehend their rights" (106). Given his adversarial model and his evident reluctance to reinforce the widespread identification of blacks with crime, it seems odd for Douglass syntactically to place "the enslaved people" in apposition (rather than opposition) to the slave "system" and its perpetrators. At midcentury the more common abolitionist gesture was, as Douglass had just done, figuratively to subpoena slave witnesses to testify against the perpetrators of slaveholding villainy before the popular tribunal. Moreover, the vast majority of the enslaved people were *not* on trial. Denied even perfunctory due process, most slaves, like Frederick and his comrades at St. Michael's, were subject to either private plantation justice or its extension, summary police power.[217]

Douglass's unexpected parallelism thus serves as a potent reminder that whereas the figuring of slave speech as testimonial was a distinctly antebellum phenomenon, the public positioning of "the enslaved people" as defendants had a much longer history in American law and print culture. With his counterintuitive claim that "the enslaved people are . . . on trial," Douglass suggests how print publication could make such a defensive posture a strategic position from which to "apprehend" African American rights, politically as well as philosophically. Such a civic agenda, of course, lay at the heart of the abolitionist slave narrative: presenting themselves as "eye-witness to the cruelty" of slavery, Douglass and other formerly enslaved activists asserted the civil personality so scrupulously obviated by the legal fiction of the slave's mixed character.[218] Figuratively challenging the increasingly widespread legal practice of restricting slave courtroom speech to confession (or the inculpation of fellow African Americans), their testimonial narratives broadened the forensic scope of the literary genre—the gallows narrative—that had for so long compounded even as it complicated the legal restriction of slave personhood to criminality.

Well aware of the legal and literary paper trail stretching out behind the black print subject, Douglass appreciated that to concede that "the enslaved people are also on trial" was to access a kind of literary due process. To address the bar of public opinion, even from the rhetorically disadvantageous position of defendant, was nevertheless to claim the hearing (fair or otherwise) that until very recently had been accorded primarily to the published speech attributed to black criminals. In a characteristic rhetorical flourish, Douglass's play on the word "apprehend" highlights that seemingly vulnerable defensive posture as a strategic literary stance. By publishing this, his second personal narrative in a decade, Douglass seeks to apprehend the rights of the enslaved by consolidating black civic presence in order to assert the civil personality requisite to citizenship.[219] With this brilliantly post-confessional gesture Douglass reverses the flow of African American legal-literary authority back to its source.[220]

Frederick Douglass published *My Bondage and My Freedom* less than a decade before the Emancipation Proclamation, at the cultural moment when the classic slave narrative is supposed to have heralded the fugitive's shedding of his chains upon entry into the republic of letters. But, by making a lengthy detour down the "pathway . . . of insult and mortification" and depicting Frederick and his co-conspirators "like felons," Chapter 19 points to the skeleton dangling in the closet of African American literary history. Retracing the steps of the black condemned on Execution Day, Douglass redirects the ritual's literary effects by broadening the culpable slave's recognized legal personhood into a newly political black print persona. Four years earlier, Douglass had summoned that civic selfhood when, citing his "duty" as an "American citizen," he announced his rejection of William Lloyd Garrison's view that the Constitution was a proslavery document.[221] It was this autonomous sense of selfhood that led Douglass in this revised edition of his textualized life to replace authenticating documents by white abolitionist leaders Garrison and Wendell Phillips with an endorsement from fellow black public intellectual James McCune Smith. Just as noteworthy, however, is the fact that Smith's introduction is *itself* prefaced by the unsigned "Editor's Preface" featuring Douglass's long letter stating his authorial intentions. With *My Bondage and My Freedom*, then, Douglass joined those autobiographers who, on both sides of the Atlantic, had in effect begun "acting as their own ordinaries—composing and publishing their own confessions, by their individual . . . authority, without the support of patrons."[222] Lest the comparison seem strained, we would do well to recall the indictment that leaped to Garrison's lips on learning of Douglass's apostasy. "There is roguery somewhere!" exclaimed the erstwhile patron of the man who, in print as in practice, was transforming himself from fugitive "American slave" into conscientious "American citizen."[223]

The question that emerges, then, is not how a slave was made a man by writing classic American literature—but, much more precisely now—how Douglass and his African American contemporaries could fashion themselves as full members of the imagined national and transatlantic communities conjured by Anglo-American print culture and thus as eligible citizens.[224] How could they so confidently presume to occupy a shared civic space with their imagined readers? How did they come to believe that writing and publishing personal narratives would enable them to make apprehensible, on several levels, the rights of their fellow African Americans, the enslaved people?

This book seeks more fully to address these and related questions by examining the criminal posture and the confessional voice that Douglass— indeed, the slave narrative genre—so painstakingly disavows. For, in an irony worthy of Douglass at his best, the same legal regime that made black person-hood legible primarily in terms of criminality itself acquired meaning in a popular print culture built on stories of individual encounters with law, from the popular colonial and early national gallows literature to antebellum trial accounts and fiction.[225] As unpropitious as they seem today, these were the indispensable legal and literary resources out of which African Americans in the early republic and then the Jacksonian era began to fashion black civic authority in print. As an important site for this newly civic African American public presence, nineteenth-century American print culture increasingly registered the extent to which the normatively white citizenry was implicated in the crime of slavery. It is in this sense that we can see a new national literature and the equally novel figure of an autonomous, authoritative black protocitizen emerging from the shadow of the gallows.

PART I

Chapter 1

Contracting Guilt: Mixed Character, Civil Slavery, and the Social Compact

> What, then, is the American, this new man?
> —J. Hector St. John de Crèvecoeur,
> *Letters from an American Farmer* (1782)

With respect to citizenship, the query posed by Crèvecoeur's fictional American farmer (himself a British colonist) would go formally unanswered from the Founding to the Civil War. Until passage of the Fourteenth Amendment (1868), the Constitution did not specify the terms of U.S. citizenship. Neither did it explicitly address the race slavery that, prior to Emancipation, stood in definitive opposition to citizenship.[1] Speaking on behalf of "We the People of the United States," the document distinguished "free Persons" from those tacitly racialized "other Persons" who were to be partially enumerated for purposes of taxation and representation—as well as subject to forced "Migration or Importation" and, being "held to Service or Labour," denied freedom of movement.[2]

If many in the young republic embraced the Aristotelian notion of democracy as "the form of government in which the free are rulers" (with the unspoken assumption that democracy encompassed an unfree, ruled class), their understanding of what it meant to be a citizen was more complicated than the *Politics'* "shar[ing] in governing and being governed."[3] Positioned within a civic continuum, citizenship for most Americans denoted active political participation less than recognized membership in the polity.[4] As Rhode Island-born blacksmith Benjamin F. Cornell put it when serving as delegate to New York State's 1846 Constitutional Convention, any American familiar with "the elementary principles of our political institutions" would acknowledge "the existence of the conditions of extrageneous alienage and the various stages of *quasi* citizenship intermediate between the condition of chattel slavery, and that of complete technical citizenship."[5]

Cornell, like the rest of "the people" represented by the U.S. Constitution, was heir to a western European political tradition where citizenship had signified not so much a specific set of political rights as disparate bundles of legal and civil duties and privileges that varied according to an individual's status, natal origin, residence, and economic standing, as well as familial and social affiliations.[6] During the colonial and early national periods, historian James H. Kettner argues, English understandings of subjectship, in which "bonds of personal allegiance" were rooted in "blood" and "land," came to be replaced by a notion of citizenship phrased in innovative contractarian "terms by which civil and political rights in the community were to be exchanged for support for republican principles, adherence to the Constitution, and responsible and virtuous behavior under enlightened forms of self-government."[7] This shift reflects the influence of social contract theory, which imagines people in a state of nature voluntarily compacting to form a polity. Centered on "the model of the naturalized subject," America's abstract concept of citizenship acquired greater corporeal specificity through the Naturalization Acts of 1790 and 1795: with their preliminary limitation of the eligible alien to the "free white person," the Acts racialized citizenship, at least among the foreign born.[8] Theoretically more inclusive than the common law's birthright citizenship, in practice the consensualist approach proved doubly ascriptive, denying some native-born inhabitants citizenship on the basis of their (or their ancestors') exclusion from the founding compact while simultaneously rendering them "noncitizens ineligible for naturalization."[9] For African Americans in particular, contractarianism posed a daunting hurdle to citizenship.

The few African Americans who did manage to attain recognition as state citizens in places like New York and Massachusetts found their access to a broader national citizenship (however ill-defined) stubbornly blocked. Even if judges had not been determined to ignore the applicability of Article 4 of the Constitution on precisely this point, free blacks' legal disabilities rendered them ineligible for protection under the privileges and immunities clause in the eyes of many authorities.[10] Pervasive legal restrictions on African Americans' full participation in civil society (to say nothing of the polity) thus became the pretext for denying the expansion of formal state citizenship into a more plenteous, substantive national citizenship.[11] From the passport office to the courtroom, political scientist Rogers M. Smith concludes, government officials and legal authorities "treated race as legally more basic than citizenship."[12]

In this way, municipal regulations, state statutes, court decisions, and constitutional conventions combined to offer a composite sketch of a normative American citizen characterized by his whiteness and masculinity.[13] If, in Jacksonian America, the comparatively full range of political rights accorded the white, male citizen had come to represent an important aspirational ideal, on the eve of the Civil War citizenship continued to be anything but monolithic, experienced by and assigned to different people in different ways. Decisive as the Supreme Court's culminating rejection of black citizenship was in *Scott v. Sandford* (1857), the panoply of concurring and dissenting opinions revealed a continued lack of consensus regarding the precise content of the citizenship from which African Americans were excluded.[14] Nevertheless, where questions of political belonging were concerned, the slippage from condition to race was frequent and all too easy. In the "broad sense of participation in political and social life," legal historian Ariela Gross concludes, "only white people could become—and were seen as *capable* of becoming—citizens."[15]

American writers rushed to fill the Constitution's awkward silence over slavery and citizenship. From Charles Brockden Brown to Ralph Waldo Emerson and Frederick Douglass, the republic's writers conducted an ongoing dialogue with the nation's founding legal documents.[16] Others found inspiration in controversial laws, as when the Fugitive Slave Act of 1850 prompted Harriet Beecher Stowe to write her bestselling *Uncle Tom's Cabin* (1852). The era's closely watched court cases resurfaced in numerous literary works, with *State v. Mann* (1829) fictionalized in Stowe's *Dred* (1856), and the *Creole* (1841) and *Amistad* (1841) cases looming behind Douglass's "Heroic Slave" (1853) and Melville's "Benito Cereno" (1855).[17] Plotting their narratives around such landmark legislation and litigation, these canonical authors answered the call for a distinctively American literature by meditating on the unique dilemmas faced by a slaveholding republic.

Unquestionably, the original Constitution's celebrated refusal to speak the name of slavery evinced a foundational reluctance to acknowledge racism's constitutive importance to the national compact. Just as revealing as the Framers' reticence on race and slavery, however, was the utter inability of state and local legislators and jurists to *ignore* black public presence. As abolitionists never tired of pointing out, statute books devoted what appeared to be inordinate attention to—and thus recognition of—African Americans as persons in their criminal capacity.[18] It is this contradiction that Publius seeks to resolve in *Federalist* 54. Making the provisional acknowledgment of slaves' legal liability as culpable persons a matter of doctrine, Publius reads in Article 1, Section 2 of the Constitution a local, state, and national consensus regarding slaves' "true character" that was as fictive as that character itself.[19] As if to remind us that it was not just "rights talk," but "responsibility talk" that filled the air in America's long nineteenth century, Publius (ironically) turns our gaze from legal and literary elites who dominated the national scene toward the less exalted figures who regularly participated in routine, local proceedings.

Printed locally and attributed to vagrants, servants, and slaves, the flimsy pamphlets and broadsheets prompted by Execution Day rituals did not, like the belletristic books and periodicals emanating from the urban Northeast, seek to found an enduring national literature. But, with their everyday allocation of legal responsibility, these gallows texts, too, answered Crèvecoeur's query. For, as these ephemera registered the culpability that mandated minimal, usually punitive, official recognition of personhood under law, they also helped limn the new American man in print. From the colonial Boston of convicted murderer Joseph Hanno to the antebellum Northampton of condemned slave insurgent Nat Turner, local, occasional inscriptions of black personhood contributed to a popular crime literature that, over the years, straddled a professionalizing legal culture and an industrializing print culture whose shared nationalizing tendencies only intensified their growing interdependency.[20]

This chapter commences the literary critical reorientation from constitutional to criminal constructions of black personhood and political belonging—from questions of rights to those of responsibility—by demonstrating how one of the nation's guiding civic myths, that of the social compact, worked productively at cross-purposes with the legal fiction of the slave's mixed character.[21] Punitive recognition of slave personhood by local jurisdictions increasingly amounted to a retroactive, formal acknowledgment of the criminous slave's membership in the polity.[22] Complicating both recent Black Founders scholarship and an emergent necropolitical narrative of Afro-diasporic subjectivity, the chapter contends that because the fiction of slaves' mixed character located their personhood in their punishable acts, criminality formed the conceptual basis for that legal person's expansion into the modern liberal citizen.

To clarify the logic of this counterintuitive claim, we begin with a discussion of how the sovereignty of the U.S. citizen lay in the constitutive "inclusive exclusion" of the enslaved (to adapt the influential phrasing of philosopher Giorgio Agamben's *Homo Sacer*).[23] Slaves' abandonment by the founding compact was, as early national and antebellum literature illustrates, most vividly evident in the summary, often private, punitive measures to which they were subject. From a literary survey of the treatment meted the merely transgressive (as opposed to the criminous) slave, we turn to consider how the slave's mixed character as incapacitated civil subject and culpable legal person was discursively applied to the growing free African American population over the course of the protracted First Emancipation. Meliorist commentaries on slavery by Noah Webster, Thomas Jefferson, and St. George Tucker reveal how the early national racialization of crime and criminalization of race precluded free African Americans' smooth passage into the polity. Because the limited personhood ascribed to blacks under slavery was literally and definitively *un*civil, it could not, in freedom, automatically be enlarged into the civil standing upon which political qualification for citizenship rested. Consigned to what Tucker termed "civil slavery," free African Americans collectively were held to lack the requisite civil personality to convert the slave's fractional, culpable legal personhood into political membership. (This explains why African Americans' unremitting efforts to make the transition from slavery to citizenship through conventional displays of civic virtue, whether understood in classical republican terms as disinterested public service or in the liberal sense of exemplary industry, could not ultimately succeed on their own.)[24] Surprisingly, the solution to this dilemma lay neither in covert acts of transgression nor in public performances of virtue, but in publicized criminality. Under the terms of the social compact, punitive recognition of the slave's legal personhood amounted to tacit acknowledgement of his (retroactive) membership in the polity. The legal fiction of the slave's mixed character perversely resuscitated the legal personhood of the criminous slave, inadvertently countering the necropolitics that would consign slave and convict to separate civil deaths. Furnishing the condemned with civic presence, early America's popular crime literature created the further opportunity for the literary, public performance of black civil personality.

Like All Other Persons?

If Crèvecoeur's American farmer initially replies to his own question by affirming in Letter III that the new American man "is either an European or the descendant of an European," his provocative query finds its most decisive answer in Letter IX's unflinching display of what an American man is *not*.[25] As he passes through "a pleasant wood" en route to dinner with a Charles-town planter, Farmer James hears "a sound resembling a deep rough voice" forming "a few inarticulate monosyllables" (177). It is "a Negro, suspended in [a] cage and left there to expire" (178). The "birds," we are told, "had already picked out his eyes; his cheek-bones were bare; his arms had been attacked in several places; and his body seemed covered with a multitude of wounds. From the edges of the hollow sockets and from the lacerations with which he was disfigured, the blood slowly dropped, and tinged the ground beneath" (178). When James scares off the scavenging birds with a blast of his gun, "swarms of insects covered the whole body of this unfortunate wretch, eager to feed on his mangled flesh and to drink his blood." Recounting how the "living spectre" begged for water "in his uncouth dialect," James reflects: "Humanity herself would have recoiled back with horror; she would have balanced whether to lessen such reliefless distress, or mercifully with one blow to end this dreadful scene of agonizing torture! Had I had a ball in my gun, I certainly should have dispatched him." (Upon receiving the water, the slave himself pleads, "Tanky you, white man; tanky you; puta some poison and give me.") Having finally "mustered strength enough to walk away," James learns "that the reason for this slave's being thus punished was on account of his having killed the overseer of the plantation" (178–79). The "laws of self-preservation," James is instructed, "rendered such executions necessary" (179).

Set before the Revolution and published upon its conclusion, this grim tableau distinguishes the literary farmer *as* "American" from the caged slave. Inspired by the grotesque scene, James's prefatory "melancholy reflections" on the nature of human evil affirm that he is, in Aristotlean terms, "a political animal" whose verbal skills enable him not merely to indicate "pleasure and pain" as "other animals do" but to articulate "the just and the unjust."[26] By contrast, the "uncouth dialect" of the "inarticulate" slave reduces him to mere existence, devoid of political agency.[27] ("A state," Aristotle maintained, "exists for the sake of a good life, and not for the sake of life only; if life only were the object, slaves and brute animals might form a state, but they cannot, for they have no share in happiness or in a life based on choice.")[28] As James appreciates, to kill such a creature in an act of mercy is not to commit murder but to affirm one's own "humanity."

Crèvecoeur's caged slave is revolutionary America's *homo sacer*: he whom, in Agamben's terms, "*it is permitted to kill without committing homicide and*

without celebrating a sacrifice."[29] Unable to lay claim to the politically qualified life of his master and Farmer James, he exists in an exceptional state of
"bare life."[30] Uniting in a social compact to form the new republic, the *Letters'*
emblematic Carolina planter and Pennsylvania farmer would neither recognize slaves as citizens nor bar them as foreigners.[31] Present at the Founding
without being a party to it, slaves stood on the threshold of the politico-
juridical order whose sovereignty is constituted by their abandonment.[32] For
this reason, legal scholar Devon W. Carbado argues, it is a mistake to see
blacks as having been barred from American society or consigned to second-
class citizenship. Rather, their intelligibility *as* Americans resides in their
constitutive exclusion: "American identity" refers to "the capacity, as a racial
subject, to be a representative body—figuratively and materially—for the nation."[33] With its subtitular designation of the author as "an American Slave,"
Douglass's 1845 *Narrative* encapsulates this contradictory phenomenon.[34] The
operative distinction is not between the normatively white American and the
black alien, but between the *Letters'* "American . . . man" and the *Narrative's*
"American slave"; this is why Douglass makes it his literary project to show
how (American) slave became (American) man. What was at stake in the
transformation from one position to the other was not national identity but
legal personhood, civil standing, and political membership.

It makes sense, then, that Douglass and other antislavery authors should,
like Crèvecoeur, define this new (African) American man as sovereign
subject against a black *homo sacer*—in Douglass's case, the slave Denby. A
"powerful young man, full of animal spirits," and "among the most valuable
of Col. Lloyd's slaves," Bill Denby, Douglass recounts in *My Bondage and My
Freedom*, resisted a flogging from the overseer, Austin Gore, by submerging
himself in a creek and disobeying orders to come out—"whereupon, for this
refusal, *Gore shot him dead!*"[35] Gore, Douglass adds, "was continued in his
office on the plantation. His fame as an overseer went abroad, and his horrid
crime was not even submitted to judicial investigation. The murder was committed in the presence of slaves, and they, of course, could neither institute
a suit, nor testify against the murderer" (202). Because "his bare word would
go further in a court of law, than the united testimony of ten thousand black
witnesses," Douglass explains, "all that Mr. Gore had to do, was to make his
peace with Col. Lloyd. This done, and the guilty perpetrator of one of the
most foul murders goes unwhipped of justice, and uncensured by the community in which he lives" (202). Killed not by Col. Lloyd, his legal owner, but
by Gore, Lloyd's employee, Denby embodies "the one with respect to whom

all men act as sovereigns."[36] Just as the inarticulate caged slave affirms Farmer James's status as "an American," Denby's silent dissolution marks Frederick's own transition from one among masses of legally unrecognized "black witnesses" to the nation's foremost authorial "eye-witness" to the crime of slavery.[37]

Foils for antebellum print culture's nascent African American protocitizen, black *homines sacri* are ubiquitous in the abolitionist writing that bespoke America's new literary independence even as it took up the well-established "mortuary politics" of British antislavery rhetoric.[38] In *Uncle Tom's Cabin* (1852) the wraith-like Prue is locked in a cellar all day as punishment for drinking, with the result, as slave rumor would have it, that "the *flies had got to her,—* and *she's dead!!"*[39] "Sketches of Neighboring Slaveholders," the chapter that reformer Lydia Maria Child urged Harriet Jacobs to add to the manuscript for *Incidents in the Life of a Slave Girl* (1861), tells the story of James, who, "receiving the treatment of a dog" under his new master, flees, only to be recaptured and subjected to "hundreds of lashes."[40] This punishment deemed "too mild for the poor slave's offence," James is "cut with the whip from his head to his feet, then washed with strong brine," and finally "put into the cotton gin, which was screwed down" (48–49). When "a horrible stench came from the gin house" four days later and "the press was unscrewed, the dead body was found partly eaten by rats and vermin" (49). In all three accounts, as in *My Bondage and My Freedom*'s "Run-Away Plot," the offending slaves are, as objects of property, subjected to private plantation justice. Denied due process for their own offenses, they are dispossessed of the legal personhood that would mandate their publicly authorized punishment under law. Killed with impunity outside the official rites of legal execution, Crèvecoeur's caged slave, Douglass's Denby, Stowe's Prue, and Jacobs's James each represents "a life that may be killed by anyone—an object of a violence that exceeds the sphere both of law and of sacrifice."[41]

These scenes of extralegal plantation justice, in which the slave offender dissolves into nature following a killing that is neither a murder nor an execution, are the antithesis of the elaborate legal rituals by which, from classical antiquity through the mid-nineteenth century, animals and inanimate objects were punished for taking human life.[42] (Think of *The Merchant of Venice*'s "wolf . . . hang'd for human slaughter" on "the gallows.")[43] Ritual hangings of "infanticidal swine" and the like expiated wrongful death through due process of law and its attendant ceremonies.[44] Part of a Christian tradition centered on human life's transcendent value, such sacrificial legal rites affirmed the political as well as spiritual worth of the condemned creature.

Suffused with animal imagery, these fictional and firsthand accounts of slaves' transgressions and punishments illustrate how *homo sacer* stands at "a threshold of indistinction and of passage between animal and man, *physis* and *nomos*, exclusion and inclusion."[45] The figure of *homo sacer* challenges social contract theory's mythic rendering of the state of nature's chronological priority to the civil state by illustrating how the foundational gesture of the ban instead incorporates the state of nature into the polity as "a state of exception" betokening its dissolution.[46] These slaves, assigned animal attributes or consumed by vermin, are subjected to extravagant punishments that, in their extralegality, invoke the absent presence of law—as made explicit by each author's recourse to juridical terminology. Exhibiting "animal spirits" and treated like dogs, the slaves lack political qualification for personhood, and through their extrajudicial deaths are reabsorbed into the surrounding nature, from the creek into which Denby's "mangled body" sinks, to the birds, insects, and rats that feast on the caged slave, Prue, and James.[47]

It is in its manifestation as bandit (one who is banned, banished, outlawed) that *homo sacer* comes to legal as well as literary life in American print culture.[48] Since the colonial period, slaves could be consigned to "the ultimate alienation" through a legal proclamation of outlawry placing them "completely outside the law" in the extralegal zone of force and thus allowing them to "be killed by anyone."[49] Even more than the African Americans sweepingly designated by Chief Justice Taney's obiter dictum in *Scott v. Sandford* (who, as defendants in criminal proceedings, would still have received formal due process and custodial protection), "outlaws had no rights others were bound to respect."[50] In her *Key to Uncle Tom's Cabin* (1853), Stowe quotes a notice from the Wilmington *Journal* affirming that "any person or persons may KILL AND DESTROY" outlawed slaves "by such means as he or they may think fit, without accusation or impeachment of any crime or offence for so doing, and without incurring any penalty or forfeiture thereby."[51] Stowe, whose subsequent novel *Dred* dramatizes the outlawing of the noble, Douglass-like slave Harry, finds "an inkling of history and romance about the description of" a runaway slave "who is thus publicly set up to be killed in any way that the negro-hunters of the swamps may think the most piquant and enlivening."[52]

Affirming the sovereignty of even the lowliest member of society, outlawry statutes were particularly important in establishing extra-constitutional (and thus highly controversial) police powers in the face of an amorphous black security threat. As Stowe's newspaper clipping illustrates, such enactments address themselves to citizens, not the outlaw; so doing, critic Bryan Wagner has demonstrated, such enactments signal the difference between preventative summary police powers and the punitive due process of criminal prosecution. Accompanied by "the foreclosure" of the black subject's "point of view," this simultaneously legal and journalistic "suspension of recognition" rejects the formal presumption of innocence—to say nothing of the corollary commitment to distinguish acts from intents—and thus even the fractional legal personhood accorded the accused criminal.[53] The dehumanization of the black outlaw throws into relief the personhood accorded the criminous slave. (Killed with impunity, such outlaws, Vincent Brown observes, nevertheless acquired a "significant afterlife" through their entry into "popular history," resurfacing as romantic antiheroes and noble dying negroes.)[54]

Whether abandoned or banned by law, the black *homo sacer* embodied the civil death of the slave. Articulating America's exceptional legal metaphysics of (non)personhood, Bouvier's *Law Dictionary* defines a "slave" as "a man who is by law deprived of his liberty for life, and becomes the property of another."[55] In the nation's first legal lexicon, Enlightenment contractarianism finds a rationale in the new liberal contractualism: the slave "has no political rights, and generally has no civil rights," given that "he can enter into no contract, unless specially authorized by law" and that "what he acquires generally, belongs to his master."[56] The effective denial of civil rights to the slave renders him dead in law, as indicated by Bouvier's entry for "death." Whereas "natural death" is "the cessation of life," civil death "is the state of a person who, though possessing natural life, has lost all his civil rights, and, as to them, is considered as dead"; thus, "a person convicted and attainted of felony, and sentenced to the state prison for life, is . . . to be considered as civilly dead."[57] The fictive quality of this death in law confirms that the slave, like the prisoner, is *not expelled from but included in* the polity by which he is mortified. Contrary to making him a "double outlaw," conviction brings the criminous slave *into* law.[58] After all, the word "civil," Bouvier explains, citing Montesquieu, Blackstone, and Story, acquires its meaning "in contradistinction to *barbarous* or *savage*, to indicate a state of society reduced to order and regular government; thus we speak of civil life, civil society, civil government, and civil liberty."[59] No barbarians at the gate, the civilly dead slave and prisoner are incapacitated legal insiders.

However exposed and threatened by the constitutive legal abandonment that mandated their exclusion from the political status of "free Persons," American slaves did not, as we have seen in *Federalist* No. 54, lack the potential for legal personhood. Madison's elaboration of the slave's mixed character under state laws, published in defense of the federal constitution's three-fifths clause, separates slaves' lack of civil standing ("classed with those irrational animals which fall under the legal denomination of property") from their recognized legal personhood (punitively "regarded by the law as a member of the society, not as a part of the irrational creation"). Acknowledging the fictive nature of slaves' legal status as property, Madison locates slaves' residual legal personality in their roles as "protected" victims and "punishable" offenders.

Madison's assertion that, in his legally recognized status as victim, the slave was "regarded by the law as a member of the society" would seem to belie portrayals of the enslaved *homo sacer*. The oft-repeated but largely optimistic claim that slaves were protected "against the violence of all others" in their capacity as persons was challenged by Madison's fellow legal publicist, William and Mary law professor St. George Tucker. In his "melancholy review" of Virginia legal history from 1669 to 1788, Tucker concluded that, for the enslaved, "even the right of personal security, has been, at times, either wholly annihilated, or reduced to a shadow" by law.[60] The relevant statutes, Tucker explained, provided that "if any slave resist his master, or others, by his master's orders correcting him, and by the extremity of the correction should chance to die, such death should not be accounted felony: but the master or other person appointed by his master to punish him be acquit from molestation: *since it could not be presumed that the prepensive malice, which alone makes murder felony,* should induce any man to destroy his own estate."[61] By Tucker's account, victimization historically had led to legal nullification—rather than legal recognition—of even the resistant slave's personhood: the deadly "correction" administered by the master or his agent effectively restored the slave's property status as part of the master's "estate"— as that which may be killed without being murdered.[62] Those instances when slaves were legally protected from assault thus served further to reinforce their property status.[63] Moreover, because slave ownership solidified masters' social status and legal standing, economist Jenny Bourne Wahl notes, "assaulting a slave, like damaging any valuable property, tended to carry far more serious legal consequences than assaulting a free person."[64]

Misleading as they were, claims for the enslaved victim's legal personhood were a necessary rhetorical expedient in a society whose laws' authority derived from contractarian principles. Tucker's original scenario recalls the "death-contract" Locke envisions the slave having struck with his master: "whenever he finds the hardship of his slavery outweigh the value of his life, it is in his power, by resisting the will of his master, to draw on himself the death he desires."[65] However contradicted by Locke's own role in legislating New World slavery, the *Second Treatise* recognized as legitimate slaves only those "taken captive in a just war," and not those unjustly conquered or consigned to hereditary slavery; on the contrary, it was precisely the denial of legal recourse to particular individuals or groups that Locke found justifiably instituting a state of war within the polity.[66] The same logic that made the authorities reluctant to treat slaves as internally alien enemies led Madison and legal commentators to insist on legal protection of slave victims in their capacity as persons.[67]

In any case, the *Federalist* constructs the slave's legally recognized agency as persons exclusively in terms of punishable criminal acts ("violence committed against others"), with victimhood presented as a purely passive condition (in which the slave is "protected . . . against the violence of all others").[68] Depriving the slave of most of the rights and privileges that for the legal person had, in the Roman tradition, become tantamount to citizenship in even its most attenuated form, this preliminary reduction of the slave's legal personhood to the anti-civic acts of the criminal precludes its enlargement into liberal citizenship. "If the laws were to restore the rights which have been taken away," Madison avers, "the negroes could no longer be refused an equal share of representation with the other inhabitants." Fictive as the liberal citizen that emerged from the expanded legal person may have been, it is precisely such citizenship that Madison's counter-fiction of the slave's mixed character seeks to obviate. Rendering the slave civilly incompetent and restricting his or her recognized agency as a person to punishable criminality, the fiction effectively foreclosed the civil standing that at once enabled and was affirmed by citizenship.[69]

In keeping with his professional agenda, Madison's tidy legal fiction obscured a messier legal-historical reality, as a centralized rights-regime replaced the patriarchal colonial legal order. In early America the slave's legal personality did not necessarily rest on a sharp theoretical distinction between his or her civil incapacity (as property) and criminal responsibility (as person).[70] "It was not the universal denial of personhood to slaves that distinguished slavery," notes historian Joanne Pope Melish, "but the assumption of power to deny it arbitrarily or, . . . to ignore, sanction, encourage, or even demand personhood if such a position served the purpose of the slaveowner or the state."[71] This "instrumental alternation between person and thing," what Dayan calls the slave's "retractable personhood," enabled the sovereignty of American citizens by facilitating the broader constitutive dialectical oscillation in the three-fifths clause's partially suppressed racial provisions.[72]

Publishing an avowedly sectional defense of the proposed federal constitution in the New York press, Madison effectively nationalized slaves' "mixed character" ("in fact their true character") even as he grounded that newly doctrinal character in the emergent opposition of civil to criminal agency. The retractability of slave personhood, what proslavery Georgian legal treatise writer Thomas R. R. Cobb would call the slave's "double character of person and property," was particularly apparent in criminal cases against slaves.[73] In order to explain how "the law, upon high grounds of public policy, pretermits, for a moment" the master-slave relationship, Tennessee Supreme Court Justice William B. Reese in *Elijah, a Slave v. The State* (1839) vividly described how such a proceeding restored the defendant's personhood: it "takes the slave out of the hands of the master, forgets his claims and rights of property, treats the slave as a rational and intelligent human being, responsible to moral, social and municipal duties and obligations, and gives him the benefit of all the forms of trial which jealousy of power and love of liberty have induced the freeman to throw around himself for his own protection."[74] This amnesiac withdrawal of the slave from the circuit of private property relations activates his relationship with the broader public as an individual member of the polity.

For Louisiana attorney George S. Sawyer this legal move offered the perfect rebuttal to abolitionist outrage. "One of the most hideous features of the American system . . . in the estimation of anti-slavery people," he acknowledged, "is, that it is termed chattel-slavery; that it makes merchandize of human beings, and reduces men to mere things."[75] In his *Southern Institutes* (1859), Sawyer patiently explained to lay readers that "the idea of a person becoming property, a mere chattel or thing, as a brute, a bale of merchandize and the like, is but a fiction of law, for mere form or convenience, that has no counterpart in reality" (312). He went on to prove that "the person of the slave is not subject to ownership from the fact that he is individually held amenable to law; which, if he violates, he is taken from the control of the master and punished; *like all other persons*, he must atone for a transgression of the law by suffering the penalty, and all the master can claim from the civil authorities is remuneration for the loss of his services" (313; emphasis added). Unintentionally echoing the three-fifths clause, Sawyer highlights the (literal) terms of slaves' inclusive exclusion in the nation: euphemistically designated by the Constitution as "all other Persons" (as opposed to "free Persons") in civil contexts of taxation and representation, slaves are nevertheless held criminally responsible "like all other persons" in the polity.

Rendered Highly Criminal

The agonizing gradualness of the First Emancipation ensured that this coupling of civil incapacity with criminal culpability would be extended to free blacks in the early national North. This state of affairs was not inevitable. Since the early seventeenth century free blacks throughout colonial America had been active in civil as well as criminal proceedings, obtaining documentation for their property and debts, notarizing their wills, suing and being sued, testifying, and petitioning, even in the post-*Dred Scott* South.[76] By the 1850s, however, the legal limitations on black political belonging were such that Frederick Douglass could reference the common allegation that blacks were "unconscious of their wrongs, and do not apprehend their rights," and Chief Justice Taney could assert that "they had for more than a century before been regarded as . . . so far inferior, that they had no rights which the white man was bound to respect."[77] Regardless of individual status, collectively African Americans were understood to lack the political membership, and often the civil personality, that even the most limited forms of citizenship presupposed. When, upon emancipation, African Americans finally attained formal freedom and the corresponding recognition of their capacity as responsible civil actors, critic Saidiya Hartman finds, "the guilty volition enjoyed by the free agent bore an uncanny resemblance to the only form of agency legally exercised by the enslaved— . . . criminal liability."[78]

The possibility that African Americans, rather than metamorphosing from property into citizens, might instead mutate into a permanent class of social outsiders within the polity—criminals, in fact—had its roots in the classical republican model of citizenship. The slave, characterized by Aristotle as "the reverse of independent," lacked the liberty that enabled civic virtue.[79] Kant, writing as the First Emancipation was occurring, included among those who "lack civil personality" and thus find "their existence . . . only [in] inherence" not only minors and "all women," but those who filled the service occupations to which, in the early national North, free blacks were largely constricted.[80] The correlation between personal independence and political membership was further intensified by the American Revolution's rhetorical rejection of enslavement to England.[81] With the rare exception of figures like privateer-turned-Philadelphia entrepreneur James Forten, free African Americans could not convincingly exhibit the independent virtue that for Aristotle had called into question the slave's unfree status and, by extension, exclusion from the *polis*.[82] The widespread tendency to group all blacks together regardless of condition had the further effect of racializing the lack of autonomy that defined slavery.[83] Seen as "freed" rather than "free," as "acted upon, not acting," in the context of civil society and the state, blacks appeared to even the most sympathetic Northern whites as dependent and potentially disruptive social outsiders.[84] Proof that African Americans were perceived not simply as noncitizens, but as "'anticitizens' to be excluded from civic affairs" were Republican and Federalist attempts to reveal the opposing party's lack of virtue by portraying "blacks in the service of the other"—by publishing hoax "Negro" letters to the editor or by artificially inflating black participation in parades and other celebrations.[85] In early racial identity cases, Gross has found, it was "civic performance" more than biology that was held constitutive of whiteness: "a person who was *not* white was presum[ed] incapable of performing the acts of civic participation that white men performed."[86]

During the long prelude to the Revolution this perception of blacks as profoundly uncivil, anti-civic threats to American society was already sufficiently established to provide a single, capacious frame for competing accounts of the events leading to the Boston Massacre. On the same page as it memorializes "Crispus Attucks, a molatto, killed on the spot, two balls entering his breast," *A Short Narrative of the Horrid Massacre in Boston* (1770) lists as one of the more grievous impositions of the British troops "Cap't Wilson's . . . exciting the negroes of the town to take away their masters lives and property, and repair to the army for protection."[87] Whereas in the patriot pamphlet the specter of black criminality passed among less threatening visions of African American dependency and martyrdom, it was central to John Adams's successful defense of the British soldiers in *Rex v. Wemms* (1770). "This Attucks," Adams noted in his summation, "appears to have undertaken to be the hero of the night; and to lead this army with banners."[88] Lest his audience be deceived by this appearance of militant patriotism, Adams insisted that "if this was not an unlawful assembly, there never was one in the world" (268). Rather than a paragon of republican virtue, Attucks becomes, in Adams's account, "a stout Molatto fellow, whose very looks, was enough to terrify any person" and "to whose mad behaviour, in all probability, the dreadful carnage of that night, is chiefly to be ascribed" (269). Rather than leading an act of organized political resistance, Attucks and Irish leather worker Patrick Carr merely "sally out upon their thoughtless enterprizes, at the head of . . . a rabble of Negroes" (269).

In the new nation, this tendency to incriminate African American political activity and thus to view black public presence as inherently anti-civic would only intensify with the gradual abolition of slavery in the Northern states.[89] With free African Americans standing as both cause and effect of disorder, "accusations of 'disturbing the public peace' and 'disorderly conduct' against people of color increased dramatically between 1784 and 1830."[90] Just as the Thirteenth Amendment would simultaneously abolish slavery in the United States and authorize a new, penal form of bound servitude in the convict-lease system, the First Reconstruction legislatively eased the transition from enslavement to imprisonment in the early national North. Although the criminous slave was legally liable for his or her crimes in most jurisdictions, private plantation justice, the police power, and summary magistrates' proceedings made more formal legal prosecution comparatively rare.[91] Following the First Emancipation, many African Americans for the first time became legally visible subjects on the landscape of criminality.[92]

The transition from enslavement to racial criminalization was strikingly apparent in Pennsylvania, where the trend was, in effect, institutionalized. A decade after enacting the nation's first abolition law in 1780, Pennsylvania passed legislation authorizing the country's first modern state prison, the Jail and Penitentiary House at Walnut Street in Philadelphia. Upholding Section 4 of the Act for the Gradual Abolition of Slavery, which terminated the separate criminal justice system for defendants of African descent and subjected them to the same procedures and punishment as the state's other inhabitants, the 1790 Act's principled colorblindness ironically directed greater scrutiny toward black criminality, due to African Americans' disproportionately high incarceration rates.[93] The prison's outsized black presence provoked comment by numerous contemporary observers.[94] Notorious white felon Ann Carson published an 1822 memoir recounting "her Sufferings in the Several Prisons"—not least of which, from her perspective, was the fact that "blacks . . . formed a large majority of our female republic" in Walnut Street Prison's women's wing.[95] When the Pennsylvania State Penitentiary for the Eastern District opened in 1829, "Prisoner Number One" in the world's most closely watched penal experiment was eighteen-year-old Charles Williams, a literate black farmer from Harrisburg sentenced to "two years confinement with labor" for the theft of "one twenty-dollar watch, one three-dollar gold seal," and "a gold key."[96] And when the first female prisoners were received in 1831, all four were African American.[97]

Free African Americans' increased visibility on the criminal law landscape underwrote efforts to rationalize and articulate what had hitherto been amorphous racial fears and impressions. In his *Effects of Slavery on Morals and Industry* (1793), intended to demonstrate the virtues of gradual emancipation over immediatism or colonization, Noah Webster parsed (and ultimately affirmed) the logic that associated blacks, through their collective servitude, with crime. Blackness, asserted the abolitionist author of early America's ubiquitous Blue-Backed Speller, or *Grammatical Institute of the English Language* (1783–85), was rapidly becoming a synonym for crime. Noting that "*oppression is the mother of crimes*," Webster traced "*villain* and *knave*," words denoting criminality, back to their "ancient" designation of, respectively, the "bondman" and the "domestic servant."[98] Given "*the proneness of men in a degraded sphere of life to contract vicious habits*," the lawyer and lexicographer explained, the meaning of words that "anciently conveyed no idea of dishonesty, more than *bondman* and *servant* do now," was transformed through "the complete transfer of their signification from the destination of the *persons*, to their *properties*" (10). (As Douglass and his fellow bondsmen suspected, the slave could "own nothing" but guilt.) Webster found his environmentalist etymology "verified by the general character of the negroes in the United States of America," notably their propensity for social disorder (12). "Destitute of that openness of character that marks the wild freedom of savages" in Africa and elsewhere, "the blacks in this country, are, with few exceptions, addicted to the practice of committing little clandestine frauds," he observed (13). Moreover, "a large proportion of capital crimes, will on examination, be found to be perpetrated by the same race of men," Webster contended, noting that "not a year passes, but we hear of the burglaries, the rapes, or the murders committed by the blacks in the United States" (13). Webster thus rationalizes the inevitable linguistic conflation of criminal conduct and black character by referring to anecdotal impressions of disproportionate criminality among the black "race of men" that could in turn be proven "on examination." In the process, he alerts us to the way in which race became an interface for the celebrated disciplinary technologies employed in the early national North's new penitentiaries and the biopolitical

techniques targeting recently emancipated blacks for governmental management as a deviant population that posed a security threat.[99]

It was the (unsuccessful) attempt to encompass the new disciplinary
strategies within the existing legal order of sovereignty, Michel Foucault suggests, that informed Enlightenment articulations of social contract theory.[100]
And indeed, Webster's allusion to blacks' propensity *"to contract vicious
habits"* recalls Thomas Jefferson's attribution of slaves' criminality to their
exclusion from the social compact: "that disposition to theft with which they
have been branded," Jefferson maintained in *Notes on the State of Virginia*
(1784), "must be ascribed to their situation, and not to any depravity of the
moral sense."[101] Attributing slaves' lawlessness to their political outsidership,
the Sage of Monticello did not seek to redress this state of affairs by incorporating free blacks into the polity through a revised social contract.[102] Instead,
like so many of his contemporaries, he marshaled fears about the lingering
environmental impact of slavery on black character, manifested not only as
dependency but as criminality, by advocating their more absolute exclusion
through mandatory emigration. Such colonizationist discourse depended
upon a logic of deferral that, while acknowledging African American civic
potential, maintained that the fulfillment of black citizenship—which itself
would finally fulfill the revolutionary promise of American liberty—could
only occur at some future date, outside the United States.[103] What remains
unremarked, however, is the extent to which imputations of black criminality framed early national visions of a future American republic unclouded
by slavery.

Emblematic as the *Notes'* tidy exchange of white immigrants for black
emigrants may be of Jefferson's penchant for mathematical social engineer-
ing, it is his fellow Virginian St. George Tucker's *Dissertation on Slavery
with a Proposal for the Gradual Abolition of it, in the State of Virginia* (1796)
that offers valuable insight into the process of emancipation as it was actually unfolding in the North.[104] If Tucker enthusiastically participates in what
David Kazanjian terms Jefferson's "colonizing trick," his scheme displays far
greater dexterity in the racial sleight of hand by which it was to be accomplished.[105] Read against Jefferson's more famous plan to establish "a free and
independant" black colony, St. George Tucker's proposal is distinguished by
the means by which it would induce voluntary black migration.[106] The difference lay in the "encouragements" Tucker deemed "proper."[107] Beginning with
two widely held premises, the antidemocratic nature of bound servitude and
the desirability of a free white republic, Tucker seeks to remove from the

nation "a stigma, with which our enemies will never fail to upbraid us, nor our consciences to reproach us" (11), while at the same time offering relief from "those apprehensions which are naturally excited by the detention of so large a number of oppressed individuals among us" (41). Once again, these ends are to be accomplished through the removal of blacks themselves. But Tucker rejects the *Notes'* plan, and direct colonization in general, as impractical and expensive. Moreover, sharing Jefferson's misgivings about blacks' capacity for self-governance, Tucker suggests that, unlike "European emigrants," who "have been accustomed to the restraint of laws, and to respect of government," blacks, "accustomed to be ruled with a rod of iron, will not easily submit to milder restraints" and would doubtless "become hordes of vagabonds, robbers and murderers" (86).[108] In light of these concerns, Tucker advances a plan to encourage African Americans' voluntary, gradual colonization through unapologetic governmental repression of black civil liberties.

Defining civil liberty as "natural liberty so far restrained by human laws, and no farther, as is necessary and expedient for the general advantage of the public" (18), Tucker reduces it to, essentially, "the right of personal security; the right of personal liberty; and the right of private property" (49). Tucker, drawing on Blackstone's *Commentaries*, finds civil slavery occurring wherever civil liberty is "further restrained than is necessary and expedient for the general advantage," noting that such civil slavery may either "affect the whole society" or occur "whenever there is an inequality of rights, or privileges, between the subjects or citizens of the same state" (18). Distinguishing, as Montesquieu did, among political, civil, and domestic slavery, Tucker differs from him (and Webster) in classifying American race slavery under the final rather than the penultimate term.[109] In this redefinition, domestic slavery is "that condition in which one man is subject to be directed by another in all his actions," a state in which "all the incapacities and disabilities of civil slavery are incident, with the weight of other numerous calamities superadded thereto" (22). Whereas political slavery was "the state of united America before the revolution" and domestic slavery is that of blacks currently in bondage, civil slavery, "notwithstanding the maxims of equality which have been adopted in their [the states'] several constitutions, . . . exists . . . in the persons of our free Negroes and mulattoes; whose civil incapacities are almost as numerous as the civil rights of our free citizens" (17, 19).

For Tucker the denial of the civil rights of personal liberty and private property to the slave illustrates "how perfectly irreconcilable a state of slavery is to the principles of a democracy" (50). In practice, this theoretical state

of affairs has only been worsened by the fact that, in Virginia legal history
at least, "even the right of personal security," the last vestige of civil liberty
normally allowed to the slave, "has been, at times, either wholly annihilated,
or reduced to a shadow" (57). Consideration of slaves primarily in their legal
capacity "as a distinct class of *persons*, whose rights, if indeed they possess
any, are reduced to a much narrower compass" leads Tucker to their imputed
criminality (49). Requiring slaves to function within this more restricted
range of legal activity, law criminalizes behavior normally deemed civil.
"Many actions, indifferent in themselves, being permitted by the law of nature to all mankind, and by the laws of society to all free persons," Tucker
notes, "are either rendered highly criminal in a slave, or subject him to some
kind of punishment or restraint" (57). The *Dissertation*, delivered at William
and Mary as "part of a course of Lectures on Law and Police," understands
slave criminality as the product neither of blacks' innate moral depravity, nor
of slavery's corrupting influence, nor even of slaves' exclusion from the social
compact, but, in effect, as itself a legal fiction (i).

Restoration of civil liberties to former slaves was not the remedy, however. Far from it. In Tucker's view, the greatest danger posed by immediate
large-scale emancipation was its potential to convert legal fiction into social
reality. Rather than being nullified by freedom, black criminality would become a historical inevitability thanks to slavery's corrosive impact on both
personal character and race relations. Hence the need to "find some middle
course, between the tyrannical and iniquitous policy which holds so many
human creatures in a state of grievous bondage, and that which would turn
loose a numerous, starving, and enraged banditti, upon the innocent descendants of their former oppressors" (90). When Tucker turned briefly to
consider slaves in their legal capacity as property (rather than persons), he
found further reason for such a middle course. Acknowledging the perennial
tug-of-war between the slaveholder's property rights and the slave's natural
right to liberty, Tucker grants greater pull to the latter, admitting that the
"claims of nature . . . are stronger than those which arise from social institutions, only" (81). With the caveat that "nature also dictates to us to provide for
our *own* safety, and authorizes all *necessary* measures for that purpose," however, Tucker cautions that "our own security, nay, our very existence, might
be endangered by the hasty adoption of any measure for the *immediate* relief
of the *whole* of this unhappy race" (81–82).[110] Even the most benevolent legislator had a responsibility to ensure public security and safeguard the existence of the republic by circumventing the social disorder that the sudden,

practical realization of a hitherto fictive black criminality would doubtless occasion.

To prevent this eventuality, Tucker advocated the strategic institutional-ization of the largely ad hoc civil slavery to which the small number of free people of color had already been consigned. In Virginia, "we have seen that emancipation does not confer the rights of citizenship on the person eman-cipated; on the contrary, both he and his posterity, of the same complexion with himself, must always labour under many civil incapacities" (75). Allud-ing to Jefferson's account of black inferiority and following the logic of the state constitutional convention in 1776, Tucker agues that social contract theory permits blacks' "exclusion from a society in which they have not yet been admitted to participate in civil rights; and even to guard against such admission, at any future period, since it may eventually depreciate the whole national character" (89).[111] On this consensualist basis, Tucker decisively re-jects the common assumption that "in abolishing" domestic slavery "we must also abolish" its "scion," civil slavery (88). Noting, moreover, that the "experi-ment so far as it has already been made among us, proves that emancipated blacks are not ambitious of civil rights," Tucker offers an eight-point plan that, by replacing bound servitude with institutionalized civil slavery, would "prevent the generation of such an ambition" in free blacks (90). Tucker's proposal, which combines the usual schedules for gradual emancipation, apprenticeship, and registration with detailed provisions for the curtailment of African American civil liberty, resembles contemporary mid-Atlantic legislative initiatives to attach repressive black codes to abolition bills.[112] Such pernicious legislative pairings would permit "the creation of an order of citizens, who are to have no legislative or representative share in the govern-ment"—or so New York's Council of Revision predicted as it rejected one such act, explaining that it "necessarily lays the foundation of an aristocracy of the most dangerous and malignant kind, rendering power permanent and hereditary in the hands of those persons who deduce their origin through white ancestors."[113]

But rather than an insidious side effect, such a hierarchically racialized civil order was the *purpose* of Tucker's plan. What preserved his scheme from the "dangerous and malignant" antidemocratic tendencies of the New York bill was the fact that any emancipated domestic bondman-turned-civil slave who did become "ambitious of civil rights" would have recourse to migra-tion: "Possessing the liberty of loco-motion, which was formerly denied him, it is in his choice to submit to that civil inferiority, inseparably attached to his condition in this country, or seek some more favourable climate, where all distinctions between men are either totally abolished, or less regarded than in this."[114] Civil slavery and emigration would alike be voluntary in the new Virginia. "By denying" free blacks "the most valuable privileges which civil government affords" and thereby endeavoring "to render it their inclination and their interest to seek those privileges" elsewhere, Tucker could retain a principled opposition "to the banishment of the Negroes" while gratifying the shared "wish not to encourage their future residence among us."[115] The trick (a warm-up for Kazanjian's "colonizing trick") was to ratify the continued banning of blacks from the social contract by decoupling emancipation from civil standing and freedom from equality. Through such racial legerdemain, emancipation would lead not to African American citizenship but to black civil slavery as (ideally) a first step toward voluntary emigration and the consolidation of a free white republic.

Tucker, like Jefferson, devised his emancipation and colonization scheme for his home state. His reference to preserving the integrity of (a free, white) "national character" serves as a reminder, however, of the well-established precedent for making Virginia a model for the larger American republic. More to the point, as discussed in Chapter 3, many in the North shared not only Tucker's sense of the national dilemma posed by slavery but his appreciation of the need for any solution to that dilemma to grapple with the perceived problem of black criminality. Tucker's proposal differed from Northern schemes for emancipation and reconstruction not in its colonizationist impulse (which many Northerners would share well into the nineteenth century), nor even in its provocative injunction to replace so-called domestic slavery with its civil analogue, but in the frankness with which it would pursue such an attenuation of black civil liberty. Where Northern reality departed from the Virginian's fantasy was in its piecemeal, largely informal implementation of what came to look like Tucker's civil slavery: a form of civil inferiority that was authorized by grounding blacks' alleged incapacity for citizenship in their imputed criminality. Envisioning an idealized future for slaveholding Virginia, Tucker came close to describing the emancipating North's strained present. Forty years later, reviewing civil restrictions on free African Americans in his *Commentaries on American Law* (1836), chancellor of New York James Kent observed that "the African race," even when free, "are essentially a degraded caste, of inferior rank and condition in society."[116] Released from the state of bondage, these undeniably "human creatures" could be prevented from becoming Tucker's "numerous, starving, and enraged banditti" by being reduced to a state of de facto, if not de jure, civil slavery.

From Status to Contract?

Jefferson and Tucker appreciated the philosophical as well as political threat posed by slavery to a republic whose authority derived, at least in part, from the notion of the social compact. By the late eighteenth century, slavery had become an indispensable, if sometimes indecipherable, touchstone for contractual logic. Slaves were widely held incapable of entering into valid contracts; conversely, self-possessed individuals were believed incapable of contractually binding themselves into slavery.[117] "As soon as compact enters," Locke affirmed, "slavery ceases."[118] Tellingly, however, Locke made this assertion to rebut the persistent argument that slavery itself was contractual in nature, a condition arising from legitimate self-sale for either protection or maintenance.[119] For a later generation, the notion of enslaving so as to maintain the self surfaced in protests against the Industrial Revolution's new "wage slavery."[120] Further complicating the opposition of bondage to contract was the scattered state legislation permitting free African Americans to sell themselves into slavery and the recognition, both formal and informal, accorded some slave contracts.[121] After the Civil War, restrictive labor contracts extended bound servitude beyond the Emancipation Proclamation and the Reconstruction Amendments.[122]

Despite these contradictions, early national and antebellum Americans widely understood emancipation to enact modern Western society's broader shift *"from Status to Contract,"* in Sir Henry Maine's classic formulation.[123] Evoking the enduring Enlightenment myth wherein individuals in the state of nature compact together to form a law-bound polity, Maine's decidedly Victorian thesis also reflected assumptions of nineteenth-century contract law.[124] Contract promised to usher in an era of consensualism that would extinguish not only hereditary status but the coercion, sentimentalism, and paternalism that accompanied it, introducing in its place transitory exchange relationships characterized by volition, consent, and, above all, self-ownership.[125]

In such a climate, depictions of black contractualism spoke to much more than African Americans' business acumen. Appreciating the indispensability of property ownership (especially property in oneself) not only to emancipation but to civil standing, free blacks sought to prove their eligibility to sign on to the social contract through (usually liberal) displays of virtue. "The reader may here see," the Preface to the *Narrative of the Life and Adventures of Venture, A Native of Africa* clumsily promised, "a Franklin and a Washington, in a state of nature, or rather in a state of slavery."[126] If the scarcity of chances for military valor or disinterested public service prevented most blacks from patterning themselves on the republican model of Washington, they had ample opportunity to display the exemplary industriousness exhibited by Franklin.[127] Smith's "narrative," the anonymous Preface observes, "exhibits a pattern of honesty, prudence and industry, to people of his own colour," pointedly adding, "perhaps some white people would not find themselves degraded by imitating such an example."[128] If enslaved "black Ben Franklin[s]" from Smith and Equiano to antebellum businessmen Lunsford Lane and Moses Grandy could accumulate significant personal wealth through their conscientious fulfillment of their economic commitments, then surely, as free men, they would be qualified to sign on to the larger social contract.[129]

Yet contract almost inevitably failed to live up to its epochal promise. Just as emancipation did not guarantee entry into the social compact, contractualism was not necessarily liberating for the enslaved.[130] Seeking to release themselves from commodity status, former slaves in their personal narratives negotiated the fault line between the actual legal contracts that conferred free black personhood and the mythic social compact that would confirm black political membership. Entrepreneurial slave narratives' portrayals of black contractualism almost inevitably culminate in, and are thus belied by, the trope of the self-purchase fraud: those repeated scenes where the industrious slave scrupulously pays to emancipate himself, only to be betrayed by his white owner or treasurer.[131] The self-purchase fraud blocks the narrative trajectory wherein slave becomes free man through virtuous industry, thereby revealing, in Edlie Wong's words, "the hermeneutic limit of an emergent liberal discourse of contract premised on universalized notions of will and free choice in a partially free world."[132] In mounting such a critique of liberalism, however, the trope effectively affirms the slave's civil incapacity and, by extension, his ineligibility to join the larger social compact as an autonomous legal person. For, beyond cruelly depriving the slave of his hard-earned funds and viciously exploiting his hopes for freedom, the fraud exposes the false premise underlying *all* the preceding transactions. Due to the enslaved businessmen's lack of civil standing, their agreements with whites are grounded not in self-interested mutual consent but in the latter's honor, pity, or deceit. Rather than demonstrations of the slave's competence to enter into contractual relations, these subsidiary agreements turn out to be status relations in disguise.

However illusory, such "contracts" sometimes achieved their purported ends. Like Smith, both Grandy and Lane recount purchasing their own freedom, as well as that of family members. But even successful contractualism tended to perpetuate rather than terminate the black subject's identification with property. Ensnaring their narrators in what Philip Gould calls the "epistemological trap" of liberalism, these entrepreneurial narratives depict the conundrum of a free status acquired through contractual relations which, even as they emancipated the quondam slave, reinforced the newly freed man's prior (and thus ongoing) equivalency with the consideration—property—exchanged for his or her manumission.[133] Stymied in his attempts "to convert himself," through property relations, "out of the Madisonian paradox in the *Federalist*," the industrious early black autobiographer "never fully narrates his life out of it."[134]

By the same token, the contractual exchange of slavery for freedom inhibited as much as it enabled freedpeople's belated entry into the polity. In the personal narratives of Equiano and Smith as well as of fellow black mariners Briton Hammon, John Jea, Boston King, and George Henry, this trace element of materiality is what ensures the political exclusion of even free blacks in a world where citizens, not unlike commodities, were defined by their abstract interchangeability.[135] Having been once exchangeable for other commodities, their national or ethnic identities reduced to "mere product labels," free blacks could never quite lay claim to the dematerialized political fungibility of citizens.[136] Their own rights claims even more evidently "born of the market" than those of the bourgeois citizen, they could not enact what Julie Stone Peters sees as their white counterparts' "double and contradictory move" of identifying those rights "as autonomous from the market."[137]

The vexed history of race and contract documents the difficulty encountered by blacks, both enslaved and free, in gaining recognition as civil persons and thus as members of the polity, whether in *potentia* or in actuality. Rather than being swept, as legally free persons, into the broader stream of American political life, African Americans in the early national and antebellum United States found themselves caught in the riptide of liberal and classical republican understandings of citizenship. Under such conditions, they could fight the current through displays of civic virtue, but their exertions could not ensure political survival. No matter how industrious, pious, heroic, or disinterested, black founders' virtue could not stop Americans from seeing free blacks collectively as the slaves many had once been or the criminals whites feared most were destined to become. To appreciate this point, one need only to consider (as Chapter 3 does in greater depth) that microhistory of black civic virtue, Absalom Jones and Richard Allen's *Narrative of the Proceedings of the Black People*, published to refute Matthew Carey's widely circulated *Short Account of the Malignant Fever*, which, rather than honoring Philadelphia's black nurses and carters for their valiant public service during the yellow fever epidemic, instead charged them with extortion and "plundering."[138] The dilemma can be traced to the "Madisonian paradox" articulated in *Federalist* No. 54 and embedded in the nation's founding legal document. Just as Article 1, Section 2 was integral to the federal constitution (as both political process and textual product), the fiction of slave character was a key clause in the racial contract materialized therein.[139] The definitive (albeit fictive) restriction of slave agency to punishable criminality made such local demonstrations of black civic virtue practically illegible in law and popular print culture.

Their civil personality compromised by their ongoing identification with racialized human property and their public acts construed as criminal rather than civic, free blacks in the early republic seemed destined perpetually to tarry at the threshold of citizenship, affirming others' political qualification through the denial of their own. But if the doctrine of the slave's mixed character impeded even free blacks' entry into the polity as virtuous or self-possessed citizens, the combination of this foundational legal fiction with the civic myth of the social contract inadvertently created an opening for imagining a more capacious black personhood.[140]

Contracting Guilt

Punishment stood at the definitive core of contractarian understandings of the polity. The central terms of *Federalist* No. 54's elaboration of the slave's mixed character—property and punishment—had been the hallmarks of Locke's *civitas*. Although Locke is celebrated for defining the protection of property as the compact's impetus, the *Second Treatise*'s definition of "political power" foregrounds punishment. Locke opens the second part of his rebuttal to Robert Filmer by distinguishing "political" from other forms of power, glossing it as the "right of making laws with penalties of death . . . and of employing the force of the community in the execution of such laws" (along with devising and enforcing lesser property laws and protecting the commonwealth from external threat).[141] The derogation to the commonwealth of punishment, primarily capital punishment, separates the polity from the state of nature, with the authority to execute such a penalty constituting political power. Over a century later, Kant would concur that "the mere idea of a civil constitution among human beings carries with it the concept of punitive justice belonging to the supreme authority."[142] If we amend conventional readings of social contract theory in which "the state is narrativized as guaranteeing the citizen's right to property" to emphasize how the state is first and foremost narrativized as deriving from the punishability of its citizens, we see that culpable subjects are at least as constitutive of the polity as "propertied subjects."[143]

Discussing criminal responsibility in his *Commentaries on the Laws of England* (1765–69), Blackstone refers in passing to "the capacity of doing ill, or contracting guilt."[144] This revealing apposition, legal historian Holly Brewer notes, serves as a reminder that "guidelines for accountability were defined during the same era as guidelines for political participation and political rights" and that "questions of accountability for crime and of membership in the political community were asked and answered in the same breath."[145] In his 1790–92 law lecture series for the College of Philadelphia, James Wilson, who like St. George Tucker aspired to be the American Blackstone, observed that the "science" of criminal law (not unlike the new nation) was "as yet, . . . in a weak and infantine state."[146] Nevertheless, Wilson based society's right to punish individual offenders more firmly in the social contract than his English counterpart.[147] In keeping with the contemporaneous shift toward calculating criminal responsibility on the basis of intent rather than proximate cause or status, Wilson locates "the true meaning of felony" in "the principle and disposition from which it proceeds," the intention to deceive society (1101). Noting that "without mutual confidence between its members, society . . . could not exist," Wilson identified "this mutual and pervading confidence . . . as the attractive principle of the associating contract." Whereas "to place that confidence in all the others is the social right, to deserve that confidence from all the others is the social duty, of every member"; conversely, "to entertain a disposition, in which that confidence cannot with propriety be placed, is a breach of the social duty, and a violation of the social right: it is a crime inchoate." Thus, "when an injury, atrocious in its nature, or evil in its example, is committed voluntarily against any one member, the author of that voluntary injury has, by his conduct, shown to all, that their right is violated; that his duty is broken; that they cannot enjoy any

longer their right of placing confidence in him; that he entertains a disposition unworthy of this confidence; that he is false, deceitful, and treacherous:
the crime is now completed." Through his careful elaboration of *mens rea* and
actus reus as crime's component parts, Wilson locates the authority to punish
felony in the social contract: the other members of the compact punish the
offender when, by actively breaking his social duty through the commission
of an injury, he violates their right to confidence in him.[148] Without such
contractual reciprocity, "society . . . could not exist."

But, of course, the punishment of the slave offender is the exception that
proves Wilson's contractarian rule. The purpose of the legal fiction of slave
character was to remove the enslaved as civil actors from the circuit of reciprocal relations that inaugurated and maintained the polity. The criminally responsible slave is held accountable for his breach of social duty in the marked
absence of the corresponding civil right to place such confidence "in all the
others." Montesquieu, whom Wilson cites on a different point of criminal
law in the same lecture, addresses this very issue in *The Spirit of the Laws*
(1748). "What makes the death of a criminal lawful is that the law punishing
him was made in his favor," he explained, citing the example of the murderer
condemned by the same law whose deterrent effects had hitherto preserved
his own life. "It is not the same with the slave," Montesquieu insists: "the
law of slavery has never been useful to him; it is against him in every case,
without ever being for him, which is contrary to the fundamental principle
of all societies."[149]

Unlike Montesquieu, to whom the slavery of the "Negroes in [the French]
colonies" must have seemed a distant phenomenon, Wilson lived in—and, as
Founder, helped to create—a polity in which slavery was omnipresent.[150] (The
Slaveholder-in-Chief, President Washington, attended Wilson's inaugural
lecture.) And yet the nation's first legal expositor does not address the complications posed to contractarian criminal law by the slave's anomalous status
as both culpable legal person and civil nonentity. Given that Wilson does not
even paper over the difficulty with the usual claims about legal protection for
slave victims, his silence might be seen as yet another instance of the kind
of willful oversight that frequently characterizes the lectures' treatment of
slavery. But, here, in "Of the Nature of Crimes; and the Necessity and Proportion of Punishments," to acknowledge the slave's mixed character would be to
raise troubling questions about a legal regime unauthorized by or exceeding
the social contract. Better to preserve the ties that bind society—and which
legitimate law's punitive measures—than to defend the equally fictive (and

contradictory) basis of the criminally responsible slave's civic exclusion. As philosopher Charles W. Mills observes of the actual, historical "racial contract" and the mythic social contract it encompasses, although "the nonwhite subset of humans" cannot be "genuinely consenting" participants, "it may be sometimes politic to pretend that this is the case."[151] Wilson's law lectures for the new nation offered an occasion for such expediency. If the price of such politic pretense was the retroactive, tacit recognition of the criminous slave as a member of the polity, so be it.

Wilson's lecture series ends with an unsettling image of the citizen-turned-condemned criminal: upon sentencing, "law puts him out of its protection, considers him as a bane to human society, and takes no farther care of him than barely to see him executed: he is already considered as dead in law."[152] Conviction and sentencing in Wilson's account effectively affirm the offender's erstwhile political belonging by mandating his exemplary exclusion from the society of which he had previously held a right and a duty of membership. Typical of Foucault's late eighteenth-century "reforming jurists," Wilson and other exponents of contractarianism "saw punishment as a procedure for requalifying individuals . . . as juridical subjects."[153] Wilson's account of civil death echoes Rousseau's insistence that the condemned or banished former citizen loses his political qualification and effectively returns to bare life: "when the guilty man is put to death, it is less as a Citizen than as an enemy. The proceedings, the judgment, are the proofs and declaration that he has broken the social treaty, and consequently is no longer a member of the State. . . . for such an enemy is not a moral person, but a man."[154] A product of the social contract, the citizen as moral, or legally constructed, person fails to exist as such when his crime and punishment bring him into a state of civil death and thus to mere humanity.[155] But for the *Federalist*'s Publius, recall, it is precisely that punishment that acknowledges the slave as a "moral person." In Rousseau, the tell-tale phrase is "no longer" ("*n'est plus*"); for it is precisely in this eligibility for punishment that *The Social Contract* locates political freedom.[156] Although it may well result in civil death and exclusion, due process is what enables the citizen's freedom and affirms his membership in the state.

The condemned citizen's exceptional state of legal abandonment and civic exclusion bears a striking resemblance to that of the slave as *homo sacer*. For Kant, the convict's loss of civil personality was what authorized him to be consigned to prison labor and thus "reduced to the status of a slave for a certain time, or permanently if the state sees fit."[157] If the erstwhile citizen is reduced to civil death by his own breach of the social contract, what of the slave offender? Or those de facto civil slaves, free blacks? Unquestionably, as Brewer suggests, the eighteenth- and nineteenth-century reorientation away from status and proximate cause to intent in assessments of criminal accountability produced a double standard in which children, women, the poor, and the enslaved, "could not exercise political authority" but "could be punished regardless."[158] Yet however predictably it compounded African American civil incapacity, punitive recognition also had the unexpected effect of affirming black political belonging. Under the legal fiction of slave character, criminality formally marked slaves' movement out of the legal abandonment that characterized their position as *homines sacri* in the state of exception so fundamental to U.S. sovereignty. Temporarily released as a recognized legal person from property status, the criminous slave moved from private or summary penalty into the rule of law, repressive as the latter may have been. Rather than the commencement of the black felon's civil death, the period before execution could mark its suspension. As a prelude to Chapter 2's discussion of how print activated this dormant side effect of the black prisoner's seemingly redundant civil death, this chapter closes by clarifying how the fiction of slave character might open an unanticipated loophole in the founding inclusive exclusion of blacks from America's social contract.

Beyond the Death Contract

"Black lives are expendable, can disappear, click, just like that."[159] With these words, novelist and social critic John Edgar Wideman glosses the necropolitics of racial subjectivity for which the slave is the inaugural figure.[160] But that figurative "click," in its lethal, thoughtless immediacy, is exactly what sets black malefactors of gallows literature apart from the enslaved *homines sacri* and noble dying negroes with which they are often grouped. However significant, even ritualistic, the deaths of the latter may be, it is only the black condemned whose deaths are authorized by the opposite of Wideman's click: due process of law. Peremptory and unjust though that process may be in a white supremacist legal order, such procedural deliberation and public justification prohibit the expenditure of black life from taking the form of an instantaneous disappearance (however posthumously memorialized).

Due process serves this purpose because, as legal historian Mark S. Weiner has suggested, the hinge joining citizenship to a broader sense of civic belonging in America has been "the need for groups seeking full civic membership . . . to be widely perceived as being 'a people of law'" and thus "to overcome a perception of their legal incapacity."[161] Weiner maintains that "more than for any other racial or ethnic minority, the life and identity of black Americans have for centuries been inextricable from law and legal ideas."[162] Hence the persistent American fascination with what Weiner calls "black trials." As "legal events that figure symbolically and dramatically in American culture by making public certain basic ideological conflicts about race and civic life," black trials become referenda not simply on African American political inclusion, but on the meaning of American citizenship itself.[163]

Before and after the Founding, the execution of the condemned slave was unequivocally "the ritual killing following a death sentence."[164] Punished criminality inverted the slave's position from inclusive exclusion to exclusive inclusion. To be convicted and sentenced as a criminal with recognized legal personhood through due process of law was to gain entry into the polity, for contractarian logic derives the legitimacy of such punishment from the defendant's antecedent membership.[165] Retroactively inserting the enslaved accused into the social contract, the most perfunctory due process removed him from slavery's constitutive "death-contract."[166] It is in this sense that the thoughtlessly extinguished lives of slave victims like Denby and outlaws like Louisiana's Bras-Coupé—or even such martyrs as Crispus Attucks or Stowe's Christlike Uncle Tom—distinguished them from judicially executed malefactors like Cotton Mather's "miserable African," condemned murderer Joseph Hanno.

To perceive this distinction we need only adopt the perspective of Paul Revere on his famous midnight ride of April 18, 1775. In a close call, Revere encountered two British officers as he paused near Charlestown Neck, "nearly opposite where Mark was hung in chains."[167] Along with his fellow slave Phillis, Mark had been convicted of petit treason twenty years earlier in the poisoning death of his Massachusetts master, Captain John Codman.[168] After Mark was hanged in Cambridge on September 18, 1755, the Boston *Evening Post* reported the following week, his "Body . . . was brought down to *Charlestown* Common, and hanged in Chains, on a Gibbet erected there for that purpose."[169] Encased in bars of iron and exposed to dissolution by the elements, birds, and vermin, only to be symbolically restored as a landmark on Paul Revere's sovereign ride, Mark would appear to differ from Crèvecouer's caged slave only in his grotesque corporeal endurance. In 1758 Dr. Caleb Rea marveled that the dead man's "skin was but very little broken, although he had hung there near three or four years"; Rea's colleague Dr. Josiah Bartlett confirmed that "the gibbet remained till a short time before the revolution."[170] In fact, these offhand comments by decades of passersby point to the exemplary legal publicity that sets Mark's officially sanctioned death apart from those of black *homines sacri*.

Displayed in a gibbet on the Common rather than hidden away in a cage on an estate, Mark posthumously serves not only to terrorize the blacks held as private property by local slaveholders but to provide an object lesson to the larger society. "What sad and awful Scenes are these / presented to your View," begins *A Few Lines on Occasion of the Untimely End of Mark and Phillis* (1755), admonishing the observing reader: "Let every one Example take, / and Virtue's Ways pursue." Explicitly applying the lesson to "Servants black and white," the broadside concludes with a more expansive caution to "every Soul who views the Sight, / be careful how they View; / Lest while they do remain in Sin / Eternal Death pursue." Tragic as their lives may have been and horrifying as their ends undoubtedly were, the condemned, exemplifying both legal guilt and the possibility of spiritual redemption, were *homo sacer*'s diametric, indeed dialectic, opposite.[171] In the case of the criminous slave, and especially of the condemned slave subject to ritual killing by law and thus no longer in the exceptional state of one "who may be killed by anyone without committing homicide, but never submitted to sanctioned forms of execution," the role of exemplar (however negative) displaces that of *homo sacer*.[172]

Anything but thoughtless, the expenditure of black life recorded in *A Few Lines* is presented as the final stage in a coordinated theological and legal process:

> God's Vengeance cries aloud indeed,
>   And now his Voice they hear,
> And in an Hour or two they must
>   before his Face appear.
>
> To answer for their Master's Blood,
>   which they've unjustly spilt;
> And if not Pardon'd, sure they must,
>   Remain with all their Guilt.
>
> Their Crimes appear as black as Hell,
>   and justly so indeed;

And for a greater, I am sure,
   there's none can this exceed.

Three were concerned in this Crime,
   but one by Law is clear'd;
The other two must suffer Death,
   and 'tis but just indeed.[173]

Celebrated as a communal civic rite, the macabre state-sanctioned deaths of
Mark (drawn to the gallows, hanged, and then gibbetted) and Phillis (drawn
to the place of execution and burnt to death) prevent them from being *homines sacri*. Raising the legally, politically, and philosophically fraught question
of how slaves might "unjustly" spill "their Master's Blood"—what is justice to
a piece of property?—the broadside, like the trial, locates their personhood
in that very criminal act by holding them accountable for another's death.[174]
State-administered death, the procedural outcome of their culpability as
moral agents, confirms rather than negates their legal personhood.

In place of the punishment privately or summarily administered to the
disobedient slave by the citizen or the police, the legal proceedings invoked
here publicly authorize the purging of the slaves from a legally constructed
political community of which, as human property, they had not heretofore
been recognized members. Identifying the conviction and execution of
the malefactors as the necessary communal expiation of sin even as it acknowledges the rumor that Mark and Phillis's fellow slave Phebe escaped
punishment by turning state's evidence, the broadside locates the (thrice-
mentioned) justice of these particular black deaths in the due process denied
the martyr, the victim, and the outlaw.[175] The broadside strives to justify that
legal proceeding's lethal results to the same community it seeks to admonish with the slaves' exemplary deaths. After directly addressing the reader
regarding the "sad and awful Scenes / . . . presented to your View" and cau-
tioning, "here you see what Vice has done," the broadside joins its audience to
observe (however tritely) that "the Sight is shocking to behold, / and dismal
to our Eyes; / And if our Hearts are not o'er hard, / will fill us with Surprize."[176]
Like the ensuing display of Mark's juridically killed body on Charlestown
Common, the broadside stresses the black criminals' public visibility. More
than mere spectacle, such legally initiated publicity endows the condemned
slaves with the civic presence denied them as Captain Codman's property.
Under the combined fictions of slave character and the social compact, the

conviction and sentencing of the already civilly dead slave did not amount to a redundancy but rather a productive contradiction that, by exposing the fictive nature of the slave's nonpersonhood, created an unanticipated occasion for black civic presence. Crucially for our purposes, that presence is manifest not only in the terrifying form of Mark's body rotting in irons on the Common but in the poetic broadside that finds in Mark and Phillis's crime evidence of their membership in the community of persons.

Conclusion

Because "to be 'free' instead of determined is to perceive oneself, or one's choices and actions, as causes instead of effects"—in other words, "to perceive oneself as an uncaused cause"—Thomas L. Haskell points out, "we stumble over the problem of freedom every time we attribute causal status to ourselves, other persons, things, conditions, or events."[177] By locating the slave's personhood in criminality, the legal fiction of mixed character necessitated a radical reassessment of classical republicanism's inclusive exclusion of the slave in the polity as "the reverse of independent." For Aristotle, the master-slave relation naturally assigns the dominion of him who can "foresee by the exercise of mind" (and therefore is "by nature lord and master") over "that which can with its body give effect to such foresight" ("a subject, and by nature a slave").[178] As James Wilson's emphasis on intent indicates, the slave's crime affirms his status as self-willed person rather than as "a living instrument" or "a living possession."[179] Under Wilson's revised definition of felony, the criminous slave's legal accountability not only registers his (belated, punitive) inclusion in the social contract but also acknowledges his possession of the foresight necessary to independent action.[180] The new emphasis on intent as consent's criminal analogue ironically liberates him (through his imputability) from being the tool of another—a slave, a human thing, a household object. For Kant the "capacity to set oneself an end" distinguished humans from other animals.[181] Suggestively, his inquiry into political philosophy begins by defining, in the context of that "*intentional transgression . . . called a crime,*" a "*person*" as "a subject whose actions can be *imputed* to him," in contradistinction to a "*thing,*" or "that to which nothing can be imputed."[182]

At the same time, by reducing contract's promise to sanction, the slave's mixed character and social contract theory together offer one way around liberalism's epistemological trap. In contrast to the virtuous industry that risked affirming the black subject's equivalency to the property exchanged for self-ownership, criminal accountability retroactively (albeit punitively) included the black self in the polity, endowing him with a presumptive prior political membership that shared its fictive origins with that of the (culpable rather than propertied) citizen-subject.[183] Holding the enslaved offender responsible for the autonomous agency that he, by definition, lacked, punishment of the criminous slave mandated a profound redefinition of the black subject.[184]

Undeniably, as with the temporary assignment of free will to (once and future) slaves in free jurisdictions, the dubious authority of an increasingly liberal legal system that nonetheless accommodated slavery was reinforced by the retrospective attribution of responsible personhood to enslaved criminals.[185] But in contrast to the freedom suits that presented such free will as either a legal fiction or the product of the slaveholder's actions (or, as was usually the case, both), here the agency originated with the enslaved person, retracting if not terminating his or her status as incapacitated thing. It bears noting, moreover, that the gradual legal reorientation from proximate cause to intent coincided with the decline in the criminal prosecution of nonhuman agents. From the late eighteenth into the nineteenth centuries, in Anglo-American law as in continental philosophy, to commit a crime was to enact one's personhood as never before.

Reading the legal fiction of the slave's mixed character against the civic myth of the social contract, we begin to appreciate how for the enslaved and the free blacks so often identified with them as elements of social disorder, criminal responsibility offered a kind of access—however formal, punitive, and fleeting—to political membership. The very legal regime that allowed the slave to be killed, but not to kill, with impunity was, perversely, that which recognized his agency as a legal person—in the *Federalist*'s phrasing, "as a member of the society, not as a part of the irrational creation; as a moral person, not as a mere article of property"—and thus his potential for a politically qualified life. Given the repressive and largely theoretical nature of the condemned slave's retroactive entry into the polity, it is tempting to echo Dayan's grim observation regarding legal acknowledgment of the enslaved victim's personhood: "the dead slave gets the protection of positive law, but at great cost."[186] But a cost-benefit analysis of the punitive legal recognition dispensed to the condemned slave cannot renegotiate the terms by which the early black subject entered the public sphere.

Rather, this study seeks to assess how those terms shaped print articulations of African American subjectivity contemporaneously as well as over time. In the feedback loop of (African) American literary history, the fictive, theoretical construction of the black subject both under state laws and in national politico-legal discourse conditioned the African American and abolitionist refashioning of that subject in early national and antebellum print culture. Clearly, it was not enough for early black authors to "trade" their writing for recognition of "their humanity."[187] Nor was it sufficient for black founders to mount impressive displays of civic virtue. This was because the recursive interplay of early American law and print culture made it extraordinarily difficult for many in the early republic to perceive black publicity in civil rather than criminal terms. If the persistent incrimination of the black subject rendered criminality a uniquely viable alternative to virtue as a means of asserting personhood, it also meant that print was equally indispensable to the process by which culpable black personhood would be transmuted into African American civic presence, even civil personality.

Chapter 2

Black Catalogues:
Crime, Print, and the Rise of the Black Self

"Own nothing!" said I. *"Own nothing!"* was passed around
and enjoined, and assented to.
—Frederick Douglass, *My Bondage and My Freedom* (1855)

Writing for the abolitionist *National Era* newspaper five years after Harriet
Beecher Stowe's *Uncle Tom's Cabin* had debuted in its pages, prolific Southern novelist and death penalty critic E.D.E.N. Southworth concluded one of
her popular serialized "nouvellettes" with a tableau that vividly illustrates
the belated penal political membership accorded the enslaved condemned.[1]
"The Brothers" tells the story of Valentine, the cosmopolitan, Shakespeare-
reading, mixed-race slave who kills Oswald Waring, his half-brother, childhood companion, and now master, in a fit of enraged self-defense. When
Execution Day arrives, Valentine is joined on the gallows by his fellow slave
Governor, a "jet-black" naïf who has committed the equally justifiable crime
of killing an overseer in flagrante delicto with Governor's enslaved wife
Milly.[2] The "very high" scaffold, "reached by a flight of more than twenty
steps," has been "erected upon a gentle elevation" on the outskirts of the
Southern "city of M———."[3] Facing "a crowd of many thousands, each moment augmented," so as finally to become a virtual "forest of human beings,"
the men "stood in full view of every individual of that vast concourse of
people"—some of whom, at least, would have perceived a telling anomaly:
"The prisoners were not prematurely clad in the habiliments of the grave, as
is usual upon such occasions, but were attired in ordinary citizens' dress."[4]
With this one detail, Southworth captures how the rites of execution fleet-
ingly resurrect the civilly dead slave into political and civic life prior to his

bodily destruction. If Valentine and Governor had been the "usual" victims
of the gallows (that is, white male citizens), their sepulchral clothing would
mark the final stage in their descent from the civil death of the prisoner into
the physical death of those terminally excluded from the social compact. But
the unusual execution of a capital sentence upon slaves occasions a change in
the ritual's sartorial trappings. Governor, we are told, wears "his best Sunday
suit of 'pepper and salt' cassinet," while Valentine is clad in "a suit of black
broadcloth, with a white cravat and gloves." Possessed, if not owned, by the
quondam slaves, their clothing is transformed by the extraordinary occasion
into "ordinary citizens' dress," marking the men's corresponding metamorphosis into members of the polity, the requisite preliminary to their legally
authorized hanging.

Discrepancies in skin tone and education notwithstanding, the condemned men are united by their vestiture in the habiliments of citizenship,
from dark woolen suits to execution "cap[s]" and "cords." Yet, only for Valentine does this spectacular penal affirmation of political membership coincide
with the emergence of a personality that, without attaining civil standing,
nevertheless transcends formal legal personhood, achieving plenitude
through a pervasive civic presence. The divergence between the two men
is not spiritual in origin. Both are genuinely penitent, with Governor—as
romantic racialism would lead us to expect—the more expressively soulful
of the two. Rather, the unworldly Governor differs from his well-traveled
companion in his failure to realize and thus internalize the transformative
publicity of his apprehension and conviction. Misled by his own experiences
of slaveholding paternalism and the presiding judge's physiognomic display
of the profession's vaunted moral-formal dilemma, Governor confuses the
criminal trial's due process with the plantation's summary disciplinary measures.[5] "Ole marse up dere on de bench put a black nightcap on his head, an'
said somethin' 'r other 'bout hangin'," Governor acknowledges after his brief
trial, "but I reckon he only did it to scare me, 'case I saw by his face how his
heart was a *saftening* all de time." Unable to "understand one-half of what
had been done or said during the whole course of his trial," Governor cannot
apprehend, in Frederick Douglass's dual sense of the word, that the proceedings have formally converted him from human property into legal person
in order to hold him accountable for his crime. Thus, seeking to console
Valentine, Governor obstinately reassures him: "Dey's only doin' dis to scare
we! Sho! dey's no more gwine to hang *we*, nor dey's gwine to heave so much
money in de fire! Sho! we's too *walable* . . . ! I heern de gemmen all say what

fine walable men we was—'specially *me*! Sho'! *dere's* muscle for you!' said Governor, drawing himself up, jerking forward both arms . . . and then clapping his hands upon his nether limbs. 'Sho! *You* think dey's gwine to let all dat dere go to loss? . . . Sho! what de use o' dead nigger? What good dat do em?" In his self-commodification, Governor fails to follow up his forced removal from the plantation with a corresponding psychic departure from that enclosed, private economy. However much it may shield him from the terrors of the gallows, his inability to assimilate his new, definitively public status as person indicates a fundamental absence of selfhood. "It was known," the narrator recalls, "that *two* slaves were to be tried for similar offenses. But every one was interested in Valentine, and no one, except his master, seemed to care one farthing for Governor"—and with "no one except his master and Valentine . . . the least interested in him," Governor, "poor wretch . . . was not even interested in himself!"[6]

By contrast, Valentine becomes *a* self, if not more fully *him*self, through the public attention he attracts as first defendant and then convict. (The anonymous disinterestedness of this publicity is precisely what distinguishes it from the "care" manifested by Governor's master, whose benevolent paternalism mingles with economic self-interest to ensure that he cares a great deal more than a "farthing" for the fate of his "*walable*" slave.) Upon Valentine's apprehension, "the news of the arrest . . . spread rapidly over the city and surrounding country, creating everywhere an intense excitement" and drawing an ecumenical flock of clergymen to the "condemned cell" in which, with "slight irregularity" but "for greater security," Valentine has been incarcerated pending his trial.[7] As the days pass, this potentially ominous "excitement" coalesces in neither a lynch mob nor a rescue attempt, but in the sympathetic "local notoriety" accorded to the enslaved defendant.[8] "The better Valentine was known, the deeper this interest grew," notes the narrator, explaining how, "in advance of his trial, the press took up his case, and the papers were filled with accounts of visits that this or that gentleman had made him; conversations that one or another clergyman had held with him in his cell; and with descriptions of his good looks, graceful manners, intelligence, knowledge, conversational powers, and eloquence—all 'so remarkable in one of his race and station.'"[9] Yet, however much "it would seem . . . as if, unhappily, the good points of the unhappy young man had never been known or suspected, until crime had brought him prominently before the public," the very press coverage that acquaints the outside world with Valentine's personal strengths inhibits the self-knowledge that comes from penitential introspection. Although he had "already repented" well before his capture, Valentine's sudden celebrity "prevented the self-recollection and sobriety that befitted the solemnity of his situation."[10]

Constraining his inner self from fully preparing to quit its human tenement, this publicity delineates Valentine's print self in ever greater detail as Execution Day approaches. Upon sentencing, "again the papers were filled with this 'extraordinary boy,' as Valentine was called. Interviews held with him by clergymen were reported at length. His likeness was taken in prison, and wood-cutted in a pamphlet report of his trial," recounts the narrator, concluding that this remarkable "notoriety" was "ascribable, not to the nature of the catastrophe . . . but to the individuality and character of the condemned."[11] Any uncertainty as to whether Valentine's "individuality and character" originate in the flesh-and-blood human being or its print avatar seems about to be resolved when Valentine composes "an address that he wished to deliver upon the scaffold." "Intended to illustrate the mutual trials in the relation of master and slave" and comprising "experiences, as they are already known to the reader," this "address embodied a great portion of Valentine's life"; upon being "finished in manuscript, it was submitted to the perusal of the attendant clergymen," who either immediately "declared it . . . the most eloquent appeal they had ever met" or "afterward asserted that it was the most powerful Anti-Slavery sermon that they had ever seen or heard." But no one hears Valentine vocalize these hand-written—and carefully vetted—traces of his lived life. In anticipation of the hangings, we are told, "the authorities [had] published a card in the daily papers, formally inviting the masters of the city and the surrounding country to give their slaves a holyday . . . to enable the latter 'to attend the execution,'" but "so numerous was the multitude of negroes that gathered in from all parts of the country, and so great was the excitement that prevailed among them, that the powers saw the mistake they had made in issuing this general invitation, and felt great alarm as to the result." Fearing a "rescue," if not a full-scale race war, the marshal unceremoniously truncates the proceedings, abruptly dropping "the fatal trap-door" before Valentine can read "the manuscript address that he wished to make to the assembly."

Under pressure of the suddenly materialized—and ominously racialized—public sphere convened by print publication, Valentine's oral transmission of his manuscript autobiography is silenced by his abrupt demise. The personal life "embodied" in various paper texts and the notoriety "ascribable" to his "individuality and character" are now unambiguously lodged in a single scriptive self. And here the story comes full circle. From the outset the narrative premise of "The Brothers" has been to disclose the privately recounted "domestic tragedy" behind public events that "probably never got beyond 'mere mention' in any but the local papers."[12] But, unlike the oral narrative Othello offers in his own defense, the "round, *unvarnished* tale" the narrator offers as a supplement to the brief "item" in "the columns of a Southern paper" serves only further to figuratively flesh out the Valentine of that print milieu, whose personal life becomes "known to the reader" through a published—and thrice republished—newspaper novella.[13] Compounding, rather than stripping away, the accumulated layers of print, the story merely reconstitutes the condemned man's public persona, affirming the inaccessibility of its human referent.

With "The Brothers" Southworth demonstrates how the tenuous legal person recognized by even the most racially compromised due process could expand, through the medium of print, into the abundant civic presence of the notorious black criminal.[14] As the negative example of Governor underscores, publicized legal proceedings were insufficient to accomplish this augmentation; it was print publication, combined with official recognition accorded by the criminal trial, that credited the black offender with personhood—indeed, an individualized personality—in the eyes of "the public" as well as those of the law.[15] Attuned to how the black condemned were, in Cotton Mather's words, "puffed up" by their ostensible participation in print culture, Southworth shows an equally canny appreciation for the subtle ways the rites of execution could at once differentiate condemned African Americans from their racial opposites and identify them with those white citizens.

Well over a century of hindsight informs the novella, whose belated quality seems as apparent to its author as it would have been to the *National Era*'s subscription list. "The execution was to be a public one," clarifies the narrator to readers who by 1856 might well have presumed otherwise.[16] As we shall see, however, "The Brothers" was not alone in having its condemned black protagonists tarry on the scaffold as their white literary counterparts retreat into the confines of the penitentiary. In order to understand what was accomplished by keeping the culpable black subject "in full view" of the antebellum reading public, this chapter provides the legal-literary backstory to Southworth's vivid gallows tableau by analyzing the transformative effects of broadsides and pamphlets attributed to African American criminals from the colonial period through the Jacksonian era.

(Temporarily) leaving behind the idealized world of the nineteenth-century romance for the grittier one of early American scaffold confessions, we find that it was typically property crime, not principled acts of violent resistance, that made the man. Personal narratives attributed to condemned African Americans skirted liberalism's epistemological trap by distinguishing the legally responsible narrator from the chattels that circulate through gallows texts. Like the clothing of the condemned in "The Brothers," the same popular crime ephemera that usually charted the normatively white citizen's declension into civilly dead convict could also plot the black print subject's extraordinary ascension from the civil death of the slave (or the civil slavery of the free African American) into legal personhood. At times, first-person articulation of individual black selfhood could even fill out this meager guilty legal personhood with an incipient civil personality. To be the narrator of one's own historical life is to claim responsibility for and authorship of that life.[17] However ventriloquized, first-person black subjectivity would acquire greater interiority and authenticity as, with greater and greater specificity, it voiced its accountability to a print culture increasingly concerned with the individual self. Accordingly, whereas incrimination in print set the black condemned apart both from other first-person black subjects in colonial and early national America and from the more generalized, mythic Africanist presence of the nation's founding literature, the gallows tradition's increasingly interiorized, responsible black self contrasted sharply with a guilty white citizen-subject whose lack of accountability revealed the fictive nature of normative civil selfhood.

Tempting as it is to begin to illustrate these claims with an exceptional work like the exuberant transatlantic rogue's narrative, *Sketches of the Life of Joseph Mountain, A Negro* (1790), this chapter instead begins by reading *The Life, and Dying Speech of Arthur, a Negro Man; Who Was Executed at Worcester, October 10, 1768. For a Rape Committed on the Body of One Deborah Metcalfe* (1768).[18] This typically brief, formulaic broadside, standing at the furthest remove from any plausible black consciousness, offers a worthy test case for the death of the condemned black author. The value of the confession attributed to Arthur lies not in its revelation of an authentically transgressive black self nor in its illumination of the fraught dynamics of textual collaboration across lines of race, class, and condition. Rather, *The Life, and Dying Speech*, like so many other works of black gallows literature, acquires literary historical significance for the way that it repositions the (newly individualized and responsible) black print subject within the property relations that structured both personhood and chattelhood in early America.

With hangings and other forms of punishment moving indoors, gallows texts like those attributed to Arthur and Joseph Mountain were no longer elicited by public Execution Day rituals. But, as Southworth's midcentury novella illustrates, the black condemned did not vanish from the American printscape with the rise of the penitentiary; they persist in a range of antebellum texts, from the era's sensational crime ephemera to Herman Melville's "Benito Cereno." As it turned out, the era's penal reform and antislavery movements only furthered the divergent civic trajectories of incriminated black and white subjects. For when the captive black protagonist finally did step down from the scaffold, he did not follow his white counterparts into the new genre of prison writing. Instead, as Chapter 4 considers in greater depth, he reappeared in that other literary innovation of Jacksonian America, the slave narrative.[19] It was by lingering on the gallows in the waning days of public execution, the current chapter argues, that the black print persona attained the requisite civic presence to authorize his reemergence in the slave narrative as African American protocitizen.

Black Catalogues

Here, then, is Arthur as he nears the end of his criminal career—and his life:

> On . . . the 30th of March 1767, [I] was discovered, and committed to *Worcester* Goal, where I continued 'till the 20th of April following; at which Time I broke out with the late celebrated *FRASIER*, and a young Lad, who was confined for stealing. After which, at *Worcester*, we broke into a Barber's Shop, from whence we stole a Quantity of Flour, a Comb, and a Razor: We then set off for *Boston*. At *Shrewsbury*, we stole a Goose from Mr. *Samuel Jennison*; and from the Widow *Kingsley*, in the same Place, we stole a Kettle, in which we boiled the Goose, in *Westborough* Woods. At *Marlborough*, we broke into a Distill-House, from whence we stole some Cyder Brandy: In the same Town we broke into a Shoe-maker's Shop, and took each of us a pair of Shoes. . . . At *Watertown* we stole a Brass Kettle from one Mrs. *White* of that Place. My Companions now left me; upon which I went to Mr. *Fisk's* in *Waltham*, who knew me: And having heard of my Escape from *Worcester* Goal, immediately secured me, and with the Assistance of another Man, brought me back again, where on the 17th of September following, I was tryed and found guilty. Upon which,

by the Advice of my Counsel, I prayed for the Benefit of the Clergy; which after a Year's Consideration, the Court denied me: And accordingly I was, on the 24th of Sept. last, sentenced to be hanged, which I must confess is but too just a Reward for my many notorious Crimes.[20]

The *Life, and Dying Speech* provides a wealth of historical data. Like much early gallows literature, this account refers to people, places, and events likely familiar to its readers from local press coverage, gossip, or personal acquaintance—and thus not easily susceptible to outright fabrication.[21] It describes the mid-eighteenth-century movements and activities of an escaped Massachusetts slave and offers information about specific households, their inhabitants, and their contents.[22] Particularly noteworthy is Arthur's literacy, his recourse to legal counsel, and the interracial collaboration of "persons in low circumstances" (to quote the words attributed to Arthur's better-known colleague in the popular *Brief Account of the Life, and Abominable Thefts of the Notorious Isaac Frasier*, published the same year).[23] Clearly, early American crime literature has a great deal to offer historians in American and African American studies.[24]

But this same passage also indicates why literary critics, notably African Americanists, find these early texts far less appealing.[25] For one thing, notwithstanding the broadside's first-person voice and Arthur's earlier claim to have learned to write as well as to read before running away, we can be excused for wondering whether the man hanged for raping Deborah Metcalfe actually wrote or even narrated this text. His closing acknowledgment that his hanging "is but too just a Reward for my many notorious Crimes" sounds less like the slippery, twenty-one-year-old jail-breaking repeat offender portrayed here than the clerical and state authorities who helped produce Execution Day rituals. This admission, along with Arthur's stated reluctance to close his "Narrative, without gratefully acknowledging the unwearied Pains that was taken by the Rev. Mr. *McCarty*" to prompt Arthur's "own sincere Endeavours after true Repentance" suggests that we might better look to the Reverend, not the condemned man, as the source of this text.[26] Indeed, this portion of the confession recalls the tripartite Puritan sermon's final, "application" section: the repentant Arthur expresses his "earnes[t] desire that this Recital of my Crimes, and the ignominious Death to which my notorious Wickedness has bro't me, may prove a Warning to all Persons," particularly admonishing "those of my own Colour . . . to avoid Desertion from their Masters, Drunkenness and Lewdness."[27] And in fact, McCarty's colleague, the Reverend Aaron

Hutchinson of the Church of Christ in Grafton, quoted these very lines from Arthur's "printed confession" in his own "Sermon Preached . . . the Sabbath after the Execution of Arthur, a Negro Man."[28] Even if it is Arthur's voice we hear in the broadside, we can be excused for sharing Hutchinson's suspicion "that one who had been so arch and hypocritical in his wickedness, might not be without some degree of dissimulation in his repentance"—after all, the successful performance of such "sincere Endeavours after true Repentance" was known to be determinative in the pardon process (20).[29]

What literary critical payoff can prosaic broadsides like *The Life, and Dying Speech of Arthur* possibly be expected to offer? "If all his enormous villainies, and wrongs to men, could be enumerated," Rev. Hutchinson speculated in his sermon on Arthur, "what a black catalogue would there be of his crimes . . . !" (19). To enumerate one's villainies was to generate monitory or (increasingly) sensational black catalogues, not to compose great literature. These highly formulaic texts are narratives in only the strictest sense of the word, apparently more committed to inventorying stolen goods than telling the condemned malefactor's story. (As a note in Frasier's *Brief Account* explains, such lists "are particularly mentioned at his desire, that the owners may know the articles taken by him, in order to exculpate others.")[30] An inspired critic might find in these pedestrian lists of stolen rum, kettles, and shoes a Whitmanesque catalogue of early American transgression, but the rest of us can be forgiven for finding ourselves at a bit of a loss as to what literary hay to make of these documents.

Further complicating matters is the fact that, like *The Life and Confession of Johnson Green, Who Is To Be Executed This Day, August 17th, 1786, for the Atrocious Crime of Burglary; Together with His Last and Dying Words* (1786), and the *Life, Last Words and Dying Speech of Stephen Smith, a Black Man, Who Was Executed at Boston This Day Being Thursday, October 12, 1797 for Burglary* (1797), *The Life, and Dying Speech of Arthur* differs little in content and style from the confessions attributed to condemned white malefactors like Arthur's colleague Isaac Frasier.[31] The prevalence of captivity and forced servitude in the eighteenth-century Atlantic world may make it more useful to think in terms of degrees of unfreedom than binaries of race and condition.[32] (This point is borne out by a quick comparison of the narratives of Green and Frasier. Green, the son of a "negro . . . servant" and "an Irish . . . widow" claims to have been "used very tenderly" as an agricultural apprentice and "instructed in the principles of the Christian Religion" before succumbing to "drunkenness, the keeping of bad company, and . . . correspondence . . . with lewd women"; Frasier, on the other hand, was born in "low circumstances," and, when he stole a "watch and money" was "whipt" and had his time "sold at public vendue" in partial restitution for his theft.)[33] Given the apparent similarities of the texts attributed to colonial condemned—and of the lives depicted therein—why focus on *black* gallows literature? The answer lies in the peculiar relationship among race, crime, property, and personhood in early America.

This Was the Beginning . . .

The *Life, and Dying Speech of Arthur* devotes little space to depicting the rape for which its putative author was hanged. After acknowledging that "the Devil put it into my Head to pay a Visit to the Widow *Deborah Metcalfe*, whom I, in a most inhumane manner, ravished," Arthur adds that "the Particulars of which [rape] are so notorious, that it is needless for me here to relate them."[34] Typical of colonial gallows literature, the broadside stresses not the condemned man's rare capital crime but the petty offenses more commonly practiced in the larger community. Specifically, it joins other freestanding eighteenth-century confessions attributed to the black condemned in focusing on the various property offenses that define the malefactor's career. By this identification of the black felon with crimes against property, gallows texts confounded prevailing representations of slave character in early American law and print culture.

Consider the advertisement that appeared in *the Boston Gazette, or, Weekly Advertiser* in early May 1754: "To be Sold at public Vendue on Thursday the 23d Instant, at the House where the late Mr. *Henry Darrell*, deceas'd, dwelt, the Household Furniture and Goods of said Deceased, consisting of Feather Beds, Bedsteads, Chairs, Tables, Desks, China, Earthen & Glass Ware, Looking Glasses, Pewter, Brass & Copper Ware, 2 Turkey Carpets, a parcel of Ironmongery and Tin Ware, sundry Pieces of Plate, Men's Apparel, and a Collection of Books; also a Negro Man and Women, and a Horse and Chaise."[35] In this jumble of goods, the enslaved people are set apart only by the semicolon that seems to mark them not as living beings (like "a Horse") but as particularly valuable items (like "a Horse and Chaise"). Even posthumously, "the late Mr. *Henry Darrell*, deceas'd," possessed of a name, an address, and "Household furniture and goods"—including other humans—lays claim to the legal personhood denied the "Negro Man and Women" who survive him.[36] (Indeed, even when he resurfaces as "*Mr.* Henry Darrell, *late of* Boston,

Merchant, deceased, represented Insolvent," he remains, through the disposition of his estate, accountable to "the *several Creditors*" he left behind.)[37] And it is this point that helps us to see how the similar inventories of stolen goods ostensibly provided by confessing criminals like Arthur and Isaac Frasier reveal a subtle but signal difference between even the most formulaic print portrayals of the black condemned from those of their white partners in crime, as well as from other contemporary forms of black life-writing.

The *Life, and Dying Speech of Arthur* opens:

> I Was born at *Taunton*, January 15, 1747, in the house of *Richard Godfrey*, Esq., my Mother being his Slave, where I lived fourteen Years; was learned to read and write, and was treated very kindly by my Master; but was so unhappy as often to incur the Displeasure of my Mistress, which caused me then to run away: And this was the beginning of my many notorious Crimes, of which I have been guilty. I went first to *Sandwich*, where I lived two Months in a very dissolute Manner, frequently being guilty of Drunkenness and Fornication; for which crimes I have been since famous, and by which I am now brought to this untimely Death.
>
> At *Sandwich*, I stole a Shirt, was detected, and settled the Affair, by paying twenty Shillings. My Character being now known, I thought proper to leave the Place; and accordingly shipped myself on board a Whaling Sloop. . . .[38]

With its definitive project of recounting and taking responsibility for past offenses, confession is a particularly retrospective form of narrative. Yet, looming over these backward-looking accounts is the long shadow of the gallows. Anticipating its putative author's death as well as its own posthumous circulation, the printed confession constructed a past overshadowed by events in the near future. Imminent execution and publication structure the order and meaning of prior actions ("crimes . . . by which I am now brought to this untimely Death"). The published confession's time frame is structured by criminality: anticipated future punishment (or pardon) elicits the present admission of past crimes. Nevertheless, its very narrative form, in conjunction with the legal fiction of slave character and the genre's preoccupation with property disposition, provides an alternative framework for black subjectivity. As it tells the conventional story of Arthur's descent, through crime, to death on the scaffold, the *Life, and Dying Speech* simultaneously recounts his ascent, also through property crime, from the civil death of the slave, via the culpable legal personhood of the felon, to the civil standing of the self-possessed, contracting individual. Mutually oriented toward the future, property and narrative impel each other forward.[39] Best understood not physically, as specific objects, but metaphysically, as a particular set of rights, property structures relations as much among persons as between persons and things.[40] The ability to assert and maintain such relationships before law is in fact an important aspect of legal personhood. To his family, friends, and acquaintances, the "Feather Beds," "Collection of Books," and "Apparel" owned by "the late Mr. Henry Darrell," along with other less fungible items (a wedding ring, perhaps, or bundles of private correspondence) were things that helped to establish his individuality, both prior to and after his death.[41] But equally constitutive of Darrall's personhood, the ad also suggests, was the disposition of such items either in the course of his lifetime or posthumously. Understanding "personhood" as "a continuing character structure" over time, we can appreciate "why protecting people's 'expectations' of continuing control over objects seems so important," for, as property theorist Margaret Jane Radin explains, "if an object you now control is bound up in your future plans or in your anticipation of your future self, and it is partly these plans for your own continuity that make you a person, then your personhood depends on the realization of these expectations."[42] Disposition of property, including property in the person, is central, possibly even essential, to any narrative of progressive selfhood. [43] The advertised probate proceedings in Darrall's case offer a pithy illustration of this point: had death not interrupted his plans in 1753, the man who in 1750 was advertising goods freshly imported from London might not have been "represented Insolvent" on his demise.[44]

Typically associated with the period after Emancipation, this emphasis on expectation as an aspect of property rights is of crucial importance to eighteenth- and nineteenth-century narratives of black personhood.[45] For it was not his status as the object of property, but his inability to be the formally recognized subject of property relations, that defined the slave.[46] Douglass thus locates the origins of "The Run-Away Plot" in Frederick's determination to cast himself as a continuous character in the narrative of his own life: "the thought of only being a creature of the *present* and the *past,* troubled me, and I longed to have a *future.*"[47] The right to the future disposition of oneself and one's property distinguished the self-possessed individual from other "creature[s]."[48] This dynamic becomes clearer when we turn from young

Frederick and the redundantly "late Mr. Henry Darrell, deceased" back to the condemned Arthur.

Claiming to have committed the first of his "many notorious Crimes" by running away, Arthur commences life anew as an autonomous person with a future as well as a past and a present.[49] "This was the beginning," he says, dramatizing how, by asserting criminal culpability, the first-person black narrator simultaneously takes responsibility for the plotting of his life. And the same capacity for self-disposition that will ultimately make Arthur answerable for the criminal career that supported his "Drunkenness and Fornication" enables him to project himself into that future through contractual relations: "My Character being now known, I thought proper to leave the Place; and accordingly shipped my self on board a Whaling Sloop."[50] That the former bondman's criminality at once provides the impetus to go whaling and the "Character" to do so under his own authority alerts us to how Arthur's illegal acquisition and disposition of various chattels creates the narrative possibility from which the broadside's speaking self emerges.

References to "character" abound in gallows texts.[51] If Isaac Frasier's "mother tho' poor, yet always had the character of an honest person among her Neighbours," her son would gain a different reputation: although he was initially "in good credit" with the inhabitants of Newtown, it was not long before a series of thefts ensured that Frasier's "true character was known," prompting him to move to Goshen, Connecticut.[52] His "character . . . entirely lost," Frasier embarks on property crimes that lead him to be treated in a manner virtually indistinguishable from a slave: "tried, convicted and sentenced to be whipt, cropt and branded as punishment for the first offence of Housebreaking," he was "sold to [the plaintiff,] Mr. Hopkins to defray cost and damages."[53]

What sets the formulaic gallows texts of condemned criminals of color apart is the way in which the recounted property crimes irrevocably distinguish their black perpetrators from the things they steal. Arthur's thefts of chattels from the inaugural shirt in Shrewsbury to the culminating brass kettle in Watertown establish a fundamental, insistent difference between the person and the objects he appropriates. If, like "those irrational animals which fall under the legal denomination of property," slaves could resist, run away, or destroy things, by law they differed from livestock in the criminal responsibility that elevated them to the status of legal personhood.[54] Brass kettles didn't steal brass kettles—and neither did livestock. "Would it not be an anomaly in judicial proceedings," proslavery lawyer George S. Sawyer would ask in his *Southern Institutes*, "to organize a court for the trial and punishment of unruly horses and horned cattle?"[55] It is this personhood, grounded in Arthur's narrated criminal actions, that ultimately blocks his narrative reversion to chattel status. Following another spate of thefts (during which he was jailed, only to escape again), Arthur recalls having "shipped my self on board a Vessel bound to *Swanzey*, where I was discovered, taken on Shoar, and whip'd sixteen Stripes; being then set at Liberty, I returned to *Taunton*, after one Year's Absence, where my Master received me kindly, whom I served three Years."[56] Capture and punishment as a fugitive from justice, not from service, only affirm Arthur's autonomy and individuality; "set at Liberty" on completion of his sentence, Arthur returns to servitude under his old master on a seemingly voluntary, temporary basis. Thus established, Arthur's responsible, individualist personhood cannot be compromised by his subsequent sale. (Ironically, in this and subsequent slave narratives, repeated references to "my master" obscure the actual economic fungibility of the bondman with the semantic interchangeability of those who lay claim to him: here the first-person possessive construction consolidates Arthur's continuous selfhood as the referent for "master" shifts inconsistently among "Mr. *John Hill*, of *Brookfield*," "Capt. *Clarke*, of *Rutland* District," and "a Dutch Gentleman, whose name I have since forgot.")[57] For Arthur, having a criminal "Character" was quite different from the loss of reputation it represented to a white man—even an indentured servant whose time was subject to public sale, as Frasier's had been. The slave's acquisition of such a public criminal "Character" marked the *attainment* rather than the diminution of recognized personhood. For the white man such a reputation brought the loss of civil standing, but for the erstwhile slave, criminal character marked the ascension from human thing to person.

Just as the divergent effects of incrimination distinguish the confessions of the black condemned from those of their white counterparts, the narration of such property crimes differentiates these figures from other authors of early Black Atlantic personal narratives. Virtuously and industriously laboring to purchase their freedom, Olaudah Equiano, Venture Smith, and John Marrant confront the liberal dilemma outlined by Gould (discussed in Chapter 1): "The necessity to demonstrate individuality in market culture actually translates into the need to possess property. Yet for a slave to own property that can free him is to become reduced to property in a post-Lockean culture."[58] Arthur too must pay to release himself from captivity, but in his case the money is equivalent not to himself but to the shirt he has stolen.

Far from ensnaring him as fungible commodity in a seemingly inescapable circuit of property relations, Arthur's restitution for the stolen shirt has the opposite effect: acknowledging his responsibility for the crime, the payment affirms rather than negates his personhood.[59] Through his property offenses, the criminous slave nimbly sidesteps the epistemological trap of liberalism. Official recognition of Arthur's thefts changes his position in the web of relations among people and things, doubly consolidating his personhood as property holder and responsible agent.

Held in View

Arthur, though, is the relic of a period before transatlantic antislavery and penal reform movements sought to transform contemporary attitudes about race, crime, and punishment. How are we to understand the interplay of black criminality and publicity in a period when, on the one hand, both convicts and executions were increasingly hidden behind prison walls and, on the other, abolitionists indicted the perpetrators of slaveholding villainy before the court of public opinion? Reading Melville's "Benito Cereno" and Douglass's "The Heroic Slave" alongside a series of gallows pamphlets devoted to condemned pirates Charles Gibbs and Thomas J. Wansley, we will see, in the next two sections, how these and other forces in nineteenth-century law, politics, and society effectively broadened the transverse arcs inscribed by gallows literature's ascending black and descending white protagonists into more generalized itineraries of racialized subjectivity in antebellum print culture.

Like the public Puritan testimonies from which they were in part derived, colonial criminal confessions indicate how the preparationist practice of taking stock of the individual life paradoxically fostered within the deterministic framework of Calvinism a transitive understanding of selfhood in terms of responsible individual agency.[60] Notions of accountability and imputation as external constraints quickly led in the late eighteenth and nineteenth centuries to more subjective concerns, such as moral responsibility.[61] Thus even the most terse crime narratives move almost irresistibly from the official assignment of legal culpability to an interest in the responsible individual and his emergent self, whether as stock Puritan penitent, picaresque rogue, or Romantic outlaw.[62] Complementing law's discernment of the slave's personhood, and thus political belonging, in his answerability, crime literature confirmed the black felon's individuality within the larger civil society of which he was a member. Such recognized selfhood would become indispensable to antebellum African American print activism; it was what enabled the individual known as "Frederick Douglass" first to fashion himself as a representative "American Slave" in his 1845 *Narrative* and thereafter to politicize "*My* Bondage and *My* Freedom."

Such individualization was of course integral to the disciplinary processes that Michel Foucault found replacing punitive juridical procedures in the nineteenth century. Inverting its usual function of displaying sovereign power and commemorating the heroic deeds of the few, "biographical investigation" now served to document and describe, and thus to control and dominate, the many.[63] Not accidentally, the first-person black subject entered Anglo-American print culture as the political axis of life-writing tilted from the "ascending" individualization of the epic hero to the "descending" individualization of the abnormal juvenile, madman, patient, or delinquent.[64] The development of the antebellum slave narrative out of the colonial and early national criminal confessions attributed to the black condemned occurred in this changing penal environment, as Chapter 5 discusses in more detail. Yet, if personal narrative, long the African American canon's preeminent genre, contributed to the disciplinary supervision of the black subject, it also asserted that subject's right to membership in the polity on the basis of his sovereign—because culpable—individual personhood. Ever susceptible to descent, the black persona was nevertheless, from the eighteenth through the mid-nineteenth century, an individual on the ascendant.

The reconstructed prison became an important landmark on the divergent trajectories of the white and the black criminal in print.[65] However much the penal reform movement may have walled off the felon from society, its principles were developed, promoted, assessed, and refined in a nineteenth-century print culture that put both actual convicts and the imagined figure of the prisoner constantly before the eye of a public deeply concerned with questions of liberty and captivity.[66] "Disembodied, colored white, isolated, and inward looking," the prisoner stood at the center of a "poetics of the penitentiary," which, Caleb Smith contends, drew on Christian ascetic traditions, Enlightenment social contract theory, gothic representational strategies, and nineteenth-century liberalism to recapitulate the polity's triumph over the state of nature in the citizen's exemplary carceral dissolution and reconstitution.[67] In order to stage the citizen's contractarian acquisition of personhood and political membership through relinquishment of his natural, animal existence, this primal drama required a lead actor whose once and future citizenship could be assumed: a normatively white, male prisoner whose civil death unambiguously arose from his breach of the social contract (rather than his racial status or condition of servitude).[68] Only he could embody the highly interiorized rite of civic regeneration in which the abjected rights-bearer was reborn as a citizen.[69] Unqualified to perform this ritual, the black convict appeared to remain on the gallows well after punitive incarceration and prison yard executions had replaced the death penalty and public hangings throughout much of the United States.

Withdrawing convicted citizens in order to restore them to civil society, the new republican penitentiary offered a secular modification of colonial Execution Day rituals that strove at once physically to purge and spiritually to reintegrate condemned malefactors. Yet, however race may have skewed the "justice" that brought them to the scaffold, the black condemned were welcomed as candidates for heaven on roughly equal terms as their white partners in crime.[70] "Canst thou *Love* thy *Negro*, and be willing to see him ly under the Rage of Sin, and the Wrath of God?" Cotton Mather asked his Puritan readers in *The Negro Christianized* (1706).[71] Two decades later, reporting the Plymouth, Massachusetts, hanging of "molatto" infanticide Elizabeth Colson, Boston's *New-England Weekly Journal* noted that Colson, having knelt in the cart during the Rev. Mr. Leonard's sermon on her behalf, "made an Excellent Prayer her self, which greatly affected the numerous Throng of People gathered together on that sad occasion: in a word, her carriage was such, as begat in the Spectators a charitable hope that she dyed a true Penitent."[72] But when reintegration into the community was to take place in the here and now rather than the hereafter, spiritual equality did not translate into civic parity. Still enthusiastically embraced as redeemable sinners in early national and antebellum America, black convicts were perceived as considerably less eligible than white prisoners for individual civic reformation. Everyone who mounted the scaffold was a legal person with a human soul; not everyone who entered the prison was a citizen.

Blacks' ineligibility for the transformative civic mortification and re-animation wrought by the penitentiary resulted not so much from their absorption into plantation slavery as an alternative site of captivity as from their presumptive status as a deviant population of noncitizens. In 1843 persistent doubts about black prisoners' capacity for civic regeneration received scientific confirmation in a widely circulated pamphlet by Dr. Benjamin H. Coates. Published fifty years after Noah Webster's *Effects of Slavery on Morals and Industry*, Coates's *On the Effects of Secluded and Gloomy Imprisonment*

on Individuals of the African Variety of Mankind in the Production of Disease
(1843) once again positioned race as the interface between disciplinary and
biopolitical techniques.[73]

As the title's reference to "secluded and gloomy imprisonment" suggests,
Coates conducted his research at Philadelphia's Eastern State Penitentiary,
whose introduction of a strict program of silent "solitary confinement at
labor" in 1829 made it the nation's most celebrated penal reform experiment.[74] The essay's impetus was the disproportionately high mortality rate
of black inmates as measured against both Pennsylvania's larger black population and the white inmates (who appeared to thrive in contrast to their
free counterparts). After discussing the interiorized transformation of individual citizen-convicts housed in multiple solitary cells, Coates addressed
the statistical impact of imprisonment on the black inmate as the embodiment of a population shaped by biological and environmental forces. Black
prisoners' abnormal death rates revealed not the failure of the disciplinary
apparatus—after all, Eastern State's *white* inmates had a lower mortality
rate than Pennsylvania's white population—but a racial incapacity for civic
reformation, individually and collectively. Influenced by the romantic racialism of the day, Coates noted that "the negro, or even the mulatto, is a very
different person, in his physical and psychical conformation from that one
who may be presumed to have been held in view in our legislation, the white
Anglo-Saxon, Celt, or German."[75] Hence the radically different effects of incarceration on the black prisoner: "it is not by remorse and anguish that he
is affected, so much as by intellectual and mental weakness and decay" (268).
Because he is "constitutionally free from that deep, thoughtful anxiety for
the future, so conspicuous in his paler neighbour," the black prisoner cannot
engage in the civically regenerative reflective process the penitentiary (and
Pennsylvania's renowned "silent system" in particular) was designed to promote. Instead, "gloomy confinement becomes thus to him, mentally as well
as physically, a nearer approach to the punishment of death." Incapable of
the necessary combination of penitential retrospection and future-oriented
civic self-projection, the black prisoner could not prepare to reclaim what
had always been an elusive, if not entirely illusory, civil standing and civic
belonging. Unable to emerge from the prison as a (re)born citizen, the black
prisoner dies either mentally or physically within its walls. Constitutionally
incapable of keeping pace with America's rapid social reforms (indeed, not
being "held in view" in its melioritive "legislation"), the black prisoner cannot progress but, in a sure sign of his political retrogression, experiences the

era's new rehabilitative imprisonment as the death penalty it was devised to replace.

This racialized penal poetics finds realization in the verses of abolitionist missionary and political prisoner George Thompson, who followed his diaristic *Prison Life and Reflections* (1847) with *The Prison Bard; Or, Poems on Various Subjects. Written in Prison* (1848). Along with two fellow seminarians from the Mission Institute in Quincy, Illinois, Thompson had arranged to escort some Missouri slaves across the Mississippi river onto free soil, only to be betrayed and taken up on charges of slave-stealing. Convicted in September 1841 of grand larceny and sentenced to twelve years of hard labor at Missouri State Penitentiary, Thompson was pardoned in June 1846.[76] Notwithstanding his tendency to equate the abolitionist martyrs' temporary captivity with slaves' hereditary bondage, Thompson, too, figures the mind-body split that preserves the (white) prisoner in racialized terms, as he proclaims of "the *Spirit* immortal—the MIND— / A Slave it disdaineth to be."[77] Actual slaves, apparently incapable of such psychic resistance, can find relief only in death. So, at least, suggests another poem, "The Slave's Hope," which Thompson explains, "was suggested by a Slave's coming into the Prison, whom I asked, 'When are *you* going to be free?' [upon which] He replied, '*After I'm dead!*' Repeated twice in three refrains through four stanzas, the phrase appears twenty-four times in the thirty-two-line poem ("I shall be free from their scorn and contempt, / After I'm dead—After I'm dead. / They, to their malice, may give a free vent, / After I'm dead—After I'm dead"), a haunting sing-song of black fatality.[78]

Ventriloquizing the slave's first-person voice in support of his own abolitionist critique of Missouri's repressive regime, Thompson alerts us to the invisibility in American letters of the enslaved convict for whom imprisonment itself is punishment, rather than a prelude to state-administered death. (Indeed, Thompson's prefatory note makes it impossible to discern whether the slave has come to the prison on an errand, for summary punishment, or as a result of criminal prosecution.) Although, due to post-Reconstruction developments in penal practice, twentieth-century American prison writing has come to be predominantly associated with incarcerated African American authors from Chester Himes, Iceberg Slim, and Donald Goines to Eldridge Cleaver, George Jackson, and Angela Davis, antebellum prison literature was essentially a white phenomenon.[79] During this period Eastern State and other penitentiaries became home to a new kind of prison writing, as gallows pamphlets like *Brief Account of the Life and Abominable Thefts*

of the Notorious Isaac Frasier were being supplanted by volumes of poetry
or memoirs similar to those published by Thompson, notably prison poet
Harry Hawser's *Buds and Flowers, of Leisure Hours* (1844) and James A.
Clay's *A Voice from the Prison* (1856).[80] These real-life voices from the prison
found their analogues in fictional characters created by Melville, Hawthorne,
and Poe.[81] But one only need to turn from Clifford Pyncheon and Bartleby
the Scrivener to Nat Turner and Babo (or, for that matter, to Valentine and
Governor) to appreciate the normative whiteness of the prisoner in contrast
to the condemned black convicts who continued to populate the literature
of the period.[82] Like Paul Revere recalling the gibbetted slave Mark on his
midnight ride, antebellum Americans could not easily rid themselves of the
afterimage of the black condemned hanging before their eyes.

Fixed on a Pole in the Plaza

As formulated by Douglass in *My Bondage and My Freedom*, the dilemma
facing the antebellum black author was to deploy personal narrative to apprehend the rights of the enslaved in a culture that historically had apprehended
African Americans in print primarily as chattels or criminals. That the
challenges of this undertaking were themselves apprehensible to non-black
writers is suggested by the conclusion to Herman Melville's "Benito Cereno,"
published serially in *Putnam's Monthly Magazine* over the final three months
of 1855—the second installment appearing in the same issue as a laudatory
review of Douglass's second autobiography.[83]

Near the novella's conclusion, Melville presents, in the form of the eponymous Spanish captain's deposition to the vice-regal court at Lima, an account
of the events preceding American captain Amasa Delano's day-long encounter with the *San Dominick*, a slave ship, now in distress, that unbeknownst to
him has been taken over by its insurgent captives. Appearing near the story's
end, the deposition effectively serves as "as the key to fit into the lock of the
complications which precede it," not only by exposing the slave rebel Babo's
"plot"—and thus that of the narrative itself—but also by assigning names and
identities to the novella's background characters, the *San Dominick*'s slaves,
crew, and passengers.[84] Noting the novella's uniqueness as Melville's one
maritime text not to include "a voice from before the mast," critic Maurice
S. Lee observes that, by the time one gets through the dry deposition, "one
might not give a wilted pumpkin for the names of the other rebels, any more
than give a basket of fish for the rest of the gentleman and tars."[85] But if, as

Lee notes, "in the absence of sustained characterization, of personal history and voice, the minor players . . . remain stubbornly inaccessible," it is all the more significant that the legal occasion of the trial is what yields the few details we do get.[86] For, in the process of individuating these characters, the deposition itself documents criminal law's racialized construction of individual personhood.

Having provided "a list of some fifty names, descriptions, and ages" of the ship's human cargo (a "catalogue" derived from "recovered documents" of the murdered "Don Alexandro Aranda, gentleman," to whom the slaves "mostly belong[ed]"), the deposition then offers "a partial renumeration of the negroes, making record of their individual part[s] in past events, with a view to furnishing, according to the command of the court, the data whereon to found the criminal sentences to be pronounced" (104, 111; emphasis omitted). Whereas the initial inventory lists the slaves according to their marketable skills (José, fluent in "Spanish"; Dago, "a grave-digger"; "four old negroes, . . . calkers by trade"), the blacks' criminal actions prompt the court to document their individual roles in the uprising (104). Aranda's manservant José is the informer; the Ashantee Lecbe "wounded" Delano's "chief mate" (111); Yau, with Lecbe, "riveted the skeleton [of Aranda] to the bow" (112); and of course, "Babo was the plotter from first to last" with "Atufal . . . his lieutenant in all" (112). If the insurgents' rebellious actions ultimately do not prevent their recapture and death, their documented crimes nevertheless have the effect of transforming scriptive representation of the blacks, from chattel in Aranda's ledger and the court's initial catalogue, to responsible persons in the court's records.[87] This transformation occurs on the level of the narrative exposition as well, as those who had appeared to Delano (and the reader) largely as undifferentiated "blacks"—at most, clusters of "unsophisticated Africans" or "Ashantee conjurors"—acquire individual names and identities in the deposition (70, 50, 60).

The *San Dominick*'s "nondescript crew" undergoes a similar metamorphosis in both the story and the deposition it encloses (50). Those whites whom Delano had viewed largely in generational, national, and occupational terms—"two Spanish boys," "a young Spanish sailor," "an aged sailor," and so on—emerge in the deposition as named individuals (59, 64, 75): the clerk "Hermenegildo Gandix," tried to hint to Delano "the true state of affairs" (112); sailor "Luys Galgo . . . sought to convey" similar tokens to the obtuse American (112), and another clerk, "Don Joaquin, Marques de Arambaolaza" "secreted" from his captors "a jewel" originally intended as a votive offering to "the Shrine of our Lady of Mercy in Lima" (113).

The deposition's contrasting lists of characters follows the established racial logic of American law and print culture, with white subjects acquiring individuality largely through their recognized civic deeds, while for black subjects such public recognition often depended upon imputations of criminality. (That "the negresses" who "used their utmost influence to have the deponent made away with" and encouraged the revolutionary violence with their "melancholy songs" nevertheless remain an anonymous collective, identified only by race and gender and not by individual names, is consistent with a larger tendency to focus concerns about *both* civic and criminal agency on masculine subjects [112].) Yet even as it singles out the white crew members and passengers for their civic acts, the deposition confirms Douglass's sense of law's tendency to misapprehend black civic agency as criminal activity. How, for instance, does the communication by "the negro, José" to "the negro Babo, about the state of things in the cabin" differ fundamentally from the parallel efforts by the captive white sailors to inform the Yankee captain of "the true state of affairs" on the ship (111)? Like Douglass recounting "The Run-Away Plot," Melville (albeit with greater cynicism) leaves it to the reader to see what law cannot: that those whom the court records as "felons" are in fact would-be Patrick Henrys.

Or Madison Washingtons. For Melville also resembled Douglass in finding literary inspiration in well-publicized court cases involving revolts on slave ships.[88] The difference is that "The Heroic Slave," Douglass's fictionalization of the 1841 uprising led by Washington on the domestic slave ship *Creole*, concludes not with the slave rebels' recapture but their liberation on free British soil in the Bahamas. Whatever the discrepancies between their envisioned outcomes of violent black resistance, Douglass and Melville both offer fictional narratives that chart the African American print subject's transformation from chattel to person. "The Heroic Slave" opens by contrasting the scriptive treatment accorded to the "statesmen" who have made "the State of Virginia . . . famous in American annals" ("history has not been sparing in recording their names, or in blazoning their deeds") with the "undeserved obscurity" assigned to Madison Washington, the titular heroic slave, who "holds now no higher place in the records of that grand old Commonwealth than is held by a horse or an ox."[89] The story thus seeks to erase Washington from "the chattel records of his native State" and reinscribe him in the annals of American history by rendering as black heroism what many would see as criminal activity (483). (Reviled as a "murderous villain" by Tom Grant, the *Creole*'s "sturdy mate," Washington pauses mid-combat to correct this classic misapprehension of black civic virtue as *mens rea*: "You call me a *black murderer*. I am not a murderer. . . . LIBERTY, not *malice*, is the motive for this night's work" [518, 515, 518]). Along with clarifying Washington's motives, Douglass accomplishes this revision by placing his black hero beyond the punitive and discursive reach of American law. Upon arrival in Nassau, Grant sends the consul "a statement of facts, requesting his interference," with a view to securing the slaves who, "by the laws of Virginia and the laws of the United States . . . were as much property as the barrels of flour in the hold"; when, however, "by order of the authorities, a company of *black* soldiers came on board . . . and said they did not recognize *persons* as *property*," the former captives "formed themselves into a procession on the wharf" and "marched" off "under the triumphant leadership of their heroic chief and deliverer, MADISON WASHINGTON" (520). Having, through violent acts of criminalized resistance, reached a jurisdiction where their personhood is no longer retractable, the blacks assert their public presence in an emphatically civic display.

With less personal and political stake than Douglass in fashioning an unambiguously heroic slave, Melville more straightforwardly identifies criminality as a means by which the black print subject can escape chattel status and achieve recognized (however misapprehended) personhood. His novella's ghastly ending follows the court's racialized constructions of criminal and civil capacity to their logical conclusions. "Three months after being dismissed by the court, Benito Cereno" is "borne on the bier" to a monastery at the aptly named Mt. Agonia in an image of deathly repose mirroring that of "the recovered bones of Aranda" as they sleep in the vaults of St. Bartholomew's church (117). By contrast, "dragged to the gibbet at the tail of a mule, the black met his voiceless end" (116): with his "body . . . burned to ashes," Babo's "head, that hive of subtlety, fixed on a pole in the Plaza, met, unabashed, the gaze of the whites" even as it "looked towards" the buried remains of his white enemies (116–17).[90] In its macabre staging of the divergent fates meted out to black slaves and white masters by a slaveholding legal regime, the story's conclusion nevertheless points to execution as an inaugural site of black civic presence. The head of the former slave convict stands at the center of the Plaza, posthumously scrutinizing both his captors and the surrounding "whites." Silent, dead, dismembered, and demeaned, Babo does not achieve this presence on his own terms, as a successful uprising might have accomplished. But if the executed Babo is no heroic slave, he *is* an unavoidable—and, Melville's phrasing suggests, critical—civic presence in white civil society.[91] It is from that presence, the grim legacy of the legally executed slave, that neither black nor white antebellum writers could entirely avert their eyes as they set about the project of creating a distinct American literature in a slaveholding nation.

Sheltered from the dehumanizing spectacle that Babo silently endures, the two slaveholders, Aranda and Cereno, nevertheless disappear from civic space and thus, perhaps, from public consciousness. That such obscurity may not have been altogether a desirable fate for the white citizen-subject is suggested by the ephemera surrounding the comparatively late public execution of an interracial pair of convicted pirates and murderers, Charles Gibbs (white) and Thomas J. Wansley (African-American). Reluctant participants in the time-honored Execution Day ritual (itself soon to be terminated in many states), Gibbs and Wansley acquired highly individualized public identities that nonetheless appeared to affirm the increasing authority and autonomy of the black persona and its criminal white counterpart's corresponding civic declension.

A Difference of Treatment

On Friday April 22, 1831, on Ellis (a.k.a. "Gibbet") Island, Gibbs and Wansley were executed for piracy and the murder of, respectively, the captain and the mate of the brig *Vineyard*.[92] Fifty-five years before the Statue of Liberty would come to dominate views of that spot, hundreds of boats bobbed in New York Harbor, their passengers having disembarked to watch as, in unison, the African American and the white man were jerked upward to their deaths, the white-garbed black man briefly folding his hands as if in prayer while the white man, clad in navy-blue duck, desperately clutched at his execution cap and his mouth for several awful minutes. Even if they couldn't attend in person, vicarious spectators from as far away as Hanover, New Hampshire, and Easton, Maryland, could read about the execution in newspaper accounts and the fifteen or so pamphlets depicting the men's crimes, capture, confessions, trials, sentencing, and, finally, deaths. And, if the copiously illustrated pamphlets were insufficiently graphic, the curious could view Gibbs and Wansley alongside other famous criminals and their victims in a traveling exhibition of "Eighteen Wax Figures as Large as Life."[93]

In a nineteenth-century version of the interracial buddy picture, some pamphlet engravings depicted Gibbs and Wansley diligently disposing of their victims and burying their booty together[94] (see Figure 9). These images of racially egalitarian criminal labor find their visual completion in the many woodcuts portraying the executed Wansley and Gibbs hanging side by side on the gallows or enclosed in twin coffins (Figures 4 and 6). The former images' stark symmetry, enhanced in some instances by the black and white figures' contrapuntal light and dark outfits, presented a vivid graphic rebuttal to Wansley's widely reported protest at sentencing that "a difference of color produced a difference of treatment, where white men were judges."[95] Prompted by Circuit Court Judge Samuel Rossiter Betts's conventional query ("have you any thing to say, why the sentence of law should not be passed upon you?"), Wansley placed his criticism of the American justice system's racial bias in the larger context of transatlantic slavery: "They had taken the blacks from their own country, and scattered them over their own settlements, and treated them differently than those of their own country. There was an antipathy, as he knew, entertained by the whites against the colored persons. He had found it so himself, both as regarded the witnesses and jurors in this case, and at the hands of the District Attorney."[96] Even as the pamphlets faithfully reproduced variant versions of Wansley's protest, the accompanying woodcuts visually endorsed Judge Betts's insistence that "whatever prejudice he [Wansley] might imagine existed, growing out of the distinctions of color, the utmost impartiality had been observed in his case."[97]

Images of paired coffins notwithstanding, published accounts of the condemned pirates suggest that however equal their usage was supposed to have been under law, the black man and the white man received markedly different narrative treatments. Although Wansley's widely reported trial included testimony that he was from Delaware, the black man's specific origins remained obstinately obscure. "Wansley, it is by some asserted, was born on a plantation on the Mississippi; by others that he was a native of one of the West India Islands; while others, again, as confidently, locate his birth-place in a number of dissimilar positions," an account published a decade after the execution noted, adding, "we are not enabled to give anything certain on this point, nor it is important, as it is known that he and Gibbs never met until on board the Vineyard."[98] However irrelevant Wansley's origins may have been to the monitory tale so many sought to fashion from the pirates' lives, those of Gibbs were crucial (if ultimately equally obscure).[99] Said to have been born in 1794 "on the farm of his father, an opulent agriculturalist of Rhode Island," and erroneously rumored to have been "the son of a former Governor" of that state, Gibbs (later revealed to be James D. Jeffers) reportedly embarked on a number of abortive middle-class careers with full paternal support and was thus easily typed as "the prodigal."[100] Seemingly destined to contribute to the new nation, Gibbs was diverted from productive citizenship by his life of crime, whereas Wansley, a virtual nonentity, could only gain public recognition through criminality.

When the two men's paths crossed on the *Vineyard*, their criminal conspiracy sent them on radically different trajectories. Launched from obscurity into public consciousness by his trial, conviction, and impending execution, Wansley attained a degree of critical civic authority, as his widely circulated comments on racism in the judicial process attest. (Despite having "naturally a sullen smile on his countenance," Wansley is characterized during his protest at sentencing as "quite coherent in his remarks, and distinct in his utterance; but [with] nothing impudent in his demeanor."[101]) Gibbs acquired even greater publicity. Regaling jailhouse visitors with his pre-*Vineyard* adventures as a pirate responsible for (as several pamphlets had it) "nearly FOUR HUNDRED HUMAN BEINGS MURDERED," the larger-than-life Gibbs dominated print coverage of the trials and execution.[102] But while Gibbs actively sought to enlarge his notoriety with what many saw as dubious tales of murder on the high seas, print coverage of the condemned men depicted Wansley's mounting civic presence and textual authority against the steady erosion of these traits in his white co-conspirator.

The discrepancy was most immediately apparent in reports of the sentencing. After Wansley protested the proceedings' racial injustice, Gibbs chimed in, claiming that two other white crew members had murdered the mate while he watched helplessly. Perhaps in response to Wansley's criticism, Judge Betts credited the interracial pair with not only a common legal personhood, but (increasingly elusive in Jacksonian America) equal political membership. Not only had the victims "trusted in them as able and good citizens, and confided to them their lives and property," but as "American citizens" who "had shown, in what they had said in court this day, that they were possessed of a more than ordinary share of common intelligence, and must have participated to some extent, in the blessings of education so widely scattered over this country," Gibbs and Wansley were entirely responsible for their actions.[103]

But if the men were united in their legal accountability as American citizens, that responsibility acquired significance along distinctly racial lines. Addressing the prisoners' final appeals, Judge Betts located the black man's culpability in his criminal actions, reminding Wansley that "he was a free, voluntary, and active agent in depriving two fellow human beings of their lives."[104] By contrast, he located Gibbs's guilt in his *failure* to take action, noting even if he had not "throw[n] the mate overboard . . . the very reaching of his hand would have saved him."[105] Other accounts echo the Court's logic. In one of many dying speeches attributed to Gibbs, the condemned man unpersuasively attempts to distinguish his lack of agency from culpability: "It is true, I stood by and saw the fatal deed done, and stretched not forth my arm to save him: the technicalities of the law believe me guilty of the charge—but in the presence of my God, before whom I shall be in a few minutes, I declare I did not murder him."[106] If, by his own admission, Wansley was executed as "a pirate, a robber, and a murderer," Gibbs, it would appear, was condemned for a criminal evasion of his civic duty.[107] Whereas Wansley's crimes, followed by his measured criticism of the American justice system, endowed the black man with a new degree of civic presence, Gibbs's efforts to exonerate himself effectively confirmed the white man's civic declension.

The disparity between the responsible black actor and his increasingly passive white counterpart finds its most dramatic evocation in the widely reprinted *Visit to the Condemned Criminals Gibbs and Wansley. By a Layman*.[108] The anonymous "Layman" describes his prison visit with Wansley and Gibbs "three short days" before "the hand of justice" was scheduled to "terminate their earthly career."[109] The visitor calls first on Wansley, remarking the changes wrought in him by his apparently sincere religious conversion. At the trial, Layman, like so many other observers, "thought his countenance indicated that sullenness and hardihood which naturally associates with it the idea of a character stained with the commission of those horrible crimes with which he stood charged" (1). Struck, even "on that occasion," by Wansley's "general appearance and the symmetry of his well proportioned person," Layman is moved by his personal encounter with the condemned man to elaborate that "his complexion is that of a light mullatto and the general cast of his features and physiognomy approach but little towards those which distinguish the African race." "His well knit limbs convey[ing] the idea of great personal strength," Wansley prompted in his visitor "no hesitation in saying that I have seen but few persons of any colour who to my mind bear a more striking resemblance to the statute of the Apollo Belvidere, which I have seen, and which, has been considered as the most perfect model of manly beauty."[110] Given "the opinion" he had "previously formed of this convicted criminal," the visitor's "pleasing emotions" upon "witnessing his entirely altered appearance and manners" are intensified as he converses with a penitent Wansley regarding the condemned man's calm, sincere hopes for the hereafter.[111] (The contrast between Wansley and Coates's black Eastern State Penitentiary inmates is noteworthy: condemned to death rather than punitive incarceration and tasked with a spiritual rather than civic conversion, the black felon thrives behind prison walls.)

Having "departed highly gratified with my visit, and under a feeling of pleasing emotions arising from a conviction that there was a well-founded assurance of hope in his case"(2), Layman giddily heads to his meeting with Gibbs who, as another visitor observed, while still evincing "the air of his bold, enterprising and desperate mind," had "since his trial," become "somewhat enfeebled" in frame, "his face paler, and his eyes more sunken."[112] Layman, upon reaching Gibbs's cell, is horrified not so much by the physical and spiritual differences between the two men—no penitent Apollo Belvedere, the sallow pirate Gibbs—as by the contrasting circumstances in which he finds each. Encountering the white man "here, in his narrow cell," Layman quickly loses the good cheer generated by his visit with Wansley, for "considering the awful condition of civil death in which he was placed, I could not help regarding [it] as a living grave" (3). The shift from the spiritual to the civic register as Layman travels from Wansley's to Gibbs's cell bears noting. Notwithstanding the promising state of Wansley's soul, he too of course occupies "the awful condition of civil death," but Layman does not perceive this condition as a loss to the black man.

After his discovery of Gibbs in his "living grave," Layman seems much more concerned with the salvation of the white man's civic identity than with his immortal soul. Having earlier disavowed "morbid curiosity" as his motivation, Layman now divulges the real reason for his visit (1). On a tip that Gibbs "was in possession of facts respecting persons and circumstances" pertaining to "our intercourse with the West Indies," "the knowledge of which would be important to our government and useful to society," Layman hopes to "elicit something from him on the subject, that might be useful to the United States and the world" (4). Specifically, Layman wants Gibbs to finger his erstwhile pirate colleagues who continue to wreck havoc on American shipping in the Caribbean. Despite his intransigence with Layman, it was widely reported that Gibbs, before his death, "made a full disclosure of all the accomplices, aiders and abettors in his piracies, and that it is the intention of the person who has the information in his possession to proceed to Washington and communicate it without delay to the President."[113] "When published," these reports confidently averred, "*it will astound the people of this nation.*"[114] Such a disclosure promised not only to restore the smooth flow of trade disrupted by Caribbean piracy but also to resuscitate, in the condemned Gibbs, the self-possessed individual believed to emerge from such market relations by posthumously rendering him civically "useful." If, for the condemned Gibbs, civil death did not precede reentry into the polity, the white prisoner's civic reanimation could be accomplished symbolically, through print publication.

But Gibbs's much-anticipated tell-all was never published.[115] Instead, a very different pamphlet appeared following the executions: *The Life and Confession of Thos. J. Wansley, One of the Pirates, concerned with Charles Gibbs, alias James Jeffers, in the Murder and Piracy Committed on Board the Brig Vineyard. Written by Himself.* (1831; see Figure 9). Offered as "a correct copy, from papers, written by Wansley himself, since his condemnatation [*sic*], and handed to his attending Minister, the Rev. Joseph Carter," the *Life* claimed to have "been merely corrected in orthography and punctuations, at the request of the author."[116] Tellingly, the Preface continues, the same minister also had "many letters, together with the life of CHARLES GIBBS, written and presented by Gibbs himself, but of which he [Rev. Carter] doubts the veracity; therefore, at present, he deems it proper to withhold them from the public."[117]

The two pirates' print legacies correspond, in the secular realm, to the divergent trajectories that many anticipated for the condemned men after they had been launched into eternity.[118] A virtual nonentity (who may or may not have been a slave), Wansley only emerges as an individualized person at the nexus of antebellum law and print culture when he is tried and sentenced to death for the crimes of piracy and murder. But whereas Wansley's criminality boosts his ascent into individual subjectivity, Charles Gibbs—alias J. Jeffers, scion of a respectable Rhode Island family, who still promises on the eve of his execution to "be useful to the United States and the world"—descends as a result of his criminal passivity into "civil death" prior to his actual death.

Rather than producing a document "important to our government and useful to society," Gibbs leaves only spurious accounts of criminal activity.[119] "Upon what principle . . . that ordinarily governs mankind, even those of the most hardened and obdurate," agonized the mystified Layman, "could he act, by seeking to increase the public horror of his crimes, and their indignation against him, by adding to the list of dreadful deeds he had actually perpetrated, others, which had no existence but in his own murderous imagination[?]"[120] Layman's question finds its answer in the account of another jailhouse visitor: "He often asks," that observer noted of Gibbs, "if he should not be murdered in the streets, if he had his liberty, if he was recognized."[121]

Fearing not violent physical dissolution but the civil death that so unsettled Layman, Gibbs fantasizes about his own killing at the hands of the mob as an appealing alternative to execution under the supervision of the authorities. Such public "recognition" offered a desirable adjunct to "liberty," even if purchased by equally public death. Better to have one's head on a pole in the plaza than buried away where no one can see it.

Conclusion

Gibbs and Wansley were tried and executed at a turning point in American culture. While the two men were imprisoned at Bellevue awaiting trial, William Lloyd Garrison brought out the first copy of *The Liberator*; four months after their hanging, Nat Turner would lead the bloodiest slave insurrection in American history, which in turn generated widespread press coverage and legislative efforts to suppress both slave literacy and abolitionist print propaganda. Authentic or otherwise, *The Life and Confession of Thos. J. Wansley, . . . Written by Himself* anticipated not only the *Confessions of Nat Turner*, published the same year, but also *Narrative of the Life of Frederick Douglass, Written by Himself*, published the following decade. It is perhaps significant, then, that even as the *Life and Confession* elevates Wansley from "one of the pirates, concerned with Charles Gibbs" to an "author" with alleged control over his published *Life*, the manuscript "life of CHARLES GIBBS" is withheld from the public, its source having gone to his grave not merely a criminal but what may have been a worse fate in antebellum American print culture: a frustrated, unpublished writer of derivative fiction.

PART II

Chapter 3

The Ignominious Cord: Crime, Counterfactuals, and the New Black Politics

But where does Negro crimes exceed the Crimes of White Men?

—Warner Mifflin, *The Defence of Warner Mifflin against Aspersions Cast on Him on Account of His Endeavors To Promote Righteousness, Mercy and Peace, among Mankind* (1796)

The remarkable *Address of Abraham Johnstone, A Black Man, Who Was Hanged at Woodbury, in the County of Glocester, and State of New Jersey, on Saturday the the [sic] 8th Day of July Last; To the People of Colour. To Which Is Added His Dying Confession or Declaration. Also, a Copy of a Letter to His Wife, Written the Day Previous to His Execution* (1797) opens with an urgent invocation of temporality. "Brethren," begins the emancipated Delaware slave and convicted murderer, "I address you at this (to me, and not only to me but to all mankind) solemn important and truly aweful and momentous time, a time when I am on the verge of eternity, and that there is but a few short fleeting hours for me to remain in this world, and of that short time every moment spent by me even in addressing you my dear brethren, shortens."[1] Packed with seven temporal references, this preliminary sentence establishes Johnstone's conventional position as a condemned man entering print culture—authorizing him as one en route to the divine tribunal. In keeping with generic expectations, Johnstone, his "heart overflowing with love and humble hope in my God and Redeemer," exhorts his "dear friends, and brethren" to consider "what a miserable and unhappy fate awaits me in a few days" (3).

But the Johnstone depicted in the *Address* was no ordinary penitent criminal, and the pamphlet would not offer the standard gallows confession. Published fifteen years after the close of the American Revolution, the anti-confessional *Address* evinces the subversive tendencies of the era's most widely circulated crime literature. As the title page indicates, the interpolated personal narrative is more a "Declaration" of Johnstone's view of his case than a "Confession" of his guilt. Like the evangelical Whiting Sweeting or the roguish Stephen Burroughs, Abraham Johnstone articulates a broader popular resistance to the criminal law as a particularly coercive arm of an overreaching state power.[2] Structurally, the composite text revises an earlier form of gallows literature in which the malefactor's dying confession was appended to or published alongside the minister's monitory sermon. Here the condemned man usurps the clergyman's role, prefacing his exculpatory personal narrative with his own "series of wholesome admonition" (2).

In similar fashion, the *Address* evokes the genre's eschatological framework only to reinsert Johnstone in historical time. The two understandings of temporality were of course intimately connected in early America—and perhaps nowhere more visibly than in the Execution Day ritual, which joined individual repentance to communal expiation by mingling prayers and sermons with legal punishment. In his opening allusion to the "few short fleeting hours for me to remain in the world," Johnstone appears to commence the traditional labor performed by the condemned by offering, through his untimely death, a timely warning to his fellow sinners that it is never too soon to prepare for the hereafter. But, as this chapter will argue, the time and place of its publication ensured that the *Address*'s sense of urgency was a primarily political one.

Scheduled to be executed on July 8, 1797, four days after the annual Independence Day celebrations, Johnstone stood on the verge of eternity at a time when many in the United States felt themselves to be standing on the brink of a national future.[3] The Revolution behind them, the Constitution ratified, Americans were poised to enact an autonomous history even as they continued to refine the myth of their national past. "The time of Anglo-America," Stephen M. Best notes, "is a future perfect, a time not yet arrived, whose contingency and idealism remain the privileges granted to those on the road of history."[4] This sense of futurity was particularly intense in Johnstone's North, which in the 1790s was putting a period to two kinds of dependency at once: colonialism and slavery. Many in the North seized the occasion to consolidate their nation's exemplary identity as a free (white) republic by willfully forgetting slavery's history in the region and either ignoring or seeking to eradicate the continuing presence of African Americans in their towns and cities.[5] Others sought to safeguard the nation's future through social control efforts centering on the region's growing free black population. If, as critic Jared Gardner finds, "race helped provide the terms and the metaphors by which the first generations could stabilize national identity by giving it a past and a future" through the invocation of "narratives of origins, histories of change, and fantasies about the futures of peoples," these stories often turned on questions of individual and national responsibility.[6] It is thus emphatically "in this world" that the occasion of Johnstone's impending execution attains its significance, becoming a "solemn important and truly aweful and momentous time"—"not only to" the condemned speaker and his local community, "but to all mankind," and the new nation in particular. Evincing a reluctance to engage in the retrospective act of confession even as it narrates revisionist national and personal histories, the hortatory, forward-looking *Address of Abraham Johnstone* itself represents a powerful attempt to redirect America's racial future at a crucial historical moment—the 1790s—and from an evocative location—the gallows.

It is hard to say whether the fascinating, critically neglected *Address* garnered any more attention in its day than in our own. In this sense, Abraham Johnstone offers a rather extreme example of the black subject as a back formation of the gallows text.[7] No legal or print records documenting his trial, execution, or involvement in prior civil proceedings have been discovered, and the circumstances of the *Address*'s authorship, editing, publication, and circulation remain a mystery.[8] Daniel A. Cohen is one of the few scholars to appreciate the significance of the pamphlet's abolitionist stance, its apparent lack of an amanuensis, and its proleptic articulation of "several of the central liberal arguments in the discourse of race and crime as it would develop over the next two hundred years," yet even he sees Johnstone "exhort[ing] his fellow African Americans to adopt conventional virtues of bourgeois Christians."[9] Suggesting an alternative reading, this chapter finds in the *Address* a rare (and subtle) print critique of what historian Richard S. Newman has called the "patron-client politics" of early national racial reform initiatives.[10] In an era when an emerging cadre of African American publicists deferentially appealed to white civic leaders by deploying a rhetoric of moral reform and racial uplift in the interest of black inclusion, the *Address of Abraham Johnstone* simultaneously engaged in and ironized (or signified on, in Henry Louis Gates, Jr.'s classic formulation) this politics of respectability to offer one of the period's most insightful assessments of "the present situation of those of his colour."[11] Even as the *Address* appears to join the chorus of black and white reformers admonishing African Americans to prove their eligibility for citizenship through performances of virtue, its gallows perspective reveals that the persistent misapprehension of black civil activity as criminal behavior renders such civic displays not only futile but dangerous.

Although the pamphlet shares the future orientation of the era's other addresses to the people of color, Johnstone's own imminent removal from that future inflects the syntax in which he offers his forward-looking vision and thus the vision itself. In the 1780s and 1790s, abolitionist invocations of free blacks' role in the national future employed the optative and the imperative as well as the future perfect to evoke a black citizenship that was at once deferred and highly contingent. Because Johnstone's impending execution necessarily reduced any anticipation of the future on his part to its counterfactual essence, the *Address* calls into question his contemporaries' assumption that African American civic membership was conditional upon exemplary black deportment. Instead, by coupling a subjunctive counterfactual glimpse of Johnstone's future with declarative fact-based counternarratives of both his own and the nation's pasts, the *Address* demonstrates how the widespread tendency among white citizens and legal authorities to see racialized criminality in black civility preempts African American political inclusion.

Reading *The Address of Abraham Johnstone* in this way does not simply offer a more inclusive Black Atlantic canon or a more plebeian Black Founding era. The task here is not primarily to supplement scholarship "on the protest tactics of an elite black leadership class" by disclosing "the community struggles of nonelite reformers."[12] Virtually unique in African American gallows literature for its explicit endorsement of such a communalist, reformist ethos, *The Address of Abraham Johnstone* acquires significance on its own distinctly penal terms. Characterized by a temporal consciousness that highlights narrative's historicizing and projective functions—functions that also link individual, race, and nation in and through time—that penality also exposes the racialized logic of citizenship and criminality that ensured the continuity of black political exclusion, from slavery through the nominal freedom enacted by the First Emancipation, to today's incursions on African Americans' Fourth Amendment rights.[13] To understand that logic as it unfolded in the early republic, we must remind ourselves of the world from which the *Address* emerged.

Hanged at Woodbury, Printed in Philadelphia

According to the *Address*, Abraham Johnstone, originally named Benjamin, was born in Delaware, the slave of Dr. John Skidmore, at "Johnnycake landing Possom town, in Mother Kind-Hundred" in "County of Sussex."[14] Owned by five masters in fairly rapid succession, Johnstone was offered manumission (in exchange for financial remuneration) by his last master, James Craig, as a token of appreciation for having saved the white man from stabbing by another slave. Because Craig "owned that he owed his life to" Johnstone, he was willing, it seems, to give Johnstone the chance to own his own life—by owing Craig (33). As Johnstone explained, "he sold my time to myself, and gave me a considerable length of time to pay the money in," at which point Johnstone "staid away a whole year with a woman, and then was taken up as a run away, and put into Baltimore jail" (33). After acquainting Craig with his situation, Johnstone was moved to the jail in Dover, presumably so that Craig could arrange for his release. Unfortunately, Craig "died drunk" while Johnstone was still incarcerated (33). Craig's "executors then wanted to have me a slave," Johnstone recalled, "but being informed of my master's agreement with me, they did not attempt it" (33). Johnstone's release was arranged and paid for by "Mr. James Clements, merchant." After Johnstone had reimbursed Clements with his labor, Craig's executors sent him to chop some wood in a forest where they suddenly appeared "with two Georgia men" (slave traders, in Chesapeake vernacular) to whom they had sold him (33).[15] Bound and taken to a tavern eleven miles away for food and rest before continuing the southward journey, Johnstone managed to secrete a dinner knife and cut the cords that bound him while his captors slept. When Johnstone returned to Clements "and informed him of the business," the merchant "advised" him "to apply to Warner Mifflin, Esq. in Dover," which Johnstone "instantly did" (34).

Clements, whom the *Address* locates "at Mifflin's cross roads near Dover," gave Johnstone excellent advice (33).[16] The mercantile Crossroads where Clements and Johnstone worked was owned by first Warner and then brother Daniel Mifflin (with whom the *Address* places Johnstone's free thirteen-year-old son on his father's departure for New Jersey).[17] Born into a slaveholding Quaker family from Accomack County, Virginia, Warner Mifflin manumitted his twenty-one slaves in 1774–75, and quickly became one of the early republic's foremost abolitionists, cofounding the Delaware Society for Promoting the Abolition of Slavery in 1788 and sending an early

antislavery petition to Congress in 1792.[18] It was during this later period that
the *Address* places Johnstone's encounter with Mifflin, whose involvement
in freedom suits made him the subject of gossip and slander in the states
where he pursued his antislavery agenda.[19] "Knowing the footing I was on
with my late master," Johnstone explains, Mifflin "stood my fast friend on
the occasion, and obtained for me the manumission which I have got, as yet
and which protected me" (34).[20] Documentation notwithstanding, Johnstone
was still in danger from his now "extremely dissatisfied" would-be captors.
"To avoid trouble," Johnstone, knowing that "my poor colour had but few
friends in that country, where slavery is so very general, and if one negro was
befriended, it was feared to be setting a bad example to the others," followed
"the advice of all my friends, both black and white" and "came by water up
the Delaware to Philadelphia," moving quickly on to New Jersey, where he
settled in 1792, taking his brother's name of Abraham.[21]

The former slave's troubles did not, however, end with his arrival in
slaveholding New Jersey. The *Address*'s account of the tense circumstances
leading to Johnstone's conviction for "the murder of Thomas Read, a Guinea
negro" is cryptic. Johnstone asserts that, following his settlement on a leased
Gloucester County farm, he was "improving the place fast, and doing well
for myself, which made me an object of envy and hatred" in the local community—as evidenced by persistent rumors that he'd stolen carpets from
the boarding house keeper and quantities of meat from a number of local
smokehouses and slaughterhouses (39). Johnstone alleged that his landlord
and another man effectively framed him for the murder of Read, an African
man who had previously sued him. The unsigned editorial preface to Johnstone's *Address* insists that his was "a singularly uncommon and peculiar case,
as there was not positive evidence of the fact; the proof being founded on
presumption"—and, Johnstone would claim, false testimony (2).

Whatever Johnstone's transgressions (he acknowledges only "a too great
lust after strange women"), in the pamphlet attributed to him the condemned
man musters the authority to protest his innocence, impugn those whom he
accused of swearing falsely against him, and compare his imminent suffering
on the gallows to that of Christ on the cross (40).[22] Comprising the "Address
of Abraham Johnstone . . . to the People of Colour," "His Dying Confession or
Declaration," and "A Copy of a Letter to His Wife," plus the anonymous preface, the *Address* sheds even less light on the path that brought it to a Philadelphia printer than that which led its putative author from Delaware servitude
to the New Jersey scaffold.[23] The pamphlet lacks the explicitly white-authored

documents that typically authenticated early African American publications from Phillis Wheatley's *Poems on Subjects, Religious and Moral* (1773) and Jupiter Hammon's *Address to the Negroes in the State of New-York* (1785), to the *Narrative of the Life of Frederick Douglass*.[24] Written in the editorial first-person plural, the prefatory note "To the Public" refers to Johnstone in the third person, claiming that his "dying confession is a full and impartial account of himself from his birth unto the time of his execution[,] He having handed it out of the dungeon he was confined in on the morning of his execution; before a number of truly respectable persons, and declared that all that was therein contained was the truth, and nothing but the truth" (2). Maintaining that "the account of his life is strongly corroborated by a Mulatto man and his wife, both of respectable characters, and now living in Haddonfield," the anonymous compiler proposes to leave the question of the pamphlet's authenticity and the veracity of its ostensible author with the reader, who, "by having the whole of the pieces left by the unfortunate convict, . . . may be enabled to form an opinion of the true character, and guilt of the man independent of the malignant assertions, and innumerable falsehoods that have been propagated on this occasion by prejudiced persons."

However it reached the printer, the *Address of Abraham Johnstone* appeared at the very place and time at which the intersecting futures of race and punishment in America were being charted. Philadelphia, the temporary seat of the federal government, was also the "capital of free black life."[25] With its gradual emancipation law of 1780, Pennsylvania became the first state legislatively to enact abolition—although proslavery forces fought hard in subsequent years to weaken the act's effectiveness and comprehensiveness.[26] By the 1790s the Quaker city had established itself as the organizational and publishing center of a new print-based black politics, a nascent antislavery movement, and a budding international penal reform movement.[27] Early in the decade the city saw the publication of "the first federally copyrighted essay by African American writers," prominent activist ministers Absalom Jones and Richard Allen, both of whom, like Johnstone, had been enslaved in Delaware.[28] The first African American congressional petition also originated in the city, signed by manumitted North Carolina emigrants and reprinted in Philadelphia's *American Universal Magazine*. All this occurred while Benjamin Rush was becoming America's answer to Cesare Beccaria and Walnut Street Prison the experimental basis for the renowned Pennsylvania System.[29]

In the same decade, though, the home of the Free African Society, the Pennsylvania Abolition Society, the American Convention for the Abolition of Slavery, and the Philadelphia Society for Alleviating the Miseries of Public Prisons also became a haven for the masses of white slaveholders who, with their bondpeople, fled the revolution in Saint Domingue. Dramatizing Philadelphia's conflicting sympathies, "many white city dwellers reneged on their [financial] pledges to the African Church" founded by Jones and Allen "in order to help the destitute slaveholders now taking refuge in their city."[30] In that same year, the city watched as the resident Congress passed the first Fugitive Slave Act.[31] When, three years later, William and Mary law professor St. George Tucker wanted to publicize his plan to replace slavery and its inevitable criminal aftermath with legislated "civil slavery" for emancipated blacks, it was anything but incongruous for him to place his *Dissertation on Slavery . . . in the State of Virginia* with Philadelphia publisher Matthew Carey.[32] Throughout the 1790s, as local reformers commenced the civic regeneration of the new republic's (normatively white) prisoners, the city fairly hummed with debate over African Americans' prospective role in the nation's future.

That African Americans would enter that future as free people (even in the severely circumscribed freedom of the Pennsylvania Abolition Act) was by no means certain.[33] The transition from slaveholding colonies to "free" states was freighted with uncertainty and ambivalence, to say nothing of determined opposition. Although nostalgic sectional pride, growing disapproval of Southern slavery, and a desire to efface black presence altogether would inspire antebellum New Englanders, and Northerners more generally, to craft a triumphal narrative of post-Revolutionary liberty, the historical experience of African Americans and their white captors-turned-neighbors was far more complicated.[34] The complexities of the agonizingly gradual emancipation process were most evident in neighboring New York and New Jersey, where slavery was still not only legal but thriving when Abraham Johnstone was hanged in 1797.[35] When freedom finally came to those states, it was the sharply curtailed result of protracted and disconcerting legislative battles which, as in Pennsylvania, coupled emancipation with new penal regimes.[36]

While Johnstone awaited hanging in Gloucester County, his adopted state of New Jersey and his home state of Delaware were each vigorously debating yet another gradual emancipation bill.[37] New Jersey had seen extensive public controversy on the question of slavery and abolition over the past decade, previous bills having been defeated in 1792 and 1794. Belatedly founded in 1793, the New Jersey Society for Promoting the Abolition of Slavery finally introduced a gradual emancipation amendment to a proposed revised slave code in January 1797.[38] In the months leading up to Johnstone's execution New Jerseyites wrangled over the ensuing emancipation bill—particularly the "disgraceful penal sections" prohibiting slave testimony and prescribing whipping for minor offenses.[39] Four months after Johnstone's death, the bill was narrowly defeated.[40]

Despite its willingness to contemplate emancipation, the state still had all the trappings of a slaveholding society. The Wednesday following the hanging—little over a week after Independence Day—ads for runaway slaves James and Syphax appeared in the *New-Jersey Journal* alongside a notice for "a pair of *Brindle Stears* . . . and a *Red Heifer with Calf*" that had likewise "STRAYED."[41] Rather than abating, racism mounted throughout the 1790s. Freehold's Old Tennant Church opened the decade by introducing segregated gallery seating for its black congregants, while the Methodists, Johnstone's own preferred sect, amended their 1782 ban on slaveholding members.[42] Even in trailblazing Pennsylvania, emancipation was beginning to look more like a prelude to civic exclusion than to citizenship. "There exists a penal law," English travel writer Henry Bradshaw Fearon would observe of Philadelphia early in the new century, "deeply written in the *minds* of the whole white population, which subjects their coloured fellow-citizens to unconditional contumely and never ceasing insult. No respectability, however unquestionable,—no property, however large,—no character, however unblemished,—will gain a man, whose body is (in American estimation) *cursed* with even a twentieth portion of the blood of his African ancestry, admission into society!!!"[43]

Twenty years before Fearon's visit and a mere seven months prior to Abraham Johnstone's hanging, the first African American congressional petition called the federal government's attention to this very problem. Submitted by a Philadelphia-based group of four North Carolina ex-slaves, the "PETITION and REPRESENTATION of the undernamed FREEMEN" explained how, due to the combined forces of the 1793 federal fugitive slave law and a North Carolina statute allowing for the recapture of manumitted former slaves who remained in the state, they were treated more like property and criminals than free people.[44] Despite being "restor[ed] . . . to our native right of freedom" through manumission, the petitioners found themselves denied a civil existence (182). Once emancipated, Jupiter Nicholson spent two years "employed as a seaman" in North Carolina before moving with his legally manumitted wife to Virginia, where he became a sawyer; committed to his own extended family, Jacob Nicholson remained in the state with his old master; Job Albert lived with his wife, also manumitted, in the house provided by his former North Carolina master (182). Similarly, Thomas Pritchet's former master "furnished me with land to raise provisions for my use, where I built myself a house, cleared a sufficient spot of woodland to produce ten bushels of corn" the first year, "fifteen" the year after, and an anticipated "thirty" in the third year (184). But, Pritchet continued, he was deprived of the fruits of his labor when "I was obliged to leave one month before it was fit for gathering, being threatened by" the new husband of his master's widow, "that if I would not come and serve him, he would apprehend me and send me to the West-Indies," while another man "also threaten[ed] *to send me to gaol, and sell me for the good of the country*." Just as, "being thus in jeopardy," the industrious, prosperous Pritchet was forced to leave "my little farm with my small stock and utensils, and my corn standing," in order to escape "by night into Virginia" and thence to the North, the other three men were, one by one, driven to Philadelphia by threats to their liberty and livelihoods (184). Jupiter Nicholson was "pursued by men with dog and arms"; Jacob Nicholson, "pursued day and night," was "obliged to leave [his] abode, sleep in the woods, and stacks in the fields, &c. to escape the hands of violent men, who, induced by the profit afforded them by law, followed this course as a business" (183). Despite having "a house to accommodate me and my wife," Job Albert found himself, ironically, relieved that his "wife was by my kind master locked up under his roof" after the couple were "night and day hunted by men armed with guns, swords and pistols, accompanied with mastiff dogs." His white pursuers were the ones guilty of breaking into and entering his house (making away with "but small booty"), but it was Albert who was "discovered and seized" by men who, "armed with guns and clubs," bound him with "a rope round [his] arms and body" and took him to "prison."

Gainfully employed, with families and sometimes substantial property of their own, these men found the primary impediment to black civil life to be "violent men, who, induced by the profit afforded them by law," made a business of converting free people back into property—or, failing that (as in Albert's case), stealing property accumulated through free black labor. When the petitioners alluded to the plight of "a fellow black now confined in the gaol of this city, under sanction of the act of general government, called the Fugitive Law," they made it clear that, whether in North Carolina or Pennsylvania, African Americans, freed from bondage to individual masters, found themselves criminalized or relegated to a version of St. George Tucker's civil slavery (184). Recounting their viciously thwarted efforts to live as free people, the petitioners offer their personal stories as "flagrant proof how far human beings, merely on account of colour and complexion, are through prevailing prejudice out-lawed and excluded from common justice and common humanity, by the operation of such partial laws, in support of habits and customs cruelly oppressive" (184).

If those who read the petition in Philadelphia's *American Universal Magazine* had any doubt about this last claim, confirmation came with the following week's edition, which, as promised, published congressional debate over the petition. Ignoring the main issue of whether the 1793 fugitive slave law unconstitutionally restrained the liberties of free men, the House focused on the procedural question of what to do with the petition—and specifically, whether its formerly enslaved authors had the civil standing to be heard by the legislature. (In a rare moment of clarity, Congressman Aaron Kitchell of New Jersey reminded his colleagues that "the question was not now, whether they are or are not slaves, but it is on a law of the United States," specifically the petitioners' claim "that this law does act injuriously to them.")[45] Representatives from New York and Massachusetts, seeking to preserve the right of petition as a form of redress traditionally open to "any class of men," cautioned against setting a dangerous precedent that "the house should not receive a petition without an evidence to prove it was from a free man!" (276, 279).[46] Those who favored tabling the petition or ignoring it altogether maintained, in the words of South Carolina's William Smith, that the petitioners "*were not entitled to attention* from that body" and that "to encourage slaves to petition the house, would have a tendency to invite continual applications: indeed . . . it would act as an 'entering wedge,' whose consequences could not be foreseen'" (279). Torn between treating the petitioners as "*a kind of property*," as Representative Smith would have it, and acknowledging that, in the words of Massachusetts's exasperated George Thatcher, "THEY CERTAINLY . . . ARE FREE PEOPLE," Congress ultimately disregarded not only the petitioners' political membership in the new nation but their civil standing as legal persons (279, 276). By a robust margin of seventeen votes, the House refused to receive the petition. The debate dramatized even as it officially denied the legitimacy of the petitioners' complaint that law conspired with oppressive racial "habits and customs" to refuse African Americans recognition as anything but property or criminals in the wake of slavery.

A Cause Why We Ought Not To Be Free

"What further is to be done with them?" Thomas Jefferson had asked in *Notes on the State of Virginia* after ascribing blacks' thievishness to their enslaved "situation" rather than an innate "depravity."[47] American slaves' racial alterity prohibited their inclusion into the social compact, Sally Hemmings's bedmate maintained, arguing that free blacks should "be removed beyond the reach of mixture" (151). Accordingly, a proposed amendment to the revised legal code that Jefferson helped draft for the Virginia legislature directed that, following mandatory emancipation, former slaves "should be colonized to such place as the circumstances of the time should render most proper" (145). Employing the future perfect, the author of the Declaration of Independence goes on to defer black citizenship indefinitely as he proposes "sending them out with arms, implements of houshold and of the handicraft arts, feeds, pairs of the useful domestic animals, &c. to declare them a free and independant people, and extend to them our alliance and protection, till they shall have acquired strength" (145).[48] Nominally sovereign and free but civilly incapacitated, the former slaves, unable even to declare their own independence, remain under American custodianship "till" the unspecified and apparently distant day when "they shall have acquired strength" necessary to assert and maintain political autonomy.

Northern abolitionists concurred with Jefferson and Tucker that, as Noah Webster put it in his *Effects of Slavery*, "the practice of enslaving men, which, in the first instance, is the most attrocious act of villainy," was virtually guaranteed to become "introductive of every species of crimes."[49] Attuned to the anecdotal evidence that manstealing begat further crime—to "the black catalogue of the public and private evils flowing from the practice of enslaving men"—Webster, as seen in Chapter 1, shared Tucker's conviction that "the restoration of freedom" did not "in general correct the depravity" inculcated by involuntary servitude (14, 13). Webster, who based his own assertions not on anxious projection but on anecdotal evidence, affirmed of free blacks that "manumission, instead of destroying their [slavery-derived] habits and repressing their corrupt inclinations, serves to afford them more numerous opportunities of indulging both" (13). It was in this sense, he reluctantly concluded, that "an act of strict justice to the slave often renders him a worse member of society" (13). Believing themselves faced with the same predicament outlined by Tucker's *Dissertation on Slavery*—emancipation's tendency to effectuate rather than eliminate black criminality—Webster and his North-

ern white abolitionist colleagues proposed a different tack from those advocated by the Virginians. In light of the perceived black propensity for crime
in slavery's aftermath, they saw the supervision, regulation, and instruction of
free(d) African Americans as indispensable components of emancipation.[50]
Instead of excluding free blacks from the polity outright, these reformers
would make African American citizenship highly conditional.

Accordingly, in the mid-1790s, responding to what they perceived as both
the promise and the threat of black emancipation, the mid-Atlantic abolitionists who made Philadelphia their organizational hub began to redirect
their reform efforts from enslaved to free African Americans.[51] Whereas antislavery societies had previously devoted themselves to seeking manumission
through colonial and then state legislatures and courts, now the prospect of
a rapidly growing free black population inspired a concerted attempt to supervise and regulate those African Americans no longer under direct white
control.[52] Gathering in Philadelphia for their second convention in January
1795, delegates from all-white abolition societies in the states of Connecticut,
New York, New Jersey, and Pennsylvania as well as from cities in Maryland
and Virginia recognized the need to "take into consideration the means of
improving the condition of the Blacks, who are, or may be, made free in the
different states, and of preventing the inconveniences that may arise from
the degraded state of the Negroes in the United States."[53] To this end, the
delegates requested member organizations to submit "an exact account of the
persons who have been liberated by the agency of your Society, and of those
who may be considered as signal instances of the relief you have afforded;
and, also, a statement of the number of free blacks in your state, their property, employments, and moral conduct."[54]

Such accurate registers of manumissions provided valuable evidence for
subsequent freedom litigation.[55] But the abolitionist impulse to document
the free black population bore a chilling resemblance to the registration
systems and expanded police powers that Southern state legislatures and
municipalities were developing throughout the 1780s and 1790s in order to
exert ever tighter control over free African Americans.[56] Closer to home,
such efforts recalled New England's well-established transient examination
system even as they corresponded to newer carceral practices, both of which
incorporated biographical record-keeping into broader governmental supervisory strategies that, in cities from Providence to Philadelphia, increasingly
and disproportionately focused on poor people of color.[57] Pointing out that
in 1784, New York's Common Council "sought to develop a ward-by-ward

accounting of 'the Names Ages & Places of Abode of every Negro & Molatto,'" historian David N. Gellman has traced the superintendence enjoined
by early national abolitionist organizations back to municipal regulations
grounded in "the presumption that African Americans should be treated as
criminal suspects to be carefully monitored."[58]

Along with more formal record-keeping, white abolitionists sought to
supervise those whom they considered their black charges. "Keep a watchful
eye over the conduct of such Negroes as have been and may be liberated,"
the New York Manumission Society (NYMS) urged its members in 1785, "to
prevent them from running into immorality or sinking into idleness."[59] Failing to establish the proposed Committee for Preventing Irregular Conduct in
Free Negroes and thus to create a registry of New York's free African Americans, the NYMS did conduct supervisory home visits so as to gauge the
moral standing of prospective students for its African Free School, founded
in 1787.[60] For the Pennsylvania Abolition Society (PAS), compliance with the
Convention's calls for supervision meant simply "resum[ing] the house calls
that Quakers had initiated in the 1780s" among Philadelphia's black population in order "to warn against 'disorderly meetings' and to give 'friendly
admonitions against such improprieties in their conduct.'"[61]

Such supervisory strategies became integral to the politics of respectability that, with its deferential tone and its moral reform rhetoric, characterized
early abolitionist activism in the 1790s. If we parse the grammar of print discussions of race and slavery, we can discern how the various moods adopted
by the early national participants in this future-oriented discourse disclose
not only their divergent views of the prospective role of African Americans
in the United States, but also their conflicting understandings of the national
and racial past and present. For whereas the future perfect of Jeffersonian
colonizationist discourse figured an exported black citizenship as at once
providentially ordained and conveniently deferred, Northern white abolitionists tended to articulate their view of African American civic inclusion
in the optative—even as they shared Jefferson's tendency to objectify "the
emancipated." Anticipating a day when their efforts "will gradually produce
an entire abolition," the Convention of Delegates from the Abolition Societies Established in Different Parts of the United States was quick to note in its
annual minutes: "Yet, even should that great end be happily attained, it cannot put a period to the necessity of further labor. . . . When we have broken
his chains, and restored the African to the enjoyment of his rights, the great
work of justice and benevolence is not accomplished—The new born citizen

must receive that instruction, and those powerful impressions of moral and religious truth, which will render him capable and desirous of fulfilling the various duties he owes to himself and to his country."[62] The infantile black "new born citizen" does not emerge fully formed from the emancipated "African," that passive beneficiary of white abolitionist agency; rather his citizenship is conditional upon his successful socialization into his civic "duties."

In an effort to ensure the African American civil subject's correct maturation, the Convention resolved to "address the free black people, in the United States, exhorting them, by suitable arguments and motives, to such conduct and behaviour as may be judged most proper to promote their own happiness, and render them useful members of society," appointing a committee to draft such a document for publication.[63] The ensuing appeal *To the Free Africans and other Free People of Color in the United States*, an unrecognized but key source for Johnstone's *Address*, begins by urging the value of public worship, education (for manual labor in particular), and exemplary Christian deportment, then proceeds to discourage drinking and frolicking, while encouraging frugality and legal documentation of birth, deaths, and marriages[64] (see Figure 10).

To its designated free black audience, the Convention explained its motives for "undertak[ing] to address you upon subjects highly interesting to your prosperity."[65] "They wish," the broadside began, "to see you act worthily of the rank you have acquired as Freemen, and thereby to do credit to yourselves, and to justify the friends and advocates of your color in the eyes of the world." The nine "articles of Advice" that followed quickly shifted from the preamble's optative into the imperative. After the first two articles (which modestly begin "WE earnestly recommend to you" and "WE advise . . . you"), five of the remaining six articles, dropping the first-person plural subject, commence with a capitalized command: "TEACH your children useful trades"; "BE diligent in your respective callings"; "REFRAIN from the use of spirituous liquors"; "AVOID frolicking"; and "ENDEAVOUR to lay up as much as possible of your earnings." Republishing a slightly expanded version of the broadside in May 1797, the Convention followed a new closing injunction (against "gaming") with a final promise: "Go on in these paths of virtue: By persevering in them you will justify the solicitude and labors of your friends in your behalf and furnish an additional argument for the emancipation of such of your brethren as are yet in bondage in the United States and other parts of the world."[66]

Expressive of white reformers' desire simultaneously to nurture and to

TO THE

Free Africans and other free People of color

IN THE

UNITED STATES.

THE Convention of Deputies from the Abolition Societies in the United States, affembled at Philadelphia, have undertaken to addrefs you upon fubjects highly interefting to your profperity.

THEY wifh to fee you act worthily of the rank you have acquired as Freemen, and thereby to do credit to yourfelves, and to juftify the friends and advocates of your color in the eyes of the world.

As the refult of our united reflections, we have concluded to call your attention to the following articles of Advice. We truft, they are dictated by the pureft regard for your welfare, for we view you as Friends and Brethren.

In the firft place, WE earneftly recommend to you, a regular attention to the important duty of public worfhip; by which means you will evince gratitude to your CREATOR, and, at the fame time, promote knowledge, union, friendfhip, and proper conduct amongft yourfelves.

Secondly, WE advife fuch of you, as have not been taught reading, writing, and the firft principles of arithmetic, to acquire them as early as poffible. Carefully attend to the inftruction of your children in the fame fimple and ufeful branches of education. Caufe them, likewife, early and frequently to read the holy Scriptures; they contain, among other great difcoveries, the precious record of the original equality of mankind, and of the obligations of univerfal juftice and benevolence, which are derived from the relation of the human race to each other in a COMMON FATHER.

Thirdly, TEACH your children ufeful trades, or to labor with their hands in cultivating the earth. Thefe employments are favorable to health and virtue. In the choice of mafters, who are to inftruct them in the above branches of bufinefs, prefer thofe who will work with them; by this means they will acquire habits of induftry, and be better preferved from vice, than if they worked alone, or under the eye of perfons lefs interefted in their welfare. In forming contracts, for yourfelves or children, with mafters, it may be ufeful to confult fuch perfons as are capable of giving you the beft advice, who are known to be your friends, in order to prevent advantages being taken of your ignorance of the laws and cuftoms of our country.

Fourthly, BE diligent in your refpective callings, and faithful in all the relations you bear in fociety, whether as hufbands, wives, fathers, children or hired fervants. Be juft in all your dealings. Be fimple in your drefs and furniture, and frugal in your family expenfes. Thus you will act like Chriftians as well as freemen, and, by thefe means, you will provide for the diftreffes and wants of ficknefs and old age.

Fifthly, REFRAIN from the ufe of fpirituous liquors; the experience of many thoufands of the citizens of the United States has proved, that thofe liquors are not neceffary to leffen the fatigue of labor, nor to obviate the extremes of heat or cold; much lefs are they neceffary to add to the innocent pleafures of fociety.

Sixthly, AVOID frolicking, and amufements that lead to expenfe and idlenefs; they beget habits of diffipation and vice, and thus expofe you to deferved reproach amongft your white neighbours.

Seventhly, WE wifh to imprefs upon your minds the moral and religious neceffity of having your marriages legally performed; alfo to have exact regifters preferved of all the births and deaths which occur in your refpective families.

Eighthly, ENDEAVOUR to lay up as much as poffible of your earnings for the benefit of your children, in cafe you fhould die before they are able to maintain themfelves—your money will be fafeft and moft beneficial when laid out in lots, houfes or fmall farms.

Ninthly, WE recommend to you, at all times and upon all occafions, to behave yourfelves to all perfons in a civil and refpectful manner, by which you may prevent contention and remove every juft occafion of complaint. We befeech you to reflect it is by your good conduct alone, that you can refute the objections which have been made againft you as rational and moral creatures, and remove many of the difficulties, which have occurred in the general emancipation of fuch of your brethren as are yet in bondage.

WITH hearts anxious for your welfare, we commend you to the guidance and protection of that BEING who is able to keep you from all evil, and who is the common Father and Friend of the whole family of mankind.

By order, and on behalf, of the CONVENTION,

Theodore Fofter, Prefident.

Philadelphia, January 6th. 1796.

Atteft.

Thomas P. Cope, Secretary.

PHILADELPHIA: PRINTED BY ZACHARIAH POULSON, JUNIOR, NUMBER EIGHTY, CHESNUT-STREET.

27

Figure 10. Convention of Delegates from the Abolition Societies Established in Different Parts of the United States, *To the Free Africans and Other Free People of Color in the United States* (Philadelphia, [1796]). The Library Company of Philadelphia.

police the North's growing free black population, the broadside's uneasy mingling of the optative with the imperative conveyed the conflicting moods of
the era's interracial patron-client politics. This collaboration, framed by the
same language and rituals of deference that continued to shape early republican politics more broadly, assumed reciprocal duties from and offered respective benefits to each party. Advocating racial advancement through collective
moral reform, African American leaders "drew common inspiration from the
prospect of free people of color 'uplifting' themselves to conditions of 'respectability,' an approach to securing equality that stressed patient incrementalism,
strenuous self-improvement, deference from ordinary community members,
and the guidance of patriarchal leaders."[67] "Respectability" meant different
things to different racial (and class) constituencies in the early republic.
Rather than echoing their white counterparts' injunctions, the moral reform
rhetoric of such black "mediators," took aim at racism and slaveholding as
much as any lapse in African American deportment.[68] In this way, Newman
and Finkenbine suggest, such "black founders" cultivated "a translocal black
identity" that they developed and articulated in part through an oppositional
discourse of civic inclusion designed to "persuade Americans that they were
equal citizens of the Republic in theory if not reality."[69] The shared rhetoric
of respectability thus obscured the often discrepant goals of early national
white and black activists, with the former seeing in "respectability" a form of
accommodation to the dominant culture and the latter viewing it as a means
to achieve both cultural autonomy and political equality.[70]

Newman views this patron-client politics of respectability as an integral
component of the "new black politics of public engagement" that emerged
in the 1790s throughout the urban Northeast when African Americans side-
stepped exclusionary "rules of party politics" and their proscription from "the
very sites of political venues" by "seizing print" as a medium that "provided a
public voice to a politically powerless people."[71] Along with "establishing autonomous institutions, claiming an independent voice in print, and securing
the services of white printers," a key element of the new black politics was
the development of a cadre of leaders who could serve as "spokesmen for the
race" in these novel institutional and print forums.[72] Piety, thrift, temperance,
dignified deportment, and education were indispensable, but, James Brewer
Stewart maintains, "above all, 'respectability' connoted the possession of
the intellectual and literary skills necessary to allow African Americans to
contribute their own authoritative political voices as equals to the nation's
ongoing civic discussions."[73]

Appropriately, then, one of the earliest print exponents of moral reform was not a member of the professional or educated elite, but the "Servant of John Lloyd, jun, Esq; of the Manor of Queen's Village, Long-Island."[74] As America's first published black poet, the enslaved Jupiter Hammon could authorize his monitory *Address to the Negroes in the State of New-York* on the basis of his "age," piety, and literary reputation, as well as his "nation and colour" (6). Published in New York and Philadelphia, Hammon's *Address* acknowledges "that liberty is a great thing, and worth seeking for, if we can get it honestly, and by our good conduct, prevail on our masters to set us free" (13).

Seven years later, in their own exhortation "To the People of Colour," Absalom Jones and Richard Allen, "having been ourselves slaves, and as desirous of freedom as any of you," similarly urge the enslaved portion of their audience not to "sink at the discouraging prospects you may have" but rather to "put your trust in God," keeping in mind that, "as your hearts are inclined to serve God, you will feel an affectionate regard toward your masters and mistresses . . . this will be seen by them, and tend to promote your liberty."[75] A shared racial identity meant a common destiny, regardless of condition. Jones and Allen reminded those "who are favoured with freedom" that "much depends upon us for the help of our colour . . . if we are lazy and idle, the enemies of freedom plead it as a cause why we ought not to be free, and say we are better in a state of servitude, and that giving us our liberty would be an injury to us, and by such conduct we strengthen the bands of oppression, and keep many in bondage."[76] Such vigilance was indispensable at a time and a place at which the "enemies of freedom" might well include abolitionists who, like Noah Webster, seemed all too ready to concede that "liberty would be an injury to us." Authoritatively instructing their own social subordinates even as they deferentially appealed to white civic leaders, Jones and Allen made clear that liberty was not merely elusive but highly contingent upon the patron-client politics of respectability.

The great irony, of course, was that these defensive warnings appeared in the appendices to Jones and Allen's exhaustive documentary account of black civic virtue, *A Narrative of the Proceedings of the Black People, during the Late Awful Calamity in Philadelphia in the Year 1793: and a Refutation of some Censures, Thrown upon Them in some late Publications.* The even greater irony was that all this abstract discussion of whether and on what terms African Americans would be included in the social compact was emanating from Philadelphia in the mid- to late 1790s. For if the First Emancipation

had commenced just too late to incorporate blacks on equal terms into
the newly drafted federal and state constitutions, recent events in the city
seemed almost providentially designed to force such an experiment. During "the late awful calamity" alluded to by Jones and Allen—the 1793 yellow
fever epidemic—Philadelphians descended into a near-Hobbesian state of
nature before entering a renovated social compact. At least, that is how things
appear in the "Publication" that prompted Jones and Allen's print "Refutation," Mathew Carey's influential and widely circulated *Short Account of the
Malignant Fever, lately prevalent in Philadelphia* (1793).[77] The regeneration of
the nation's capitol—coming as it did a mere three years after Pennsylvania's
groundbreaking emancipation act—was perfectly timed to allow free blacks'
inclusion into the new social order as scripted by Carey. But by focusing on
the civic exertions of the middling and entrepreneurial white men whose
extralegal Committee on Malignant Fever filled the vacuum in city government, the striving Irish publisher largely ignored or underrated the substantial contributions of African Americans, women, and the so-called lesser
orders. Worse, as Jones and Allen point out, Carey's exclusion of blacks from
the revised social compact turned on the *Short Account*'s insistent misin-
terpretation of their recent display of civic virtue as evidence of a collective
propensity for criminality.

Along with Dr. Benjamin Rush's ill-considered commitment to copious
purging and bloodletting as a cure, the epidemic is remembered largely
for the print debate it provoked between the white publisher and the black
churchmen. As leaders of the Free African Society, Jones and Allen were
approached by both Rush and abolitionist Anthony Benezet early in the
epidemic to recruit the city's African American community to attend to the
sick and the dead—a request grounded on an erroneous belief in blacks'
immunity to the disease. Benezet published a newspaper notice offering a
broad "hint to the black people, that a noble opportunity is now put into
their hands, of manifesting their gratitude to the inhabitants of that city,
which first planned their emancipation from slavery, and who since afforded
them so much protection and support, as to place them, in point of civil and
religious privileges, upon a footing with themselves."[78] The carefully considered decision of Jones, Allen, and others to comply with white civic leaders'
requests meant, as Phillip Lapsansky points out, that the "humblest of Philadelphians, many recently slaves, helped administer what was effectively the
government of the city" at a time of almost complete municipal and social
disintegration.[79] Jones and Allen enlisted black Philadelphians to nurse the

sick, cart away corpses, and dig graves. In this early national instance of
white flight, the city's wealthiest denizens (and the republic's political leaders)
fled to the more salubrious suburbs and countryside while black volunteers
"patrolled the streets, checked abandoned properties, and tried to maintain a
semblance of social order." [80] This black-organized civic order was instituted
over a week prior to the founding of the all-white Committee memorialized
by Carey's pamphlet. [81]

Carey's *Short Account* did more than crop out people of color from its
"inspiring image of 'public-spirited citizen,'" for, as Jones and Allen immediately perceived, it is only by criminalizing black civic action that Carey,
in historian Sally F. Griffith's words, "reserves his central roles as founding
fathers of the new social compact for white, male middle-class citizens." [82]
Recollecting how, "at an early stage of the disorder, the elders of the African
church met, and offered their services to the mayor, to procure nurses for the
sick, and to assist in burying the dead," Carey alleged in the passage made
famous by Jones and Allen's subsequent print dissent, "the great demand
for nurses afforded opportunity for imposition, which was eagerly seized by
some of the vilest of the blacks. They extorted two, three, four, and even five
dollars a night for attendance, which would have been well paid by a single
dollar. Some of them were even detected in plundering the houses of the
sick." [83] "But," he concluded, "it is wrong to cast a censure on the whole for
this sort of conduct, as many people have done. The services of Jones, Allen,
and [William] Gray, and others of their colour, have been very great, and
demand public gratitude." [84] Carey's seemingly conscientious identification of
exceptionally virtuous African American individuals enacts the very racial
slur that the passage ostensibly eschews, effectively casting "a censure on the
whole" for its allegedly criminal "conduct."

Outraged by Carey's inability to view black public activity as anything but
extortion and theft, Jones and Allen published their "refutation." This microhistory of black civic virtue helps us to understand how what Lapsansky
characterizes as the "first account of a free black community in action" was
necessarily also "the first African American polemic in which black leaders
sought to . . . directly confront an accuser." [85] "By naming us," Jones and Allen
note, Carey "leaves these others, in the hazardous state of being classed with
those who are called the 'vilest.'" [86] Maintaining that "the few that were discovered to merit public censure, were brought to justice, which ought to have
sufficed, without being canvassed over in his 'Trifle' of a pamphlet," Jones and
Allen deplore Carey's arraignment of Philadelphia's black community before

the bar of public opinion (13). Whereas a formal indictment would have allowed recourse to due process, Carey's print allegations exposed black Philadelphia to the very real hazards of extrajudicial censure and punishment.

Promoting the new provisional government's managerial containment of
the biopolitical crisis of the yellow fever epidemic, Carey figured Philadelphia's
black population as an amorphous, anonymous, mass security threat to both
city and nation. In response, Jones and Allen presented capsule narratives
recounting the disinterested civic acts of, among others, "a poor black man,
named Sampson," "Sarah Bass, a poor black widow," "a woman of our colour,"
"an elderly black woman," "a young black woman," and "Caesar Cranchal,
a black man" (11–12).[87] Much as the testimonial slave narrative would do in
the antebellum period, these brief accounts individualize African Americans
while decriminalizing black public presence. And, like that later genre, the
pamphlet's articulations of African American civility at once refute and rest
upon the pervasive association of black publicity with criminality.

The Carey/Jones-Allen controversy has helped scholars to reconstruct
the political, scientific, economic, theological, and philosophical discourses
of race and slavery in the early republic.[88] Yet, beyond examining how Jones
and Allen refute Carey's allegations by exposing white misconduct, elaborating the market forces governing response to the epidemic, and noting Carey's
own opportunistic print exploitation of the epidemic—"Is it a greater crime
for a black to pilfer, than for a white to privateer?" they asked (8)—scholars
have paid scant attention to criminality's central role in this early national
debate over race and civic inclusion. All too aware of the illegibility of African American civic virtue as such, these black founders did not hesitate to
exert the print leverage that had long been enabled by punitive recognition
of black malefactors.

Jones and Allen's well-known pamphlet opens with a telling corrective
that has received surprisingly little critical commentary. After summariz-
ing the events leading to organized African American involvement in the
epidemic, Jones and Allen embark on their rebuttal of Carey by quoting not
his aspersions on black nurses but his approbation for the city's prison population: "Mr. Carey . . . has observed, that, 'for the honor of human nature,
it ought to be recorded that some of the convicts in the gaol, a part of the
term of whose confinement had been remitted as a reward for their peaceable, orderly behavior, voluntarily offered themselves as nurses to attend to
the sick at Bush-hill; and have, in that capacity, conducted themselves with
great fidelity'" (4). Whereas later Jones and Allen will criticize Carey for

indiscriminately incriminating other black caregivers, in this first instance they protest his *failure* to identify the convicts as African American. "Here it ought to be remarked, (although Mr. Carey hath not done it)," the *Narrative* continues, "that two-thirds of the persons, who rendered these essential services, were people of colour, who, on the application of the elders of the African church . . . were liberated, on condition of their doing the duty of nurses at the hospital at Bush-hill; which they as voluntarily accepted to do, as they did faithfully discharge, this severe and disagreeable duty" (4–5). It is only after this initial identification of Carey's exemplary convicts as predominantly people of color that Jones and Allen go on to recount their training into and administering of Dr. Rush's methods; render a financial account of the losses incurred by the Free African Society; provide the contrasting anecdotes of white misconduct and black heroism; and present a close-up account of the illness's devastating physical and social impact on the city's inhabitants. Given the pamphlet's exculpatory purpose, why commence the refutation of Carey's censures by highlighting the disproportionate number of African Americans in the city's prison population?[89] Why open an exoneration of African American conduct with the image of black convicts, however exemplary? Were Jones and Allen so desperate for even grudging white approval that they were willing to compromise their defense of black civic behavior by reinforcing the widespread belief in African Americans' predisposition to crime?

Rather than a confirmation of the black origins of social disorder, Jones and Allen's first corrective to Carey can be read as a template for the counter-assertion of African American aptitude for citizenship in a nation that increasingly seized black criminality, real or imagined, as a pretext for political exclusion. In the *Short Account*, Carey's convicts are defined less by the crimes that land them in gaol than by the civic duties they undertake at Bush Hill. Their ability to do so, Carey's digressive encomium on Walnut Street Prison insists, is attributable to the success of such Enlightenment penal experiments, which "prove that jails may be easily converted from sinks of human depravity and wretchedness, into places of reformation" and their inmates into "useful members of society."[90] Whereas under "the old system . . . these men's lives would have been long since offered up as an atonement to society for the injury they had done it," Carey notes, under "the improved plan, they and great numbers of others are restored to society and usefulness once more."[91] One of the Committee's first administrative triumphs, the convicts' "peaceable, orderly behavior" as Bush Hill nurses marks their successful disciplinary reintegration into society even as it affirms the provisional authority's successful management of its superfluous waste populations by having the civilly dead minister to the physically dead and dying.[92] Instead of casting a shadow of self-interest on their exemplary virtue, the convicts' exchange of civic services for remitted sentences demonstrates their eligibility to participate in the new social contract occasioned by the epidemic, in which an entrepreneurial liberalism advanced the republican commitment to civic virtue.[93] As they trade the "severe and disagreeable duty" of nursing for release from prison, the ex-convicts are initiated into the contractualism on which that compact is premised.

Jones and Allen commence their *Narrative* with this enlightened, liberal exchange of "confinement" for "liberat[ion]" in consideration for civic duties, endorsing Carey's view of the epidemic as inaugurating a renovated social order governed by a revised compact that includes those excluded from or marginalized in the previous regime. In the process, they highlight blacks' eligibility for the regeneration heretofore envisioned for a normatively white prison population. More subtly, by insisting that those whose prior "peaceable, orderly behavior" qualified them to be "liberated" from (a perhaps unjust) "confinement" were disproportionately "people of color," Jones and Allen open their refutation of Carey with a clear-eyed acknowledgment of how black criminality could be turned to account. Cognizant that "an ill name is easier given than taken away" (especially when given in print), Jones and Allen preface the nation's first black-authored exposition-cum-exoneration of African American civic behavior by demonstrating how punitive recognition of black public presence could be converted into a civil "capacity" (in Carey's word) that in turn could be cited to justify African American citizenship.

The neglected opening to Jones and Allen's refutation of Carey's "Censures" suggests that if the black founders' print tactics opened a new door into the public sphere, the old one remained in steady use. Ideally, respectable, articulate, educated leaders would now, in an appropriately deferential tone, use print to activate the era's patron-client politics through a display of black uplift that would enlist elite white support to reject calumny from unenlightened "enemies of freedom" determined to impede black citizenship. Failing that, African Americans (of whatever qualifications) could always do as the inmates of Walnut Street Prison had recently done—and as Frederick Douglass would still be doing sixty years hence: expand the recognized legal personhood granted to criminals of color into an altogether different kind of black public presence, one that just might lay the groundwork for claims to full citizenship.

That *The Address of Abraham Johnstone* was published in Philadelphia a mere three years after the *Narrative of the Proceedings* appeared in that city suggests that Jones and Allen's successful modeling of both elite and everyday black virtue had not eliminated the need to leverage the publicity that accrued to black crime. The challenge, of course, was to do so at a time when the new black politics rested so heavily on the interracial patron-client politics of respectability. The *Address* rose to this challenge by deploying the era's moral reform rhetoric to expose that politics' underlying racist assumptions while at the same time revealing the emancipating North's persistent misapprehension of black civic behavior for criminality as the false premise upon which African American political exclusion was increasingly predicated in the early republic. Attuned to, yet wary of, the era's uplift ideology, this dense but richly suggestive pamphlet intervenes in contemporary debates over the nation's racial future by counterfactually revealing the extent to which African American citizenship was contingent on (American) political and legal reform, not (black) moral reform.

The Address of Abraham Johnstone

Mindful of the influence of (white) "men of genius, spirit and candour," the *Address of Abraham Johnstone* exhorts the people of color "to endeavour by your irreproachable conduct to ripen [their] good disposition towards you into esteem," promising that "by so doing you will make yourselves not only respectable but beloved, and also will thereby furnish your friends with strong arguments and inducements to endeavour the relief of the rest of our breth[re]n, as yet in thraldom."[94] Such invocations of the era's interracial deference politics have prompted speculation that the pamphlet may have been "written by a white missionary" or that Johnstone, "guided by the abolitionist project of his amanuensis/editor, or by his own concern for the emancipation of 'his brethren['], . . . is only explicitly critical of racism from the distance of history or geography," expediently directing "those blacks who remain" to be "civilly obedient."[95] And indeed, Johnstone echoes black preachers like Hammon, Allen, and Jones as, addressing his "dear friends and breth[re]n," he dispenses counsel "not only . . . absolutely necessary to promote your prosperity and welfare, in this life, but essentially necessary to your future happiness," expressing hope that his advice "will be treasured up in your minds."[96]

Yet notwithstanding his concern lest he "become too speculatively refined in my sentiments, and too tedious to my hearers," Johnstone occupied
a markedly different position from the era's eminent reformers, addressing
his fellow people of color not from the pulpit or the lecture platform but "on
a stage beneath [the] gallows" (23, 40). With his spotty church membership,
"too great lust after strange women," alleged string of thefts, and murder
conviction, Abraham Johnstone more closely resembled the wayward constituents to whom such venerable black founders directed their monitory
addresses—men like John Joyce and Peter Mathias, whose 1808 execution
for the murder of an elderly white Philadelphia shopkeeper would prompt
Richard Allen to publish the first black-edited gallows pamphlet.

But if Johnstone's murder conviction precluded the requisite display of
respectability, its unique circumstances also enable the pamphlet to reject
for him the conventional roles that Joyce and Mathias would soon fill, those
of negative exemplar or penitent sinner. More than just twelve miles of road
separated Joyce and Mathias's Philadelphia from Johnstone's Woodbury, New
Jersey. In place of the "midnight dances and frolics" that figure so prominently in Allen's account of urban social disorder, *The Address of Abraham
Johnstone* depicts a world where former slaves did agricultural work alongside white yeomen and African laborers, threshing grain for local farmers
and occasionally managing to raise crops and husk corn of their own.[97] Far
from being snatched from the "midnight revel, the polluted couch" like Joyce
and Mathias, Johnstone found himself "tied, coming to jail," near "a piece of
buck-wheat" that he might well have worked.[98] ("Would'st thou O man avoid
the gallows?" Allen admonished his fellow people of color, "labour with thy
hands and thou will provide things that are honest, and with a good conscience enjoy them.")[99] Johnstone's legal troubles had their origin in neither
"the tavern" nor "the chambers of the harlot" (4), but in literally the most civil
of circumstances: either a previous lawsuit (as the prosecution contended)
or a disputed lease (as Johnstone maintained). Instead of confirming what
Allen feared to be a pernicious racial "tendency of dishonesty and lust, of
drunkenness and stealing" (5), Johnstone's conviction and execution, like the
experiences of the four congressional petitioners earlier that year, dramatized
the risk that even the most mundane civil acts imposed on nominally free
blacks in the early national United States.

Sensitive to the rhetorical disadvantages of the condemned man's status,
the embedded—and intriguing—"Address of Abraham Johnstone . . . to the
People of Colour" puts the conventional printed gallows speech in service

to the new black politics by suggesting that, rather than compromising his
integrity, Johnstone's impending execution heightened both the relevance
and the urgency of his appeal. Johnstone commences his "Address" with
an exhortation "to be upright, and circumspect in your conduct" before
(windily) explaining: "I must the more earnestly urge this particular from a
combination of circumstances that at this juncture of time concur to make
it of importance to our colour[,] for my unfortunate unhappy fate however
unmerited or undeserved, may by some ungenerous and illiberal minded
persons, but particularly by those who [o]ppose the emancipation of those
of our breth[re]n who as yet are in slavery, be made a handle of in order to
throw a shade over or cast a general reflection on all those of our colour, and
the keen shafts of prejudice be launched against us by the most active and
virulent malevolence."[100] Confident, on second thought, that "such general reflections or sarcasms, will be only made by the low minded illiberal and sor-
did persons who are the enemies of our colour, and of freedom," Johnstone
acknowledges that another, more pressing "circumstance that renders my fate
peculiarly unhappy at this crisis, is that it [his condemnation] happens at a
time when every effort is using for a total emancipation of all our brethren
in slavery within this state" (7). Verging on eternity, Johnstone is nevertheless
explicit that the "juncture of time" in question is as historical as the current
"crisis" is political: "'Tis thence my dear friends and breth[re]n that I esteem
it so peculiarly unfortunate, as it may be made a handle of to retard the truly
laudable endeavours of such generous and worthy persons" (8).

Identifying Johnstone's own prosecution with a more general racial
persecution, the *Address* combines the two genres deployed in the project
of black social control, the confession and the address to the people of
color, in order to expose the devastating tendency of American racism to
misapprehend civil activity as criminal behavior. Johnstone's position on
the gallows, the *Address* implies, gave him an unsurpassed view of this phenomenon as it first unfolded in the early republic. If his condemned status
kept him from ascending the Olympian heights from which black founders
sometimes seemed to survey their communities, his *Address* indicates that in
the urgent political "juncture" of the 1790s, the gallows offered more than a
still-serviceable platform from which to project even the humblest African
American voice into the public sphere. In light of the criminalization of the
free black population, Johnstone suggests, the scaffold may well have offered
the best vantage point from which to assess the racial past, present, and future. Johnstone's "Address," rather than invalidated by being "handed . . . out

of the dungeon . . . on the morning of his execution," gained authority from that grim tableau (2).

Even if its penal origin did not deprive his "Address" of its legitimacy, it did place Johnstone in a profoundly different relationship to the future that preoccupied both black founders and white civic leaders. Whether offering blueprints for a post-emancipation republic or guiding the people of color in the transition from slavery to freedom, early national commentators on race and slavery shared the forward-looking orientation of their fellow Americans, who, faced with the "perishability of revolutionary time," saw the problem of slavery as central to their efforts to construct the national future in the political present.[101] The gallows, however, was a singular location from which to scan the future. Its sole function, after all, was to extract the viewer from that future. Accordingly, Johnstone's admonitions necessarily differ from those of contemporary reformers; no longer merely indicating desires or stipulating commands regarding some contingent or hypothetical state of affairs, they express wishes contrary to fact.

Soon to be violently withdrawn from the future with which he is so deeply concerned, Johnstone engages in counterfactual logic—"expressing" in the OED's definition "what has not in fact happened, but might, could, or would, in different conditions."[102] Reviewing the circumstances surrounding his execution, Johnstone explains that "the following short but necessary council" to the people of color results from the author "conceiving it a duty incumbent on me at this time to admonish and counsel you with respect both to your present and future welfare, which God knows has always been next my heart, for I ever and always took a lively interest and pride in forwarding the affairs and assisting all those of my colour that I could, and had God been pleased to have spared me and granted me a length of days I fondly tho' alas! vainly hoped to have rendered myself useful to all."[103] Counterfactualism provides a remedy for any lingering discomfort with Johnstone's problematic status as a condemned man inserting himself into the politics of respectability. With his state-authorized execution as a murderer thus transformed into the martyrdom of a would-be black founder, the "Address" converts Johnstone's (mis)apprehension as a criminal into proof of his unrealized potential for wider political leadership. Interrupting his progress on the path of civic virtue, the historical contingency of Johnstone's hanging prompts an alternative chronology based on the subjunctive claim that, had he been "granted . . . a length of days," Johnstone (not unlike Walnut Street Prison's reprieved convict nurses) would have "rendered [him]self useful to all."

Through the alchemy of counterfactualism, Johnstone's gallows text—a genre traditionally authorized as much by its putative author's imminent execution as by his retrospective confession of past crimes—yields an alternative future in which the black subject, rather than being purged from society, becomes the model citizen envisioned by contemporary addresses to people of color.

The *Address of Abraham Johnstone* offers a valuable early example of what Best in his analysis of *Plessy v. Ferguson* (1896) has characterized as "the utility of the counterfactual's subjunctive mood to musings on race, causation, and historical responsibility."[104] Surfacing in legal and philosophical efforts to discern causation and thus to assign responsibility, counterfactuals follow a "Y-shaped narrative logic" in which, as Catherine Gallagher explains, "a unified root or trunk of historical time is imagined to have preceded the juncture at which the branches diverge"—which in turn encourages "undoing" narratives through which remediation is accomplished.[105] Given that, on the one hand, "optative reflections are . . . constitutive possibilities of subjectivity" in personal as well as national history, and, on the other, that our individual and collective lives are full of paths not taken, Andrew Miller asks why counterfactual self-assessment becomes more pressing at some moments than others.[106] "The optative becomes important," he concludes, on those occasions that "encourage us to understand our lives as determinate, bounded (as by a body), *separate* from others" and "at the same time . . . encourage us to abstract from that separateness, to treat lives as comparable, perhaps in some sense exchangeable."[107]

Prompted by counterfactuals in film, photography, and fiction since the late nineteenth century, these insights indicate why, from the colonial through the antebellum period, Execution Day was America's counterfactual occasion par excellence. "O Young People . . . Oh! That you were duely terrified!" Cotton Mather remonstrates in his sermon for condemned murderer Joseph Hanno, asking, "have you not seen many of your Companions in Sin, distressed, yea, destroyed by the Stupendous Judgments of GOD, and brought unto *Untimely Ends*? But what? . . . Have not their *Groans* been, *Oh! That I had not been led away with such wicked Company! And, Oh! That I had not put off my Conversion to GOD! And, Oh! That I had not thrown away my Time, and my Soul, in those things whereof I am now ashamed!"*[108] As Mather's prosopopoeial optative lamentations indicate, gallows texts locate responsibility for the current political crisis of crime and punishment not in the death-dealing state but in individual choice and action. (Had the condemned not allowed himself to be led astray, none of us would have to be here today for his hanging.) Identification of a past, irrevocable moment of personal error demonstrates the present inevitability of execution as a necessary remedial intervention by the authorities. "You are now to Dy," the minister reminds Hanno, for "the Land where you now Live, would be polluted, if you should be spared from *Death*; —— for an horrible *Murder*" (33). With its shift in focus from the individual to the collective, this corollary counterfactual authorizes the terrifying rite of execution by explicitly envisioning and rejecting an alternative future in which, having allowed the pollution to remain uncleansed, the community and the malefactor together stray even farther from the path of righteousness. Execution Day thus becomes a second historical juncture which symbolically undoes the first, recuperating the counterfactual past of the malefactor by enabling the community as a whole to resume the journey toward the righteous future from which he and thus it had been diverted by individual wrongdoing. As Mather addresses "all the *Wicked-doers*, who (*Except they Repent!) must be cut off from the City of GOD*," he reminds his audience that the current occasion simultaneously offers an analogical turning point for each unconverted member of that community (29). Imaginatively exchanging places with the condemned man even as they savor the horror and the relief of a violently truncated life separate from but perhaps comparable with their own, they are urged to redirect themselves individually toward a different future than that which awaits Hanno. Execution Day counterfactuals adumbrate "lives unled"—wicked *and* saintly, individual *and* collective, on earth *and* in heaven or hell—so as to bond members of the community to each other through a constant narrative remediation that rejects a range of undesirable pasts and presents so as to reinstate a preferable shared futurity.[109]

The fact that Joseph Hanno, already "a pretty noted Fellow," had not been just any wicked, unrepentant youth inspired Mather to delineate all the more sharply the counterfactual road that the condemned man had failed to follow.[110] In *Tremenda: The Dreadful Sound with which the Wicked Are To Be Thunderstruck*, Mather observes that "it adds doleful Murmurs to the *Dreadful Sound*, That this Wretched *Ethiopian* has been so distinguished from the most of his Complexion; and been admitted unto such very *Distinguishing Privileges*."[111] "Favoured with a Religious Education, which Enabled him to Read the *Oracles* of GOD" (even if he chose not to do so in jail) "and learn the *Principles* of Christianity," Hanno "then had an Emancipation into a *Liberty* . . . made a Profession of Religion, and was *Baptised*, and stood a Candidate for *Communion* in the Church" (23). "For One who so *Knew the*

Will of our Glorious Master, to do as he has done; for One under such Obligations, to be a Pattern of all Goodness unto other *Ethiopians*, to prove of
so Doubly and so Deeply *Black* a Character," suggests to Mather less a racial
propensity for sin (all punning aside) than a prime pastoral opportunity
(23). That the once "favoured," now "Wretched," black ex-bondman finds
himself not en route to the City of God but on the highway to hell allows
Mather to draw a particularly pointed lesson to "the *Ethiopian*, and Other
Slaves among us" (27). Noting their too prevalent "*Fondness* for *Freedom*,"
Mather urges them "to take warning" from Hanno's example, citing the "Fate
of their Unhappy Brother" as chilling proof of the minister's counterfactual
assertion that "if you were *Free*, many of you would not Live near so well as
you do" (27). The only alternative to slavery is a life of criminality cut short
by execution, Mather implies, foreclosing any possibility of free black civil
existence.

Seven decades, two Great Awakenings, and three revolutions later, the
Address of Abraham Johnstone figures forth that perennially absent form of
black subjectivity with a counterfactual that reorients Execution Day's usual
vectors of temporality and accountability. As *Tremenda* illustrates, gallows
counterfactuals bind the fate of the condemned to that of the country, both as
a collective and as individuals, through the initially retrospective allocation
of responsibility. But by evoking the condemned man's *future* (rather than
his imaginary past), Johnstone's *Address* reverses the sequence of causality.
To conjure a counterfactual future is necessarily to envision an alternative
state of affairs in the present; no longer inevitable, the current political
state appears even more contingent when Johnstone presents his factually
insistent counternarrative of American history. The account of the nation's
guilty racial past in the "Address" suggests that until white Americans collectively take responsibility for past crimes by rectifying their treatment of
blacks, African Americans are best advised to accommodate themselves to an
unjust present so as to ensure some form of future survival. Performing his
counterfactual identity, Johnstone presents the ensuing "series of wholesome
admonition" to his fellow people of color not as a penitent malefactor taking
responsibility for his past but as martyred black founder leading his people
into an uncertain future. When in this alternative role Johnstone urges other
blacks to learn from his mistakes, the effect is not to make him individually
accountable for the current regrettable state of affairs but to foreground the
instability of a present in which blacks are routinely denied civil status by
enemies and friends alike.

"The Address of Abraham Johnstone" is organized under five "heads": it opens with the initial call to the people of color "to be upright, and circumspect in your conduct," recommends "serious, and regular attendance on divine worship every Sabbath day at least," moves on to discourage both litigiousness and lying (with pointed reference to "false swearing, and perjury"), and, finally, concludes with a generalized appeal for black decorum.[112] In each instance the "Address" enjoins respectable behavior not simply for its own sake, but, crucially, as a means of refuting imputations of racial inferiority. For example, as an external manifestation of unassailable black virtue and morality, punctilious black church attendance decisively counters "the cavils raised by some against us," specifically "the foolishly chimerical notion that . . . because we are black, we are not to enjoy a future state, nor be admitted to inherit the kingdom of God, and that our Saviour did not die for us, therefore we cannot hope a redemption" (to say nothing of the imputation by "some other speaking idiots" that people of color are "the seed of Cain") (16). Concurring with the abolitionist Convention on what its 1796 broadside called "the important duty of public worship," a Franklinesque Johnstone pragmatically suggests that, along with its considerable spiritual value, visible piety served crucial political ends by confuting the religious rationales that had so long lent support to both slavery and racism.[113]

Just as the occasionally blunt phrasing of the "Address" gainsays its otherwise deferential tone, the pamphlet's contribution to moral reform rhetoric goes well beyond contemporary black founders' carefully worded calls for racial uplift, to expose the exclusionary logic at the heart of the patron-client politics of respectability. Crucially—and a point overlooked by the few scholars to write about Johnstone—the *Address* reproduces and radically reconfigures the broadside *To the Free Africans and other Free People of Color in the United States*, published by the abolitionist convention the prior year (see Figure 11).

Through his call "to be punctual, upright, and just in all your contracts, engagements and dealings" (27), Johnstone supplants the 1796 Convention's more paternalistic suggestion that, while "forming contracts, for yourselves or children, with masters, it may be useful to consult such persons as are capable of giving you the best advice, who are known to be your friends, in order to prevent advantages being taken of your ignorance of the laws and customs of our country." Unlike the "Free Africans and other Free People of Colour" conjured by the Convention but very much like the convict nurses at Bush Hill, Johnstone's brethren—still perhaps subject to "masters" under

Thirdly, ... In forming *contracts*, for yourselves or children, with masters, it may be useful to consult such persons as are capable of giving you the best advice, and who are known to be your friends, in order to prevent advantages being taken of your ignorance of the laws and customs of our country.

Fourthly, *BE diligent in your* respective *callings*, and *faithful in all the relations you bear in society, whether as husbands, wives, fathers, children or hired servants. Be just in all your dealings.* Be simple *in your dress* and furniture, and *frugal* in your family *expenses.* Thus you will act like Christians as well as freemen, and, *by* these *means, you will provide for the* distresses and *wants of sickness and old age.*

Fifthly, *REFRAIN from the use of spirituous liquors*; the experience of many thousands of the citizens of the United States has proved, that those liquors are not necessary to lessen the fatigue of labor, nor to obviate the extremes of heat and cold; much less are they *necessary to* add to the *innocent pleasures of society.*

Sixthly, *AVOID frolicking, and amusements that lead to expense and idleness; they beget habits of dissipation and vice,* and thus expose you to deserved reproach amongst your white neighbours.

My dear breth[re]n I earnestly pray ye, to *be diligent* and industrious *in all your callings,* manners of business and stations in life, be punctual, upright and *just in all your contracts,* engagements, and *dealings* of what kind or nature soever, *be faithful* tende[r, a]nd affectionate *in all the relations ye bear in society whether as children, servants, husbands, wives, fathers or mothers.* Be decent *in your dress* and *frugal* in all your *expences,* for *by* that *means you will provide for the wants and of sickness and old age, refrain from the* two great *use of spirituous liquors* a little is serviceable, but by all means beware of too much, for that irreparably injures the constitution, and cannot add to the enjoyment of those *innocent pleasures* and recreations *necessary* to ye as human beings and members *of society.* But above all my dear friends *avoid frolicking, and* all *amusements that lead to expence, and idleness* for, *they beget habits of dissipation and vice,* and lead ye into many inconveniences ....

Figure 11. Left column: Excerpt from Convention of Delegates from the Abolition Societies Established in Different Parts of the United States, *To the Free Africans and Other Free People of Color in the United States* (Philadelphia, [1796]). Emphasis added; original emphasis omitted.
Right column: Excerpt from Abraham Johnstone, *The Address of Abraham Johnstone, a Black Man, Who Was Hanged at Woodbury, in the County of Glocester, and State of New Jersey, on Saturday the the [sic] 8th day of July Last; to the People of Colour. To Which Is Added His Dying Confession or Declaration; also, a Copy of a Letter to His Wife, Written the Day Previous to His Execution* (Philadelphia, 1797). Emphasis added.

conditions of quasi-freedom—are nonetheless capable of the contractualism requisite to full participation in the social compact.[114]

Similar to its elision of the Convention's assumption of black servility, civil dependency, and legal incapacity, the "Address" modulates the abolitionists' call for abstinence into a plea for temperance. Whereas the Convention bids free blacks learn from the "experience of many thousands of the citizens of the United States" who have found alcohol unnecessary to labor, health, or pleasure—effectively relegating free blacks to the sidelines of American citizenship—Johnstone merely maintains that drink cannot enhance "those innocent pleasures and recreations necessary to ye as human beings and members of society" (28). Affirming his audience's humanity and civic membership, Johnstone implicitly rejects the ambiguous outsider status to which the broadside repeatedly consigns them.

With racial surveillance an integral part of white reformers' vision of the transition from slavery to citizenship, the imperative call for black respectability presumed white supervision. But as the *Address*'s revisions suggest, such surveillance potentially threatened African American citizenship by denying people of color the autonomy and independence that republican self-government requires. The pamphlet's emendation of white abolitionist rhetoric treats African American civic participation itself not as a dubious contingency, but as a given (albeit embattled) reality. A set piece of Gatesian signifyin(g), "The Address of Abraham Johnstone" repeats much of the counsel, often the very words, of the white citizens who dispensed their advice to free blacks not from "Woodbury jail" but from Philadelphia's City Hall (31).[115] The signal difference is that the *Address*, while conceding "there are some very bad" black people, leaves no question that the nation, rather than its black inhabitants, must take responsibility for moral improvement (29).

The urgency of this demand for accountability helps to explain the astounding counterhistory that awkwardly erupts in the midst of Johnstone's carefully reasoned admonitions to the people of color. Johnstone elaborates his opening injunction "to be upright, and circumspect in your conduct" by historicizing the need for such exemplary deportment with a frankly digressive account of "the vicissitudes of fortune our colour have generally encountered, from their first introduction into this county, as also the present hardships many of them endure at this moment" (8). Fulfilling his role as would-be black founder, Johnstone lays the groundwork for an alternative African American future by reconstructing a narrative of the American past that runs distinctly counter to (even as it acknowledges) what had already become the standard account of the nation's founding. "Shortly after" the English settlement of Jamestown, Johnstone's seemingly conventional interpolated history begins, "religious dissensions caused very many to leave their native country and come hither with their families and goods where they might enjoy a liberty of conscience uncontroled and free from the danger of the religious persuasions that then raged in England" (9). But the obverse side of the civic myth linking American freedom ("liberty of conscience") to the possessive individualism underwritten by individual property rights ("with their families and goods") is revealed with Johnstone's next, rushed sentence. Recalling how "those truly respectable emigrants settled in that part of this country now called New England, and named their first place of settlement New Plymouth," he immediately (and awkwardly) adds that "it was a very considerable time after before that part of Africa called Guinea was discovered, and a much longer time before they attempted to traffic in human beings, and tho' at that time their earliest and best writers mentioned with abhorrence their cruelties to each other there, yet they did not hesitate to barter and traffic for them, as for other animals, and what is shocking to humanity to relate[,] raise fortunes out of the price of blood, even in this country in latter years" (9). After a pause to censure the rape of slave women and the sale of their biracial offspring, Johnstone in another breathless sentence traces the founding of both the United States and the antislavery movement to the interlinked rise of global capitalism, Native American dispossession and genocide, and African enslavement:

> The continual wars and dissentions between the Aborigines and the settlers left the settlers but little time to cultivate their lands, and besides they were too few to carry on husbandry with any success, at least not so extensively as to enable them to benefit themselves by trade in the staple commodities of the country, and Guinea Negroes having some short time before been introduced into the West Indies and found extremely serviceable, they were next introduced into this country for they having tried in vain to make slaves of the Aborigines, but having found their attempts fruitless they next turned their thoughts to the importation of our colour, particularly to the southward, and it increased astonishingly until the colonies declared their independance, and from that time the importation annually decreased until at last the finishing blow was given to that most in-

human and diabolical trade by an act of Congress, which expressly
prohibits the further importation of negroes into any part of the
United States, so [to] that ever memorable æra when the doctrine
of non-resistance was exploded, the unalienable rights of man were
asserted, and the United States of America were declared sovereign
free and independent, we may ascribe our present dawning hopes of
universal freedom. (10)

Although Johnstone apologizes for being "longer on this head than I first intended," his historical digression is anything but tangential (15). For whereas
the Convention's broadside arose from white abolitionists' felt need to prepare the freed slave as "new born citizen" to "fulfill[] the various duties he
owes to himself and to his country," and gallows texts like *Tremenda* exhorted
people of color to take warning from the negative example of the black malefactor by reconciling themselves to servitude, Johnstone's fact-based counterhistory reallocates responsibility from blacks (individually *or* collectively)
onto the nation itself.[116] Only by fulfilling its neglected duties to "our colour,"
Johnstone suggests, can the newborn United States redirect itself to a future
of "universal freedom."

Without such a reorientation, the nation's anticipated glorious future will
be as counterfactual as that of the condemned man. Presciently gauging the
tendency of American civic mythology to fuse what Brook Thomas identifies
as the two basic myths of patriotism—"the myth of unique national origin,
and . . . the myth of unique national destiny"—into a "myth of democratic
revolution" as "a perpetually renewing democracy," Johnstone's counterhistory highlights the precarious future of the United States by calling attention to the undemocratic effects of its unfinished revolution.[117] Although it
was in the Revolutionary era "that the prospect of total emancipation from
slavery which now begins to brighten upon us had birth" (10), Johnstone la-
ments, "still my dear brethren we were forgotten, or we were not conceived
worthy their regard or attention, being looked on as a different species" (11).
However injurious to African Americans, such "contradictory" biopolitical
"conduct" on the part of patriots "justly exposed" the United States "to the
scoff and derision of their enemies both at home, and abroad." Here it is the
young nation, not African Americans, that, having strayed from the path of
righteousness, must redirect its course.

With its forked narrative logic, the *Address*'s fashioning of Abraham
Johnstone as black founder manqué identifies the condemned man's conviction

and execution as the pivotal historical "juncture" that separates the counterfactual future (in which Johnstone "would have rendered [him]self useful
to all") from the imminent one in which the formerly enslaved convicted
murderer will have been forcibly eliminated from the national landscape.
Although this counterfactual vision offers a convenient remedy for Johnstone's present disadvantageous rhetorical position, this remedial impulse is
more typical of counterfactual history, with its efforts to "identify past events
whose alteration or undoing would lead to a substantially different present."[118] When activated in juridical practice through remediation (or through
the execution rite) such counterfactualism seeks, according to Gallagher, to
"actualize the future of an alternative past"—a gesture that, Best cautions,
requires "the evacuation of historical consciousness."[119] But in the "Address,"
Johnstone's counterfactual future self-fashioning prompts a counternarrative
of the nation's founding that restores the very historical consciousness that
was being evacuated during the First Reconstruction. In contrast to the films
and court cases analyzed by Best and Gallagher, Johnstone's project is not an
undoing mission that seeks to rectify past errors by instantiating admirable
liberal principles in the place of regrettable historical facts. Poised on the
cusp of eternity and sharing his fellow Americans' sense of the revolutionary
moment's finitude, Johnstone looks backward not to install the preferable future of an alternative past but to review the country's formative racial history
and prevent its continuation into the present and future by placing responsibility for the criminal past with the nation and its normatively white citizens.
The goal is not the retroactive remediation sought by civil lawsuits and the
execution ritual but a politicized version of the forward-looking assessment,
correction, and redirection that Puritan ministers urged on Execution Day
crowds.

The *Address* replaces the counterfactual gallows tale of irrevocable individual error with an emphatically factual revisionist history of the national
past. In this way, it counters the "triumphant narrative of free, white labor"
that, "commonplace by the time of the Constitutional Convention," cast a
mythic New England as "a region within which free people of color could
be represented as permanent strangers whose presence was unaccountable
and whose claims to citizenship were absurd."[120] With its counterhistory of
white colonialism, Native American dispossession and genocide, race slavery, and sexual terrorism, the pamphlet anticipates the interracial antebellum
abolitionist movement's effort to remove culpability from blacks and place it
onto slaveholding whites.[121] More to the point, through its stress on the vexed

interplay of race, causation, and historical responsibility in early America, Johnstone's corrective counternarrative called on its readers to envision a present and future in which black criminality, not African American political membership, would appear contrary to fact.

Taking as its point of departure the condemned man's counterfactual future (not past), the *Address* reveals the political present as contingent (not inevitable) by recounting an emphatically factual (not imaginary) national history that traces answerability for the current situation to the criminal acts of the government and its citizens (not the convict), urging that the nation (not the execution's black audience) must reform itself. Only after the vectors of temporality and responsibility have been redrawn along these lines does the *Address of Abraham Johnstone* present "The Dying Words of Abraham Johnstone." For, having recounted the nation's guilty history in place of that of the condemned man and imagined his forsaken virtuous future rather than past, the *Address* opens up a new narrative space for Johnstone's exculpatory first-person account. And just as the "Address" offers a revisionist counterhistory of the nation's founding, "His Dying Confession or Declaration" questions rather than restores the (racial) status quo by disputing the official version of past events, here the facts leading to his arrest, trial, and condemnation.[122] As with Jones and Allen's pamphlet and the North Carolina freemen's congressional petition, Johnstone's narrative corrective demonstrates how African American civil activity, and here the actor himself, have been misapprehended as criminal. Thus, in keeping with the counterfactual fashioning of Johnstone as black founder in his radically signifyin(g) address to the people of color, the critique of American legal process that "His Confession or Declaration" offers in tandem with the "Address" enacts the civic participation that his conviction and execution should have rendered contrary to fact.

A Devoted Victim

Johnstone, who will later allude to murder as a "crime of the blackest dye," sounds like a stock Puritan penitent when he opens the *Address* with a highly conventional affirmation of his trial and conviction.[123] Characterizing himself "a devoted victim to the just resentment of the laws of my country and the rules of society," Johnstone reiterates the key phrase, elaborating, "—just resentment—because, after a candid and impartial trial I have been convicted by a jury of my peers, twelve truly good and worthy men whose integrity and love of truth I so well know that had they not conceived themselves clear of all doubts and scruples, they would not have consigned a fellow creature to death, and to so ignominious a death" (3–4).

At the moment when the conventional penitent would have gone on to justify his hanging by confessing his crime, however, Johnstone defers the question of his guilt until the day of execution, "when my pitiable situation and the solemnity and horror of the spectacle I shall be exhibiting shall add weight, and death give a sanction to my assertions" (4).[124] Detaching his culpability from the process by which it was adjudicated, the pamphlet endorses the trial as an institution without nullifying Johnstone's own civic posture. Like any good American citizen, Johnstone defends the jury trial on principle, even though a particular trial may produce unjust results, as it has here. Just as his execution provides counterfactual proof of his unfulfilled potential as black founder, Johnstone's conviction certifies his fellowship, as God's "creature," with his "peers," the "twelve truly good and worthy" (and presumptively white) men who fulfill their civic duty by serving on his jury. And like Hanno before him, Johnstone, assenting to his conviction, affirms his punitive, retroactive entry into the social contract. In this case, however, the rote (albeit express) consent elicited by the criminal confession genre provides the condemned former slave with the authority to criticize the new nation from within. In the process of deploring the specific procedural flaws (excessive dependence on oaths and circumstantial evidence) that yielded his own unfair conviction, Johnstone offers a more radical critique of his American peers' failure to acknowledge the civil status of people of color.

Appropriately penitent for his sexual misconduct yet innocent of the crime of which he has been convicted, Johnstone brackets the question of his criminal culpability to assert his civic membership by granting the overall justice of the trial and consenting to its verdict. When, in the ensuing "Declaration or Confession," Johnstone does finally offer his version of the events leading to his murder conviction, his account is obscure. The *Address* substitutes a series of refutations of the purportedly false testimony against him for a more coherent narrative, replacing the conventional criminal confession with a "declaration" of his innocence. The only undisputed facts appear to be that Thomas Read, having previously sued Johnstone, went "missing" and that the Delaware ex-slave was charged for and eventually convicted of the African's murder on the basis of circumstantial evidence in the form of testimony from his New Jersey neighbors, both black and white (37).[125] Johnstone, apparently responding to an allegation that the earlier lawsuit supplied his murder motive, insists that he did not "collar Tom the deceased after the trial between him and me, nor did I say a word to him except that I told him I hoped we were good friends notwithstanding our law suit, and asked him to come with me to the tavern to take a drink" (36). Condemned by a prosecutorial narrative that located the crime's origins in civil litigation between the two black men, Johnstone presents a counternarrative of Afro-diasporic civility.

If we understand civility not simply as courteousness but as "conformity to the principles of social order, behaviour befitting a citizen," Johnstone might be said to join his adversaries in tracing his legal troubles back to such black civility.[126] To solve the mystery of Read's disappearance, John-stone suggests, one must look not for an ex-slave whose crimes bespeak his political disqualification but for those white citizens who are dangerously apprehensive about displays of black civil standing (and the economic stand-ing that necessarily underwrites such performances). "Samuel Huffsey and William Nicholson have long persecuted me with the utmost rancour and malice," Johnstone notes, pointedly stopping just short of assigning them "blame . . . for Tom's death" (39, 40). "But," he continues, "this in justice to my conscience I must declare on the solemn assertions of a dying man; that I think Samuel Huffsey procured Tom to steal my lease, as I then could have no title to shew for the place I held from him and lived upon, nor for the crop then growing on it, as I was improving the place fast and doing well for my-self, which made me an object of envy and hatred" (39). Adding that Huffsey and Nicholson "both know that it was at their instigation that Tom sued me, and they also know that they accompanied him and acted as his attorneys, at the magistrates," Johnstone questions how, "on the unfortunate night" in question, "they came to know at what instant of time Tom came to my house, and the particular conversation that passed between Tom and myself" if they did had not "seen Tom later than I did" (39–40). It could hardly be a coinci-dence that "the day after Sam. Huffsey brought a witness with him and called upon me to produce my lease, or else quit, &c" (40). Murky as this account of the events leading to Johnstone's trial may be, it is crystal clear that in this case allegations of black criminality emerged not from a racial underworld of social disorder but from the workaday world in which property, contracts, and litigation mediated relations between and among New Jersey's white and black inhabitants.

As he refutes what he claims to be false testimony against him at trial, Johnstone implies that *American* blacks are particularly qualified to participate in such officially sanctioned civil actions. Earlier Johnstone, determined to "speak to" his fellow people of color "on a crime, that alas! too many of you are guilty of" (acknowledging, that "indeed, it is not confined to our colour alone"), remonstrated with his hearers to resist false swearing, and perjury ("such as have, alas! robbed me of life"), deploring the prevalence of these and other forms of lying as a threat to the "security" of "life" and "property" (20, 25). Now, having magnanimously forgiven two other witnesses for their incriminating perjury, Johnstone notes that "Richard Skinner also swore to a fals[e]hood, but I cannot nor can any body blame him, for he being a Guinea negro, and not speaking the English language well, it could not be expected that he knew the nature of an oath" (36). Johnstone exempts Skinner from criminal responsibility for perjury on the basis of his cultural alienness: "if whites whose educations should make them know better, are capable of committing such crimes," he wonders, "what must be expected from a poor Guinea negro[?]" (37). Johnstone asserts his own and other native-born blacks' political membership by distinguishing those foreigners whose civil incompetence arises from their cultural ignorance from those "whose educations should make them know better" ("whites" or Johnstone's free black audience) and therefore can be held responsible for "such crimes." Having thus aligned Johnstone with the "citizens" whose "estates and lives" are threatened by the general public's inclination toward perjury and casual oath-taking, the "Address" urges, "surely, if it be viewed only in a political light, it is the interest of every state to render oaths as inviolable as words and ceremonies can make them, and must be highly and essentially necessary for the government to keep up the sanctity of an oath in the opinions of men" (26). The *Address* transcends the question of Johnstone's own guilt, transforming his wrongful conviction under allegedly perjured testimony into an opportunity to encourage the nation's legislatures to undertake some much-need legal reform. Johnstone transmutes self-exoneration into civic authority as he dispenses "political" counsel to the "government" under the rubric of moral advice to the people of color. Consistent with the broader effects of black gallows literature, the exhortation serves less to highlight the urgent need for racial self-improvement than, by assuming African Americans' culpability for any such criminal behavior, to affirm their responsibility as legally recognized persons subject to (if unprotected by) American law. Prompted by a capital conviction that occasions not civil death but a public performance of African American leadership, the pamphlet here offers an even more audacious counterfactual, simultaneously asserting and performing black civic participation and political membership through the condemned man's disinterested criticism of the government.

Johnstone's disparagement of Guinea negroes' civil competence would appear to mint African American political inclusion in the coin of nativist exclusivity.[127] With the recent federal naturalization acts of 1790 and 1795 affirming African Americans' (non)status as "nonforeign, noncitizen," Johnstone asserts the qualifications of native-born people of color against such black outsiders.[128] The pamphlet appropriates the logic of what Devon Carbado has called "racial naturalization" when it uses Guinea negroes' alienness to convert the unquestioned national identity of African Americans into (counterfactual) proof of their civil capacity and responsible political membership.[129] Johnstone's intraracial application of the discriminatory logic by which historically the civil standing of blacks as a collective had been denied or circumscribed serves as a reminder of what Brook Thomas cautions is "the always present danger of the need to define the citizen against the noncitizen."[130] But this seemingly exclusive gesture is countered by the *Address*'s portrayal of Guinea negroes and African Americans as joined in, rather than divided by, a variety of civil activities. Suing and being sued, testifying in court, and entering into labor and housing contracts, the *Address*'s blacks at first glance would appear not only to refute Johnstone's aspersions on non-native blacks' civil competency, but also to demonstrate a general racial qualification for the duties of citizenship. Yet in Johnstone's Woodbury, New Jersey, none of these activities is sufficient to confer or affirm black civil personality.[131] Johnstone's own involvement in the lawsuit with Thomas Read becomes a possible murder motive, whereas Read sued Johnstone at the "instigation" of his "attorneys," and Skinner, however "actuated by rancour and malevolence" of his own, got the "answer he gave in the court . . . by note from [Johnstone's] persecutors."[132]

Faced with a legal system in which blacks, acting in their civil capacity, are consistently misapprehended as either criminals or tools to be manipulated by white citizens, Johnstone calls for the people of color to withdraw at least provisionally from a state that cannot (or will not) credit blacks with the civil capacity requisite to citizenship. In the fourth "admonition" in his "Address," Johnstone pleads, "for your own ease, peace of mind, worldly . . . welfare, and future happiness, I most earnestly beg, exhort, and intreat ye, my dear brethren, to avoid all strifes, quarrels, contentions, animosities, law-suits or litigations of any kind" (27). "Rather chuse," he counsels, "when any misunderstanding shall arise, to refer it for decision to two or three

respectable neighbours; and avoid, by all means, the frequent appearing before Justices of the Peace to be sworn, for there is an old saying, that familiarity breeds contempt" (27). The "old saying" is invoked here to illustrate how
frequent swearing can deprive oaths of their "sanctity," but it also intimates
the risk of too much exposure to a judicial system that viewed with growing
contempt post-emancipation blacks' increasing visibility on the landscape
of legal claims.[133] If the pamphlet urges Johnstone's fellow people of color to
shun the representatives and institutions of law for informal arbitration by
"respectable neighbours," it by no means endorses the kind of custodial white
supervision and regulation advocated by the abolitionist Convention. (That
such "respectable neighbours" need not have been white is affirmed on the
Address's opening page, which, recall, authenticates Johnstone's "account of
his life" by reference to a "respectable" "Mulatto" couple [2].)[134] Avoiding the
representatives and institutions of American law while developing their own
civil procedures and resources, Johnstone's community of color could consolidate its civic presence beyond the ken of punitive legal scrutiny.[135] Rather
than offering a vision of a future black citizenship conditional upon racial
uplift, the *Address* directs its designated audience to seek civic fulfillment
outside the state, in civil society. Even when he delegates Quaker and other
"friends of freedom, and our colour" to "us[e] every effort in their power to
render the emancipation of our colour general, and have us admitted to the
rights of freedom as citizens in this state" (12), Johnstone does not so much
confirm the black dependency assumed by the abolitionist Convention as
acknowledge whites' responsibility to enact any remediation and the impossibility of any effective direct political engagement by those whose civil
standing and civic authority was shaky at best.[136] It is only away from the
institutions and representatives of American law, and in the persuasive public
sphere of print, the *Address* at once admonishes the people of color and demonstrates by its own example, that African Americans can reject both the civil
death assigned to the criminal and the civil slavery increasingly meted to free
blacks. Instead of limning yet another conditional black citizenship—even
one contingent upon independence and activism rather than deference—the
Address of Abraham Johnstone deploys print to leave that future literally in the
readers' hands.

Johnstone, anticipating that "the solemnity of the spectacle I shall exhibit
as also the novelty of this address at present, may make some little impression
on ye for a moment, and then alas! it will be gone, and forgot," counters the
evanescence of his execution with his published *Address*:

But my dear breth[re]n and friends, I beg of ye by frequent readings to impress it on your minds, and early instill those precepts I have laid down unto your children by frequent reading and relating it to them, for as the water by continual and incessant dropping makes an impression on the stone, so will these my admonitions make an impression on your minds by frequent readings and recourse to them, which I the more earnestly recommend as I think them calculated to promote your prosperity in this world, and ensure you that everlasting happiness in the next, which that ye may all obtain is the sincere wish, and shall be the dying prayer of your truly affectionate, but deplorably distressed friend.

ABRAHAM JOHNSTONE
Woodbury jail, July 2d. 1797 (30–31)

Print, which will enable Johnstone posthumously to fulfill his leadership role, will also foster the cultural transmission and the collective political commitment indispensable to the achievement of independent black civility. Once the judicial process has endowed black authorship with political authority, print publication becomes the technology that can convert the counterfactual into the actual—to make a condemned man a civic leader after his own execution and to render black economic and political "prosperity in this world" the plausible sequel to American slavery.

Conclusion

Speaking from his anomalous but authoritative position as "a devoted victim to the just resentment of the laws of my country and the rules of society"— that is, as a good citizen willingly sacrificed to a fundamentally fair but procedurally flawed legal system—Abraham Johnstone does far more than exculpate himself in his *Address . . . to the People of Colour.* For, "with the ignominious cord round [his] neck, and standing on a stage beneath [the] gallows," Johnstone is perfectly positioned to make "some general observations on the present situation of those of his colour." (Indeed, in the absence of "positive evidence of the fact" of murder, the verdict that "established a *presumption* of [Johnstone's] guilt" might be said merely to formalize the presumptively criminal status assigned to free blacks everywhere [2, 4].) A firsthand observer of the process whereby black civil activity is consistently misapprehended as criminal behavior, Johnstone simultaneously criticizes and inverts that process by turning such imputed criminality into an occasion for civic participation and redirecting critical scrutiny from the people of color to the national polity of which they are emphatically (if precariously) a part. Like Absalom Jones and Richard Allen in the wake of the yellow fever epidemic and the formerly enslaved North Carolinian exiles who petitioned Congress, the Johnstone of the *Address* leaves little doubt that if African Americans are currently "out-lawed and excluded from common justice and common humanity" it is due not to their own moral deficiency but to the "prevailing prejudice" authorized by "partial laws, in support of habits and customs cruelly oppressive."

But even as the *Address of Abraham Johnstone . . . to the People of Colour* echoes contemporary addresses by white civic leaders and black founders in its title, tone, rhetoric, and mood, what sets Johnstone apart from both black and white moral reformers is his gallows perspective on the future. Inflected by his condemned status, Johnstone's subjunctive appeal does not make African American citizenship conditional upon the successful display of black respectability. Rather, it reveals the extent to which, at "this juncture," in the 1790s, *any* attempt to articulate black citizenship entails uttering a statement contrary to fact. This is because, from apologists and meliorists to abolitionists, white Americans' collective failure to take responsibility for slavery leads them not simply to understand black social disorder as a regrettable impediment to full citizenship but persistently to misapprehend black civil activity as criminality and thus actively preempt such citizenship. From Johnstone's scaffold prospect, the danger appeared to be less that African Americans would be erased from the nation's past through the myth of free, white New England origins, or even that they would be removed from the nation's future through colonization schemes, than that, like the condemned man, they would be removed from *any* future civil existence, collectively consigned to civil death, as criminals or through a de facto civil slavery. Hence the need to replace the conventional acknowledgment of criminality through which so many blacks had entered print culture—the confession—with a declarative counterassertion of black civic identity. If Johnstone could not entirely refute, as Jones and Allen had, allegations that misread black civil activity as crime—nursing as extortion, a lawsuit as a murder motive—he could, like them, seize the responsibility and publicity generated by such allegations to recast such allegedly base behavior into the shining currency of civic belonging and political membership.

The pamphlet's redaction of the politics of respectability's moral reform rhetoric reveals the extent to which free blacks' abolitionist allies participated in the era's growing racism by cloaking their own resistance to African American citizenship in fictions of black criminality. For the *Address of Abraham Johnstone*, as for "The Petition and Representation of the Undernamed Freemen," the integrity of black citizenship was imperiled not by the failure of free African Americans to "be upright, and circumspect in [their] conduct," but in the national failure to answer for the crime of slavery. Holding blacks rather than themselves accountable, white Americans continued to turn a blind eye to African American civil conduct. No longer viewed as objects of property in the emancipating North, blacks were increasingly scrutinized through the lens of crime. Like Jones and Allen's defense of Philadelphia's black community, like the convicts' nursing at Bush Hill, and like the petition that appeared in *American Universal Magazine* a week after it was dismissed by Congress (thereby attaining for the petitioners in print the civic recognition denied them at law), the *Address of Abraham Johnstone, A Black Man, who Was Hanged at Woodbury* presented an opportunity to transform perceived black criminality into an occasion for African American civic participation. Moreover, through its assertion of black legal responsibility as tantamount to civic inclusion, the *Address* envisioned in print the future political actualization of an African American citizenship built on black autonomy rather than white coercion or patronage.

Chapter 4

The Work of Death: Time, Crime, and Personhood in Jacksonian America

> Lord what is Man? Or rather what are not brutes?
> —*The Address of Abraham Johnstone* (1797)

Faced with the dilemma race slavery and its legacy posed to the new republic, such prominent Americans as Noah Webster, Thomas Jefferson, and St. George Tucker suggested that a slavery-engendered propensity for crime precluded blacks' belated entry into the social compact. For his part, condemned ex-slave Abraham Johnstone held accountable not African Americans but the citizens who had yet to answer for their nation's guilty past. The *Address of Abraham Johnstone* seized penal scrutiny of imputed black criminality as an occasion to call for political and legal reform, thereby anticipating antebellum abolitionists' efforts to redraw the lines connecting slavery, crime, responsibility, and political membership. "The enslaved people" may still have been figuratively "on trial" in nineteenth-century America, but by the time Frederick Douglass made that observation in 1855, twenty-five years of abolitionist print agitation had also placed the slave "system . . . at the bar of public opinion . . . for judgment."[1] Supplanting gallows literature's confessing malefactor with the slave narrative's testifying "eye-witness to the cruelty," abolitionist publicists sought to display African Americans' civil potential (and thus eligibility for citizenship) while making slaveholders and all American citizens answerable for the national crime of slavery.[2]

With its highly interiorized account of the birth, growth, and maturation of the leader of the bloodiest slave uprising in American history, Thomas Gray's *Confessions of Nat Turner* broke with the black catalogues of the early

American scaffold tradition while looking forward to the fugitive slave narratives promoted by the antebellum abolitionist movement. The scandal that
greeted the first such publication, the *Narrative of James Williams, An American Slave*, suggests the difficulty many Americans still had in conceiving of
a civic, rather than criminal, black public presence. After spending much of
1838 responding to print allegations that Williams was a fraud, an imposter, perhaps even a murderer, the American Anti-Slavery Society formally
withdrew from circulation his sensational "testimony" to the brutality of
southwestern slavery.[3] As AASS Executive Committee members were trying
to decide how best to dispose of Williams's *Narrative*, newspapers along the
Eastern seaboard were following the unsuccessful insanity defense mounted
by Edward Coleman, who in a paroxysm of jealousy had all but decapitated
his wife Anne in full view of passersby on New York's Broadway. Press coverage of the enraged razor-wielding African American murderer apparently
inspired literary nationalist Edgar Allan Poe to craft a new kind of crime
literature with his detective story about a wrathful razor-wielding killer ape.
"The Murders in the Rue Morgue" appeared in *Graham's Magazine* in April
1841, just as an eloquent Maryland fugitive was embarking on the public
autobiographical performance that would yield the *Narrative of the Life of
Frederick Douglass, An American Slave*.[4]

Like the runaway-turned-lecturer, the abolitionist slave narrative's exemplary black protocitizen was an antebellum phenomenon. In the genre's
first decade, however, its fugitive narrator was an unstable persona, easily
confounded with the Africanist presence conjured by a white romancer like
Poe or with a condemned black criminal such as Turner. The confusion lay
as much in the new literary abolitionism's transatlantic penal origins as in
the slave narrative's more local gallows provenance. Turning both fictional
and autobiographical storytelling into antislavery propaganda, antebellum
publicists injected Anglo-American abolitionism's anxiety for appropriate
punishment into a prose tradition historically concerned with the allocation of responsibility. The result, in Jacksonian America, was a literature
that, preoccupied with penality and answerability, employed extended prose
narrative to evoke a continuous, individual, and, above all, *responsible* black
civil self. Twenty years on, with the publication of Harriet Beecher Stowe's
bestselling *Uncle Tom's Cabin*, this convergence would resonate powerfully
with readers on both sides of the Atlantic (and, indeed, around the world).
Initially, however, it risked compromising a movement whose representative

black subject recounted a first-person story of crime and punishment that bore an uncanny resemblance to the confessions so long attributed to condemned criminals of color.

Throughout this period, the temporal progression so essential to narrative remained instrumental to the apportionment of blame. In the *Essay Concerning Human Understanding* John Locke observes that "personality extends it*self* beyond present existence to what is past, only by consciousness, whereby it becomes concerned and accountable, owns and imputes to it*self* past actions."[5] The "name" for this continuous and therefore responsible "*self*," Locke explains, is "Person," which, as "a forensic term appropriating actions and their merit . . . belongs only to intelligent agents capable of a law."[6] For Locke, the passage of time manifests the responsibility that renders the self-conscious human being a legal person. Accordingly, scaffold orations like Cotton Mather's *Tremenda* justify present practices—the rites of execution—by, on the one hand, tracing responsibility back to the malefactor's once avoidable, now irrevocable choices and, on the other, envisioning the future danger the community and its members would invite by failing to take remedial action. The *Address of Abraham Johnstone* restructured Execution Day's hegemonic temporality by recasting spiritual exigency as political urgency so as to hold the nation and its citizens, rather than the condemned "Black Man" and his Afro-diasporic community, accountable for criminal wrongdoing and its redress. Overlaying the preparationist gallows confession with the forward-looking address to the people of color, the pamphlet appeared as older, Puritan views of time were vying with the early republic's emergent civic temporality.[7]

This shift in temporal sensibility accelerated with the industrial revolution's technological and managerial innovations, which complicated, even as they intensified, calls for individual and national accountability. Causes may have lost their proximity to effects in the industrialized workplace, but, Trish Loughran finds, an emergent "abolitionist culture industry" overcame the republic's "spatial and temporal fragmentation" to demand that U.S. citizens "take responsibility for remote practices" by acknowledging their complicity "in the national crime of slavery."[8] With their huge outlays on steam printing and postal distribution, abolitionist publicists sought to produce, on a mass scale, individual consciousness of slavery's "criminality"; in the process, Edlie Wong notes, they also "invested in the manufacture of acceptable forms of slave agency."[9]

The fugitive slave narrative sought to retain the confessing black felon's radical individuality and deepening interiority while shifting the blame to slaveholders. Yet by sundering the black persona from the criminality in which recognized legal personhood had so long inhered, the abolitionist tactic of reassigning culpability to the white American citizen could also fortify the "average racism" fostered by a fabulist like Edgar Allan Poe, to say nothing of the scientific racism being developed by proslavery professionals like Dr. Samuel A. Cartwright.[10] Separating *mens rea* from *actus reus*, criminal intent from wrongful deed, the diverse array of antebellum publications considered in this chapter—crime ephemera, abolitionist propaganda, literary fiction, and medical report—probed the increasingly racialized terms by which, in Locke's concise formulation, Jacksonian Americans understood "punishment [to] be annexed to personality, and personality to consciousness."[11] Written and published during the crisis of accountability that was the national slavery debate, these works survey the havoc wreaked by irresponsible actors, from homicidal cats, dogs, and apes, to their apparently unmotivated but equally dangerous enslaved human counterparts. Reformers' efforts to transfer culpability from slave to master may well have yielded the newly civil self of the black protocitizen, but, these works suggest (and as Chapter 5 explores further), that persona's rhetorical decriminalization also raised the specter of an incapacitated agent whose lack of accountability precluded not only personhood, but now, finally, humanity.

Reading the *Confessions of Nat Turner* as an extraordinarily time-conscious document, we begin to see the complications that both slavery and industrialization posed to the allocation of responsibility.[12] Gray hurried his pamphlet into print in the truncated interval between Turner's long-awaited arrest and expeditious execution, nearly three months after the Virginia slave had led the Southampton uprising that culminated in the deaths of fifty-five whites, prosecutions of nearly as many suspected insurgents, and extralegal reprisals against countless other African Americans throughout the South. The protracted manhunt had served to widen the temporal interlude that always, however infinitesimally, separates intent from action. In print coverage of the insurrection, the agonizing delay between the bloody predawn events of August 22 and Turner's late autumn capture split the slave rebels' exhaustively detailed acts from their elusive leader's inscrutable purposes. Rather than providing narrative closure by uniting the horrific actions to newly disclosed motives, however, the *Confessions* only deepened this disconcerting rupture. The alternative temporal frame of Turner's interpolated first-person account decouples—and thus decriminalizes—the insurgents' violent acts and their leader's bloody intentions. Turner, pleading "*not guilty*; saying to his counsel, that he did not feel so," disavows legal culpability while taking full narrative responsibility for what both he and Gray repeatedly refer to as "the work of death."[13] Executed in the slaveholding antebellum South rather than the emancipating early national North, Turner inverts the persistent white tendency to misapprehend black civility as criminality, presenting the Southampton massacre as the perhaps inevitable product of efficient, productive slave labor.

Depicting its first-person subject not simply as "an American Slave," but one "who was for several years a driver on a cotton plantation in Alabama," the *Narrative of James Williams* portrays the labor of slavery as itself the work of death—a work in which slaves, like the plantation's animals but unlike its free, white overseer, are mere (if deadly) tools. This separation of the slave's violent acts from any criminal intent, faltering though it may be in this early abolitionist-sponsored slave narrative, is what will enable black life-writing to emerge from the shadow of the gallows in the decades leading up to the Civil War. With antislavery propaganda ascribing the motives for black violence to the increasingly criminalized slaveholder, the slave narrative offered unprecedented access to a newly blameless black secular self. That the taint of criminality was not so easily purged in Jacksonian America is suggested as much by the *Narrative*'s antislavery content as by its anti-abolitionist reception. The *Narrative* consistently implicates the fugitive in, rather than clears him of, the criminality inculcated by slavery, marking the ambivalence of reformers' efforts to shift the burden of guilt from black victim to white perpetrator.

What happens when Locke's formula for responsible human personhood is broken into its component parts—when the self admittedly concerned in past actions is not accountable for them? Failing to own and impute to itself the merit of such actions (punishment as well as reward), can such a being be deemed an intelligent agent capable of a law? If not, then, what position could such a creature possibly hold in the polity? The black persona's instability as it made the transition from gallows confession to antislavery testimony demonstrates culpability's importance to legal personhood and political membership. If, as the slave's abolitionist advocates argued, slavery itself was a crime, how could its victims be held responsible as criminals? Did exonerating the enslaved for their participation in slavery's many crimes reduce them to will-less tools in the hands of white citizens? How did those citizens' (direct or indirect) complicity in the crime of slavery confirm their own freedom and autonomy?

These questions are obliquely addressed by Poe's "Murders in the Rue Morgue" and Cartwright's "Report on the Diseases and Physical Peculiarities of the Negro Race." By revealing the culprit in the nation's first detective story to be a homicidal Ourang-Outang—patterned on a deranged free black murderer—Poe anticipates Cartwright in elucidating how the denial of criminal responsibility to a violent actor might be tantamount to the denial of personhood, even human status. In a post-Enlightenment United States where the dual fictions of the slave's mixed character and the social compact ran up against medico-jurisprudential rationales for both individual and racial incapacity, African Americans more than ever before faced allegations "that they are, naturally, inferior; that they are *so low* in the scale of humanity, and so utterly stupid, that they are unconscious of their wrongs, and do not apprehend their rights."[14] Keenly aware of this state of affairs, the fugitive Frederick Douglass would outdo the condemned Abraham Johnstone in making this defensive posture into a position from which to enact African American civility. While Douglass and a new generation of activist publicists were assiduously severing criminality from black personhood in the young republic's legally inflected print culture, more conservative writers like Poe and Cartwright seemed to offer *mens rea*, with its attendant legal and civic perquisites, as the preserve, perhaps even the preservation, of sovereign white manhood. Probing the limits of both race and criminality, Gray's *Confessions*, Williams's *Narrative*, Poe's story, and Cartwright's "Report" reach remarkable consensus in setting aside for white citizens the answerability traditionally held to be constitutive of legal personhood. Resonant as abolitionist invocations of individual and collective responsibility were in an increasingly democratic slaveholding republic, the unresolved issue of black accountability would pose daunting literary and political challenges to subsequent efforts to assert a civil, autonomous African American self in print.

Let Time Answer

In the antebellum United States, the suddenly prevalent timepiece was both literally and figuratively a sign of the times. Mass production of American clocks had commenced in 1806, with mechanical timekeeping entering parlors and kitchens as well as factories and offices.[15] Seemingly an urban, industrial phenomenon, mechanical time consciousness quickly came to structure life on the South's plantations and yeoman farms. Accompanied by its aural and corporeal adjuncts, the bell, horn, and whip, the clock ordered labor and discipline under slavery. Slavery's time-discipline did not entirely escape abolitionist notice. Slaveholders "not only rob [slaves] of all they get, and as fast as they get it," Theodore Dwight Weld protested, "but rob them of *themselves*, also; their very hands and feet, all their muscles, and limbs, and senses, their bodies and minds, their time and liberty and earnings."[16] Like their bodies, slaves' time was integral to their selfhood. Largely excluded from possession of watches and clocks, as well as from the literacy to read them, slaves could not claim the same proprietary relationship to time as masters and overseers.[17] As Weld's allegation suggests, slavery, deplored since biblical times as "manstealing," now appeared criminal in its theft of a "time" that Jacksonian Americans were learning to value on its own terms. If, as antebellum commentators feared, industrial labor deprived workers of the requisite time for character formation, under plantation slavery it was the master who, "filching all their time," inhibited blacks' moral and intellectual development.[18]

Mechanical timekeeping and capitalist industrialization could not impose a homogeneous temporal sensibility.[19] But for many contemporary observers, the multiple temporalities now widely identified as a characteristic of modernity appeared as indices to historical change itself. The deepening political divide over slavery, in particular, seemed manifest in sectional asynchronism, as the South, with its traditional rhythms of agrarian labor and feudal social structure, appeared to fall further and further behind the rapidly industrializing, democratic North. Thus, as sectional tensions were peaking, doggedly neutral *New York Ledger* editor Robert Bonner sought to boost intersectional goodwill excursions as a kind of time travel: "The Northern man who goes South makes a journey into the Past. The Southern man who comes North beholds the living, realized Future. Go five hundred miles south, and then get ten miles from the railroad, and you have arrived at Fifty Years Ago."[20]

The section's perceived time lag seemed most evident in its outmoded penality.[21] Bonner's fellow editor, Virginia-born slaveholder-turned-abolitionist moderate Joseph Evans Snodgrass, designated slavery one of "the causes which retard the progress of Criminal Reform in the Southern States"; years later Snodgrass's best-known literary discovery and Bonner's valued contributor, E.D.E.N. Southworth, would illustrate his claim by having Valentine, her condemned black protagonist, await trial in a Southern prison where, "evidently, reform had not even looked upon its outer walls, far less opened one of its doors or windows."[22] Replacing the gallows' eschatological timeframe with the civic one of the penitentiary, reformers on both sides of the Atlantic were redeploying temporality to accomplish what was now seen as the primarily secular redemption of the nation's convicts.[23] Virginia's first penitentiary may have opened in 1800, with states like Tennessee and Mississippi constructing prisons in the 1820s and 1830s, but public execution (to say nothing of lynching) would remain a Southern ritual well into the twentieth century.[24]

Under the new penology, as with slavery, temporality was racialized. Deemed incapable of penitential reflection, the Northern black prisoner, we have seen, was perceived to be ineligible for the carceral regeneration requisite to civic reintegration. In the South, the reforms that did make it into statute books and penal procedure were effectively reserved for whites, with the effect that blacks were executed in disproportionately high numbers.[25] Inhabiting a penal time warp, nineteenth-century African American convicts, as discussed in Chapter 2, appeared in print as antiprogressive throwbacks to early America's antiquated rituals of crime and punishment. Acquiring (rather than losing) political membership through their apprehension, conviction, and sentencing, condemned blacks like the penitent pirate Thomas Wansley continued to be portrayed as finding spiritual (and not civil) rebirth en route to a gallows that (unlike the prison) offered symbolic (rather than physical) release.

Under that earlier penal regime, time had been a key component of the civic and religious stagecraft by which the "*Tragick* Scene" on the scaffold was "strangely *changed into a* Theater *of* Mercy."[26] Due process of law, combined with the timely exertions of ministers and lay spiritual advisors, ushered the repentant criminal from the here into the hereafter, from the political present into the spiritual future. Alluding to this ritual, the court in the *Confessions of Nat Turner* visits its most exacting retribution upon the slave insurgent not when it condemns him to death but when it denies him time to prepare for execution. In Gray's imaginative scripting of Turner's sentencing, real-life magistrate Jeremiah Cobb's fictional obiter dictum reveals the retributive logic by which the antebellum Court reconciles its scrupulous observance of legal form with its glaring departure from the eschatological temporal rituals that validated state violence.[27] Lamenting that the uprising has "deprive[d] us of many of our most valuable citizens . . . when they were asleep, and defenceless," Cobb goes on to direct Turner's "attention to the poor misguided wretches who have gone before you," insisting that "the blood of all cries aloud, and calls upon you, as the author of their misfortune.

Yes! You forced them unprepared, from Time to Eternity."[28] Fulfilling the judicial branch's duty to "deal pain and death," Southampton County's Court of Oyer and Terminer had in the months between the August 22 killings and Turner's November 5 trial been busy with its own work of death.[29] Holding the slave defendant answerable not only for the deaths of his uprising's white victims, but for those of his black "bosom associates," Gray's Cobb transfers the death-dealing Court's responsibility to Turner.[30] So doing, the Court goes beyond mere recognition of the slave's culpable personhood, holding him not just legally but politically answerable as (in the *Confessions* subtitle) "The Leader of the Late Insurrection in Southampton, Va."[31]

Having the Court of Oyer and Terminer authorize the denial to Turner of the usual time of repentance by transferring to him its own accountability for the other Southampton insurgents' deaths, the *Confessions* highlights the importance of the rhetorical manipulation of temporality to the allocation of blame for crime and its redress. Execution Day's counterfactual evocation of lives unled held the individual responsible for his own state-administered death as a recuperative exercise that would return the community (and ideally, each of its members) back to the path toward a righteous future in this world and beyond. A similarly remedial impulse drove some antebellum observers to trace blame for the Southampton uprising to its timing. Anti-abolitionists connected incendiary cause to deadly effect by pointing out that the nation's largest slave insurrection occurred soon after the appearance of inflammatory abolitionist publications such as David Walker's *Appeal* (1829) and Garrison's *Liberator*. Summoning counterfactual logic in their own criticism of abolitionist print agitation (had there been no Garrison or Walker, there would be no Turner), apologists for slavery sought, like the minister at the scaffold, to restore a social order disrupted by crime through narratives that unfolded in alternative timelines—in effect, turning time to their own political ends.

Reformers disavowed responsibility for "the late sanguinary proceedings in Virginia" by correcting anti-abolitionists' temporal frame of reference.[32] Remarking that "men are too ready to ascribe sudden and violent eruptions of evil to the operation of temporary causes," the correspondent "O. L." insisted that any familiarity with "ancient or modern history" would confirm "that conspiracies and insurrections have always been frequent among slaves . . . long before the invention of printing, and in places where newspapers never circulated."[33] O. L. refuted counterfactual allegations with factually insistent narratives of past crimes. Like the *Address of Abraham*

Johnstone, the *Liberator* offers this revisionist counterhistory in an effort to set the nation on an alternative path toward a just future by cultivating a collective sense of culpability. And, like the *Address*'s Johnstone, antebellum reformers could not entirely resist indulging in their own counterfactuals. "What we have so long predicted has commenced its fulfillment," Garrison all but gloated as he published the first reports from Southampton: "We have exerted our utmost efforts to avert the calamity. We have warned our countrymen of the danger of persisting in their unrighteous conduct."[34] (Had the nation only heeded Garrison, there would be no Turner.) And now what? "Let time answer," the immediatist editor's jeremiad ominously concluded.[35]

Time was made to answer for much in a nation where, Thomas M. Allen finds, the responsible use of time was coming to define a new "market-oriented personhood."[36] If most Americans still lived diurnal lives ordered by Sabbath observance and seasonal change, industrialism's widening reach (as evidenced by ever more prevalent gas lighting and clocks) was recasting time as a "productive resource" to be spent, conserved, invested, wasted, and even redeemed.[37] Print, disseminated through translocal networks that united readers in what Lloyd Pratt has called "a technologically enabled national common time," became a figure for this networked temporality.[38] In this urgent temporal economy mediated and symbolized by print, crime reporting played an important role by more closely linking criminal cause to punitive effect.[39] In the first extant newspaper report of the Southampton uprising, for example, Richmond's *Constitutional Whig* corrected rumors by citing an "express" from Southampton, reassured readers that "prompt and efficient measures are being taken by the Governor," assuaged fears of more widespread danger by noting that "the deluded wretches have rushed on assured destruction," and concluded by affirming that "the insurrection . . . will be quickly suppressed."[40] A particularly overdetermined example of how, as Hal Gladfelder puts it, "the immediacy of printed representations helped to secure the ideological centrality of the law, making possible the instantaneous and broadly dispersed publication of its rituals and proceedings," the *Constitutional Whig* also illustrates how journalistic crime reporting created a demand for gallows literature.[41]

Since the days of Cotton Mather, time had been nearly as important to the endeavor to textualize the rites of execution as it had been to the conversion process dramatized in the pamphlets and broadsides sold at or just after public hangings.[42] Now, however, positioned at "opposite ends of a single narrative continuum," the execution account provided reassuring closure to the anxious story initiated by crime news.[43] Whereas this drama had unfolded on a local level in the late colonial and early national periods, by 1831 the rapid dissemination of printed news ensured that gallows ephemera were, in Pratt's phrasing, "organized around a punctual temporality . . . necessarily addressed to the national 'moment.'"[44] Gray acknowledges as much in his opening remarks "To the Public." Noting that "the late insurrection in Southampton has greatly excited the public mind, and led to a thousand idle, exaggerated and mischievous reports," Gray observes that the uprising "could not fail to leave a deep impression, not only upon the minds of the community where this fearful tragedy was wrought, but throughout every portion of our country, in which this population is to be found."[45] Supplanting such "idle . . . reports" with his own rapidly produced, authoritative account, the newly disinherited scion of Virginia's plantocracy and recent defense counsel for several of Turner's co-conspirators promised instant "gratification" to an understandably impatient "public" whose "curiosity has been on the stretch to understand the origin and progress of this dreadful conspiracy, and the motives which influences its diabolical actors."[46] With any luck, the pamphlet would appeal to the masses of American consumers snapping up Franklin Clocks emblazoned with manufacturer Silas Hoadley's "TIME IS MONEY" label.[47]

The down-at-the-heels Virginia lawyer-turned-entrepreneurial publicist found Hoadley's adage literalized as he negotiated an industrializing capitalist print culture that reified time into a productive resource.[48] After all, the Court had given *both* Turner and Gray a disconcertingly "short" time to prepare for the execution.[49] Turner was admitted to jail on October 31, 1831, tried on November 5, and hanged within a week, on November 11. Accordingly, Gray "visited NAT on Tuesday the 1st November," had a complete "statement" by "the evening of the third day," spent a week editing the manuscript, began his journey northward to the nation's publishing centers, and, finally, deposited the title in the Washington, D.C., copyright office on the day preceding Turner's execution.[50]

As noted, the pamphlet's timing affected more than just its marketability. The delay between the August uprising and its leader's November trial and execution (and the publication of the *Confessions*) occasioned the attribution of an unprecedented degree of interiority to the condemned slave. By the time Gray had hustled *Confessions* into print, the uprising's basic contours had become well drawn after months of extensively reprinted newspaper reports based on eyewitness accounts and the ongoing trials of suspected insurgents. The inevitable minor discrepancies aside, most of the main points had been established: who was killed, when, where, how, and even by whom. As a result, the belated capture of the man who had gradually emerged as the uprising's leader only further separated *actus reus* from *mens rea* in print coverage of the event. Rampant speculation about the perpetrators' intent had sharpened the usually blurry line between act and motive. When it became clear that the uprising was motivated by much more than "a design to plunder," the enslaved killers were portrayed as Aristotelian extensions of another's will, either "two white leaders," as originally reported, or the mysterious "Captain Nat" who soon became the focus of the investigation.[51]

It was by giving the American public an interiorized account of that will that the *Confessions of Nat Turner* promised to provide "general satisfaction" to its readers.[52] Here Nat Turner's legal transformation, upon arrest, from demonized outlaw into accused person was crucial. As Gray noted in his introductory remarks, "the insurgent slaves had all been destroyed, or apprehended, tried and executed, (with the exception of the leader,) without revealing anything at all satisfactory, as to the motives which governed them. . . . Every thing connected with this sad affair was wrapt in mystery, until Nat Turner, the leader of this ferocious band, whose name has resounded through our widely extended empire, was captured" (40). Newspaper reports and an earlier pamphlet by Samuel Warner had vied to provide (in the shortened title of the latter) an *Authentic and Impartial Narrative of the Tragical Scene which was Witnessed in Southampton County*.[53] Rather than offering yet another exteriorized view of the "Tragical Scene," the *Confessions* presented the first-person narrative of a slave with "motives" all his own. As "the contriver and head" of "the insurrectory movements of the slaves," Gray emphasized, Turner "makes no attempt (as all the other insurgents who were examined did,) to exculpate himself, but frankly acknowledges his full participation in all the guilt of the transaction" by means of the extrajudicial "full and free confession" that Gray promised to have published "with little or no variation" (40–41). With almost nothing new to be said about the actions comprised in the uprising, the *Confessions of Nat Turner* promised a portrait of the slave as pure *mens rea*.

Gray cleared a space for his unwonted composition by casting aside preliminary sketches of Turner as a slave who, driven perhaps by petty "motives of revenge or sudden anger" (42), acted with "the purpose of obtaining money to make his escape" (54). Lacking the "advantages of education" but far from "ignorant and cowardly," Turner is, Gray affirms, "for natural intelligence and quickness of apprehension . . . surpassed by few men I have ever seen" (54). Of course, to emphasize the mental capacity that transformed human property into culpable person was to risk conceding that the slave's motives for killing slaveholders were not only rational but justified. Submitting "to the public" Turner's "own account of the conspiracy" as "an awful, and it is hoped, a useful lesson, as to the operations of a mind like his, endeavoring to grapple with things beyond its reach," Gray proffers a narrative of the mind of the criminous slave—"how it first became bewildered and confounded, and finally corrupted and led to the conception and perpetration of the most atrocious and heart-rending deeds" (41).

No black catalog of shoes, gooses, and kettles stolen, the interpolated first-person narrative is a story of intentions, not acts. Mindful of the instrumentality of other slaves ("Jack, I knew, was only a tool in the hands of Hark"), the young Turner emerges as a sort of itinerant criminal mastermind (48). "I was not addicted to stealing in my youth," he recalls, "yet such was the confidence of the negroes in the neighborhood, even at this early period of my life, in my superior judgment, that they would often carry me" along "on any roguery, to plan for them" (45). Foreshadowing the "atrocious and heart-rending deeds" of August 22, 1831, which he also directed but only minimally participated in, Turner's reminiscence credits him with the forethought necessary to put any "roguery" into action. Here, though, as in the account of the uprising itself, the persistent disjuncture between planning and deed, between intent and act, makes it extraordinarily difficult to assess blameworthiness. It is in this sense that the pamphlet finally fails to deliver on its promise. Making the bloody events seem "the results of long deliberation, and a settled purpose of mind," the shifting temporality that here lends gothic overtones to Gray's prose will, in Turner's first-person account, rid the insurgents' acts of their criminality (42).

The Work of Death

A time-sensitive document in more ways than one, the *Confessions of Nat Turner* provides a striking example of how, in Pratt's words, nineteenth-century American literature "both documented and compounded a conflict of times that inhibited the consolidation of U.S. national and racial identity."[54] Gallows literature not only exemplifies this process but demonstrates how these temporal collisions stymied the allocation of liability so central to the period's competing accounts of American selfhood. With its quintessentially antebellum layering of temporal modes, the *Confessions* confounds any straightforward attribution of criminal culpability.

In a temporally obsessed genre and culture, Gray's pamphlet stands out. "Having arrived to man's estate," Turner is addressed by "the Spirit that spoke to prophets in former days."[55] After "several years rolled around" Turner receives a "revelation in the year 1825" that "the Spirit" would reveal to him "knowledge of the elements, the revolution of the planets, the operation of tides, and changes of the seasons" (46, 47). Then, on "the 12th of May, 1828," Turner received several indications that "the time was fast approaching when the first should be last and the last should be first" (47–48). With the eclipse of the sun in February 1831 indicating that "I should arise and prepare myself, and slay my enemies with their own weapons," Turner "communicated the great work laid out for me to do" to four enslaved confidants, intending "to have begun the work of death on the 4th July last" (48). Upon this proliferation of signs in biological, typological, calendrical, natural, eschatological, and national time, Turner began to fulfill his "great purpose" (46).

The slave rebel appears to hail from a different age than his white interlocutor as he tells his story "in the condemned hole of the prison . . . still bearing the stains of the blood of helpless innocence about him; clothed with rags and covered with chains; yet daring to raise his manacled hands to heaven" (54–55). Gray, as he races from jail to writing desk to copyright office in order to turn out his pamphlet in less than a fortnight, is a paragon of the modern entrepreneur who efficiently and profitably manages time, print, and markets to address (and thus call into being) a newly cohesive translocal, contemporaneous imagined U.S. community. Yet Nat Turner, for all his scripture quoting, heaven scanning, and leaf reading, was no premodern foil for the frantic Virginia lawyer and his impatient readers. Quite the contrary: Gray's Turner is the embodiment of the temporal mashup that has become the hallmark of modernity. Ranging among a multiplicity of temporalities, the Turner of the *Confessions* fashions an enslaved black self whose radical individualism both derives from and is manifested by a unique relationship to time.

In the first lines attributed to him, the slave rebel turns the (time)tables on Gray. "SIR," he parries, "you have asked me to give a history of the motives which induced me to undertake the late insurrection, as you call it—To do so I must go back to the days of my infancy, and even before I was born" (44). Giving the lie to Gray's introductory assertion that "NAT . . . without being questioned at all, . . . commenced his narrative," Turner identifies the primary selling point of the *Confessions*—as a first-person "history of the motives" prompting the uprising—even as he alters the temporal frame through which culpability is conventionally assigned to the acts arising from those motives (44). Like Johnstone before him, Turner reclaims the temporality through which gallows literature assigns responsibility so as to question the meaning of and thus answerability for crime under a slaveholding legal regime. Although his account of the uprising will accomplish this by adapting the temporal economy of the capitalist workplace to the work of death, the preliminary autobiographical narrative achieves the same end by associating Turner's political leadership with his special relationship to time. Turner eschews the generic imperative to produce an incriminatory confessional narrative that will locate the roots of the recent crisis in "the recesses of his own dark, bewildered, and overwrought mind" (41). "I was thirty-one years of age the 2d of October last, and born the property of Benj. Turner, of this county," he commences, exchanging the role of mental alien for that of local slave (44).[56] Replacing Gray's time frame with his own, more comprehensive one, Turner suggests that the uprising's origins predate his own existence, making the crisis coextensive with and traceable to the ongoing history of slavery itself. As with O. L.'s appeal in the *Liberator* to "history, ancient or modern," Turner's initial statement places recent events in a much longer political continuum, locating the uprising in a history that transcends personal biography. He thus joins the *Liberator* in turning back the narrative clock to shift responsibility for the crisis from specific enslaved actors to a society wherein one human can legitimately be "born the property" of another.[57]

This adjustment made, the Turner of the *Confessions* displays a chronological precision at odds with abolitionist (and critical) accounts of the dehumanizing effects of temporal deprivation on the enslaved.[58] As the leader of an uprising that Gray accurately predicts "will be long remembered in the annals of our country," this Turner fashions a self defined by its superhuman mastery of historical time (42). "Being at play with other children, when three or four years old," he recalls, "I was telling them something, which my mother overhearing, said it had happened before I was born—I stuck to my story, however, and related somethings which went, in her opinion, to confirm it—others being called on were greatly astonished, knowing that these had happened, and caused them to say in my hearing, I surely would be a prophet, as the Lord had shewn me things that had happened before my birth" (44). Under a regime that deprived slaves of historical existence, to prophesy was to look backward. As with his prophetic access to the past, young Nat's spontaneous literacy affirmed his chosen status even as it offered yet another instance of his exceptional relationship to time. "Fully confirmed . . . in the impression that I was ordained for some great purpose in the hands of the Almighty" and "knowing the influence I had obtained over the minds of my fellow servants," the adult Turner begins "to prepare them for my purpose" (46). In a world where mastery was both displayed by and dependent on absolute control over time—and especially, perhaps, the future—a slave with a plan for himself, his fellow bondpeople, and their white enslavers was dangerous indeed. The uprising's horror, as Gray underscores, lay in its terrifying simultaneity: "whilst every thing upon the surface of society wore a calm and peaceful aspect; whilst not one note of preparation was heard to warn the devoted inhabitants of woe and death, a gloomy fanatic was revolving . . . schemes of indiscriminate massacre to the whites" (41).[59]

Yet even this most exceptional of slaves was mastered by the slaveholder's clock. In the narratives of Douglass and Solomon Northup, Pratt has found, any separation of "premodern and modern ways of being in time . . . collapses," as scenes of temporally disciplined slave labor unfold on "a terrain indistinguishable . . . from that of the Lowell mills."[60] It is against the backdrop of slavery's "laboring time" that the Turner of the *Confessions* fashions a radically individual self.[61] As a child, Turner recalls, "all my time, *not devoted to my master's service,* was spent either in prayer, or . . . in attempting to make paper [and] gunpowder."[62] Upon reaching maturity, Turner "for two years prayed continually, *whenever my duty would permit*" (46; emphasis added). Having begun "the first steps of righteousness" that will acquaint him with the planetary, tidal, and seasonal forces that govern temporality, Turner, still subject to the master's time discipline, "withdrew myself *as much as my situation would permit*, from the intercourse of my fellow servants" (46–47; emphasis added).

Notably, then, the narrative that documents Turner's portentous relationship to time also recounts his Franklinesque manipulation of temporal appearances in order to consolidate and augment his power within the slave community. "Having soon [been] discovered to be great," he explains, "I must appear so, and therefore studiously avoided mixing in society, and wrapped myself in mystery, devoting my time to fasting and prayer" (45). When Turner mentions in passing that he arrived at "about three o'clock" for the initial dinner meeting in the woods to plan the uprising, Gray (revealing himself to be a man very much of his time) asks Turner why he was "so backward in joining them" (48). The reply—"the same reason that had caused me not to mix with them for years"—is telling. Like his industrial, domestic, and Transcendentalist counterparts throughout antebellum print culture, the Turner of the *Confessions* appreciates that, as Allen puts it, "time has the power to produce personhood, but only when it is spent well and invested wisely."[63] Whereas the bourgeois businessman, his conscientious helpmeet, and the Concord eccentric asserted their self-possessed individualism through careful time management, the prophet eschews such mundane existences through a temporal self-mastery that, in the antipodal world of the slaveholding South, is appropriately "backward," manifesting itself in lateness rather than punctuality.[64]

Some Americans moved beyond the equation on Hoadley's Franklin Clocks, seeing "time, rather than money, as the fundamental measure of value."[65] The *Confessions*, having debunked rumors of any financial motive, depicts Turner's leadership of the uprising as, above all, an attempt to gain time. As he races against increasing daylight and the growing likelihood of capture, Turner directs the insurgents to dispatch the local slaveholding families with, well, dispatch. Apprehensive about their inevitable apprehension, Turner urges his followers to transform the quick into the dead as quickly as possible. With no hope of victory or escape, the insurgents perform the work of death with maximum speed and efficiency, capitalizing on the interval of freedom that separates the captivity of the slave from that of the apprehended suspect. The massacre described in the *Confessions* observes the same urgent temporal economy as the pamphlet's production and reception. Like the harried Gray and his edgy readers, the insurgents are, to borrow the *Constitutional Whig*'s description, "rushed." Although the rising sun, not the sweeping hands of a clock, indicates the passage of time, what the *Confessions* repeatedly refers to as the "progress" of the uprising closely resembles the frenetic internalized time-consciousness that Max Weber identified with the Protestant work ethic and rise of capitalism.[66]

In fact, the interpolated confession has no time for the brooding mental alien conjured by Gray's gothic introductory remarks. Rather, the Turner who directs the massacre is an uncannily familiar figure: the model American whose temporal discipline enables him to govern himself while leading others in efficient, productive labor.[67] Commencing at the Travis household, the insurgents make "the murder of this family, five in number, . . . the work of a moment" (49). (Having recollected that "there was a little infant sleeping in a cradle, that was forgotten," Henry and Will, weighing diligence against speed, "returned and killed it" [49].) At the Whitehead house, temporarily

diverted by his mistaken pursuit of a fleeing slave, Turner "returned to commence the work of death, but they whom I left, had not been idle; all the family were already murdered, but Mrs. Whitehead and her daughter Margaret"
(50). That remaining task is quickly accomplished. "By this time," Turner's
group is rejoined by "the six who had gone by Mr. Bryant's," who "informed
me they had done the work of death assigned them." Not long afterward, on
learning that "the alarm had already spread," Turner is gratified to discover
his subordinates' efficiency to surpass his own: "I immediately pursued the
course taken by the party gone on before; but knowing that they would complete the work of death and pillage, at Mr. Francis' before I could get there, I
went to Mr. Peter Edwards', expecting to find them there, but they had been
there also" (50).

The martial language and imagery interspersed throughout the time-
conscious account of the uprising's progress confirms rather than negates
Turner's managerial persona. After seizing guns owned by the (slaughtered)
Travis family, Turner recalls, the men "paraded" with their newly acquired
weapons; then, having "formed them in a line as soldiers, and after carrying
them through all the manoeuvers I was master of," Turner "marched them
off" to their next engagement (49). Turner's army of slaves look most martial
when engaged in behaviors that would, in other circumstances, confirm well-
established stereotypes of black criminality. Following his "company," now
divided for maximum efficiency, to the home of (the escaped) Captain Newit
Harris, Turner finds "some . . . in the yard, loading their guns, others drinking" (49–50); on seeing him they report that they had destroyed "the property
in the house . . . , robbing [Harris] of money and other valuables," whereupon
Turner "ordered them to mount and march instantly" (50). The military trope
effectively decriminalizes the killers by placing them in a state of war with the
slaveholding Virginians. Standing outside the social compact and doing their
duty, Turner's "soldiers" conduct acts of war rather than perpetrate crimes.

But in the *Confession's* rendition of their motiveless, almost mechanical
killings, Turner's "soldiers" finally appear less the "army of oppressed men,
fighting for liberty" idealized by reformers than an impressively disciplined
labor force legitimately employed in the efficient production of dead bodies.[68]
If here as in Thoreau's *Walden*, "the rhetoric of temporal economy" works, as
Allen suggests, "to extend the logic of the market into a venue where it might
be appropriated and put to the service of another social agenda," it bears
recalling that Virginia in the 1830s was precisely the place and time where
the military industrial management techniques intrinsic to the "American

system" of manufacture were being developed and transferred to the private sector.[69] Rationally and systematically directing his underlings in the "work of death assigned them," the Nat Turner portrayed here is ultimately more general manager than prophet-revolutionary—and a highly effective one at that. Given that his "object" was "to carry terror and devastation wherever we went," efficient administration requires that Turner oversee rather than perform the job himself.[70] In the routinized labor of killing, Turner typically "placed fifteen or twenty of the best armed and most to be relied on, in front, who generally approached the houses as fast as their horses could run" (50–51). It was "on this account," he explains that "I never got to the houses . . . until the murders were committed" (51). Noting that "I sometimes got in sight in time to see the work of death completed," Turner recalls experiencing the supervisor's gratification at a job well done as he "viewed the mangled bodies . . . in silent satisfaction." His inspection complete, Turner, losing no time, "immediately started in quest of other victims" (51).

Newspaper coverage highlighted Turner's administrative expertise. Published alongside a "list of the victims . . . compris[ing] 58 persons of all ages," an early report emphasizing the insurgents' ruthless efficiency appeared in the same issue of the *Liberator* as a filler item offering a "minute calculation as to the amount of cloth manufactured at Lowell in different portions of time: '. . . 12 to 14 millions yards . . . annually—equal to 44,000 per day—3,000 per hour—60 per minute—or a yard every second!'"[71] Evoking, in their disciplined, productive labor, the Southern slaves who involuntarily produced the massive quantities of cotton that would be processed into those millions of yards of cloth, the Southampton insurgents, with their rapid output of white corpses, likewise kept pace with Northern factory workers. (It was Eli Whitney, after all, who had facilitated the early national knowledge transfer from military to commercial enterprise.)[72]

With no qualms about treating one slave insurgent as "only a tool in the hands of" another, the managerial Turner of the *Confessions* differed from both the lords of the lash and the lords of the loom in his lack of a profit motive. As he follows the divine call to "slay my enemies with their own weapons," Turner is the supreme Weberian capitalist: working within a closed economy of deadly destruction, he assiduously reinvests any windfall back into the "work of death and pillage." Thus even as it confirms Gray's depiction of Turner as the "contriver and head" of the "insurrectory movements of the slaves," the account of the uprising is structured by a familiar industrial capitalist temporality in which Turner finally appears more as supervisory taskmaster than evil genius. Effectively decriminalizing the insurgents with this separation of *mens rea* from *actus reus*, the *Confessions* also decouples the noble motives that abolitionists had attributed to Turner from their bloody outcome in the slaves' speedy, efficient slaughter of scores of white men, women, and children. Regardless of whom one held responsible, print coverage of the Southampton uprising left little doubt that the problem with the slaveholding South was not that it lagged behind the industrialized North, but that it produced the wrong thing. Rather than the virtuous Christian citizens that disciplined free labor was supposed to yield, the peculiar institution appeared to be in the business of speedily and efficiently churning out criminals and victims.

Witnesses and Participants

The *Narrative of James Williams*'s unremitting scenes of intraracial as well as interracial violence confirmed that impression. Upon publication in early 1838, this new kind of abolitionist propaganda "excited a great deal of interest everywhere," claimed AASS Executive Committee members James Gillespie Birney and Lewis Tappan.[73] This was "not so much because it revealed" slavery's atrocities, "but because it brought many such together, and connected them in the form of a regular narrative, in which the narrator himself was the principal actor, and to most of the particulars of which he could himself testify." Transcribed and edited by Quaker poet John Greenleaf Whittier, the *Narrative* went through three print runs in its first six months before being compromised by charges of fraud and, formally at least, withdrawn.[74] A brief survey of literary abolitionism's penal ancestry suggests that the *Narrative*'s downfall lay in its historically and generically novel approach to antislavery print agitation.

Responsibility, criminal and otherwise, was at the core of the conjoined national and individual selfhood that accompanied the novel as it arose amidst cognate print forms like popular trial reports, criminal biographies, and scaffold speeches.[75] Changes in criminal procedure and penal reform, on the one hand, and in the technology and influence of a legally inflected print media, on the other, contributed to the emergence in the early national and antebellum United States of a definitively "juridical self-fashioning" akin to that Jonathan Grossman sees emerging in Britain.[76] From Charles Brockden Brown and James Fenimore Cooper to Nathaniel Hawthorne and Herman Melville (to say nothing of Kate Chopin, Mark Twain, Albion Tourgée, and

Charles Chesnutt), American fiction has since its inception proven consistently attentive to the most subtle alterations in legal discourse and practice.[77] As their British colleagues had since the mid-eighteenth century, American writers appealed to the popular legal consciousness of a readership increasingly imagined as forming a national community governed by law.[78] Such appeals were particularly powerful in a nation where legal standards of responsibility were changing, with the criminal law's reorientation toward intent and the civil law's turn from strict liability toward a new sense of universal responsibility ("of all the world to all the world" in Oliver Wendell Holmes's maxim).[79] As indicated by the popularity and influence of reform writing from temperance stories to anti-polygamy fiction, American literary fabulists had, as Lisa Rodensky observes of English novelists, attained an "unofficial yet undeniable" authority regarding social issues with their "authoritative" if not "authorized" appropriations of legal discourse, especially as it pertained to criminal answerability.[80]

The long-standing designation of slavery as "manstealing" in transatlantic print propaganda eased the assimilation of these developments by America's new antislavery literature.[81] Like the eighteenth- and nineteenth-century British audiences described by Grossman, Americans were encouraged by crime and trial reporting to understand themselves as "answerable member[s] of a law-bound state" while novel-reading heightened their consciousness of themselves as living "individual accountable lives" within "a republic of justifying citizens."[82] But in the United States the foundational principle of self-government made Americans "a people tensed toward (narrative) answerability" not only abstractly, but with specific reference to the crime of slavery.[83] "No other proof is required" of the particular evil of slavery in the United States, maintained Whittier, "than an examination of the statute books of the American slave states. Tested by its own laws, in all that facilitates and protects the hateful process of converting a man into a '*chattel personal*;' in all that stamps the law-maker, and law-upholder with meanness and hypocrisy, it certainly has no present rival."[84]

Significantly, Whittier's depiction of slavery as a grotesque perversion of law (as opposed to, say, an outmoded labor system or a sin against God) appears in his preface to the *Narrative of James Williams*. The *Narrative*'s immediate success and the genre's continued popularity in the 1840s and 1850s indicate that American readers found the first-person testimonial voice of the slave at least as compelling as Alexander Welsh maintains English audiences did the Victorian novel's third-person narrator. For if, like that narrator, the slave's white advocates mimicked the era's professionalizing lawyers in their management and presentation of disparate pieces of evidence in their novels and factbooks, the fugitive slave's first-person account became Exhibit A in abolitionist propagandists' "strong representations" before the bar of public opinion.[85] "Heretofore, the wrong-doer alone has introduced *all the testimony* in his case—or, he has been, himself, the only witness," explained Birney and Tappan regarding the Society's decision to publish the *Narrative of James Williams*.[86] It is precisely because "the slave has had no forum at which he could implead the wrong doer," they elaborate, that "the abolitionists have at length instituted one" by publishing the fugitive's firsthand account of slavery. In the slave narrative, Birney and Tappan maintain, abolitionists established print publication as "the only tribunal before which the slave can bring his cause against him from whom he has suffered the mightiest trespass that one human being can commit against the property, the life, the liberty, the happiness of another."

Over the years, the mildly adversarial torts proceeding imagined by Birney and Tappan would be refigured by Garrison and his ilk as a criminal indictment, with "manstemasteraling" rather than mere "trespass" as the wrong at issue. This was, perhaps, inevitable, given that transatlantic antislavery propaganda shared Anglo-American prose narrative's preoccupation with penality. Analyzing the tandem emergence of "the two abolitions" in late eighteenth- and early nineteenth-century Britain, Mark Canuel finds the rhetoric of the anti-death penalty movement shaping the language, imagery, and logic of the contemporaneous print campaign against slavery and the slave trade. In particular, penal reform rhetoric resurfaced in "abolitionist discourses that made the freedom of slaves inseparable from their punishability."[87] Canuel examines antislavery publicists' tendency to focus on the inappropriateness of slaveholding penality, contending that "the entire discourse of antislavery depends upon the horrors and excesses of the slave's punishment, which are not to be removed but simply alleviated and systemized" (152).[88] As both agents and victims of punishment, slaves are "portrayed as the perpetrators of lawlessness—injury and death" (148), resulting in an abolitionist "fantasy that depends upon the slave's presumed guilt" (151).[89] Rhetorically "criminalizing the slave," this first wave of antislavery "writers make it clear that both masters and their slaves need to be punished for their crimes" (154).

Ideally positioned to activate both the penal logic of such earlier antislavery propaganda and the sense of accountability inculcated by the novel, antebellum literary abolitionists urged their fellow Americans to take moral and political responsibility for the crime of slavery.[90] ("But, what can any individual do?" Stowe asks in the conclusion to *Uncle Tom's Cabin* before admonishing readers: "there is one thing that every individual can do,—they can see to it that *they feel right*.")[91] If English literature during this period can be said to have made "a jump from criminal biography to the novel," in the racialized literary history of the United States that leap is perhaps best figured by the syncopated rhythms of double-dutch.[92] When the other foot hit the ground, it completed the parallel bound from criminal confession to slave narrative. Thus even as antislavery propaganda joined the novel in holding its readers individually accountable, abolitionist rhetoric frequently depicted slaves as, in Canuel's phrasing, "instruments of pain and death detached from any agent."[93] This separation of the (often involuntary) acts performed by enslaved blacks from the intentions of their (often physically passive or absent) white masters, latent as it was in earlier transatlantic antislavery discourse, became indispensable to the political viability of the abolitionist-sponsored slave narrative.

If the Victorian novel's superiority to law inhered in its ability to expose the relationship of hidden motives to visible acts, in the United States a different kind of literary engagement with the *mens rea/actus reus* dyad enabled the slave narrative to slip out from the shadow of the gallows.[94] Antebellum abolitionism's rhetorical splitting of (white) intent from (black) act helped to authorize what would otherwise have been the deeply suspect, if not downright incriminating, evolution of the testimonial slave narrative from the gallows confession. With slaveholding *mens rea* hived off from the unmotivated *actus reus* of the enslaved, the new genre could continue to offer a first-person account of theft and violence—now attributed to the white perpetrators of slaveholding villainy rather than the black speaker—while opening up the inner African American self for readerly inspection.[95] Exposure of this newly expansive, accessible black interiority was in itself exculpatory, for it consistently disclosed principled mental resistance to (despite actual physical complicity in) slavery's crimes. Hence Douglass's figuration of young Frederick's disturbingly passive, even voyeuristic, childhood observation of his Aunt Hester's sexualized whipping as "the blood-stained gate, the entrance to the hell of slavery."[96] Douglass adopts the movement's juridical rhetoric to designate the scene "the first time I ever witnessed this horrible exhibition," presenting his aunt's flogging as "the first of a long series of such outrages, of which I was doomed to be a witness and a participant."[97] Bifurcating observed acts and interior motives, slavery "doomed" its victims to be *both* witnesses to and participants in its outrageous criminality—even if the slaves themselves were understood to be (as) innocent (as) children. As Chapter 5 demonstrates, the problem with denying black responsibility was that doing so risked importing the custodial relations of slavery into this new era of universal liability, thereby distinguishing suddenly irresponsible African Americans from Jacksonian America's self-governing citizens.

As one of literary abolitionism's early public relations blunders, the *Narrative of James Williams* serves as a reminder that the racial division of print labor between the autobiographical testimony of ex-slaves and the strong representations of their white advocates did not spring fully formed from the founding of the *Liberator* and the AASS in the early 1830s.[98] Nor was that division absolute: in 1853 Douglass would take a break from his journalism and life-writing to publish a work of historical short fiction in "The Heroic Slave"; the same year, William Wells Brown melded novel and personal narrative in *Clotel, or, The President's Daughter: A Narrative of Slave Life in the United States* (1853). These midcentury texts, along with dialogue-laden personal narratives like *Incidents in the Life of a Slave Girl*, may well mark the transition toward the realist novel.[99] But in the 1830s, the pressure for fugitives to establish their eligibility for inclusion in American society as truth-telling, promise-keeping, self-governing free laborers through the publication of authentic nonfiction personal narratives ensured that, in Ann Fabian's words, "licenses to invent would be long in coming."[100] As the Williams scandal illustrates, the perceived generic instability of the early slave narrative threatened its value as abolitionist propaganda. The difficulty was that the ingredients for the slave narrative's political effectiveness also offered a recipe for political vulnerability. Featuring an interiorized black first-person narrator who recounts a series of atrocities, the slave narrative appeared to critical antebellum audiences to hover suspiciously between the white-authored romances of the day and the ephemeral gallows literature attributed to the black condemned.

Both sides of the Williams controversy registered anxieties about the slave narrative's generic indeterminacy. When J. B. Rittenhouse's *Alabama Beacon* challenged the authenticity of "the lying Abolition pamphlet" in the spring of 1838, it deplored the *Narrative* as "a foul fester of falsehood, a miserably 'weak invention of the enemy,'" implying that the book "was written by 'some peddling Yankee preacher.'"[101] In his preface Whittier, in a customary but perhaps ill-advised allusion to the first-person storytelling of Othello, Shakespeare's black killer, characterized Williams's narrative as "the simple and unvarnished story of an AMERICAN SLAVE."[102] His confidence in the *Narrative*'s authenticity and its enunciator's veracity rested on "the perfect accordance of [Williams's] statements (made at different times and to different individuals) one with another."[103] The *Narrative*'s detractors rejected such claims, referring to Williams as "the hero of this profligate romance," every bit as much a "fabulous character" as the other personages in the dubious tale.[104]

With the fugitive narrator out of reach, in transit through the British empire, the AASS sought to corroborate his story by supplementing its informal pre-publication "cross-examination" of Williams with information solicited from correspondents in Alabama and elsewhere. Finally, the AASS Executive Committee published a lengthy statement in the *Emancipator* that, although it stopped short of retracting the *Narrative*, sought to distance the organization from the compromised document. Making the best of a bad situation, Birney and Tappan maintained that even as "pure, unmixed *fiction*," the *Narrative*, like other novels, "may well portray the prevailing manners of a people, although it does not relate a single transaction . . . as it has actually taken place among them." Otherwise, they asked, "shall we say to the scores and hundreds and thousands of Abolitionists, who have been made such, by reading this thrilling Narrative—be ye *unmade*— . . . there's nothing bearing the least resemblance to its filthy details among the happy laborers, and the gallant chivalry of the South?"[105]

Birney and Tappan did not rest content with defending the political value of antislavery fiction by opposing the questionable slave narrative's verisimilitude to what would soon be the familiar types of the plantation romance; they grounded their claims for the pamphlet's authenticity in the implausibility of a slave composing a work of extended prose fiction. Had the *Narrative* been fabricated by Williams out of whole cloth, it would be "one of the most successful and remarkable efforts of the *imagination* of which the times bear witness," Birney and Tappan readily acknowledge. "But," they insist, "this cannot be; it is saying too much for the powers of the *man*, to suppose that James, in his circumstances, could bring out such *creations*." Birney and Tappan effectively endorsed their print antagonists' tacit assumption that such imaginative, original, literary creativity could be expected of a John Whittier, not a James Williams, when they failed to acknowledge the allegation that the fictional narrative might indeed be attributable to the white reformers, not their black protégé.

Pressed by the abolitionists to address the specifics of the disputed *Nar-*

rative, the *Alabama Beacon* had also switched hermeneutic tacks, treating the pamphlet as a black criminal confession rather than a white-authored romance. In a reprinted letter to the editor, a "Geo. T. F. Larimer" (whose name resembled that of Williams's putative master, George Larrimore) claimed that the *Narrative*'s Williams was in fact his mother-in-law's "former carriage driver, who call[ing] himself Shadrack Wilkins," had been "sold by her in consequence of having been detected" in a conspiracy to poison a local doctor and his family. When his "accomplices . . . were tried," Larimer reports, "one . . . was transported, and the other was sentenced to be hanged, and afterwards reprieved, and likewise transported," adding that had Williams/ Wilkins "been tried, there is scarcely a doubt, but that he would have been hanged" as "the principal mover in the business." Instead, having escaped from his new owner "in company with an abolitionist," Williams/Wilkins was said to have been fraudulently sold by the latter to a Baltimore "trader, who . . . put him in jail, when Shadrack confessed every thing." Larimer's elaborate counterfactual counternarrative effectively returns the subject of the abolitionists' inaugural slave narrative to the gallows literature tradition: no longer testimony to the trespasses of white wrong-doers, the slave's first-person account reverts to a self-incriminating jailhouse confession by an enslaved murderer and imposter.

Conscious as they were of "adding a new department to the literature of civilization," Williams's antislavery sponsors awkwardly negotiated the same hurdles as their antagonists with respect to the slave narrative's generic—and thus political—integrity.[106] Sectional challenges to the *Narrative* may have renewed lingering suspicions about its fictive qualities, but the reformers' own tendency to associate slavery with crime had from the beginning led them to cast Williams's first-person account in a penal light. Whittier's preface mines statute books, Southern newspapers, and planters' manuals for examples of harsh disciplinary measures, following up its jeremiad on slaveholding American law with an account of the dangers of plantation justice. In a world where the slave "only knows his master as lawgiver and executioner," Whittier quotes meliorist slaveholder Rev. Thomas S. Clay as lamenting, "*offences against the master* are more severely punished than violations of the law of God, a fault which affects the slave's personal character a good deal."[107] Whittier leaves little doubt about the long-term consequences of slavery's perversion of divine and civil law. "Calling on all the world to shake off the fetters of oppression, and wade through the blood of tyrants to freedom," the hypocritical American slaveholder "has been compelled to smother, in darkness and silence the minds of his own bondmen, lest they too should hear and obey the summons, by putting the knife to his own throat" (v). If the image evokes "the insurrection of Nat Turner" (explicitly referenced in the opening paragraph of Williams's narrative), Whittier's preface calls attention less to how tyrannous oppression prompts revolutionary resistance than to how, in his words, American slavery "encourages crime" among its victims (27, vi).

That both bondmen and masters are implicated in slavery's many crimes is suggested by the incongruously carceral figure with which the Quaker poet introduces Williams's narrative. Having supported his opening argument with the self-incriminating "testimony and admissions of slave-holders" like Rev. Clay, the prosecutorial Whittier contends that "for a full revelation of the secrets of the prison-house, we must look to the slave himself" (vi–vii, xvii). The metaphor is prompted by Whittier's identification of American slaves, bearing "the marks of the whip . . . the gun-shot wounds, and the traces of the branding iron," with "the escaping heretic," who "with his swollen and disjointed limbs, and bearing about him the scars of rack and fire," exposed Spanish Inquisitors "to the gaze and abhorrence of Christendom" (xvii). Sympathetic as this comparison would have been for Whittier's predominantly Protestant readers, abolitionists' ongoing fascination with slaveholding penality gave their ubiquitous references to "the prison-house of bondage" the collateral effect of incriminating the African Americans figuratively consigned to this imaginary carceral space.[108] (A decade later, Ephraim Peabody would temper his appreciation of the fugitive slave narrative by expressing regret that "these books give the impression that the Slave States constitute one vast prison-house, of which all the whites without exception are the mere keepers.")[109] Depicting the South's peculiar institution as a "prison-house," works like the Narrative of James Williams risked suggesting that its black inmates were not merely *victims* of the crime of slavery.

To Some Purpose

However much the Narrative of James Williams differed from the jailhouse confession that the Alabama Beacon attributed to Shadrack Wilkins, scape-gallows poisoner, it is noteworthy that the first narrative published by the AASS should tell the story of a slave *driver*. In contrast to later, more unambiguously "innocent" narrators such as Lewis and Milton Clarke ("Sons of a Soldier of the Revolution"), Solomon Northup ("a Citizen of New-York, Kidnapped in Washington City"), Linda Brent ("A Slave Girl"), or James W.

C. Pennington ("The Fugitive Blacksmith"), "James Williams, an American Slave, who was for Several Years a Driver on a Cotton Plantation in Alabama" offers a testimonial first-person narrative that implicates its speaker in the violent acts described therein.

To what degree—if any—is James Williams responsible for his actions? The question haunts the *Narrative*, made even more troubling by the fact that Williams's stint as driver coincides with his first real experience of slavery's brutality, which in turn coincides with his maturity. Williams, who voluntarily (and he believes, temporarily) leaves his wife and children behind to accompany his young master to Alabama, is horrified to be abandoned there by "the man . . . whose slightest wish had been my law."[110] Portrayed as a descent into atemporal lawlessness, Williams's sojourn as a driver is also the first time the reader sees him performing labor. And when Williams finally does commence the work of slavery as a driver on the anomic estate, it is unambiguously the work of death.

In the *Narrative*'s Alabama, a slaveholding economy that treats human beings as fungible objects of property is translated into a disciplinary regimen whose endless cycle of violence renders perpetrators and victims interchangeable. Williams is introduced to this penal logic when the white overseer, Huckstep, informs him that "a Virginia driver generally had to be whipped a few times himself before he could be learned to do justice to the slaves under his charge" (42). Tasked by Huckstep with "keeping the lazy hell-hounds, as he called the slaves, at work," Williams finds himself in the agonizing position of "a driver set over more than one hundred and sixty of my kindred and friends, with orders to apply the whip unsparingly to every one, whether man or woman . . . myself subject at any moment to feel the accursed lash on my own back, if feelings of humanity should perchance overcome the selfishness of misery, and induce me to spare and pity" (42–43). One cannot "do justice to the slaves" without having first "learned" the dangers of equity. The black driver, schooled by whipping to appreciate his potential interchangeability with his victims, will endeavor to preserve his distinctness from them by unsympathetically wielding the lash himself.

The overseer's plantation jurisprudence is soon put into penal practice. A series of five interlocking scenes form a metonymic chain in which the perpetrators and victims of punitive violence vacate and fill each other's positions in succession. Reluctant to whip Sarah, a light-skinned, pregnant woman rumored to be the old master Larrimore's daughter, Williams, "told that my business was to obey orders," finally "gave her fifty lashes" (61).

When, after repeated whippings, Sarah pleads illness, Huckstep vows, "Very well! . . . I shall bleed you then, and take out some of your Virginia blood," before tying her to a tree and torturing her to death (63). When a second Sarah takes her dead namesake's place, the recalcitrant driver furtively disobeys by striking the tree instead. Discovering the subterfuge, Huckstep, assisted by three slaves, fulfills his threat to Williams that "the blows intended for Sarah should be laid on my back" (66). Upon his return to work, Williams recalls, "almost the first person that I was compelled to whip . . . was the man who pushed at my back when I was tied up to the tree," noting that "all thought he pushed me much harder than was necessary; and they expected that I would retaliate upon him the injury I had received" (67). With the man himself now bound to the trunk and the overseer once more conveniently absent, Williams defies expectations, again striking the tree instead of the slave. The gory cycle comes full circle when, as Williams recalls, soon after the overseer orders yet another pregnant slave woman "to be tied up against a tree, in the same manner that I had been" and "whipped until *she was delivered of a dead infant, at the foot of the tree*" (74–75), Huckstep himself is found, following a drunken fall from his horse, inert "at the foot of one of [the] trees," his "face . . . black" from "a frightful contusion" (76). The overseer, Williams reports, was "carried into the house, where, on my bleeding him, he revived" (76). Under slavery's inappropriate penalty, perpetrators and victims switch places in a dizzying series of substitutions, breaking down subject positions of gender, race, and condition. "Black," bruised, and incapacitated, the indiscriminately brutal overseer, having "made no distinction between the stout man and the feeble and delicate woman" who take each other's places at the whipping tree, now himself becomes indistinguishable from his enslaved victims (64). As he lies helpless at the base of a tree, the blackened overseer takes the place of the stillborn slave. Having sarcastically characterized punitive whipping as medicinal bleeding in the earlier scene, the tyrant now has his own blood therapeutically shed by one of his erstwhile victims.

Huckstep's recovery prompts Williams's fellow slave Little Simon to reproach the "fool" driver that "if *he* had bled" the overseer, "he would have done it to some purpose" (77; emphasis added). Confirming Whittier's warning that slavery "encourages crime" by making every bondman a knife-wielding Nat Turner-in-waiting, Little Simon's optative claim throws into relief the exceptional virtue of the black AASS protégé. James Williams's displays of Christian forbearance toward both white and black antagonists and his empathetic treatment of his fellow bondpeople would seem to poise the AASS's first representative "American slave" to emerge from bondage as exemplary protocitizen. Rather than producing crime, slavery here seems to generate, in Christopher Castiglia's words, "black citizens as abstract markers of civic virtues."[111] Yet, as Castiglia demonstrates, in antebellum reform rhetoric the crucible of slave suffering tended to yield an "always alienated civility," in which "black Americans rhetorically marked a civility that they, by definition, did not possess," while endowing white abolitionist luminaries like Garrison with a new kind of "civic depth."[112] Having established in its preface the deleterious effects of slavery's penal regime on "the slave's personal character," the Narrative of James Williams does not, finally, hold up the virtuous former driver as a foil either for less principled blacks or for a corrupted nation. Instead, this first testimonial slave narrative illustrates how the potential meaninglessness of criminality in a slaveholding polity threatens not merely white and black moral development but responsible personhood itself. This dilemma is encapsulated by the Narrative's repeated transitive use of the verb "bleed" to denote an act that is by turns punitive, restorative, and murderous. "Purpose," Little Simon's waggish remark underscores, is what imbues the sanguinary act with criminality. But under slavery's rampant penality, the Narrative asks, how can accountability be assessed when the everyday "business" of masters and slaves alike is the motiveless work of death?[113]

The question is an important one, given the decisive role played by culpability in political-philosophic definitions of personhood and particularly in the legal fiction of slave character. Here it seems significant that the central Alabama segment occurs in a temporal as well as legal vacuum. "It is not in my power to give a narrative of the daily occurrences on the plantation," notes Williams after recounting yet another bloody scene: "the history of one day was that of all."[114] Frozen in an endless cycle of violence, those on the Alabama plantation are not only excluded from progressive history but from the personhood that, at least since Locke, had inhered in a continuous, and therefore accountable, human consciousness. Located at the intersection of temporality and answerability, modernity's forensic person is—unlike Whittier's "human chattels"—both free and discernible from other animals (100). Notably, then, in the Narrative of James Williams the illegibility of mens rea under slavery's workaday violence has the effect not merely of egregiously interchanging men and women, whites and blacks, adults and infants, living and dead, free and enslaved, but, far more disturbingly, of undermining the foundational opposition between persons and animals from which these other distinctions exert their ideological sway.[115]

Animal imagery is a commonplace in depictions of American slavery, from Crèvecoeur's buzzard-tormented bondman to Douglass and Jacobs's serpentine masters and overseers.[116] Yet by implicating animals in the everyday crimes of slavery, the *Narrative* exceeds the abolitionist truism that slavery brutalizes master and slave alike. The malicious violence of the *Narrative*'s nonhuman animals not only makes them handy tools in slavery's work of death, but troubles conventional assumptions about culpability's definitive function in establishing personhood. In one instance, the overseer subjects a recidivist runaway to a punishment involving "two large cats," in which "the enraged animals extended their claws, and tore his back deeply and cruelly as they were dragged along it."[117] Whereas the "enraged" cats inadvertently kill the recaptured fugitive by "cruelly" tearing the flesh on his back, the bloodhounds in a previous scene actually "seem to enjoy the sport of hunting men" (50). Upon another slave's escape, Williams recalls, "the dogs were started on his track"; having "met the dogs returning" later the same evening, Williams and the overseer, joined now by neighbors, defer their search for the fugitive until the following morning, when they find his body "dreadfully mangled and gnashed by the teeth of the dogs" (50–51). Given his initial use of the passive voice, the hounds' independent movements, and the men's belated discovery of the corpse, Williams's later reference to "the murdered young man" leaves uncertain whether the dogs are merely the instruments or the self-motivated (even sportive) agents of death (51).

With its malevolent animals, pliant slaves, reluctant black driver, besotted overseer, and absentee owner, the AASS's inaugural slave narrative stages the accountability crisis at the heart of the national slavery debate. It is suggestive that Huckstep's intoxication is responsible for his being found, incapacitated, at the foot of the plantation's tree, in the position of one of his slave victims. As overseer, Huckstep could have been every bit as much a tool as the cats, dogs, and slaves he uses to accomplish the plantation's lethal labors. That it is specifically during "the overseer's periodical fits of drunkenness" that "neither life nor limb on the estate were secure from his caprice or violence" might likewise appear to mitigate his culpability (52).[118] But by holding Huckstep responsible for the alcoholic atrocities he commits while in another's employ, the *Narrative* makes it clear that the overseer is neither wage slave nor incapacitated inebriate. If Huckstep recalls Locke's drunkard (whom "human judicatures justly punish . . . because the fact is proved against him, but want of consciousness cannot be proved for him"), Williams's garrulous overseer need not await "his conscience accusing or excusing him" on Judgment Day.[119] Huckstep, who once whipped a slave to death only to realize that the man "was wholly innocent of the offence charged against him," reveals his guilty conscience when he confesses to Williams that the unjustly punished slave "had haunted him ever since."[120] "Tell[ing] long stories about hunting and shooting 'runaway niggers,' and detail[ing] with great apparent satisfaction the cruel and horrid punishments which he had inflicted," the overseer himself presents these violent acts not as private penal sanctions but self-motivated crimes that subvert rather than fulfill his employer's orders (49). Warned by Larrimore "to beware how he attempted to punish" Big Harry, the overseer profligately kills the notoriously "indomitable" but "excellent workman" (53–54). Unlike Douglass's Covey, Williams's Huckstep does not have the prudence to restrain his violence so as to protect his reputation—and employability—in a slave economy that must carefully balance profitable discipline against wasteful mortality. Huckstep's violence, unmotivated by profit, ultimately distinguishes him from the slaves by affirming his position as, in Haskell's terms, "an uncaused cause."[121] When Huckstep disregards his employer's admonitions and even his own best interests, his deadly acts establish their perpetrator as a free, *because* culpable, agent. Unlike white convicts—but like other American citizens?—Huckstep's answerability consolidates rather than compromises his autonomous personhood.

Contractualism brings out the contrast between the overseer whose autonomy derives from his accountability and the enslaved driver under his command. Unaccountable for his motiveless physical coercion of the other slaves, the driver is a civil cipher. In order to disguise his efforts to subvert Huckstep's unrelenting attacks on Big Harry, Williams is "compelled to promise to obey his directions."[122] Performing contractualism's illocutionary acts against his will, Williams can consent only to obey. The slave's civil incapacity is most evident, however, when he confronts his master and erstwhile confidante during the latter's rare visit to the Alabama estate. The chastened Larrimore responds to Williams's recriminations with an ineffectual bargain. "If I would stay ten years," Williams recalls Larrimore proposing, "he would then give me a thousand dollars, and a piece of land to plant on my own account" (69). The impossibility of a labor contract between master and slave is evident when, upon Williams's feeble protest ("But . . . my wife and children . . ."), Larrimore himself promises, "I will do my best to purchase them, and send them on to you" (69). Williams, unable to claim possession of himself, can do nothing on his "own account," from contracting for employment to governing his family. Held captive indefinitely on "1500 acres of wild land" in what looks to be a perpetual state of war, James Williams is in no state of nature, Hobbesian or otherwise (36). Owned by another man and "compelled to promise to obey," Williams can no more enter into a new social contract than he can gain retroactive, punitive entry into the existing compact through a violence lacking criminal intent.

What, then, of absentee planter and slave master George Larrimore, Junior? When, on that same visit, Larrimore interrogates first his overseer and then his driver about the deaths of Big Harry and Sarah, he seems "much affected and shed tears" upon learning of "the manner of Harry's death" (69). Held accountable by Williams for decoying him to the plantation, Larrimore incongruously responds, "well, well, it was too bad, but it could not be helped—you must blame Huckstep for it" (68). When Williams instead persists in urging Larrimore's responsibility on him ("I was not his servant; I belonged to you, and you could do as you pleased"), the genteel white man lamely replies, "well . . . we will talk about that by and by" (68). Larrimore, an obvious proxy for the Northern white reader, is able to sentimentalize the slaves' suffering by assigning blame to its proximate cause, indefinitely deferring any discussion that would expose a culpability otherwise obscured by his distance from the scene of slavery's crimes.

In keeping with the *Narrative*'s ever-shifting subject positions, however, Whittier's concluding "Note by the Editor" compares the reader to neither the self-possessed proprietor nor his white employee. "Better would it be to forego, at once, this mockery of freedom, and wear the acknowledged chains of slavery ourselves," the abolitionist admonishes his fellow American citizens, "than thus to stand ready at the beck of our masters to howl in the track of the fugitive, in concert with the trained bloodhounds of the South" (102). The mockery lies in Americans' refusal to take responsibility for slavery. Without such accountability, the *Narrative* suggests, U.S. citizens risk not only losing their own fictive freedom but their personhood, possibly even their humanity, becoming indistinguishable from the civilly dead, brutalized slaves who, like trained bloodhounds, stand ready to perpetrate the motiveless violence that transacts their political and economic fungibility. Seen in this light, the "judges, sheriffs, constables, and citizens of the free states" who "are bound by the constitutional law of the land, to hunt men like wild beasts" seem less like consenting members of the social compact than they do the slave who promises obedience under compulsion (102). (Just who, Whittier's ambiguous phrasing leaves us wondering, is "like wild beasts" here—the hunted "men," or their hunters?)

The *Narrative of James Williams* registers how the process of making the generic conversion from criminal confession to slave narrative temporarily destabilized print constructions of black personhood. For if the slave—like a domestic animal and unlike an inebriate or an employee—cannot be held responsible for his violent acts, how can he attain the personality that, from Locke to Kant, arose from that answerability? Contending that slavery begat criminality, abolitionist print propaganda came dangerously close to hinting that it also aborted the capacity requisite for black political membership.

That Startling Absence of Motive

The enraged cats and lethal bloodhounds in the *Narrative of James Williams* find their fictional analogue in the simian killer who stands at the center of Poe's "Murders in the Rue Morgue." Set in motion when the narrator and his friend Monsieur C. Auguste Dupin read in a Paris newspaper of the murders of Madame L'Espanaye and her daughter Camille, this classic locked-room mystery sets the scene of the women's deaths in their own fourth-story apartment, which is littered with gold, jewelry, and other objects of wealth. The all-but-decapitated mother is found in the paved yard below, whereas her daughter is discovered head-down in the chimney, bruised, scratched, and apparently strangled. The narrator is forced to "agree with all Paris in considering [the murders] an insoluble mystery," after the *Gazette des Tribunaux* publishes summaries of the depositions of witnesses.[123] Hailing from "the five great divisions of Europe," all testify, in essence, to hearing "two voices in loud and angry contention—the one a gruff voice, the other much shriller," the former decidedly "that of a Frenchman," the latter only identifiable as "that of a foreigner" (550, 540). As Dupin explains, the difficulty with the witnesses' testimony regarding the shrill voice was "not that they disagreed—but that . . . each one spoke of it as that *of a foreigner* . . . sure that it was not the voice of one of his own countrymen," leading to the possibility that "it might have been the voice of an Asiatic—of an African" (549–50). (Dupin, "without denying the inference," merely notes that "neither Asiatics nor Africans abound in Paris" [550].) Visiting the crime scene and working with print sources ranging from the sensational *Gazette* to the zoology of Georges Cuvier, Dupin solves the mystery by revealing the homicidal intruder to be "a *very large, tawny Ourang-Outang*" that had escaped from its sailor-owner (560).

However uncommon it may have been to encounter members of the

African diaspora (to say nothing of escaped apes!) in Dupin's Paris in "the summer of 18—," an Africanist presence pervaded the Philadelphia where, in the late 1830s and early 1840s, Poe lived and composed "The Murders in the Rue Morgue" (531). Unsettled by the anti-abolitionist riots that resulted in the historic burning of Pennsylvania Hall in May 1838, Poe's Philadelphia was also, Dayan notes, "a city infatuated with prisons," as evidenced by the looming gothic presence of Eastern State Penitentiary, with its disproportionately (and morbidly) black population.[124] After some print detective work of his own, Poe scholar Richard Kopley has identified key newspaper sources for the story in a series of items that appeared in the *Philadelphia Saturday News and Literary Gazette* from May through December 1838, notably an article featuring a "hideous Negro with ourang-outang face."[125] Kopley, noting an earlier article on an "Ourang Outang," suggests that "Poe's transmutation" of the newspaper's ape "into the murderous orangutan of the Rue Morgue would have been significantly assisted by a subsequent *Saturday News* piece . . . concerning the murderous behavior of a human, Edward Coleman" (32). Like Poe's fictional killer, the real-life Coleman, a black Philadelphian, nearly decapitated a woman (his wife Ann, whom he suspected of infidelity) by slitting her throat with a razor. The newspaper article, published adjacent to a review of Poe's *Narrative of Arthur Gordon Pym* (1838), recounted the Coleman murder case in "distinctly similar language" to that in the detective story (33). The *Saturday News* circulated in a community that was at once fascinated with simians' human-like attributes and pervaded by a racist discourse that associated blacks, who dominated the barbering profession, with apes. ("At the time Poe's tale was published in Philadelphia," historian Elise Lemire points out, "the city's own Peale's Museum displayed stuffed monkeys dressed and arranged so as to depict the life of the barbershop," transparently legible as "parodies of black barbers.")[126] In these restored print contexts, the story's climactic razor scenes offer a gauge for the impact of Poe's "average racism" on both his writing and his literary nationalist agenda.[127]

In the story, the sailor returns to his lodging only to find "the beast" (his erstwhile "prisoner") loose in his rooms, mimicking "the operation of shaving, in which it had no doubt previously watched its master through a keyhole of the closet" in which it had been locked.[128] Instantly "terrified at the sight of so dangerous a weapon in the possession of an animal so ferocious, and so well able to use it," the sailor brandishes the whip he had previously used "to quiet the creature" (565). Catching "sight of it," the Ourang-Outang flees with the razor, followed by the sailor. The ape enters the Rue Morgue, climbs into the L'Espanaye apartment, seizes the elder woman by the hair, "and was flourishing the razor about her face, in imitation of the motions of a barber," when the sailor glimpses it through the window (566). When "the screams and the struggles of the old lady" have "the effect of changing the probably pacific purposes of the Ourang-Outang into those of wrath," it cuts her throat "with one determined sweep of its muscular arm" (566–67). Then, "the sight of blood" having "inflamed its anger into phrenzy," the ape kills the swooning daughter (567). On seeing the face of its horrified "master" in the window, "the fury of the beast, who no doubt bore still in mind the dreaded whip, was instantly converted into fear. Conscious of having deserved punishment, it seemed desirous of concealing its bloody deeds," shoving the younger woman up the chimney and the elder out the window (567).

By imitating the shaving techniques of his captor, critics suggest, the escaped beast seeks to purge itself of the hirsutism that distinguishes ape from human.[129] But if the razor forges the missing link here, surely it does so as the implement, not of civilized man's grooming behavior, but of his equally characteristic malice. For it is only after reproducing the (presumably unobserved) motions of a (normatively black) barber that the ape, no longer wielding the razor for "pacific purposes," is credited with a distinctly human "wrath." Crime, once again, would appear to make the man. Crucially, however, the ape acquires the qualities of a human person not in the act of killing but in the *narration* of that act, the narrator's summary exposition of the sailor's firsthand account. Compelling as it is, this narrative can offer only fictive access to the ape's presumed criminal intent by melding the description of the Ourang-Outang's visible behavior (*actus reus*) with the sailor's conjectural attribution of motives (*mens rea*) to the ape's actions. Significantly, this fictive narrative interpretation of the women's violent deaths is opposed by Dupin's own strong representation of the circumstantial evidence at the crime scene.[130] In direct opposition to the sailor's transcribed account, Dupin's discovery of the nonhuman killer—like Poe's story itself—depends on his discerning appreciation for "that startling absence of motive" that has, from the beginning, constituted the mystery (557).

Dupin characterizes the crime as "a butchery without motive" (558), illuminating the developmental gulf that separates the ape as, literally, a mere mimic-man, from the supremely rational "analyst" Dupin (530). For Lindon Barrett this contrapuntal pairing "redact[s] entrenched figurations of the racial animus of 'blackness' and 'whiteness'" in Western modernity.[131] Yet unlike so much subsequent detective fiction, which pits the mind of the sleuth against that of the criminal, the drama of Poe's story lies in the opposition not of Dupin to Ourang-Outang, but of the imagined murderer (a person) to the actual killer (an ape). At this point, the legal, as well as historical, philosophical, and print contexts for Poe's story become important. A salient manifestation of racialized Enlightenment "Reason," criminal intent differed markedly from other kinds of motive in the slaveholding legal regime in which Poe lived and wrote. Like the enraged cats in the *Narrative of James Williams*, the escaped ape displays survival instincts that read as intentionally violent acts. And like the overseer's sportive hounds, the quasi-domesticated primate seems to harbor even more sophisticated purposes, such as physically transforming himself into a man through the gestures and effects of shaving. But also like those animals—and their human counterparts under Huckstep's control—the ape cannot lay claim to the *mens rea* that constitutes legally responsible personhood for slave and freeman alike. This is why the story of his actions must be told by others; without motive, the inarticulate ape lacks the inner self that confession simultaneously discloses and constructs.[132] And it is "that startling absence of motive" that enables Dupin to deduce that the killer is an Ourang-Outang ("without denying the inference," of course, "that it might have been" an "Asiatic" or an "African"), rather than a human person of European origin.

The same "absence of motive" requires this crime narrative to end not with legally sanctioned punishment but with a sale. In a process not unlike that which lodged the pass-forging Frederick Bailey and his fellow conspirators in jail as commodities rather than criminals; put James Williams's alter-ego, enslaved poisoner Shadrack Wilkins, beyond the reach of the hangman; and authorized the transportation and sale of many of the Southampton insurgents, Poe's killer Ourang-Outang "was subsequently caught by the owner himself, who obtained for it a very large sum at the *Jardin des Plantes*."[133] Inscribed in a print culture that routinely recorded the sale of transgressive slaves as an alternative to the state-sanctioned punishment administered to criminal persons (including criminous slaves), the killer ape's fate underscores rather than erases the text's association of blacks with nonhuman primates.[134] This reading becomes even more suggestive in light of an increasingly influential abolitionist rhetoric that implicated blacks in the crimes of slavery even as it denied them the culpability that had so long activated legal recognition of black personhood and the corresponding retroactive, punitive inclusion of the African American criminal in the social compact. The Ourang-Outang, betrayed by "that startling absence of motive" that characterizes its violence, must be sold rather than punished, in a final proof of its lack of legal responsibility and ineligibility for personhood.

Awareness of *mens rea*'s role in constituting black personhood under slave law allows us to see the underappreciated consistency of Dupin's logic.[135] Taken together, Dupin's refusal to deny the linguistic inference that would incriminate nonwhites; the accretion of symbolic and quotidian identifications of African Americans with simians in Jacksonian America; and Poe's persistent fictional evocation of law's artificial construction of persons,[136] all support a reading that finds in "The Murders in the Rue Morgue" a desire to exclude those ambiguously identified as nonhuman—and just as unambiguously identified as non-European—from the category of recognized persons. Under the legal fiction of slave character, denial of criminal intent is precisely what would make personhood and, by extension, the polity, an all-white preserve.

By the same token, in order to maintain the distinction the story has established between the violent, irresponsible, depersonalized non-European actor and its opposites, Poe cannot allow any of the white characters to descend into the civil death so elaborately conjured by his other works of fiction.[137] Hence the insistent, almost excessive, exculpation of the story's most prominent property-holder, the sailor. The seaman, decoyed into the apartment shared by Dupin and the narrator, is urged to tell his part of the story. Faced with a locked door and a drawn gun, the sailor "flushed up as if he were struggling with suffocation," jumping up and seizing "his cudgel," only to collapse into a chair "with the countenance of death itself" and "spoke not a word."[138] He "recover[s] his presence of mind" and commences his eyewitness narrative of the killings only when Dupin assures him, "I perfectly well know that you are innocent of the atrocities in the Rue Morgue," adding, "it will not do, however, to deny that you are in some measure implicated in them" (563–64). Reiterating, "you have done nothing which you could have avoided—nothing, certainly, which renders you culpable. You were not even guilty of robbery, when you might have robbed with impunity," Dupin reminds the sailor that he is "bound by every principle of honor to confess all" he knows, given that "an innocent man is now imprisoned, charged with that crime of which you can point out the perpetrator" (564). (Dupin alludes to falsely accused bank clerk Adolphe Le Bon.) Much like the slaves who were appearing with greater and greater frequency in abolitionist print propaganda, the sailor is "implicated in" yet not "culpable" for the "atrocities" in question; like them, he must "confess all" in a first-person narrative which, as testimony against another, will also confirm that he is "innocent" of (in Dou-glass's phrasing) the "series of . . . outrages, of which [he] was doomed to be a witness and a participant." If, like the testimonies of the bondmen who were finding a new civic existence on the lecture stage and the printed page, the sailor's first-person narrative arrests his declension into a deathlike state, Poe repeatedly reminds us that he is not slave but "master," not property, but "the possessor"—and thus already a legally recognized person (561). ("Above all, *I am known*," Dupin imagines the sailor reflecting upon reading the detective's false newspaper notice [561].) He can only be reduced to the civil death of the slave (and the killer beast?) if convicted of a crime. "Bound by every principle of honor," not chains or penal laws, even a lowly sailor can preserve his own personhood and that of his countryman by telling his story. Like the other racially charged Jacksonian narratives of crime and punishment discussed here, Poe's story insistently separates *mens rea* from *actus reus*: capable of a criminality that he does not enact, the property-holder of European extrac-tion distinguishes himself from the Africans, Asiatics, and nonhuman ani-mals who potentially engage in "butchery without motive."

Conclusion

Poe's fictional preservation of criminal intent for whites as an indicator of legal personhood in "The Murders in the Rue Morgue" finds its medical ana-logue in Dr. Samuel A. Cartwright's account of the etiology, symptoms, and treatment of "Dysæsthesia Æthiopis, . . . a disease peculiar to negroes—called by overseers, 'rascality.'"[139] Blacks' infantile respiratory systems, Cartwright explained, resulted in "a hebetude or torpor of the intellect—from blood not sufficiently vitalized being distributed to the brain" (711). Without careful management, "the negro" slips into this unhealthful torpor. Then, aroused by hunger, "he takes anything he can lay his hands on, and tramples on the rights, as well as on the property of others, with perfect indifference as to con-sequences" (711). Likewise, "when driven to labor by the compulsive power of the white man," blacks suffering from this untreated condition "break, waste and destroy everything they handle,—abuse horses and cattle,—tear, burn, or rend their own clothing, and paying no attention to the rights of property, they steal other's to replace what they have destroyed" (711, 710). In short, "they raise disturbances with their overseers and fellow servants without cause or motive" (710). Sounding a great deal like his colleagues who (as we shall see in Chapter 5) were serving with growing frequency and volubility as expert witnesses in the era's burgeoning capacity litigation, Cartwright cautioned against treating symptoms of illness as criminal acts. "From the careless movements of the individuals affected with the complaint," Cartwright explained, "they are apt to do much mischief, which appears as if intentional, but is mostly owing to the stupidness of mind and insensibility of the nerves induced by the disease" (710). Although "the overseers call it 'rascality,' supposing that [it] is intentionally done," Cartwright's research proved that "there is no premeditated mischief in the case" (711).

Not coincidentally, the "complaint" was most prevalent "on badly-governed plantations, and . . . universal among free negroes, or those who are not governed at all" (710). Although the colder climate of the North was healthier for negroid respiratory systems, the section's sociopolitical environment lessened its salubrious effects. "The northern physicians and people have noticed the symptoms, but not the disease from which they spring . . . ignorantly attribut[ing] the symptoms to the debasing influence of slavery on the mind, without considering that those who have never been in slavery, or their fathers before them, are the most afflicted, and the latest from the slave-holding South the least." Flourishing "among free negroes living in clusters by themselves," Dysæsthesia Æthiopis, Cartwright contended, "is the natural offspring of negro liberty" (709, 710).

Cartwright acknowledged the widespread tendency, evinced by Southern overseers and sympathetic Notherners alike, to misapprehend a negro medical peculiarity as a racial propensity for crime (whether innate or environmental in origin). Hence his call for diagnosis and therapy rather than judgment and punishment. (His prescribed treatment, administering a broad leather strap to a slave's skin before consigning him to hard labor, itself mimics the discipline of slavery.) The appropriate medicalization of trangressive, but emphatically *not* criminal, black behavior promises to redeem slavery as the most salutary political-economic arrangement possible in a biracial society. For if "both parties are benefitted—the negro as well as his master . . . there is a third party benefitted—the world at large," given that "the three millions of bales of cotton, made by negro labor, afford a cheap clothing for the civilized world," leaving "the laboring classes of all mankind . . . more money to spend in educating their children, and in intellectual, moral and religious progress" (714). Reaching James Henry Hammond's mud-sill theory of intellectual productivity by an alternative, medical route, Cartwright defends the South against Anglo-American reformers' charges that, rather than a democratizing abundance of cheap cotton, what slavery really produces is crime.[140] Ironically, he can only do so by adopting their strategy of detaching criminal intent from violent or destructive acts. Little surprise then that, like the exteriorized depictions of the motiveless black laborers who conduct the work of death in both the *Confessions of Nat Turner* and the *Narrative of James Williams*, this peculiarly "Negro" disease has the effect, by Cartwright's own account, of "making man like an automaton or senseless machine" (710).

Cartwright's vision of an irresponsibly transgressive and unmotivated black actor had already found grotesque realization a decade earlier in a gothic scene worthy of—and perhaps suggestive to—Edgar Allan Poe. On January 12, 1839, Dr. J. R. Chilton applied his Galvanic Multiplyer to the corpse of Edward Coleman, who just thirty minutes earlier had been hanged for the "Wilful Murder" of his wife Ann.[141] Like the *Confessions*' Nat Turner, Coleman had pleaded "Not Guilty" to a homicide he did not deny having committed.[142] But unlike Poe's Ourang-Outang and the countless slaves subject to plantation justice, Coleman, a free black laborer, was tried, not sold. Yet Edward Coleman never accepted responsibility for the crime; as the Baltimore *Sun* wryly reported: "the plea of insanity was set up, but it was no go."[143]

The Coleman defense's separation of act from intent was gruesomely, posthumously materialized by Dr. Chilton's Galvanic Multiplyer.[144] The device's electric charges produced the eerie effect of making parts of the black man's corpse move involuntarily. In one experiment that doubtless would have fascinated Cartwright, "the muscles used in respiration were thrown into violent action"; in another, Coleman's "leg was flexed, then . . . became forcibly extended"; a final experiment, on the tongue, produced a current by which "the mouth was forcibly closed, and the wire was so firmly held by the teeth that the head was raised quite off the table."[145] It is hard to imagine a stronger representation (whether medical, legal, or literary) of the black subject as the embodiment of horrific acts directed not from within but by external white agents.

Writing under (and supportive of) a legal regime whose fiction of slave character was supplemented by a popular literature that often correlated responsible black individuality to criminality, Poe with "The Murders of the Rue Morgue" presents a cautionary tale against assigning personhood to just any perpetrator of a violent act. At a time when an increasing sense of responsibility for the national "crime" of slavery was prompting American writers and readers alike to probe the guilty implications of American citizenship, Poe published a story in which white male citizens are preserved from the specter of civil death through a radically exteriorized account of unmotivated killings that in turn safeguards criminal intent as the marker of a now racially exclusive responsible legal personhood and eligible political membership.[146] Concurring with abolitionists that blacks' seemingly criminal behavior could not be attributed to malicious intent even as it joined Poe in preserving the capacity for such intent to whites, Cartwright's "Report" illustrates the danger that exculpation, rather than assuaging concerns about African Americans' post-emancipation inclusion into the social compact, could instead authorize further custodial administration of blacks through racialized science.

In an antebellum print culture where the colonial gallows literature tradition and early national legal doctrine contended with new medico-legal discourses of race and crime, it was insufficient to exculpate the black subject. To retain personhood while attaining recognition as a potential citizen, the African American self had not merely to be exonerated but to deflect charges of criminality in the first place. To that end, the *Narrative of the Life of Frederick Douglass*, like the *Address of Abraham Johnstone* before it, offered a first-person narrative that revealed how African American civility was persistently misapprehended as black criminality. Otherwise, as we have seen in the *Confessions of Nat Turner*, the *Narrative of James Williams*, "The Murders in the Rue Morgue," and Cartwright's "Report," decoupling *mens rea* from *actus reus* in a nation struggling with the legacy of slavery had the effect of pathologizing both race and crime, binding the two more closely than ever before.

Chapter 5

How Freeman Was Made a Madman:
Race, Capacity, and Citizenship

> Ignorance and depravity, and the inability to rise from
> degradation to civilization and respectability. . . . The
> evils most fostered by slavery and oppression, are precisely
> those which slaveholders and oppressors would transfer
> from their system to the inherent character of their
> victims. Thus the very crimes of slavery become slavery's
> best defence.
>
> —Frederick Douglass, *The Claims of the Negro*
> *Ethnologically Considered* (1854)

In contrast with the thousands who flocked to early American Execution Day rituals, only about three hundred people attended the prison-yard hanging of Edward Coleman, and doubtless fewer still watched Dr. Chilton apply his Galvanic Multiplyer to the murderer's corpse.[1] All the more important, then, that Edgar Allan Poe and others were able to follow the proceedings in print.[2] Withdrawn from the civic landscape, convicts more deeply penetrated the national imaginary.[3] In keeping with the gradual legal reorientation from "individual lives to individual rights," published crime accounts extended their reach beyond the communities directly affected by a particular offender's acts to a national audience that tended to attach broader political significance to local instances of social disorder.[4] Thus the enslaved man known to Southampton whites simply as "Nat" entered American consciousness as the "Nat Turner" of Gray's *Confessions*. "Having the true negro face," did Turner represent the true negro race as, "in the recesses of

Figure 12. *Freeman Stabbing Child*, 1847–1850, unidentified artist, oil on bed ticking, H: 7N x W: 8N11O, F0111.1954. The Farmers' Museum, Cooperstown, New York.

his own dark, bewildered, and overwrought mind," he revolved "schemes of indiscriminate massacre to the whites"?[5]

Rural New York families may have feared so as they gazed upon a series of oil paintings commissioned by antebellum impresario George J. Mastin. Done on mattress ticking, the four larger-than-life images depict the "Murder of the Van Ness [*sic*] Family by the Negro Freeman, which took place in Cayuga County, NY."[6] The paintings toured Central New York in a traveling show that also featured "sentimental and comic singing, a double clog dance and a lecture by Mr. Mastin on phrenology."[7] Even without the clogging, the story of the killings was compelling: on March 12, 1846, William Freeman, an ex-convict of color, had senselessly slaughtered a white family ranked

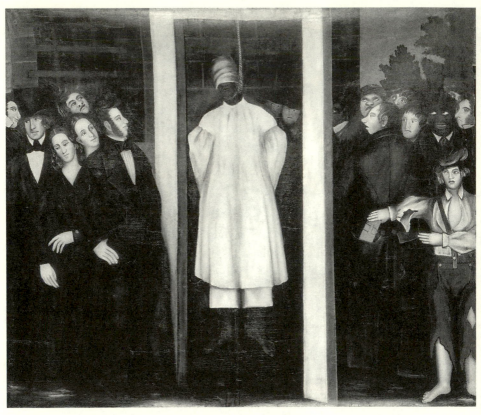

Figure 13. *Hanging Freeman*, 1847–1850, unidentified artist, oil on
bed ticking, H: 7 ½N x W: 8 ½N, F0110.1954. The Farmers' Museum,
Cooperstown, New York.

"among the most respectable people in the county."[8] Night after night audiences, guided by Mastin's narration, viewed the macabre scenes under
dramatically flickering candlelight. There was the black man at the bedside
of little George Van Nest, the two-year-old's pale, gleaming chest awaiting the knife that hung in the air before him, his father John lying dead on
the floor (see Figure 12); next, outside the stately Van Nest house, Freeman
contended with Phebe Wyckoff, the boy's blood-soaked grandmother, while
her daughter, pregnant Sarah Van Nest, tottered in the background, bleeding
from a stab wound; inside, two female survivors formed a tragic group with
the dead infant and the mortally wounded hired man as the killer peered in

from a window, eyes and knife blade gleaming against the exterior darkness. *Hanging Freeman*, the final painting in the series, depicts the story's predictable end: a crowd of townspeople look on as the murderer hangs limply from a tightened noose, his dark skin set off by the white execution cap and robe (see Figure 13).

But, as Mastin's voiceover acknowledged, the condemned murderer "had a new trial Granted and Was not hung."[9] Most likely, the paintings had been completed before the New York Supreme Court had granted abolitionist lawyer William H. Seward's appeal on behalf of his allegedly insane client.[10] Inaccurate as it was, the final painting offered iconographic compensation to Cayuga County communities shaken by the puzzling killings and their unsatisfying resolution. Mastin's haunting visual fiction graphically affirms the continuing power of the outmoded execution rite in framing the black subject in the popular imagination.

Critical as criminality had become to the assertion of a more expansive, civil form of African American subjectivity, the black felon's persistence in the national mind's eye posed, as we saw in Chapter 4, a serious public relations challenge to antebellum abolitionists. Distinguishing the coerced, involuntary acts of slaves from their masters' malicious intentions, the new nationally oriented, print-based movement presented the slave narrative's decriminalized first-person subject as more representative of African Americans' collective civic potential than individuals like Edward Coleman and Nat Turner. Thus, even when Frederick Douglass, whom a decade of interracial collaboration had taught to be wary of a white reformer like William Lloyd Garrison "taking me as his text," replaced the *Narrative*'s prefatory remarks by Garrison and Wendell Phillips with those of fellow "radical" African American abolitionist James McCune Smith in *My Bondage and My Freedom*, the effect was merely to widen the scope of his exemplary selfhood.[11] No longer just the *Life of Frederick Douglass, An American Slave*, McCune Smith informed readers, Douglass's more comprehensive autobiography recounted the life of "a Representative American man—a type of his countrymen."[12]

However successfully it may have portrayed an interiorized, civil African American self, the slave narrative was framed by Southern bondage and Northern freedom.[13] What of those who had not been enslaved? Those for whom the "free" North was origin, not destination? What did the (nominally) free black persona look like, stripped of the culpability that had for over a century occasioned the black print subject's entry into the public sphere? For an answer, this chapter suggests, we might look to William Freeman—not as he appears in the anachronistic, fictive gallows tableau with which the naïve paintings in Mastin's rustic regional show culminate, but in nationally circulated print accounts of his case.

The Cayuga County court's injunction against publishing testimony during the trial may have temporarily curtailed newspaper coverage, but the case was discussed thoroughly in the periodicals of the day, from the luridly illustrated *National Police Gazette* to reform publications like the *Liberator* and the *Prisoner's Friend*.[14] Reverend Anson Winfield's condemnatory *Sermon at the Interment of the Bodies of John G. Van Nest, Mrs. Sarah Van Nest, G.W. Van Nest, Their Son, and Mrs. Phebe Wykoff, Who Were Murdered March Twelfth Inst., By a Colored Man Named William Freeman* (1846) supplanted the conventional execution sermon. Pamphlet trial reports were followed by legal reporter and lawyer Benjamin F. Hall's 508-page *Trial of William Freeman* (1848), a handsome octavo volume in "half law, sheep."[15] As Hall's title indicates, William Freeman was granted the due process that was being withheld from many of his class, race, and youth as, with greater frequency, they entered almshouses, mental institutions, and houses of refuge. Tellingly, however, insight into the black killer's actions and possible motives came not from the defendant's printed confession but from the era's burgeoning medical and legal publications. With this shift from first-person narrative to professional examination, the increasingly irresponsible free black deviant, protected from the gaze of Execution Day crowds, took up residence in the era's new asylums—and the American psyche.

Or so McCune Smith suggested in 1852 when he observed that for most Americans, "the *negro* . . . is not an actual physical being of flesh and bones and blood, but a hideous monster of the mind, ugly beyond all physical portraying, so utterly and ineffably monstrous as to frighten reason from its throne, and justice from its balance."[16] Denied political membership and removed from civic space, this racialized specter "haunts . . . the precincts of this republic," which it can enter neither as flesh-and-blood human nor as legal person (86). Although McCune Smith made these comments in a review of lesser American School ethnologist Ephraim George Squier's *Nicaragua* (1852) for *Frederick Douglass' Paper*, his ongoing public and private criticism of Seward's handling of the Freeman case suggests his belief that it was not hostile whites alone who had lodged this "grim presence" in the mind of the nation (86). A few years later, in a letter to white abolitionist Gerrit Smith, McCune Smith recalled, "my spiritual quarrel with Seward began in the very act for which you commend him. In defending Freeman, he used an expression about 'inferiority of race' which I can forgive in no man; and I gave up all hope of him when I read that sentence, because no man can fight the true Anti-Slavery fight that does not believe that all men are equal *socii*."[17] In fact, Seward had used the expression only in rebuttal, but the abolitionist lawyer's account of the horrific effects of racism on his deranged African American client had indeed conjured a blackness sufficiently monstrous to imbalance the scales of justice.[18] The Freeman case had, to adapt the words of McCune Smith's *Nicaragua* review, illustrated how "a constructive negro . . . a John Roe and Richard Doe negro . . . shaking his gory locks over legislative halls and family prayers" could supplant the "actual negro" who, from the colonial criminal confession to the antebellum slave narrative, had made "himself manifest by word or blow."[19] McCune Smith's invocation (and inversion) of those ever-present courtroom personae, John Doe and Richard Roe, suggests that whereas once self-articulating black subjects had elicited punitive recognition through the law and its fictions, now they were in danger of being replaced altogether by stock racial characters.

In keeping with his surname, mass murderer William Freeman fulfilled many white Northerners' fears about the social legacy of the First Emancipation. Said to have been born in 1824 "of parents recently emerged from slavery," the crazed ex-convict and accused murderer seemed to be living proof of "some bad blood running in the veins of the Freeman tribe."[20] His mother, of mixed Mohican and African American parentage, was rumored to be "a woman of violent passions, severe discipline, and addicted to intemperance" (395). His father, who "became a free man in 1815, by purchase of his time, under the act for the gradual abolition of slavery in New-York" (17), died, Freeman's lawyers claimed, "of *delirium tremens*, leaving his children to the neglect of the world" (395).[21] "*Hereditary insanity* was added to the Prisoner's misfortunes" (395): reportedly, a brother had for twelve years been "a wandering lunatic" (17); a sister was "for many years immediately preceding her death, insane" (17); an uncle "got crazy in prison" (238); and an aunt was said to be "raving crazy" (45). Young William, whose own sanity would become a pressing question at the murder trial, was sent into service at seven or eight years old. At sixteen, Freeman was convicted of stealing Martha Godfrey's horse. "Ever ready for a frolic or a dance," Freeman would leave the penitentiary five years later a changed man (18). As his mother put it: "When he came out of prison he didn't say any thing, and didn't appear as if he knew any thing" (44–45).

This transformation was not the rehabilitative one the state prison was designed to effect. Incarcerated in the institution that put his hometown on the map, Freeman was subject to the nation's second great penal experiment. Antebellum New York's answer to Pennsylvania's controversial "separate" system of penitential solitary confinement, Auburn State Prison in 1825 introduced a "congregate" regimen wherein prisoners lived in silence, working, eating, and marching in groups during the day before retiring to separate cells at night.[22] By the time William Freeman arrived in 1840, Auburn's flaws were evident. As Francis Lieber explained in the preface to his translation of Gustave de Beaumont and Alexis de Tocqueville's *On the Penitentiary System in the United States* (1833), silence was enforced "with the whip, which, it must be allowed, is not a very intellectual or moral means of discipline."[23]

Auburn's trademark combination of enforced silence and corporal punishment was applied to the black teenager in a peculiarly personal, harsh, and permanent way. When Freeman complained about the substandard tools assigned him in the prison workshop, Benjamin Van Keuren, his foreman, threatened to report him for insubordination. Another keeper, James E. Tyler, then "punished" Freeman "by showering"—Auburn's version of water-boarding.[24] Some time afterward, Freeman attacked Tyler as the keeper was seeking a cat-o'-nine-tails to flog him. Forgoing the cat and wielding "a basswood board, two feet long, fourteen inches wide, and half an inch thick," Tyler "struck [Freeman] on the head, flatwise"; the impact, Tyler recalled, "split the board, and left a piece in my hand four inches wide" (65). In self-justification, the keeper explained that a "black man's hide is thicker than a white man's, and I meant to make him feel the punishment" (263). Foreman Van Keuren (who would later urge a mob to lynch Freeman) affirmed that the attack "did not hurt the negro" (327). Freeman, however, maintained that the blow to his forehead "knocked all the hearing off, so that it never came back to him again" (20).

That the blow also knocked much of the sense out of the young man was suggested to many by his erratic behavior following his September 1845 release.[25] Persistently and quite plausibly claiming that he had been falsely imprisoned (the actual horse-thief had turned state's evidence against him), Freeman became obsessed with obtaining legal as well as financial redress. His monomania, if that's what it was, took a peculiarly civil turn. When, upon release from Auburn "he received the usual gratuity of two dollars, for which he was required to sign a voucher," Freeman answered, "I have been in Prison five years unjustly, and ain't going to settle so" (389).[26] Back at home in New Guinea, Auburn's black neighborhood, he repeatedly voiced his determination that "somebody had got to pay him" (37). In the week prior to the killings, he went to the offices of the local lawyer and the magistrate seeking warrants against those responsible for falsely imprisoning him, only to be rebuffed. Then, in the second week of March, having "prepared a butcher knife, and a club with a knife inserted into the end" (474), Freeman commenced what he called "his work" by proceeding to the Fleming, New York, home of well-to-do farmer John G. Van Nest, a man with no discernible link to his conviction (274). Upon arrival, Freeman stabbed to death Van Nest, his pregnant wife, her elderly mother, and the Van Nests' sleeping toddler. Startled by an accidental encounter with hired man Cornelius Van Arsdale, Freeman reportedly paused to ask, "Is there a man there?" before knifing him in the chest.[27] Sustaining a bad hand wound himself, Freeman absconded with a feeble horse and rode away, a single cent in his pocket, only to be captured and eventually arrested for the murders. When asked how he came to commit the crime, Freeman replied to Abram A. Vanderheyden, his arresting officer on this and previous occasions, "You know there's no law for me."[28]

Narrowly escaping lynching, Freeman was tried for the murder of John Van Nest following a preliminary hearing on the issue of his mental competence. The inherent sensationalism of the Freeman case was compounded by its celebrity counsel and its parade of expert medical witnesses. District attorney Luman Sherwood received high-profile assistance from attorney general John Van Buren, son of the recent president, Democrat Martin Van Buren. And, in the eleventh hour, the indigent, mentally challenged prisoner himself got some much-needed help when prominent abolitionist lawyer, progressive Whig, and former New York governor William H. Seward volunteered to lead the defense. Freeman was convicted and sentenced to hang on September 18, 1846. Seward's appeal was more successful than his defense, however: reversing the lower court ruling, the New York Supreme Court granted the motion for a new trial. In legal limbo, suffering from tuberculosis, pus oozing from his ear, twenty-four-year-old Freeman died in his cell on August 21, 1847.

Everyone involved in the Freeman case agreed that the legal proceedings were of tremendous importance. What they disagreed over was why. For the prosecution, the question of capacity extended beyond the killer to the communities touched by his trial. "Insanity as constituting legal incompetency or irresponsibility," Van Buren's closing argument insisted, "must be within the comprehension of any ordinary man of fair capacity" (427). At stake was whether the local community, represented by the jury, would be guided by established legal principles, or—along with the rising legal profession—be forced to cede authority over criminality to a new cadre of medical specialists.[29] Rumors of Freeman's rapt attendance at Seward's insanity defense for fellow Auburn inmate and accused murderer Henry G. Wyatt the month before the Van Nest massacre intimated the risk of allowing an apparent madman to kill with impunity.[30]

Whereas Van Buren cast Freeman as "an *unlearned, ignorant, stupid* and *degraded negro*" to caution against the dangers that lurked when "men of *learning* and of *science* may be deceived by converting natural imbecility and taciturnity into strong '*symptoms*' of mental derangement" (173–74), the defense presented a narrative in which "an ignorant colored boy . . . had been confined in the stateprison [*sic*] for an offence of which he was innocent, and driven to lunacy by a sense of the injustice of his punishment, and by inhumanity in the exercise of penitentiary discipline."[31] Concurring with the prosecution that Freeman's was "the most important trial that has occupied the courts of this country for the last half century," Seward's co-counsel David Wright urged the jury to pause and consider why.[32] Pointing out that "there is no property at stake," he reminded his courtroom audience that no outcome could "resuscitate or reanimate the forms of the slaughtered victims" and that conviction would only take "the life of one . . . conceded" by the prosecution "to be of very low intellect, indeed—scarcely above the brutes that perish" (217). Alluding to the "demon thirst for blood" and "unchristian thirst for revenge" that led to his client's near-lynching on capture, Wright insisted that "it is important to ascertain whether, under all these disadvantages, we can obtain for this once a man, this now but a clod, a fair and impartial trial, by and before a jury of our country," concluding, "it is this, and this only, that renders this cause important" (218). For those involved in Freeman's defense, several of whom advocated abolition of slavery, capital punishment, or both, this landmark black trial seemed perfectly timed to demonstrate the triumph of law and order over mob justice, expose the dangers of the death penalty, demonstrate the ongoing need for penal reform, and dramatize the high social costs of racism.[33]

New York State had abolished public hangings in 1835, but popular interest in capital punishment had recently flared up again, this time in a distinctly literary form. In December 1841 William Wordsworth published in the *London Quarterly Review* the poems that would become *Sonnets upon the Punishment of Death* (1842), providing *United States Magazine and Democratic Review* editor John O'Sullivan the opportunity to cast his literary nationalist Young America principles in an anti-death-penalty mold.[34] Earlier that year, in his role as New York State assemblyman, O'Sullivan had made his commissioned *Report in Favor of the Abolition of the Punishment of Death by Law* (1841) available to lay readers by printing an influential second edition in book form.[35] Extending the magazine's criticism of Wordsworth's *Sonnets* over two years, O'Sullivan made capital punishment a matter of cultural as well as political concern, printing his own anti-gallows essays alongside similarly themed poetry and prose by the likes of Lydia Sigourney, John Greenleaf Whittier, James Russell Lowell, Walt Whitman and even Nathaniel Hawthorne.[36] From his editorial chair at the *Brooklyn Eagle*, Whitman wrote and published a steady stream of articles on what he derisively termed "the present popular (?) system of legal strangulation."[37] Back in Manhattan, transplanted New Englander Lydia Maria Child made the gallows a recurrent site in her column for the *Anti-Slavery Standard*, which when revised and republished as *Letters from New York* (1842) went through eleven print runs before decade's end.[38] (That the two abolitions did not always align was suggested not only by the anti-gallows fiction of proslavery novelist William Gilmore Simms, but by the published debate in the *Democratic Review* between colonizationist O'Sullivan and the Reverend George B. Cheever, prolific death penalty activist and antislavery immediatist.)[39]

If the Freeman case seemed uncannily to coincide with New York's renewed participation in the ongoing national dispute over the death penalty, in Cayuga County, timing would once again decisive in the apportionment of blame. Tellingly Whitman followed up his initial report on the Van Nest murders—sardonically titled "Hurrah for Hanging!"—with two articles protesting the execution of Freeman's fellow Auburn inmate, Henry G. Wyatt, for the murder of another prisoner in the state penitentiary.[40] In mid-February 1846, in the same courtroom where Freeman would soon be tried, Seward had presented a controversial moral insanity brief on behalf of his white client. Supported by expert medical testimony obtained at his own expense, Seward argued that Wyatt "had so often been whipped brutally across the spinal cord that he had become insane and irresponsible."[41] Seward's defense was persuasive enough to produce a hung jury, with a retrial scheduled for June. When in the interim Freeman, whom several witnesses placed at the Wyatt trial, killed the Van Nest family, the two cases became irrevocably linked. Heard by Judge Bowen Whiting during a special term of the Court of Oyer and Terminer, both trials pitted the Democrat attorney general against the Whig former governor over an insanity defense based on alleged mistreatment at Auburn State Prison. The Van Nest murders made Wyatt's conviction and execution—far from certain in February—a foregone conclusion by June. "Wyatt is made to answer for the murder committed by Freeman," Seward's wife Frances wrote bitterly to her sister on learning of the guilty verdict, adding, "it is more than probable that Freeman . . . will be another victim to satisfy popular vengeance."[42]

Counsel's opposing views of Freeman centered on widely divergent understandings of the black convict's relation to law and its attendant narratives: was he *non compos mentis*, incompetent to follow the proceedings on his behalf, much less be held responsible for his incomprehensible (and uncomprehending) actions? Or a scheming murderer whose premeditation of and culpability for the Van Nest murders were evidenced not only by his procurement of the murder weapons beforehand and his flight afterward, but also by his attendance at the Wyatt trial the month prior to the murders and his convenient insensibility in the period since? Was he not only the undisputed author of the killings both sides attributed to him but also, as Van Buren implied, "the *author* of the disease imputed to him"?[43]

The Heads of the Colored People

The Freeman case has been recognized for its importance to the history of the insanity defense, either as an early instance of the "black rage defense" or as an example of the nineteenth-century understanding of the murderer as "mental alien."[44] As a highly publicized, racialized, criminal-law instance of the capacity litigation that seemed to swell American dockets throughout the nineteenth century, however, the case became an antebellum forum on the politico-legal legacy of slavery and the possibility of black citizenship.[45] In this respect, too, the case's timeliness was striking. Two years before phrenologists came to William Freeman's cell to measure the black prisoner's head with string and calipers, Samuel George Morton, a leading American school ethnologist, had followed up his *Crania Americana* (1839) with *Crania Aegyptiaca* (1844), which asserted the biological (and thus unalterable) basis of human diversity, with the corollary that race was fixed and racial inferiority a matter of fact.[46] That same year, statistician, public health pioneer, and insane asylum superintendent Edward Jarvis published *Insanity among the Colored Population of the Free States* (1844) to protest the dangerous inaccuracy of the controversial 1840, or Sixth, Census. Documenting mental illness in the nation for the first time, the census had found African Americans in the free states eleven times more likely to be insane than their Southern (and predominantly enslaved) counterparts.[47] Such statistics carried great political import in an era when state constitutional conventions were removing tax, property, and nativity requirements for white male voters while disenfranchising the mentally ill, inmates of public asylums, convicts, and nonwhites.[48] In the very months that lawyers and expert medical witnesses in Auburn were wrangling over Freeman's mental capacity, delegates across the state in Albany debated whether African American men should retain voting rights under New York's revised constitution.[49] Eight years earlier, Pennsylvania's constitutional convention had disenfranchised that state's African Americans. In a grim irony, the 1838 census that Philadelphia abolitionists had conducted to disabuse delegates of the notion that "the free colored people" were "fit only to fill almshouses and jails" had, by 1846, become a source of "authentic statistics exhibit[ing] a vastly greater ratio of crime for the Coloured than for the White race," making it the perfect fundraising tool for the nation's first asylum for "Colored Juvenile Delinquents"—whose organizational meeting was held the week of Freeman's bloody rampage at the Van Nest household.[50] Those seeking to understand such disturbing instances of social disorder could turn to the recently published American edition of Marmaduke Blake Sampson's *Rationale of Crime, and its Appropriate Treatment* (1846). With "Notes and Illustrations by E.W. Farnham, Matron of Mount Pleasant State Prison" in Ossining, New York, this expanded version of the British journalist's phrenological foray into criminology featured engravings of inmates from New York's Blackwell's Island Penitentiary and the nearby Long Island Farm School— a disproportionate number of which depicted incarcerated blacks—made from daguerreotyped head portraits by future Civil War photographer Mathew Brady.

As phrenology was giving way to cranial ethnology and environmentalist takes on African American criminality were becoming caught up with scientific debates about black mental competence, Americans were devoting greater attention to what James McCune Smith would, in a series of satirical character sketches for *Frederick Douglass' Paper*, would call "The Heads of the Colored People" (1852–54).[51] The first African American to receive a medical degree, a vocal critic of both phrenology and Seward's defense of Freeman, and a committed advocate for racial equality, McCune Smith appreciated the dangers of approaching the "colored" mind from an exterior, normatively white perspective. For the radical black abolitionist, as for others concerned with race and citizenship in the United States, the Van Nest murder case posed disturbing questions that reached well beyond the Central New York courtroom. What if, viewed as racialized objects rather than as individual subjects, the heads of colored people attested not to African Americans' eligibility for citizenship but to their civil incapacity? How would slaves become men in a nation where even free African Americans could not be held responsible for their inevitably anti-civic behavior? Was personhood tantamount to humanity after all?

Framed by the transatlantic death penalty debate, national controversy over the Sixth Census, statewide wrangling over African American citizenship, municipal asylum initiatives, and, more immediately and locally, the Wyatt murder trial, the Freeman case centered, as Frances Seward appreciated, on the issue of answerability.[52] In both trials, the attempt to exonerate an apparently incapacitated offender was countered by the community's outraged demand for accountability. Rejecting an insanity defense that would have located responsibility for the white convict's actions in social conditions (namely, his abuse in the state prison), the jury in the Wyatt case returned a guilty verdict, ensuring that at least one individual was "made to answer" for a local murder. As this seepage into the Wyatt verdict indicates, the simmering tensions between individual and communal culpability boiled over in the Freeman case. Even the most confused accounts located the origins of the Van Nest killings in William Freeman's own obsessive if futile quest for redress: his sense that "somebody had got to pay" for the time and labor unjustly extracted from him through false imprisonment.[53] As misguided as his effort to exact remuneration by stabbing members of the Van Nest household may have been, the defense mounted on Freeman's behalf effectively formalized his disoriented demand for social accountability, if not justice. For if, as in the Wyatt case, immediate blame for the individual offender's insanity was traceable to Auburn State Prison's routine brutality, Freeman's defense counsel maintained that the racist local community should be held responsible for the social conditions that led to his imprisonment, abuse, insanity, and, finally, homicidal acts. ("Be it remembered," enjoined the *Prisoner's Friend* in the same issue it reported Freeman's death, "they will not allow colored children to go to school in Auburn!")[54]

This second Auburn murder trial, with its protracted inquiry into whether a combination of physical and environmental factors mitigated the black defendant's criminal responsibility, asked not only if Freeman could be held answerable for the Van Nest killings but also, if he could not, then where exactly the responsibility for social disorder lay. After the census controversy, which framed this question specifically in terms of racialized insanity and criminality, many Americans believed that finding the correct answer would also provide the solution to the much larger and more vexing problem of the future of race and slavery in the United States. A lavishly produced encore to the well-attended debate over the Sixth Census, the Freeman case urged Americans once again to consider whether the nation would benefit most from continuing the process of emancipation begun in the early national North or from expanding the custodial captivity of African Americans from the plantations of the antebellum South to the nation's new carceral institutions.

In the process, the case also dramatized the difficulty of presenting the public with a black subject who, relieved of criminal liability, nevertheless stood ready to shoulder the responsibility of full citizenship. Insanity, after all, represents an incapacity for self-government or, in an equally resonant phrase, self-mastery.[55] From classical antiquity to the late nineteenth-century rise of the reasonable man, the insane have been considered, to an important extent, outside law's purview.[56] This history of legal outsidership becomes particularly salient in the specific context of race slavery in the United States where, under the legal fiction of the slave's mixed character as person and property, the punitive attribution of criminal responsibility necessitated recognition of legal personhood. For although capacity litigation tends to focus on its subject's mental competence at the time of performing the act under dispute, in criminal contexts this attention to the conditions controlling the commission of the offense was influenced by the problem of punishment. If insanity negated *mens rea*, it also nullified one of the primary reasons for punishment: deterrence. A madman should not be held answerable for his offense because he could not plausibly serve as an example to society.[57] Thus the question arises, if the punished, and especially the condemned, criminal stands as a negative exemplar to the society from which he must be expelled, what of the offender who is acquitted on the basis of insanity? Absent the conviction and execution that retroactively ratify his prior membership in the social contract, what does he exemplify? In the mid-1840s a possibly mad black repeat offender like William Freeman represented not political membership in the breach but African Americans' ineligibility for even such minimal citizenship.

Pointing to the risks involved in abolitionist publicists' efforts to exculpate the black subject, the Freeman case offers a gauge for the impact of antislavery rhetoric on the broader politics of race in antebellum America.

For in the same years that Frederick Douglass's 1845 *Narrative* was helping American citizens to see how a slave might be made a man, press coverage of the killings and their legal aftermath provided a cautionary tale about how easily Freeman had been made a madman. While the slave's white advocates were indicting "the perpetrators of slaveholding villainy" and their Northern "abettors" at the bar of public opinion, Seward returned to the court of law in order to make the case that in the North, as in the South, American citizens, rather than the victims of racial injustice, should be held accountable for the crimes committed in their midst.[58] Like his more literary counterparts, Seward strove to cabin the intent that determined culpability from the act that provoked punitive scrutiny and redress. In the slave narrative this decoupling ideally produced a newly autonomous civil self, emphatically untainted by criminality. In the Freeman case, as in Poe's fiction and Cartwright's "Report," it had the opposite effect: detaching *actus reus* from *mens rea*, defense counsel presented a black subject who, lacking criminal responsibility, relinquished legal personhood and political membership—perhaps even human status.

A year before the Van Nest murder trial, William Lloyd Garrison, the best-known advocate for the slave, had introduced Douglass's testimonial *Narrative* with a powerful opening statement. "Let it never be forgotten," Garrison admonished, "that no slaveholder or overseer can be convicted of any outrage perpetrated on the person of a slave . . . on the testimony of colored witnesses, whether bond or free. By the slave code, they are adjudged to be as incompetent to testify against a white man, as though they were indeed a part of the brute creation."[59] Fashioning himself as "an eye-witness to the cruelty" of slavery, Douglass performed in print the civil standing routinely denied to African Americans in courtrooms both North and South. Threatened with recapture, the famous fugitive took his performance of black civility on the road, modeling (African) American citizenship for audiences on both sides of the Atlantic during his exhaustively covered British book tour of 1845–47.[60] In the reform press, such print displays of civic worth were compromised when William Freeman appeared in neighboring columns as a free black killer with "a mental organization but a little superior to the brute creation."[61]

A perverse echo of Garrison's introduction, this description of Freeman by Universalist minister John Austin in the *Auburn Daily Advertiser* was excerpted in the *Prisoner's Friend* before being reprinted in the *Liberator*. In a reminder of the continuing overlap of "the two abolitions," Charles and

John M. Spear's anti-death penalty journal was supported by proceeds from the "Narrative of Frederick Douglass," advertised alongside other "Books on Capital Punishment &c." available for purchase at the Spears' office just down Boston's Cornhill Street from the *Liberator*'s premises.[62] This tight publishing circuit extended beyond reform-minded Boston: the Auburn-based firm that put out the *Trial of William Freeman* in 1848 would publish *My Bondage and My Freedom* seven years later. Reorganized as Miller, Orton, and Mulligan, the firm retained Derby, Miller and Company's 107 Genesee Street offices, located just down the street from the Cayuga County Courthouse, around the corner from Seward's family home, and across the river from Auburn State Prison.[63] This proximity spatializes the encroachment of what one antebellum editor called "the typographical tribunal" upon courts of law, whose cultural authority at midcentury seemed to decline in direct proportion to their evident complicity with a corrupt slaveholding legal regime.[64] This discursive change of venue may have authorized an adjudicative American reading public to censure the national crime of slavery, but Austin's unfortunate characterization of Freeman suggests the limited portability of the abolitionists' exculpatory brief by revealing its inappropriateness to the larger suit for racial justice.

James McCune Smith highlighted this difficulty when, a full decade after the Van Nest murder trial and within a year of publishing his introduction to *My Bondage and My Freedom*, he rejected a prospective William H. Seward / Horace Greeley Republican presidential ticket in the pages of *Frederick Douglass' Paper*. Seward's "defense of Freeman," by divulging his "belief in the inferiority of the negro to the white man," had proved he was not "morally fitted to advance the cause of Human Freedom"—which, McCune Smith reminded his readers, was merely "the case before us" in the greater "cause of Human Brotherhood."[65] McCune Smith forcefully suggested the political danger in transferring anti-slavery rhetoric from one venue to another or, indeed, from one cause to another, when he used the movement's by-then hackneyed juridical idiom to question the abolitionist lawyer's credentials as a reform candidate on the national level.

Shuttling between the court of law and the court of public opinion and between "the cause of Human Freedom" and the "cause of Human Brotherhood," Seward inadvertently demonstrated how abolitionists' forum-shopping could not only reconfigure but distort African American public presence by altering the black subject's relationship to narrative. Douglass identified this dynamic when, in *My Bondage and My Freedom*, he showed how reformers' practice of relegating participants in the slavery debate to established courtroom roles produced a racial hierarchy in which the slave's white advocates marshaled the testimonial "facts" of the fugitive's "simple narrative" into a more comprehensive forensic "philosophy."[66] That the abolitionist author, editor, and orator leveled this criticism in a work that he himself figured as having been subpoenaed before "the bar of public opinion" suggests Douglass's own appreciation for the influence he had attained as the movement's most credible witness. For, whatever its limitations, extrajudicial black personal narrative had the potential to represent, in McCune Smith's words, the "majestic self-hood" of actual African Americans who made themselves manifest by word or by blow.[67]

The growing visibility of people of color, women, the poor, and the otherwise disenfranchised in transatlantic print culture contrasted sharply with social subordinates' diminishing presence in American courtrooms.[68] As a professionalizing cadre of lawyers exercised their new managerial function, witnesses, plaintiffs, and defendants fell silent, while circumstantial evidence acquired greater probative force.[69] Thus, at the very moment when abolitionist writers were assuming the prosecutor's adversarial stance, the real-life attorney was coming to resemble the Victorian novel's third-person author-narrator, assembling disparate pieces of evidence into a persuasive, coherent narrative.[70] Accordingly, in the move from the criminal confession and the slave narrative to the trial transcript and the novel, authority shifted from the self-articulating black subject, who, from Arthur to Nat Turner, had coupled violence with first-person speech to attain a degree of civic presence, to the slave's white advocates who, from Seward in the Freeman case to Harriet Beecher Stowe in *Dred*, put "a constructive negro . . . a John Roe and Richard Doe negro" at the center of their stories of black legal incapacity.[71] Disencumbered of his traditional burden of guilt, the black print subject could, like Douglass, tell a story that disclosed even as it created a civil self whose civic belonging and political eligibility were affirmed by his participation in the republic of letters. But, deprived of accountability, he could, like Freeman, become the object of others' narratives, losing even the fractional personhood and punitive political membership accorded the criminous slave. On a good day in antebellum America, the exculpation of the black persona yielded the protocitizen of the slave narrative; on a bad day, it produced an unprecedentedly incapacitated racial subject who could be confined, it seemed, by everything *but* the borders of the printed page. In either case, narrative capacity correlated closely with competent personhood.

The Sublime Catastrophe of Emancipation

Readers eager to learn more about the "most brutal murder of several persons by the hand of William Freeman . . . a young colored man," may well have come across a "Letter from Governor Seward" which, in anticipation of New York's upcoming constitutional convention, called for truly universal manhood suffrage.[72] As Seward explained, the combined effects of the Constitution's three-fifths clause and race-based voting restrictions in the nominally free states made abolition virtually impossible. "Slavery continues in the South," he maintained, "because the negroes there are represented in the Public Councils, and virtually vote, through their masters, for perpetual Slavery, while northern allies disfranchise free negroes, whom nature would oblige to cast their votes for freedom."[73] Restoring "the right of suffrage to freemen" would "draw after it in due time the sublime catastrophe of emancipation."[74] Enfranchised black Northern men, Seward reasoned, could help resurrect enslaved Southerners from civil death.

As Seward's letter anticipated, the state's constitutional debate over "Negro Suffrage" exposed core questions in American political philosophy, such as the distinctions between subjecthood and citizenship, natural rights and political privileges, humanity and personhood.[75] Those who embraced the "unpopular side of the question" (1017), urged unrestricted black manhood suffrage on the basis that, in fellow delegate George Simmons's words, "political slavery" in the North "was but one remove from" the race slavery of the South, warning that such "a course should ultimately result in insurrection" (1035). Conversely, Maryland-born delegate John A. Kennedy blamed "the menacing attitude, and boisterous tongue" of that "pitiless ruffian," Nat Turner, for making him wary of both abolitionism and black suffrage (1028). Hopeful in his youth that "the African race . . . had evidently been much improved in transportation from their native wilds, where they were but little superior to the mimic man, their co-inhabitant," Kennedy now disavowed a "fanaticism . . . that would take to their bed and board, the extreme link of humanity, simply because it is the extreme link of humanity" (1028). Tellingly, Kennedy grounded his opposition to the black vote not only in the new racial science, but also in the crime statistics that were becoming de rigueur in any argument for African American political exclusion. Exhaustively citing data from the recent 1845 New York State census, Kennedy calculated that "the relative proportion of infamous crime is nearly thirteen and a half times as great in the colored population as in the white," clear "evidence of a criminal disposition in the race" (1029).[76] This racial propensity for crime, combined with the scientific division of "the human family" by "physiologists," convinced Kennedy that the elective franchise, as a "political privilege" rather than "natural right," should not be extended to "every human being who might happen to be on our soil on election day" (1027). Delegate John L. Russell concurred, rejecting any proposal to include in "the governing class" another "class, who, for 4000 years have never yet been found capable of sustaining our political institutions, under any circumstances, or in any country" (1018). This despite the fact that the Committee on the Elective Franchise had heard testimony from a "colored delegation" whose members modeled the very political qualification that Russell now called into question (1028). Rather than listening to these particular black New Yorkers, delegate John L. Hunt assumed unmediated access into the heads of colored people— or at least "all sane negroes"—asserting that "they knew and felt . . . that they were negroes and aliens by the act of God, and there was no remedy" (1030).

Speaking barely two weeks after Freeman's condemnation, Hunt may not have intended to evoke the state's most famous *in*sane negro. But his comment, taken in the context of the larger discussion of black disenfranchisement, reveals the stakes of Seward's hugely unpopular decision to represent Freeman, which may have jeopardized any chance of universal suffrage in the state.[77] If the abolitionist lawyer's apparently conscientious defense of Freeman imperiled the political advancement of New York African Americans by tarnishing his party's image, his well-publicized advocacy for a black man said to have "a mental organization but little superior to the brute creation" threatened to undermine the new civic authority that African Americans, from Frederick Douglass to the New York Constitutional Convention's Colored Delegation, were consolidating through their publicized participation in antebellum politics and print culture.[78] Seward's conduct of the Freeman case, like the suffrage debate on the Convention floor, illustrates how recent developments in law and medicine could complicate the abolitionist strategy of separating (racial) character from (sometimes violent) conduct. With "no remedy" for a black alienness traceable to either divine, scientific, or environmental causes, many Americans might have concurred with delegate Russell in rejecting Seward and his fellow reformers' calls for racial equality as "a mock philanthropy, which requires them [white citizens] to share their own dear-bought political privileges with any class of men, who are not intellectually and morally competent to appreciate our institutions, and faithfully sustain them" (1019).

In light of this midcentury preoccupation with African Americans' collective "competence," understood in "intellectual," "moral," political, civil, or criminal terms, it is crucial that Freeman was not himself a slave, but the progeny of both slavery and the First Emancipation. At a time when the new medico-legal scholarship was arguing, as one antebellum book reviewer put it, "that what is commonly called crime is to be referred to physical organization, in combination with external influences" (the tack taken by Freeman's defense), the criminality widely imputed to free blacks seemed attributable to the combustive interaction of their distinctive "physical organization" with similarly racialized "external influences" to which they were exposed under slavery and in its aftermath.[79] With crime increasingly understood as "the inevitable consequence of the mental condition of the criminal, and the circumstances in which he is placed," and the criminal himself thus effectively in "the same state of irresponsibility with the insane," professionals and lay readers alike found themselves asking, "But where does responsibility end, and irresponsibility begin?"[80]

This is the question that, to a large extent, opposing counsel in the Freeman case strove to answer as they disputed the black defendant's mental state. Availing himself of the era's new theories of insanity to resolve this dilemma (and to shield his client from the gallows), Seward uncovered a larger conundrum for those who, like him, were committed to ending slavery and promoting African American enfranchisement. The seemingly sharp ideological divisions between the Democratic prosecution and the Whig defense in the Freeman case obscure the fact that it was the *latter*, not the former, who repeatedly impugned Freeman's humanity as well as denied his personhood.[81] For the D.A. and for Attorney General Van Buren, Freeman was unquestionably "an *unlearned, ignorant, stupid* and *degraded negro*," but he was, just as unquestionably, a person legally responsible for his crimes against other persons and society as a whole. By contrast, contending that Freeman was "once a man," originally "made in the image of his Maker, and might have so continued" if not for racist neglect and abuse, the defense nevertheless insisted that he was "now but a clod." In these and similar characterizations, Freeman's counsel thrashes about in the alluvium of a rapidly progressing medical jurisprudence only to be sucked into the sedimented discourse of black subhumanity.

"In America . . . insanity is said to be more common than anywhere else," observed Tocqueville in 1835, struck by "that strange melancholy which oftentimes will haunt the inhabitants of democratic countries in the midst of their abundance."[82] Understood as a disease on the rise, insanity was also seen by both the fledgling psychiatric profession and lay people as, in Jarvis's words, "the price we pay for civilization."[83] Jacksonian Americans' vaunted ambition unquestionably took its toll, but so did republican liberty, especially, maintained Isaac Ray, author of the influential *Medical Jurisprudence of Insanity* (1838), the stress imposed by responsible political membership.[84] Thus, whereas Western religion and medicine had traditionally associated the insane with blackness and wildness, antebellum Americans like reformer Dorothea Dix now found those blacks and Indians who were largely segregated from civilized American society comparatively untouched by the disease.[85] Focusing on bourgeois and working-class whites, those most vulnerable to the debility, contemporary efforts to institutionalize the mentally ill made the insane asylum, in critic Benjamin Reiss's formulation, "a happy twin of slavery."[86] "Both institutions," Reiss explains, "revoked the civil liberties of a confined population in the name of public order and the creation of an efficient labor force, and both housed a purportedly subrational population that was deemed incapable of handling the complexities of life in a modern democracy. Lunatics, like slaves, were deprived of the right to vote, to sign contracts, to make wills, and to hold property" (15). Yet, Reiss notes, "unlike slaves" and very much like the normatively white citizen-convicts envisioned by the era's other great carceral reform movement, "the insane had their rights and freedoms revoked in the name of restoring them to citizenship" (16). (Thomas Cooper, secessionist preceptor and author of the first American treatise in the field, *Tracts on Medical Jurisprudence* [1819], held that, as "an inferior variety of the human species," blacks were "not capable of the same improvement as the whites.")[87] The parallel broke down in another way, for just as isolation from the pressures of American democracy preserved enclaves of blacks and other uncivilized people from insanity, integration into U.S. society was almost certain to render them particularly susceptible to mental illness.[88] Samuel L. Cartwright would soon provide a physiological explanation to demonstrate that "[the negro's] physical organization, and the laws of his nature, are in perfect unison with slavery, and in entire discordance with liberty."[89] Indeed, the Sixth Census had already provided documentary proof for this theory with its stark correlation of black madness to freedom.

With the "science" of statistics on the rise at home and in Europe, Americans had held high expectations for the census of 1840. Designed to collect detailed data with an eye toward legislation, the census would also contrib-

ute to the ongoing construction of the nation in a more symbolic sense. As
"a federal action that was both nonpartisan and nonsectional," historian
Patricia Cline Cohen notes, the census promised to yield "a full-dress inventory of the greatness of America," thereby promoting the "cause of national
harmony" after the heightened sectionalism of the 1830s.[90] As it turned out,
the controversial census added fuel to the conflagration over the future of
slavery, and thus of African Americans, in the nation.[91] Like the census itself,
the debate reached every corner of the nation. Analyzed in medical, financial,
and literary periodicals, census results were also reprinted in newspapers at
home and abroad. It didn't help when the State Department justified its dubious statistics by citing similarly disproportionate rates of black imprisonment
in the free North. "Throughout the civilized world," Edward Jarvis lamented,
"the statement has gone forth that, according to the experience of the United
States . . . slavery is more than ten-fold more favourable to mental health
than freedom." [92] If true, Jarvis and others feared, "this apparent exemption
of the slave from one of the most terrible disorders that has visited humanity,
and the ten-fold liability of the free black to the same, may become not only
a fundamental principle in medical science, but also one of the elementary
principles in political economy."[93]

One of the earliest and most inflammatory contributions to the census
debate appeared in the June 1843 issue of the Richmond-based *Southern
Literary Messenger*. Opening with the sunny "picture" of national strength
and prosperity painted by the census, the unsigned article ominously noted
the "dark shades" cast by the insanity statistics.[94] Acknowledging the physical component of mental illness, the *Messenger* posited that the disease arose
"most frequently from moral causes, acting on physical predisposition," and
was thereby "greatly increased in times of public distress" (342). This environmentalist approach enabled the *Messenger* to identify "the controlling causes"
in the "extraordinary contrast" between the rates of insanity among free
blacks in the North and their enslaved counterparts in the South as "moral"
(that is, social rather than physical) in nature—and thus to attribute the
sectional epidemic of black madness to both the historical fact of emancipation and the more recent emergence of abolitionist politics (342). Given the
"remarkable fact, that where slavery has been the longest extinguished, the
condition of the colored race is worse" (344), the *Messenger* concluded not
only that "the free colored race, in the free States, have been for many years
deteriorating" (340), but that "the free negroes of the northern states are the
most vicious persons on this continent, perhaps on the earth" (346). Then, in

a gesture that would become commonplace in the Sixth Census debate, the *Messenger* collated the insanity statistics with a random sampling of figures on conviction and imprisonment, also subdivided by race.

This conflation of racialized insanity and criminality fostered a nightmare vision of the national impact of immediate abolition. "Let us then suppose a half of a million of free negroes suddenly turned loose in Virginia, whose propensity it is, constantly to grow more vicious in a state of freedom," the *Messenger* proposed, echoing the anxious early national prognostications of meliorists like Noah Webster, Thomas Jefferson, and St. George Tucker (346–47). If recent reports were to be believed and free African Americans "are now perishing from want" in "Philadelphia, so distinguished for its benevolence," then, shrilled the *Messenger* in a rising crescendo of racial panic, "what would be their fate where they exist in such numbers? Where should we find Penitentiaries for the thousands of felons? Where, lunatic asylums for the tens of thousands of maniacs? Would it be possible to live in a country where maniacs and felons met the traveller at every cross-road?" (347).

The author expressed confidence that, in a fair fight, the South's virulent commitment to white supremacy would ensure swift, merciless extermination of "the negro race" (347). But "with the aid of the abolitionists," free blacks could triumph, "extirpate the white race," and transform the South into "a savage wilderness where the strong would rob and murder the weak" (347). Deploring the South's peculiar institution as "the greatest evil that could have been inflicted on our country," the article lamented slavery "not for the sake of the black race," for whom its salubrity the Sixth Census had just conclusively documented, "but of the white" (350). Still, voicing a utilitarian dedication to settling on the solution "most promotive of human happiness," the *Messenger* deferred further serious "consideration" of "the subject of general emancipation" until "it can be shown . . . that the free blacks of any of the 'free states' are as happy as the slaves" (350). That day would be a long time coming. For now, "so long as [free blacks] furnish little else but materials for jails, penitentiaries and mad-houses," the nation's founding commitment to the pursuit of happiness mandated the continued denial of liberty and equality to its African American population (350).

These were exactly the kind of conclusions that the reform-minded New Englanders who had founded the American Statistical Association (ASA) feared the 1840 Census would encourage. A perceived underreporting of the total number of insane people initially led ASA member Jarvis to question the accuracy of the published census. Over the course of several medical

journal articles and a pamphlet, Jarvis revised his view of the census dramatically. After espousing a reformist version of the *Messenger's* conclusion
that the greater stress on Northern free blacks produced their disproportionate insanity rates, Jarvis came to reject wholesale "that fallacious and
self-condemning document, the 'sixth census' of the United States."[95] Jarvis's
pamphlet reveals the census's egregious reporting and tabulation errors. Repeatedly emphasizing that the document was "corrected at the Department
of State," then under the direction of notorious Fire-Eater and Nullifier John
C. Calhoun, Jarvis joined other ASA members in petitioning Congress, with
the active support of John Quincy Adams, to investigate and issue a revised
report (4).

Calhoun, who had already cited the census in support of Texas's annexa-
tion as a slave state, issued *Errors in Sixth Census. Letter from the Secretary
of State* (1845). Like the *Southern Literary Messenger*, the State Department
corroborated the evidence of black insanity with statistics enumerating, by
race, the convicts in state prisons. Whereas the *Messenger* implicitly justified
this dubious move by noting that prisons often accepted those inmates whom
overcrowded insane asylums could not accommodate, Calhoun airily noted
the widely held assumption that "there is an intimate connexion between
extreme physical wretchedness and crime" and that the "same causes which
produce the one, will the other."[96] The resulting information, graphically presented in an entirely new statistical chart, "strongly confirms the correctness
of the late census, by showing the prevalence of crime among the negroes of
the non-slaveholding States, compared with the slaves of the slaveholding
States" (2). With this additional overlay of criminality, the Sixth Census tabu-
lated the direct correspondence between freedom and black social disorder
all the more decisively. Verifying its accuracy, Calhoun presented the census
as a vindication of his section's peculiar institution. Emancipation, "so far
from bettering the condition of the negro or African race," the Secretary of
State concluded in his official letter to Congress, "would render it far worse.
It would be, indeed, to them, a curse instead of a blessing" (3).

The slippage from insanity to criminality was as instrumental to Calhoun's proslavery agenda as it was revelatory of a broader white supremacist
mindset. Conducted from "house to house," and leaving "no dwelling—neither mansion nor cabin—neither tent nor ship [—] unvisited and unex-
amined," the census was itself a powerful act of national inclusion.[97] And,
explicitly providing for the enumeration of both "free coloured and other
coloured persons," the census as a federal undertaking offered a striking

contrast to the Constitution and its infamous three-fifths clause by constructing a nation in which slaves were counted individually rather than fractionally represented by proxy. As the subsequent controversy indicates, the danger was that, in a textbook example of biopolitical inclusive exclusion, African Americans would be both literally and symbolically counted as part of the nation, only, through the instrumentality of the same document, to have Northern free blacks automatically *discounted* from political membership on the basis of their statistically proven mental incompetence and thus civil incapacity. Refusing to address in any substantive manner the key issue of misreporting or incorrect tabulation of black insanity, the State Department affirmed the dubious Sixth Census results by resorting to an asymmetrical (albeit culturally resonant) comparison: the disproportionate prevalence of criminality among Northern free blacks confirmed, both analogically and metonymically, the corresponding epidemic of black insanity.

The State Department's statistical shell game did more than merely distract a national readership's attention from errors in the Sixth Census by directing its gaze toward black criminality. Whatever public relations problems the census and its government-sponsored vindication may have created for embattled Northern free blacks and the unpopular abolitionist movement of the 1840s, the superimposition of prison data on the insanity figures forwarded a more subtle proslavery objective. The same sleight of hand that turned insanity into criminality—a gesture that the Freeman defense would soon seek to halt in mid-air—also enacted another form of racial legerdemain. This is because, when faced with slave offenses, slaveholders and authorities alike tended to respond with summary penalty rather than due process.[98] As a result, few slaves would have appeared as convicts in the data provided by state prison administrators. The South's lower conviction and imprisonment rates reflected not the section's lower incidence of black criminality, but the ineligibility of the majority of its African American population for such enumeration. The data's irrelevance to the urgent question of black insanity aside, the State Department's recourse to prison statistics tacitly withdrew the enslaved from the population pool from which such figures were drawn, effectively reprivatizing them as property. Absent the punitive recognition that conviction represented, slaves simply did not count for the purposes of the government's reassessment (however flawed) of the census findings. Whether in the *Southern Literary Messenger* or in the State Department's report, the resort to figures drawn from a population in which slaves did not, for the most part, figure as legal persons served to denigrate the civil capacity of free blacks and thereby invalidate all African Americans' eligibility for political membership. In this way, the statistically higher rates of social disorder attributed to free Northern blacks disqualified both them and their (seemingly more docile) enslaved counterparts from being reckoned as full citizens, in either the present or the future.

Wild Beasts

Just as the public debate over the Sixth Census was moving off center stage, the Van Nest murder trial once again raised the curtain on issues of race, capacity, and political membership by presenting them in that popular antebellum genre, the printed courtroom drama.[99] With an allegedly insane free African American repeat offender from Auburn in its starring role, the Freeman case could not avoid addressing how one of the elementary principles in the nation's political economy, race slavery, heightened the crisis of attribution that occurred when the fundamental principles of medical science confronted those of law.

Perhaps wary of provoking uncertain responses, neither the prosecution nor the defense explicitly connected the case to the recent census-driven controversy over insanity and criminality among Northern free blacks. Nevertheless, the closely watched, extensively covered legal proceedings showed how thoroughly African American political inclusion continued to be entangled with culpability in the antebellum United States. In his efforts to protect from execution a client he genuinely believed to be mentally incompetent, Seward sought to replace conviction, law's acknowledgment of responsible personhood, with an exoneration that instead would mandate therapeutic custodial confinement characterized by segregation and supervision.[100] From the perspectives of legal history and the history of science, Seward's defense epitomizes the broader cultural move away from punishing particular acts and toward treating individual offenders.[101] But when read in the history of race, slavery, and abolitionism, it advocates the same strategies of social control that, since the colonial period, had been proffered as alternatives to the kind of full African American citizenship that Seward and the New York Convention's Colored Delegation supported through their advocacy of universal suffrage.

An important factor in the dispute over Freeman's sanity was the matter of his racial representativeness. Police officer Thomas F. Munroe succinctly voiced the prosecution's position when he testified of Freeman, "I think if he is insane most of the negroes in Auburn are."[102] In his closing statement, Seward, protesting that "an inferior standard of intelligence has been set up here as the standard of the Negro race," urged the jury (373): "Hold him then to be a MAN. Exact of him all the responsibilities which should be exacted under like circumstances if he belonged to the Anglo-Saxon race, and make for him all the allowances which, under like circumstances, you would expect for yourselves" (374). But even as the defense rejected differential racial standards for mental capacity and cautioned against bias in the proceedings, it joined the prosecution in casting Freeman as representative of the larger African American collective, and specifically the North's post-emancipation black community (375). Their varying degrees of racial sensitivity notwithstanding, counsel on both sides concurred that Freeman's own individual mental condition (sane or insane, responsible or irresponsible) reflected the social conditions in which the mass of free blacks lived—whether those conditions were seen as the result of racial "degradation" or racist "neglect" (222, 396).

Because opposing accounts of Freeman's capacity centered upon the question of whether or not his core identity had undergone a profound transformation at the time of his imprisonment, counsel offered competing biographies of Freeman. The prosecution's narrative was straightforward: "He was a mischievous boy; and, utterly uncared for and unrestrained, he naturally ends up being a criminal man" (443). By contrast, the defense (more than a little disingenuously, given the concurrent debate over black suffrage in New York) cast the young Freeman as a "bright, cheerful, happy child, destined to become a member of the social state, entitled by the principles of our Government to equal advantages for perfecting himself in intelligence, and even in political rights, with each of the three millions of our citizens" (395). This civic potential was irrevocably lost when, "confined in prison" under a false conviction, Freeman "was abused, ill treated and flogged . . . and was so altered upon returning to the world, that his friends scarcely knew him" (222). Designating Freeman's insanity and the resulting Van Nest tragedy "the fruits of this unmanly and criminal prejudice," Seward expressed confidence in his twelve-hour closing argument that "this neglect will plead powerfully in his excuse" before the divine tribunal, if no other (396).

Instead of individualizing Freeman, the defense's environmentalist biography rendered him a dehumanized cipher. From the opening statement onward, the effects of racism impinge not only on Freeman's mental competence but also on his lawyers' ability to identify their client as a fellow human:

"notwithstanding all his ignorance, and stupidity, and degradation," Wright asserted, "he *has been* a brother man, made in the image of his Maker, and *might have so continued* but for the brutal treatment received by him amongst this Christian community" (222–23; emphasis added). Here Freeman's "brutal treatment" by a canting society discontinues not his fraternal belonging, but his status as one made in God's image—as, in the well-worn abolitionist motto, "a Man and a Brother." It is the legal incapacity entailed by Freeman's insanity and not the moral insensibility evinced by his transgressions that prompts the defense repeatedly to deprecate his humanity. Mere moments after Seward has exhorted the jury to "hold" Freeman "to be a MAN," his African American client returns as "this stupid, senseless fool, almost as inanimate as the clay moulded in the brick-yard"—far less promising stuff, apparently, than that from which God made Adam (374). Figuring the black defendant as a "clod" in its opening argument and "inanimate . . . clay" in its close, the defense framed Freeman's criminal irresponsibility in terms not just of his mental impairment but—more disconcertingly, given their own participation in the controversy over slavery and African American suffrage outside the courtroom—of his allegedly subhuman status.

It was, of course, in the prosecution's best interest to deploy race as a means of decreasing Freeman's human worth to a jury faced with applying the death penalty. But the prosecution tenaciously maintained that, "degraded" though he might be, Freeman was nevertheless a responsible member of society. This logic finds colloquial expression in the testimony of prosecution witness Stephen S. Austin. Dismissing the defendant as a "mischievous, cunning kind of a darkey," Austin emphatically rejected the possibility that Freeman was "a fool," disarmingly affirming that "he knows as much as either of my dogs" (62). Canine competence aside, it is significant that, rather than eschewing such dehumanizing comparisons, the *defense* repeatedly offered them as proof of Freeman's incapacity. Assessing Freeman to have "as much capacity as a brute beast," Auburn prison keeper Theron Green surmised that, in any case, he had "none to spare more" (289; see also 283). Witness Ira Curtis doubted that Freeman felt "any more compunction than a dog or a cat," who "may know they have done wrong, but yet know nothing of the character of an act" (261). If Freeman were convicted and sentenced to hang, defense witness and attorney Warren T. Worden anticipated, "he would probably know as much as a dumb beast that was taken to the slaughter house, as to what was to be done with him" (227).

Their remarkably similar phrasing makes it unclear whether witnesses

were coached by counsel or were merely drawing on established cultural associations that identified both the insane and those of African and indigenous
descent with animals.[103] Far from distancing himself from such vernacular
portrayals of Freeman as subhuman, Seward confirmed them in his closing
argument with a series of progressively more demeaning comparisons: "My
child, with an affectionate smile, disarms my care-worn face of its frown
whenever I cross my threshold. The beggar in the street obliges me to give,
because he says 'God bless you,' as I pass. My dog caresses me with fondness
if I will but smile on him. My horse recognizes me when I fill his manger"
(371). Then, directing attention to his benighted client, Seward plaintively
asked, "but what reward, what gratitude, what sympathy and affection can
I expect here?" (371). At best, Freeman could "repeat like a parrot a consent
that I should defend him" (400). Well below most domesticated animals (to
say nothing of children and beggars), the incapacitated black man prompted
Seward to an even more mordant simile. Pointing to Freeman's disconcerting lack of "human curiosity" regarding the legal proceedings on his behalf,
Seward observed that an "oyster, shut up within its limestone walls, is as in-
quisitive as he" (397). The figure was well chosen. After all, cats may scratch,
birds peck, dogs bite, and horses trample, but the supremely passive and
unthreatening mollusk has the further advantage of being naturally confined
in its own "limestone walls."

No matter how benign the referent, the pervasive recourse of lawyers and
witnesses on both sides to such animal imagery indicates the larger representational crisis the Freeman case created for the racially egalitarian principles
espoused by the defense. The entrenched associations of blackness and bes-
tiality that attended (indeed, facilitated) western modernity have been well
documented.[104] The timing and nature of the Van Nest killings ensured that
the Freeman case would be severely buffeted by the countervailing rhetorical
winds that had shaped the contours of race and insanity in Anglo-American
law, science, and print culture. The trial occurred just as the centuries-old
"wild beast" theory of culpability was being replaced by the more liberal
test of criminal responsibility known as the McNaughtan Rules. Established
as early as 1256 by jurist Henry de Bracton, the previous doctrine's classic
formulation came in 1724, with English Judge Robert Tracy's instructions to
the jury in the trial of Edward Arnold that a madman "must be a man that is
totally deprived of his understanding and memory, and doth not know what
he is doing, no more than an infant, than a *brute*, or a *wild beast*, such a one
is never the object of punishment."[105] The doctrine not only set an almost

impossibly high legal standard but, when added to the age-old identification of insanity with demonic possession, also fostered assumptions about the savagery and carnality of the mentally ill. By contrast, the McNaughtan Rules required only proof of incapacity at the moment of the crime's commission.[106] Many on the vanguard of medical jurisprudence found even this looser standard lamentably insufficient, however, and recent rulings by Massachusetts Supreme Court Chief Justice Lemuel Shaw and New York Judge John Worth Edmonds in the trials of Abner Rogers (1844) and Andrew Kleim (1845), respectively, incorporated more progressive theories of moral insanity into American jurisprudence.[107] Often quite rational and otherwise intellectually sound, the morally insane lacked control of the will or the emotions, leading to immoral, antisocial, or criminal behavior. Manifested as seemingly motiveless offenses against society, symptoms of the disease looked a lot like crime.[108]

Seward marked the prosecution's abandonment of McNaughtan for a narrower, retrograde definition of insanity by protesting a legal standard that "requires that by reason either of natural infirmity or of disease, the wretched subject . . . shall have no more reason or thought than a brute beast."[109] Yet the defense's own identification of Freeman with creatures ranging from pigs and horses to parrots and oysters makes Seward's criticism appear not a little disingenuous.[110] For even as the defense urged the jury to accept a more flexible moral insanity approach to the prisoner's mental state, counsel and witnesses alike fell back on the vivid (and disturbingly multivalent) imagery of an earlier doctrinal regime. The defense sought to have it both ways medico-jurisprudentially speaking: by making the novel case for Freeman's partial insanity while retaining the culturally resonant "wild beast" terminology, counsel dishonored its own egalitarian call to "hold him to be a MAN." For, in the antebellum United States, the rhetoric set in motion by the defense could not stop once it had conveyed Freeman's incapacity but, rather, collided with reformers' insistence on his (and other African Americans') right to a "fair and impartial trial" as members of the polity. The defense drew on current psychiatric theory to replace nineteenth-century causal narratives of individual responsibility with what early twentieth-century legal realists would figure as a "web of circumstances," making its portrayal of Freeman as "scarcely above the brutes that perish" both a forensic and a rhetorical necessity.[111] Depicting Freeman as subhuman enabled the defense to exploit the enduring cultural currency of the archaic "wild beast" theory of insanity while rejecting its narrow legal applicability.

Outside the courtroom, the spokesman for the defense's environmentalist view was the Rev. Austin who, true to his Unitarian anti-gallows principles, appears to have played an important behind-the-scenes role in arranging representation for Freeman.[112] In addition to securing Seward's services, Austin published articles on the case in the daily and weekly versions of the Whiggish *Auburn Advertiser* which, through reprinting, reached a national audience. Excluded from white institutions and "unable to sustain" their own, Austin lamented, Auburn's free blacks are "almost wholly without the benefits [of] moral, religious, or intellectual culture."[113] Turning from the free people to Freeman, the minister asked: "To these causes must we not trace the guilt of the miserable wretch whose hands are now reeking with the blood of murdered worth and innocence?" Austin's biography of the black killer recalls Poe's gothic excess even as it anticipates Richard Wright's naturalism: "Born in ignominy . . . raised in total ignorance—what little mind he naturally possessed unimproved, unenlightened by religion or education—falling early and easily into crime—incarcerated in prison to work out a long sentence—*while there, beaten with bludgeons into deafness and comparative idiocy*—at length released, with faculties shattered or benumbed, every evil passion magnified, and burning with revenge against those whom he believed had injured him— . . . he rushes to an act which destroys an interesting and valuable family, fills the community with alarm and terror, and seals his own ignominious death!!" Austin's redundant diction underscores the inevitability of the cycle of racism in which Freeman is trapped: "born in ignominy," Freeman can only take actions that will lead, inexorably, to "his own ignominious death." Although at trial the defense would downplay the vengefulness that Austin here attributes to Freeman, it shared his conclusion that the black offender could not be held liable for his destructive acts. "I ask," Austin demanded of his readers, "is not society, in some degree, accountable for this sad catastrophe? Is it not to be traced as one of the legitimate effects of the utter indifference and neglect manifested toward the colored population of this place?"

In court, the prosecution cross-examined Austin carefully, determined not to let this widely circulated print portrayal of Freeman as a victim of racist circumstances block conviction. Queried as to whether he had "charge[d] this community with the crimes of this man" in his article, the minister affirmed that its members "were, to a certain extent, responsible for the crimes committed in their midst."[114] Pressed as to whether he deemed "this murder the legitimate consequence of the neglect of the colored people in this place,"

Austin assented, with the proviso that social "neglect is no justification for the crime" (253). Asked, "What signature did you append to your article published in the Advertiser?" Austin answered simply, "Justice." Here again, the question emerges: given "the neglect of the colored population," where did responsibility end and irresponsibility begin? By holding the local Auburn community morally (but not legally) answerable for the racism that made Freeman insane (and thus legally irresponsible), Austin's article in the *Advertiser*, like Seward's defense, opened a frightening vacuum in the logic of legal causality. If the task of the judiciary is to allocate responsibility by dispensing punishment, what kind of "Justice" traces crimes to their pernicious causes without requiring punitive action?

In remarkable consensus over the black defendant's status as the embodiment of "the general neglect of the colored race," his homicidal acts as emblematic of "the crimes which this race commits," and, finally, the need to try Freeman "like a white man," the prosecution and the defense diverged in the attribution of responsibility (466). Van Buren maintained that the social factors that often contributed to both mental illness and criminality did not annul legal accountability. Seeking Freeman's conviction, the prosecution rejected what it understood as a distinctively "abolitionis[t]" tendency "to hold society, and not the individual, responsible" for the seemingly unavoidable manifestations of endemic black criminality. Such criminality may well suggest a society in desperate need of reform. But under the racial status quo, in which free blacks were denied many of the rights of citizens, yet still subject to the nation's laws, the black offender was responsible to the society of which he was only marginally a member. Such an offender may, like Freeman, "levy War on Society and kill the first man he meets;—and yet HE IS NO LESS AMENABLE TO PUNISHMENT" (436). This criminal responsibility affirmed that, wherever moral culpability may lie and however justifiably antagonistic their relations to American society, African Americans were answerable members of that society. The liberal project of social reform may or may not occur. In the meantime, the solution was not therapeutic treatment of those whom it was too late to prevent from committing offenses against society and whose own reform was, in any case, preempted by the nation's deep-rooted racism. Their status as members of society must be negatively ratified through punishment. After all, the defense's medical jurisprudential argument, however well-intentioned, left open the troubling question: if the race-based neglect and brutality that for many free blacks had followed in the wake of Northern emancipation effectively divested the black offender of responsibility for his acts, how could he or other African Americans be, in James Madison's words, "regarded by the law . . . as a moral person" and therefore "as a member of the society, not as a part of the irrational creation"?

Materials for Jails, Penitentiaries, and Mad-Houses

Seward addressed this question indirectly when, in his closing statement, he sought to relieve the jury of immediate responsibility for the communal crisis posed by the Van Nest slayings. "If you acquit the Prisoner," Seward assured jurors, "he cannot go at large, but must be committed to jail, to be tried by another Jury, for a second Murder"—and so on, until Freeman would finally be made "to answer a fourth Murder"; then, "whether the fourth Jury acquit or convict, your dwellings will still be safe; for if they convict, he will then be cut off, and if they acquit, he must, according to the law of the land, be sent to the Lunatic Asylum, there to be confined for life" (378). However much the extravagant due process Seward envisioned for his client contrasted with the summary procedures by which other young, poor, disabled, and nonwhite Americans were routinely incarcerated in the antebellum United States, Freeman nevertheless represented the contemporary penal trend toward treating institutionalized confinement as an alternative to state-administered death.[115]

The racial logic of this trend is literally illustrated in a book that received prominent notice from the nation's first successful law magazine while Freeman's case was under appeal. Reviewed in the *Law Reporter* as editor Peleg W. Chandler was preparing a Freeman-inspired multi-issue forum on "the medico-legal relations of insanity," Sampson's *Rationale of Crime* rested on the same phrenological theory that undergirded the defense's expert testimony.[116] Seeking to "adapt" Sampson's 1841 treatise "to the purpose of interesting the popular mind—for it is emphatically on the popular mind in republican America that such a work must exert its chief influence," controversial reformer Elizabeth Farnham worked with famed phrenologist Lorenzo Fowler to select representative Blackwell's Island and Long Island Farm School inmates from to sit for daguerreotypes by Mathew Brady.[117] These images were accompanied by brief narratives of each sitter's life whose textual origin lay, no doubt, in the comparatively new practice of carceral biographical record-keeping. Ranging from the terse entries in Walnut Street Prison's 1795 Sentence Docket to the more detailed life stories of 173 Auburn inmates included in the prison's 1829 and 1830 annual reports, these institutional narratives replaced the public, first-person confessions elicited by Execution Day rituals.[118] Of the nineteen "Accurate Portraits of Criminals" that adorned the American *Rationale*, five—over a quarter—featured sitters of African descent.

The reason for this disproportionate visual representation of African Americans is suggested in a footnote in which Farnham cites sources designating the "peculiar" "form of the head possessed by all dangerous and inveterate criminals" while identifying that distinctive cranial structure with "the brains of savage tribes, and the degraded characters of even civilized populations," as well as "the brains of those found in the prisons, at the galleys, [and] the penal colonies" (7).[119] Physiology wasn't entirely destiny, though. Consistent with the Enlightenment Common Sense philosophy from which it arose, the theory of moral insanity (and its correlate practice of phrenology) held individuals responsible for their cultivation or neglect of higher faculties such as morality and intellect.[120] A lack of positive social influences, notably education, leaves the innate "animal propensities" to triumph over the underdeveloped "moral sentiments" (67).[121] Accordingly, whereas the economically and socially privileged could be held accountable for a lack of self-cultivation, the disadvantaged were not answerable for their condition. Given that "the ignorant, who constitute by far the larger class of criminals in all countries . . . have differed little from the brute animal, to whose mental constitution their own is so nearly assimilated," Farnham asked, "who can doubt that their responsibility is as positively lessened, we will not say destroyed, as that of the insane patient?" (xxvi–xxvii). Even as they moved away from the "wild beast" theory of insanity, such experts did not hesitate to associate nonwhites and the poor with "the brute animal." In the absence of the requisite education to fortify such individuals against their bad impulses, the best solution was (as Cartwright would argue in the coming decade) not to hold them responsible as legal persons but to remove them from aggravating external influences by segregating them from society and putting them in protective custody.[122] For Foucault, this nineteenth-century reorientation from conduct to character, from motive to instinct, and from criminal to deviant, established a "region of juridical indiscernibility . . . around the author of the offense."[123] Untrodden as this region may have been for the normatively white citizens-in-waiting now designated lunatics and delinquents, it was familiar territory to African Americans. If the new prisons, houses of refuge, almshouses, and insane asylums can be seen, like the antebellum plantation, as "total institutions," they threatened, where African Americans were concerned, to extend that peculiar institution's custodial supervision and summary penality into nominal freedom.[124]

For Matron Farnham, protective incarceration affirmed the insane offender's "right as one of [society's] members" to "such treatment at its hands
as will enable him to exercise his membership safely and happily."[125] The
difficulty, as illustrated in both Brady's profiles of criminality and Seward's
narrative of racial neglect, was that in the case of free blacks it was the denial of such rights of membership that necessitated incarceration in the first
place. In this sense, it is less the patently racist efforts to document African
Americans' greater physiological disposition for criminality than the liberal
environmentalist views articulated by Farnham, Seward, and other white
reformers that have the makings of a viciously self-justificatory cycle of black
civic as well as political exclusion.

Philadelphia House of Refuge superintendent Elisha Swinney captured
the problem as he described the unique "difficulties" involved in running his
institution's Colored Department: "To a white boy, inducements may be held
out to make efforts to elevate himself to some important position in life. Not
so with these colored children. We cannot say, you may attain to such a high
calling or position in life; to that of a physician, lawyer, legislator, governor."[126]
Apparently modeled on Auburn's congregate system, this "school" was "like
the prison, [in that] it secludes its inmates from society, and subjects them to
the care of officers and the discipline appointed by law."[127] Yet, unlike both the
prison and the white House of Refuge, the Colored Department emphasized
social control to the *exclusion* of preparing its inmates to reenter society as
model citizens.[128] Concerned with "vagrant and delinquent children of color,"
not with the phrenological basis of homicidal insanity, white Philadelphians
characterized their target demographic in language strikingly similar to that
deployed by Freeman's counsel.[129] "In right of birth they are men, entitled to
reason's large discourse," Judge William D. Kelley affirmed of the city's free
black youth, echoing Seward's account of his client's lost civic potential.[130]
But, like the Van Nest killer and like Farnham's inmates, "their nobler faculties lie all undeveloped" (24). This was because, Kelley explained, "they have
been loved as the bear loves her cub," aspiring only "to live as well fed animals" (24). But if the House of Refuge sought to elevate its inmates of color
to the level of human beings, its advocates' own aspirations for its racially
segregated populations were as separate as the buildings that housed them.[131]
Pointing to the White Department's most exemplary graduates, Kelley expressed satisfaction that "hundreds of them are now filling, with propriety,
the responsible positions of husband, wife, and parent, master, friend, and
citizen."[132] Kelley conjured no such civic visions for the disenfranchised in-

mates of the separate and manifestly unequal Colored Department (12). The best he could imagine is that, having become qualified "for usefulness and duty," these former "pests of society" would be suffered to leave the institution when they had learned "to bow the knee in grateful acknowledgments to God for blessings liberally bestowed" (24).

With dubious access to the status of "citizen," to say nothing of "posts of public trust and honor," free blacks could not be reformed as long as society itself remained unreformed (8–9). To incarcerate individuals who, like Freeman and Philadelphia's black juvenile delinquents, were particularly susceptible to the debilitating effects of racism, without addressing—or redressing—the unhealthy social climate that mandated such segregation was to engage in an enterprise that could only be "preventative," never "reformatory" (6). Given these circumstances, the carceral impulse seems not unlike that which had, in the early republic, made colonization an appealing alternative to both slavery and full African American citizenship. Whether the destination was a colony or one of the nineteenth century's asylums, the removal of a potentially dangerous free black population from American society would protect the nation—if not from crime, then at least from the need to eliminate its foundational racism.

The *Rationale*'s first Brady portrait is an icon of this conundrum of reform, racism, and social disorder (see Figure 14). M. B., the caption notes, "is a negro man, under confinement for petit larceny"; "born in slavery," he "freed himself, and has lived at the north several years."[133] As his personal history would suggest, M. B. "possesses great strength of purpose, strong powers of reason, and much capacity to plan, as well as energy to execute" (156). Predictably, his "head," phrenologically speaking, "indicates very strongly all these characteristics": "with a very powerful temperament, are combined a large brain, well developed in the intellectual region, particularly the superior faculties, large self-esteem, firmness, caution, and secretiveness." The formerly enslaved Blackwell's Island prisoner evinces the key traits of responsible citizenship: "a man of great determination and fixedness of mind and character," M. B. "can scarcely be thrown off his guard, or induced to do any thing" he "does not deliberately consent to." "He has," the caption concludes portentously, "the capacity to be made a very useful or a very desperate and dangerous man."

But how could someone like M. B. be anything but "desperate and dangerous" in a polity that seeks not his "deliberat[e] consent" but his involuntary servitude? How can he possibly live up to his civic potential to be

M. B.

M. B. is a negro man, under confinement for petit larceny, born in slavery; freed himself, and has lived at the north several years. He is a man of great determination and fixedness of mind and character; can scarcely be thrown off his guard, or induced to do any thing which his own mind does not deliberately consent to. He possesses great strength of purpose, strong powers of reason, and much capacity to plan, as well as energy to execute. He is esteemed by his officers an obliging, good man.

The head indicates very strongly all these characteristics. With a very powerful temperament, are combined a large brain, well developed in the intellectual region, particularly the superior faculties, large self-esteem, firmness, caution, and secretiveness. He has the capacity to be made a very useful or a very desperate and dangerous man.

Figure 14. "M.B.," engraving from daguerreotype by Mathew Brady, in Marmaduke B. Sampson, *Rationale of Crime, and Its Appropriate Treatment: Being a Treatise on Criminal Jurisprudence Considered in Relation to Cerebral Organization. By M. B. Sampson. From the Second London Edition. With Notes and Illustrations by E. W. Farnham, Matron of Mount Pleasant State Prison. Embellished with Numerous Accurate Portraits of Criminals and Other Persons* (New York, [1846]). The Library Company of Philadelphia.

"very useful" under a legal regime that recognizes him only as property or a criminal? These, of course, are the questions posed by Frederick Douglass's "The Heroic Slave." With his "capacity to plan, as well as energy to execute," M. B. uncannily prefigures Douglass's Madison Washington, who likewise possesses "the head to conceive, and the hand to execute."[134] As "one to be sought as a friend, but to be dreaded as an enemy,"[135] the fictional Washington shares with not only M. B. but Douglass, William Freeman, and perhaps all antebellum African Americans, the "capacity to be made a very useful or a very desperate and dangerous man" or woman. In a slaveholding polity that stunted or destroyed black civility, "capacity" could only be realized as criminality. Like the historical Madison Washington, who led a successful slave revolt on the *Creole* and escaped to Nassau in the British Bahamas, Douglass's fictional heroic slave romantically chooses insurrection and exile over bondage and criminal prosecution. For Northern free blacks like Freeman, M. B., and Philadelphia's juvenile delinquents, however, segregation and supervision in the new carceral institutions could seem the sole alternative to slavery in a nation where full citizenship was not a possibility.[136]

No Reason at All

"They have made WILLIAM FREEMAN what he is, a brute beast," protested the defendant's brother-in-law John DePuy from the witness stand, "they don't make anything else of any of our people but brute beasts; but when we violate their laws, then they want to punish us as if we were men."[137] To prosecute Freeman for murder in the debilitating white supremacist climate of antebellum New York, the African American farm laborer suggested, was to extend the slave's mixed character to all black freemen and -women. DePuy's vague "they" obscures an important discrepancy, however. The construction of the slave as "a mere chattel or thing, as a brute, a bale of merchandize and the like" was, as even an apologist like George S. Sawyer admitted, "but a fiction of law"—one that abruptly ended with the apprehension that held the criminous slave responsible "like all other persons."[138] But in the wake of the First Reconstruction, DePuy implied, those who oppress free blacks turn them into "brute beasts" by actually rather than rhetorically nullifying their human potential. A legal fiction no more, this brutalization is now the very real effect of race-based social neglect and political exclusion. (This was exactly Walt Whitman's point when, in an examination of "the murderer's life," he attributed environmental factors to Freeman attaining a "character . . . of the most blindly brutal cast—a mere human animal . . . in whom the brute had been allowed to rule the man.")[139] Challenging the appropriateness of punishing members of this oppressed population "as if [they] were men," Freeman's defense team replaced the criminal as "juridical subject" with his Foucauldian twin, the incapacitated deviant.[140] Pervasive racial discrimination and the insalubrious environments to which most free blacks were consigned suggested the injustice of their execution, incarceration, or other forms of punishment as criminals.

The lament that "they don't make anything else of any of our people but brute beasts" was belied, of course, by the distinctly unbrutish DePuy himself. At trial Seward effused to his courtroom audience that DePuy "claims your respect as a representative of his people, rising to that equality to which it is the tendency of our institutions to bring them."[141] Proclaiming, "I have heard the greatest of American Orators. I have heard Daniel O'Connell and Sir Robert Peel, but [I] heard JOHN DE PUY make a speech excelling them all in eloquence," Seward risked undermining his case for the devastating effects of racism in Auburn's New Guinea neighborhood. But his fulsome encomium underscores how vital "intelligently given" black "testimony" was to both antebellum abolitionism and McCune Smith's more elusive "doctrine . . . of Social Equality . . . of slaves or Free Blacks."[142] What made John DePuy's testimony so eloquent in the Cayuga County Courthouse—and that of Douglass at the bar of public opinion—was his principled oppositional posture as one critical of and engaged in, *not* incapacitated and ensnared by, American society. Freeman differs from Douglass and DePuy neither in his greater exposure to the debilitating effects of American racism nor in a resulting tendency to manifest himself in brutish blows, but in his very different relationship to the "words" through which not only these men, but Freeman's equally violent predecessors, had historically countered the "constructive negro" of white racial imaginings with the "actual" black selves of published first-person speech.

The prevailing legal view of relations among selves, words, and blows—that is, between first-person narrative and criminal responsibility—had been decisively stated in neighboring New Jersey during the First Emancipation. "The capacity to commit a crime," ruled Judge Samuel L. Southard in *State v. Aaron, slave of L. Solomon* (1818), "necessarily supposes the capacity to confess it."[143] In *State v. James Guild* (1828), New Jersey Supreme Court Chief Justice Charles Ewing echoed his colleague's words in affirming Guild's death sentence on appeal, possibly making the "coloured boy" the last person under age fourteen to be executed in the United States.[144] "He who is a rational and moral agent and can merit the infliction of legal sanctions," Ewing had quoted Southard approvingly, "must be able to detail his motives and acts; and must be judged by them."[145] Like its predecessor, the case involved the admissibility of confessions extracted from adolescent African American murder suspects. If the earlier case's inaccurate title bespeaks the North's uncertain transition from slavery to freedom (crucially, under New Jersey's gradual emancipation statute, eleven-year-old Aaron was Levi Solomon's servant, not his slave), both cases point to the treacherous divide between criminal accountability and political authority that yawned open for people of color, as well as for women, children, and the poor, in the seismic shift from a status-based patriarchal legal order to a contractarian rights regime.[146]

It was to this racial abyss that John DePuy had gestured in his impassioned courtroom outburst—and from which Seward endeavored to save Freeman. But a strategy that sought to change the legal status of the offender, rather than the conditions that produced crime, only worsened the problem. In Seward's hands, black personal narrative may no longer have been reduced to the self-incriminating utterance of the criminal confession, but neither did it articulate a responsible inner self. In the Freeman case, first-person black speech instead became evidence of racial incapacity—subjected, like the heads of African American prisoners and the skulls of exhumed Africans, to scientific scrutiny.

The prosecution and the defense concurred that Freeman's legal culpability lay in his narrative answerability. Van Buren exploited experts' claims that the mad are "disconnected in conversation and narration" to turn testimony regarding the defendant's words and storytelling acts against him (449). "Does he not detail . . . the minutest circumstances of his early as well as his later life?" the prosecutor demanded, "Does he not narrate . . . all the circumstances of his imprisonment, escape, flight and capture?" (449). For his part, Seward asked the court: "How else," if not by the fact of insanity, "will you explain the mystery that he, who seven years ago had the capacity to relate connectively any narrative, however extended, and however complex in its details, is now unable to continue any relation of the most recent events, without . . . prompting . . . ?" (397).

Explaining that "the circumstances of the massacre . . . were themselves indicative of insanity rather than depravity," Freeman's defense counsel echoed Poe's Dupin in asserting that the startling "absence of motive on the part of the prisoner for the commission of an act so dreadful and revolting"

was decisive in tracing the homicide of an innocent white family to an irresponsible killer (34). The prosecution flagged the irrelevancy of this line
of argument in its closing statement, reminding the court that criminal intent matters in those cases where tenuous "circumstantial evidence is vastly
strengthened by proof of a strong motive actuating the accused" (440). "But
where, as here, the testimony is direct and conclusive that the bloody deed
was performed by the Prisoner, his motive ceases to be material," Van Buren
continued with increasing vehemence, "the illegal act being proved, the Law
declares the motive. THAT MOTIVE IS MALICE—A WICKED, DEPRAVED
HEART" (440). No mere technicality, the prosecution maintained, this one
procedural feint was part of a larger dodge. Whereas, due to the (sometimes
counterintuitive) effects of the privilege against self-incrimination, normally
"the declarations and acts of the prisoner" are inadmissible in court, "the
defence of insanity differs from all others" in that those very "declarations
and acts . . . constitute this defence" (426).[147] In these two manipulations of
legal procedure, Van Buren implied, lay the defense's duplicitous strategy:
insisting that Freeman's motiveless killing of the Van Nests implied his insanity, his lawyers created an opening to introduce the otherwise inadmissible
"declarations and acts" of the accused—not as direct evidence (testimony),
but, in effect, as the very circumstantial evidence that would have required
a (now absent) motive for conviction. The defense shielded their client from
the legal presumption that his killings betokened malice by treating Freeman's words and actions not as traces of human agency but as objects for
analysis.

Consistent with its environmentalist claims, Seward's insanity brief had
the effect of objectifying Freeman himself. In the void of legal responsibility
the case had opened up, the authority of circumstances threatened to super-
sede that of persons, with people in danger of becoming reduced to things.
Instead of producing a first-person narrative of the racial neglect, harass-
ment, and brutality he experienced in his youth—much as slave narratives
offered "testimony . . . [to] what Slavery really is"[148]—and thereby simultaneously establishing his civil subjectivity and the circumstances that impeded
its development, Freeman, like the speech and actions that emanate from
him, instead becomes (in more than one sense) "material" evidence of the
very circumstances that deprive him of subjectivity.

For their part, rather than allowing the defense to locate insanity in the
lack of a clear motive, the prosecution turned the tables by identifying insanity—or the legal irresponsibility that recently had been so publicly attached

to it—as *itself* a motive for the murders. Positioning Seward as, in effect, an accessory before the fact, the prosecution implied that Freeman's real motive was a criminal desire to kill with impunity—a motive inspired by his presence, as "an attentive listener" (albeit one "hard of hearing") to the suggestive insanity defense Seward mounted on Wyatt's behalf in the murder trial that immediately preceded Freeman's homicidal rampage (461).[149] Seward emphatically rejected the implication that "he listened to me on that occasion, in regard to the impunity of crime, and that he went out" from Wyatt's trial "a ripe and complete scholar" (422). "This stupid idiot," Seward insisted, gesturing, no doubt, to Freeman, "who cannot take into his ears, deaf as death, the words which I am speaking to you . . . and who even now is exchanging smiles with his and my accusers, regardless of the deep anxiety depicted in your countenances," simply could not be the "mischievous, cunning kind of a darkey" portrayed by the prosecution (422–23). A nonpareil of ignorant passivity, incapable of self-representation much less of criminal intent, Freeman was pathetically dependent on counsel who "plead for him a plea that he cannot understand" (35).

During Freeman's case, narrative's complicated relationship to civil personality and criminal responsibility was dramatized outside the courtroom by a proposal made to Seward by Henry Wyatt. The indigent white Auburn prisoner, "after receiving his sentence, anxious to afford Governor Seward some compensation, offered to narrate his 'life' for publication, the profits of which should go to Governor S."[150] More than calling into question the link between narrative incapacity and mental incompetence (or, indeed, the murderer's own insanity), Wyatt's proposal underscores how the punitive recognition of criminal responsibility could, through the medium of print publication, enable the condemned to affirm his status as a civil person. Here, the condemned Wyatt seeks to convert his life into a *Life*, in the conventional form of the criminal confession, and, thereby, to transform not only his relationship with Seward but to society. For if, as in Seward's insanity defense for Freeman, Wyatt's declarations and acts—and, by extension, the allegedly insane defendant himself—were reduced at trial to inert evidentiary facts, the condemned man's offer to remunerate Seward with the proceeds from the sale of his personal narrative seeks to restore his civil capacity by transforming him from an object of forensic analysis into a legal subject capable of entering into a contract, by (belatedly) providing financial consideration in exchange for Seward's services as an attorney. As important as a minimal degree of mental competence undoubtedly was to such an enterprise, Wyatt's conviction was crucial: without his impending execution, there would be no opportunity to contract for and publish a gallows narrative.

That unlike Wyatt—or, for that matter, Joseph Hanno, Abraham Johnstone, Thomas J. Wansley, and Nat Turner—William Freeman could not acquire an autonomous, interiorized civic presence through the attribution to him of a confessional personal narrative is arguably due less to his more legitimate or advanced mental illness than to the legal limbo in which the insanity defense, followed by Seward's successful appeal, placed him.[151] For despite Freeman's alleged incapacity for narrative, trial testimony reconstructed not only Freeman's words and actions, but also, as the prosecution pointed out, scenes in which he told the story of the killings. In an unguarded moment, an incensed Seward himself recounted how, after seeing prosecution witness "Dr. BIGELOW on the stand swearing away his life, upon confessions already taken," Freeman, "followed" by the doctor "from the Court to his cell . . . with child-like meekness, sat down on his bench and confessed further for hours, all the while holding the lamp by whose light Dr. BIGELOW recorded the testimony, obtained for the purpose of sealing his fate beyond a possible deliverance."[152] As he confesses to Dr. Bigelow, the incapacitated Freeman, more lamppost than author, is not the self-generating subject of his own story but the object of another's representations. Regardless of his ability to produce coherent narratives, Freeman lacked the requisite personhood out of which to form such a confession. Saved from the gallows, Freeman was also denied the civic presence that punitive recognition of his criminal responsibility would have engendered. Instead, in a process for which the scene with Dr. Bigelow serves as a set piece, Freeman became the focus of disciplinary scrutiny in professional journals from the *Law Reporter* to the *American Journal of the Medical Sciences*, *New York Journal of Medicine and the Collateral Sciences*, *American Journal of Insanity*, and *American Quarterly Retrospect of American and Foreign Practical Medicine and Surgery*.[153]

Even more telling than this panoply of medico-legal representations is the Mastin-commissioned folk painting of Freeman on the scaffold. Circulating among the same local and regional audiences who might have eagerly snapped up a pamphlet confession by Freeman, the painting is finally notable less for its fictiveness than for the emphatically exteriorized view it provides of the event and its black subject. Framed by the gallows, the William Freeman of the painting is also framed by the execution's spectators, whose expressive gazes evince a range of interpretive responses.[154] Missing here is the first-person perspective that even the most formulaic, ventriloquized criminal confessions purported to offer: rather than viewing the world through the killer's eyes, the painting covers those eyes—so hauntingly illuminated in depictions of the killings—with the condemned man's cap.

Conclusion

When the *Liberator* first reported on the Van Nest killings and Freeman's near-lynching, it anticipated that, "as Freeman happened to have a colored skin, no doubt the wicked persecutors of the colored people will hold them all responsible for it."[155] Freeman's "deed was his own," the article insisted, "and the consequences should be confined to him alone." But appreciation for the way Freeman's offense would be used to tar the entire race drove the anonymous writer him- or herself to racial generalizations. "Surely, the colored population of this country have given the strongest evidence of possessing incomparably more humane feelings, of having a much stronger aversion to the shedding of blood, than their white enslavers," the article continued in a transparent attempt to stave off the predictable charges of widespread black criminality: "When it is remembered how many years they have been robbed, scourged, bought and sold like cattle, subjected to every outrage that cruelty could invent or tyranny inflict,—thousands of them having been flogged to death, stabbed, mutilated, and shot down by those monsters who have possessed unlimited and irresponsible control over them,—the marvel is, that where only one has become revengeful, there have not been hundreds among them driven by desperation to commit the most shocking atrocities, by way of retaliation." Shifting its focus from the free black killer to the victims of slaveholding villainy, the *Liberator* sought to counteract the inevitable politicization of Freeman's case by assigning an alternative meaning to the murders. The source of such social disorder lay not in an inherent black criminality and thus incapacity for freedom but in slavery and its dehumanizing legacy of racism. Anomalous as his "revengeful" violence may have been, the *Liberator* implies, Freeman succumbed to the same retaliatory impulses that his fellow African Americans had so admirably suppressed. Full emancipation, not continued slavery, was the only way to ensure against such shocking atrocities.

Employing print publication to channel attention away from the black criminal toward slave victims, the *Liberator* implied that the long-suffering African American collective was at least as eligible for citizenship as the members of the Auburn lynch mob whose calls for the black man to be "*strung up without judge or jury*" betrayed "a state of mind quite as horrible as that which Freeman exhibited, and certainly equally lawless." In this way the article adopts the by-now familiar abolitionist strategy of decoupling the public recognition of African American political membership that flowed from the black malefactor's crime from the offense itself. But here the specific application to "Crazy Bill" Freeman illustrates that strategy's pitfalls.[156] If Freeman is, thankfully, atypical in acting on a widespread "desperation" and justifiable desire for "retaliation" among disenfranchised and enslaved African Americans, then the larger black collective's admirable restraint itself bespeaks a high degree of civic virtue. The problem, of course, is that according to Freeman's abolitionist-led defense team, no such racialized intentions motivated the senseless killing of the white Van Nest family; rather, as reporting in the *Liberator* affirmed, the black madman "had 'no reason at all.'"[157] Without reason—understood here as both motive and the sanity that enabled such criminal intent—Freeman could not do the symbolic work typically performed by the black condemned who entered American print culture: serve as a kind of human switching station through whom the dangerous current of criminal responsibility could be transformed into a civic presence that itself could be converted into civil standing. Instead Freeman, rendered irresponsible by a form of insanity clearly traceable to racial neglect and abuse, could only represent a kind of civic impasse in which the African American collective seemed increasingly to be caught. (What Seward's twentieth-century successor, New York Senator Daniel Patrick Moynihan, would infamously figure as a "tangle of pathology.")[158] As unjust as it might have been to hold those denied the right of citizenship subject to the laws, as the prosecution advocated, the defense's alternative of custodial isolation seems even more troubling at a time when the ongoing project of inclusive racial exclusion was being institutionalized in the prison and other antebellum asylums.

The undisputed identification of Freeman's hotly disputed capacity with that of the nominally free African American collective makes it tempting once again to adapt Douglass's insight in *My Bondage and My Freedom*: "Not only is Freeman on trial, but . . . the free people are also on trial. It is alleged, that they are, naturally, inferior; that they are so low in the scale of humanity, and so utterly stupid, that they are unconscious of their wrongs, and do not apprehend their rights."[159] If, as with all offenses against society, the offense imputed to William Freeman was itself attributable in the medico-legal thought of the day to his distinctive "physical organization" (whether his color or his head injury) "in combination with external influences" (whether social neglect or social degradation), and if that condition placed the accused black criminal in "the same state of irresponsibility with the insane," then, again, where did responsibility end, and irresponsibility begin? If the racially determined physical and external factors that produced both criminality and insanity in someone like Freeman also blocked the "apprehensive power" long held to separate most humans from animals, then how could other freemen, manifesting a similarly racialized physical organization and subject to the same corrupting external influences, ever possibly apprehend (in Douglass's dual sense of understanding and seizing) the full rights of American citizens?[160]

Chapter 6

Who Aint a Slaver? Citizenship, Piracy, and Slaver Narratives

20th Nov., My expedition . . . found exploring the Congo
in search of brig [*Windward*] to be very much like hunting
for fugitive slaves in the Dismal Swamp.
—Correspondence of African Squadron Commander
William McBlair (1857)

As initial reports of the Van Nest murders appeared throughout the spring of 1846, the press was also publicizing the seizure of the American slave ship, *Pons*, and the landing of its nearly nine hundred sick and dying African "recaptives" in Liberia.[1] Not long after papers had corrected initial, erroneous reports that the Auburn, New York, killer was "some one in disguise of a negro" by confirming that the suspect was in fact "a full-blooded negro named Wm. Freeman," news began to trickle in from Monrovia that "the citizens of Liberia have suffered severely on account of the depredations of the recaptured Slaves of the Pons," with "cattle . . . stolen, sheep and swine driven off at night, hen-roosts robbed and cassava and potato patches dug up."[2] Revealing the suspected blackface killer to have unambiguously "negro" features and the slave trade's most piteous victims to be common thieves, antebellum newspapers retraced the heavily scored line connecting blackness with crime.

While coverage of the Freeman case eddied into professional journals, print portrayals of the illegal slave trade spread from newspaper reports to magazine fiction to full-length books. Published as popular interest in the democratic figure of the American seaman peaked, these stories appeared in the midst of the midcentury controversy over federal designation of the international slave trade as piracy.[3] Unlike the articles above, these legal, reportorial, and literary narratives focused on offenders who were not only white but guilty of a crime that produced the very concept of racial whiteness. Centering on the plebeian sailors, bourgeois merchants, and professional captains who fit the normative profile of white, male citizenship, these slaver narratives unexpectedly helped reconfigure the lineaments of race and criminality in antebellum print culture. "The laws should pry out every man who helps the slave-trade,—not merely the sailor on the sea, but *the cowardly rich villain, and speculator on the land*—and punish *him*," fulminated Walt Whitman on the *Pons* capture.[4]

Accounts of international slave traffickers portrayed the one group of Americans held criminally responsible for their participation in slavery—and, conversely, the one group of active criminals whose liability for prosecution turned on their status *as* U.S. citizens. Much as the legal fiction of slaves' mixed character recognized black political membership and legal personhood only in the breach, federal anti-slave trafficking legislation and litigation gave punitive content to the U.S. citizenship that would remain formally undefined until passage of the Fourteenth Amendment. Partaking of their fellow Americans' mixed character as state and federal citizens, the slaver narrative's mariners and merchants personified a U.S. citizenship that appeared to be legible only through the lens of culpability.

The slave trade had informed articulations of national political identity since the founding. From the beginning, American critiques were prompted more by concerns about national sovereignty than African suffering. Writing the Declaration of Independence, Thomas Jefferson sought to exonerate the new republic of historical responsibility for slavery by blaming that "piratical warfare" on the "*Christian* king of Great Britain."[5] In keeping with the Founders' decision to strike the passage from the Declaration's final draft, the Constitution protected slave importation at least until 1808. Thirteen years after illegalizing imports, and decades after imposing restrictions on American participation in the carrier portion of the trade, Congress passed the Atlantic world's harshest anti-slave trade legislation when it designated international traffic piracy a capital offense.[6] An initial burst of successful enforcement in the 1820s led to a relaxation of vigilance into the 1840s, when prosecutions of slavers under the 1820 statute once again began to appear with some regularity on federal dockets and in the columns of the country's newspapers.[7] Although only one person, Nathaniel Gordon, was executed under the law (and that during the Lincoln administration), a steady stream of cases provoked national as well as local commentary in the two decades leading up to the Civil War.[8]

The opening lines of "The Slaver," a novella published serially in *Graham's American Monthly Magazine of Literature and Art* in 1847, hailed the literary opportunity presented by the slave trade's changed legal status.[9] Too many "modern authors," the writer lamented, "take for the hero of their story some horrible and bloody pirate, or daring and desperate smuggler, of the sixteenth or seventeenth century; characters that the increased number, strength and vigilance of armed cruisers, and the energy of the excise officers, have long since driven from the face of the ocean, in these capacities."[10] The realities of modern law enforcement ensured that such romantic characters "now can only be found in that lawless traffic, the Slave Trade" (1). Thus, the trade's comparatively recent designation as piracy proved a boon to the romancer who would provide a spice of the real to his story. "Whilst we are quietly perusing some thrilling tale," the writer marveled, "events equally startling, deeds as dark and desperate, scenes as horrible, may be transpiring at that instant, on the bosom, or the borders, of the same ocean, that laves with its salt waters the shores of our own happy land" (1).[11] Whatever gains and losses accrued to its practitioners and victims, illegal slave trafficking held out great dividends for American authors.

Today's novelists and scholars tend to place fugitive slave cases at the epicenter of the combustive interaction of politics, law, and literature that the slavery crisis ignited in the urban North.[12] But even as Boston and New York were rocked by highly publicized hearings involving James Hamlet, Shadrach Minkins, Thomas Sims, Anthony Burns, and other runaways, these cities were shaken by less well remembered cases implicating merchant slavers Charles Kehrman, James Smith, Joseph Smith, and William C. Valentine.[13] Just as fugitive slave cases offered a legal correlate to the slave narrative, these trials found their counterparts in published slaver narratives. Whereas the attempted rendition of fugitives exposed sectional tensions over the South's peculiar institution, the jurisdictional emphasis of slave trade legislation, policing, and litigation ensured that legal proceedings and press coverage centered on questions of national sovereignty and U.S. citizenship, as well as the related problem of civil capacity. Because enforcement pivoted on the Americanness of the ports, men, and ships involved in the illegal traffic, public discussion tended to focus less on specific offenses than on slavers' answerability as U.S. citizens and knowing, voluntary actors. At issue was not the crime of forcibly kidnapping human beings in Africa and transporting them for sale in the New World, but whether the accused were identifiably American—and, if so, whether they could be said to be in control of their own actions.

As in the Freeman case, the minutiae of legal procedure encapsulated more abstract political and cultural issues. Following separate rules of evidence, civil and criminal slaver cases yielded strikingly different outcomes. Proceedings *in rem* ("*against the thing*") sought only forfeiture of the ship and its cargo. In these admiralty cases judges tended to find circumstantial evidence probative, ensuring a 60 percent success rate in the 1840s and 1850s.[14] Criminal proceedings against persons were far less straightforward. Because international slave trafficking "was an old practice but a new crime," as historian Don E. Fehrenbacher put it, "the United States, more than any other nation . . . struggled with the problem of using criminal sanction against the slave trade."[15] Lacking clearly defined legal precedent and activating common-law protections for the accused, print-grabbing, predominantly Northern trials generated what many saw as scandalously low conviction rates.[16]

In contrast to other white offenders, slavers' descent into criminality arguably resulted not from a breach of the social compact but from the illegalization of a commerce that had hitherto been not only legitimate but foundational to the young republic's political economy. Literary populist George Lippard reminded readers of *The Bank Director's Son* (1851) that, until very recently, "the slave trade was as legal, moral, and religious, as stock gambling at the present day."[17] Little surprise, then, that slaver narratives should evince the cultural anxieties that Priscilla Wald associates with two Supreme Court cases framing the antebellum period: *Cherokee Nation v. the State of Georgia* (1831) and *Scott v. Sandford* (1857). Demonstrating how American law did not merely protect but created its citizens' personhood, the cases implicitly posed "the anxious question of what keeps a government from making white men slaves," as well as "the equally anxious . . . query of what keeps a government from making white men (legally) disappear."[18] These misgivings only intensified when the legal focus shifted from Cherokee or African American *rights* to the legal *responsibilities* of white citizens, for it is in the realm of criminal law that governmental authorities routinely consigned the latter to a civil death not unlike that of slaves, making them disappear by means of the gallows or the penitentiary.

The two previous chapters discussed new antebellum views of the constitutive relations among crime, race, responsibility, personhood, and citizenship primarily in connection with rhetorical strategies deployed in the slavery debate. When abolitionists called slaveholding a crime, their charges were directed not at the comparatively few Americans who held slaves illegally, but the legions who did so under sanction of law. But what of those citizens who were literally as well as figuratively criminalized by their participation in slavery? Those whom federal law, not abolitionist rhetoric, deemed criminals? What happened when a previously licit business became illegal? How did federal statutes transform not the act of slave trading (which, after all, persisted) but the persons targeted by that legislation? What did the criminalization of historically tolerated money-making activities of common seamen, ships' officers, and merchants portend for their fellow citizens, who increasingly found themselves held accountable for the crime of slavery in the court of public opinion? These were the questions insistently impressed upon midcentury audiences by slaver narratives, whether they took the form of naval dispatches, published trial transcripts, modern pirate stories, or literary fiction.

Like its better-known opposite, the slaver narrative probes the meaning of political belonging and civil capacity under a slaveholding legal regime. Together, these two antebellum literary modes extend the transverse arcs inscribed by early American gallows literature. We saw from the examples of Isaac Frasier and Charles Gibbs how criminality could initiate the white print subject's decline from presumptive political membership to civil death. During the same period, however, from Joseph Hanno and Arthur, to Abraham Johnstone, on to Thomas J. Wansley and Nat Turner, first-person articulations of criminal culpability mandated penal recognition of black personhood, required retroactive (although purely formal) acknowledgment of political belonging, and provided access (however fictive) to the public sphere through print publication. In the Jacksonian period, the slavery controversy intervened to direct the black persona on one of two disparate itineraries: protocitizen or incapacitated outsider. Holding American citizens culpable for the national crime of slavery and seeking to exonerate African Americans from volitional complicity in slavery and its subsidiary crimes, abolitionist reformers joined social conservatives like Edgar Allan Poe and Samuel Cartwright in isolating the immediate, violent *actus reus* ascribed to blacks and nonhuman animals from the remote, even passive *mens rea* that was increasingly reserved for white persons. With enslaved African Americans thus relieved of responsibility for coerced or otherwise involuntary actions, the classic slave narrative could present a highly interiorized, individual black self. Yet this separation of (black) acts from (white) intents also threatened to prolong rather than curtail African American civic and political exclusion after emancipation. Whether the product of racial pathology or environmental racism, the incapacity newly assigned to the "free" black custodial subject made African Americans appear less civilly competent and more ineligible for political membership than ever. The tendency to imagine not only citizenship, but crime and punishment, as a preserve of normative white personhood is indicated as much by the sale of Poe's homicidal Ourang-Outang as by the real-life death in custody of incoherent, twenty-four-year-old multiple killer William Freeman. While the testimonial slave narrative was replacing the criminal confession as the legally inflected form of life-writing that distinguished its speaking subject from "the brute creation," these other antebellum publications suggested how elusive had become the recognized criminality that for over a century had decisively placed African Americans "above the brutes that perish" in American law and print culture.[19]

Enter the slaver narrative's inscrutable white, masculine subjects. Part of a larger Jacksonian cohort that included Susanna Blumenthal's eager incompetents and Dana D. Nelson's evanescent national fraternity, as well as the necro-citizens of Russ Castronovo's public sphere and the inarticulate innocents of Nancy Ruttenburg's American Renaissance, the slaver narrative's merchants, captains, and sailors bore the particular impress of anti-slave-trade legislation and litigation.[20] In response to jurisdictional requirements, defense briefs for slavers were centrally concerned not with affirming or denying the commission of specific offenses but, rather, with demonstrating the inapplicability of the legislation in question by constructing selves that constantly retreat in law's presence. Published during "the boom years of American nautical writing (1840–60)," few literary slaver narratives speak in the first-person voice that Hester Blum finds at once aligning sailors' documentary accounts with those of former slaves while distinguishing these sea narratives from their British analogues.[21] At the same cultural moment when African Americans like Frederick Douglass and William Wells Brown were adopting the slave narrative's juridical idiom to claim the comprehensive personhood and full political membership denied them as slaves, slaver narratives depicted ship captains and their merchant collaborators disclaiming American citizenship as their seafaring subordinates displayed remarkable civil incapacity.

These narratives of denationalized or irresponsible white manhood appeared as the "legal model of the self" was undergoing considerable

reassessment and revision.[22] Post-Revolutionary legal thought, rejecting the
status-based English law of persons and emphasizing individual as well as
collective self-government, sought to delineate the contours of legal personhood for the new nation. Such efforts, Blumenthal argues, were complicated
by the sharp rise in capacity litigation. Although slaver cases did not turn
on the specific question of mental illness, these "courtroom performances"
of disavowed citizenship and disclaimed agency became, when rendered in
print, similarly "unsettling affairs, conjuring up vivid images . . . of deluded
minds, overborne wills and moral insensibility."[23] Far from consolidating the
legal personhood of male citizen-subjects, such printed encounters with law
threatened to break it down altogether.

International slave trading offers an extreme instance of how competi-
tion in the antebellum market economy blocked connections across lines of
gender, race, nation, and culture at the expense of those outside the imagined
brotherhood of white American men.[24] Here, though, the promised fraternal
unity of white male citizens is not just tantalizingly deferred. As we shall
see, depictions of slave-trading pirates as everyday businessmen hinted at
the precarious political identity of these most representative (if unsavory)
American citizens, whereas the collateral portrayal of common seamen as
will-less subjects highlights these white working men's tenuous claim to
autonomous selfhood in a slaveholding, industrializing, commercial nation.
Respectively relinquishing the two constitutive components of that fraternity,
national identity and legally recognized personhood, traders and sailors in
these accounts lose their grasp on the very qualities that separate them from
the civilly dead human beings in whom they traffic.

That involvement in the slave trade could destabilize the personhood
and political membership of not only Africans, but U.S. citizens themselves,
is tantalizingly suggested by Chief Justice John Marshall's decision in the
Antelope case (1825), the only U.S. Supreme Court case to involve (apparently) American slavers. Discussing the Africans whose fate the case would
decide, Marshall did not follow Georgia's acting district attorney Richard
Wylly Habersham in referring to them as "persons of color from some Eastern Kingdom of Africa"; instead, Marshall speaks of the recaptives as the
"residue" derived from an elaborate calculus that applied a new "ratio" to
reach a revised "apportionment" of Africans.[25] The inverse of the court's stub-
born refusal to acknowledge individual black persons was its persistent but
finally unsuccessful struggle to identify the mysterious Portuguese national
on whose behalf the case had, for five years, been conducted.[26] The failure of

the vessel's title-holder to materialize led Marshall to conclude that the "long, and otherwise unaccountable absence, of any Portuguese claimant furnishes irresistible testimony that no such claimant exists and that the real owner belongs to some other nation and feels the necessity of concealment." In a pattern that would be repeated in slaver cases over the next three decades, circumstances yielded the "irresistible testimony" that unforthcoming witnesses could not or would not provide. "Who is that individual?" Marshall asked of the presumptive U.S. citizen who privately held title but disavowed any public identity, finally ruling that "no such person is shown to exist, and his existence . . . cannot be presumed." Marshall's unanswered question recalls the query hovering over the Freeman proceedings. "Is there a man there?" print coverage of slaver cases also asked. If the man in question was a U.S. citizen, the answer, more often than not, was a silent "No." The antithesis of the slave narrative's advancing black print persona, the slaver narrative's recessive white subject results from the genre's profoundly aconfessional quality. Self-effacing witnesses all but vanish before the evidence of things seen, and observed actions speak louder than stifled words.

Attending to this neglected archive of the print controversy over slavery, this chapter returns to "Benito Cereno" as one among many slaver narratives to surface in the 1840s and 1850s. As with Graham's "Slaver" and Lippard's *Bank Director's Son*, the renewed policing and prosecution of slave-trading pirates prompts Melville's novella to examine the relationship of slavery to national identity, holding all Americans (rather than just Southerners) responsible for their complicity in acts that were legally (rather than figuratively) criminal. Like reportorial and courtroom accounts of international slave traders, these late antebellum fictions suggest that the nation's failure to assume responsibility for the crime of slavery threatened to expose not simply the vacuity of sovereign American identity, but, perhaps even more disturbingly, the requisite civil incapacity upon which such a guiltless (if ultimately empty) U.S. citizenship was premised.

"Benito Cereno" introduces a new twist into our analysis of temporality's significance to assessments of criminal liability. For, by tampering with horologicals and chronometricals, Melville ensured that the gap between the setting and the publication of his historical romance synchronized tellingly with the timeline of federal slave trade legislation and enforcement. Approached in its own midcentury print and legal contexts, Melville's version of Amasa Delano's encounter with Benito Cereno stages many of the central preoccupations of popular legal spectatorship over slaver cases: questions about the dubious relationship of Yankee seafarers to Spanish "paper captains"; concerns about the probative value of testimony versus circumstantial evidence; doubts about the semiotics of national identity; and, above all, difficulties discerning piracy from slave trafficking. With this last issue as its core interpretive crisis, the story points to the slaver narrative's disconcerting generic indeterminacy. Just as the early slave narrative was troubled by uncertainty as to whether the narrator was the perpetrator or the victim of the crimes to which he testified, the instability of the slaver narrative as a literary genre arose from its subject's changing legal status. Were slavers swashbuckling corsairs or criminally corrupt entrepreneurs?

Taking up this question, the chapter next examines *Graham's* "Slaver" from the perspective of press accounts portraying the international slave trade as a business—right down to its exploitative labor practices—in order to demonstrate how slave-trading pirates' insouciant disregard for national sovereignty could not, finally, dispel the quintessentially Jacksonian anxiety about claiming "freedom" in a slaveholding republic. If, as Blum reminds us, "sailors . . . were always inter- and transnational figures," and, as historian Paul Gilje has shown, American mariners' pursuit of "liberty" had often put individual or collective interests before patriotic principle, it was nevertheless in the antebellum period that the new nineteenth-century "idea that the common seaman represented the democratic man" reached an apotheosis in popular first-person sailors' narratives.[27] Yet, as we turn from masters to men, it becomes evident that the aconfessional slaver narrative exhibited not only civic estrangement but a disquieting evacuation of selfhood. In a literary historical epoch when humans legally defined as objects of property accessed the public sphere through eloquent first-person testimonies, slaver narratives instead relied on the evidence of things seen, effectively reducing their human subjects to civil nonentities. The only hope for restoration, George Lippard intimates in the pamphlet novel he published alternately as *The Killers* and *The Bank Director's Son*, was for Americans to answer for their complicity in the crime of slavery. Without such collective accountability, his and other slaver narratives warn, U.S. citizens could be reduced to unprosecuted "Killers" (like slave traders) or civilly dead ciphers (like slaves).

Rhetorically and often ideologically at odds with antislavery propaganda, slaver narratives inadvertently joined the abolitionist appeal to popular legal consciousness by probing how white male citizens' abjuration of legal responsibility literally alienated them from the American polity while betokening an alarming absence of inner selfhood. Read in light of the legislation, enforcement, and litigation of the international slave trade, these stories articulate widely held fears that the pervasive denial of accountability for slavery threatened to deprive both American identity and normative white personhood of any meaning, leaving only a set of external signs as its place-holders. In this sense, Melville's novella, itself anything but straightforward, provides a revealing point of entry into an illicit commerce that by the early antebellum period had become, in the restrained phrasing of one naval historian, "logistically complex."[28]

An Everyday Occurrence

"Benito Cereno" opens with Melville's fictional Captain Delano facing a crisis of interpretation: he must divine whether the "strange sail" that he sees coming into the secluded harbor of a desert island is a pirate ship.[29] Because "the stranger . . . showed no colors," even Delano, "a person of a singularly undistrustful good nature, not liable, except on extraordinary and repeated incentives" to impute "malign evil in man," must be persuaded that the stranger "could be no wonted freebooter on that ocean" (46–47). The craft's erratic movements convince the benevolent American captain that he has instead encountered "a ship in distress" (47). His relief is augmented when, "upon a still nigher approach," the San Dominick's "true character . . . was plain—a Spanish merchantman of the first class; carrying negro slaves, amongst other valuable freight, from one colonial port to the other" (48). Supported by the ship's initial appearance and its captain's subsequent testimony (official and unofficial), this reassuring conclusion is nevertheless unsettled, during the long day that follows, by contradictions emerging from both Benito Cereno's story and Delano's own observations. Accordingly, while his crew delivers provisions, Delano invests his own small store of critical resources in collecting and evaluating evidence that the San Dominick is, in fact, a slave ship and not a pirate ship.

If contemporary readers shared Delano's apparent blindness regarding the actual state of affairs aboard the San Dominick—the slave rebellion—critics have argued that this confusion can be attributed in no small part to the ideological blinders supplied by American racism.[30] What has not been addressed, however, is how the temporal gap that separates the novella's 1799 setting from its composition and publication in the mid-1850s contributes to the interpretive predicament by creating a discrepancy between Delano's perspective and that of the antebellum reader. The novella's source text, Amasa Delano's *Narrative of Voyages and Travels in the Northern and Southern Hemispheres* (1817), details the "Particulars of the Capture of the Spanish Ship Tryal, at the island of St. Maria" in February 1805, and provides "Documents relating to that affair."[31] Antedating Amasa Delano's encounter with the Spanish vessel and renaming the ship the *San Dominick*, the novella evokes the Saint-Domingue slave rebellion of the 1790s.[32] It also gestures to uprisings on the slave ships *Creole* and *Amistad*, which generated court cases and exhaustive press coverage in the years between Delano's narrative and Melville's story.[33] But this cluster of dates has particular relevance in the legislative history of the international slave trade.[34]

However much Melville's readers might have shared his Yankee captain's views of race and slavery, they necessarily had radically different perspectives on the slave trade's legal status. For it was during the period between 1799 and 1855 that the dilemma that stymies Melville's "American"—slave ship or pirate ship?—ceased to be an either/or proposition under federal law.[35] In the legal regime under which both the fictional Delano and his real-life counterpart pursued their calling, to identify a strange ship as a slaver was virtually to guarantee it was *not* a pirate ship; by the time Melville began to draft his novella in late 1854, however, to be a slaver *was* to be a pirate.[36] "The only pirates that infest these waters now," a correspondent wrote the antislavery *National Era* from Cuba, "are the slavers."[37] No wonder Melville's Delano is confused.

The timing of the story's composition and publication ensured that Melville's contemporaries would not read "Benito Cereno" simply as a tale of a bygone epoch in the history of the slave trade. Published serially in *Putnam's Monthly Magazine* over the final three months of 1855, the novella would have resonated with renewed concerns about American involvement in the international traffic. Melville had embarked on the story as a wave of slave trade publications crested in the United States. The first of four antebellum editions of Henry C. Carey's political economic treatise, *The Slave Trade, Domestic and Foreign; Why It Exists and How It May be Extinguished*, appeared in 1853, followed by Brantz Mayer's widely read *Captain Canot; or, Twenty Years of an African Slaver* (1854). Not to be outdone, Lieutenant Andrew Hull Foote published *Africa and the American Flag* (1854) to promote and defend the embattled African Squadron, America's answer to the much-larger and better-funded British force patrolling for the likes of Captain Canot on Africa's west coast.[38] All three books received prominent editorial notice.[39] Although many read Mayer's racy tale with a splash of salt water, Commander William McBlair, Lieutenant Foote's naval colleague, took *Captain*

Canot seriously enough to pass it along to the officers of his sloop-of-war as it cruised for slave-trading pirates on the African coast.[40] No yarn from "a distant era," "Benito Cereno" was, like its predecessor "The Slaver," very much "A Tale of Our Own Times."[41]

These works were published just as Southern hostility toward federal legislation was voicing itself in calls to reopen the trade—even though, as *Uncle Tom's Cabin* had recently shown, demand for imported Africans had been drastically reduced by the thriving domestic trade in American-born men, women, and children.[42] Like its successor, *Dred: A Tale of the Great Dismal Swamp* (1856), to which Commander McBlair alludes in the epigraph to this chapter, Stowe's novel portrayed slavery as the South's peculiar institution. But Americans' involvement in and profits from transatlantic slavery by no means depended upon the presence of slave ships on Southern shores. For, if the practice of slaveholding had long been associated with that section, the equally lucrative traffic in slaves had always been a distinctly Yankee enterprise.[43] Unable to "say that New England and New Englandmen were free from this deep pollution," U.S. Supreme Court Justice (and Bay Stater) Joseph Story had to acknowledge that "they who drive a loathsome traffic, 'and buy the muscles and the bones of men,' are to be found here also."[44]

Restricted since 1794, American participation in international slave trafficking had, by the 1840s and 1850s, become centered in the "free" North.[45] "The thing is getting to be an every day occurrence," the *New York Herald* remarked in 1839 upon a U.S. slaver's capture.[46] In March 1846 the seizure of "four vessels . . . in about as many days" led the *Brooklyn Eagle's* anti-gallows editor Walt Whitman to opine, "the laws are sharp enough—too sharp. But who ever hears of their being put in force, further than to confiscate the vessel, and perhaps imprison the crews a few days?"[47] Predictable though their verdicts may have been, slaver trials "excite[d] universal interest" among American audiences fascinated by the possibility that a fellow citizen could be hanged for what had been, over much of the nation's history, a legitimate form of commerce.[48] As these reports reflect, the Atlantic slave trade was headquartered in Melville's hometown. In rare agreement with its archrival, Horace Greeley's reformist *New York Tribune*, the conservative, proslavery *New York Times* complained that "*scarcely a month passes in which there are not one or more vessels cleared at this port, which embark at once in the Slave-trade and land their cargoes on the coast of Cuba.*"[49] Proof of local—and national—complicity in illegal slave trafficking came with the arrests of the *Julia Moulton's* captain, James Smith, and marine outfitter, New York merchant William C. Valentine, prompting U.S. district attorney John McKeon to designate the city "the very depot of this nefarious traffic."[50] Word spread across the Mason-Dixon line and to Canada West. "New York," affirmed Captain Smith in a widely reprinted jailhouse interview, "is the chief port in the world for the slave trade," reiterating "two or three times, '*It is the greatest place in the universe for it.*'"[51]

The Smith and Valentine trials were extensively reported from November 1854 well into January 1855, the months when Melville, in steady contact with New York family, friends, and editors, was composing his only sustained fictional treatment of slavery.[52] (The *Times* singled out the Smith proceeding as "the most important [criminal] case which has come to trial during this year," funding its lengthy, closely printed transcripts and trial reports in part through advertisements for *Captain Canot* as a "most amusingly readable and most freshly instructive book"—"NOW AVAILABLE IN ITS TENTH EDITION.")[53] Seeking, somewhat desperately, to lighten pressing financial and familial burdens, including a debt to his father-in-law, Massachusetts Supreme Court Chief Justice Lemuel Shaw, Melville published "Benito Cereno" in the insistently nationalist—and politically neutral—*Putnam's*.[54] We would be mistaken, however, to read in Melville's decision not to openly criticize Southern slavery an instance of self-serving quietism or a disappointing lack of imagination in the financially imperiled sailor-turned-author.[55] Quite the contrary, recalling that the justice's cold formalism in resolving slave cases had left William Lloyd Garrison's *Liberator* "unable to perceive . . . wherein the guilt of Judge Shaw differs from that of the slave pirate on the African Coast," it is noteworthy that, with "Benito Cereno," Melville joined the motley crew of antebellum authors who at midcentury were probing the national and international implications of Americans' continuing involvement in the transatlantic slave trade.[56] In 1850, market-savvy George Lippard expanded an earlier pamphlet novel on urban crime by having his corrupt Philadelphia bank director finance slave-trading pirates operating out of New York. At the other end of the decade (and of the literary spectrum), Stowe relocated *The Minister's Wooing* (1859) from the slaveholding antebellum South of her previous abolitionist fiction to the slave-trading early national North.[57] With its Spanish masters, African-born slaves, and a representative "American" captain from "Duxbury, in Massachusetts," "Benito Cereno" similarly eschews a Southern setting and characters for cosmopolitan, seafaring ones.[58] To read Amasa Delano and Benito Cereno allegorically as "Yankee" and "Cavalier" is to risk overlooking how, in its pointed allusions to the slave trade controversy, the novella brings together two Melvillean preoccupations: the high seas and American law.[59] Replacing the stock characters of the plantation romance with a New England captain and his Spanish counterpart and setting the story on a turn-of-the-century slave ship rather than an antebellum estate, Melville positioned "Benito Cereno" alongside the decade's closely watched slaver cases. The novella, like those proceedings, serves as reminder that Southerners weren't the only Americans who had benefited from—and were thus responsible for—this "loathsome traffic."

Africa and the American Flag

Much like "Benito Cereno," enforcement of federal anti-slave-trade statutes obsessively circled back to two related issues: the legibility of national identity and the reliability of different forms of evidence. Exploiting the legislation's jurisdictional limits as well as the political constraints limiting American cooperation with British-led suppression efforts, a transnational cabal of slavers manipulated the semiotics of sovereignty, most notably by cloaking their illegal activities under the American flag. Yet, however deceptive appearances may have been, words often proved more so. As with many a slaver case, the novella raises perennial questions about the status of circumstantial evidence—here, by juxtaposing a compromised form of positive proof, Benito Cereno's deposition, against the presumptive proofs Delano (along with the reader) gathers aboard the San Dominick. As we shall see, this emphasis on circumstantial evidence correlates with the novella's susceptibility to being read anachronistically, in the context of the contemporary controversy. Under such a reading, the American and Spanish captains move in and out of roles that would have been familiar to audiences intrigued by the tricks of the (slave) trade. At the same time, the story dramatizes concerns about national sovereignty posed by enforcement efforts at sea and under federal law.

Of course, if Delano's conjecture, supported by Benito Cereno's verbal account and subsequent deposition, is correct, and the San Dominick is merely "a Spanish merchantman," captained and crewed by Spaniards and Portuguese, "carrying negro slaves . . . from one colonial port to the other," its activities would not have constituted piracy any more than did the U.S. coastal slave trade.[60] But as any student of "Benito Cereno" knows, neither the Spanish captain's representations nor the American captain's conclusions are to be taken at face value. Given this uncertainty, Melville's readers, unlike the vice-regal court at Lima but very much like the antebellum authorities responsible for enforcing federal anti-slave-trade statutes, find themselves uncomfortably dependent upon "*circumstantial* evidence, or the doctrine of *presumptions*."[61]

Historically considered a lower order of proof than positive evidence, "where the witness swears distinctly to the commission of the act or crime which forms the subject of the trial," presumptive evidence, explained a nineteenth-century treatise, "is that conclusion which the jury draw for themselves, from circumstances or minor facts, as sworn to by the witnesses."[62] "Benito Cereno" follows its source text, Delano's *Narrative of Voyages and Travels*, when it offers positive evidence in the form of the Spanish captain's deposition.[63] But Melville's version stipulates that "some disclosures" in the deposition "were, at the time, held dubious," given that Cereno "raved of some things which could never have happened"; yet because "subsequent depositions of the surviving sailors, bearing out the revelations of their captain in several of the strangest particulars, gave credence to the rest," the vice-regal "tribunal . . . rested its capital sentences upon" these otherwise inadmissible "statements."[64] By omitting the text of the sailors' corroborative accounts and by enclosing the incapacitated Cereno's deposition in a larger literary narrative, "Benito Cereno" calls the available testimony into question, necessitating a turn to circumstantial evidence.

In Melville's story this move from positive to presumptive proof (and back again) is enacted by Amasa Delano, whose vacillation between the two corresponds to his larger dilemma as to whether to judge the *San Dominick* a slaver (on the basis of Don Benito's testimony) or a pirate ship (on the basis of his own past experiences and immediate observations). In this sense, Delano resembles the naval officers whose task it was to board suspicious ships and ascertain, by comparing the verbal accounts provided by captain and crew with what they saw around them, whether or not a ship was a slaver and thus guilty of piracy. Such presumptive proof was critical to the identification and apprehension of international slave traffickers, although U.S. statutes departed from other slave trade legislation in failing to specify incriminating equipment. The Navy Department prepared Lieutenant-Commander William W. Hunter to penetrate slavers' "artful character" by supplying him with a list of "signs" by which a slaver's "true character . . . may, at all times be conjectured."[65] For their part, civilians could turn to press accounts that accompanied similar inventories with helpful explanatory glosses. Seized on its departure from New York, the *Falmouth* turned out to be "open under deck from cabin to stern, and boards were found to erect, it is supposed, a

slave deck that would hold, as one of the officers remarked, 'about six hundred niggers.'"[66] The boarding party further discovered that "between decks
were over fifty hhds. of water, large stores of rice, beans, farina and preserved
meats, such as are used by slavers," along with "large copper pots and pans for
boiling large masses of food at a time, with ladles and spoons to match, and
many other questionable appurtenances."[67] Finally, and most damning, "in
the cabin were found charts of the west coast of Africa, and a large quantity of
bunting to make American flags." Under such "curious circumstances" seemingly innocent items like lumber, rice, beans, and copper pots attained an
irresistible cumulative narrative logic. The need quickly to adduce such presumptive proof upon boarding a suspicious ship led Lieutenant-Commander
Hunter's naval superiors to warn him that "nothing but the utmost vigilance
and caution will enable you to detect" a slaver, even as they expressed confidence that "your own observations and sagacity will soon discover other
contrivances for deceiving and escaping you."[68]

Procedural discrepancies between civil and criminal actions intensified
the pressure to read shipboard circumstances accurately. "The difficulty" in
prosecutions of slavers, the New York Commercial Advertiser acknowledged,
"has been to convict the parties on legal evidence[,] however strong the
moral proof of their nefarious designs."[69] That suspected captains and owners
often returned to the trade the next season suggests the odds against winning
criminal cases on the basis of presumptive proof—especially given slavers'
practice of relying on seemingly innocent supply ships or "auxiliaries" to
transport incriminating cargo separately.[70] It was a different procedural matter, however, when property (including African "cargo"), rather than the lives
of American citizens, was at stake. Because admiralty cases often featured
"men . . . swearing under the pressure of pecuniary interests, or the terror
of personal penalties," Judge William Peter Van Ness of the District Court
of Southern New York explained in Case of the Schooner Plattsburgh (1822),
"their aberrations and evasions must be corrected by a careful consideration
of the plain facts and circumstances of the case."[71] The authority granted to
circumstantial evidence in such proceedings was even more significant given
that, unlike criminal cases, the burden of proof lay with the defendant. When
a vessel "is found under suspicious circumstances," Van Ness maintained,
"it is reasonable that the owner should be held to develop the mysteries that
surround it, and the innocence of his object."[72]

Untroubled by procedural niceties, press accounts presented incriminating circumstances as evidence against the captain and crew of suspected

slavers like the *Falmouth*. To assert the probative value of things seen in this way was not only to assign objects and their circumstances an authority on par with first-person narrative, but also to foreground the process of seeing itself—a process, inevitably, of interpretation.[73] In his *Theory of Presumptive Proof* (available in a New York edition since 1816), English treatise writer Samuel March Phillipps noted that the "principles of evidence are founded on our observations of human conduct, on common life, and living manners," adding that "it has been found, from common observation, that certain circumstances warrant certain presumptions. Thus, that a mother shall feel an affection for her child,—that a man shall be influenced by his interest, . . . —are laws of our general nature, and grounds of evidence in every country."[74]

Encountering the *San Domick* under suspicious circumstances and frustrated in his reasonable expectation that Benito Cereno will develop the mysteries surrounding his vessel and the innocence of his object, the fictional Delano repeatedly turns to just such culturally based presumptions—only to judge incorrectly time and again. Indeed, two of Delano's best-known conclusions correspond to Phillipps's examples of maternal affection and manly self-interest.[75] He is distracted from musing on "any wickedness on board" the *San Dominick* by the sight of a "doe"-like "negress" nursing and kissing her "fawn" in "maternal transports" in a tableau of "naked nature."[76] Soon afterward Delano quells his renewed suspicions of Benito Cereno by adverting to the Spanish captain's presumed racial self-interest, asking himself, "who ever heard of a white so far renegade as to apostatize from his very species almost, by leaguing in against it with negroes?"[77]

If, in his anxious turn to presumptive proof—in his awkward efforts to construct a coherent, authoritative narrative from evident circumstances and the conclusions arising from them—Delano resembles the naval officers, federal judges, and jurors tasked with determining whether or not their fellow citizens were slavers, readers found themselves in a similar position. Immersed in print accounts of the illegal international slave trade (in which "a low, suspicious looking brig was" often "discovered . . . steering for land, but without showing any colors," "the conduct of the Captain and passengers exceedingly suspicious," and thus offering "altogether a very piratical[-]looking concern in appearance whatever she may be in reality"), Melville's contemporaries had already assimilated Delano's wary reading practices.[78] Rather than confirming the novella as a sectionalist allegory, the story's paranoid hermeneutics were consistent with the doctrine of presumptive proof that had repeatedly, in the extensive print coverage of slaver cases, exposed the grim reality of Northern complicity in the international traffic in human beings.[79]

As Delano's initial concern that the approaching sail "showed no colors" suggests, the shipboard object that attracted the most intense scrutiny was a vessel's flag.[80] In an enforcement context where the evidence of things seen often supplanted eyewitness testimony, slavers did not hesitate to manipulate the appearances that spoke on their behalf. And, given jurisdictional constraints on efforts to suppress the trade, the slave ship's flag spoke with particular urgency. The ship's standard thus became a tell-tale in more than the conventional nautical sense, as those policing international waters struggled to discern what story the slaver's fluttering ensign actually told. "The way these American clippers are engaged in the business is this," explained the *New York Herald* in 1839: vessels built and fitted in U.S. ports "sail with American papers and crews" to the West Indies, where the ships "are sold, the American crews discharged and a mixed crew of Spanish, Portuguese and Americans shipped, and a Spanish Captain goes out as passenger. The American commander runs her across to the west coast of Africa"; then, "when all is completed . . . they are away at sea with the Spanish flag flying, and the American captain a passenger in place of the Spanish."[81] Accordingly, "nearly every slaver that has been recently captured, has had an American ship master on board."[82] The choice of flag followed the vagaries of slave trade legislation, as we shall see.[83] But whichever banners slavers chose at a particular moment, they cast national identity to the winds.

As contemporary observers and slavers alike appreciated, the same sensitivity to American sovereignty that shaped federal slave trade laws served as the primary obstacle to their enforcement. After its own belated about-face on slavery, Britain maintained an active, dedicated fleet of cruisers on the coast of West Africa in an effort to suppress the Atlantic trade. In the decades following the Congress of Vienna, European powers evinced a growing willingness to cooperate, signing treaties that allowed, to various extents, right of search to British officers and provided for hearings before mixed tribunals.[84] The United States stood out against this backdrop of concerted action, both for its comparatively severe legislation and its incongruous reluctance to enforce it (much less allow anyone else to do so). Prickly about any maritime incursions on national sovereignty by its former colonial master, recent wartime enemy, and current commercial rival, the United States persistently refused to cooperate with British authorities in the search, seizure, or trial of suspected slavers, thereby encouraging countless American slavers to glide by otherwise vigilant British cruisers.[85] The Webster-Ashburton Treaty of 1842, establishing "a system of joint patrol," temporarily soothed but did not resolve persistent Anglo-American tensions over the slave trade.[86]

Humanitarianism could not be allowed to trump sovereignty, U.S. officials insisted to the ever-larger numbers of Americans whose heartstrings were vibrating in response to sentimental appeals on behalf of the suffering slave. "Every person interested in upholding the rights of humanity, or concerned in the progress of Africa, will sympathize with the capture and deliverance of a wretched cargo of African slaves from the grasp of a slaver, irrespective of his nationality," Commander Foote acknowledged.[87] "But," he felt compelled to instruct his incautiously benevolent countrymen, "it is contrary to national honor and national interests, that the right of capture should be entrusted to the hands of any foreign authority," for "American commerce [would] suffer materially from a power which keeps afloat a force of armed vessels, more than four times the number of the commissioned men-of-war of the United States"—a pointed allusion to Great Britain (300).[88] "The deck of an American vessel under its flag," Foote reminded his readers, "is the territory of the United States, and no other authority . . . must ever be allowed to exercise jurisdiction over it" (300–301).

Ongoing tensions over the rights of search and visit of American vessels by British authorities mounted as the young nation struggled to maintain its political sovereignty and nurture its new economic prowess.[89] In spring 1858 a series of notorious incidents in which English naval officials appeared to make the Webster-Ashburton Treaty a pretext to harass U.S. commercial shipping prompted some to assess, as *Harper's Weekly* put it, the "Cost of a War with England."[90] If, after the War of 1812, Americans ceded the right of search to that "nursery of despotism and despotic habits . . . the English navy," the *National Era* warned, "England will indeed become the mistress of the seas" and the United States (currently "the second Commercial Power in the world") "shall navigate them at her pleasure; our flag will cease to command respect."[91]

By the 1850s, however, any coupling of "our flag" and "respect" in maritime contexts required some rather undignified backpedaling. "Grant that our flag is abused," the writer stubbornly continued, "it is not for them [the English] to correct the abuse."[92] The problem, as the *National Era* knew (and the title of Foote's *Africa and the American Flag* advertised), was that due to U.S. policy and lack of enforcement, the star-spangled banner now flew over the decks of not only American vessels but virtually any slaver seeking to avoid international scrutiny. "The chief obstacle to . . . the suppression of the slave-trade on the coast," Liberia's Governor Thomas H. Buchanan observed in 1839, "is the *American flag*. Never was the proud banner of freedom so extensively used by those pirates upon liberty and humanity as at this season."[93] Thus, in 1842, when the United States finally established its own meager African Squadron, the impetus once again was less to protect African humanity than to assert national sovereignty.[94] ("There need be no conflict between Patriotism and Philanthropy," the *National Era* temporized, "contending for the rights of others, we should jealously guard our own rights.")[95] With American naval officers now policing American commerce, both legal and illegal, British authorities should have no more pretense to board U.S. ships than foreign slavers would have cause to hoist the stars and stripes.

But the African Squadron was no magic bullet for suppression of the slave trade. Neither philanthropy nor patriotism could stop its officers from whiling away their hardship post on Madeira Island and otherwise neglecting their duties. "Oh monotony thy name is coast of Africa," sighed Master's Mate John C. Lawrence to his journal after six months of cruising on the Squadron's *Yorktown*.[96] As Commander Foote's less conscientious colleague Horatio Bridge unapologetically acknowledged, his *Journal of an African Cruiser* (1845), "records not the capture of a single slave-vessel, either by our own ship or any other belonging to the American squadron."[97] (Edited with "pretty large license" by Melville's future friend and neighbor, Nathaniel Hawthorne, Bridge's *Journal* was the inaugural work in that literary nationalist endeavor, Wiley and Putnam's Library of American Books.)[98] The Navy's lack of zeal did not escape public notice: "Why is it that American ships of war never capture a slaver?" the *Colored American* had asked four years earlier, adding "It looks very suspicious."[99]

In this enforcement climate, slavers donned and discarded national ensigns with abandon so as to avoid scrutiny and capture by an international fleet of cruisers. An anecdote from Captain Theodore Canot's nose-thumbing memoir reprinted in the *National Era* played up slavers' dependence on the ubiquitous "flag chest" with its "ample supply" of standards from seafaring nations.[100] When U.S. officers boarded the *Rachel P. Brown* off the West African coast in January 1853, they found "a portion of an American naval officer's uniform" and "bunting sufficient and suitable for a Spanish flag," leading to the surmise that, "had [the slavers] succeeded in getting a cargo of slaves on board, and been overhauled by a vessel of war of any other nation, one of them would put on the American uniform, and pass himself off as an

American officer in charge of a prize; and if spoken by an American, would have shown the Spanish flag."[101]

Anticipating the "juggling play" staged by Babo and Benito Cereno, such mummery was not beneath the U.S. Navy.[102] In 1857 Commander McBlair recounted to his wife how, having fallen in with some "English ships" who "daily display their flags to me . . . I, to disguise the character of my ship, hoist an English flag & pennant," planning, "if we get so near as to speak . . . I must be Captain Smith of Her Majestys Ship *Rose*."[103] Sent to coastal West Africa to protect national sovereignty from the perceived British threat by safeguarding the American flag from misuse by slave traders, the African Squadron only exacerbated the problem when it resorted to slavers' tactics in a sham pageant of British authority. In their efforts to make slavers Fast-Fish, Squadron commanders ensured that American identity remained a Loose-Fish.

Masquerading in the costumes and ensigns of the Western world's maritime powers, slavers also unsettled notions of sovereignty in their very persons, raising questions about the content and borders of national identity. If, in Manhattan, the business end of the trade was handled by John Albert Machado, native Azorian turned U.S. citizen, and William de la Figaniere, naturalized American citizen and son of Portugal's minister to the United States, on the high seas it was conducted by men like Theodore Canot, whom one reviewer described as "an Italian by birth, a Frenchman by descent, a Spaniard by semi-naturalization and trade, an African in habit, and somewhat an American by early association and apprenticeship."[104]

Lubberly legislative assumptions about the transparency of national sovereignty proved to be the Achilles heel of much slave trade litigation. Press coverage of slaver trials makes clear that, more than piracy's legal status as a capital offence or the slaver's moral status as one who had deprived countless people of liberty and even life, the central concern of such litigation was political membership. One such trial, of the *Glamorgan*'s Captain Kehrman, appeared in Boston newspapers in spring 1854, just as the excitement over the trial and rendition of fugitive slave Anthony Burns was winding down. The coincidence is apt, for trials of accused slavers followed a logic that corresponded to, even as it inverted, that of hearings for alleged fugitives. Just as testimony in the Burns case centered less on the act of escape from bondage than on establishing the fugitive's prior slave identity, Kehrman's and other slavers' trials pivoted not on whether the accused had seized, decoyed, received, or otherwise brought "any negro or mulatto" into slavery but on whether the accused was a U.S. citizen or had been in the service of an American-owned or -operated vessel.[105] Due to the exceptional nature of the U.S. statute defining international slave trafficking as piracy, defendants in slaver cases were well advised to disavow their status as American nationals.[106] If slave trading was piracy, went the standard defense brief, the accused was not a U.S. citizen: and, if he were not a U.S. citizen, slave trading was not the capital crime of piracy (at least not under international law). Thus despite James Smith's previously sworn U.S. citizenship and eminently Anglo name, the *Julia Moulton*'s captain furnished testimony that "proved that the prisoner was born in the village of Beden Keser, about 50 miles from Hamburg, in the kingdom of Hanover; . . . that his name was not James but Julius, and that he could not be a citizen of the United States," having emigrated too recently to have been naturalized.[107] At trial First Mate James Willis testified that, although Smith "belonged to [German] Hanover," "sometimes he used English, and sometimes Spanish and Portuguese."[108] Subsequent coverage of a related trial revealed that young "Willy" himself had been born and raised in Amsterdam.[109] A few years later, when things were looking particularly desperate for Captain Nathaniel Gordon, lawyers for that scion of a well-known Yankee seafaring family raised the possibility that Mother Gordon had given birth on the high seas, thereby nullifying her slave-trading son's established U.S. citizenship.[110]

At first, "Benito Cereno" appears to suffer no such ambiguity, consistently designating its characters by nationality. Along with Amasa Delano and Benito Cereno, who are repeatedly referred to as "the American" and "the Spaniard," there are, for example, "a Portuguese oarsman," "a young Spanish sailor," and even "Ashantee conjurors."[111] Such authoritative markers of national origin are belied, however, by the cosmopolitan seafaring world in which the characters meet. Most of the shipboard dialogue occurs in Spanish: "thanks to his frequent voyages along the Spanish main," the Yankee captain could "converse with some freedom in [the] native tongue" of "the strangers" and even receive prompt obedience when "issuing his orders in his best Spanish" (51, 92). All the more discomfiting, then, when drawn by the sight of "such a knot [as] he had never seen in an American ship, or indeed any other" in the hands of an "old sailor," resembling "an Egyptian priest, making gordian knots for the temple of Ammon," Delano finds the man throwing "the knot towards him, saying in broken English,—the first heard in the ship,—something to this effect—'Undo it, cut it, quick,'" in such a way "that the long, slow words in Spanish, which had preceded and followed, almost operated as covers for the brief English between" (76). In the mystifying tangle of identities aboard the *San Dominick*, the confused American captain can no longer maintain the national boundaries that structure his thought, Spain and Phrygia slipping into Egypt just as the sailor's Spanish slides into and out of English.

On boarding the slave-transporting "Spanish merchantman" that suspiciously "showed no colors," Delano is greeted by "a clamorous throng of whites and blacks" who "in one language, and as with one voice, all poured out a common tale of suffering" (49). Rather than offering clarity, this seeming unanimity proves disconcerting to Delano, "perhaps" due to "some such influence" as the following:

> Always upon first boarding a large and populous ship at sea, especially a foreign one, with a nondescript crew such as Lascars or Manilla men, the impression varies in a peculiar way from that produced by first entering a strange house with strange inmates in a strange land. Both house and ship . . . hoard from view their interiors till the last moment; but in the case of the ship there is this addition; that the living spectacle it contains, upon its sudden and complete disclosure, has, in contrast with the blank ocean which zones it, something of the effect of enchantment. The ship seems unreal; these strange costumes, gestures, and faces, but a shadowy tableau just emerged from the deep, which directly must receive back what it gave. (49–50)

The deck of a nation's vessel may have been considered domestic territory, as Commander Foote maintained, but a ship exists in radical isolation from the surrounding cultural contexts that simultaneously give meaning to and authorize displays of identity. Enclosed not by a vibrant national culture (however "foreign" or "strange") but by "the blank ocean," the "living spectacle" disclosed by the ship, unlike that of the house, becomes "unreal" due to the absence of local referents for signifiers like "costumes, gestures, and faces." Thus decontextualized, markers of national identity lose their substance at sea, becoming expressive only of the surrounding oceanic blankness. Jurisdiction notwithstanding, the cosmopolitan setting of such moments of maritime contact call national sovereignty into question by reducing its performance to "a shadowy tableau."[112]

The costumes of those aboard the *San Dominick* are strange indeed, sending mixed messages about class and nation. "Though on the present voyage sailing from Buenos Ayres," Benito Cereno "had avowed himself a native and

resident of Chili" (57); nevertheless, "there seemed something so incongruous in the Spaniard's apparel, as almost to suggest the image of an invalid
courtier tottering about London streets in the time of the plague" (58). Along
with the impotent captain and his "artificially stiffened" scabbard (116), there
is "Don Juaquin, Marques de Arambaolaza," who, in the story's climactic
battle scene, with "a hatchet tied edge out and upright to his hand, was made
by the negroes to appear on the bulwarks; whereupon, seen with arms in his
hands and in a questionable attitude," he "was shot for a renegade seaman"
(113). Similarly "degraded to the office and appearance of a common seaman"
(113), another clerk, Hermenegildo Gandix, confounds Delano by sporting a
"frock, or shirt, of coarse woollen, much spotted with tar" while "revealing a
soiled under garment of what seemed the finest linen, edged, about the neck,
with a narrow blue ribbon, sadly faded and worn" (66). And, of course, there
is the shackled Atufal, whose clanking chains belie his regal origins.

If the *San Dominick*'s captain, passengers, and crew resemble the Anacha-
rsis Cloots congress of witnesses and defendants whose indeterminate
national identities perplexed prosecutors and juries in the era's slave trade
cases, nowhere is there a more equivocal display of sovereignty than in the
novella's famous shaving scene, which first appeared in the same issue of
Putnam's Magazine as the positive review of Frederick Douglass's *My Bondage and My Freedom*.[113] "The mode of shaving among the Spaniards," we are
told, "is a little different from what it is with other nations," due to the use
of a special basin (84). Accordingly, "combs, brushes, and other implements
of the toilet" rest on a washstand opposite a "flag locker" standing "in one
corner, open, exposing various colored bunting, some rolled up, others half
unrolled, still others tumbled"—recalling, in its jumbled, irreverent excess
the similarly "ample supply" of slavers' indispensable flag chests (83).[114] And
of course it is Babo's peculiar requisition of the Spanish flag that endows the
scene with its starkly deflated nationalism.[115] In a passage frequently read as
evidence of Delano's blind acceptance of romantic racialism, the American
captain is "amused with an odd instance of the African love of bright colors
and fine shows, in the black's informally taking from the flag-locker a great
piece of bunting of all hues, and lavishly tucking it under his master's chin for
an apron" (84).[116] Soon afterward,

the agitation of the Spaniard had a little loosened the bunting from
around him, so that one broad fold swept curtain-like over the chair-
arm to the floor, revealing, amid a profusion of armorial bars and

ground-colors—black, blue, and yellow—a closed castle in a blood-red field diagonal with a lion rampant in a white.

"The castle and the lion," exclaimed Captain Delano—"why, Don Benito, this is the flag of Spain you use here. It's well it's only I, and not the King, that sees this," he added with a smile, "but"—turning towards the black,—"it's all one, I suppose, so the colors be gay;" which playful remark did not fail somewhat to tickle the negro. (85)

As even dim Delano appreciates, the significance of such displays lies in the eye of the beholder. Subject to scrutiny by the nation whose flag it exhibits, the suspicious vessel is safe under the American captain's gaze, which, like that of his counterparts in the African Squadron or, indeed, on the federal bench, is narrowed by jurisdictional blinders. As Delano's condescending closing remark registers, however, for virtually everyone else involved in suppressing or conducting the slave trade on the high seas in the 1850s, the semiotics of national sovereignty had become largely moot: "it's all one . . . so the colors be gay." (Hence "the vagary, that in the black he saw a headsman, and in the white, a man at the block" can be dismissed as an "antic conceit . . . appearing and vanishing in a breath" [85].)

If, for the notorious Charles Gibbs and others roving the high seas, the turn to piracy was marked by a collective decision "*to hoist the Black Flag, and declare war against all nations*," transatlantic slave traders—"the only pirates that infest these waters now"—found it more prudent to wave another nation's banner as they waged war simultaneously on African humanity and on national sovereignty.[117] Whereas American slave traffickers had once skirted federal prohibitions by "throng[ing] to the Coasts of Africa under the stained flags of Spain and Portugal," by the 1850s the Stars and Stripes had become the preferred emblem of these modern pirates.[118] Appropriately, then, the famous shaving scene in "Benito Cereno" closes with "the standard of Spain removed, tumbled up, and tossed back into the flag-locker."[119] For, presumably, "during the long, mild voyage to Lima" the San Dominick, now under Delano's command, would have sailed its captive cargo of human beings and its erstwhile Spanish captain, crew, and passengers under the American captain's national ensign (114).

For some readers, the very circumstances of that voyage, combined with Delano's impression of Benito Cereno as "a commander who has little of command but the name," might confirm the Spaniard as "one of those paper captains" that for decades had been featured in press accounts of the illegal slave trade (59). The same December 1820 issue of *Niles' Weekly Register* that featured an article on the Nantucket "Whale Fishery" (including Melville's inspiration for *Moby-Dick*, the ill-fated *Essex*) published court documents from the case of the slaver *Science* stipulating that "the Spanish captain . . . shall only have the title" of his position, while "the command" of the vessel was to remain with his American counterpart.[120] As Judge Van Ness explained in the *Plattsburgh* case covered in the same article, "a *capitan de papel*, as the Spaniards call him, [is] a mere man of straw" furnished with fraudulent paperwork that allowed him to stand in for American principals seeking to avoid federal prosecution.[121]

But if, on the *San Dominick* as on the *Science* and the *Plattsburgh* and other piratical slavers, "the Spaniard" is "only *capitan de papel*," then who is responsible for the ship?[122] The American who supplies captain, crew, and slaves alike with much-needed water and other provisions? The American who "secured" the "surviving negroes" and refitted the ship before piloting it to various South American ports?[123] The American who stands to profit from the safe return of the slave ship and its precious human cargo?[124] "Considering the lawlessness and the loneliness of the spot and the sort of stories, at that day, associated with those seas," could an antebellum reader—a reader far more willing than Delano "to indulge in alarms . . . involving the imputation of malign evil in man," especially "in view of what humanity is capable"—be blamed for seeing in Melville's American captain less a resemblance to Commander Foote than to Captain Canot?[125] Or for discerning in the Spanish slave ship's apparently accidental encounter with the U.S. vessel a striking reenactment of preconcerted meetings of slavers with American auxiliaries?

"There is certainly something in these proceedings," Judge Van Ness intoned in the *Plattsburgh* admiralty case, "that exposes them to decided and just suspicions."[126] But if, like the jury at a slaver's trial, the novella's readers cannot ultimately create a sufficiently incriminating narrative out of such an accumulation of suspicious circumstances, they too nevertheless may have found themselves left with unsettling questions about American complicity in the slave trade, the illegibility of national identity, and, perhaps most disturbing, the fickleness of legal personhood in a slaveholding nation.

Inhuman Beings

Provoking hermeneutic crises from Africa's shores to America's parlors, the federal designation of international slave trafficking as piracy also posed a

generic predicament. For the 1820 statute did not merely increase the criminal sanction for what had once been a well-established form of maritime
business and labor; it risked romanticizing slavers as the embodiment of the
anti-authoritarian, democratic ethos that made pirate stories so appealing in
an era of rapid industrialization and proletarianization. Recast as a pirate,
would the slave-trading merchant seaman become a paragon of masculine
agency who, unconfined by statutes or borders, glamorously represented "a
culture of masterless men"?[127]

Master's Mate John C. Lawrence of the African Squadron seemed to
think so. After months of mind-numbingly dull "philanthropic cruising,"
Lawrence's ship, the Yorktown, finally seized a prize in late September 1845.[128]
It is admiration, not repugnance, that the twenty-one-year-old naval officer
must suppress upon meeting his first slave-trading pirates. The Patuxent's
captain and mate, Lawrence enthused to his diary, are "two as bright and
intelligent looking men as I have seen for a long time" (236)—although the
young naval officer is careful to remind himself that "they are men arrived
at the years of discretion and of course fully aware of the chances against
them in this precarious and, I must conscientiously add, nefarious game"
(236). Three months later, when the Yorktown captured the Pons, Lawrence
made a similar conscientious addition as he described "the wretched slaves
(created my fellow beings) confined on board" (276). Whereas the slaves'
captivity mitigates their humanity, the slavers' answerability, combined with
their intelligence and physicality, only heightens their appeal for the young
New Yorker. The Patuxent's mate in particular, Lawrence gushes, "is a man
about as well calculated for an enterprise where danger and daring and action were necessary to the achievement of any object as I can now think of
or remember ever having seen. He is all vivacity and perception apparently,
with a frame that indicates the utmost of muscular power to be expected in
the human frame" (236). Driven to redundancy in his breathless appreciation for these masculine American embodiments of "danger and daring and
action," the young naval officer articulates his countrymen's ambivalence
toward those whose slave trafficking, however "nefarious," resembled a
high-stakes "game" that awe-struck American spectators followed through
the medium of print. The opposite of "the wretched slaves" whose abjection
obscures their humanness, the pirate's powerful "frame" limns human capacity at its "utmost."

It is precisely to block such unwholesome identification that Henry
K. Brooke claimed to have published his luridly illustrated pocket-sized

compilation, *Book of Pirates: Containing Narratives of the Most Remarkable Piracies and Murders, Committed on the High Seas* (1841). Knowing that his book would meet with disapproval from "well disposed persons" concerned that in such works "vice is depicted in colours of so specious a hue that it is rather calculated to fascinate than disgust," Brooke defended his publication's "strictly moral" value for "the youth of this country" even as he sought to slake the "popular taste for the curious and horrible."[129] The trick, Brooke insisted, was to be careful "in all cases to visit crime with its punishment" (x).

However monitory Brooke's young—or seafaring—readers may have found the grisly execution accounts that usually concluded his sensational tales of murder, mutiny, and robbery on the high seas, their newspaper-reading counterparts would have looked in vain for such punitive endings to real-life stories of slave-trading piracy in the years before the Civil War.[130] Far from being "deter[red . . .] from the commission of some direful enormity," aspiring slave traders might well have found encouragement in the failure to visit crime with its punishment in such cases (x). Prior to Nathaniel Gordon's execution, most slave traders indicted for piracy easily skipped bail, were acquitted, received light sentences, or were pardoned. Whatever moral satisfaction American public opinion derived from seeing the 1820 piracy law "proudly incorporated into our statute book" clearly did not translate into support for its enforcement.[131] And yet, the dangers of young men growing up to become pirates, and slave traders in particular, would have been apparent to anyone observing the trials of James Smith, Joseph Smith, or Charles Kehrman—for the very reasons that explained more famous pirates' heroic allure.

The sincerity of Brooke's faith in the didactic worth of exemplary punishment aside, his elaboration of the source of popular "interest" in pirates provides insight into contemporary anxieties arising from the recent move to prosecute slave traders as pirates. "Pirates, robbers, and murderers, from the days of Robin Hood . . . to the present time," Brooke observed, "have been *heroes* in the mind of the old and young, rich and poor, the learned and the illiterate" (x). Brooke, whose preface concludes with lengthy extracts from Byron's "Corsair," asserts the universal attractiveness of such rogues to a nineteenth-century American culture steeped in Romanticism: "We are all of us alike in one point,—we all admire that which is active and enterprising, however destructive, in preference to that which is passive and perhaps at the same time more beneficial" (x). Master's Mate Lawrence doubtless would have agreed.

As noted earlier, it was a sense that such maritime derring-do "now can only be found in that lawless traffic, the Slave Trade" that prompted *Graham's* to promote the slaver narrative as a true-to-life modern-day pirate story. Beyond the occasional odd resonance with Melville's "Billy Budd, Sailor" (c. 1886-91), "The Slaver" merits attention for its revealing solution to the narrative challenges posed by the author's self-conscious attempt to update, combine, and Americanize the literary figures of the pirate and the slave trader. Set fifteen years after passage of the 1820 statute, the tale tells the story of the mysterious man behind "the celebrated slaver 'La Maraposa;' who, for three years, had been setting at defiance the whole naval force on the African station."[132] Charles Willis lives an untroubled double life until he meets the lady of his dreams. Passing in Cuban society as "a young American, high in the confidence of the government, who had been sent out to the West Indies on a special mission," Willis suffers growing internal anguish as "the dark thought of his present position obtruded itself. He was a slaver—an outlaw! and in the estimation of many in the world, worse than a pirate" (10). The nemesis of "the handsome slaver" is Captain De Vere, an aristocratic British naval officer (117). Captured by De Vere, tried and condemned in Havana, and then rescued by his beloved Francisca (and her father's gold), Willis embarks on "one more voyage in the slave trade" with "the old Spaniard's money," planning to use "the capital remaining" to "begin a new and honorable career, and win . . . the hand of Francisca" (68). Once again facing capture on this final trip, the escaped convict, "determined never again to be in chains," blows up his ship off the African coast. Surviving the blast, Willis is rescued by a passing vessel—captained, of course, by De Vere, with Francisca and her family for passengers (116). When De Vere is conveniently dispatched by Willis's delusional, vengeful Spanish first mate, the young American is free to return to Cuba and relinquish the trade for cozy domesticity with his new family.

In keeping with his ship's name (Spanish for "Butterfly," a footnote informs us), Willis undergoes a series of metamorphoses that seem consistent with earlier Anglo-American portrayals of the barbaric European trader debased by his participation in the international traffic in slaves (3).[133] The most dramatic occurs when, having exploded his ship near the West African coast, the American captain, "grimed and black with powder," becomes racially unrecognizable (116). The *Graham's* blackface trader differs from his eighteenth-century counterparts, however, in that his declension is a civil rather than a cultural one.[134] For in antebellum narratives like "The Slaver," the trade's new and exceptional legal status as piracy ensured that the figure of the American slaver provoked, rather than transcended, urgent questions of national identity and civil capacity. A federal statute establishing that pirates "throw off their national character" was passed in 1790, just one month after the nation's first naturalization act restricted eligibility for citizenship to "any free white person."[135] The question was, having thrown off their American character in a strategic bid to evade federal law, did slavers reveal an underlying nationality?[136] Or did they, like the defense's image of infant Nathaniel Gordon, bob about in a sea of nationlessness, as blankly void of authentic civic identity as the "nondescript crew" manning Melville's "unreal ship"—or, for that matter, poor Pip in *Moby-Dick*? The slaver narratives of the 1840s and 1850s consistently register the risk of these unaccountable white male selves losing the citizenship and civil capacity that had hitherto protected them from the civil death to which they consigned their human cargo. Having chosen a life of exile over death on the gallows, the "begrimed, sunburnt, blood-stained, and skeleton figure" of Charles Willis evokes less the "white savage" of Hannah More and Philip Freneau than the dirty, emaciated, ailing slaves who populated antebellum reports of captured slavers.[137]

The narrative resolution of "The Slaver" illustrates how the terms of the trader's declension had shifted from cultural debasement to political exclusion. Captain Charles Willis, the scape-gallows pirate turned family man, undergoes the kind of civic transformation envisioned by the era's penal reformers. "In all that vicinity," the story concludes, "no one has a higher character for kindness, charity, or benevolence, than Don Carlos Willis; . . . but none know that the good man, whose name they all unite in praising, was formerly the notorious slaver! the outlaw! the desperado of the 'MARAPOSA!'" (120). What appears to be a romance of sentimental redemption and national vindication can attain closure only by insisting on Willis's ultimate illegibility as a U.S. citizen. The reformed slaver's expatriate reputation for civic virtue cannot compensate for the citizen's failure to take responsibility for his crimes. Thus the same notorious American who, following an encounter with a British man-of-war, had once hoisted "a large white burgee, with 'Willis' on it, in conspicuous blue letters, to let her antagonist know to whom she was indebted" (5), has metamorphosed into the unrecognizable "Don Carlos Willis." Having gained his dark-eyed lovely, her father's well-stocked plantation, a male heir, and a new Spanish name, the slaver has lost not only his ship with its signature burgee, but also (and here it bears recalling that "burgee" is thought to derive from the Old French *burgeis*, or citizen) the

unquestionably American "character"—criminal or otherwise—that the slaver's flag had defiantly signaled.[138]

If the slaver, "compris[ing] all the wickedness and blood-thirstiness of
the pirate; the recklessness and determination of the smuggler; with the
coolness, skill, and knowledge of the merchant captain," proved irresistible
to antebellum romancers, the changing literary fate of the trader-cum-pirate
lay in the very nature of his business (1). Both Henry K. Brooke and Master's
Mate Lawrence celebrated the pirate's "enterprise" in an era when "the bold,
arduous, or momentous undertaking" denoted by the term was increasingly
connoting a "commercial or industrial undertaking," especially "one involving risk; a firm, company, or business."[139] Ironically, it was this recent liberal
configuration of business, law, and individual agency that deprived antebellum slavers of the pirate's definitive autonomy in midcentury print culture.
The "egalitarian," "collectivist" ethos of eighteenth-century pirates, historian
Marcus Rediker maintains, arose in response to an increasingly exploitative
merchant marine that anticipated subsequent forms of industrial capitalism
by aggregating and commodifying labor in a tightly disciplined hierarchical
structure.[140] Pirates may have romantically declared war *against all nations*
and in turn been deemed *"hostis humani generis"* under international law,
Rediker suggests, but piracy also mounted an important challenge to the inhumanity of maritime commerce and labor. In his modern-day incarnation
as a slave-trafficking bourgeois, the antebellum pirate embodied the exploitative, authoritarian, disciplinary, hierarchical excesses he would have once
avenged. A far cry from the swashbuckling freebooters who dashed across
the pages of Brooke's *Book of Pirates*, American captains and merchants
flouted federal law not out of a renegade scorn for middle-class society but,
on the contrary, to gain a solid footing in the United States' highly competi-
tive market economy.[141]

Although still depicted as a "fierce and remorseless captain," or a "fiend,"
the nineteenth-century slave trader increasingly appears as that quintessentially American type, the ambitious businessman with his eye on the
main chance.[142] When, in a jailhouse interview with the New York *Evangelist*,
Captain James Smith recollected his reluctant decision to ship on the *Julia
Moulton*'s last, fateful voyage, he sounded less like a vicious slaver than a conscientious professional: "I tried to get another captain to take charge of my
ship," he explained, "I wanted to stay at home and get married. *But good men
in our business are scarce.* And I had to go."[143] Indeed, affirmed the *Evangelist*,
"the noble captain seemed ambitious of a higher career."[144]

That "the captain and the crew of the ship are not the only pirates engaged in" the slave trade and, in fact, "there are ship-builders and mercantile speculators involved" was driven home when, along with Captain Smith, "respectable ship chandler, Wm. C. Valentine, was also arrested, charged with furnishing supplies for the trade."[145] Illustrating the extent to which "the slave trade with Africa is a branch of the mercantile profits" of New York, the *Julia Moulton* cases revealed how "the cruelties of the darkest crimes of the darkest ages are pharisaically enacted by parties claiming to be gentlemen."[146] The city's entire business community seemed implicated: not merely those "who sell shackles," but those "who sell rice" and "persons who purchase the privilege from the Croton Water Department" of supplying "fifteen to forty thousand gallons of water" to slave ships.[147] As a result of this extensive complicity, shrilled the *Tribune*, "there are now in New York, wallowing in wealth, living in sumptuous palaces up town, and driving splendid equipages, men called merchants, who for years, uninterruptedly, have been engaged in the infernal slave trade, and who, if they had their deserts, according to law, would be swinging on the gallows as high as Haman."[148]

The same outraged public awareness that could, at least figuratively, consign professional Northern "gentlemen" to the gallows for their piratical slave-trading activities imaginatively relegated their subordinates to what many would have seen as a fate worse than death. If, as naval historian Donald L. Canney concludes, the desire for "fast, American-built vessels; immunity from search; and growing profits" ensured that "the trade was becoming 'an American business'" by midcentury, the trade offered an extreme version of the supervision and discipline to which such enterprises increasingly subjected their laborers.[149] As Jacksonian references to "white slavery" and "slavery of wages" indicate, Americans feared that such nominally "free" laborers' dependency threatened to reduce them to the status of African American bondpeople.[150] "But for the name of liberty, the slave of the United States is in the enjoyment of as much comfort and happiness as those of the domestic class, the laboring class," asserted "the Rev. Dr. Winans" to the New York Colonization Society just after the annual meeting had received a report of the capture of the "'Pons, of Philadelphia,' with her 900 slaves."[151] Winans's provocative proto-Fitzhughian claim was met with a mixture of "hisses and applause, which continued some time."[152] As this response and the minister's own qualified phrasing implied, the "name of liberty"—as opposed to the lived experience of civil liberty enabled by property ownership and manifested in personal autonomy—appeared to many in the antebellum

United States to be the one thing distinguishing so-called wage slaves from hereditary life-long bondpeople. (Slaves, after all, could look white, and free laborers certainly included people of color.)

Works like Richard Henry Dana Jr.'s *Two Years before the Mast* (1840) and Melville's *White-Jacket* (1850) focused these racially inflected class anxieties on the figure of the (white) seaman. After having "flogged" the sailor Sam "like a beast" for protesting that he is "no negro slave," Dana's brutal Captain T– turns to the crew, shouting, "'You see your condition! . . . You've got a driver over you! Yes, a *slave-driver—a negro-driver!* I'll see who'll tell me he is n't a negro slave!'"[153] But then again, asks *Moby-Dick*'s well-born Ishmael just before contracting to sail with tyrannical Captain Ahab, "Who aint a slave?"[154] The conditions of maritime employment, the denial of civil rights to common seamen, and the long-standing rhetorical association of sailors with slaves ensured that slave trade litigation both played to and aggravated contemporary concerns about the precise meaning of "the name of liberty" when applied to laboring white men at sea—especially those employed in the comparatively low-status slave trade.[155] Crimped or trepanned aboard, sailors on slave ships could find themselves shackled, flogged, refused wages, denied access to the courts, and even incarcerated in slave forts.[156] In contrast to the slave-trading merchants and captains who had long evinced bourgeois aspirations, pretensions, and values, historian Emma Christopher observes, the slaver seamen of "indeterminate legal freedom" had at once a much more direct and ambiguous relationship to the "business of 'making' slaves."[157] These men's firsthand participation in the process by which persons were transformed into commodities shaped their own struggles to define themselves as (normatively) white, free working men in an occupation that, like slavery, was characterized by debased labor, physical captivity, and corporal punishment.[158] The process of enslavement in which slave traders were so intimately involved reinforced the value of legal personhood while calling attention to its precariousness.[159] In the nineteenth-century United States this process was part of the larger phenomenon in which an emerging white working class defined itself against the nation's largely enslaved black population.[160]

Any compensatory sense of freedom and autonomy sailors may have derived from their participation in the slave trade was powerfully countered by the very real threat to their liberty posed by arrest, prosecution, and even execution under the 1820 piracy statute. Congress and the federal courts were expanding the definition of piracy to include slave trading just as state legislatures were enfranchising the full brotherhood of white men (increasingly regardless of class and even national origin) and the literary sailor was asserting his "rights as a social and accountable being."[161] Defined by their role in transforming African persons into property, slave-trafficking seamen could not simply define themselves as free white citizens against their enslaved black "cargo," for they risked losing their own civil capacity and national identities when their labor came under legal scrutiny.

The risk that American involvement in the international slave trade might lead to a Cereno-esque evacuation of agency is suggested by the era's closely watched slaver trials.[162] Noting that the *Julia Moulton* "carried a crew of . . . 15 persons, some of them boys," the prosecution's opening argument in the Smith case drew on the conventional equation of seduction with the loss of civic virtue, promising jurors: "How they came on board that ship, what were the representations made to them, and by whom they were made, will be proved to you in evidence. What inducements were held out to these men to go on board this ship and engage in this traffic, will be shown to you."[163] Counsel emphasized the crew's youth as it stoked tensions over coercive maritime practices in order to portray these callow seamen as themselves captives of slavers. And it wasn't only raw hands who were vulnerable: young Henry Fling of New London, Connecticut, testified that "I first discovered the *Julia Moulton* was going on the Slave-trade when they began laying the slave-decks" en route to the West African coast. The experienced young sailor, having "supposed we were going to the West Indies," bewilderedly "thought we were a long time getting there, as I had been there before."[164] Contemporary print accounts of such nonconsensual shipboard labor aligned the involuntary transit of these unwitting slaver sailors with that of the "live cargo" below decks.[165]

As with the courtroom repudiation of U.S. citizenship by slaver captains and merchants, such performances of incapacity served legal purposes: under the Act of 1800, crew members had to have "voluntarily serve[d]" on slavers to be convicted.[166] As they disclaimed responsibility for their presence on slavers, sailors sought to avoid self-incrimination at a time when the privilege was far from secure in practice.[167] Because prosecutors often relied on the evidence of sailors as the only positive proof available in notoriously difficult criminal cases, it was not unusual to find naïve sailor witnesses pitted against wily slaver defendants. (When the fictional Charles Willis is convicted and sentenced to death, "the rest of the crew" are "all pardoned," having testified to "their necessity to obey the commands of Willis, and that when they had

joined the Maraposa they did not know she was a slaver.")[168] Such evasive
legal strategies only ensured that press coverage of these cases would depict
those legally implicated in slave-trading piracy as eerily will-less subjects.
Portraying slavers' efforts to deny culpability, these aconfessional accounts
enacted a parallel denial of selfhood. In the *Julia Moulton* case First Mate
James Willis, the government's key witness, insisted in tense rebuttal to
another witness's testimony: "I never said that I did not know that the *Julia
Moulton* was to be used as a slaver, until after I arrived on the coast of Africa;
I never said that I did not know that she was to be used as a slaver, until a
long time after we sailed."[169] Lost in a welter of double negatives, the Mate's
emphatically repeated "I" finally enacts only its own effacement.

    "Unwilling to repose with implicit confidence on the testimony" of sus-
pected American slaver Joseph Findlay Smith, Judge Van Ness had the option
in the *Plattsburgh* admiralty proceeding to "resort to the acts and conduct
of Smith, as a better and purer source of information."[170] Such external elements of crime "cannot lie," Van Ness affirmed, voicing a conviction shared
by his novel-reading contemporaries.[171] Judge Van Ness's comments suggest
the applicability of Alexander Welsh's insights about Victorian fiction to
antebellum slaver narratives, urging us to consider how, "in novels as elsewhere, circumstantial evidence might emerge as a threat to private being."[172]
When observed actions spoke louder (and more reliably) than self-referential
words, suggested one press report, a slaver's crew could easily be reduced to
ciphers: "None of them knew how they had got aboard, who had shipped
them—where they were going to—what the captain or owners['] names were.
All on board the vessel were Portuguese, and either did not or pretended
not to understand a word of English. The captain was a myth. No one on
board acknowledged the title, or could tell who that functionary was."[173] No
wonder that "circumstances spoke for themselves," the newspaper concluded,
when "the crew on board were not so communicative, but were silent and
non-committal."[174] Refusing to incriminate themselves, slavers went beyond
forcing the authorities to rely on presumptive proof; a frieze of passivity and
silence, these men approximated the lifeless objects they let speak in their
place. Surreally ignorant and passive yet astonishingly susceptible to deceptive inducements, misleading promises, and terrifying threats, even those
whose citizenship was indisputable found that scrutiny of their participation
in the slave trade entailed a disavowal of autonomous legal personhood that,
as Jacksonian men, they should have epitomized.[175] Thus, in the context of the
era's renewed enforcement of and interest in the federal statute making inter-

national slave trafficking a capital crime, to call a slave trader an "inhuman being" (as the *African Repository* did upon the *Pons* capture) was no longer simply to judge the slaver's moral character but, increasingly, to acknowledge his unrecognizability as one of "We the People."[176] The slaver narrative's fascination ultimately lay not in its portrayal of a modern breed of uniquely American pirates, but from its unnerving depiction of those who straddled the precarious fault line separating the legal personhood of U.S. citizens from the civil death of slaves and criminals.

The jurisdictional logic seemed inescapable: to deny culpability was to yield to a self-imposed evacuation of national identity and loss of civil capacity. What, then, could Northerners do when, like *The Minister's Wooing*'s artless Miss Prissy, they realized that their nation's extensive involvement in the business of slavery mean that "there a'n't hardly any money here that's made any other way"?[177] *The Bank Director's Son*, discussed below, offers one solution. With its surprise ending, George Lippard's heavily revised pamphlet novel suggests that only by answering for their complicity in slavery's crimes could America's mortified citizen-subjects restore themselves to full political life. Without such accountability, Lippard's novel and other slaver narratives warn, Jacksonian men risked becoming insubstantial fictions.

Paper Captains

If false legal papers make the nominal Spanish commander a mere *capitan de papel*, in slaver narratives his American counterpart becomes a "paper captain" in a literary sense—the flimsy product of his own and others' fabulations.[178] More common criminal than dashing buccaneer, the slaver is nevertheless prevented from articulating an inner self by these stories' insistently aconfessional quality. Because they center on their putative narrators' culpability, even the most formulaic, ventriloquized, or coerced print confessions necessarily posit a causal human agent—Locke's forensic self. With their depictions of slave traders' sometimes ingenious, occasionally daring, but more often mundane evasions of criminal responsibility, slaver narratives create an ebbing selfhood that seems to vanish altogether when faced with law and its representatives. No longer accountable legal persons, these elusive subjects, fictional or otherwise, become impotent, commoditized characters. This process is encapsulated in a magazine interview with Captain James Smith at his cell in New York's Halls of Justice ("the Tombs") and more fully elaborated in *The Bank Director's Son*. There, Lippard presents confessional narrative as the salubrious alternative to an enervating first-person storytelling that reduces the irresponsible slave trader to the stock character of cheap fiction.

The *Evangelist* introduced its profile of Smith by attributing the convicted slaver's candidness to the fact that his case turned on the question of national identity rather than his involvement in slave trading: "though he protests against the condemnation, on the ground that he is a foreigner, and not amenable to the laws of the United States, he does not deny the fact of his share in the business. He speaks of it freely, and relates with unconcealed exultation the particulars of his wild and desperate career."[179] Smith "told his own story not like a criminal making a confession, but rather with the freedom and pride of an old soldier relating his battles," observes the interviewer, who authenticates "the truth" of Smith's narrative by noting that "his account is consistent with itself; it agrees with what was proved on the trial, and with the descriptions in Capt. Canot's book." As if to excuse publication of Smith's personal story—which would resurface in *Frederick Douglass' Paper*, the *National Era*, *De Bow's Review*, *Graham's Magazine,* and *Littell's Living Age*—the *Evangelist* goes on to insist that, as a result of the old salt's extravagant boasting, "his disclosures . . . are public property."[180]

Smith's jurisdictional challenge to his piracy conviction seems initially to preserve his political identity while staving off civil death: in the act of personal storytelling he resembles "an old soldier" rather than a confessing "criminal," and indeed expresses a desire to exchange his profession as slave-trading pirate for that of privateer. But the defensive origin of Smith's claim to be "a foreigner" undermines his assertion of *any* national identity. If it is unclear which nation James, a.k.a. Julius, Smith of Beden Keser, would represent as "an old soldier relating his battles," his counterfactual civic self-fashioning as a privateer equipped with "a well built clipper" and a (congressionally issued?) "letter of marque" seems to grope after his jettisoned membership in the American polity. The *Evangelist's* appropriation and retailing of the slaver's aconfessional narrative illustrate how such printed disavowals of U.S. citizenship threatened to strip professional white men like Smith of far more than criminal culpability. Smith only appears to "speak . . . freely" as he tells his story from his cell. For, rather than taking narrative responsibility for his acts—and thereby constructing and asserting an interior self "like a criminal making a confession"—the incarcerated Smith's larger-than-life account of "his wild and desperate career" reduces him to a fictional character in his "own story." Absent a self to claim ownership, that story and its main character, Captain James Smith, become "public property." Only apparently basking in "freedom and pride," the subject of that story is, like its enunciator, buried in the Tombs.

The *Evangelist*'s Smith is not unlike Lippard's titular bank director: as the "embodiment of indomitable energy, and grasping meanness, which in modern days is called a 'business man,'" Mr. Jacob D. Z. Hicks is "just as good a man as hundreds whom you meet every day ... in the Exchange ... and ..., withal, no better than any ninety-nine out of a hundred convicts in the Penitentiary."[181] Hicks acquires his fortune through a series of financial scams and the illegal slave trafficking that he, along with several other Philadelphia merchants, conducts through a (recently executed) Captain Velasquez. Evidence of Hicks's crimes lies in the "heavy volume, which resembled a merchant's Ledger," which the banker keeps hidden in his home office; in it "were entered ... not only those operations which are told to the world, under the head of the 'stock market'" (21–22), but also those that "implicated some four or five respectable houses in the profitable transactions of the African Slave Trade" (50).

The *Bank Director's Son*'s main characters, however, are the rival members of the "Killers" street gang who can each claim the eponymous filial identity. Cromwell Hicks, recently disowned as the bastard son of Hicks's adulterous wife, embarks on a slaving voyage from New York with Don Jorge, fellow Yalie and the son of executed Cuban slaver Don Velasquez. Cromwell returns to Philadelphia just as Elijah Watson, the banker's real but unknown biological son, has served out his prison sentence for counterfeiting a note from one of the senior Hicks's sham banks. "Condemned ... to be buried alive for the space of four years" at Eastern State Penitentiary (20), Elijah realizes upon release that his experience as Convict "Number Fifty-One" prohibits rather than enables his reentry into society (29). (Exposed as a felon, "the silent compositor" is dismissed from his hard-won printing job as he is setting type for an article on "The Gospel nature of the Gallows" [22, 24].)[182] The young men thus personify the two sides of criminality as conventionally imagined by popular fiction. Whereas his "sunburnt" slave-trading surrogate (33), now the swaggering leader of the Killers, appears to represent the enterprising masculinity of the typical pamphlet-novel pirate or gang member, Elijah, with his "corpse-like face," embodies the civil death of the felon (34).

Yet a reversal occurs when, in the Killers' den, the pair engage in an impromptu round of personal storytelling that discloses the slaver narrative's generic instability as pirate yarn even as it confirms the confession's

Self-constituting effects. The slaver Cromwell's "stirring narrative . . . spoke much of life in Havana—of life on the coast of Africa—of slave ships stored thick and foul with their miserable cargo—and of the manner in which certain mercantile houses, in the north, made hoards of money, even at the present day, by means of the Slave Trade" (35). Told in a "leisurely" fashion and "punctuat[ed] . . . with draughts of whisky and puffs of cigar smoke," Cromwell's hackneyed tale comports with his stylized public persona. By contrast, Elijah's rendition of his altogether "different story" transforms him from within: "There was something like eloquence in the manner of the Con-vict" as "his pale face lighted up, and his eyes shone" while he tells "the story of his wretched Life—a brief but harrowing story, commencing with the life of an apprentice at the work bench, and ending with the life of a Convict in the Eastern State Penitentiary" (35). Having "turned away in involuntary loathing" from the slaver as he told his tale, the "circle of 'gallows' faces" reconvenes as an appreciative audience, "shudder[ing]" sympathetically in response to Elijah's account (33, 35). Like real-life pirates Charles Gibbs and James Smith before him, "the hero of the Slave Ship" becomes attenuated to a two-dimensional character in his own swashbuckling fiction, whereas the convict's confessional narrative actively produces both an inner self and public recognition of that self (35).

Stopping Lippard's galloping plot in its tracks, this seemingly random storytelling scene recapitulates a similar duality in the novel's own com-position history. As the *Life and Adventures of Charles Anderson Chester, the Notorious Leader of the Philadelphia "Killers"* (1850), the shorter version of the pamphlet novel had fictionalized the October 9, 1849, election-day riot in which the Irish Catholic Philadelphia gang known as the Killers of Moyamensing burned down California House, a tavern which, owned by a light-complexioned African American man with a white wife, had served an interracial clientele.[183] This compressed version of the novel resembles the other "action-filled adventures about various types of wanderers or outcasts such as corsairs, freebooters, pirates, [and] criminals" that, David S. Reyn-olds reminds us, were so popular in the 1840s.[184] But Lippard literally revised the genre in the longer version of the novel, which reappeared in multiple formats: as "The Killers," an unsigned serialized novel that commenced on December 1, 1849, in *Quaker City Weekly*, a.k.a. "Lippard's Newspaper"; an anonymous 1850 pamphlet novel of the same name "by a Member of the Philadelphia Bar"; and finally *The Bank Director's Son* "by George Lippard."[185] With its comparatively cosmopolitan, intricate plot linking the city's corrupt merchants to the illegal slave trade, this more expansive (and apparently more accessible) version bucked the generic trend toward depoliticized sensationalism that, Reynolds notes, "reduced even the most serious radical-democrat themes to the flat level of diverting adventure, virtually devoid of serious political or metaphysical significance."[186] Placing the taint of criminality on slave-trading merchants rather than street thugs, Lippard politicizes this more substantial version of his novel by interweaving the gang and slave-trafficking plots to designate the "Merchant and his confederates—all Respectable Killers."[187]

Like its predecessor, the revised novel climaxes in an election-night race riot that burns down a black-owned groggery on Philadelphia's southern city limits. *The Bank Director's Son* rewrites this scene of chaotic civic dissolution, dispensing to Lippard's slave traders the justice in narrative form that they have so successfully eluded in its legal manifestation. Elijah's ghastly appearance may inspire Cromwell to compare him to "a subject on a dissecting table" (34), but it is ultimately the American "Slaver," his slave-trafficking paternal namesake, and his Cuban partner in crime, not the ex-convict, who appear in positions traditionally occupied by black corpses (41).[188] Stabbed by tavern-keeper Black Andy (whose unmotivated violence is emblematic of his racial identity), Cromwell "quivered for a moment like a man suspended on a gibbet" before collapsing "quiet and motionless" at the black man's feet (42), while, in an upper room, his quondam father, suffering from smoke inhalation, "falls upon the floor and lays there, like a bundle of 'forgotten goods'" (47). The Hicks men's charred remains soon become indistinguishable from those of the black villain in the anomic riots that occur in that civic no-man's-land, Philadelphia's "Barbarian District" (35). Meanwhile—lest we miss the point—back downtown, in Hicks's secret study, Don Jorge "lay dead upon the floor, as dead indeed, as any Negro that he had ever pitched from the deck of his Slaver; in the midst of the broad Ocean" (48). In a nice Lippardian touch, Don Jorge has been shot by a self-triggering pistol concealed in the booby-trapped box containing the bank director's incriminating financial records. The "merchant's Ledger" literally becomes the smoking gun of the business community's complicity in the crime of slavery (21).

Having paid his debt to society at Eastern State Penitentiary, Elijah is spared such compensatory literary retribution, escaping to the newly admitted state of California with his beloved, pure, and suddenly sexually available foster sister. He bankrolls their new life by using Hicks's ledger (pried from Jorge's dead hands) to blackmail the "four or five respectable houses" who are "implicated . . . in the profitable transactions of the African Slave Trade" (50). Living happily ever after upon their doubly ill-gotten gains, Elijah and sister Kate at first appear content to join their fellow Americans in exchanging complicitous silence for a share in the indirect profits of the slave trade (and thus of slavery itself). Lippard disrupts such a conclusion, however, with an incongruous footnote indicating that Elijah and Kate have restored the papers to the Philadelphia businessmen only *after* revealing the incriminating documents to the authorities.

The footnote, which features an "extract from the Message of President Taylor . . . to Congress, on the 24th of December, 1849," effectively reinscribes Elijah Watson's revivifying narrative of personal accountability on a national scale. As the president directs Congress's "attention . . . to an amendment of our existing laws relating to the African slave trade, with a view to the effectual suppression of that barbarous traffic," Taylor acknowledges that "this trade is still, in part, carried on by means of vessels built in the United States, and owned or navigated by some of our citizens," noting that it is "a customary device to evade the penalties of our laws by means of sea letters" (50).[189] The excerpted presidential address then closes with a final, tantalizing assertion that "much additional information of the same character, has recently been transmitted to the Department of State." Thanks to Kate and Elijah's intervention, Hicks's incriminating "papers" will enable federal authorities to prove the falsity of paper captains' "sea letters" in the international slave trade.

Tacking this genuine public document onto his fictional tale, Lippard does more than fraudulently authenticate his "Real . . . Revelation of City Life." The footnote further revises the plot of this extensively revised novel to suggest that it is by exposing Philadelphia's slave-trading merchants to the authorities that Elijah attains the civic resurrection that Eastern State Penitentiary, that municipal "stone coffin," so notably fails to provide (31). With the fate of the three slavers serving narrative rather than legal justice, that of Elijah Watson shows how slavery's dirty profits could be not only laundered but cleansed of their criminal taint. Businessmen, the embodiment of the slaveholding nation's bourgeois capitalist society, must, through their fellow citizens' conscientious initiative, be held as accountable for their collective crimes as the individual convict is for his comparatively petty crime against that same corrupt society. In the absence of such government scrutiny and intervention, Lippard allegorically suggests, the Northern "Merchant and his confederates" will continue to be nothing but "Respectable Killers" (50).

Conclusion

Inspired by the legal-literary twist of fate that changed everyday merchants and seafarers into pirates, *The Bank Director's Son* and "The Slaver," like "Benito Cereno," registered the cultural apprehensions attending that transformation. If slave narratives, with their testifying eyewitnesses, exposed the United States to censure before the bar of public opinion, slaver narratives, with their denationalized, incapacitated subjects, suggested an even greater threat to national "freedom and pride." Americans' refusal to accept responsibility for slavery, these aconfessional accounts intimated, might well signal the core emptiness of their shared civic identity. Even worse, the passivity and silence that these most representative citizens displayed when charged with the federal offense revealed the incapacity that slavery imposed on the nation's white, as well as its black, inhabitants.

That the loss of civic identity and legal competence depicted in print portrayals of illegal slave traders bespoke an imaginary rather than actual cession of power should be obvious. (What better proof than the persistent failure, throughout the antebellum period, to prosecute federal statutes to their fullest extent?) But if the civil declension in print of the white, male, American slaver did not reflect historical and political realities, it nevertheless illuminated pervasive antebellum concerns about the uncertain premises of personhood and belonging in a slaveholding nation. This was because the constitutive conundrum of "American slavery, American freedom" (however self-enabling) presented the young nation with far more than an embarrassing contradiction.[190] With its unstable foundational distinction between those who could claim property in themselves as persons and those whose lack of civil standing authorized others to claim them as property, the legal fact of slavery put citizens on shaky ground, placing Americans in perpetual danger of slipping into the civil death reserved for those human beings defined as property—or categorized as criminals. What made the increased policing and litigation of anti-slave-trading statutes in the 1840s and 1850s so unsettling was that, however narrowly defined, *any* federal recognition of slavery's criminality necessarily implicated all U.S. citizens.

For hadn't most citizens profited in some way from slavery? When, in "The Slaver," Charles Willis's indictment is read to him at trial in Havana, the American's second-person response addresses not only the fictional tribunal but *Graham's* real-life readers: "Guilty I am! . . . as who that hears me is not? but, that I am more worthy of condemnation than even you, my judges, or than the accuser, I deny! 'Tis true, I have been guilty of bringing negroes from Africa to this island. But wherein am I thereby more guilty than you?"[191] Bringing the charge even closer to home, Stowe in *The Minister's Wooing* unambiguously implicates the novel's quintessentially American community of folksy Yankees in the slave trading practiced by commercial elites. In the only part of Rev. Hopkins's climactic sermon to be presented in direct discourse, the minister insists that "all who have had any hand in this iniquitous business, whether directly or indirectly, or have used their infuence to promote it, or have consented to it, or even connived at it, or have not opposed it by all proper exertions of which they are capable,—all these are, in a greater or less degree, chargeable with the injuries and miseries which millions have suffered and are suffering, and are guilty of the blood of millions who have lost their lives by this traffic in the human species."[192] Lest any uncertainty remain in the minds of his—and Stowe's—Northern audience, the fictional Hopkins maintains that "not only the merchants who have been engaged in this trade, and the captains who have been tempted by the love of money to engage in this cruel work, and the slave-holders of every description, are guilty of shedding rivers of blood, but all the legislatures who have authorized, encouraged, or even neglected to suppress it to the utmost of their power, and all the individuals in private stations who have in any way aided in this business, consented to it, or have not opposed it to the utmost of their ability, have a share in this guilt."[193]

"Who aint a slaver?" Melville's Ishmael might just as well have asked his fellow Americans.

Conclusion

Let us return to the gallows portrait depicting "two sweeps, one of whom was represented as a negro, and the other as a mullato speaking the German language," at prayer before their hanging for the murders of Pennsylvania Dutch matrons Anna Garber and Elizabeth Ream[1] (see Figure 8). The illustration from *Das Manheimer Trauerspiel* (1858) is a fascinating visual artifact. The delicate steel engraving of Henry Richards and Alexander Anderson on the Lancaster County scaffold offers a more nuanced version of the crude woodcuts that, since the colonial period, had portrayed the execution ritual in print. As the English-language edition of the pamphlet reveals, however, the image also subtly marks a break from this tradition. For pasted into *The Manheim Tragedy* (1858) is the salt-print photograph on which the engraving is based. Caught in their final minutes, the condemned men seem frozen in time, memorialized by a photographic technology that belies its all but obsolete iconography (see Figure 15).

With its penal-technological asynchronism, the image captures a fleeting transitional moment in the history of race, representation, and public death in America. After the Civil War, depictions of the state-administered executions became almost exclusively verbal.[2] At the same time, photography became the medium of choice for documenting the nation's newly racialized ritual of lynching.[3] Like its predecessors, the *Manheim* portrait is dominated by the gallows that materializes the execution of a capital sentence—literally, its legal apparatus. Accordingly, from the woodcut on the *Dying Confession of Pomp* broadside and the pamphlet illustrations of the Gibbs-Wansley hangings to the mattress-ticking painting of William Freeman's fictive execution, crowds of solemn onlookers affirm the civic function of the juridically mandated ritual (see Figures 3, 6 and 13). By contrast, lynching photographs, with their improvised nooses, natural settings, and jeering crowds, convey that extralegal ritual's anti-civic purposes. What distinguishes the *Manheim* photograph from both sets of images is its carceral enclosure. Instead of an open field, a town common, or a forest, the backdrop for the Anderson-Richards

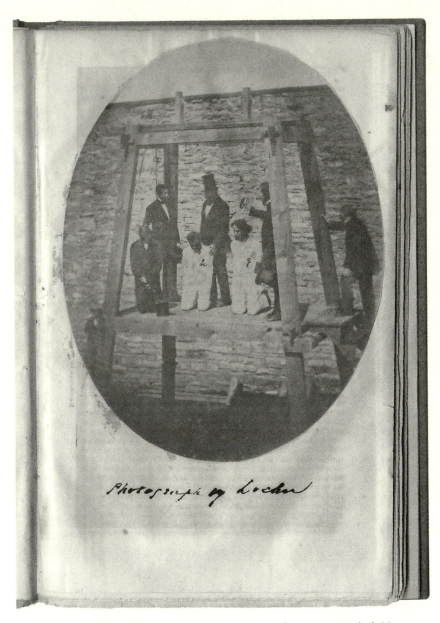

Photograph by Locher

Figure 15. Salt-print photograph by M. H. Locher, from H. A. Rockafield, *The Manheim Tragedy. A Complete History of the Double Murder of Mrs. Garber & Mrs. Ream: with the Only Authentic Life and Confession of Alexander Anderson. Together with a Correct Account of the Arrest, Trial, Conviction, Sentence, Death-Warrant, and Execution of Anderson and Henry Richards, His Accomplice; To Which is Appended some brief Reflections on the Causes and Consequences of Crime* (Lancaster, Pennsylvania, 1858). The Library Company of Philadelphia.

hanging is the high prison wall whose top aligns, not coincidentally, with that of the scaffold itself. In the Library Company of Philadelphia copy of the pamphlet, hand-inked letters designate each of the scene's actors, a reminder that the image depicted an intimate performance conducted by identifiable individuals. Absent are the anonymous, massed crowds that, in earlier images, mediate between the condemned and governmental authorities—or, in lynching photographs, replace the latter altogether.[4]

In this way, the *Manheim* photograph graphically documents the penal reform trend that, by bringing the public execution ritual "indoors," also contributed to its privatization, textualization, and eventual bureaucratization.[5] But, read alongside the pamphlet's verbal portrayal of Alexander Anderson and within a black scaffold tradition reaching from Joseph Hanno to Nat Turner, the photograph also portends the carceral confinement of the African American subject after Emancipation. The *Manheim Tragedy* marks the end of the path that this study has mapped out as an alternative to the more familiar route from plantation to prison. Inadvertently widening the gap between the contradictory fictions of the slave's mixed character and the social compact, Execution Day's printed gallows texts created an opening for a first-person subject that, having exceeded the narrow confines of culpable personhood with its civic self-assertion (however fictive), might eventually lay claim to a civil standing. Rather than confining the black subject in a succession of total institutions, this historical conjunction of penality, due process, and print publicity made conceivable the African American protocitizen conjured by the antebellum slave narrative. The challenge, as the contrasting examples of James Williams and William Freeman have shown, was to decriminalize the black print persona without ceding the legal responsibility that for over a century had elicited acknowledgment (however formal, punitive, and retroactive) of political membership. This challenge was intensified as the nineteenth-century asylum movement issued an increasingly authoritative call for the custodial supervision of a free black underclass that would only grow more populous after the Civil War and Reconstruction. The publication of *My Bondage and My Freedom* affirmed the ascendancy of the autonomous (and normatively male) African American self that would prove so indispensable to subsequent political, legal, and social activism—from Booker T. Washington's *Up from Slavery* (1901) to Alex Haley's *Autobiography of Malcolm X* (1964) to Barack Obama's *Dreams from My Father* (1995).

Published three years after Douglass's autobiography, the comparatively obscure *Manheim Tragedy* points to how, by midcentury, the path hewn by the combined forces of penality and publicity had reached an impasse in the encompassing carceral space of the prison. To understand why criminality ceased to provide access to civic presence, it helps to recall Jürgen Habermas's account of how interpersonal communication expands the physical locales where civic rituals are performed into the abstracted, shared social space known as the public sphere.[6] (For Habermas "a second-person attitude" that goes beyond mere observation to mutual address and recognition is essential to this ongoing process.)[7] Traditionally seen as the apparatus by which the physical gave way to the metaphysical, the scaffold became, through newspaper items, published sermons, and pamphlet criminal confessions, the site where the architecturally defined religious and political event of the public hanging opened into this broader discursive arena. Launching the black condemned into eternity, the legal-literary rite of execution propelled them as responsible individual subjects into the imagined community of the nation—and, sometimes, into the republic of letters.

The *Manheim Tragedy* photograph visually chronicles how, midway through the nineteenth century, this penal trajectory began to double back on itself. No longer encircled by unbounded civic space, the scaffold is enclosed by the high walls of the prison which, simultaneously excluding the general public and confining the condemned men, helped, in Austin Sarat's words, to "change execution from a public display to [a] semiprivate bureaucratic event."[8] This development was a remarkably gradual one that would not achieve full rationalization until after the Civil War.[9] Already in the *Manheim* photograph, however, critical reciprocity in even its most symbolic, attenuated form has been eliminated. Just a few years earlier, Herman Melville could still vividly imagine Babo's head "on a pole in the Plaza," posthumously meeting, "unabashed, the gaze of the whites" as it "looked towards" the graves of his enemies.[10] The 1858 photograph instead offers a unilateral sightline much like that provided by the two-way mirrors and closed-circuit televisions through which today's state-administered lethal injections are covertly observed by a select group of witnesses. With this constriction of the visual field, the *Manheim* portrait anticipates a radical shift in the semiotics of the death penalty. Rather than occasioning the articulation (however fictive or ideological) of an inner selfhood, today's executions direct scrutiny to the exterior surface of the condemned's physically restrained and pharmacologically passive body.[11]

The *Manheim Tragedy*, of course, still offers the first-person perspective of one of the condemned men in the form of the "Confession" attributed to Alexander Anderson. Every bit as rare as the salt-print photograph depicting the execution scene is the verbal image H. A. Rockafield, editor of the local Lancaster *Evening Express* and the pamphlet's compiler, presents of Anderson as condemned author. During a visit to the prisoner's cell, Rockafield finds "Anderson sitting on his stool, near the door and in front of a small writing stand, securely ironed."[12] "These irons," Rockafield explains, "secure both feet, and cause great difficulty to the wearer in moving about, the two staples which encircle the ankles being connected with a strong sliding bar, secured with set-screws at the end" (25).

Chained at, rather than to, his desk, the prisoner is presumably composing what the pamphlet's title page bills as "the Only Authentic Life and Confession of Alexander Anderson." If, as Rockafield notes, "the idea of having it published for the benefit of his wife and children seems to have occurred to him before his trial" (during which "the janitor was freely offered fifty cents a head for admission into the court room"), the packed proceedings doubtless spurred Anderson's authorial ambitions (26, 19). Apparently more concerned about his "Life" than his life, Anderson refused to be scooped by enterprising journalists like Rockafield. "The reason I did not tell the truth at the Court House, even to my lawyer, or the judge," Anderson explains in his interpolated account, "was because I knew there was some anxious to get it to publish; but as I knew I must die, I wanted it published for the benefit of my poor wife and children. I told Henry [Richards, Anderson's co-defendant] not to tell how the murder was done for the same reason. There was several who wanted to get my confession, and offered to pay me for it, but I refused them all, and they would have liked very much if I had told all about it when the Judge sentenced us, but I kept the truth to myself, for this purpose" (42).[13]

The chimney-sweep-turned-axe-murderer sits at his writing desk "securely ironed" with shackles that, through iconic and racial association, link the "mullato" convict to Anderson's enslaved brethren south of the Mason-Dixon line. Indeed, Rockafield's account invites comparison with the scene in *My Bondage and My Freedom* depicting the would-be fugitives' incarceration upon exposure of "The Run-Away Plot." Frederick and his fellow captives face "a swarm of imps, in human shape—the slave-traders . . . that gather in every country town of the state, watching for chances to buy human flesh, (as buzzards to eat carrion,)" and who, as Douglass recalls, "flocked in upon us, to ascertain if our masters had placed us in jail to be sold."[14] Confined following an informal "sort of examination" and thus only apparently treated "like felons," the slaves receive summary punishment that merely reinforces their chattel status. However brute-like the predatory slave traders themselves may be, the parallel between the slaves' commodifiable "human flesh" and "carrion" illustrates the incommensurability of the slaves' unquestioned (and highly marketable) humanity with the culpable legal personhood that would have at least temporarily retracted their property status.

Not unlike the pageant in Easton jail, a swarm of visitors descends on the imprisoned Anderson, eager to purchase his "Life." Unlike the Maryland runaways, however, the Pennsylvania felon retains, even augments, his self-possession upon apprehension by assiduously protecting his property right to that textualized "Life." When, in an uncanny echo of Frederick's whisper to his co-conspirator, Anderson urges *his* Henry to, in effect, "Own nothing," the legal and print publicity attending the formal proceedings make all the difference. For it is by owning nothing in court, the *Manheim Tragedy* suggests, that the condemned African American murderer comes to own something in prison, specifically the "profits" that, as proprietary author, prudent investor, and conscientious husband and father, he leaves to his family.[15] As if to underscore this point, the fugitive slave advertisements and bills of sale that Douglass, Harriet Jacobs, and other formerly enslaved authors reproduced as authenticating devices in their personal narratives are replaced in the *Manheim Tragedy* with another sort of facsimile legal document.[16]

With "no less than three copy-rights" issued "for titles purporting to cover confessions of Anderson and Richards," the prefatory "Word from the Publisher" establishes "this book" as Anderson's "only authentic Life and Confession" by affirming that it is "published under the following agreement, the obligations of which, on our part, will be carried out to the very letter":

> LANCASTER COUNTY PRISON, March 4, 1858.
>   Know all men by these presents, that I, ALEXANDER ANDER-
> SON, now in the Lancaster County Prison under sentence of death,
> do hereby appoint H. A. ROCKAFIELD sole agent to publish and sell
> my life and confession, at such price as he may think proper. . . . the
> profits from the sale to be . . . invested either in real estate security or
> city coupon bonds, the interest thereof to go to my wife during her
> natural life, and the principal to my children, provided they have at-
> tained their age before her demise.
>   Witness my hand and seal this fourth day of March, 1858.
>   ALEXANDER ANDERSON, {SEAL.}
> Witness present at signing: RUDOLPH RESSLER. (3)

With this ostensibly (and ostentatiously) legal document, the *Manheim Tragedy* presents not merely *A Complete History of the Double Murder of Mrs. Garber & Mrs. Ream . . . with a Correct Account of the Arrest, Trial, Conviction, Sentence, Death-Warrant, and Execution of Anderson and Henry Richards, His Accomplice*, but the equally intriguing story of how one of the "authors of the bloody deed" became a published author (6).

Transforming the condemned man's last will and testament into a publishing contract, the *Manheim Tragedy* telescopes the trajectory from early American gallows literature to professional African American authorship. A century and a half after Cotton Mather presented "a Picture of *Hell* . . . in a *Negro* then *Burnt* to *Death* at the Stake," the pamphlet depicts Alexander Anderson asserting authorial control over his personal narrative by withholding it not only from competing publishers but from the very judicial process that authorized the black malefactor's entry into print. This evocative portrayal of the shackled, scribbling, contracting Anderson might well serve as a set piece illustrating how punitive recognition by the legal system, in conjunction with the ongoing American fascination with crime publications, contributed to the process by which, under the legal regime of race slavery, criminality enabled the performance of civil personality. The Anderson figured forth by the pamphlet appears not only as a condemned criminal of color, but as a legal person competent to perform civil as well as criminal acts. In a nation where African Americans continued to be represented in law and in print primarily as human commodities, Anderson's avowed authorship of his bloody deed underwrites his civil capacity as party to the publishing agreement, as testator, and thus as patriarch. Occasioning his civic role as author of his printed confession—not to mention posthumous investor in "real estate security or city coupon bonds"!—Anderson's criminal culpability activates and publicizes in jail the civil standing that for many free African Americans remained uncertain outside its walls. Portrayed as one of the "authors of the bloody deed" *and* as a professional gallows author, the Alexander Anderson of the *Manheim Tragedy* stands as the individual embodiment of a more abstracted, protracted literary historical phenomenon.

But just as the insistent "author" of *My Bondage and My Freedom* gestures to the incriminating confessional paper trail stretching out behind the antebellum slave narrative's new black protocitizen, the *Manheim Tragedy*'s Anderson points toward a future in which black civil activity, instead of merely being misapprehended as criminality, might just become coterminous with it. Reading the pamphlet's account of Anderson's jailhouse authorship alongside the gallows photograph of Anderson and Richards, we can see how the responsible selfhood constituted by the condemned man's printed personal narrative, rather than expanding out into an open civic space and its abstracted corollary, the public sphere, is now confined within the imposing masonry that surrounds the scaffold. Especially after the Civil War, the boundaries of the prison would enclose not just increasingly private, efficient state-sponsored deaths, but ever greater numbers of African American *lives*. Here, then, is the point at which the civil death of the slave merged into that of the prisoner.[17] The *Manheim Tragedy* presaged how, after the Reconstruction Amendments, conviction would no longer offer, through punitive acknowledgment of political membership, an inadvertent occasion to complement the culpable personhood of the criminal black subject with a consummative civic presence. Instead, like the individual lives pent by the thick, high walls of the prison, African Americans' birthright citizenship could now appear to be contained by and fulfilled within such carceral spaces. For even as it releases a fictive, textualized "Alexander Anderson" to circulate posthumously in print as a self-articulating public authorial persona, Anderson's will-cum-publishing-contract also suggests how black civility might be realized under the necropolitical conditions of confinement, segregation, and supervision authorized by the *Civil Rights Cases* (1883) and *Plessy v. Ferguson* (1896). In the wake of an emancipation that was national rather than individual or sectional, the absence of the legal fiction of the slave's mixed character radically revised the racialized relationship of criminality to subjectivity in American print culture. Instead of providing entry into a broader form of recognized legal personhood through publicity, the legal processes of prosecution, conviction, and punishment now entailed the custodial isolation that for so many critics has linked the post–Civil War prison to the antebellum plantation. No longer merely providing the terms by which to apprehend African American political membership, criminality has, from the blues to hip-hop, from Chester Himes to Sanyika Shakur, and from *Cops* to *The Wire*, become the *normative* base line from which to measure African American subjectivity.

That, along with black criminality, an evacuated white civic identity might be slavery's ultimate legacy in a newly reconstituted Union is suggested by Edward Everett Hale's short story, "The Man Without a Country," published five years after the *Manheim Tragedy*. Hale's enduringly popular and influential Civil War fiction commences when the narrator, naval officer Fred Ingham, comes across an obituary for Philip Nolan, who has died at sea, prompting him to present Nolan's life story as a cautionary tale "showing young Americans" what it means to relinquish membership in the national polity.[18] As a young officer in the army's western division, Nolan is "seduce[d]" into Aaron Burr's scheme to set up a separate nation in Louisiana Territory (366). In a local version of Burr's treason trial, Nolan is tried and, when asked "whether he wished to say anything to show that he had always been faithful to the United States, he cried out, in a fit of frenzy,—'D--n the United States! I wish I may never hear of the United States again!'" (666–67). Composed largely of Revolutionary War veterans, the military court sentences Nolan to having his wish fulfilled. In practical terms, this means that "from that moment, September 23, 1807, till the day he died, May 11, 1863," Nolan is exiled to a series of government vessels and barred from hearing any discussion of or receiving any information about the United States (667). At first Nolan's punishment offers little hardship: he is comfortably provided for and, having "grown up in the West" and been "educated on a plantation, where the finest company was a Spanish officer or a French merchant," the "'United States' was scarcely a reality" for the young man (667). Through a series of epiphanies, however, Nolan comes to value his forfeited national identity, even as he himself is ultimately forgotten by his countrymen. ("Every official report relating to him was burned" in the attack on Washington, while "to the press this man's story has been wholly unknown" [665].) Dying confident that "there is not in America,—God bless her!—a more loyal man than I," Nolan is granted his deathbed request to be told "something,— . . . everything" about his homeland. In a sympathetic gush, Danforth, his keeper, "tell[s] in an hour the history of fifty years" (678). Determined as he is to tell Nolan "everything I could think of that would show the grandeur of his country and its prosperity," Danforth admits, "I could not make up my mouth to tell him a word about this infernal Rebellion!" (679).

This reticence over the Civil War makes it all the more significant that one of Nolan's epiphanies regarding his plight as stateless exile arises from a fleeting moment of identification with the enslaved. Ingham encounters Nolan "in the first days after our Slave-Trade treaty" when the narrator is serving as midshipman in the African Squadron (673). Upon "overhaul[ing] a dirty little schooner which had slaves on board" (673), the Americans are greeted with "a scene" of "nastiness beyond account, and chaos run loose in the midst of nastiness" (674). The source of the chaos is the Africans' confusion about their fate. "By way of making" them "understand that they were free, [Captain] Vaughan had had their hand-cuffs and ankle-cuffs knocked off, and, for convenience' sake, was putting them upon the rascals of the schooner's crew," when the liberated slaves surround him, "addressing him in every dialect" (674). Nolan saves the day when he volunteers to serve as Lusophone interpreter for Africans formerly employed in the slave trade who will translate "in turn to such of the negroes as could understand them" (674). "Tell them they are free," Vaughan instructs Nolan, "and tell them that these rascals are to be hanged as soon as we can get rope enough." Nolan's speech is met with "a yell of delight, clinching of fists, leaping and dancing, kissing of Nolan's feet, and a general rush . . . by way of spontaneous worship of Vaughan, as the *deus ex machina* of the occasion"—until Nolan delivers the second part of the captain's message: "'Tell them,' said Vaughan, well pleased, 'that I will take them all to Cape Palmas.'" Aware that "Cape Palmas was practically as far from the homes of most of them as New Orleans or Rio Janeiro" and that "they would be eternally separated from home there," the Africans through their Krooman translator, "instantly said, '*Ah, non Palmas*,' and began to propose infinite other expedients in most voluble language." Visibly "disappointed at this result of his liberality," Vaughan asks Nolan for an interpretation. The Man without a Country "choke[s] out" a translation: "He says, 'Take us home, take us to our own country" (674). In an "equal agony of sympathy" to that of Nolan for the Africans, the previously obdurate Vaughan promises, "they shall go home!" (675).

Unlike similar scenes in which complacent white liberals emancipate grateful slaves into a dubious freedom (think *Uncle Tom's Cabin's* young George Shelby), here the swelling music of redemption is not chorused with the slaves' servile declarations of loyalty but interrupted by their demands for white accountability. The excessive gratitude with which the Africans initially greet Nolan's announcement is cut short by their realization that freedom will not, in the early national phrasing that had all but disappeared by the Civil War, "restore the[ir] rights" through repatriation to their countries of origin.[19] No longer cargo yet still not legal persons, they risk becoming, like the *Antelope's* Africans, non-individuated recaptives. Acknowledging one of the most persistent sticking points in slave-trade suppression efforts, the story provides, through Vaughan's sympathetic speech act, an alternative to the unspoken ending of many a legal or journalistic slaver narrative, in which official intervention offers not liberty and autonomy, but exile, captivity, forced labor, statelessness, and civil death. A liminal zone on the continuum between "the condition of chattel slavery, and that of complete technical citizenship" evoked by New York State Convention delegate Benjamin Cornell, the condition of nominal freedom means little in the absence of a civic home.[20] If Hale's solution bears a remarkable similarity to colonizationist fantasies that culminate in the (deferred) restoration of black rights outside the United States, here the crucial proviso is that the ethnically and linguistically diverse group of African former slaves are to be literally rather than figuratively restored to their countries of origin and thus not only to their abstract natural rights as humans but to their civil rights as, in *Antelope* prosecutor Habersham's words, "persons of color from some . . . Kingdom of Africa."[21]

Yet Hale's embedded revisionist slaver narrative exposes similar tensions in the larger story's resolution. Much of the tale centers on official efforts to enforce a punitive silence that keeps Nolan in communicative exile from America's public sphere even as the passage of time generates a national history. The climax, then, occurs when the dying Nolan has that fifty-year history narrated to him in an hour—with the glaring omission of the Civil War. Withheld as a kindness to the repentant old man (whose agonies of remorse would only worsen with the knowledge that an entire army was following in his erring, and errant, footsteps), the erratum in the nation's history that for the reader points to the similar fates of the Man without a Country and the Confederate officers also papers over the dilemma posed by Nolan's encounter with the slave trade. Even as the passing acknowledgment that "there were not a great many of the Negroes" aboard the captured slaver renders their projected repatriation more plausible, it prompts the question: what of the millions of newly freed people stateside?[22] In contrast to the recaptives' return, delivery of emancipated U.S. slaves to Africa would be not only expensive and impractical (as foes of colonization had long maintained) but inappropriate, an act of banishment, not repatriation. Under the story's own exilic logic, such a colonizing trick could only tragically affirm the freedpeople's Americanness. Although, as discussed below, Lincoln's recent Emancipation Proclamation is strikingly absent from Hale's story, it is nevertheless tempting to see in Vaughan's intervention a model of the kind of benevolent white activism that would usher the unruly freedpeople (and the nation) through the immediate "chaos" of emancipation to the security of an internal repatriation that, occurring at home rather than abroad, would be both actual and symbolic.

Ironically, however, Vaughan's vow to return the recaptives (a transparent sublimation of his frustrated desire to repatriate his own captive fellow citizen) ensures that Nolan resembles the captured slavers far more than he does the blacks who are now bound only for home. Introduced at the beginning of the story as "the poor wretch" (665), the multilingual Nolan is linked to the polyglot blacks whom Vaughan initially refers to as "these wretches" by both his cosmopolitanism and his misery (674). Crucially, however, Vaughan's pledge effectively releases the blacks from their wretchedness, from the exile implied by the word's Old English root, whereas Nolan's banishment continues under the captain's authority. Qualified though he may be to voice the recaptives' dread of statelessness, Nolan occupies a position more akin to the arrested slavers.[23] The circle is complete when, confined in the shackles vacated by their former captives and potentially denationalized by their criminal participation in piratical manstealing, these quondam citizens are consigned to the civil death from which the slaves have just been resurrected and in which Nolan remains.

Hale's effort to include the reader in this circuit of identification is anything but subtle: escorted back to the African Squadron ship by the narrator, Nolan urges the young Ingham to learn from the traumatic scene aboard the slaver "what it is to be without a family, without a home, and without a country," admonishing him "never to look at another flag" (675). Ingham keeps the faith when, decades later, he publishes the story "as a warning . . . of what it is to throw away a country" (677). Yet, appearing when the Civil War had already made manifest the dangers of such apostasy, "The Man without a Country" seems less a cautionary tale for would-be traitors, from filibusterers to slave-trading pirates to Confederate officers, than an articulation of loyal citizens' inchoate apprehensions about the fabricated nature of American identity—indeed, of the nation itself.

That the real lesson of Hale's story is intended for constituents of the Union rather than the Confederacy is suggested by the narrator's passing observation, regarding Nolan's presence among "marines" and "sailors," that "the theory was, that the sight of his punishment did them good" (669). But if, like the condemned in early America's Execution Day spectacles, Nolan serves as a negative exemplar to those who witness his punishment, the takehome lesson here is notably different.[24] For whereas public hangings symbolically reintegrated the condemned into the spiritual life of the community through ritualized displays of repentance and forgiveness, and whereas for the black condemned in particular such punitive recognition affirmed their grim, belated entry into the polity, the punishment endured by the Man without a Country represents, finally, not the dangers of statelessness for individual citizens but for the American people as a whole.

The story's elaborate conceit belies the fact that, as actual African

Squadron Commander Andrew Foote would have been quick to point out, Nolan remains on sovereign U.S. territory as he travels on ships that assert American political and economic power throughout the world.²⁵ But, as Melville would have appreciated, Nolan's residence in this floating, satellite United States impels him to limn all the more assiduously the nation that is his psychic home. When Danforth, Nolan's keeper, finally enters the dying man's state room he "could not help a glance round, which showed . . . what a little shrine he had made of the box he was lying in" (677). Following his gaze, Nolan says "with a sad smile, 'Here, you see, I have a country!'" pointing to "a great map of the United States, as he had drawn it from memory, and which he had there" at the foot of his bed "to look upon as he lay" (677). Viewed from the young American's perspective, the map is emblazoned with "quaint, queer old [territorial] names" that betray Nolan's unfamiliarity with the contemporary United States. Denied a vocation as well as a national identity, a history, and even a name, Nolan (known as "Plain-Buttons" due to the lack of national insignia on his uniform) makes "his reading and his notes . . . his profession" (669, 673). If the "note-books" and "scrap-books" that Nolan compiles from his "methodical" Jeffersonian regimen resemble his pastiche "country" in their composite construction, both sets of texts are defined by the absent Americanness at their core (673). Rigorous as Nolan's scholarship is, it must depend on sources that "were not published in America and made no allusion to it" (669). Although such publications "were common enough in the old days, when people in the other hemisphere talked of the United States as little as we do of Paraguay," the legitimacy and relevance of Nolan's scholarship necessarily declines with the rise of the American cultural influence. Marked by its discursive absence from his sources, "the United States" is in Nolan's own texts, at best, a nostalgic, inaccurate fiction.

That the psychic crisis posed by such an ultimately false apprehension of Americanness may well extend beyond the Man without a Country to his erstwhile countrymen is intimated by the patriotic epitaph that provides the story's closing lines. Knowing he will be buried at sea, Nolan asks for a memorial stone "at Fort Adams or at Orleans" inscribed "*In Memory of* PHILIP NOLAN, *Lieutenant in the Army of the United States. He loved his country as no other man has loved her; but no man deserved less at her hands*" (679). The eulogistic assertion that Nolan "loved his country" seems to end the tale on a redemptive note by retroactively affirming his American identity. At the same time, however, the epitaph calls into question the very possibility of such an identity. If, as Nolan's map ("my country") so vividly illustrates, "his country" is a fiction, what of the possessive individualist self premised on affective identification with that fictive, absent country?

But even if (as his surname reminds us) Nolan has no land, he is not therefore a nonentity. This point becomes evident when we recall the story's title: despite his exile status, it is not "The Man," the quite fully realized "Philip Nolan," that is absent from the story, but the "Country" which he is, geographically as well as civically, "without." The country, not the man, is missing. Nolan's—and the story's—United States resembles Gertrude Stein's California: there's no there there. It could be argued that Hale, through the story's fictional narrator, Ingham, a naval officer who "had some influence in Washington," forges with his real-life readers an imagined national community that would render unnecessary, even redundant, any detailed evocation of the United States (675). After all, Danforth's inability to compromise his account of the nation's "grandeur" and "prosperity" with a single "word" about the "infernal Rebellion" that has redefined the Union as such ensures that the "United States" shared by the reader and the narrator is radically different from the one imagined by Nolan even after his sentence has been broken. But because Hale himself is similarly unable to make Emancipation part of the story (thereby anticipating the tendency to define the war in terms of Southern rebellion rather than American slavery), the "United States" conjured by the story remains fundamentally incomplete.[26]

This lacuna is all the more remarkable given an earlier scene that seems to fill in the absent Americanness at the story's core with a distinctively black civic presence. At a shipboard party an "English lady . . . called for a set of 'American dances,'" upon which, "the black band . . . conferred as to what 'American dances' were, and started off with 'Virginia Reel,'" proceeding through other "contra-dances" until, "just as Dick, the leader, . . . bent forward, about to say, in true negro state, 'The Old Thirteen,' . . . the captain's boy tapped him on the shoulder, whispered to him, and he did not announce the name of the dance; he merely bowed, [and] began on the air . . . —the officers teaching the English girls the figure, but not telling them why it had no name" (671). The early national confusion about what designates an "American" dance is cleared up when the "black band" plays the Scottish folk dances that, popular in New England, have in the South been further domesticated through the very African American cultural adaptation on display here. The danger that naming this particular dance will contravene Nolan's sentence is averted when the band leader is silenced and the piece's Americanness disappears into a set of unidentified "figures." For Dick to name "in true negro state, 'The Old Thirteen,'" would be to make the United States present in a way the English lady's call, the other songs' titles, or mere dancing could not, voicing the nation in an explicitly black, and thus authentically American, idiom. With its own silence about the Emancipation Proclamation, the story seems similarly reluctant to articulate, in place of either Nolan's absent "country" or its own more complete but still fictive Civil War nation, a United States in which both the legacy of slavery and the presence of free African Americans were definitive realities.

Furthermore, as the free speech case that inspired "A Man without a Country" demonstrated, Lincoln's wartime crackdown on civil liberties made such selective fictions safer than more realistic critical assessments of the nation.[27] As its title indicates, "The Man without a Country" is an exercise in imagining a self in the absence of citizenship. This, of course, is the task that had faced African Americans since the nation's founding.[28] But the story's immediate political context also encourages the reverse speculation: to imagine a nation lacking a political self, as it were—a United States suddenly without the constitutional (and constitutive) civil liberties guaranteed to normatively white men like the young Philip Nolan. If, in the first thought experiment, the story's silence about Emancipation precludes it from pursuing the reparative trajectory suggested by Nolan's identification with the newly freed slaves, Hale's fable nevertheless says a great deal about a national identity premised on similar omissions.

Framed by an obituary and an epitaph, the scriptive markers denoting Philip Nolan's physical death, "The Man without a Country" presents a compelling narrative of one American citizen's civil death. But the story's creative penalty offers insight into how crime and punishment inflect political inclusion in the United States. The terms of Nolan's sentence stipulate to naval captains that he is to be provided "with such quarters, rations, and clothing as would be proper for an officer of his late rank, if he were a passenger on your vessel in the business of the government"; he is, moreover, "to be exposed to no indignity of any kind, nor is he ever unnecessarily to be reminded that he is a prisoner" (668). To all outward appearances, Nolan continues to look like a common American citizen, albeit one with greater civic duties ("in the business of the government"). One of Nolan's earliest and most poignant realizations of his condition comes when the first ship to which he has been assigned finally begins its journey home, with all the usual rituals by its giddy crew. Encountering en route an "outward-bound" ship, the captain exchanges "poor Nolan and his traps" for "homeward bound men[,] letters and papers"

(670). Nolan looks "very blank when he was told to get ready to join her," his face betraying "distinct evidence of something he had not thought of, per-haps,—that there was no going home for him, even to a prison" (670). Spared the usual "indignity" meted to the prisoner, Nolan is also denied the punitive recognition that would enable him to inhabit the nation's carceral spaces.

This exceptional nullification of Nolan's political membership is literal-ized when, a decade or so after his sentencing, "they began to ignore the whole transaction at Washington" (672). Well-intentioned naval officers who, like the narrator, seek a pardon for Nolan find "it was like getting a ghost out of prison. They pretended there was no such man, and never was such a man" (675). That the U.S. government bureaucracy's determined denial of Nolan's personhood is clearly a pretense does not diminish its devastating effectiveness. The difficulty of getting a ghost out of prison, after all, lies not in architectural barriers but in the ghost's own insubstantiality. And it is here that Nolan's virtual indistinguishability from other citizens becomes not only relevant but chilling. Absent the legal recognition that due process and other civil liberties enact, not only the man but his (former) countrymen are at risk of becoming "very blank." (Old Colonel Morgan, the Revolutionary War veteran presiding over Nolan's court martial, delivers the sentence "with a face like a sheet" [667].)

Ironically, Nolan's bureaucratic erasure commences at "about the time" when his heroic (albeit unplanned) participation in "one . . . of the great frig-ate duels" of the War of 1812 leads the captain to affirm, "you are one of us to-day; you will be named in the despatches" (671–72). But more than civic virtue, what ultimately makes Nolan "one of us" may be his delusive embrace of an American identity as false as it is idealized. Nolan's actual death occurs in "the little shrine he had made of the box he was lying in," thereby materi-alizing the process in which his civil self is buried in the American identity that has been withheld from him. From this bizarre deathbed Nolan greets Danforth's (unfulfilled) promise to tell him "everything" about his country with a quietly smiling "white face" that figures, at once, his racial identity, his ongoing civil death, and his impending physical dissolution (678). Encased in its coffin-like shrine to an incorrectly imagined America and eagerly re-ceiving a national history from which both slavery and Emancipation have been deleted, that eerily smiling white face offers a ghostly warning of how "one of us" can be imprisoned—if not buried alive—in a national identity as unsubstantial as the self it constitutes.[29]

If the horror of Nolan's sentence arises simultaneously from its extravagant unorthodoxy and its uncanny familiarity, it also provides an instructive contrast to the more common but no less horrific civil death assigned to African Americans since the nation's founding. They, like Hale's liberated slaves, refused to conceive of themselves as people without a country. For to be without a country was to be, as the *Antelope*'s and other recaptives knew all too well, denied legal personhood. And so, like the "negroes" in Hale's story, African American activists "propose[d] infinite other expedients in most voluble language," often through the newly accessible medium of print. One such expedient was to expand the established civic presence of the black persona, derived in large part from colonial and early national gallows literature, into the protocitizenship of that new form of first-person black life-writing, the slave narrative.

Providing an opening wedge for the more expansive political and literary presence claimed by a subsequent generation of African American authors, the texts ascribed to the black condemned made possible a forward-looking (if counterfactual) vision of a political membership that exceeded the punitive and the formal. The difficulty of fulfilling such a vision is suggested by the fiction of Edgar Allan Poe, Herman Melville, George Lippard, and Edward Everett Hale, each of whom registered how the national failure to take responsibility for the crime of slavery threatened to make citizenship resemble civil death.

Under such apprehensions, American literature stepped forth from the shadow of the gallows.

Notes

Introduction: How a Slave Was Made a Man

1. See Berlin, *Many Thousands*, 9; V. Smith, *Self-Discovery*, 24–27; Waldstreicher, "Reading."

2. Gates, "Writing," 11–12. Acknowledging the political and cultural dangers of assigning such a role to Afro-diasporic literature, Gates does not question its instrumentality in achieving this transformation. Because "there are . . . few humanistic disciplines so completely dominated by a single scholar's ideas as African American studies is by Gates's," the current generation of critics finds it "necessary to point out" the perceived "shortcomings" of his work "more emphatically than" would be the case "were his influence less consequential." Jackson, "Talking," 293n6.

3. See Fanuzzi, *Abolition's Public Sphere*, 83–128.

4. Gates, *Figures*, 4, xxiv.

5. Here and throughout, the word "man" is used advisedly: in the contentious gender politics of race and abolitionism as well as in the context of antebellum discussions of citizenship, "man" had undeniably gendered connotations; see Leverenz, *Manhood*, 108–34; McDowell, "Making Frederick Douglass"; Gates, *Figures*, 108; Gates, "From Wheatley," 47–65; Franchot, "Punishment"; Yarborough, "Race"; Sale, *Slumbering*; M. Wallace, *Constructing*, 53–107. See also Sánchez-Eppler, *Touching*; Foster, *Written*, 76–94; C. Peterson, *Doers*; Wiegman, *American Anatomies*; Hartman, *Scenes*, 79–112; Garfield and Zafar, *Harriet Jacobs*; Zaeske, *Signatures*; Hong, "Ruptures," 3–29. Focusing on the gradual development of a normatively if often tacitly male public civic selfhood in print from the colonial through the antebellum periods, the current study eschews the scholarly tendency to impose the gender-neutral language of our era retroactively on these texts.

6. See McHenry, *Forgotten Readers*; Foster, "Narrative," 736n5; J. Brooks, "Early American"; see also McCarthy, "To Plead." For critiques of the emphasis on individualist life-writing; V. Smith, *Self-Discovery*, 34–35; Newman, Rael, and Lapsansky, *Pamphlets*, 22; J. Brooks, *American*, 12.

7. *Independent Gazetteer; or the Chronicle of Freedom* (Pa.), May 28, 1787.

8. Marr, Introduction. Less African than Arab, the Algerine passes for a French gentleman.

9. *Independent Gazetteer*, May 28, 1787.

10. Gates, *Figures*, 25.

11. In return for advertising revenue, newspapers provided special free services to their slaveholding clients, keeping inventories of slaves wanted or available for purchase, as well as making their offices available for such transactions; McManus, *History*, 31; see also M. Wood, *Blind Memory*, 80–94; Waldstreicher, "Reading," 268–70.

12. Gates, *Figures*, 24–25. Parallel structure implies false equivalencies here: animals and slaves were objectified, while human beings and citizens were credited with subjectivity, but human status neither guaranteed citizenship nor precluded enslavement. Given the tendency, discussed below, to treat human and person as synonyms, the broader transformation evoked here would appear to be that of property to person.

13. Ibid., 108.

14. *Independent Gazetteer*, May 28, 1787; for criticism of the pamphlet, see *Independent Gazetteer*, May 30, 1787.

15. *Independent Gazetteer*, May 30, 1787; *Trial of Alice Clifton*, 1, 14.

16. In the U.S., the legal fiction of the slave's mixed character (discussed below) suggests that Patterson's influential designation of the slave's "social death" should be amended to "civil death." J. Brooke, "Consent," 233; Patterson, *Slavery*.

17. Slotkin, "Narratives"; Foster, *Witnessing*, 36; W. Andrews, *To Tell*, 33; Sekora, "Black Message," 489; Starling, *Slave Narrative*, 196; D. Williams, *Pillars*; Fabian, *Unvarnished*, 49–116.

18. Bruce, *Origins*, 115; see McManus, *History*, 98; Rowe, "Black Offenders," 697; S. White, *Somewhat*, 64–65; Waldstreicher, "Reading." On these other personae, generally, Foster, *Witnessing*, and W. Andrews, *To Tell*. On the picaresque see Hedin, "American Slave Narrative"; Nichols, "Slave Narrators." On the Spanish picaresque's penal origins, see Echevarría, *Myth*; in the Anglophone tradition the rogue protagonist is more adventurous rascal than roaming criminal; but see Gates, *Figures*, 81–84. On the pious negro, see Bruce, *Origins*, 74, 112–15; B. Dain, *Hideous*, 49–54, 70. On portrayals of blacks in almanacs as sympathetic grotesqueries, see S. White, *Somewhat*, 66–73. Given the white supremacist regime in which blacks were indicted, prosecuted, convicted, and punished, it should be obvious that this book embraces "a nonpejorative definition" of crime, as "those actions that were . . . historically criminal—*i.e.*, in conflict with criminal laws of the time—even if . . . such behavior might be positively characterized as 'convictional crime,' deriving from laudable or reasonable motives or convictions" (Schwarz, *Twice Condemned*, xii; citation omitted).

19. John Saffin, *Brief and Candid Answer*, quoted in Von Frank, "John Saffin," 254.

20. Mather, *Pillars*, 71.

21. See Slotkin, "Narratives"; Bosco, "Gallows Literature"; D. Cohen, *Pillars*; D. Williams, *Pillars*.

22. Douglass, *Narrative*, 80. See W. Andrews, *To Tell*, 43–44.

23. Douglass, *Life and Writings*, 366.

24. W. Brown, *Narrative*, 148.

25. Watkins, *Struggles*.

26. Many different texts could be seen to enact this transfer. See DeLombard, *Slav-*

ery on Trial, 71–98; Ashton, "Slavery"; DeLombard, "Slave Narratives." See also Fabian, *Unvarnished*, 78.

27. Newman, *Transformation*, 131–51; see also Masur, 1831, 9–62.

28. "Alabama Beacon versus James Williams," *[N.Y.] Emancipator*, August 30, 1838.

29. See Brode, *Odyssey*; DeLombard, "Making Waves."

30. "There is no historiography of legal personhood," much less a poetics. Welke, *Law*, 160. The classic study of legal and cultural exploitation of slaves' recognized humanity is Hartman, *Scenes*. Examining how, in the context of race slavery in the U.S., liberalism produced the very concept of personhood that it appears merely to register, Riss demonstrates how "literature worked to disseminate decisive knowledge about the 'person,' assuming a prominent office in arguments both for and against slavery." *Race*, 15–16. Indispensable as this account of the slave narrative's role in this process is, the failure sufficiently to address the legal fiction of the slave's mixed character—leading to the erroneous claim that "the US slave was never a 'person' and thus never forfeited any rights"—limits the study's applicability (203n43; see also 77). For a rare treatment of the distinction between recognized black humanity and denied black personhood see Wald, *Constituting*; see 15, 17, 23, 39, 43.

31. Even the most helpful elaborations of legal personhood are susceptible to this lapse: having explained that, as "entities that have nothing to do with 'human personality,'" legal persons "take on changing capacities variously granted by the state, such as legal rights, freedoms, duties, and obligations," one study goes on to describe slaves and criminals as "degraded below the rank of human beings, not only physically and morally but also politically," composing "a class of citizens who are dead in law . . . bereft of humanity." Dayan, *Law*, 25, 45, 49.

32. Douglass, *My Bondage*, 419.

33. John Bouvier, *Law Dictionary* . . . , 1st ed. (Philadelphia, 1839), s.v. "person"; see *Dartmouth College v. Woodward* (1819).

34. John Bouvier, *Law Dictionary* . . . , rev. 6th ed. (1856), s.v. "person."

35. Edwards, *People*, 27; on the broader national trend, see 224.

36. Ibid.; Dayton, *Before*. On popular legal consciousness, see Hartog, "Constitution"; see also Kramer, *People*; Curtis, *Free Speech*; DeLombard, *Slavery on Trial*, 2–3, 23–24.

37. Douglass, *Life and Writings*, 363.

38. Ellis, "Suffering Things," 96. This difference in reception does not render insignificant the extent to which the commoditization of former slaves' published lives had the effect of reducing their enunciators to the objectified status of property; see L. Cohen, "Notes"; Rohrbach, *Truth*.

39. [V. Smith,] *Narrative*, 13.

40. Karl Marx, *Capital*, quoted in B. Johnson, *Persons*, 140.

41. This tactic often involves a shift from the legal to the religious register, as in Douglass's selection of an epigraph from Samuel Taylor Coleridge for the title page of *My Bondage and My Freedom*: "By a principle essential to christianity, a PERSON is

eternally differenced from a THING; so that the idea of a HUMAN BEING, necessarily excludes the idea of PROPERTY IN THAT BEING."

42. On the consistency of different strands of racial thought as inquiries into human diversity, see B. Dain, *Hideous*. "To try to imagine other people as nonhuman" is not necessarily to succeed; indeed, discursive efforts to dehumanize black subjects often perversely rehumanize them. Cassuto, *Inhuman*, xiii.

43. See Higginbotham and Kopytoff, "Property First," 539; see also Wren, "Two-Fold Character."

44. Pennington, *Fugitive Blacksmith*, iv; see Hartman, *Scenes*; Waldstreicher, "Reading," 261; Gross, *Double Character*; Wong, *Neither*.

45. Madison, Hamilton, and Jay, *Federalist*, 332.

46. Bouvier, *Law Dictionary*, rev. 6th ed., s.v. "person."

47. Edwards, *People*, 97; for similar observations regarding slavery in the colonial Northeast, see Greene, *Negro*, 168; Von Frank, "John Saffin."

48. "Representatives and direct Taxes shall be apportioned among the several States which may be included within this Union, according to their respective Numbers, which shall be determined by adding to the whole Number of free Persons, including those bound to Service for a Term of Years, and excluding Indians not taxed, three fifths of all other Persons." U.S. Const., art. I, sec. 2. "When the word 'persons' is spoken of in legislative acts, natural persons will be intended." Bouvier, *Law Dictionary*. . . . , 2nd ed. (1843), s.v. "person."

49. Madison, Hamilton, and Jay, *Federalist*, 331.

50. Madison's reference to the criminous slave as "moral person" highlights the now rare but previously quite common usage of "moral" as an adjective "relating to, affecting, or having influence on a person's character or conduct, as distinguished from his or her intellectual or physical nature." *Oxford English Dictionary Online*, s.v. "moral," http://dictionary.oed.com.myaccess.library.utoronto.ca/cgi/entry/50168569, accessed Jan. 18, 2010. Relevant throughout this study, this usage will be particularly important to Chapter 5's discussion of moral insanity.

51. Dayan, "Legal Slaves," 80; see Edwards, *People*, 79–80.

52. Edwards, *People*, 221. Proceedings involving slaves were often last to receive such oversight; see Waldrep, *Roots*, 16–24; Olwell, *Masters*, 73.

53. Edwards, *People*, 93–95.

54. Welke, *Law*, 3–6.

55. Madison, Hamilton, and Jay, *Federalist*, 332.

56. Glenn, *Unequal*, 6–55, especially 54.

57. Welke, *Law*; see R. Smith, *Civic Ideals*, 165–242, especially 177, 258, 268; see also C. Holland, *Body Politic*.

58. Kant, *Metaphysics*, 92. This state of affairs was even more evident in the South; see, for example, Olwell, *Masters*, 68–69.

59. D. Walker, *Appeal*, 72.

60. Garrison, Preface, 41.

61. Gates, *Figures*, 105.

62. Starling, *Slave Narrative*, 50–104; Foster, *Witnessing*, 24–43; W. Andrews, *To Tell*, 32–56; V. Smith, *Self-Discovery*, 13–14. Generally, see C. Davis and Gates, *Slave's Narrative*; Gates, *Signifying*. See also Bercovitch, *Puritan Origins*; for parallel Afro-Protestant adaptations of Puritan cultural forms, see Moses, *Black Messiahs*, 30–48, Howard-Pitney, *African American Jeremiad*, 1–14; J. Brooks, *American*. See also H. Baker, *Journey*, 3–29; *Long*, 31, 41–43, 60.

63. Foster, *Witnessing*, 36.

64. W. Andrews, *To Tell*, 33; see also Sekora, "Black Message," 489; Fabian, *Unvarnished*, 49–116.

65. Thanks to Hilary Schor for alerting me to this discrepancy. See Richetti, *Popular Fiction*; Faller, *Turned*; Schramm, *Testimony*; Gladfelder, *Criminality*; Grossman, *Art*; Mascuch, *Origins*.

66. Dayan cited in C. Smith, *Prison*, 50; for other examples, see A. Davis, *Reader*, 61–107; Dayan, "Legal Terrors," 58, 65; C. Smith, *Prison*, 108, 151; Greiman, *Democracy's Spectacle*, 26. On the Northern penitentiary's emergence as an "instrument of counter-definition" to Southern race slavery, see C. Smith, "Emerson," 230n4. Michael Hindus's classic comparative study is the exception that provides the rule's logic; see *Prison*.

67. T. Green, *From Plantation*. On the extension of the slave's civil death to nonwhite prison populations through judicial application of the Eighth and Thirteenth Amendments, see Dayan, "Held," "Legal Slaves," *Story*, and *Law*; C. Smith, *Prison*, 141–71; Oshinsky, *Worse*.

68. For a concise schematization of legal, disciplinary, and biopolitical (or governmental) penal approaches, see Foucault, *Security*, 4. With only passing mention of the earlier period, one study inadvertently participates in the scholarly "underexamination of the historical roots of modern discourses of race and crime," especially vis-à-vis statistics. Muhammad, *Condemnation*, 281n3. Focusing on print engagements with criminal due process, the current study does not take up the biopolitical police measures so brilliantly examined in Wagner, *Disturbing*.

69. Dayan, *Law*, 64. On early modern associations of race, slavery, and crime, see Jordan, *White over Black*, 51–55, 69; Nyquist, *Arbitrary*; more generally, see D. Davis, *Slavery in Western Culture* and *Slavery in the Age of Revolution*.

70. Gilroy, *Black Atlantic*, 19.

71. Carretta and Gould, *Genius*, 1.

72. See also Butterfield, *Black Autobiography*; Stepto, *Behind*; Sidonie Smith, *Where*.

73. Among anthologies, the exception is Carretta, *Unchained Voices*; otherwise, see Gates and Andrews, *Pioneers*; Potkay and Burr, *Black Atlantic Writers*; J. Brooks and Saillant, *Face Zion*. See also Bruce, *Origins*; Mackenthun, *Fictions*; Rice, *Radical*; Zafar, *We Wear*; Moody, *Sentimental*; Drexler and White, *Beyond*; Elrod, *Piety*; May, *Evangelism*. Briefly mentioning Mohegan minister Samson Occom's execution for his fellow "Indian," Moses Paul, Brooks does not discuss early black gallows texts; J. Brooks, *American*. This neglect is most striking in recent work on the centrality of death in

Afro-diasporic literature and culture; focusing largely on the twentieth- and twenty-first centuries, this scholarship often takes the slave narrative as a representative early genre; see JanMohamed, *Death-Bound Subject*, 3, 4, 298–99; S. Holland, *Raising*; Holloway, *Passed On*; V. Brown, *Reaper's Garden*. Gallows texts associated with black criminals have long been easily available. See Porter, *Early Negro Writing*, 405–26; McDade, *Annals of Murder*; Finkelman, *Slavery, Race*; D. Williams, *Pillars*. Critiques of African Americanist canon-building and anthologization abound: see Lubiano, "Constructing"; Jarrett, *Deans*, 1–27; Jarrett, *African American Literature*, 1–9.

74. See Vanessa E. Jones, "Hip-Hop's New Plot: Urban Novels Get a Read on Literary Success," *Boston Globe*, March 2, 2004; Nick Chiles, "Their Eyes Were Reading Smut," Op-Ed, *New York Times*, January 4, 2006, http://www.nytimes.com/2006/01/04/opinion/04chiles.html, accessed April 18, 2011; Early, "What"; see also Franklin, *Prison Literature*; Dietzel, "African American Novel," 162–63.

75. Sentencing Project, "Felony," 1.

76. Pew Center on the States, "One in 100," 3. For a poignant but clear-eyed account of this stark reality's painful intersection with the project of cultural criticism in the U.S., see Holloway, *Passed On*, 9–14.

77. Sentencing Project, "Felony."

78. A. Davis, *Reader*, 62; see Hartman, *Scenes*, 76–78.

79. W. Andrews, *To Tell*, 43; Gould, *Barbaric*, 145. See Pasley, Robertson, and Waldstreicher, introduction to *Beyond*, 2; Newman and Finkenbine, "Forum"; Newman, "Protest," "Chosen," *Black Founders*, and *Freedom's Prophet*. For a twist on the "black Ben Franklin," see Waldstreicher, *Runaway*, 241–44.

80. See B. Dain, *Hideous*, 48–54.

81. See Newman, *Black Founders*.

82. Aristotle, *Politics*, 1255a; see also *Nichomachean Ethics*, 1180a.

83. Otter, *Philadelphia*, 262. See also McHenry, *Forgotten Readers*, 23–83; Melish, "'Condition' Debate"; and J. Stewart, "Emergence" and "Modernizing Difference."

84. Mailloux, *Reception*, 75; see W. Andrews, *To Tell*, 7; also Pierce, "Redeeming Bondage"; Potkay, "Olaudah Equiano"; Howard-Pitney, *African American Jeremiad*, 15–52.

85. See A. Walker, *In Search*, 71–82.

86. W. Andrews, *Sisters*, 2. See also Foster, *Written*, 1–116; C. Peterson, *Doers*; Moody, *Sentimental*.

87. W. Andrews, *To Tell*, 41. "In American history, the death penalty has been, very largely, a male monopoly" (H. Allen and Chubb, *Race, Class*, 10). Where gender statistics are available, although African American women are disproportionately represented among the female condemned from 1608 to 1945, the evidence indicates that "less than 3%" of those executed "were women" during this period on average, even factoring in considerably higher numbers of female execution rates in the earlier periods (15). See also Hoffer and Hull, *Murdering*; Hull, *Female Felons*.

88. Foster, *Witnessing*, 38–39.

89. W. Andrews, *To Tell*, 39; see also Sekora, "Black Message," 489.

90. W. Andrews, *To Tell*, 43, 44.

91. Cruz, *Culture*, 89.

92. Mascuch, *Origins*, 170, 155; see Fliegelman, *Declaring*, 140–50. On the emergence of the accountable—and recounted—modern self in the religious and legal development of confession in the West, see P. Brooks, *Troubling*. Brooks builds on Foucault's account of confession's disciplinary function; see Foucault, *History*, 58–73, *Abnormal*, 184. For an early American overview, see D. Davis, *Homicide*.

93. Mascuch, *Origins*, 206; see also Habermas, *Between*, 96, 365; Gladfelder, *Criminality*, 6.

94. W. Andrews, *To Tell*, 40.

95. See Mehta, *Anxiety*, 127.

96. V. Smith, *Self-Discovery*, 13.

97. Masur, *Rites*, 25–49; Banner, *Death Penalty*, 9–13; Meranze, *Laboratories*, 19–54; see also Linebaugh and Rediker, *Hydra*, 50.

98. Banner, *Death Penalty*, 25–32.

99. On American crime literature's transatlantic origins see Towner, "True Confessions," 525–26; D. Cohen, *Pillars*, 22, 42–46; see also Langbein, *Prosecuting*, 45–54; Rawlings, *Drunks*; Terpstra, *Art*.

100. Emsley, Hitchcock, and Shoemaker, "Ordinary."

101. Samuel Danforth's *The Cry of Sodom Enquired Into* (1674) has been tentatively identified as "the first execution discourse" published in New England: D. Cohen, *Pillars*, 4; Cohen traces important changes in genre, format, and audience over time (3–38). Wherever possible I will use precise terminology when discussing specific texts, but, following Bosco, "Gallows Literature," references to gallows or crime literature are intended to be broadly inclusive, comprising the wide range of publications associated with the Execution Day ritual. See also D. Williams, *Pillars*.

102. D. Cohen, *Pillars*. On execution sermons' comparative profitability, see also Banner, *Death Penalty*, 48–51.

103. D. Cohen, *Pillars*; McDade, "Christian Brown"; on the newspaper secularization of crime accounts, see Waldstreicher, *Runaway*, 95–98.

104. McCarty, *Power*, 20.

105. D. Cohen, *Pillars*, 52.

106. Rogers, *Death*, 118.

107. Ibid.

108. D. Cohen, *Pillars*; see also McGiffert, *God's Plot*; Swaim, "Women's Puritan Evidences."

109. Halttunen, *Murder*, 21–22.

110. D. Cohen, *Pillars*, 143; see also D. Williams, *Pillars*, 19–33; Breen, "Making"; Wilf, *Imagined*, 56–104.

111. Gould, *Barbaric*, 74, 72–73. Gould does not address gallows texts; he finds the trope in texts ending with slave suicide or sale. See also Isani, "Gambia's Golden Shore,"

370; V. Brown, *Reaper's Garden*, 157–200; H. Baker "Critical," 25. For a parallel contextualization of Indian gallows literature with respect to both the enduring trope of the Dying Indian and popular colonial Indian deathbed literature, see Schorb, "Seeing," 148–49.

112. Mather, *Diary*, 2:620; *Boston News-Letter*, May 22–29, 1721; *Boston Gazette*, May 1–8, 1721; on Nanney, see M. Weiner, *Black Trials*, 36.

113. Mather, *Tremenda*, title page, 27.

114. Mather amplified the case's latent politics of slavery: presiding over Hanno's trial was Judge Samuel Sewall, who twenty years earlier engaged in America's first print debate over slavery with his colleague Judge John Saffin in conjunction with a case involving a (now emancipated) slave named Adam—with whom Hanno had done involuntary duty on a free black road crew in 1715; M. Weiner, *Black Trials*, 379n25. See also S. Kaplan, "Samuel Sewall"; Towner, "Sewall-Saffin"; M. Peterson, "*Selling*."

115. Mather, *Diary*, 2:620.

116. Gladfelder, *Criminality*, 24, 23.

117. Bosco finds 203 "sermons, moral discourses, narratives, last words, and dying sayings, and poems written for, by, and about persons executed for criminal activity" contained within 164 works published from 1674 to 1800. Bosco, "Gallows Literature," 81. Collating Bosco's figures with those in Slotkin's "Chronological Checklist" and those that surfaced during the research for the current study, we can estimate that at least sixty such publications featured criminals of African heritage before the Civil War. Slotkin, "Narratives," 28–31. See also McDade, *Annals*.

"Beginning in the early eighteenth century, a majority of those executed in most years were of African descent, and the pattern persisted" throughout American history, despite the fact that "African Americans . . . never constituted a majority of the colonial or national population"; conversely, from 1608 to 1945, "whites appear as a distinct minority of those executed," despite their relative numbers. H. Allen and Chubb, *Race, Class*, 9. Allen and Chubb offer helpful breakdowns for each period, as well as an overview of the definitional problems impeding collection and analysis of empirical data on legal executions, and those of slaves in particular; see 191–204. In a more nuanced study of serious crime in colonial Massachusetts, Hull finds that although "ethnic/racial factors did carry some weight in criminal indictments and committals . . . what emerges is a picture of substantial justice crisscrossed with lines of prejudice. Certain crimes and the race and servitude of the accused did play a role in labeling likely suspects and encouraging convictions"; overall, however, "conviction patterns showed . . . little concern for personal characteristics. On the whole, women (regardless of marital status), male blacks (charged with capital offenses), and Indians were not substantially disfavored by the courts' verdicts. . . . Eighteenth-century Massachusetts applied substantial justice to men and women." Hull, *Female Felons*, 106–7. Greater disparities appeared in sentencing: "the court was harsher toward minorities than whites in its application of the death penalty" (117). Of those convicted of capital offenses, fewer than half of white women were executed as against "black women, who were executed two-thirds of the time," and "the majority of white men, like women, avoided hanging. Male blacks fared less well: they were condemned in proportions similar to black women, not white men. Black men were hanged in 68.8 percent of their cases" (117–20). Confirming Hull's account, Kawashima offers valuable comparative statistical analyses of Indian and black encounters with law, noting the low rate of active black involvement in civil as opposed to criminal proceedings; see Kawashima, *Puritan*, 125–201; see also Towner, "Fondness"; Chamberlain, "Execution," 437–38. For a sampling from specific locales and periods, see Hindus, *Prison*; Schwarz, *Twice*; Waldrep, *Roots*; Olwell, *Masters*, 57–101.

118. Mather, *Warnings*, 74, 72. Mather's *Warnings* does not appear in Slotkin's "Chronological Checklist"; the earliest work included there, Nathaniel Saltonstall's *Continuation of the State of New-England . . . Together with an Account of the Intended Rebellion of the Negroes in the Barbadoes* (1676), offers neither an execution sermon nor the words of the condemned; it merely summarizes the measures taken by authorities following exposure of the rebellion (Slotkin, "Narratives," 28).

119. For gallows literature devoted to women of African descent, see *Few Lines*; H. Channing, *God*; D. Ripley, *Account*; Stanford, *Authentic Statement*; see also H. Warner, *Report* (which ends with the acquittal of "Susanna, a Coloured Woman"). The latter three do not appear in the lists compiled by Bosco or Slotkin. For analyses of race, crime, and print focusing on women of color before the Civil War, see Hartman, *Scenes*, 79–112; Stone, "Interracial"; Schorb, "Uncleanliness" and "Seeing"; S. Harris, *Executing*. See also Madow, "Forbidden," 479n59.

Anna Julia Cooper offers a trenchant post-Reconstruction critique of the historic absence of any testimony from, representation of, or advocacy for black women in the ongoing metaphorical "trial" over black civic belonging: "The colored man's inheritance and apportionment is still . . . the dumb skeleton in the closet provoking ceaseless harangues, indeed, but little understood and seldom consulted. Attorneys for the plaintiff and attorneys for the defendant, with bungling *gaucherie* have analyzed and dissected, theorized and synthesized with sublime ignorance or pathetic misapprehension of counsel from the black client. One important witness has not yet been heard from. The summing up of the evidence deposed, and the charge to the jury have been made—but no word from the Black Woman. It is because I believe the American people to be conscientiously committed to a fair trial and ungarbled evidence, and because I feel it essential to a perfect understanding and an equitable verdict that truth from each standpoint be presented at the bar,—that this little Voice, has been added to the already full chorus" (A. Cooper, *Voice*, i–ii).

120. See also Hunter, "Race," 72.

121. Halttunen, *Murder*, 32.

122. Contrast B. Johnson, *Persons*, 34–44.

123. V. Brown, *Reaper's Garden*, 200. On African American commemorative culture, see Holloway, *Passed On*, 7, 6. For an overview of scholarship on the cultural transformation (and transformative cultural effects of) death and mourning in America prior to the Civil War, see Nudelman, *John Brown's Body*, 178–79.

124. Fuss, "Corpse Poem," 2; on the genre of "Moriens," the dying man, within the larger *ars moriendi* tradition, see Mascuch, *Origins*, 62–70.

125. On racialized religious rhetoric, see Slotkin, "Narratives"; Jordan, *White over Black*, 200–201; Nelson, *Word*, 25–27.

126. Wilf, *Imagined*, 56; Sekora, "Red," 98. Among the vast scholarship on abolitionism, print, and corporeality, see Sánchez-Eppler, *Touching*; Franchot, "Punishment"; Levine, *Martin Delany*, 99–143; Hartman, *Scenes*; Best, *Fugitive's Properties*; Fanuzzi, *Abolition's Public Sphere*; Gardner, *Master Plots*, 160–85; Cossu-Beaumont and Parfait, "Book History"; Loughran, *Republic*, 319.

127. Notably, Katherine Grandjean's analysis of gallows literature devoted to condemned Indians finds evidence of a new corporeal notion of race in "ministers' increasingly strenuous and tortured efforts to argue against it." "Our *Fellow-Creatures*," 942.

128. Rodensky, *Crime*. On the post-Civil War shift toward a focus on the body of the condemned, see Madow, "Forbidden," 486.

129. Gray, *Confessions*, 41.

130. On recycled imagery, see M. Wood, *Blind*, 120–24.

131. The exception proves the rule: an unusually grotesque account of another interracial hanged pair recounts how decay of gibbetted African American and white corpses led them to switch not only colors but other phenotypic markers; Horsmanden, *Journal*, 233–34. Although its depiction of multiple subjects places this gallows text outside the scope of the current study, it has received extensive study in recent years; see Linebaugh and Rediker, *Hydra*, 74–110; Lepore, *New York*; Hoffer, *Great New York*.

132. Gardner, *Master Plots*, 5; B. Dain, *Hideous*, ix, 1–39; see also Downes, *Democracy*, 39.

133. Sidonie Smith, *Subjectivity*; Sánchez-Eppler, *Touching*; M. Warner, *Letters*; see also Hartman, *Scenes*; Wiegman, *American*, 21–78.

134. Wilf, *Imagined*, 6, 10. On the role of regicidal execution iconography in the formation of the democratic citizen-subject, see Downes, *Democracy*, 31–57.

135. Wheatley, *Collected Works*, 180; see Wilf, *Imagined*, 25.

136. Equiano, *Interesting Narrative*, 242, 239.

137. Marrant, *Journal*, 94.

138. H. Baker, "Critical," 15; Wagner, *Disturbing*, 223–25.

139. A. Davis, *Reader*, 62.

140. See Habermas, *Structural Transformation* and *Facts and Norms*, 360–66, 373–79; Calhoun, *Habermas*, particularly Schudson, "Reflections" and Ryan, "Gender." The classic early American application is Warner, *Letters*.

141. J. Brooke, "Consent," 230.

142. J. Brooks, "Early American"; Newman and Finkenbine, "Forum," 91; see also H. Baker, "Critical." For an example, see I. Wilson, *Specters*, 7, 13.

143. Wong, *Neither*, 7. See also Waldstreicher, "Reading."

144. Frontispiece, H. Brown, *Narrative*.

145. D. Cohen, *Pillars*, 79.

146. See, for example, the claim that "because slaves had no legal status, the criminal slave was a . . . double outlaw." Sekora, "Black Message," 489. Patterson long ago disposed with the fallacious but common "definition of the slave as someone without a legal personality." Patterson, *Slavery*, 22. On the persistence of this assumption, see Best, *Fugitive's Properties*, 300n118.

147. Habermas, *Between*, 96; see also 365.

148. Habermas is uncharacteristically, and perhaps inadvertently, exclusive in his phrasing here: leading into a discussion of literature, and life-writing in particular, he asserts, "the political public sphere can fulfill its function of perceiving and thematizing encompassing social problems only insofar as it develops out of the communication taking place among *those who are potentially affected*. It is carried by a public recruited from the entire citizenry." Habermas, *Between*, 365. This public, as I argue here, is recruited from much more than the "entire citizenry," that is, the much larger cohort of "those who are potentially affected" by such social problems.

149. The notion of the dematerialized citizen-subject has made it difficult to conceive of citizenship in terms of plenitude. We imagine that "the state forges the citizen by stripping away the skin to expose a legal person," discarding the extraneous, messy elements of embodiment so long associated with women and the enslaved in Western culture. Castronovo, *Necro*, 53; see also Riesenberg, *Citizenship*, 27–30; Mehta, *Anxiety*, 167; Wald, *Constituting*; Nelson, *National Manhood*; Castiglia, *Interior States*; Dayan, *Law*. But the dialectical opposition of the lethally embodied slave to the inert, abstracted citizen fails to take into account how legal and cultural fictions of mixed character credit the enslaved with a fractional legal personhood while rendering that personhood incommensurate with citizenship. Itself denuded of the civil standing that renders the legal person eligible for citizenship, the partial legal personhood accorded the criminous slave is decidedly lesser than, not equal to, the pared-down subjectivity granted the citizen. (By the same token, the excessive corporeal humanity ascribed to the merely transgressive slave distinguishes him from his legally apprehended counterpart; see Chapter 1.) When we recall, moreover, that much like the individuality conjured by liberalism, the citizenship figured forth by African American literature is "an aspiration, a process of coming-to-be," we can see how literary assertions of civic eligibility imply augmentation rather than diminution of black subjectivity. Mehta, *Anxiety*, 127; see also Sale, *Slumbering*, 16–25. Whatever constraints this idealized citizenship might be imagined to impose, they would impinge upon the unruly traits of the human subject and not the tiny cluster of duties, rights, and privileges that constitute his newly integral legal personhood.

150. Macpherson, *Possessive*; Moglen, "Privilege," 126; Wagner, *Disturbing*, 4–20. See also Waldrep, *Roots*, 46–50; Olwell, *Masters*, 88–101.

151. Reminding us that the distinction between public and private was itself a product of the legal reforms she documents, Edwards nevertheless emphasizes the publicity of the formal criminal proceeding; Edwards, *People*, 89–99.

152. Wagner, *Disturbing*, 18; J. Brooke, "Consent," 230.

153. Moglen, "Privilege," 117; see also Marcus, "Due"; Murrin, "Magistrates"; Edwards, *People*, 66–89; Helmholz et al., *Privilege*.

154. DeLombard, *Slavery on Trial*, 76. Tracking the "lawyerization" of the criminal trial during this period, Langbein has plotted the gradual move away from "the accused speaks" model, which centered on the defendant, to that of "testing the prosecution," in which counsel replaced the now comparatively silent accused in conducting the defense. Langbein, "Privilege," 83; see also Langbein, *Origins* and "Response."

155. Waldrep, *Roots*, 22; the case in point is Vicksburg, Mississippi.

156. Ibid., 46.

157. See Gladfelder, *Criminality*, 56.

158. See Towner, "Fondness"; M. Weiner, *Black Trials*, 33–50.

159. Mather, *Tremenda*, 39. On gallows literature's extension of the Execution Day ritual, see Banner, *Death Penalty*, 48–52; D. Williams, *Pillars*, 4–6.

160. In contrast to a reading that sees collective acceptance of the state's protection as a form of tacit consent, this more consistently Lockean analysis finds express consent in the individual's explicit acceptance of state-administered punishment; see Natanson, "Locke and Hume"; see also Lawson, "Citizenship and Slavery."

161. Mather, *Tremenda*, 32.

162. Alluding to 1 Corinthians 4:18, the phrasing—like the broader sentiment—echoes an early Christian letter on slavery from Ignatius, the Bishop of Antioch, to Polycarp: "Despise not men or women slaves. Yet let them not be puffed up, but rather bear their slavery for the glory of God, that they may win from Him thereby a better liberty. Let them not seek to be emancipated at the expense of the common fund, that they may not be found the slaves of desire." Quoted in D. Davis, *Slavery in Western Culture*, 87.

163. Mather assigned both "reason" and "stupidity" to blacks. Mather, *Negro Christianized*, 4, 23, 25; see also Nelson, *Word*, 26–29.

164. These were not, of course, mutually exclusive: see D. Hall, *Worlds*, 21–70; John Williams, "Strange"; Landsman, "Evangelists"; Lambert, "Subscribing," and *Inventing*, 22–179. The minister's encounter with Hanno occurred against the backdrop of Mather's strikingly parallel exchange with young Benjamin Franklin and his brother; see Waldstreicher, *Runaway*, 32–54.

165. In this sense Hanno resembles condemned Pequot servant Katherine Garret; see Schorb, "Writing Prisoners"; see also S. Harris, *Executing*, 45–47.

166. Linebaugh, "Ordinary"; see also Mascuch, *Origins*, 164–80; Fabian, *Unvarnished*, 49–78. References to the black condemned appear in Linebaugh, *London*, 348–70.

167. Foucault, *Language*, 138.

168. See "Usage Note," *American Heritage Dictionary of the English Language*, 3rd ed., s.v. "author." Cossu-Beaumont and Parfait, "Book History"; Jackson, "Talking"; Goddu, "Slave Narrative."

169. See Blassingame, *Slave Community*, 367–82.

170. S. Stewart, *Crimes*, 23; see also 102.

171. Ibid., 69.

172. Bruce, *Origins*, 65, xi, 32. See also Ernest, *Chaotic Justice*, 248.

173. Morrison, *Playing*, 6, 39. See also Kennedy and Weissberg, *Romancing*; Castronovo, *Necro*; Nelson, *National Manhood*; Coviello, *Intimacy*; Nabers, *Victory*, 132–72.

174. Gates, *Figures*, 115; Morrison, *Playing*, 47. See Gates, *Figures*, 16–24; H. Baker, *Journey*, 27–52; Sekora, "Black Message"; Sekora, "Red"; Riss, *Race*, 164–85; Gilmore, *Genuine*; Wagner, *Disturbing*.

175. On "judging a book by its author's skin," see Jarrett, *Deans*, 2–7.

176. Sekora, "Red," 94; see also Sekora, "Black Message," 486; W. Andrews, *To Tell*, 36.

177. See Ernest, *Chaotic*, 66.

178. Ibid., 248; see also 64–67, 87.

179. Althusser, *Lenin*, 118.

180. P. Smith, "Executing Executions"; Hunter, "Race"; Wilf, *Imagined*, 91.

181. Althusser distinguishes the process of ideological subject formation he describes from that which occurs under slavery—presumably involving the sort of refusal of recognition theorized in Hegel's master-slave dialectic and developed by Patterson; see Hegel, *Phenomenology*, 228–40; Patterson, *Slavery*, 97–101. See also Brace, *Politics*, 71–80, 163–65.

182. Although Althusser's example emphasizes the acts of writing and reading, its apostrophic framing (addressing the absent future reader) suggests that it is less important that the black condemned appear in print as authors than as historically situated first-person subjects. See also Wagner, *Disturbing*, 49–51; B. Johnson, *Persons*, 6 (for apostrophe as a form of Althusserian hailing, see 10).

183. See also Mascuch, *Origins*, 47.

184. W. Andrews, *To Tell*, 35.

185. De Man, "Autobiography," 926.

186. This line of thought is indebted to Pratt, "Lyric Public"; see also Kneale, *Romantic*, 17; Culler, *Pursuit*, 61.

187. Mather, *Tremenda*, 26; see Morrison, *Playing*. This dynamic reverses the process in which the black subject is dehumanized by a combination of summary police powers and third-person narration, neither of which interpellate their object into Althusserian subjectivity; Wagner, *Disturbing*, 49–50, 206.

188. This phrasing ("back formation") is indebted to Elizabeth Dillon. See J. Brooks, "Early American"; Sinha, "Alternative."

189. Barthes, "Death." With its preference of the "hand" for the "voice," the "scriptor" for the "author," and the linguistic "subject" for the legal "person," Barthes's critique is less relevant than Foucault's discussion of "the author-function," especially with respect to legal liability; see *Language*, 113–38.

190. See, for example, W. Andrews, *To Tell*, 32–51, 72–77; Sundquist, *To Wake*, 36–56; Hunter, "Race"; Wilf, *Imagined*, 56–137; Levine, *Dislocating*, 83–84; Wilf, *Imagined*, 56–137; S. Harris, *Executing*, 25–79; Schorb, "Seeing."

191. Levine makes this point in passing with respect to the trial pamphlet depicting the (still-controversial) Denmark Vesey conspiracy; *Dislocating*, 83.

192. See Mascuch, *Origins*, 183.

193. Hartman, *Scenes*, 94.

194. Reading gallows literature as emanating from and expressive of actual human subjects produces the opposite conclusion; Hunter, "Race," 80.

195. For an overview that foregrounds race and nation, see Levine, *Dislocating*, 1–15.

196. Emerson, *Selected Writings*, 228.

197. Peabody, "Narratives," 61.

198. T. Parker, *American Scholar*, 37; on the occasion, see 499.

199. K. Warren, "Making"; see also K. Warren, *What*.

200. See Wagner, *Disturbing*, 213, Gilmore, *Genuine*; see also Carbado, "Racial Naturalization." For contemporary analysis of this phenomenon with respect to slave songs and blackface minstrelsy, see K[ennard], "Who."

201. Morrison, *Playing*, 7.

202. Locke, *Essay*, 310.

203. For a complementary analysis of how a range of white nineteenth-century writers took up the question of a "complicity" derived "from constituency," both within and beyond the slavery controversy, see Greiman, *Democracy's Spectacle* (quotation at 17).

204. Blumenthal, "Metaphysics," 185; see also Brewer, *By Birth*, 181–229. See also Blumenthal, "Deviance," "Mind," and "Default."

205. Berlant, *Queen*, 25–54; Castronovo, *Necro*; Blumenthal, "Default," 1138; Nelson, *National Manhood*, 204. See also Ruttenburg, *Democratic*, 168; for a legal-historical consideration of related rhetorical formations around race, see Ross, "Rhetorical."

206. In this sense, this study examines and extends to the question of legal personhood "the rebound effect" Leonard Cassuto finds resulting from "the objectification conundrum that lies at the core of slavery"—examining how "the process of racial objectification . . . reverberates back to white subjects, calling their humanity into question in a different way." *Inhuman*, 6, 213, 6.

207. Kopley, *Dupin*, 42–43.

208. It may seem odd, given the literary historical narrative offered here, that this study culminates in the late antebellum mortification of the guilty white citizen-subject rather than (as one might expect) following the newly decriminalized black persona into the classic slave narrative. Although the primary critical task of Chapters 4 and 5 is to indicate how the largely successful abolitionist project of exculpating the first-person black narrator complicated as well as facilitated the print presentation of the African American self as protocitizen, other than the brief reading of *My Bondage and My Freedom* with which this Introduction closes, the testimonial slave narrative appears in this book more as a point of reference than as a subject of inquiry. This is because the current study functions as prequel to my first book, *Slavery on Trial*, which considers in depth what it meant for gallows literature's confessing malefactor to resurface as the slave narrative's testifying eyewitness. The profound literary, political, and historical

importance of this shift in black life-writing has not gone unnoticed. If "in the first fifty years . . . the slavery of sin received much more condemnation than the sin of slavery," Andrews observed, "in two or three decades abolitionists and fugitive slaves would indict slavery itself as a cause of black transgressions against morality and law." *To Tell*, 44. For Andrews, "the revolution in social attitudes toward the slave" is illustrated by "the thematic polarities between the eighteenth- and nineteenth-century fugitive slave narratives," that is, between the criminal confession and the testimonial slave narrative. To realize Andrews's insight fully, however, we cannot afford to treat black gallows literature as a stable backdrop against which to assess the cultural upheaval that would culminate in the abolitionist slave narrative, but as an elemental force in that cultural revolution.

209. Douglass, *My Bondage*, 319.

210. The earliest instance in the OED of the distinctly American colloquial use of "to own up," as "to make a full admission or confession, esp. when challenged or pressed; to confess frankly (to something)," is dated 1844. *Oxford English Dictionary Online*, s.v. "own."

211. On the effective limitation of slaves' courtroom speech to confession and testimony against other people of color, see T. Morris, *Southern Slavery*, 229–48; Moglen, "Privilege," 126. For specific statutes, see Hurd, *Law*, 1:239, 241–44, 252–53, 281, 284, 305; 2:19–20, 23, 73–75, 77, 81–82, 89–90, 97, 117–18, 128, 131, 159, 172–73, 177, 210, 217; for a summary statement, see 2:340n2.

212. Jennifer Greiman acknowledges these parallels to the gallows procession in an insightful reading of this scene as a quintessentially antebellum spectacle that, in its public, theatrical display of force, stages the tensions among sovereignty and its constitutive exceptions and thus foregrounds questions of civic belonging and political responsibility. In this sense, the present study complements her brilliant analyses of how these tensions play out in early national and antebellum literature. Yet, as my own reading of the same scene illustrates (and as Chapter 2 elaborates further), a focus on the figure of the black condemned highlights the importance of due process in distinguishing the criminous slave from those "exceptional subjects of the public": the (non-criminous) slave, the (normatively white) prisoner, and the exile (26). Far from enacting the punishments demanded by the not-so-sovereign mob, the constables protect the enslaved men from lynching and other forms of extralegal violence as Thomas Auld's property—and thus emphatically *not* as responsible legal persons—to be delivered to the jail in a typical coordination of plantation justice and police powers which together sidestep the due process also associated with law's authorities, rituals, and spaces. To adapt Tocqueville, then, the scene reminds us of us the need to distinguish the long shadow of the law from the actual proceedings that constitute that institution.

213. See Barton, "Anti-Gallows" and P. Jones, *Against*. On public treatment of the black condemned, see Banner, *Death Penalty*, 30; Masur, *Rites*, 9–24.

214. Douglass, "Capital Punishment," 245.

215. Banner, *Death Penalty*, 163–67; see also Masur, *Rites*, and D. Cohen, *Pillars*. For

contemporary commentary linking public executions in the antebellum South to slavery, see Snodgrass, "Crime"; "Capital Punishment," *Liberator*, April 24, 1846.

216. See also Castronovo, *Necro*, 34–61.

217. Challenging the assumption that "most matters involving slaves . . . were resolved within the household or on the plantation," Edwards nonetheless confirms the decreasing participation of slaves in formal legal proceedings. *People*, 304n7; see T. Morris, *Southern Slavery*, 250–51. For a detailed description of various proceedings in one jurisdiction, see Waldrep, *Roots*, 15–83. On the nineteenth-century development of the police power as an intermediary between the two spheres, see Wagner, *Disturbing*, 18.

218. Douglass, *Narrative*, 80. See Delombard, *Slavery on Trial*.

219. Charting this process, the current study complements Peters's inquiry into how the mutually constitutive development of rights discourse and literature during the period in question served to humanize the normatively white, male bourgeois reader, allowing "the citizen [to] become a 'human being.'" Peters, "Literature," 271.

220. On "the lack of the confessional in Douglass," see Moses, "Writing," 70.

221. "Change of Opinion Announced," *Liberator*, May 23, 1851, rpt. from *North Star*.

222. Mascuch, *Origins*, 188.

223. "Change of Opinion Announced"; see also Garrison's editorial in the same issue explaining his choice of words: "Constitution," *Liberator*, May 23, 1851. Thanks in no small part to his celebrity as formerly enslaved author and orator, Douglass was able to meet the high ($250) property qualification New York State imposed on African American male voters; see McFeely, *Frederick Douglass*, 208. On Douglass's unsuccessful antebellum efforts to obtain a passport against denials of his U.S. citizenship, see Wong, *Neither*, 246, 254–56.

224. See Anderson, *Imagined*; M. Warner, *Letters*.

225. In addition to previously cited sources on crime and popular print culture, see Mott, *American Journalism*, 215–52; Schiller, *Objectivity*; Papke, *Framing*; Tucher, *Froth and Scum*.

Chapter 1. Contracting Guilt: Mixed Character, Civil Slavery, and the Social Contract

1. Shklar, *American Citizenship*, 16; see also R. Smith, *Civic Ideals*, 115; D. Smith, "Citizenship"; C. Holland, *Body Politic*, 35–36; Brace, *Politics*, 168; Glenn, *Unequal*, 18–55.

2. U.S. Constitution, art. 1, sec. 2, 9; art. 4, sec. 2. See Agamben, *Homo Sacer*, 127, 177–78, 181; Fields, "Slavery," 99; Wald, *Constituting*, 14–73. It is the three-fifths clause's reference to "Indians" that, arguably, makes race specific. Indebted to Best's sharp counter-reading of the clause against the *Dred Scott* decision, my own analysis differs from his more legalistic interpretation in its presumption that the implied context of slavery would have supplied the passages in question with their absent racial significance; see Best, *Fugitive's Properties*, 79–80.

3. Aristotle, *Politics*, 1290b, 1283b. Works on U.S. citizenship are legion and the fol-

lowing account is anything but comprehensive. Along with those cited below, the most useful sources in the literary context have been Wald, *Constituting*; Castronovo, *Necro*; Nelson, *National Manhood*.

4. Shklar, *American Citizenship*, 3; see R. Smith, *Civic Ideals*, 3; Welke, *Law*; Dillon, *Gender*, 6. "In a more extended sense, under the word citizen, are included all white persons born in the United States, and naturalized persons born out of the same, who have not lost their right as such. This includes men, women, and children." Bouvier, *Law Dictionary* . . . , rev. 5th ed. (1854), s.v. "citizen."

5. Cornell was explaining his support for "revocation" of black suffrage as an "experiment" that had "failed": rather than leading to racial "improvement," it had "failed to produce any other effect than to mislead the public mind as to [blacks'] citizenship." Bishop and Attree, *Report*, 1047.

6. Riesenberg, *Citizenship*, 74.

7. Kettner, *Development*, 246–47; see also B. Thomas, *Civic Myths*, 7.

8. Kettner, *Development*, 9; Act of 26 March 1790; Act of 29 January 1795, *Stats at Large of USA*, Library of Congress, *A Century of Lawmaking for a New Nation: U.S. Congressional Documents and Debates*, http://memory.loc.gov/ammem/amlaw/lawhome. html.

9. R. Smith, *Civic Ideals*, 176; see 167–89, 230, 234–35, 255–71. "All natives are not citizens of the United States, the descendents of the aborigines, and those of African origin, are not entitled to the rights of citizens." Bouvier, *Law Dictionary* . . . , 2nd ed. (1843), s.v. "citizen."

10. R. Smith, *Civic Ideals*, 177, 258, 268; on the racial specter posed by the clause, see 188–89. See also Welke, *Law*, 34–35; Levine, *Dislocating*, 74–87.

11. The changing treatment of free blacks in James Kent's *Commentaries on American Law* is revealing. In the first edition, Kent concluded the section optimistically titled "Slaves, Domestic Slavery, and Its Extinction in this State" by noting the "disabilities" placed on black electors by New York's revised 1821 constitution. Kent, *Commentaries* (1827), 209. By the third edition, the discussion of free blacks' status was greatly expanded but, tellingly, remained under the now pared-down heading "Slaves." Noting that all American-born blacks, regardless of condition, are "natives, and not aliens," Kent concluded that "negroes or other slaves . . . are natural born subjects, but not citizens. . . . If a slave born in the United States be manumitted, or otherwise fully discharged from bondage, or if a black man be born within the United States, and born free, he becomes thenceforward a citizen, but under such disabilities as the laws of the states respectively may deem it expedient to prescribe to free persons of colour." *Commentaries* (1836), 258n.

12. R. Smith, *Civic Ideals*, 188; see also 181, 258.

13. D. Smith, *Citizenship*, 742–43; Welke, *Law*; for an overview of this process, see C. Holland, *Body Politic*, 93–103. For the evolution of this phenomenon, see Edwards, *People*.

14. Fehrenbacher, *Dred Scott*, 342–47; see also R. Smith, *Civic Ideals*, 268.

15. Gross, *Blood*, 8.

16. Looby, *Voicing*; Wald, *Constituting*; Crane, *Race*; see also R. Ferguson, *Law*; Thomas, *Cross-Examinations* and *Civic Myths*; Sundquist, *To Wake*; Best, *Fugitive's Properties*; Nabers, *Victory*; Levine, *Dislocating*.

17. Sale, *Slumbering*; Tushnet, *Slave Law*; Korobkin, "Appropriating"; see also De-Lombard, *Slavery on Trial*, 7; M. Davis, *Nat Turner*; Wong, *Neither*, 183–239.

18. H. Brown, *Narrative*, 96–109; Watson, *Narrative*, 46–48. See also Schwarz, *Slave Laws*, 1–12 and *Twice Condemned*, 16, 88. "Even in its positive sense—that of being a part of—belonging can be a negative tool." Welke, *Law*, 5.

19. Madison, Hamilton, and Jay, *Federalist*, 332.

20. See respectively Edwards, *People*; Loughran, *Republic*.

21. "Rights talk" and "responsibility talk" were by no means mutually exclusive: Fliegelman, *Declaring*, 140–50; Welke, *Recasting*; Goodman, *Shifting*.

22. For discussion of how the logic of common law, especially due process, potentially "undermined slavery" even as it "protected slave property," see Waldrep, *Roots*, 37–58 (quotation at 58).

23. Agamben, *Homo Sacer*, 7. For an excellent nineteenth-century Americanist overview of the theory and scholarship on sovereignty, the public sphere, and social and political belonging, see Greiman, *Democracy's Spectacle*, 1–35.

24. For an alternative local literary history of this phenomenon, see Otter, *Philadelphia*, 107–266, especially 115–16, 262. On the conventional dismissal of black piety, industry, and skill as mere pretense in runaway advertisements, see Waldstreicher, "Reading," 254–55.

25. Crèvecoeur, *Letters*, 69.

26. Ibid., 177; Aristotle, *Politics*, 1253a. See also Agamben, *Homo Sacer*, 7–9.

27. See also Ruttenburg, *Democratic Personality*, 275–89.

28. Aristotle, *Politics*, 1280a.

29. Agamben, *Homo Sacer*, 83. For criticism of Agamben's use of legal sources that is also attentive to how "law incipiently includes us," see Fitzpatrick, "Bare Sovereignty," 69.

30. Agamben, *Homo Sacer*, 8.

31. On the position of African Americans as "nonforeign-noncitizen," see Carbado, "Racial Naturalization," 645. On the literary dimensions of this compact, see Greeson, *Our South*, 19–41.

32. Fractionally counted for the purposes simultaneously of the taxation that affirms their status as property and of the representation that only confirms their exclusion from political existence, slaves are banned by the Constitution not in the sense of being "simply set outside the law and made indifferent to it but rather *abandoned* by it, that is, exposed and threatened on the threshold in which life and law, outside and inside, become indistinguishable." Agamben, *Homo Sacer*, 28.

33. Carbado, "Racial Naturalization," 638; see also 652–53. For an articulation of a

similar liberal logic along gender lines that does not neglect race, see Dillon, *Gender*, 3, 17–19.

34. Hence Douglass's literary marketability; see Fanuzzi, *Abolition's Public Sphere*, 211.

35. Douglass, *My Bondage*, 201.

36. Agamben, *Homo Sacer*, 84.

37. Douglass, *My Bondage*, 219, *Narrative*, 80.

38. V. Brown, *Reaper's Garden*, 200; see 157–200. See also Canuel, *Shadow*, 142–67.

39. Stowe, *Uncle Tom's Cabin*, 190.

40. Jacobs, *Incidents*, 48.

41. Agamben, *Homo Sacer*, 86; see also 102–3.

42. For an alternative reading of deodand in these contexts, see Dayan, *Law*, 127–30.

43. Shakespeare, *Merchant of Venice*, IV. i, 130–38, quoted in R. Nash, "Shylock's Wolvish Spirit," 125.

44. E. P. Evans, *Criminal Prosecution*, 157. Deriving "from *Deo dandum*, to be given to God," the legal term *deodand* "designate[d] any unhappy instrument, whether it be an animal or inanimate thing which has caused the death of a man or mischance" and whose value, under English law was usually therefore forfeit to the king. Bouvier, *Law Dictionary*, 2nd ed., s.v. "deodand." Forfeiture cases such as *United States v. One* 1963 *Cadillac Coupe de Ville Two-Door* (1966) notwithstanding, Finkelstein maintains that, perhaps due to the absence of a divine proxy in the form of a monarch, deodand "never had any standing" in U.S. law. Quaint as deodand and related proceedings may sound, their demise tends to be seen as having resulted not from progression away from a primitive embrace of *lex talionis*, but, conversely, from their renewed popularity in an era of industrial accidents as a legal remedy for wrongful death. The legal-historical turning point is usually identified as the English abolition of deodands in 1846. Finkelstein, "Goring Ox," 195. See also Dayan, "Legal Terrors," 63; W. Hyde, "Prosecution." Emphasizing the long-standing Christian reluctance to place a monetary value on human life, Finkelstein argues against the tendency to associate the decline of deodand and related proceedings with the rise of intent, stressing instead the growing acceptability, in the wake of industrialization, of the compensatory damages increasingly available through civil tort law. Finkelstein's otherwise persuasive analysis does not address how the existence of slavery complicates his claims that the nineteenth-century "survival—however attenuated—of the moral notion that the death of a person, by its very occurrence, creates a judicial climate more appropriate to a criminal proceeding than a civil one; that it still goes 'against the grain' to allow that the value of a human life is amenable to pecuniary computation and composition." Finkelstein, "Goring Ox," 196. With early drafts published in the *Atlantic Monthly* in the aftermath of slavery and during the lynching crisis (see "Bugs" and "Medieval"), Evans's *Criminal Prosecution* acknowledges the overlap in criminal prosecution of animals, things, and slaves, even as it concludes with a disturbing endorsement of criminal anthropology and reflections on the offender's bestial and especially simian qualities; see 190, 214–15. 234–37; also 51.

45. Agamben, *Homo Sacer*, 105.

46. Ibid., 109; on the body as the site where the state of nature reappears in civil society, see C. Holland, *Body Politic*, xiii–11.

47. Douglass, *My Bondage*, 201; see also Dayan, *Law*, 209–52.

48. See Agamben, *Homo Sacer*, 104–15.

49. T. Morris, *Southern Slavery*, 286.

50. Wagner, "Disarmed," 121; the fact of due process renders this formulation more accurate than the revised version, which replaces "outlaw" with "criminal"; see Wagner, *Disturbing*, 16. Emphasizing attainder in European and English contexts, scholars often characterize civil death as equivalent to or more severe than outlawry; Itzkowitz and Oldak, "Restoring," 722–25; Ewald, "Civil Death," 1060n44. But in the U.S. context where attainder is unconstitutional, the custodial state protection of defendants and convicts becomes important to the corresponding distinction between the lynching victim and the outlaw.

51. *Wilmington Journal*, December 13, 1850, quoted in Stowe, *Key*, 85.

52. Stowe, *Key*, 85; see also Stowe, *Dred*, 626–27.

53. Wagner, *Disturbing*, 50, 48.

54. V. Brown, *Reaper's Garden*, 155; see also Wagner, *Disturbing*, 51–115.

55. Bouvier, *Law Dictionary . . .* , 1st ed. (1839), s.v. "slave"; see Dayan, "Servile," 87, 100; see also her "Legal Terrors," 46, and "Poe, Persons, and Property," 116–17.

56. Bouvier, *Law Dictionary*, 1st ed., s.v. "slave."

57. Bouvier, *Law Dictionary . . .* , 3rd ed. (1854), s.v. "death." As indicated by Bouvier's full entry, this "more severe" definition of civil death appeared in the same Act of 29 March 1799 in which "the legislature set up a system of laws for the gradual abolition of slavery in New York," effectively confirming "a structural relation between slavery and civil death." Dayan, "Poe, Persons, and Property," 416.

58. Sekora, "Black Message," 489.

59. Bouvier, *Law Dictionary*, 1st ed., s.v. "civil."

60. St. George Tucker, *Dissertation*, 57.

61. Ibid., 35.

62. The most notorious example of this principle is the North Carolina case, *State v. Mann* (1829); see Tushnet, *Slave Law*. For a later Virginia case, as well as examples from antebellum Tennessee, Mississippi, and Louisiana, see Wahl, *Bondsman's Burden*, 148.

63. Wahl, *Bondsman's Burden*, 126–32.

64. Ibid., 131; see also Waldrep, *Roots*, 45–47, 58.

65. JanMohamed, *Death-Bound Subject*, 17; Locke, *Second Treatise*, 15–16. For an insightful reading of this scene as positing an always already culpable, racialized, individual subject, see Nyquist, *Arbitrary*.

66. Locke, *Second Treatise*, 47; see 13–14, 107. Alternatively, it could be argued that it was the slave's *lack* of property in his own person that required a formal legal protection that, in marked contrast to that offered the citizen, compensated for rather than delegated his (now absent rather than deputed) right to protect that property through

self-defense; see Brace, *Politics*, 174. Two persuasive recent assessments of Locke, his legislation of slavery in the *Fundamental Constitutions of Carolina* (1669), and the *Second Treatise*, include helpful overviews of the relevant scholarship; see Armitage, "John Locke," and Farr, "Locke." On Locke's nineteenth-century reception in the U.S., and particularly the antebellum proslavery rejection of both Locke's just war theory and the *Fundamental Constitutions*, see Farr, "Locke," 513–15. For a persuasive analysis of Locke's simultaneous rejection of political slavery (as tyranny) and acceptance of race slavery (as despotism), see Nyquist, *Arbitrary*.

67. For an antebellum, proslavery reiteration of Madison's claim, updated with extensive citation of relevant state statutes, see Thomas Cobb, *Inquiry*, 84–96.

68. It is important to underscore that this study focuses on the slave's responsibility for recognized criminal acts as a punishable legal person—not his or her ability to commit crimes, acts of violence, or other transgressions. This distinction between legal imputation and historical causation serves as a reminder that this study's focus is the black subject of print (including legal) discourse, not actual human actors; see Welke, *Law*, 6. On the historical usage and philosophical significance of "responsibility" and a cluster of related terms and concepts (punishability, accountability, imputability) that appear with comparatively less nuance in the current study, see McKeon, "Responsibility," and Kelsen, "Causality."

69. See *U.S. v. Amy* (1859) in Catterall, *Judicial Cases*, 1:247.

70. On the South, see Edwards, *People*; on the Northeast, see Greene, *Negro*, 167, 184; McManus, *History*, 145–46; S. White, *Somewhat*, 106–13.

71. Melish, *Disowning*, 26.

72. Dayan, "Legal Slaves," 80.

73. Thomas Cobb, *Inquiry*, 83. For a concise gloss in a civil proceeding, see *Creswell's Executors v. Walker* (1861) in Catterall, *Judicial Cases*, 3:247; for an alternative reading of its precedent, *Bailey v. Poindexter's Executor* (1858), see Dayan, *Law*, 140–76.

74. *Elijah, a Slave v. The State*, Humphreys, *Reports*, 104; see T. Morris, *Southern Slavery*, 257–58.

75. Sawyer, *Southern Institutes*, 312.

76. Berlin, *Many Thousands*, 43, 50, 78–79, 193; Breen and Innes, *Myne Owne Ground*; M. Weiner, *Black Trials*, 29; Edwards, *People*, 82; M. Jones, "Leave"; R. Smith, *Civic Ideals*, 258; see, however, 568–69n41.

77. Douglass, *My Bondage*, 106; *Scott v. Sandford*. See also Higginbotham, *Matter*.

78. Hartman, *Scenes*, 126. Referring to the post-Civil War Emancipation, Hartman's observation is just as applicable to the early national North's First Emancipation.

79. Aristotle, *Politics*, 1291a.

80. Kant, *Metaphysics of Morals*, 92.

81. L. Harris, *Shadow*, 98.

82. On Forten, see Winch, *Gentleman*.

83. L. Harris, *Shadow*, 98.

84. Melish, *Disowning*, 81.

85. Roediger, *Wages*, 100, see also 57; Waldstreicher, *Perpetual*, 209–11, 229–33, quotation at 230. See also Glenn, *Unequal*, 32, 33; C. Holland, *Body Politic*, 96; Melish, *Disowning*, 119. On the broader Jacksonian tendency to conflate dependency and (criminal) deviancy, see Rothman, *Discovery*, 164.

86. Gross, *Blood*, 54; see also R. Smith, *Civic Ideals*, 176, 267.

87. Bowdoin, Warren, and Pemberton, *Short Narrative*, 11.

88. Adams, *Legal Papers*, 268 .

89. And beyond: see, for example, the transformation of Callie House's civic pursuit of reparations for slavery into a federal mail fraud conviction; Berry, *My Face*.

90. Melish, *Disowning*, 122.

91. Waldrep, *Roots*; T. Morris, *Southern Slavery*, 250–51; Wagner, *Disturbing*, 18.

92. Phrasing adapted from K. Parker, "Making," 81.

93. Patrick-Stamp, "Numbers," 99–100.

94. Ibid., 100–101.

95. Carson, *History*, 303.

96. Patrick-Stamp, "Prisoners' Presence," 117.

97. Patrick, "Ann Hinson," 363.

98. Webster, *Effects*, 8–9.

99. On the shift from conduct to character, particularly from the criminal act to an individualized status as criminal, see Foucault, *Discipline*, 100; see also Foucault, *Security*, 4.

100. Foucault, *Discipline*, 89–90.

101. Jefferson, *Notes*, 149; see Wills, *Inventing*, 226–27.

102. See C. Holland, *Body Politic*, 35–40.

103. Kazanjian, *Colonizing*.

104. Following publication, Tucker submitted the *Dissertation* to the Virginia state legislature, where it received a "disastrous" reception in the General Assembly, which tabled the proposal. He went on to include it as an appendix, "Of the State of Slavery, in Virginia," to his edition of Blackstone's *Commentaries* (1803). Although he soon "shelved" the *Dissertation* as a "Utopian idea," during the winter of 1820–21 he conducted (uncirculated) manuscript revisions that suggest that Tucker had relinquished neither his anxieties about post-emancipation criminality nor his embrace of civil slavery for free blacks. P. Hamilton, "Revolutionary," 537.

105. Kazanjian, *Colonizing*, 89–138.

106. Jefferson, *Notes*, 145.

107. Ibid.

108. See also Schwarz, *Twice Condemned*, 194.

109. See Montesquieu, *Spirit*, 246–47, 264.

110. On the impact of Tucker's experience as a judge in a 1794 criminal case involving a free black on his views of slavery both on and off the bench, see Doyle, "Judge," 440.

111. The Virginia state constitutional convention accepted the opening clause of the

first Article of the Declaration of Rights when it was modified to include only those who had entered into the social compact; see Alden, *South*, 334–35.

112. See Zilversmit, *First Emancipation*, 139–229; McManus, *History*, 161–79; Hodges, *Root*, 162–86; Gellman, *Emancipating*, 45–55.

113. New York Council of Revision, quoted in Nordstrom, "New York."

114. St. George Tucker, *Dissertation*, 76.

115. Ibid., 94.

116. Kent, *Commentaries* (1836), 258n.

117. Locke, *Second Treatise*, 15; Montesquieu, *Spirit*, 247; see D. Davis, *Slavery in Western Culture*, 119, 406–7, 412–13.

118. Locke, *Second Treatise*, 98; see Wong, *Neither*, 39.

119. For an overview of the intellectual history of slave contracts, see Ellerman, "Inalienable," 3–7; on the case for contractual self-enslavement, see Pateman, *Sexual*, 67–68.

120. See D. Davis, *Slavery in the Age of Revolution*, 489–96; Glenn, *Unequal*, 56–92; Brace, *Politics*, 171–82.

121. See Ellerman, "Inalienable," 2n2.

122. Stanley, *From Bondage*.

123. Maine, *Ancient Law*, 174.

124. On contractarianism versus contractualism, see Pateman and Mills, *Contract*, 15–17; Darwall, *Contractarianism/Contractualism*.

125. B. Thomas, *American Literary Realism*, 1–52; Stanley, "Contract," 60.

126. [V. Smith,] *Narrative*, iv.

127. Gould, *Barbaric*, 143. See, however, Sale, *Slumbering*; Sinha, "Black Radicalism."

128. [V. Smith,] *Narrative*, iv.

129. Gould, *Barbaric*, 143.

130. Both sides in the transatlantic slavery debate used contractualism to exploit the geopolitics of mixed character—the provisional shift from slave to free, from property to (legal) person in "free" jurisdictions such as England and the North—through the fiction of the consenting slave, thereby lending support to a precarious "liberal legal structure forced to accommodate the chattel logic of slavery"; Wong, *Neither*, 92.

131. See DeLombard, "Slave Narratives."

132. Wong, *Neither*, 100.

133. Gould, *Barbaric*, 148; see also H. Baker, *Blues*, 35; Gates, *Figures*, 11–25; Fichtelberg, "Word"; Hinds, "Spirit." On gender's complication of this line of analysis in female-authored slave narratives, see C. Kaplan, "Narrative Contracts." With its aporetic invocations of consent and submission, the "Death-Contract" might be seen as the most extreme form of ensnarement in this trap; JanMohamed, *Death-Bound Subject*, 20–21, 295–96. On the perception that no amount of consideration could transform the slave's self-purchase into anything other than a token of appreciation for the master's gift of freedom, see Patterson, *Slavery*, 211.

134. Gould, *Barbaric*, 149; see also Hong, *Ruptures*, 7–8.

135. See Kazanjian, *Colonizing*, 50, 88; see also Smith-Rosenberg, "Dis-Covering," 852, and Hinds, "Spirit."

136. The reference is to the marketability of traits associated with various African groups; V. Brown, *Reaper's Garden*, 28.

137. Peters, "Literature," 267.

138. Jones and Allen, *Narrative*, 12–13; see Carey, *Short Account*, 77.

139. In *The Racial Contract* (1997), published the year before the English translation of *Homo Sacer*, Charles W. Mills deploys the contractarian language and logic of the nation's founding documents to theorize the biopolitical inclusive exclusion of nonwhites in Western liberal societies such as the U.S. (for development of this insight, see C. Holland, *Body Politic*, 96). Unlike the mythic, idealized social contract, the racial contract is "a historical actuality," materialized in legal and other documents legitimizing European conquest and the ensuing white supremacist rule. Conflating humanness with personhood, Mills underestimates the punitive recognition of criminous black personhood. Mills, *Racial Contract*, 19. Failing to distinguish between black political exclusion and black legal exclusion, Mills neglects the strategic alternation between exclusion and inclusion discussed by Agamben, Hartman, Gross, and Dayan. Defining "white men as full persons and full contractors, while white women and nonwhite men are subpersons and subcontractors," in his revised "Racial-Sexual Contract," Mills, schematically designating "nonwhite women" as "nonpersons and noncontractors," fails to take into account the strategic punitive recognition of black women's personhood for the purposes of criminal prosecution; potentially more useful, albeit less developed, is his reference to "nonsignatories." Pateman and Mills, *Contract*, 175, 262.

140. See B. Thomas, *Civic Myths*; criminality's contradictory function under the combined fictions of mixed character and the social contract help us to address the issues Fanuzzi raises regarding the formerly enslaved publicist's relationship to print culture as mediated by antebellum abolitionism: "He remained on the threshold of the public sphere . . . somewhere between the objectification of the embruted slave and the transcendence of the rational citizen." Fanuzzi, *Abolition's Public Sphere*, 210–11. Whereas Fanuzzi emphasizes Douglass's recourse to the sublime, I suggest that recognized culpable personhood in law and print was instrumental to the black persona's gradual movement out of this liminal space from the colonial period onward.

Focusing on contract's promises and failures, few scholars have devoted sustained attention to considering how the punitive provisions of social contract theory in particular might undermine as well as reveal that theory's exclusionary logic. The exception is Ellerman, *Property* (which Pateman also cites on this point in "Self-Ownership," 48). Otherwise, see Pateman, *Sexual*; Mills, *Racial Contract*; Pateman and Mills, *Contract*; Rawls, *Theory*; Nussbaum, *Justice*. In his brief discussion of crime, Mills sees racial differentials in the definition and response to criminal activity only as an effect of the racial contract and therefore does not address how criminality might complicate the contract's terms (84–89).

141. Locke, *Second Treatise*, 4.

142. Kant, *Metaphysics*, 130; emphasis omitted.

143. Hong, *Ruptures*, 11, 10.

144. Blackstone, *Commentaries*, 4:23.

145. Brewer, *By Birth*, 184; see also McKeon, "Responsibility," 28; Welsh, *Strong Representations*, 97.

146. J. Wilson, *Complete Works*, 1094; see also Edwards, *People*, 221.

147. Wilson's rejection of Blackstone's derivation of "felony" from the words for "fief, feud, or beneficiary estate" and "price or value" in favor of an etymology based on the Latin and Greek words signifying, respectively, "to deceive" and "an imposter or deceiver," places his own definition of crime more firmly in social contract theory. J. Wilson, *Complete Works*, 1096–1101.

148. For Foucault this contractarian logic rendered the criminal "a juridically paradoxical being." *Discipline*, 90, see 89–92.

149. Montesquieu, *Spirit*, 248; see also Hobbes, *Leviathan*, 141.

150. Montesquieu, *Spirit*, 249.

151. Mills, *Racial Contract*, 11–12.

152. J. Wilson, *Complete Works*, 1204; compare Blackstone, *Commentaries*, 4:373–74.

153. Foucault, *Discipline*, 130.

154. Rousseau, *Social*, 65; see also Bar, *History*, 272.

155. Rousseau's moral persons have "no physical existence . . . but owe their existence to agreements, covenants, [or] contracts." Victor Gourevitch, introduction to Rousseau, *Social*, xlv.

156. Rousseau, *Social*, 53.

157. Kant, *Metaphysics*, 106

158. Brewer, *By Birth*, 228.

159. Wideman, "Killing Black Boys" quoted in Holloway, *Passed On*, 7–8.

160. Whether studying rich Afro-diasporic cultural formations around death or the ways in which death has been wielded as a means of racialized social control, scholars have taken biopolitical theory and Patterson's *Slavery and Social Death* as twin points of departure for an analysis that places the transatlantic slave trade and race slavery at the center of a "necropolitics and necropower . . . in which vast populations are subjected to conditions of life conferring upon them the status of *living dead*." Mbembe, "Necropolitics," 40; see Dayan, *Law*; Castronovo, *Necro*, 34–45; Gould, *Barbaric*, 43–85; Young, *Black Frankenstein*; Canuel, *Shadow*, 142–67; V. Brown, *Reaper's Garden*; JanMohamed, *Death-Bound Subject*; S. Holland, *Raising*; Roach, *Cities*; Holloway, *Passed On*. The classic works on biopower/biopolitics are Schmitt, *Political Theology*; Foucault, *Society* and *Birth*; Agamben, *Homo Sacer*. For an African Americanist critique, see Wagner, *Disturbing*, 20–21.

161. M. Weiner, *Black Trials*, 9, 11.

162. Ibid., 13; see also Suggs, *Whispered*.

163. M. Weiner, *Black Trials*, xi; see also R. Ferguson, *Trial*.

164. Agamben, *Homo Sacer*, 90; see also Foucault, *Discipline*, 110–11, 130–31.

338 Notes to Pages 81–85

165. Contrast Foucault's account of the legal-theoretical crisis posed by the trial of Louis XVI; Foucault, *Abnormal*, 95.

166. JanMohamed's analysis focuses exclusively on "a whimsical and mercurial circulation of the threat of death" which "in order to affirm its sovereign power, [must] be extra-legal," requiring "that every such act falls *outside* the prevailing judicial procedures governing the death penalty." JanMohamed, *Death-Bound Subject*, 8, 9. See also Agamben, *Homo Sacer*, 83.

167. "Letter of Colonel Revere to Cor. Sec. of Mass. Hist. Soc.," quoted in Goodell, *Trial*, 30.

168. See Lemire, *Black Walden*, 41–59; see also Suggs, *Whispered*, 19–21.

169. *Boston Evening Post*, September 22, 1755, quoted in Goodell, *Trial*, 29. On usages of the word "gibbet" and racialized uses of the apparatus, see Sellin, "Philadelphia Gibbet Iron."

170. Rea quoted in Goodell, *Trial*, 30; Bartlett quoted in Sellin, "Philadelphia Gibbet Iron," 16.

171. On the criminal as exemplar of both guilt and redemption, see Halttunen, *Murder*, 21–22; C. Smith, *Prison*.

172. Agamben, *Homo Sacer*, 103; on the exemplar and belonging, see 21, 22; on social contract theory's "punitive semio-technique," see Foucault, *Discipline*, 89–114, 128–31 (quotation at 103).

173. *Few Lines*.

174. On the dilemma slavery posed to charges of both high and petit treason, see T. Morris, *Southern Slavery*, 264–65. In one notable illustration, counsel for the black defendants in the trial following the attack on the federal arsenal at Harpers Ferry successfully cited the *Dred Scott* decision to support their claim for the inapplicability of treason charges; Oates, *Purge*, 327.

175. See Goodell, *Trial*, 29–30. The distinction bears underscoring, given the scholarly tendency to conflate "outlaw" with "convict": an otherwise helpful account of the criminal prosecution of the slave as a form of legal recognition refers to "the convicted black outlaw"; Hunter, "Race," 80. To be processed by law is to have one's outlaw status terminated.

176. *Few Lines*.

177. Haskell, "Persons," 442.

178. Aristotle, *Politics*, 1252a.

179. Ibid., 1253b.

180. On the comparative importance of temporality—as either foreseeability or responsibility for past conduct—in the assessment of punishable criminal intent, see Rodensky, *Crime*, 26–30, 39–41.

181. Kant, *Metaphysics*, 154.

182. Ibid., 16; see also McKeon, "Responsibility," 17–18.

183. For implicit acknowledgment of the potential for such a fictive or artificial allocation of power through that of responsibility, especially in the interstices of criminal law and politics, see Pennock, "Problem," 19, 23.

184. Hong, *Ruptures*, 3, 4.

185. Wong, *Neither*, 77–126.

186. Dayan, "Legal Slaves," 66.

187. Gates, "Writing," 9.

Chapter 2. Black Catalogues: Crime, Print, and the Rise of the Black Self

1. Serialized over twelve weekly installments, January 31 to April 17, 1856, the work reappeared during Southworth's lifetime as "The Presentiment" in *The Haunted Homestead: And Other Nouvellettes. With an Autobiography of the Author* (1860); as *The Red Hill Tragedy: A Novel* (1877); and as *Broken Pledges: A Story of Noir et Blanc* (1891); see Homestead and Washington, *Southworth*. Notably, the revised antebellum version, "The Presentiment," omits much of the story's explicitly antislavery commentary, supporting Christopher Looby's argument regarding the relevance of print, specifically periodical, contexts to any assessment of the political investments of Southworth's fiction, even as it complicates the account of her relationship to abolitionism and challenges the surmise that "the texts of her novels are virtually identical in their serial and book forms"; "Southworth." 183. On Southworth as an anti-gallows writer, see P. Jones, *Against*, 134–59.

2. E.D.E.N. Southworth, "The Brothers," *National Era*, March 20, 1856.

3. Ibid., April 17, January 31, 1856.

4. Ibid., April 17, 1856.

5. On the judiciary's "moral-formal dilemma" under the legal regime of U.S. slavery, see Cover, *Justice*, 5.

6. Southworth, "Brothers," April 10, April 17, 1856.

7. Ibid., April 10, 1856.

8. Ibid., April 17, 1856.

9. Ibid., April 10, 1856.

10. Ibid., April 3, April 10, 1856.

11. Ibid., April 17, 1856.

12. Ibid., January 31, April 17, 1856. On tragedy in "The Brothers," see Tracey, "E.D.E.N. Southworth's Tragic Muse."

13. Southworth, "Brothers," April 17, January 31, 1856.

14. "When his case was fully investigated," Southworth writes, "it was obvious to all minds, that had the fatal encounter . . . taken place between two equals, either two white men, or two negroes, the survivor would have been scarcely arraigned," otherwise, "the verdict . . . must have been, 'Justifiable Homicide.'" Ibid., April 10, 1856.

15. The quoted newspaper item with which the original *National Era* version of the novella commences omits any print acknowledgment of Governor even as it identifies Valentine by name: "On Friday, the 24th ultimo, the mulatto boy, Valentine convicted of the murder of his master, was executed according to his sentence." Ibid., January 31, 1856.

16. Ibid., April 17, 1856.

17. Mascuch, *Origins*, 206.

18. On Mountain, see D. Cohen, "Social Injustice," 501–3; Wilf, *Imagined*, 105–24.

19. This literary history is reflected in the structure of Franklin, *Prison Literature*.

20. Arthur, *Life, and Dying Speech*.

21. D. Cohen, *Pillars*, 25.

22. It is difficult to conclude from internal evidence whether the black subjects of early personal narratives were enslaved, indentured servants, or quasi-slaves under gradual emancipation schemes; Carretta, *Unchained*, 24n3; Weyler, "Race," 51n11; Elmer, "Black Atlantic," 167. Such ambiguity is consistent with contemporaries' confusion regarding the ambiguous and often unstable condition of individual black servants. See Von Frank, "John Saffin"; but see also the distinction between "free Negro" and "Negro servant" in colonial Massachusetts in Desrochers, "Surprizing Deliverance," 174n31. Of Arthur, Breen notes that "in court documents the king's attorney described the accused as a 'labourer and servant of Edward Clark of Rutland District,' but presumably everyone knew that Arthur was in fact a slave," without explaining or documenting the latter assertion. Breen, "Making," 89. Newspaper reports of the trial refer to "a Negro Fellow named Arthur, Servant of Mr. Edward Clark." *Postscript to the Massachusetts-Gazette, Boston News-Letter*, October 15, 1767; *Boston Evening-Post*, October 12, 1767. That Arthur is supposed to have pled benefit of clergy is probably not relevant. In contrast to England, in colonial America "most everyone was entitled to benefit of clergy," including slaves in heavily slaveholding colonies like Virginia. Pestritto, *Founding*, 160n29; see also K. Hall, *Magic Mirror*, 132. References to Arthur as a slave also appear in W. Andrews, *To Tell*, 41; D. Cohen, *Pillars*, 125. Even if Arthur were not enslaved, the points made here would, at least in broad strokes, still apply, given the very ambiguity of his status, compounded by the pervasive cultural identification of nominally free with enslaved blacks in terms of civic and political exclusion and imputed criminality. See also Melish, *Disowning*, 74–79.

23. Frasier, *Brief Account*, 3.

24. Breen, "Making," 75–92; more generally, see D. Cohen, *Pillars*, 124, 131, 133, 134; S. White, "Death." In the European context, see Ginzburg, *Myths*; Linebaugh, "Ordinary" and *London*. For a literary scholar's reconstruction of the 1738 Connecticut execution of Katherine Garret (Pequot), see Schorb, "Seeing."

25. *The Life, and Dying Speech of Arthur* is mentioned but receives virtually no sustained analysis in Starling, *Slave Narrative*, 53–55; Slotkin, "Narratives," 20; Foster, *Witnessing*, 36; W. Andrews, *To Tell*, 41.

26. Differing accounts of Arthur's words on the scaffold appear in the published execution sermons as well as in the broadside; McCarty, *Power*, 28, and Hutchinson, *Iniquity*, 23.

27. Arthur, *Life, and Dying Speech*.

28. Hutchinson, *Iniquity*, 21–22.

29. Breen concludes that "the slave seems to have controlled the character and flow of his own story"; "Making," 79. On pardons, see Meranze, *Laboratories*, 41–43.

30. Frasier, *Brief Account*, 14.

31. For a reminder of the importance of distinguishing, in such generalizations, be-

tween narrative and its historical contexts we need only turn to the newspaper report of Arthur's hanging: "We hear that a negro fellow was tried at the Assizes held lately at Worcester, for a rape, and found guilty, and received a sentence of death.—A white man was also tried and found guilty of attempting the same crime and sentenced to sit on the gallows." *Boston Chronicle*, September 26, 1768, quoted in Breen, "Making," 91. Whether the different treatment lies in the convict's race, the success of his rape attempt, or some combination of the two is unclear.

32. See Linebaugh and Rediker, *Hydra*, 111; on "hierarchies of servitude," see Desrochers, "Surprizing Deliverance," 159. But see Tomlins, *Freedom Bound*.

33. J. Green, *Life and Confession*; Frasier, *Brief Account*, 3, 4.

34. Arthur, *Life, and Dying Speech*. Notwithstanding this seemingly unambiguous confession, the broadside continues: "The next Morning the unhappy Woman came and acquainted my Master of it, who immediately tyed me, to prevent me running away and told her (if she was desirous of prosecuting me) to get a Warrant as soon as possible; but she being unwilling to have me hanged, proposed making the Matter up for a proper Consideration, provided my Master would send me out of the Country; to which he agreed, and accordingly set off with me for *Albany*: But we were were overtaken at *Glasgow*, by Mr. *Nathaniel Jennison*, who it seem'd had got a Warrant for me." This was the same Jennison whose beating of the enslaved Quock Walker thirteen years later culminated in *Commonwealth v. Jennison* (1783), the court case often cited as marking the end to slavery in Massachusetts. Breen, "Making," 94; see Higginbotham, *Matter*, 91–98. On the relative absence of the soon-to-be ubiquitous image of sexually predatory African American masculinity in eighteenth- and nineteenth-century confessions attributed to convicted black rapists, see D. Cohen, "Social Injustice," 522.

35. *Boston Gazette, or, Weekly Advertiser*, May 7, May 14, 1754. An abridged version of the advertisement appears in Greene, *Negro*, 176, which cites the year as 1757.

36. A Boston merchant, Henry Darrall had a particularly prolonged posthumous print presence as, for over a year, first his commercial goods and then his personal effects were disposed of and debts and credits resolved through regularly advertised probate proceedings; see *Boston Evening-Post*, May 14, 1753; *Boston Evening-Post*, May 21, 1753; *Boston News-Letter*, November 2, 1753; *Boston Evening-Post*, May 20, 1754.

37. *Boston Evening-Post*, May 21, 1753.

38. Arthur, *Life, and Dying Speech*.

39. On property and futurity, see Best, *Fugitive's Properties*, 31–33, 88.

40. Macpherson, *Political Theory*, 142; for an overview, see Brace, *Politics*; in the racialized context of the U.S., see C. Harris, "Whiteness," 1725.

41. See Radin, "Property," 959–61.

42. Ibid., 968.

43. On the importance of private property to the early modern development of a self-possessed individualist self, see Mascuch, *Origins*, 17, 22.

44. *Boston Evening-Post*, March 5, 1750.

45. See, alternatively, Best, *Fugitive's Properties*; Underkuffler, "On Property," 136.

46. Patterson, *Slavery*, 28

47. Douglass, *My Bondage*, 304–5; for an insightful psychoanalytic reading of this question, see JanMohamed, *Death-Bound Subject*, 294–300.

48. In the African American context, see V. Brown, *Reaper's Garden*, 113–28; Penningroth, *Claims*, 89–91.

49. On running away as a racially inflected alternative to recourse to the courts in colonial Massachusetts, see Towner, "Fondness," 213–15. Crucially, Arthur's "crime" of running away was not likely to have been construed as theft. Ubiquitous scholarly references to "stealing oneself" notwithstanding, "no statute ever defined running away itself as an act of theft" due to "the conceptual problem" posed by "the intention of the act." Because runaways' intent was not to steal themselves for profit but to "transform their position from property to persons," or some other motive, such as avoiding punishment or reuniting with family, such prohibited acts were a form of disobedience. T. Morris, *Southern Slavery*, 341; see also Greene, *Negro*, 149; Higginbotham, *Matter*, 119, 121; McManus, *History*, 110–11, 120–22.

50. Community assessment of potential transgressors compensated for absence of systemic record-keeping across local, colonial, and later state borders, with predictably repressive results regarding race; Flaherty, "Crime," 347–48. See *Boston News Letter*, July 16–23, 1741; *Boston Gazette*, July 13–20, 1741.

51. On character as individual credit, a form of reputation distinct from honor or social position and thus available to subordinates, see Edwards, *People*, 111–32.

52. Frasier, *Brief Account*, 3, 5.

53. Ibid., 7.

54. Madison, Hamilton, and Jay, *Federalist*, 332.

55. Sawyer, *Southern Institutes*, 313. As discussed in the previous chapter, such proceedings in fact had an established place in Western legal history.

56. Arthur, *Life, and Dying Speech*.

57. Ibid.

58. Gould, *Barbaric*, 148; see also Fichtelberg, "Word"; and Hinds, "Spirit."

59. Criminality also confounds the paternalistic logic whereby the slave's self-purchase is understood as a token of gratitude for the master's own gift of manumission; Patterson, *Slavery*, 211.

60. Haskell, "Persons," 473–74. See Caldwell, *Puritan*; McGiffert, *God's Plot*; Swaim, "Women's Puritan Evidences."

61. McKeon, "Responsibility," 28; see also Mascuch, *Origins*, 38, 155–56.

62. These categories reflect the different literary registers in which early black rapists appear, see D. Cohen, "Social Injustice."

63. Foucault, *Discipline*, 252. The applicability of Foucault's disciplinary theory in the American context is limited by an oversimplification of the historical transition from public spectacle of the scaffold to private discipline of the penitentiary (Morris and Rothman, *Oxford*, 3–129); the focus on a European, inquisitorial rather than an Anglo-American, adversarial juridical order (Rodensky, *Crime*, 16–19, 46–47; Grossman, *Art*,

14–29); and a failure adequately to address the complicating question of race (Wiegman, *American*, 21–42, but see also Foucault, *Society*).

64. Foucault, *Discipline*, 193.

65. Americanist critiques of Foucault's epochal shift from spectacular corporal punishment to interiorized disciplinary practices emphasize the role of print in extending penal publicity into the era of the penitentiary; see Meranze, *Laboratories*, 174; Masur, *Rites*, 93–116; C. Smith, *Prison*; Schorb, "Writing," 30.

66. C. Smith., *Prison*, 111.

67. Ibid., 110, 6.

68. Ibid., 13–14, 31–32; for the argument that parties to the social compact could consent only to the forfeiture of their liberty, not their lives, see Beccaria, *Essay*, 112–13.

69. C. Smith., *Prison*, 44, 49.

70. For a similar point with respect to gallows literature devoted to condemned Indians, see Grandjean, "Our *Fellow-Creatures*," 945.

71. Mather, *Negro Christianized*, 6.

72. *New-England Weekly Journal*, May 29, 1727; see also "A Short Account of the Life of Elizabeth Colson, who now must Dye for the Monstrous Sin of Murdering her Child," *New-England Weekly Journal*, June 19, 1727; see Schorb, "Uncleanliness," 78–81.

73. See C. Smith, *Prison*, 104. Published as a Transactions of the Historical and Literary Committee of the American Philosophical Society pamphlet, the essay was reprinted in *Pennsylvania Journal of Prison Discipline and Philanthropy* (the version used here; Coates, "Effects"), and excerpted in both *Proceedings of the American Philosophical Society* (1843) and *New York Journal of Medicine and the Collateral Sciences* (1844).

74. Brightly, *Digest*, 1660.

75. Coates, "Effects," 267–68.

76. Yannielli, "George Thompson," 982–88.

77. G. Thompson, *Prison*, 156.

78. Ibid., 129–30.

79. Franklin, *Prison Literature*, 73–276; C. Smith, *Prison*, 141–71; on these developments more generally, see Dayan, "Held" and "Legal"; Oshinsky, *Worse*. A tantalizing exception is former Auburn inmate Robert Reed's manuscript memoir, *The Life and Adventures of a Haunted Convict, or the Inmate of a Gloomy Prison. With the Mysteries and Miseries of the New York House of Reffuge* [sic] *and Auburn Prison Unmasked* (c. 1857); Between the Covers Rare Books, *Catalog 145*, 56–58. Notably, this document did not appear in print.

80. Franklin, *Prison Literature*, 124–78.

81. See C. Smith, *Prison*, 27–137.

82. Particularly relevant here is the debate from the 1820s through the 1850s over the incarceration of free black seamen by South Carolina and other states: emphasizing the absence of both criminality and of the political membership that would have enabled habeas corpus proceedings, the debate yielded an influential novel by F. C. Adams, *Manuel Pereira; or, The Sovereign Rule of South Carolina* (1853). Tellingly, the imprisoned

Notes to Pages 106–111

"Pereira, caught in this prolonged interval of civil death, threatens to disappear from the story" that bears his name; Wong, *Neither,* 218, see 183–239.

83. Robbins, "Gendering."

84. Melville, "Benito Cereno," 114, 116.

85. Lee, *Slavery,* 146.

86. Ibid.

87. In a reading demonstrating Babo's lack of control of the slave rebels, Lee notes that "the more that Babo is held responsible, the more of his cohorts survive to be sold," making it clear that the court's "'partial renumeration of the negroes' . . . brings a remuneration partial to whites." Ibid., 144.

88. Sale, *Slumbering,* 146–97; Thomas, *Cross-Examinations,* 103–4, 111; Sundquist, *To Wake,* 27–221. On other points of intersection, see Levine and Otter, *Douglass and Melville.*

89. Douglass, "Heroic," 482–83.

90. On Babo's silence, see Yellin, "Black Masks," 687–89; Karcher, *Shadow,* 139–41; Rogin, *Subversive,* 217; Thomas, *Cross-Examinations,* 99, 111–12; Sale, *Slumbering,* 159–61, 170–72; Nelson, *Word,* 127–30; Sundquist, *To Wake,* 181–82.

91. See Bartley, "Creature," 467; I. Wilson, *Specters,* 142. For an instructive contrast illustrating the distinctions between police power and criminal prosecution as aligned to cultural versus political manifestations of black civic presence, see the reading of George Washington Cable's municipal repositioning of the Bras-Coupé legend in the *Grandissimes* in Wagner, *Disturbing,* 58–115.

92. Madow, "Forbidden," 476; for an excellent overview of the cultural climate in which Gibbs and Wansley were hanged in antebellum New York City, see 469–510.

93. Advertisement. *New-Hampshire Gazette,* July 15, 1834.

94. See, for example, *Lives and Trials.*

95. Wansley, *Life and Confession,* 23; see also C. Gibbs, *Mutiny,* 19; in newspaper accounts the phrasing quoted here is attributed to the *New York Commercial Advertiser:* see, for example, *Rhode-Island Republican,* March 17, 1831; *New-Hampshire Patriot,* March 21, 1831. For alternate phrasing see *Correct Account,* 21; *Norwich* [*Conn.*] *Courier,* March 16, 1831.

96. Wansley, *Life and Confession,* 24.

97. Ibid.; other versions vary slightly: see *Correct Account,* 23; C. Gibbs, *Mutiny,* 21; *Norwich* [*Conn.*] *Courier,* March 16, 1831. Following the District Attorney's motion to "submit the cause without argument, upon the charge of the Judge," and the defense's decision to "leav[e] the cause to his Honor and the jury; reserving their right to move in arrest of judgment," the jury deliberated for twenty minutes before finding Wansley guilty; by contrast, Gibbs's lawyers "occupied two hours in concluding the defence," with the jury deliberating for over two hours before reaching a guilty verdict. *Baltimore Patriot,* March 11, 1831. In any case, Wansley's protest referred less to Gibbs's trial than to the comparatively lenient treatment accorded to the two white shipmates who testified against them at the trials.

98. H. Brooke, *Book of Pirates*, 154.

99. On Gibbs's identity, see J. Gibbs, *Dead Men*, 12–35.

100. H. Brooke, *Book of Pirates*, 154–55.

101. *Lives and Trial*, 314.

102. C. Gibbs, *Confession*, 7.

103. Wansley, *Life and Confession*, 24.

104. *Norwich [Conn.] Courier*, March 16, 1831.

105. Ibid.

106. *Lives and Trial*, 327.

107. Ibid., 328. On the subsequent shift from a classical republican to a liberal mode of individual responsibility, and specifically the (ironically) titled Good Samaritan Law whose tacit racial bias lay in the race-neutral exemption of bystanders from responsibility from preventing observed injuries, thereby ignoring blacks' disproportionate historic role as both victims and self-sacrificing Samaritans, see Goodman, *Shifting*, 14, 116–32.

108. The author may have been "Newport native and career politician James Cogge-shall," who "served as a senior official in [New York] prisons" during Gibbs and Wans-ley's imprisonment and forwarded Gibbs's disclosures to President Andrew Jackson; J. Gibbs, *Dead Men*, 137.

109. Layman, *Visit*, 1.

110. On the nineteenth-century use of the Apollo Belvedere as the ideal on a physi-ognomic scale of normative human appearances against which to measure the patho-logical, see Gilman, *Seeing*, 73.

111. See also Wansley, *Life and Confession*, 10–13.

112. C. Gibbs, *Confessions*, 15

113. Reprinted excerpt from *New York Journal of Commerce* in *Haverhill Gazette*, April 30, 1831; see also *Eastern Argus*, April 26, 1831.

114. Reprinted excerpt from *New York Journal of Commerce* in *Haverhill Gazette*, April 30, 1831.

115. A letter was sent to President Andrew Jackson, who ordered an inquiry into the credibility of the information, the results of which are unknown. J. Gibbs, *Dead Men*, 136–38; Hamilton, *Reminiscences*, 218, 248–49.

116. Wansley, *Life and Confession*, iii.

117. Ibid.

118. See ibid., 10–13.

119. Questionable in their own time, Gibbs's claims have not been conclusively sub-stantiated; see J. Gibbs, *Dead Men*.

120. Layman, *Visit*, 3.

121. C. Gibbs, *Confessions*, 15.

Chapter 3. The Ignominious Cord: Crime, Counterfactuals, and the New Black Politics

1. Johnstone, *Address*, 3.

2. D. Cohen, *Pillars*, 143–63; see also Wilf, *Imagined*, 56–104.

3. On July 4 celebrations in this period, see Warren, "Fourth of July"; Waldstreicher, *Perpetual*, 108–73.

4. Best, *Fugitive's Properties*, 206; see also Castiglia, *Interior States*, 5.

5. Melish, *Disowning*.

6. Gardner, *Master Plots*, 7; see also C. Holland, *Body Politic*, 10; Fliegelman, *Declaring*, 140–50; Loughran, *Republic*, 226; Greiman, *Democracy's Spectacle*, 36–120.

7. Thanks to Michael Winship for pointing out the bibliographic and historiographic applicability of this concept specifically to the Johnstone of the *Address*, given the surprising number of extant copies in various archives, which could point to the pamphlet's reach; see Evans, *American Bibliography*, 11:217.

8. Hearn, *Legal Executions*, 63; see also Hartnett, *Executing*, 123–60. The unsigned preface reveals nothing about its author's identity, racial or otherwise. "Printed for the Purchasers," the hermetic pamphlet does not indicate who they or the printer might be. According to the Library Company of Philadelphia's catalogue entry, the pamphlet was "ascribed by Evans to the press of Robert Bell," who, however, "died in 1784, and no one else of that name is known to have printed in Philadelphia in the eighteenth century." For speculation on authorship see Hunter, "Race," 85, 92; Hartnett, *Executing*, 133; Otter, *Philadelphia*, 42. Although the current study does not turn on questions of authorial authenticity, smooth syntax often requires at least semantic attribution. Given the complexity of the *Address*'s atttentiveness to and critique of the deferential moral reform rhetoric of the patron-client politics of respectability, it does not seem necessary to pin the text's ambiguities on an imagined amanuensis. Without sliding into the verbal grotesqueries of racial caricature, the pamphlet's run-on sentences and awkward spelling suggest an author whose polemical objectives and intellectual capacity exceed the grasp of his formal education—or, in the case of the "Address," a hastily transcribed, largely unedited speech. (On early national textual racial caricature, see S. White, *Somewhat*, 66–75; Melish, *Disowning*, 163–209; J. Stewart, "Modernizing," 701.) Given the account of Warner Mifflin's involvement in Johnstone's manumission, it is possible that the wealthy, white Kent County abolitionist may have played a role in making the pamphlet available to the public by arranging for its publication or penning its preface. The possibility of Mifflin's involvement is made even more tantalizing by the Philadelphia publication, the year prior to Johnstone's *Address*, of the Quaker activist's own exculpatory personal narrative, *The Defence of Warner Mifflin* (1796). Perhaps the man who only a few years earlier had sought, "in the temper of a Christian, and the firmness of a veteran American Freeman, to plead the cause of injured innocence, and open my mouth for my oppressed brethren, who cannot open theirs for themselves," recognized in the figure of Johnstone someone even better positioned to speak on behalf of the people of color. Mifflin, *Serious Expostulation*, 11–12. Given Mifflin's own embattled position, Johnstone's less than exemplary position as a condemned man might explain the anonymity surrounding the *Address*. (Johnstone's fate renders more than a little ironic the African Methodist Episcopal Church's elegiac "hope," upon Mifflin's 1798 death of yellow fever, "that every slave he has been instrumental in freeing, is a star in his garment.")

Articles of Association, 17.) In addition to the Mifflin family, several people and places named by the *Address* appear in the historical record. On Enoch Sharp as "a member of a family that was among the colony's and then the state's oldest and most prominent landholders," see Hartnett, *Executing,* 152. Johnstone mentions being "charged . . . unjustly by William Tatem, Esq. with robbing his smoak house." Johnstone, *Address,* 35. A William Tatem was "born on 23 Jun[e] 1737 in Gloucester, New Jersey" and "died on 1 May 1820" in the same county. http://myweb.cableone.net/kevinowen3/ginnygarberancestors/pafg172.htm. Johnstone also recalls being "a chosen member of the Methodistical Society, and in William Thomas's class" while still in Delaware. Johnstone, *Address,* 36. A historical marker for Thomas's Chapel in Chapeltown, Kent County, notes that the church was renamed "to honor William Thomas, a local Methodist leader who was instrumental in securing the church building" in the late 1770s. "Kent County Markers: Thomas' Chapel," Delaware Public Archives, last modified December 30, 2009, accessed July 9, 2011, http://archives.delaware.gov/markers/kc/THOMAS%20CHAPEL%20KC%2052.shtml.

9. D. Cohen, "Social Injustice," 516. Cohen finds the pamphlet challenging the disproportionate attribution of crime to blacks; stressing systematic white supremacy; tracing existing black crime to environmental sources; and challenging prevalent views of racial inferiority. The brief reading in Starling, *Slave Narrative,* 88–89, reaches the opposite conclusion. On the pamphlet's uniqueness, see also Hunter, "Race," 85; Otter, *Philadelphia,* 42.

10. Newman, "Protest," 187.

11. Johnstone, *Address,* 2; Gates, *Signifying*; Eddie Glaude adapts Evelyn Brooks Higginbotham's "politics of respectability" to the early national period. *Exodus,* 100.

12. Newman and Finkenbine, "Forum," 91.

13. Addressing how presumptions of black criminality authorized surveillance of African Americans, fostered a deference politics of respectability, and exposed the dangers of such a politics, this chapter provides a prehistory to the account of policing and litigation in Fourth Amendment contexts offered by Carbado, "(E)racing."

14. Johnstone, *Address,* 32. Johnstone's specification of Sussex County notwithstanding, Johnny Cake Landing (now Frederica) is listed as being in Kent County, in the hundred of Murderkill, previously known as Motherkill or Motherkiln (and thus possibly the source of Johnstone's "Mother Kind Hundred"). Delaware Genealogical Society, "Delaware Towns and Places: Taken from the *Delaware Genealogical Research Guide,*" last modified September 6, 2010, accessed July 9, 2011, http://delgensoc.org/deltowns.htm. Whereas Sussex County consistently had the state's highest slave population, Kent County was home to both Quaker and Methodist abolitionist activists and sympathizers, most notably, Warner Mifflin; Essah, *House Divided,* 75–86. For possible alternative locations, see Hartnett, *Executing,* 257–58n22.

15. T. Whitman, *Challenging,* 53. The Delaware legislature illegalized out-of-state slave sales in 1787, although kidnappings of course occurred; Essah, *House Divided,* 40–41, 122–23.

348 Notes to Pages 123–125

16. Johnstone's James Clements was most likely James McClyment: "In 1787 Daniel Mifflin sold James McClyment a tract of land approximately ten acres in size at the southwest corner of Mifflin's Crossroads (Camden). . . . A house (14 South Main Street) that had been built circa 1780 on the property possibly by Daniel Mifflin was conveyed along with the ten acre plot. Records show that James McClyment and his family took up residence in this house" which "the National Register of Historic Places Inventory" refers to as "this most pretentious of eighteenth-century Camden dwellings." "South Main Street Camden, Delaware: James McClyment House Information," Friends of Historic Camden, accessed July 9, 2011, http://www.historiccamdende.org/camden-smain.php.

17. Johnstone, *Address*, 34.

18. The Delaware Society for Promoting the Abolition of Slavery was succeeded on its 1795 demise by the Wilmington-based Delaware Society for the Gradual Abolition of Slavery, which sent delegates to the Philadelphia Convention in 1795 and 1796; Essah, *House Divided*, 59–60. Dying on October 16, 1798, the year following Abraham Johnstone's execution, Mifflin was buried in the graveyard at the Murderkill/Motherkiln Friends Meeting in Kent County, Delaware—possibly near the location identified as Johnstone's birthplace.

19. See Mifflin, *Defence*, 26.

20. Johnstone's characterization of the Quaker's role carried legal as well as social connotations, given that "Mifflin . . . was frequently named as the 'next best friend' or adviser on many freedom suits, which often resulted in freedom for the slave." Essah, *House Divided*, 50.

21. Such fears were well founded: around this same time another enslaved Kent County man known to Mifflin petitioned the Court for his freedom, only to be seized, bound, and dragged behind a horse, becoming "so mangled and bruised that he died the next Morning." Mifflin, *Defence*, 25; see also T. Whitman, *Challenging*, 48.

22. See Hartnett, *Executing*, 144–45.

23. As in Hunter, "Race," italicized references to the *Address* refer to the entire pamphlet, whereas "Address" specifically indicates the first of the assembled documents, the exhortation to the people of color.

24. On authenticating documents, see Sekora, "Black Message"; Stepto, "I Rose." On similar omissions in works by Afro-British writers Ottabah Cugoano and Olaudah Equiano, see Carretta, *Equiano*, 294.

25. Newman, *Freedom's Prophet*, 25.

26. Zilversmit, *First Emancipation*, 124–37.

27. On the convergence of print and penal reform in Philadelphia, see C. Smith, *Prison*, 105; on that of abolition and penal reform in the city and beyond, see Patrick-Stamp, "Numbers," and Canuel, *Shadow*, 142–67. More generally, see Otter, *Philadelphia*.

28. Newman, *Freedom's Prophet*, 78.

29. Dumm, *Democracy*, 87–111; Meranze, *Laboratories*, 131–214; McLennan, *Crisis*, 32–52.

30. G. Nash, *Forging Freedom*, 120.

31. On the 1790s as a disappointing follow-up to the optimism of the 1780s, see Lapsansky, "Abigail," 70–74.

32. St. George Tucker, *Dissertation*, 88, 90.

33. "The most restrictive of the five gradual abolition laws enacted by northern states from 1780 to 1804," Pennsylvania's legislation "freed not a single slave; it held in lifelong bondage all children born before the law became effective; and it consigned to 28 years of servitude every child born of a slave after March 1, 1780. . . . Total abolition of slavery would not come to Pennsylvania, in fact, until 1847." Nash and Soderlund, *Freedom*, 111.

34. Melish, *Disowning*, 210–37; Gellman, *Emancipating*, 189–219.

35. Zilversmit, *First Emancipation*, 139–229.

36. See Chapter 1. In 1797, New Jersey and New York had penal laws resembling those in Pennsylvania; Dumm, *Democracy*, 106. On New York's joint introduction of a "more severe" definition of civil death and a gradual abolition scheme, see Dayan, "Legal Terrors," 75n25. The narrow defeat of a 1785 abolition bill revealed anxieties about black citizenship: when the New York Assembly's initial gradual emancipation bill severely curtailing free blacks' civil liberties failed in the Senate, a revised bill retained the original prohibition on black suffrage. Temporarily blocked in their efforts to consign free blacks to a real-life version of Tucker's civil slavery, the legislature opted for continued legal enslavement. See McManus, *History*, 161–79; Hodges, *Root*, 162–86; Gellman, *Emancipating*, 45–55.

37. Having reviewed nearly annual petitions for an abolitionist law since 1782, Delaware commenced, the month after Johnstone's execution, publishing the 1797 bill in the newspapers. Buying time under the pretense of fostering "mature deliberation," the legislature took no action the following year. Essah, *House Divided*, 52. For the terms of the print debate over slavery in Johnstone's Delaware, including the usual proslavery allegations that free blacks inevitably "must steal and rob in order to get a subsistence," see 64–66 ("Humanus," *Delaware Gazette*, October 24, 1789, quoted at 66).

38. The initial bill defeated by a close vote, a more restrictive one (which, as of 1800, would emancipate all black children at age twenty-eight) passed by a one-vote margin, prompting the house to publish the bill before proceeding farther; Zilversmit, *First Emancipation*, 184–85.

39. Joseph Bloomfield quoted in ibid., 185.

40. Further abortive efforts finally yielded a gradual abolition law which would manumit all black children born in the state after July 4, 1803, binding them in servitude until the age of twenty-one for women and twenty-five for men. Because the bill did nothing for those born before that date, in 1810 New Jersey had the dubious distinction of being the only Northern state whose slaves exceeded its free black population. The 1840s found New Jersey still debating its slave code. Even the 1846 "act to abolish slavery" ultimately offered merely "a modified form of slavery," due to elaborate postmanumission apprenticeship provisions. On the eve of the Civil War, in 1860, eighteen African Americans were still bound in New Jersey. Zilversmit, *Free Emancipation*, 193,

215, 220, 222; see also Price, *Freedom*, 51–86; Hodges, *Root*, 162–226; Hodges, *Slavery*, 113–70.

41. *New-Jersey Journal*, July 12, 1797.

42. Hodges, *Root*, 182–83. On fluctuating Methodist attitudes toward slavery in Johnstone's Delaware, see T. Whitman, *Challenging*, 70–76; Essah, *House Divided*, 56–59.

43. Fearon, *Sketches*, 168–69. Fearon's characterization of the city's unwritten law of racism as "penal" was apt, given Philadelphia magistrates' promotion of lawsuits against free blacks over minor pecuniary matters as a pretext for incarceration; see G. Nash, *Forging Freedom*, 227.

44. Humanity, "To the Editor," 182. Compare U.S. Congress, *Annals*, 4th Cong., 2d sess., 2015–18.

45. Humanity, "Sketch," 282. Compare U.S. Congress, *Annals*, 4th Cong., 2d sess., 2019–24.

46. The debate anticipated the antebellum controversy around the Gag Rule; Zaeske, *Signatures*, 20–21, 79. On abolitionist petitioning see W. Miller, *Arguing*; Curtis, *Free Speech*, 131–81.

47. Jefferson, *Notes*, 147, 149.

48. See Kazanjian, *Colonizing Trick*, 116, 118.

49. Webster, *Effects*, 12.

50. By contrast, the "regulatory sentiment" in Jefferson's colonization thought tends to operate long-distance. Kazanjian, *Colonizing Trick*, 122–23.

51. See Melish, *Disowning*, 120–22. For the argument that in the early republic "the major figures in the white-Negro debate were not really northern amnesiacs but people from the Middle Atlantic states like [Benjamin] Rush or [Benjamin] Barton who took a national perspective that denounced slavery and conceded its significance—and that of the free black presence—to 'free' territory," see B. Dain, *Hideous*, 25.

52. On publicity of black criminality as a catalyst to British attention to the problem of slavery, see Wong, *Neither*, 24.

53. Convention, *Proceedings of the Second Convention*, 11.

54. Ibid., 28.

55. This was particularly true of Johnstone's own Delaware; Essah, *House Divided*, 60–61.

56. Litwack, *North*, 93–95; Wagner, *Disturbing*, 58–73.

57. Melish, *Disowning*, 107–18, 119–39, 190–91. On Philadelphia, see Meranze, *Laboratories*, 197; for transcribed Walnut Street Prison records for 1795, see Patrick-Stamp, "Prison Sentence Docket." On the correlation of biographical detail to the specific management needs of local government, see K. Parker, "Making," 108, 116. See also Rothman, *Discovery*, 64–69.

58. Gellman, *Emancipating*, 46–47, see also 75.

59. Quoted in Rury, "Philanthropy," 233.

60. L. Harris, *Shadow*, 65; Rury, "Philanthropy," 234–36; White, *Somewhat*, 80–88.

61. March 27, 1798 Committee of Guardians Minute Book quoted in G. Nash, *Forg-*

ing Freedom, 177. Employing a similar system of domestic visits to police themselves, American Quakers from the beginning evinced a commitment to social control of black outsiders; see Nash and Soderland, *Freedom*, 44; on Quaker self-policing, see Dumm, *Democracy*, 78–79.

62. Convention, *Proceedings of the Second Convention*, 29–30.

63. Ibid., 23.

64. Convention, *To the Free Africans* (1796). With "fifteen hundred copies" scheduled "to be printed and distributed amongst the different Abolition Societies," the broadside undoubtedly reached a much larger audience; Convention, *Proceedings of the Third Convention*, 31. The PAS convened a large public meeting of free blacks at which the broadside was read aloud; in January 1798 the NYMS held a similar meeting at its African Free School, where the "address was read and explained by paragraphs, and the importance of [free blacks'] strict adherence to the advice contained therein was strongly urged"; G. Nash, *Forging Freedom*, 177; NYMS quoted in Rury, "Philanthropy," 236.

65. Convention, *To the Free Africans* (1796).

66. Convention, *To the Free Africans* (1797).

67. J. Stewart, "Modernizing," 694–95. For critiques, see J. Horton, "Comment"; Soderlund, "Comment"; Walters, "Comment"; see also J. Stewart, "Response." More generally, see Formisano, "Deferential-Participant Politics."

68. Newman, *Freedom's Prophet*, 129; see also Newman, "Protest," 187.

69. Newman and Finkenbine, "Forum," 86, 91; see also Richards, "Nationalist Themes."

70. See J. Stewart, "Emergence," 188–90.

71. Newman, "Protest," 184–85, 181.

72. Ibid., 185. On the importance of dialogue within black communities, see J. Brooks, "Early American."

73. J. Stewart, "Modernizing," 696.

74. Hammon, *Address*, ii.

75. J[ones] and A[llen], *Narrative*, 26.

76. Ibid., 27.

77. Griffith, "Total Dissolution," 50, 51. Published in four editions between November 13, 1793, and January 16, 1794, Carey's pamphlet sold over ten thousand copies along the Eastern seaboard (47).

78. Benezet, *Dunlap's American Daily Advertizer*, September 2, 1793.

79. Lapsansky, "Abigail," 63.

80. Ibid.

81. Griffith, "Total Dissolution," 54–55.

82. Ibid., 54–55.

83. Carey, *Short Account*, 76–77.

84. Ibid., 77.

85. Lapsansky, "Abigail," 61.

86. J[ones] and A[llen], *Narrative*, 12–13.

87. See also Otter, *Philadelphia*, 36, 297n16.

88. See also Powell, *Bring Out*, 94–101; G. Nash, *Forging Freedom*, 121–25; J. Bacon, "Rhetoric"; Gould, *Barbaric*, 152–89; Newman, *Freedom's Prophet*, 78–127.

89. As Chapter 5 discusses, such statistics would become a powerful argument against emancipation and for carceral supervision in antebellum America, especially in Philadelphia.

90. Carey, *Short Account*, 84–85.

91. Ibid., 84.

92. Compare Agamben, *Homo Sacer*, 159.

93. See Griffith, "Total Dissolution," 55.

94. Johnstone, *Address*, 14–15.

95. D. Epstein, *Sinful Tunes*, 111; Hunter, "Race," 92–93; see also H. Epstein, *Melting*, 164, 179n36; Lyons, *Sex*, 357n5; Starling, *Slave Narrative*, 88–89.

96. Johnstone, *Address*, 6.

97. [R. Allen,] *Confession*, 5.

98. Ibid., 23; Johnstone, *Address*, 38.

99. [R. Allen,] *Confession*, 4.

100. Johnstone, *Address*, 6–7.

101. D. Davis, *Slavery in the Age of Revolution*, 306.

102. *Oxford English Dictionary*, s.v. "counterfactual," accessed June 19, 2009.

103. Johnstone, *Address*, 5–6.

104. Best, *Fugitive's Properties*, 227; see also Gallagher, "Undoing" and "Confederate States of America"; Thomas, "Narratives."

105. Gallagher, "Undoing," 20. See also Hart and Honoré, *Causation*, lviii, 15; Collins, Hall, and Paul, *Counterfactuals*; Hawthorn, *Plausible*; N. Ferguson, *Virtual*; Gallagher and Greenblatt, *Practicing*, 49–74.

106. A. Miller, "Lives," 123.

107. Ibid.; for a consideration of how "the individuated counternarrative folds into the magical inexorability of the aggregate," see Jain, "Living," 85.

108. Mather, *Tremenda*, 29.

109. A. Miller, "Lives."

110. Marveling in his diary at "the Providence of my glorious Lord, still strangely continuing and multiplying my Opportunities to glorify Him," Mather noted with gratitude that "it comes to pass, that on my Lecture there falls out the Execution of a Negro, who has been instructed and baptised, and rendred [sic] himself a pretty noted Fellow, [and] is this day to be hanged for murdering his Wife." *Diary*, 2:620.

111. Mather, *Tremenda*, 23.

112. Johnstone, *Address*, 6, 15, 23.

113. See D. Davis, *Slavery in Western Culture*.

114. Notably, in 1797 Delaware "capped its voluntary manumission laws with an act that made freedom contracts binding and enforceable. . . . the legislature declared all verbal manumissions null and void and decreed that all freedom contracts should be

written, witnessed by a competent white citizen, attested to, and recorded by the state. These steps legally bound the slaveholder to honor the contract; in the event of a failure to do so, the slave could seek redress the courts." Essah, *House Divided*, 41.

115. See Gates, *Signifying*, xxiv.

116. In this reallocation of responsibility, Johnstone anticipates the rhetorical tactics of the "Appeal to Colored Citizens" published by the 1848 State Convention of the Colored Citizens of Pennsylvania, as discussed in Spires, "Imagining," 284–89.

117. Citing the work of Robert Michels and Max Lerner; Thomas, *Civic Myths*, 5.

118. Gallagher, "Undoing," 19.

119. Ibid., 24; Best, *Fugitive's Properties*, 213. A hallmark of early national tort law, with its compensatory damages, such remedial counterfactualism became from the 1960s onward "a collective undoing mission" expressed as "the will to compensate groups of people for the social and economic disadvantages resulting from acts of past discrimination either directly perpetrated or officially condoned by the federal government." Gallagher, "Undoing," 24; see also Jain, "Living," 85–90. See also the discussion of Pauline Hopkins's *Contending Forces* in DeLombard, "Novel."

120. Melish, *Disowning*, xiv, 3.

121. DeLombard, *Slavery on Trial*.

122. If the document evokes a common law tradition in which "a declaration was a descriptive account of grievances, not a proclamation of principles, a declaration of injuries, not of independence," it also recalls its more illustrious recent predecessor, in that "as both aggrieved narration and proclamation of rights," Johnstone's "Declaration" also "wanted it both ways." Fliegelman, *Declaring*, 151.

123. Johnstone, *Address*, 4.

124. The pamphlet thus treats the matter of Johnstone's guilt not in the long opening "Address," dated the week before his July 9 hanging, but in "The Dying Words of Abraham Johnstone," designated his "Declaration or Confession" on the title page and dated "Woodbury jail Saturday, July 8, 1797" (41).

125. Hartnett speculates that Read may have run away and that Johnstone's persecution resulted from his white neighbors' efforts to acquire either the black man's service or his crops through forfeiture proceedings. Hartnett, *Executing*, 150.

126. This early modern sense of the word had already become obsolete by the late eighteenth century; *Oxford English Dictionary*, s.v. "civility," accessed June 21, 2009.

127. Johnstone is an early example in the longer tradition of African American nativist rhetoric; see Wong, *Neither*, 247–48.

128. Carbado, "Racial," 645.

129. Ibid.

130. Thomas, *Civic Myths*, 183.

131. None of these acts exceed the boundaries of civil slavery St. George Tucker had demarcated the previous year. His plan's seventh point proposed to "Let no Negroe or mulattoe be capable of taking, holding, or exercising, any public office, freehold, franchise, or privilege, or any estate in lands or tenements, other than a lease not exceeding

twenty-one years. . . . nor, . . .be an attorney; nor be a juror; nor a witness in any court of judicature, except against, or between Negroes and mulattoes." St. George Tucker, *Dissertation*, 93–94.

132. Johnstone, *Address*, 36.

133. See K. Parker, "Making," 95.

134. Such extralegal arbitration had precedent in the courts that formed part of "the informal system of black government" in colonial New England and beyond, now on their decline with emancipation. Piersen, *Black Yankees*, 134–35. More locally, it was also consistent with the Quaker preference to resolve disputes within Friends meetings rather than through recourse to legal authorities and institutions. Tomlins, *Freedom Bound*, 227.

135. See Walzer, "Civil Society," 164.

136. In this respect, Johnstone's *Address* anticipates the similarly "counterfactual imagining of a reformed social order brought about by white civility" in David Walker's *Appeal, in Four Articles; Together with a Preamble, to the Coloured Citizens of the World, but in Particular, and Very Expressly, to Those of the United States of America* (1829). Levine, *Dislocating*, 103.

Chapter 4. The Work of Death: Time, Crime, and Personhood in Jacksonian America

1. Douglass, *My Bondage*, 106.

2. Douglass, *Narrative*, 80; DeLombard, *Slavery on Trial*.

3. "Alabama Beacon Versus James Williams," *New York Emancipator*, August 30, 1838. Williams's *Narrative* continued to be advertised and sold in abolitionist venues, including by the AASS; see Loughran, *Republic*, 508n56.

4. McFeely, *Frederick Douglass*, 83–85.

5. Locke, *Essay*, 312.

6. Ibid.; see also Dayan, "Melville, Locke, and Faith," and "Legal Terrors," 54–58.

7. See Pratt, *Archives*, 36.

8. Loughran, *Republic*, 328, 341, 342.

9. W. Channing, *Works*, 705; Wong, *Neither*, 93.

10. Whalen, "Average Racism."

11. Locke, *Essay*, 310.

12. For an alternative reading of *Confessions'* temporality, see Sundquist, *To Wake*, 54–83.

13. Gray, *Confessions*, 56, 50.

14. Douglass, *My Bondage*, 106.

15. O'Malley, *Keeping Watch*, 31; T. Allen, *Republic*, 59–113.

16. Weld, *American Slavery*, 7.

17. Mark Smith, *Mastered*, 123, 146.

18. Weld, *American Slavery*, 8; see T. Allen, *Republic*, 133.

19. See Thompson, "Time, Work-Discipline," and Anderson, *Imagined Communities*, 22–36.

20. [Robert Bonner], "The North and the South," *New York Ledger*, March 26, 1859.

21. See C. Smith, "Emerson," 230n4.

22. Snodgrass, "Crime," 27; E.D.E.N. Southworth, "The Brothers," *National Era*, April 10, 1856.

23. See Rothman, *Discovery*, xxix, 89, 106; Meranze, *Laboratories*, 202; see also Ignatieff, *Just Measure of Pain*; Dumm, *Democracy*, 113–40; Rothman, "Perfecting," 123–24; Rothman, *Discovery*, xxiv–xxxvi; McLennan, *Crisis*, 53–86.

24. Schwarz, *Twice Condemned*, 25; Banner, *Death Penalty*, 140; Oshinsky, *Worse*, 6. On the mediating role played by the summary police powers derived from the regulation of slavery, see Wagner, *Disturbing*, 58–73.

25. Banner, *Death Penalty*, 141. See also Hindus, *Prison*, 210–14.

26. Rogers, *Death*, 113.

27. On Virginia authorities' investment in the appearance of due process, see Tragle, *Southampton Slave Revolt*, 173. Snodgrass's later account of slave rebels' hangings in Charleston registers the continued perceived anomalousness of "*death on the gallows . . . with less than a week's* preparation for the fearful event!" "Crime," 29. Here again, Southworth illustrates his point: on a Southern scaffold, slaves Valentine and Governor "without one instant's warning, or one word of prayer or benediction . . . fell, and swung between sky and earth," to the consternation of "the terribly-shocked minister who," like the condemned, "was altogether unprepared for the suddenness of the execution." Southworth "Brothers," April 17, 1856.

28. Gray, *Confessions*, 56–57. For the court transcript, see Tragle, *Southampton*, 221–23; on discrepancies with *Confessions*, see 397–414.

29. Cover, *Narrative*, 213.

30. Gray, *Confessions*, 56.

31. On the political nature of the term "insurrection" as associated with "treason" (and implication of perpetrators' duty for allegiance as citizen-subjects), see Tragle, *Southampton*, 21–22; T. Morris, *Southern Slavery*, 262–88. For a discussion of the case in the context of a Virginia legal regime that had historically tended to depoliticize transgressive black acts (often through criminalization), see Schwarz, *Twice Condemned*, 255–79.

32. O. L., "Causes of Slave Insurrections," *Liberator*, September 17, 1831.

33. Ibid.

34. "The Insurrection," *Liberator*, September 3, 1831.

35. Ibid. For readings of temporality in Garrisonian abolitionism, see Fanuzzi, *Abolition's Public Sphere*, 1–42; Loughran, *Republic*, 328–61; Goddu, "Antislavery," 136.

36. T. Allen, *Republic*, 117.

37. Ibid., 119.

38. Pratt, *Archives*, 38.

39. Gladfelder, *Criminality*, 45.

40. *Constitutional Whig*, August 23, 1831, reprinted in Tragle, *Southampton*, 35–36.

41. Gladfelder, *Criminality*, 47.

42. See ibid., ix–x, 47, 50, 233n14.

43. Ibid., 46.

44. Pratt, *Archives*, 29; on this broader transition see Loughran, *Republic*.

45. Gray, *Confessions*, 40.

46. Ibid.

47. T. Allen, *Republic*, 94

48. Ibid., 94–95; see also 118–19.

49. On the economic and political incentives for expeditious legal prosecution of slaves, see Olwell, *Masters*, 73–74.

50. Gray, *Confessions*, 44, 54, 39.

51. "Insurrection in Virginia!" September 3, 1831; "Extract of a Letter," *Liberator*, September 17, 1831. See also "Remarks of Editors," *Liberator*, September 10, 1831.

52. Gray, *Confessions*, 42.

53. These may have included an earlier *Constitutional Whig* letter, possibly by Gray himself, which closely resembles the *Confessions*; Tragle, *Southampton*, 406–9.

54. Pratt, *Archives*, 3; see also T. Allen, *Republic*, 3.

55. Gray, *Confessions*, 45–46.

56. On the murderer as mental alien see Halttunen, *Murder*, 208–40.

57. See also Wong, *Neither*, 155.

58. Gates, *Figures*, 88–93, 100–101; for a critique, see Pratt, *Archives*, 162–63.

59. See Sundquist, *To Wake*, 54–55 (and the sources cited therein).

60. Pratt, *Archives*, 167.

61. Ibid., 6.

62. Gray, *Confessions*, 45, emphasis added.

63. T. Allen, *Republic*, 128.

64. See ibid., 114–45.

65. Ibid., 140.

66. Gray, *Confessions*, 40; Weber, *Protestant Ethic*, 106–7.

67. In Weberian terms, a shift from charismatic to rational-legal authority; see Weber, *Theory*, 329–63.

68. "The Crisis," *The Genius of Temperance*, reprinted in "Comments of Editors" *Liberator*, September 3, 1831. In this sense, the insurgents recall Foucault's disciplined "soldiers" fulfilling the "military dream of society" that serves as an alternative to the juridical one of the "primal social contract," with "permanent coercions" replacing "fundamental rights." *Discipline*, 169.

69. T. Allen, *Republic*, 139–40. See Merritt Smith, "Army Ordnance"; DeLanda, "Beyond."

70. Gray, *Confessions*, 50.

71. "Insurrection in Virginia!" and "Lowell," *Liberator*, September 3, 1831. On numeracy as narrative's predecessor in early abolitionism, see Goddu, "Antislavery."

72. Merritt Smith, "Army Ordnance," 47–49, 51.

73. "Alabama Beacon Versus James Williams."

74. W. Andrews, *To Tell*, 87–88.

75. Watt, *Rise*, 31; Richetti, *Popular Fiction*; Faller, *Turned*; Bender, *Imagining*; Schramm, *Testimony*; Mascuch, *Origins*; D. Davis, *Homicide*; Halttunen, *Murder*; Boudreau, *Spectacle*.

76. Grossman, *Art*, 36.

77. See R. Ferguson, *Law and Letters*; Wald, *Constituting*; Dimock, *Residues*; Thomas, *Cross-Examinations*; B. Thomas, *American* and *Civic Myths*; Goodman, *Shifting*; Crane, *Race*; Nabers, *Victory*.

78. Grossman, *Art*, 24; see Anderson, *Imagined*; L. Edwards, *People*, 35–40; Loughran, *Republic*.

79. Holmes quoted in Goodman, *Shifting*, 6–7; see also Margolis, *Public*, 81–106.

80. Rodensky, *Crime*, 4, 5. For example, on anti-polygamy fiction, see Gordon, *Mormon Question*, 29–54; on temperance fiction, see Castiglia, *Interior States*, 136–67.

81. For this history, see DeLombard, *Slavery on Trial*; Brophy, "Humanity" and "Over and Above." See also Nabers, *Victory*, 132–72; Dayan, "Poe."

82. Grossman, *Art*, 33, 172.

83. Ibid., 173.

84. James Williams, *Narrative*, iii; see also iv.

85. See Welsh, *Strong*.

86. "Alabama Beacon Versus James Williams."

87. Canuel, *Shadow*, 159.

88. For an American example, see Snodgrass, "Crime," 29. On the pornographic quality of such imagery, see Hartman, *Scenes*, 3–112; Wood, *Slavery*.

89. See also Hartman, *Scenes*, 126.

90. In the United States the abolitions' overlap would be most apparent in the 1840s; see Chapter 5.

91. Stowe, *Uncle Tom's Cabin*, 385.

92. Grossman, *Art*, 35.

93. Canuel, *Shadow*, 154.

94. See Rodensky, *Crime*.

95. On abolitionism's exposure rhetoric, see Henry, "Angelina"; Shamir, *Inexpressible*, 97–146.

96. Douglass, *Narrative*, 51.

97. Ibid.

98. Another blunder occurred when well-meaning antislavery lawyer-turned-author Richard Hildreth anonymously published his first-person novel, *The Slave: or Memoirs of Archy Moore* in 1836; for a discussion of the two incidents as a turning point in the facticity of the genre, see Starling, *Slave Narrative*, 227–32.

99. W. Andrews, *To Tell*, 265–91.

100. Fabian, *Unvarnished*, 100.

101. "Alabama Beacon Versus James Williams."

102. J. Williams, *Narrative*, xvii.

103. Ibid., xviii.

104. "Alabama Beacon Versus James Williams."

105. Ibid.

106. P[eabody], "Narratives of Fugitive Slaves," 61.

107. Clay quoted in James Williams, *Narrative*, viii; see also B. Dain, *Hideous*, 152.

108. Garrison, Preface, 33; see also W. Brown, *Narrative*, 23, 24.

109. P[eabody], "Narratives of Fugitive Slaves," 64; for the term "prison-house," see 2 Chron. 16:10, King James Version.

110. J. Williams, *Narrative*, 41.

111. Castiglia, *Interior States*, 130, 131; see also Fanuzzi, *Abolition's Public Sphere*, 237.

112. Castiglia, *Interior States*, 131.

113. For imagery and analysis of abolitionists' "assembly-line trope" of punishment, see Goddu, "Antislavery," 138.

114. J. Williams, *Narrative*, 52.

115. Gates, *Figures*, 80–98.

116. See ibid., and Titus, "Poisonous."

117. J. Williams, *Narrative*, 51–52.

118. On the perennial legal dilemma regarding the civil and criminal responsibility of drunkards and the nineteenth-century U.S. trend away from English common law, toward treating intoxication as civil incompetence, see Blumenthal, "Default," 1228–30.

119. Locke, *Essay*, 310.

120. J. Williams, *Narrative*, 49.

121. Haskell, "Persons," 442.

122. J. Williams, *Narrative*, 56.

123. Poe, *Tales*, 544.

124. Dayan, "Poe," 107.

125. Kopley, *Dupin*, 42.

126. Lemire, "Murders," 183, 184; on Poe's likely familiarity with Joseph Marzetti's performances (perhaps as early as 1836) as "Jocko! the Brazilian Ape," who both "hangs himself by the neck" and "apes the good citizen" by saving "a few orphans in a shipwreck," see Bryant, "Poe's Ape," 31.

127. Whalen, "Average Racism," 30. On race in Poe generally, see Kennedy and Weissberg, *Romancing*; Frank, "Evolutionary Reverie"; Harrowitz, "Criminality"; Dayan, "Amorous" and "Poe"; Ginsberg, "Slavery"; E. White, "Ourang-Outang."

128. Poe, *Tales*, 565; Mabbott notes the variant here as "his prisoner"; 565nn.

129. Harrowitz, "Criminality," 185; Lemire, "Murders," 182–83.

130. On the story's resolution as merely "a romance, a plot in the mind of C. Auguste Dupin," see Frank, "Evolutionary Reverie," 186.

131. Barrett, "Presence of Mind," 159; see also Bryant, "Poe's Ape," 33.

132. See P. Brooks, *Troubling*, 97.

133. Poe, *Tales*, 568.

134. Compare Lemire, "Murders," 188.

135. Crucially, criminal intent is distinct from other motives for killing: to under-

stand "outrageous violence" as a "rational and predictable response to the brutality of slavery" is to take it out of the realm of the criminal, into that of the civil (as justifiable self-defense) or the civic (as equally justifiable revolution). E. White, "Ourang-Outang," 104.

136. See Dayan, "Poe."

137. Ibid., 108, 121.

138. Poe, *Tales*, 563.

139. Cartwright, "Report," 709.

140. See Hammond, "Mud-Sill."

141. "Trial of Coleman," from *New York Journal of Commerce* as reprinted in *Dedham (Massachusetts) Norfolk Advertiser*, November 24, 1838 (emphasis omitted); "Execution of Coleman," *Pennsylvania Inquirer*, January 16, 1839.

142. *The People v. Edward Coleman.*

143. "Murderer Convicted," *Baltimore Sun*, November 19, 1838. The *New York Times* reported the "marked change" in the hitherto "perfectly cool and unconcerned" Coleman's "deportment and conversation," to a "very remarkable kind of stupidity and languor" on learning from his lawyer "that no kind of defence, save that of insanity, could be of any use in his behalf"; reprinted in *Waldo (Maine) Patriot*, August 7, 1838; see also "Coleman the Murderer," *Philadelphia Inquirer*, August 1, 1838; "A Rogue's Trick," *Baltimore Sun*, August 2, 1838; "Things in New York," *Baltimore Sun*, August 4, 1838. There is no mention of insanity in the indictment, to which Coleman pled not guilty; *Coleman.* The *New York Journal of Commerce* reported on expert testimony from a Dr. G. Bedford regarding the defendant's "monomania"; reprinted as "The Trial of Coleman," *Dedham Norfolk Advertiser*, November 24, 1838.

144. For galvanic corpse experiments in Poe's fiction before and after the Coleman execution, see "Loss of Breath," *Tales*, 61–82; "The Premature Burial," 953–72; and especially "Some Words with a Mummy," *Tales*, 1175–1201, in which a technologically superior (and quite jaded) ancient Nubian converses with the benighted scientific gentlemen who have galvanically resurrected him in nineteenth-century America. See also C. Smith, "Bodies." Like those of the condemned, the corpses of African Americans seem uniquely vulnerable to this electrical form of medical experimentation, as suggested by Poe's fellow Philadelphia-based author Robert Montgomery Byrd in his *Sheppard Lee* (1836) and by antebellum rumors that John Joyce's gallows-mate Peter Mathias had been thus resurrected; see Otter, *Philadelphia*, 99, 151.

145. "Execution of Coleman," *Pennsylvania Inquirer*, January 16, 1839.

146. Analyzing three later Poe works in light of two insanity defense cases with white defendants, John Cleman demonstrates how, by embracing the outmoded "wild beast" standard of insanity (discussed in Chapter 5, below), these aconfessional first-person crime stories display their narrators' insanity as judged by contemporary medico-jurisprudential thought—even as this rather deterministically conceived madness effectively replaces the sort of divine retribution it has in another sense supplanted. The racialization of both the Coleman case and "Murders," combined with the absence of

confession, suggest that rather than the "radical restoration of . . . moral consequences" through which "Poe's deterministic forces lead the guilty to the hangman," the earlier tale affirms criminal culpability as marker of normatively white personhood. Cleman, "Irresistible Impulses," 640.

Chapter 5. How Freeman Was Made a Madman: Race, Capacity, and Citizenship

1. "Execution of Coleman," *Pennsylvania Inquirer*, January 16, 1839. Coleman was executed the year after New York City hangings were relocated to the Halls of Justice; the *Inquirer* estimate is consistent with other accounts of Tombs executions as described in Madow, "Forbidden," 512–26.

2. Masur, *Rites*, 114–16; Madow, "Forbidden," 519–23.

3. On the normatively white prisoner's entry into the national imaginary, see C. Smith, *Prison*.

4. Edwards, *People*, 238.

5. Gray, *Confessions*, 54, 41.

6. Quoted in Arpey, *William Freeman*, ix.

7. Mastin broadside quoted in Arpey, *William Freeman*, ix; Arpey reproduces all four paintings; for analysis, see ix–xx. See also Gilman, *Seeing*, 112–15.

8. B. Hall, *Trial*, 67.

9. Arpey, *William Freeman*, xvi.

10. The New York Court of Appeals, a product of the 1846 New York State Constitutional Convention, would not be established until July 1847; hence the references to the New York Supreme Court in coverage of Freeman's November 1846 appeal.

11. Douglass, *My Bondage*, 364–65; McCune Smith, Introduction, 125.

12. McCune Smith, Introduction, 132.

13. Sekora, "Black Message," 502.

14. "Freeman, the Murderer of the Van Ness [*sic*] Family" [portrait engraving] and "Freeman the Negro Murderer," *National Police Gazette*, April 11, 1846; "Case of Freeman, the Murderer," *National Police Gazette*, January 2, 1847.

15. Blake, *American Bookseller*, 263. Pamphlets of varying lengths offered printed versions of Seward's argument; see Seward, *Argument* and Seward, *Argument . . . Reported by S. Blatchford*.

16. McCune Smith, *Works*, 86.

17. James McCune Smith to Gerrit Smith, March 1, 1855, in Ripley, *Black Abolitionist Papers*, 4:275.

18. See B. Hall, *Trial*, 373.

19. McCune Smith, *Works*, 86.

20. B. Hall, *Trial*, 395; *Syracuse Journal* quoted in *Morning Journal and New York Enquirer*, March 20, 1846, quoted in Arpey, *William Freeman*, 32. The pun turned in part on Sally Freeman's indigenous heritage. Although both legal and journalistic sources sought to criminalize those of Freeman's traits—taciturnity, vengefulness, and a resistance to physical restraint—thought traceable to his maternal lineage (specifically "the

Stockbridge tribe") and despite apparent references to him as "the young Indian" in his childhood, Freeman is most consistently depicted, in print and in visual representations, as an African American; B. Hall, *Trial*, 17, 18.

21. James Freeman is described elsewhere as having died of a head injury sustained during a fall on an Albany dock; B. Hall, *Trial*, 17.

22. See Rothman, *Discovery*, 64–71, 94–108; Colvin, *Penitentiaries*, 88–99; McLennan, *Crisis*, 54–85.

23. Lieber, introduction to Beaumont and Tocqueville, *Penitentiary*, ix.

24. B. Hall, *Trial*, 326.

25. On the antebellum etiology of insanity, including "blows on the head," see Rothman, *Discovery*, 110–19 (quotation at 111).

26. If Freeman's name suggests an allegorical reading of the black man's allegedly insane demand for financial reparations and legal redress for his unjust captivity, that narrative is played out, right down to the head injury, in No. VIII of McCune Smith's "Heads of the Colored People" series, discussed below; see McCune Smith, *Works*, 222–23.

27. "Appalling Murder," *Milwaukee Sentinel and Gazette*, April 3, 1846.

28. B. Hall, *Trial*, 331.

29. See Arpey, *William Freeman*, 92–97; see also "Medical Jurisprudence"; Blumenthal, "Mind"; Foucault, *Abnormal*.

30. See Arpey, *William Freeman*, 15–18; *Report of the Trial of Henry Wyatt*. After an initial hearing that ambiguously found Freeman competent to stand trial (that ambiguity would become the basis for his acquittal on appeal and scheduled retrial), Seward did not enter a plea of not guilty by reason of insanity but, rather, supported his not guilty plea on Freeman's behalf with arguments regarding the defendant's incapacity both at the time of the killings and during the legal proceedings.

31. G. Baker, *Life*, 113.

32. B. Hall, *Trial*, 217.

33. See Canuel, *Shadow*, 142–67; Reiss, *Theaters*, 16–17, 103–41; Weiner, *Black Trials*, xi.

34. P. Jones, *Against*, 34–64.

35. Barton, "Anti-Gallows," 160–62.

36. P. Jones, *Against*, 34–64; Barton, "Anti-Gallows," 162–73.

37. W. Whitman, *Journalism*, 1:435.

38. Karcher, *First Woman*, 305; Barton, "William Gilmore Simms," 235–38; Greiman, *Democracy's Spectacle*, 121–56.

39. Barton, "Anti-Gallows" and "William Gilmore Simms."

40. W. Whitman, *Journalism*, 1:300–301; see also 1:438–39, 2:24.

41. Bancroft, *Life*, 174.

42. Frances Seward quoted in Seward, *Autobiography*, 813.

43. B. Hall, *Trial*, 173.

44. See D. Davis, *Homicide*, 59–83; Spiegel and Spiegel, "Insanity Plea"; Hawkins-Léon, "Literature," 415–16; P. Harris, *Black Rage*, 9–30; Halttunen, *Murder*, 220.

45. See Blumenthal, "Deviance," "Mind," and "Default."

46. B. Hall, *Trial*, 504. On phrenology, faculty psychology, and race, see Cooley, *Ivory Leg*, 16–43, 60–65. On Morton, see B. Dain, *Hideous*, 198.

47. "In the southern states, the ratio of insane or idiotic among Negroes stood at 1 to every 1,558; in the northern states, it was 1 to every 144.5" in the 1840 census; Litwack, *North*, 41.

48. R. Smith, *Civic Ideals*, 214–25.

49. In 1821, with the assistance of Martin Van Buren, a racial property qualification was inserted into the state constitution restricting black suffrage to those men with taxable property worth $250. At issue in the 1846 constitutional convention was whether to eliminate the racial qualification and/or the property qualification, a decision which, at either extreme, would entirely enfranchise or disenfranchise male African American New Yorkers. Subject to four different votes within the Convention, the terms for African American male enfranchisement remained unchanged, as they did after the discriminatory property qualification was submitted to the broader electorate in November 1846, when "equal suffrage was overwhelmingly defeated by a . . . margin of 2.6 to 1" in a referendum where "voter interest was strong." Field, *Politics*, 61; on Van Buren's role, see 78.

50. Needles, *Ten Years*, 3; *Appeal* [pamphlet], 4. For an abolitionist critique, see Pennsylvania Society, *Review*. On preliminary efforts dating back to 1841, see Frey, "House," 13–15. Thus, it was not "with the publication of the 1890 census," but its predecessors, local and national censuses of the 1830s and 1840s, that "prison statistics for the first time became the basis of a national discussion about blacks as a distinct and dangerous criminal population." Muhammad, *Condemnation*, 3.

51. Reprinted in McCune Smith, *Works*, 185–241; see B. Dain, *Hideous*, 239–62.

52. Print coverage of the case joined "the profusion of treatises and tracts at midcentury, which addressed . . . the attribution of responsibility" in medico-legal terms. Blumenthal, "Mind," 100.

53. B. Hall, *Trial*, 37.

54. *Prisoner's Friend*, September 1, 1847; compare B. Hall, *Trial*, 395.

55. Wiener, "Judges," 477.

56. Robinson, *Wild Beasts*, 43.

57. Platt and Diamond, "Wild Beast," 355.

58. Douglass, *My Bondage*, 367; Frederick Douglass, "Letter from a Fugitive Slave," *[Albany] Evening Journal*, reprinted in the *Liberator*, January 16, 1846.

59. Garrison, Preface, 41.

60. See Rice and Crawford, *Liberating*; see also Tamarkin, *Anglophilia*, 178–246.

61. *Auburn Daily Advertiser* excerpted in "William Freeman," *Prisoner's Friend*, April 8, 1846; for discussion of John Austin's article as it appeared in the newspaper's weekly edition, the *Auburn Journal and Advertiser*, on March 18, 1846, see Arpey, *William Freeman*, 35–36.

62. Canuel, *Shadow*, 142; "Books on Capital Punishment," *Liberator*, September 11, 1846; *Prisoner's Friend*, August 5, 12, 1846.

63. See "Obituary" and *New-York Mercantile Union Business Directory*, 57. In 1847 the firm, intermediately reorganized as J. C. Derby & Co., was advertising Hall's *Trial* alongside other works in its law list such as *The New Clerk's Assistant*, a legal and business manual, and *Benedict's Treatise*, a New York justice-of-the peace handbook, each available with "an Appendix containing the New Constitution of New York." "Publisher's Circular: Announcements," *Literary World*, September 4, 1847.

64. Lambert A. Wilmer, *Our Press Gang* (Philadelphia, 1859), quoted in DeLombard, *Slavery on Trial*, 40.

65. McCune Smith, *Works*, 146. See B. Dain, *Hideous*, 238–39, 247; McCune Smith, *Works*, 61.

66. Douglass, *My Bondage*, 367. See DeLombard, *Slavery on Trial*, 101–49.

67. McCune Smith, Introduction, 126.

68. Edwards, *People*; Dayton, *Women*.

69. Langbein, *Origins*; Welsh, *Strong*.

70. Welsh, *Strong*.

71. DeLombard, *Slavery on Trial*, 151–76.

72. "From the Prisoner's Friend. William Freeman" and "Letter from Governor Seward," *Liberator*, April 24, 1846; see also "From the Washington Union. Free Suffrage" and "From Bennett's Herald. Black Suffrage—Its Consequences," *Liberator*, April 10, 1846.

73. "Letter from Governor Seward," *Liberator*, April 24, 1846.

74. On race and catastrophism, see B. Dain, *Hideous*, 210–12.

75. Bishop and Attree, *Report*, 220; see 269–70, 1018–30.

76. Kennedy specifically refuted charges by the Colored Delegation (see below) that such statistics were attributable to the institutional racism of the criminal justice system.

77. Seward to Thurlow Weed, May 29, 1846, in Seward, *Autobiography*, 810; see also G. Baker, *Life*, 104. Seward may have understood his defense of Freeman as a kind of outreach to potential newly enfranchised black voters, despite the consternation of more astute political players like Weed, Seward's friend and fellow progressive Whig. Sincere as Seward's political and philanthropic motives may have been, the debt-ridden former governor hoped, as he put it in a letter to Weed, "to profit professionally by the enormous outlay of time in my late murder trials," as "they have given me very effective advertisement" during the transition from public service to private practice; quoted in Arpey, *William Freeman*, 59; see also 50–51.

78. See Spires, "Imagining"; for a contemporary perspective, see "William H. Seward," 635.

79. C. S., "Notices," 378.

80. Ibid.

81. Contrast Arpey, *William Freeman*, xviii, 101.

82. Tocqueville, *Democracy*, 664.

83. Jarvis quoted in Rothman, *Discovery*, 112.

84. Rothman, *Discovery*, 117; Blumenthal, "Mind," 103.

85. Gilman, *Difference*, 131–49; Gilman, *Seeing*, 2–6. On Dix, see Rothman, *Discovery*, 112.

86. Reiss, *Theaters*, 15.

87. Dr. Thomas Cooper to Sen. Mahlon Dickerson, March 16, 1826, in T. Cooper, "Letters," 729; see Blumenthal, "Mind," 137.

88. See Reiss, *Theaters*, 69.

89. Cartwright, "Report," 714; see Washington, *Medical Apartheid*, 35–37.

90. P. Cohen, *Calculating*, 177.

91. See Stanton, *Leopard's Spots*, 58–66.

92. Jarvis, *Insanity*, 6; see Grob, *Edward Jarvis*.

93. Jarvis, *Insanity*, 7.

94. "Reflections," 340.

95. Jarvis, *Insanity*, 7; see P. Cohen, *Calculating*, 191–96.

96. U.S. Department of State, *Errors*, 2. The State Department had contacted "the proper State authorities, with a view to obtain authentic statements as to the number of white and colored convicts, including both sexes, in their respective State prisons, for the year 1840 and subsequent years"; ibid.

97. Jarvis, *Insanity*, 4.

98. Waldrep, *Roots*; T. Morris, *Southern Slavery*, 250–51; Wagner, *Disturbing*, 58–73.

99. Gilman, *Seeing*, 112; see also Gilman, *Difference*, 136–38.

100. B. Hall, *Trial*, 378.

101. See N. Dain, *Concepts*, 157–59, 199–201; Spiegel and Speigel, "Insanity Plea"; Foucault, *Abnormal*.

102. B. Hall, *Trial*, 61.

103. See respectively Platt and Diamond, "Wild Beast," 362–66; Jordan, *White over Black*, 28–32, 228–39. In any case, having heard many of the same witnesses make similar comparisons during the preliminary hearing, defense counsel clearly did not discourage them from voicing them when they were recalled for the murder trial; see B. Hall, *Trial*, 38, 41, 48.

104. Jordan, *White over Black*, 28–32, 228–39; Fitzpatrick, *Mythology*, 63–87.

105. Tracy quoted in Platt and Diamond, "Wild Beast," 359–60.

106. Platt and Diamond, "Wild Beast," 355. The rules derived from a parliamentary inquiry into Daniel McNaughtan's controversial 1843 acquittal for the murder of Edward Drummond, the secretary of McNaughtan's intended target, Prime Minister Robert Peel; see also Robinson, *Wild Beasts*, 163–82.

107. On Rogers, see Arpey, *William Freeman*, 47–49; on Kleim, see B. Hall, *Trial* 141, 375–78, 471; on the 1845 trial of Abner Baker, see [Chandler,] "Trial." See also D. Davis, *Homicide*, 59–83.

108. Blumenthal, "Mind," 131–32. For Foucault the medico-legal obsession with motiveless crimes marks a key turning point from criminality to deviancy; Foucault, *Abnormal*, 109–34.

109. B. Hall, *Trial*, 379; for these tests see Robinson, *Wild Beasts*, 118.

110. See B. Hall, *Trial*, 38.

111. See Thomas, "Narratives," 13.

112. On Austin's role, see Arpey, *William Freeman*, 25–26, 55.

113. Reprinted in "From the Prisoner's Friend. William Freeman," *Liberator*, April 24, 1846.

114. B. Hall, *Trial*, 252.

115. Suggestively, the pamphlet, *An Appeal to the Public on Behalf of a House of Refuge for Colored Juvenile Delinquents* (1846), concludes by reprinting the Supreme Court of Pennsylvania's decision in *Ex Parte Crouse* (1839), a habeas corpus proceeding initiated by the father of Mary Ann Crouse against "the keeper and managers of the House of Refuge" to which she had been committed by her mother, Mary Crouse, finding that the statutes authorizing "the committal of infants to the House of Refuge, . . . and their detention there, without a previous trial by jury, are not unconstitutional." *Appeal* [pamphlet], 10. Given the absence of racial designation and that, "after the first year, no black child was admitted" to the House of Refuge (founded in 1828), Mary Ann Crouse presumably was white. Frey, "House," 12.

116. [Chandler], "Plea I," 2. Omitting other slated material "on account of the space occupied by the case of *Freeman v. The People*," Chandler seized the occasion to publish a pair of lead articles on the "Plea of Insanity in Criminal Cases"; [Chandler], "Hotch-Pot," 46 . The forum did not dwell on the Freeman case's racial aspects, treating it as one of many that were appearing with "unprecedented frequency" on court dockets; [Chandler], "Plea I," 1. Published in November 1846, the American version of Sampson's study was not available for Seward to consult as he prepared for the Wyatt and Freeman cases during a Mississippi cruise in May 1846. Stern, "Brady," 131. Seward's key expert witness, Dr. Amariah Brigham, sent him contemporary treatises by James C. Prichard, Jean-Etienne D. Esquirol, and Isaac Ray, all three of which were mentioned at trial; Spiegel and Spiegel, "Insanity Plea," 233; see also Arpey, *William Freeman*, 45–48, 72. On the Quaker Prichard's involvement in the era's ethnological racism, see B. Dain, *Hideous*, 204–62. On Esquirol, see Gilman, *Seeing*, 76–82. On the antebellum influence of Brigham and Ray, see, respectively, Reiss, *Theaters*, 23, and Rothman, *Discovery*, 112–23. See Gilman, *Seeing*, 116–17.

117. Sampson, *Rationale*, xiii. Farnham's American edition "met a storm of denunciation by such newspapers as [James Watson] Webb's *Courier and Enquirer* and the New York *Observer*" on the basis that, as Farnham supporter and Sing Sing inspector John Bigelow wrote in his diary, "it destroys accountability." Quoted in Lewis, *Newgate*, 240; see also Stern, "Brady," 132. On Lorenzo Fowler and his brother Orson Squire Fowler in the context of race, see Cooley, *Ivory*, 19–20, 60–63. On daguerreotypy in the context of race, crime, and antebellum authorship, see Gilmore, *Genuine*, 138–46.

118. Patrick-Stamp, "Prison Sentence Docket"; Rothman, *Discovery*, 64–71.

119. Farnham quotes Robert Macnish and Robert Verity respectively.

120. Blumenthal, "Mind," 113–19.

121. These words are attributed to an unnamed Farnham protégé, an African American woman inmate.

122. Washington, *Medical Apartheid*, 35–37.

123. Foucault, *Abnormal*, 21.

124. Goffman, *Asylums*, 4–5.

125. Sampson, *Rationale*, xvii. For an Indianapolis case addressing this question in the context of race, see "The Colored Insane," *Frederick Douglass' Paper*, April 1, 1852; Reiss, *Theaters*, 16–17.

126. Swinney quoted in Frey, "House," 17–18. On (normatively white) houses of refuge, see Rothman, *Discovery*, 206–36.

127. Kelley, *Address*, 6. The regimen is reminiscent of Auburn; see Span, "Educational," 115; Frey, "House," 16.

128. On disfranchisement, see Litwack, *North*, 84–87. The critical tendency to treat civic preparation as social control obscures the fact that ideological indoctrination did not require reciprocal recognition of black youth as future citizens; thus the greater concern for Irish over African American youth may be attributable to the former's greater eligibility for civic integration rather than perception of their higher criminal propensity; see Span, "Educational," 115; see also Frey, "House," 13

129. *Appeal* [broadside].

130. Kelley, *Address*, 24.

131. See *Appeal* [pamphlet], 6–7 .

132. Kelley, *Address*, 8–9,

133. Sampson, *Rationale*, 156.

134. Douglass, "Heroic Slave," 485.

135. Ibid.

136. Prior to the advent of the Colored Department of Philadelphia's House of Refuge, the city's "poor and delinquent black children" were typically "indentured out to masters in the country" (and presumably away from local ties), placed in the disproportionately black almshouse, or imprisoned. Frey, "House," 12–13; see also Span, "Educational," 113.

137. B. Hall, *Trial*, 421. Although Seward implies that the statement appears in "testimony" by DePuy that he characterizes as "conclusive in this case," the published transcript omits any statement of the kind, summarily truncating the words attributed to DePuy as it did that of other apparently redundant testimony; see ibid., 47.

138. Sawyer, *Southern Institutes*, 312, 313.

139. W. Whitman, *Journalism*, 1:300. I credit Whitman with less originality in his environmentalism than does Paul Jones, to whom I remain indebted for this source; see *Against*, 104–106.

140. Foucault, *Abnormal*, 23.

141. B. Hall, *Trial*, 420.

142. Ibid.; James McCune Smith to Gerrit Smith, March 1, 1855, in Ripley, *Black Abolitionist Papers*, 4:275: the full passage reads: "Hence I have waged war against the

Garrisonians, and will, until they admit this doctrine. It is a strange omission in the Constitution of the American Anti-Slavery Society that no mention is made of Social Equality either of slaves or Free Blacks, as the aim of that Society."

143. *State v. Aaron, slave of L. Solomon,* "The Law of Slavery in New Jersey," compiled by Paul Axel-Lute, *New Jersey Digital Legal Library,* Center for Law and Justice, Rutgers University Library, rev. October 8, 2009, http://njlegallib.rutgers.edu/slavery/cases/4njl231.html, accessed July 19, 2011.

144. Guild was convicted for the murder of sexagenarian Catherine Beakes. *State v. James Guild,* "Law of Slavery in New Jersey," rev. October 8, 2009, http://njlegallib.rutgers.edu/slavery/cases/10njl163.html, accessed July 19, 2011. See Brewer, *By Birth or Consent,* 222.

145. *James Guild.*

146. Brewer, *By Birth,* 228; see also Edwards, *People.* Convicted of murdering two-year-old Stephen Conelly by throwing him into a well, Aaron was granted a new trial on appeal, on grounds of the exclusion of testimony from his master, to whom he stood in the relation not of slave but, as with others covered by the gradual emancipation statute, "in the situation of persons bound to service by the overseers of the poor." *Aaron.*

147. See Helmholz et al., *Privilege,* 15, 166, 267n107.

148. Jacobs, *Incidents,* 2.

149. Several witnesses, including Freeman's own previous defense lawyer, Daniel Andrus, placed Freeman in that trial's audience; Hall, *Trial,* 76, 80, 324, 327, 334.

150. G. Baker, *Life,* 102. When Wyatt's personal narrative "was found to be of doubtful moral bearing and influence," Seward "refused to permit its publication, or participate in any profits arising therefrom." Not everyone held such scruples: "a spurious copy . . . was afterward surreptitiously obtained, and brought in a pamphlet, which yielded a net profit of six hundred dollars to the publisher."

151. However unsuccessful, Wyatt's insanity defense and prisoner status placed him in a position more akin to the black condemned than to mentally competent white citizen-convicts, in that his death sentence and ensuing engagement in the public sphere of print through gallows literature represented an ascension to rather than a declension from legal personhood, civil personality, and civic belonging. On disability, race, and legal incapacity, see Welke, *Borders.*

152. B. Hall, *Trial,* 400.

153. Along with "Medical Jurisprudence," see Fosgate, "Case"; originally published in *American Journal of the Medical Sciences* (October 1847), Fosgate's article was republished in *New Jersey Medical Reporter and Transactions of the New Jersey Medical Society* (January 1848), *American Quarterly Retrospect of American and Foreign Practical Medicine and Surgery* (April 1848), and, with supporting documents, *American Journal of Insanity* (October 1848). See also Arpey, *William Freeman,* 122.

154. Arpey, *William Freeman,* xiv–xvi.

155. "Shocking Atrocity," *Liberator,* March 27, 1846.

156. B. Hall, *Trial,* 38.

157. "Shocking."

158. The phrase appears as the title of Chapter 4 in U.S. Department of Labor, *Negro Family*. For analysis of how twentieth-century "racial liberalism foundered on the shoals of black criminality," see Muhammad, *Condemnation*, 13.

159. See Douglass, *My Bondage*, 106.

160. Thomas Aquinas, *Summa Theologica*, quoted in Platt and Diamond, "Wild Beast," 361.

Chapter 6. Who Aint a Slaver? Citizenship, Piracy, and Slaver Narratives

1. "Slaves Liberated," 130. See, for example, "Capture of an American Slaver," *Amherst [New Hampshire] Farmer's Cabinet*, March 12, 1846; "Murder of the Van Nest Family," *Amherst Farmer's Cabinet*, March 26, 1846; "The Slave Ship," *Amherst Farmer's Cabinet*, April 2, 1846.

2. "Atrocious Murders," *Barre [Massachusetts] Gazette*, March 20, 1846 (reprinted from *Albany Argus*); "Murder of the Van Nest Family," *Amherst Farmer's Cabinet*, March 26, 1846; "From Africa," *Pittsfield [Massachusetts] Sun*, May 21, 1846.

3. See Gilje, *Liberty*, 234–58; Blum, *View*. Neither specifically addresses the midcentury print controversy over American mariners' roles in international slave trafficking.

4. W. Whitman, *Journalism*, 1:289.

5. "Declarations," 377. See Roediger, *Wages*, 31; see also Fliegelman, *Declaring*, 140–50.

6. Act of 15 May 1820, *Stats at Large of USA* 3:600–601; see also Act of 22 March 1794, *Stats at Large of USA* 1:348–49; Act of 10 May 1800, *Stats at Large of USA* 2:70. See Howard, *American Slavers*, 26; Du Bois, *Suppression*, 80–84.

7. Fehrenbacher, *Slaveholding Republic*, 154–204.

8. Soodalter, *Hanging*.

9. The story is attributed to "a Son of the Late Dr. John D. Godman." "Slaver," 1. A respected physician and naturalist, John Davidson Godman in 1821 married Angelica Peale, a daughter of Rembrandt Peale, with whom he had three children. It is tempting, despite *Graham's* consistent spelling of the surname, to speculate that the story was in fact written by John Codman, born in 1814, son of John Codman, Doctor of Sacred Theology (College of New Jersey, 1822). The younger Codman left Amherst College "in his junior year to ship before the mast," became a merchant sea captain, and was a prolific maritime author. *The Biographical Dictionary of America*, ed. Rossiter Johnson (Boston, 1906), s.vv. "Godman, John Davidson," "Codman, John, clergyman," "Codman, John, author." Codman published his first book, *Sailors' Life and Sailors' Yarns* (1847) under the pseudonym "Captain Ringbolt." Melville reviewed the book in the March 6, 1847, *Literary World*, just months before "The Slaver" appeared in *Graham's*, emphasizing how Codman's "quarter deck" perspective leads him to defend the sea captain, "almost den[ying] that the sailor has any wrongs and more than insinuat[ing] that sea-captains are not only the best natured fellows in the world but that they have been sorely maligned." Melville, *Piazza Tales*, 210.

10. "Slaver," 1.

11. See also [Lippard,] *Bank Director's Son*, 8.

12. The best-known novels are Toni Morrison, *Beloved* (1987) and Lorene Cary, *The Price of a Child* (1995), based on cases involving fugitives Margaret Garner and Jane Johnson. See also Von Frank, *Anthony Burns*; Collison, *Shadrach Minkins*; DeLombard, *Slavery on Trial*; R. Wallace, "Fugitive."

13. Howard, *American Slavers*, 189–91.

14. Bouvier, *Law Dictionary.* . . . , 2nd ed., s.v. "in rem"; Fehrenbacher, *Slaveholding Republic*, 195–96, 197.

15. Fehrenbacher, *Slaveholding Republic*, 191–97.

16. For a critique of scholarly consensus on the inefficacy of the 1820 statute, see ibid., 191, 197, 200.

17. [Lippard,] *Bank Director's Son*, 11.

18. Wald, *Constituting*, 36.

19. Garrison, Preface, 41; B. Hall, *Trial*, 217.

20. Blumenthal, "Default," 1138; Nelson, *National Manhood*, 204; Castronovo, *Necro*; Ruttenburg, *Democratic*, 168.

21. Blum, *View*, 14.

22. Blumenthal, "Default," 1158; see also Brewer, *By Birth*, 338–67.

23. Blumenthal, "Default," 1142.

24. See Nelson, *National Manhood*, ix.

25. Habersham quoted in Noonan, *Antelope*, 158; *The Antelope*, "U.S. Supreme Court Center," http://supreme.justia.com/us/23/66/case.html, accessed July 20, 2011. That the people to be thus liberated were not determined by name but chosen by lots only confirmed the ongoing unrecognizability of the now free blacks' personhood; see Noonan, *Antelope*, 65, 98, 101, 116–17.

26. The absent claimant was represented by the vice-consul of Portugal; see Noonan, *Antelope*, 131; also [Van Ness], *Case*, 289–90.

27. Blum, *View*, 52–53; Gilje, *Liberty*, 234.

28. Canney, *Africa Squadron*, 21.

29. Melville, "Benito Cereno," 46; see Tawil, "Captain Babo's Cabin," 49.

30. Yellin, "Black Masks"; Bartley, "Creature"; Tawil, "Captain Babo's Cabin"; Colatrella, *Literature*, 85; more generally, see Otter, *Melville's Anatomies*.

31. Delano, *Narrative*, 318. For comparative readings, see Scudder, "Melville's *Benito Cereno*"; Rogin, *Subversive*, 211–20; S. Weiner, *Law*, 113–38; Sale, *Slumbering*, 161–72; Downes, "Melville's *Benito Cereno*."

32. Nelson, *National Manhood* 1, 239n1; see Franklin, *Wake*, 144–46; Levine, *Conspiracy*, 203; Emery, "Topicality," 320.

33. Sale, *Slumbering*, 161–72.

34. Du Bois attributes the first wave of American anti-slave trade legislation, from 1787 to 1807, to the influence of the Haitian Revolution; Du Bois, *Suppression*, 70–93; see also Fehrenbacher, *Slaveholding Republic*, 201.

35. Melville, "Benito Cereno," 51.

36. See Parker, *Melville*, 2:242, 272. On the previous relationship of piracy to the slave trade, see Christopher, *Slave Ship Sailors*, 117–20; Du Bois, *Suppression*, 2–6; Gould, *Barbaric*, 94.

37. W. H. H., "Familiar Letters from Cuba," *National Era*, May 26, 1853.

38. Howard, *American Slavers*, 20; see Canney, *Africa Squadron*, 138–39, 154–55, 226–27; Spencer Tucker, *Andrew Foote*.

39. Carey's *Slave Trade* received two editorial notices in *Putnam's*, in June and July 1853; see reviews of *The Slave Trade*. *Putnam's* reviewed *Captain Canot* in the same November 1854 issue that featured an installment of Melville's *Israel Potter*; a puff for that very issue of *Putnam's* appeared the previous month in the *National Era*, alongside another lengthy review of Mayer's biography; see review of *Captain Canot*; "Literary Notices," *National Era*, October 26, 1854.

40. See review of *Captain Canot* in the *North American Review*, 160. One of two unidentified clippings in the American Antiquarian Society's copy refers to "doubt having been expressed as to the authenticity of Capt. Canot's 'Twenty Years of an African Slaver'"; McBlair, "Commander," 1; see also Canney, *Africa Squadron*, 183. On naval libraries and maritime book culture more generally, see Skallerup, *Books*; Blum, *View*, 1–45.

41. "Slaver," 1. See also Otter, *Philadelphia*, 278.

42. See Du Bois, *Suppression*, 168–71; Calonius, *Wanderer*; *Charleston Mercury* article reprinted as "Southern View of the British Right of Search," *New York Times*, May 26, 1858; Fehrenbacher, *Slaveholding Republic*, 180–83, persuasively argues against any such influx of African slaves in the 1850s.

43. Du Bois, *Suppression*, 27–69.

44. Story, *Charge*, 5.

45. Fehrenbacher, *Slaveholding Republic*, 202.

46. "The Slave Trade—More Developments," *Colored American* [New York], July 13, 1839 (reprinted from the *New York Herald*).

47. W. Whitman, *Journalism*, 1:289; see P. Jones, *Against*, 95–133.

48. "The Trial of Capt. Smith," *New York Times*, November 7, 1854.

49. "The Slave-Trade. An Important Trial," *New York Times*, November 10, 1854; for the *Tribune's* coverage, see Howard, *American Slavers*, 52.

50. See "From the New York Tribune. The Slave Trade," *Provincial Freeman [Canada West]*, November 25, 1854.

51. "The Slave Trade in New York. (From the *Evangelist*)," *National Era*, December 21, 1854.

52. See Howard, *American Slavers*, 192–99; on Melville, see Parker, *Melville* 2:231–42.

53. "The Year in the Law Courts," *New York Times*, January 2, 1855; "*Captain Canot*," *New York Times*, November 7, 1854. The advertisement ran throughout the *Times's* coverage of the Smith trial. See also "Important Trial. The African Slave Trade. Trial of Capt. James Smith for Piracy," *New York Times*, November 7, 1854; "Important Case. Trial of the Captain of an African Slaver," *New York Times*, November 9, 1854; "Impor-

tant Case. Trial of the Master of an African Slaver—His Conviction," *New York Times*, November 10, 1854; "The City in 1854," *New York Times*, January 1, 1855.

54. Parker, *Melville*, 2:162–254.

55. See also Lee, *Slavery*, 133–64; on Melville and the literary market, see Post-Lauria, *Correspondent Colorings*.

56. *Liberator*, November 4, 1842 quoted in R. Wallace, "Fugitive," 48. Having discovered that in 1818 Shaw prepared the contract for the second edition of Delano's *Narrative*, which specifically stipulates Southern distribution of the work, Wallace raises "the possibility that he may have had a role" in familiarizing his son-in-law with the book (43). For a persuasive reading of a seemingly pointed allusion to Shaw in "Benito Cereno," see 63.

57. See also Lee, *Slavery*, 84–89. Almost literally on the same page with the controversy, Stowe published serial installments of *The Minister's Wooing* from December 1858 to December 1859 in *Atlantic Monthly*. Chapter 8 followed a satirical essay whose Swiftian proposal for cannibalism commences by proclaiming "it is the destiny of the middle of the nineteenth century . . . unhesitatingly to defend the African slave-trade, and to smile at what sickly philanthropists used to consider the unutterable woe, the unmeasured crime, and the diabolical hard-heartedness of that traffic"; "Plea for the Fijians," 343. Four months later, Stowe's chapter portraying the community's response to Rev. Hopkins's anti-slave trade "Sermon" appears several pages before a review of *To Cuba and Back* (1859), which noted that Richard Henry Dana's treatment of "the institution of slavery and the slave-trade" in Cuba "give[s] a practical value to the book at this time for all thinking and patriotic citizens." Review of *To Cuba*, 132.

58. Melville, "Benito Cereno," 46.

59. Taylor, *Cavalier and Yankee*; see also Yellin, "Black Masks," 683. On "Benito Cereno"'s legal contexts, see Yellin, "Black Masks"; Rogin, *Subversive*, 211–14; Thomas, *Cross-Examinations*, 93–112; Sale, *Slumbering*; R. Ferguson, "Untold Stories"; Konefsky, "Accidental"; S. Weiner, *Law*, 113–38.

60. On the domestic slave trade, see Pacheco, *Pearl*; Lightner, *Slavery*; Deyle, *Carry Me Back*; W. Johnson, *Chattel Principle*; Gudmestad, *Troublesome Commerce*. The novella begins, moreover, in coastal Chile and ends in Peru—which, however, borders the preeminent midcentury slave-trading nation, Brazil.

61. Giles Jacob, *Law-Dictionary . . .* , ed. T. E. Tomlins, 1st American from 2nd London ed., vol. 2, s.v. "evidence."

62. [Phillipps], *Theory*, 15–17.

63. Delano also includes the deposition of Midshipman Nathaniel Luther: see *Narrative*, 332–46.

64. Melville, "Benito Cereno," 103. On the legal documents' questionable authority, see Sundquist, *To Wake*, 179; S. Weiner, *Law*, 130–34; DeLombard, "Salvaging."

65. Navy Department instructions, quoted in Howard, *American Slavers*, 86. Not until the Anglo-American Treaty of 1862 was such an equipment clause introduced; Fehrenbacher, *Slaveholding Republic*, 162, 176, 190.

66. "Further Particulars of the Seizure of the Schooner *Falmouth*," *Provincial Freeman [Canada West]*, April 12, 1856.

67. Ibid.

68. Navy Department instructions, quoted in Howard, *American Slavers*, 86–87.

69. "The Slave Trade from New York," *Provincial Freeman [Canada West]*, April 12, 1856 (reprinted from *New York Commercial Advertiser*). See, for example, "The African Slave-Trade," *New York Times*, March 12, 1855. See also Canney, *Africa Squadron*, 93–94, 194, 209.

70. On auxiliaries, see J. W., "The Slave Trade in Brazil, Correspondent of the [New York] Tribune," *North Star*, October 5, 1849. On the difficulty of obtaining convictions with circumstantial evidence, see Howard, *American Slavers*, 8, 22–24, 78.

71. [Van Ness], *Case*, 284.

72. Ibid., 285.

73. See Welsh, *Strong*, 2–42; Rodensky, *Crime*, 21–23.

74. [Phillips], *Theory*, 12.

75. See, for example, Yellin, "Black Masks," 684–86; Emery, "Topicality," 326; Nelson, *National Manhood*, 1–3, 17, 50; Sundquist, *To Wake*, 170, 178.

76. Melville, "Benito Cereno," 72, 73.

77. Ibid., 75.

78. The *Anti-Slavery Standard* quoting the *London Standard*, reprinted in "Slaves Re-Captured," *North Star*, June 27, 1850; "From the *Norfolk Beacon*. The Alleged Slaver *Rachel P. Brown*," *Frederick Douglass' Paper*, April 15, 1853; "Further Particulars of the Seizure of the Schooner *Falmouth*," *Provincial Freeman [Canada West]*, April 12, 1856.

79. See D. Davis, *Slave Power*. On paranoia and "Benito Cereno" as sectional allegory, see Levine, *Conspiracy*, 165–230; Lee, *Slavery*, 136–42. On paranoia in connection with historical agency and individual and national responsibility in the context of early national slavery, see Fliegelman, *Declaring*, 140–41; see also G. Wood, "Paranoid Style."

80. Melville, "Benito Cereno," 46.

81. "The Slave Trade—More Developments," *Colored American [New York]*, July 13, 1839 (reprinted from *New York Herald*).

82. Ibid. Such stratagems became even more necessary after an 1835 Anglo-Spanish treaty, which by "authorizing the seizure of vessels patently equipped for slave trading even if they had no Africans aboard . . . greatly enhanced the value of American cover" in that "fraudulent use of the flag of the United States . . . served to nullify" the treaty's equipment clause. Fehrenbacher, *Slaveholding Republic*, 162.

83. Generally speaking, the slave traffic "floated under the flags of France, Spain, and Portugal, until about 1830; from 1830 to 1840 it began gradually to assume the United States flag; by 1845, a large part of the trade was under the stars and stripes; by 1850 fully one-half the trade, and in the decade, 1850–1860 nearly all the traffic, found this flag its best protection." Du Bois, *Suppression*, 143. For more nuanced accounts, see Canney, *Africa Squadron*, 22–25; Fehrenbacher, *Slaveholding Republic*, 155–91.

84. Du Bois, *Suppression*, 134–50. In the Quintuple Treaty, signed December 1841,

Britain, France, Austria, Prussia, and Russia agreed to mutual right of search and declared the slave trade piracy; Fehrenbacher, *Slaveholding Republic*, 166.

85. Du Bois, *Suppression*, 133–50; Fehrenbacher, *Slaveholding Republic*, 157–72.

86. Fehrenbacher, *Slaveholding Republic*, 168–72 (quotation at 169).

87. Foote, *Africa*, 300.

88. On the priority of American commerce over slave trade policing, see Canney, *Africa Squadron*, 57, see also 207–8.

89. On the devolution of the right of search into the corollary right of visit, see Fehrenbacher, *Slaveholding Republic*, 157–72.

90. "Cost"; see also "Rights of Our Flag"; "John Bull"; "British Aggressions"; and "Visit.'" See Fehrenbacher, *Slaveholding Republic*, 184–85.

91. "The Slave Trade and Right of Search—Patriotism and Philanthropy," *National Era*, May 27, 1858. For other Anglophobic accounts of the British navy's African force, see "Slaver"; "Doom"; Lawrence, *Voyage*.

92. "The Slave Trade and Right of Search—Patriotism and Philanthropy," *National Era*, May 27, 1858.

93. Buchanan quoted in Foote, *Africa*, 152.

94. See H. Jones, *Webster-Ashburton*; on the close ties—and federal funds—linking the African Squadron to the American Colonization Society, see Canney, *Africa Squadron*, 8–9, 50; Fehrenbacher, *Slaveholding Republic*, 153–54, 187–89.

95. "The Slave Trade and Right of Search—Patriotism and Philanthropy," *National Era*, May 27, 1858.

96. Lawrence, *Voyage*, 143.

97. [Bridge], *Journal*, 177.

98. Hawthorne to Evert Duyckinck, March 2, 1845, quoted in Brancaccio "Black Man's Burden," 30; see Greenspan, "Evert Duyckinck," 684.

99. "Slavers Captured," *Colored American*, May 1, 1841.

100. "Literary Notices," *National Era*, October 26, 1854; Mayer, *Captain Canot*, 250–51.

101. "From the *Norfolk Beacon*. The Alleged Slaver *Rachel P. Brown*," *Frederick Douglass' Paper*, April 15, 1853.

102. Melville, "Benito Cereno," 87.

103. McBlair, "Commander," 16. See also Canney, *Africa Squadron*, 161–62, 166, 185; Howard, *American Slavers*, 74, 287n2. U.S.S. *Yorktown* Commander Charles H. Bell credited his capture of the *Pons* to similar stratagems; "Extract," 118.

104. Unidentified clipping in the American Antiquarian Society's copy of *Africa and the American Flag*, apparently from a Baltimore newspaper.

105. See, for example, Stevens, *Anthony Burns*, 85–90, 92–95, 109–12.

106. As "enemies of the human race," pirates were "amenable to the tribunals of all civilized nations for their crimes," but because, as Chief Justice Marshall's *Antelope* decision explained, the African slave trade "has been sanctioned in modern times by the laws of all nations who possess distant colonies, each of whom has engaged in it as

a common commercial business . . . . That trade could not be considered as contrary to the law of nations which was authorized and protected by the laws of all commercial nations." *Antelope.*

107. "Important Case. Trial of the Captain of an African Slaver," *New York Times,* November 9, 1854.

108. Ibid.

109. "Charges against Mr. Valentine," *New York Times,* December 29, 1854.

110. Howard, *American Slavers,* 201.

111. Melville, "Benito Cereno," 51, 99, 64, 60. Otter finds Melville "twice exchanging national terms ('Spaniards,' 'Spanish') for racial ones ('whites,' 'white')" when revising the work for book publication. *Philadelphia,* 268.

112. For a contrasting reading, see Levine, *Conspiracy,* 203.

113. R. Wallace, "Fugitive," 63.

114. Mayer, *Captain Canot,* 251.

115. See J. Baker, "Staging," 96; I. Wilson, *Specters,* 134–35;

116. See Bartley, "Creature," 461; Tawil, "Captain Babo's Cabin," 50.

117. *Confessions and Executions,* 6. On eighteenth-century Anglo-American use of the Jolly Roger, see Rediker, *Devil,* 278–81; on alternative nineteenth-century pirate flags, including non-slaver use of national ensigns, see J. Gibbs, *Dead Men,* 54, 55.

118. Story, *Charge,* 5.

119. Melville, "Benito Cereno," 87.

120. "Slave Trade," *Niles' Weekly Register,* December 2, 1820; see also "Slave Trade," *Boston Daily Advertiser,* November 7, 1820; Du Bois, *Suppression,* 128, 128n3; "The Slave Trade," *Niles' Weekly Register,* April 20, 1822. "Whale Fishery," *Niles' Weekly Register,* December 2, 1820; on the *Essex*'s 1820 voyage as a source for *Moby-Dick,* see Philbrick, *Heart.*

121. [Van Ness], *Case,* 293.

122. "Slave Trade," *Niles' Weekly Register,* December 2, 1820.

123. Melville, "Benito Cereno," 102.

124. Although treatment of African recaptives varied widely, most were not freed; they were often indentured under terms barely distinguishable from slavery with a percentage of their value as "prizes" (along with the ship and its fittings) going to captain and crew. See Lawrence, *Voyage* 144; Canney, *Africa Squadron,* 3–7. See also Akehurst, "Sectional Crises."

125. Melville, "Benito Cereno," 47.

126. [Van Ness], *Case,* 288.

127. Rediker, *Devil,* 286.

128. Lawrence, *Voyage,* 223.

129. H. Brooke, *Book of Pirates,* ix, x.

130. Brooke's *Book of Pirates* may have appeared alongside its popular predecessor, *The Pirates Own Book* (1837), among the literary "trash made for seamen" sold by waterfront book peddlers. Quoted in Gilje, *Liberty,* 213; see also Skallerup, *Books,* 209.

131. Story, *Charge*, 5.

132. "Slaver," 3.

133. See Gould, *Barbaric*, 45–62; see also Canuel, *Shadow*, 145–50.

134. Compare Gould, *Barbaric*, 45.

135. Act of 26 March 1790, *Stats at Large of USA*; Act of 30 April 1790, sec. 8–17, *Stats at Large of USA*; for gloss, see "An Act to Protect the Commerce of the United States, and Punish the Crime of Piracy," March 3, 1819, 511n(a).

136. On the controversial right of expatriation, see R. Smith, *Civic Ideals*, 153–59, 169–70, 192–94, 228–30.

137. "Slaver," 117; More, "Slavery," quoted in Gould, *Barbaric*, 61 (capitalization omitted).

138. *American Heritage Dictionary of the English Language*, 3rd ed., s.v. "burgee."

139. The earliest documented OED usage in the second sense above is dated 1862; *Oxford English Dictionary Online*, s.v. "enterprise," but see Hawthorne, *House*, 32, 35, 38, 40, 47.

140. Rediker, *Devil*, 287.

141. Brooke's chapter on the *Amistad* leaves unclear whether it is the Africans' uprising or their captors' slave trading that justifies their inclusion in the *Book of Pirates*. The confusion is augmented by the previous chapter, in which a slave-trading Spanish captain and first mate set off in late August 1832 "on the ordinary course for the coast of Guinea" only to be distracted by "another object . . . *piracy*." H. Brooke, *Book of Pirates*, 172; for the *Amistad*, see 184–96.

142. "Correspondence of the *Commercial Advertiser*: A Winter in the West Indies," *Colored American*, November 9, 1839; "Drowning of Six Hundred Slaves. An Incident of the Slave Trade. Related in the *Universe* Newspaper," *North Star*, December 3, 1847.

143. "From the N.Y. Evangelist. The Slave Trade in New York," *Frederick Douglass' Paper*, December 22, 1854.

144. Ibid.

145. "The Slave Trade," *National Era*, December 7, 1854 (reprinted from the *New York Tribune*); "Arrest of Alleged Slave-Traders," *National Era*, September 28, 1854.

146. "The Slave Trade," *National Era*, December 7, 1854.

147. "From the New York Tribune. The Slave Trade," *Provincial Freeman [Canada West]*, November 25, 1854.

148. "The Slave Trade," *Frederick Douglass' Paper*, December 1, 1854.

149. Canney, *Africa Squadron*, 22.

150. Roediger, *Wages*, 72–74.

151. "New York State," 192, 189.

152. Ibid., 192. See Fitzhugh, *Cannibals All*.

153. Dana, *Two Years*, 153, 152, 156.

154. Melville, *Moby-Dick*, 6. See Huntress, "Guinea," 641; Konefsky, "Accidental," 1182; Levine, *Conspiracy*, 168–82. On the 1842 scandal surrounding summary floggings and execution on the African Squadron's *Somers*, which involved Melville's cousin Guert

Gansevoort and inspired *Billy Budd*, see McFarland, *Sea Dangers*; Hayford, *Somers Mutiny*; Parker, *Herman Melville*, 1:241–44, 266–67, 293–97, 358.

155. Gilje, *Liberty*, 216–19, 245–47.

156. Christopher, *Slave Ship Sailors*, 91–117, 125–27.

157. Ibid., 213, 167.

158. Ibid., 91–117, 125–27.

159. Ibid., 229.

160. See Roediger, *Wages*.

161. Joseph G. Clark, *Lights and Shadows of Sailor Life . . .* (Boston, 1848), quoted in Gilje, *Liberty*, 248; see R. Smith, *Civic Ideals*, 170–73.

162. See DeLombard, "Salvaging."

163. "Important Trial. The African Slave Trade," *New York Times*, November 7, 1854; see C. Hyde, "Outcast," 920.

164. "The Alleged Slaver Case," *New York Times*, January 26, 1855; see also "Important Case. Trial of the Captain of an African Slaver," *New York Times*, November 9, 1854.

165. "On Board," 347; see also "Execution of Gordon"; "From the *Norfolk Beacon*. The Alleged Slaver *Rachel P. Brown*," *Frederick Douglass' Paper*, April 15, 1853.

166. Sec. 3, *Stats at Large of USA* 2:70.

167. H. Smith, "Modern Privilege."

168. "Slaver," 66.

169. "The Alleged Slaver Case. Before United States Commissioner Morton," *New York Times*, January 18, 1855.

170. [Van Ness], *Case*, 291.

171. Ibid.

172. Welsh, *Strong*, 40.

173. "Further Particulars of the Seizure of the Schooner *Falmouth*," *Provincial Freeman [Canada West]*, April 12, 1856.

174. Ibid.

175. On the "passive enervation" of Melville's sailors, see Bell, *Development*, 213; see also Levine, *Conspiracy*, 187–98; C. Hyde, "Outcast," 919–23.

176. Lugenbeel, "Letter," 112.

177. Stowe, *Minister's Wooing*, 140.

178. For complementary analysis of the phenomenon whereby the white criminal narrator "disappeared into his fictional self" by cultivating "literary infamy," see Downes, *Democracy*, 108–11 (quotation at 108).

179. "From the N.Y. Evangelist. The Slave Trade in New York," *Frederick Douglass' Paper*, December 22, 1854. Retried and pleading guilty to the far less onerous Act of 1800, Smith received the comparatively light sentence of two years imprisonment and a (subsequently remitted) fine of $1,000; Howard, *American Slavers*, 192–97, 227.

180. See "The Slave Trade in New York. (From the *Evangelist*)," *National Era*, December 21, 1854; "The Slave Trade in New York"; "From the Evangelist"; "Editor's Table."

181. [Lippard,] *Bank Director's Son*, 11, 21.

182. On the anti-gallows themes in Lippard's fiction, see P. Jones, *Against*, 11–15, 77–79.

183. For full literary and historical contexts, see Otter, *Philadelphia*, 131–252.

184. Reynolds, *Beneath*, 208.

185. Building on preliminary work by Lapsansky, Faflik has reconstructed the novels' publishing history. On the basis of Lippard's prior compositional practice, Faflik tends to assume that the *Life and Adventures*, filed for copyright on December 4, 1849, was expanded into the lengthier work; see Faflik, "Authorship," 152, 154, and "Case," 5. For Otter, the speed of the serialized version's publication suggests the *Life and Adventures* resulted from editorial condensation; see *Philadelphia*, 187. The longer work's multiple incarnations, literary and textual substance, and association with Lippard's authorial persona complicate Faflik's admirable effort to rethink individual proprietary authorship at midcentury, while suggesting that it is the "The Killers"/*Killers*/*Bank Director's Son*, not *Life and Adventures*, that represents Lippard's artisanal republican "pledge . . . to the reading public for a better *re*-public," as argued below. Faflik, "Authorship," 162. For title pages, see the on-line exhibit, "Philadelphia Gothic," guest curated by Neil K. Fitzgerald, http://www.librarycompany.org/gothic/Lippard.htm, accessed July 15, 2011.

186. Reynolds, *Beneath*, 208.

187. [Lippard,] *Bank Director's Son*, 50.

188. In the unfinished *Nazarene* (1846), Lippard has Philadelphia's Southern medical students, faced with a barroom brawl with black antagonists, reference the well-known practice of racial medical experimentation by threatening to "dissect these subjects!" Quoted in Otter, *Philadelphia*, 184.

189. The quotation is accurate: compare U.S. Congress, *Message*, 7–8.

190. See Morgan, *American*.

191. "Slaver," 66.

192. Stowe, *Minister's Wooing*, 143. Like Melville, Stowe resets her narrative clock to coincide with federal slave trade legislation; the source for the titular minister's 1790s sermon is Samuel J. Hopkins's *Dialogue Concerning the Slavery of the Africans* (1776); see Walters, "Stowe," 183–84.

193. Stowe, *Minister's Wooing*, 143.

Conclusion

1. Rockafield, *Manheim Tragedy*, 6.

2. See Madow, "Forbidden"; Banner, *Death Penalty*, 195. On the legal prohibition of photographic and televisual images of execution, including the distinction between writing implements and cameras, see *KQED, Inc. v. Vasquez*, 1991; Angeja, "Televising"; Lesser, *Pictures*; Sarat, *When*, 187–208.

3. See J. Allen, *Without Sanctuary*; Apel, *Imagery*; Apel and Smith, *Lynching*; A. Wood, *Lynching*.

4. The specific form of lynching as it emerged in the aftermath of Reconstruction—a

terrorist act conducted against informally and, typically, falsely charged African Americans—strategically inverts the process analyzed in the current study. In the historical epoch when African Americans finally were to be included in the revised American social compact—not merely in punitive retrospect, as partial, culpable legal persons, but as persons with birthright citizenship under the Fourteenth Amendment—it is not surprising that a backlash should occur that would reject *any* legal recognition of black personhood and civic belonging. Denying its victims even fractional personhood or retroactive political membership, this new, extralegal form of racial terrorism willfully misapprehended black civility as transgression so as to make the private spaces of African American life and the civic spaces of the United States alike coextensive with a zone of force. (Beyond these concluding observations, however, further analysis of lynching lies outside the scope of this paper; in addition to the works cited above, see Goldsby, *Spectacular.*)

5. See Masur, *Rites*; Banner, *Death Penalty*, 144–68; Madow, "Forbidden"; Sarat, *When*, 187–208; C. Smith, *Prison*. The hanging of "Henry Smith (colored)" on "May 11th, 1838, for the murder of Benjamin Peart, . . . took place in the jail yard" and was thus Lancaster County's "first" death penalty "carried into execution after the passage of the law abolishing public executions." A. Harris, *Biographical History*, 340n1.

6. Habermas, *Between*, 361.

7. Ibid.

8. Sarat, *When*, 193.

9. Madow, "Forbidden."

10. Melville, "Benito Cereno," 116.

11. Sarat, *When*, 198; see also Dayan, *Law*. Photographer Lucinda Devlin's photographs of empty execution chambers powerfully evoke this trend; see *Omega Suites*.

12. Rockafield, *Manheim Tragedy*, 25.

13. See also ibid., 26. Prompted by publishers' overtures to serial killer David Berkowitz in 1977, so-called Son of Sam laws represent something of a Book History watershed (however currently eroded) in seeking to prevent criminals from reaping profits from published or broadcast depictions of their crimes. See Tracey Cobb, "Making."

14. Douglass, *My Bondage*, 322.

15. How much control Anderson was finally able to exert over his text (to say nothing of its proceeds) is uncertain; the copyright is in H. A. Rockafield's name; see also Slaughter, *Bloody Dawn*, 231n19.

16. See Douglass, *My Bondage*, 376–77; Jacobs, *Incidents*, 97.

17. See Franklin, *Prison Literature*; C. Smith, *Prison*; Dayan, *Law*.

18. Hale, "Man," 666. For a reception history, see C. Hyde, "Outcast," 916–17.

19. See Madison, Hamilton, and Jay, *Federalist*, 332.

20. Bishop and Attree, *Report*, 1047.

21. Habersham quoted in Noonan, *Antelope*, 158.

22. Hale, "Man," 674.

23. Contrast Kerber, "History," 731–32.

24. See also C. Hyde, "Outcast."

25. Kerber, "History," 727.

26. See Blight, *Race*.

27. Seen as a thinly veiled rationale for Lincoln's suspension of habeas corpus, the story is typically read as a defense of the summary conviction and imprisonment of Ohio lawyer and Copperhead Democrat politician Clement L. Vallandigham for an oration criticizing the administration's abuse of the right to free speech. See Curtis, *Free Speech*, 300–356; Thomas, *Civic Myths*, 55–101.

28. See, for example, K. Parker, "Making"; Wong, *Neither*, 240–62.

29. As Blum's reading of the introduction of caskets into the sea fiction of Melville and Poe would suggest, Hale's evocation of the coffin, as ubiquitous in land-based funeral rites as it was extraneous to martime ones, underscores Nolan's association with stateside American citizens; *View*, 158–92.

Bibliography

Adams, John. *Legal Papers of John Adams*. Ed. L. Kinvin Wroth and Hiller B. Zobel. Vol. 3, *Cases 63 and 64: The Boston Massacre Trials*. Cambridge, Mass.: Belknap Press of Harvard University Press, 1965.

Agamben, Giorgio. *Homo Sacer: Sovereign Power and Bare Life*. Trans. Daniel Heller-Roazen. Stanford, Calif.: Stanford University Press, 1998.

Akehurst, Hazel. "Sectional Crises and the Fate of Africans Illegally Imported into the United States, 1806–1860." *American Nineteenth Century History* 9, 2 (June 2008): 97–122.

Alden, John Richard. *The South in the Revolution, 1763–1789*. Baton Rouge: Louisiana State University Press, 1985.

Allen, Howard W. and Jerome M. Chubb. *Race, Class, and the Death Penalty: Capital Punishment in American History*. Albany: State University of New York Press, 2008.

Allen, James. *Without Sanctuary: Lynching Photography in America*. Santa Fe: Twin Palms, 2000.

[Allen, Richard.] *Confession of John Joyce, Alias Davis, Who Was Executed on Monday, the 14th of March, 1808. For the Murder of Mrs. Sarah Cross; With an Address to the Public and People of Colour. Together with the Substance of the Trial, and the Address of Chief Justice Tilghman, on His Condemnation. Confession of Peter Mathias, Alias Matthews, Who Was Executed on Monday, the 14th of March, 1808. For the Murder of Mrs. Sarah Cross; With an Address to the Public and People of Colour. Together with the Substance of the Trial, and the Address of Chief Justice Tilghman, on His Condemnation*. Philadelphia, 1808.

Allen, Thomas M. *A Republic in Time: Temporality and Social Imagination in Nineteenth-Century America*. Chapel Hill: University of North Carolina Press, 2008.

Althusser, Louis. *Lenin and Philosophy, and Other Essays*. Trans. Ben Brewster. New York: Monthly Review Press, 2001.

Anderson, Benedict. *Imagined Communities: Reflections on the Origin and Spread of Nationalism*. London: Verso, 1983.

Andrews, Dee E. "Reconsidering the First Emancipation: Evidence from the Pennsylvania Abolition Society Correspondence, 1785–1810." *Pennsylvania History* 64 (Summer 1997): 230–49.

Andrews, William L., ed. *African-American Autobiography: A Collection of Critical Essays*. Englewood Cliffs, N.J.: Prentice Hall, 1993.

———, ed. *Sisters of the Spirit: Three Black Women's Spiritual Autobiographies*. Bloomington: Indiana University Press, 1986.

———. *To Tell a Free Story: The First Century of Afro-American Autobiography, 1760–1865*. Urbana: University of Illinois Press, 1986.

Andrews, William L., Frances Smith Foster, and Trudier Harris, eds. *The Oxford Companion to African American Literature*. New York: Oxford University Press, 1997.

Angeja, Jeff. "Televising California's Death Penalty: Is There a Constitutional Right to Broadcast Executions?" *Hastings Law Journal* 43 (1991–92): 1489–1516.

Apel, Dora. *Imagery of Lynching: Black Men, White Women, and the Mob*. New Brunswick, N.J.: Rutgers University Press, 2004.

Apel, Dora and Shawn Michelle Smith. *Lynching Photographs*. Berkeley: University of California Press, 2008.

An Appeal to the Public on Behalf of a House of Refuge for Colored Juvenile Delinquents. Philadelphia. 1846. [Broadside.]

An Appeal to the Public on Behalf of a House of Refuge for Colored Juvenile Delinquents. Philadelphia, 1846. [Pamphlet.]

Aristotle. *Nicomachean Ethics*. Ed. and trans. Roger Crisp. Cambridge: Cambridge University Press, 1988.

———. *The Politics*. Ed. and trans. Stephen Everson. Cambridge: Cambridge University Press, 1988.

Armitage, David. "John Locke, Carolina, and the *Two Treatises of Government*." *Political Theory* 32, 5 (October 2005): 602–27.

Arpey, Andrew W. *The William Freeman Murder Trial: Insanity, Politics, and Race*. Syracuse, N.Y.: Syracuse University Press, 2003.

Arthur. *The Life, and Dying Speech of Arthur, a Negro Man; Who Was Executed at Worcester, October 10, 1768. For a Rape Committed on the Body of One Deborah Metcalfe*. Boston, 1768.

Articles of Association of the African Methodist Episcopal Church, of the City of Philadelphia, in the Commonwealth of Pennsylvania. Philadelphia, 1799.

Ashton, Susanna. "Slavery, Imprinted: The Life and Narrative of William Grimes." In Cohen and Stein, *Early African American Print Culture*, 127–39.

Bacon, Benjamin C. *Statistics of the Colored People of Philadelphia*. Philadelphia, 1856.

Bacon, Jacqueline. "Rhetoric and Identity in Absalom Jones and Richard Allen's *Narrative of the Proceedings of the Black People, during the Late Awful Calamity in*

Philadelphia." *Pennsylvania Magazine of History and Biography* 125, 1–2 (January/April 2001): 61–90.

Baker, George E., ed. *The Life of William Seward, with Selections from His Works.* New York, 1855.

Baker, Houston A., Jr. *Blues, Ideology, and Afro-American Literature: A Vernacular Theory.* Chicago: University of Chicago Press, 1984.

———. "Critical Memory and the Black Public Sphere." *Public Culture* 7 (1994): 3–33.

———. *The Journey Back: Issues in Black Literature and Criticism.* Chicago: University of Chicago Press, 1980.

———. *Long Black Song: Essays in Black American Literature and Culture.* Charlottesville: University Press of Virginia, 1972.

Baker, Jennifer Jordan. "Staging Revolution in Melville's *Benito Cereno*: Babo, Figaro, and the 'Play of the Barber.'" *Prospects* 26 (2001): 91–107.

Bancroft, Frederic. *The Life of William H. Seward.* 2 vols. New York: Harper and Brothers, 1900.

Banner, Stuart. *The Death Penalty: An American History.* Cambridge, Mass.: Harvard University Press, 2002.

Bar, Carl Ludwig von. *A History of Continental Criminal Law.* 1916. Union, N.J.: Lawbook Exchange, 1999.

Barrett, Lindon. "Presence of Mind: Detection and Racialization in 'The Murders in the Rue Morgue.'" In Kennedy and Weissberg, *Romancing*, 157–76.

Barthes, Roland. "The Death of the Author." In *Image—Music—Text: Essays*, ed. and trans. Stephen Heath, 142–48. New York: Hill and Wang, 1977.

Bartley, William. "'The Creature of His Own Tasteful Hands': Herman Melville's 'Benito Cereno' and the 'Empire of Might.'" *Modern Philology* 93, 4 (May 1996): 445–67.

Barton, John Cyril. "The Anti-Gallows Movement in Antebellum America." *REAL: Yearbook of Research in English and American Literature* 22 (2006): 145–78.

———. "William Gilmore Simms and the Literary Aesthetics of Crime and Capital Punishment." *Law and Literature* 22, 2 (Summer 2010): 220–43.

Baucom, Ian. *Specters of the Atlantic: Finance Capital, Slavery, and the Philosophy of History.* Durham, N.C.: Duke University Press, 2005.

Beaumont, G[ustave] de and A[lexis] de Tocqueville. *On the Penitentiary System in the United States and Its Application in France; with an Appendix on Penal Colonies, and also Statistical Notes.* Trans. Francis L. Lieber. Philadelphia, 1833.

Beccaria, Cesare. *An Essay on Crimes and Punishments.* Philadelphia, 1778.

Bell, Michael Davit. *The Development of American Romance: The Sacrifice of Relation.* Chicago: University of Chicago Press, 1980.

Bender, John. *Imagining the Penitentiary: Fiction and the Architecture of Mind in Eighteenth-Century England*. Chicago: University of Chicago Press, 1987.

Bercovitch, Sacan. *The Puritan Origins of the American Self*. New Haven, Conn.: Yale University Press, 1975.

Berlant, Lauren. *The Queen of America Goes to Washington City: Essays on Sex and Citizenship*. Durham, N.C.: Duke University Press, 1997.

Berlin, Ira. *Many Thousands Gone: The First Two Centuries of Slavery in North America*. Cambridge, Mass.: Belknap Press of Harvard University Press, 1998.

———. *Slaves Without Masters: The Free Negro in the Antebellum South*. New York: New Press, 1974.

Berry, Mary Frances. *My Face Is Black Is True: Callie House and the Struggle for Ex-Slave Reparations*. New York: Knopf, 2005.

Best, Stephen M. *The Fugitive's Properties: Law and the Poetics of Possession*. Chicago: University of Chicago Press, 2004.

Best, Stephen M. and Saidiya Hartman. "Fugitive Justice." In Best and Hartman, *Redress*, 1–15.

———, eds. *Redress*. Special issue, *Representations* 92 (Autumn 2005).

Between the Covers Rare Books. *Catalog 145: African-Americana*. Gloucester City, N.J.: Between the Covers, 2009.

Bishop, William G. and William H. Attree. *Report of the Debates and Proceedings of the Convention for the Revision of the Constitution of the State of New-York*. Albany, 1846.

Blackstone, William. *Commentaries on the Laws of England: A Facsimile of the First Edition of 1765–1769*. 4 vols. Chicago: University of Chicago Press, 1979.

Blake, Alexander V., comp. *The American Bookseller's Complete Reference Trade List, and Alphabetical Catalogue of Books Published in this Country, with the Publishers' and Authors' Names and Prices Arranged in Classes for Quick and Convenient Reference*. Claremont, N.J., 1847.

Blassingame, John W. *The Slave Community: Plantation Life in the Antebellum South*. Rev. ed. New York: Oxford University Press, 1979.

Blight, David W. *Race and Reunion: The Civil War in American Memory*. Cambridge, Mass.: Belknap Press of Harvard University Press, 2001.

Blum, Hester. *The View from the Masthead: Maritime Imagination and Antebellum American Sea Narratives*. Chapel Hill: University of North Carolina Press, 2008.

Blumenthal, Susanna L. "The Default Legal Person." *UCLA Law Review* 54 (2006–7): 1135–1265.

———. "The Deviance of the Will: Policing the Bounds of Testamentary Freedom in Nineteenth-Century America." *Harvard Law Review* 119 (2005–6): 960–1034.

———. "Metaphysics, Moral Sense, and the Pragmatism of the Law." *Law and History Review* 26, 1 (Spring 2008): 177–85.

———. "The Mind of a Moral Agent: Scottish Common Sense and the Problem of Responsibility in Nineteenth-Century American Law." *Law and History Review* 26, 1 (Spring 2008): 99–159.

Bolster, W. Jeffrey. *Black Jacks: African American Seamen in the Age of Sail*. Cambridge, Mass.: Harvard University Press, 1997.

Bosco, Ronald A. "Early American Gallows Literature: An Annotated Checklist." *Resources for American Literary Study* 8 (1978): 81–107.

———. "Lectures at the Pillory: The Early American Execution Sermon." *American Quarterly* 30 (1978): 156–76.

Boudreau, Kristin. *The Spectacle of Death: Populist Literary Responses to American Capital Cases*. Amherst, N.Y.: Prometheus, 2006.

Bowdoin, James, Joseph Warren, and Samuel Pemberton. *A Short Narrative of the Horrid Massacre in Boston, Perpetrated in the Evening of the Fifth day of March, 1770. By Soldiers of the XXIXth Regiment; which with the XIVth Regiment were then Quartered There: with Some Observations on the State of Things prior to that Catastrophe*. Boston, 1770.

Brace, Laura. *The Politics of Property: Labour, Freedom, and Belonging*. New York: Palgrave Macmillan, 2004.

Brancaccio, Patrick. "'The Black Man's Paradise': Hawthorne's Editing of the *Journal of an African Cruiser*." *New England Quarterly* 53, 1 (March 1980): 23–41.

Breen, T. H. "Making History: The Force of Public Opinion and the Last Years of Slavery in Revolutionary Massachusetts." In Hoffman, Sobel, and Teute, *Through a Glass Darkly*, 67–95.

Breen, T. H. and Stephen Innis. *"Myne Owne Ground": Race and Freedom on Virginia's Eastern Shore, 1640–1676*. New York: Oxford University Press, 1980.

Brewer, Holly. *By Birth or Consent: Children, Law, and the Anglo-American Revolution in Authority*. Chapel Hill: University of North Carolina Press, 2005.

[Bridge, Horatio.] *Journal of an African Cruiser; Comprising Sketches of the Canaries, the Cape de Verds, Liberia, Madeira, Sierra Leone, and Other Places of Interest on the West Coast of Africa*. Ed. Nathaniel Hawthorne. New York, 1845.

Brightly, Frank F. *A Digest of the Statute Law of the State of Pennsylvania from the Year 1700 to 1894*. Vol. 2. Philadelphia, 1895.

"The British Aggressions upon American Commerce." *Harper's Weekly*, May 29, 1858, 342.

Brode, Patrick. *The Odyssey of John Anderson*. Toronto: University of Toronto Press, 1989.

Brooke, Henry K. *Book of Pirates: Containing Narratives of the Most Remarkable Piracies and Murders, Committed on the High Seas; Together with an Account of the Capture of the* Amistad; *and a Full and Authentic Narrative of the Burning of the* Caroline. Philadelphia, 1841.

Brooke, John L. "Consent, Civil Society, and the Public Sphere in the Age of Revolution and the Early American Republic." In Pasley, Robertson, and Waldstreicher, *Beyond*, 207–50.

Brooks, Joanna. *American Lazarus: Religion and the Rise of Native American and African American Literatures*. Oxford: Oxford University Press, 2003.

———. "The Early American Public Sphere and the Emergence of a Black Print Counterpublic." *William and Mary Quarterly* 3rd ser. 62, 1 (2005): 67–98.

———. "John Marrant's *Journal*: Providence and Prophecy in the Eighteenth-Century Black Atlantic." *North Star: Journal of African American Religious History* 3, 1 (Fall 1999): 1–21.

Brooks, Joanna and John Saillant, eds. *"Face Zion Forward": First Writers of the Black Atlantic, 1785–1798*. Boston: Northeastern University Press, 2002.

Brooks, Peter. *Troubling Confessions: Speaking Guilt in Law and Literature*. Chicago: University of Chicago Press, 2000.

Brophy, Alfred L. "Humanity, Utility, and Logic in Southern Legal Thought: Harriet Beecher Stowe's Vision in *Dred: A Tale of the Great Dismal Swamp*." *Boston University Law Review* 78, 4 (October 1998): 1113–61.

———. "'Over and Above . . . There Broods a Portentous Shadow, the Shadow of *Law*': Harriet Beecher Stowe's Critique of Slave Law in *Uncle Tom's Cabin*." *Journal of Law and Religion* 12, 2 (1995–96): 457–506.

Brown, Henry Box. *Narrative of the Life of Henry Box Brown, Written by Himself*. Manchester, 1851.

Brown, Vincent. *The Reaper's Garden: Death and Power in the World of Atlantic Slavery*. Cambridge, Mass.: Harvard University Press, 2008.

Brown, William Wells. *Narrative of William W. Brown, an American Slave. Written by Himself*. London, 1849.

Bruce, Dickson D., Jr. *The Origins of African American Literature, 1680–1865*. Charlottesville: University Press of Virginia, 2001.

Bryant, John. "Poe's Ape of UnReason: Humor, Ritual, and Culture." *Nineteenth-Century Literature* 51, 1 (June 1996): 16–52.

Butterfield, Stephen. *Black Autobiography in America*. Amherst: University of Massachusetts Press, 1974.

C. S. "Notices of New Books." Review of *Rationale of Crime and its Appropriate Treat-*

ment, being a Treatise on Criminal Jurisprudence, Considered in relation to Cerebral Organization. By M. B. Sampson. *Law Reporter* 9, 8 (December 1846): 377–78.

Caldwell, Patricia. *The Puritan Conversion Narrative: The Beginnings of American Expression.* Cambridge: Cambridge University Press, 1983.

Calhoun, Craig, ed. *Habermas and the Public Sphere.* Cambridge, Mass.: MIT Press, 1992.

Calonius, Erik. *The Wanderer: The Last American Slave Ship and the Conspiracy That Set Its Sails.* New York: St. Martin's, 2006.

Camp, Stephanie M. H. *Closer to Freedom: Enslaved Women and Everyday Resistance in the Plantation South.* Chapel Hill: University of North Carolina Press, 2004.

Canney, Donald L. *Africa Squadron: The U.S. Navy and the Slave Trade, 1842–1861.* Washington, D.C.: Potomac Books, 2006.

Canuel, Mark. *The Shadow of Death: Literature, Romanticism, and the Subject of Punishment.* Princeton, N.J.: Princeton University Press, 2007.

Carbado, Devon W. "(E)racing the Fourth Amendment." *Michigan Law Review* 100 (March 2002): 946–1044.

———. "Racial Naturalization." *American Quarterly* 57, 3 (September 2005): 633–58.

Carey, Mathew. "Address of M. Carey to the Public." Philadelphia, 1794.

———. *A Short Account of the Malignant Fever, Lately Prevalent in Philadelphia: With a Statement of the Proceedings that Took Place on the Subject in Different Parts of the United States.* 2nd ed. Philadelphia, 1793.

Carretta, Vincent. *Equiano the African: Biography of a Self-Made Man.* Athens: University of Georgia Press, 2005.

———, ed. *Unchained Voices: An Anthology of Black Authors in the English-Speaking World of the Eighteenth Century.* Lexington: University Press of Kentucky, 1996.

Carretta, Vincent and Philip Gould, eds. *Genius in Bondage: Literature of the Early Black Atlantic.* Lexington: University Press of Kentucky, 2001.

Carson, Ann. *The History of the Celebrated Mrs. Ann Carson, Widow of the Late Unfortunate Lieutenant Richard Smyth, with a Circumstantial Account of her Conspiracy against the Late Governor of Pennsylvania, Simon Snyder; and of her Sufferings in the Several Prisons of that State. Interspersed with Anecdotes of Characters now Living, Written by Herself.* Philadelphia, 1822.

Cartwright, Samuel A. "Report on the Diseases and Physical Peculiarities of the Negro Race." *New Orleans Medical and Surgical Journal* 7 (May 1851): 691–715.

Cassuto, Leonard. *The Inhuman Race: The Racial Grotesque in American Literature and Culture.* New York: Columbia University Press, 1997.

Castiglia, Christopher. *Interior States: Institutional Consciousness and the Inner Life of Democracy in the Antebellum United States*. Durham, N.C.: Duke University Press, 2008.

Castronovo, Russ. *Necro Citizenship: Death, Eroticism, and the Public Sphere in the Nineteenth-Century United States*. Durham, N.C.: Duke University Press, 2001.

Catterall, Helen Tunnicliff, ed. *Judicial Cases Concerning American Slavery and the Negro*. 5 vols. Washington, D.C.: Carnegie Institution, 1926–1937.

Chamberlain, Ava. "The Execution of Moses Paul: A Story of Crime and Contact in Eighteenth-Century Connecticut." *New England Quarterly* 77, 3 (September 2004): 414–50.

[Chandler, P. W.] "Hotch-Pot." *Law Reporter* 10, 1 (May 1847): 46.

———. "Plea of Insanity in Criminal Cases." *Law Reporter* 10, 1 (May 1847): 1–12. [Cited as 'Plea I.]

———. "Plea of Insanity in Criminal Cases." *Law Reporter* 10, 3 (July 1847): 97–112.

———. "The Trial of Abner Baker." *Law Reporter* 9, 8 (December 1846): 335–43.

Channing, Henry. *God Admonishing His People of their Duty, as Parents and Masters. A Sermon Preached at New-London, December 20th, 1786. Occasioned by the Execution of Hannah Ocuish, a Mulatto Girl, Aged 12 Years and 9 Months, for the Murder of Eunice Bolles, Aged 6 Years and 6 Months*. New London, 1786.

Channing, William E. *The Works of William E. Channing, D.D.* Boston, 1888.

Christopher, Emma. *Slave Ship Sailors and Their Captive Cargoes, 1730–1807*. Cambridge: Cambridge University Press, 2006.

Cleman, John. "Irresistible Impulses: Edgar Allan Poe and the Insanity Defense." *American Literature* 63, 4 (December 1991): 623–40.

Coates, B. H. "On the Effects of Secluded and Gloomy Imprisonment on Individuals of the African Variety of Mankind in the Production of Disease." *Pennsylvania Journal of Prison Discipline and Philanthropy* 1, 3 (July 1845): 259–70.

Cobb, Thomas R. R. *An Inquiry into the Law of Negro Slavery in the United States of America*. 1858. Athens: University of Georgia Press, 1999.

Cobb, Tracey B. "Making a Killing: Evaluating the Constitutionality of the Texas Son of Sam Law." *Houston Law Review* 39, 5 (2002–3): 1483–1515.

Cohen, Daniel A. *Pillars of Salt, Monuments of Grace: New England Crime Literature and the Origins of American Popular Culture, 1674–1860*. New York: Oxford University Press, 1993.

———. "Social Injustice, Sexual Violence, Spiritual Transcendence: Constructions of Interracial Rape in Early American Crime Literature, 1767–1817." *William and Mary Quarterly* 3rd ser. 56, 3 (July 1999): 481–526.

Cohen, Lara Langer. "Notes from the State of St. Domingue: The Practice of Citation in *Clotel*." In Cohen and Stein, *Early African American Print Culture*, 161–77.

Cohen, Lara Langer, and Jordan Alexander Stein, eds. *Early African American Print Culture*. Philadelphia: University of Pennsylvania Press, 2012.

Cohen, Patricia Cline. *A Calculating People: The Spread of Numeracy in Early America*. Chicago: University of Chicago Press, 1982.

Cole, David. *No Equal Justice: Race and Class in the American Criminal Justice System*. New York: New Press-Norton, 1999.

Colatrella, Carol. *Literature and Moral Reform: Melville and the Discipline of Reading*. Gainesville: University Press of Florida, 2002.

Collins, John, Ned Hall, and L. A. Paul, eds. *Causation and Counterfactuals*. Cambridge, Mass.: MIT Press, 2004.

Collison, Gary. *Shadrach Minkins: From Fugitive Slave to Citizen*. Cambridge, Mass.: Harvard University Press, 1997.

Colvin, Mark. *Penitentiaries, Reformatories, and Chain Gangs: Social Theory and the History of Punishment in Nineteenth-Century America*. New York: St. Martin's, 1997.

Confessions and Executions of the Pirates, Gibbs and Wansley. An Interesting and Correct Account of their Lives. New York [?], 1831.

Convention of Delegates from the Abolition Societies Established in Different Parts of the United States. *Minutes of the Proceedings of the Second Convention of Delegates from the Abolition Societies Established in Different Parts of the United States. . . .* Philadelphia, 1795.

———. *Minutes of the Proceedings of the Third Convention of Delegates from the Abolition Societies Established in Different Parts of the United States. . . .* Philadelphia, 1796.

———. *To the Free Africans and other Free People of Color in the United States*. Philadelphia, [1796].

———. *To the Free Africans and other Free People of Color in the United States*. Rev. ed. Philadelphia, [1797].

Cooley, Thomas. *The Ivory Leg in the Ebony Cabinet: Madness, Race, and Gender in Victorian America*. Amherst: University of Massachusetts Press, 2001.

Cooper, Anna Julia. *A Voice from the South*. Xenia, Ohio, 1892.

Cooper, Thomas. "Letters of Thomas Cooper, 1835–1832." *American Historical Review* 6, 4 (July 1901): 725–36.

Cornelius, Janet Duitsman. *When I Can Read My Title Clear: Literacy, Slavery, and Religion in the Antebellum South*. Columbia: University of South Carolina Press, 1991.

Correct Account of the Trial and Sentence of Thos. Wansley and Charles Gibbs, for Murder, Piracy, and Robbery. On board the Brig Vineyard. [New York], 1831.

"Cost of a War with England." *Harper's Weekly*, June 12, 1858, 370.

Cossu-Beaumont, Laurence and Claire Parfait. "Book History and African American Studies." *Transatlantica* [Online] 1 (2009). http://transatlantica.revues.org/4280.

Coval, Jennifer L. and Andrea J. Reidell. "List of Fugitive Slaves/Former Slaves at Eastern State Penitentiary." Handout, Roundtable: Raise Every Voice: Research and Interpretation at Eastern State Penitentiary. In Incarceration Nation: Voices from the Early American Gaol Conference, McNeil Center for Early American Studies, Philadelphia, April 3–4, 2009.

Cover, Robert M. *Justice Accused: Antislavery and the Judicial Process*. New Haven, Conn.: Yale University Press, 1975.

———. *Narrative, Violence, and the Law: The Essays of Robert Cover*. Ed. Martha Minow, Michael Ryan, and Austin Sarat. Ann Arbor: University of Michigan Press, 1995.

Coviello, Peter. *Intimacy in America: Dreams of Affiliation in Antebellum Literature*. Minneapolis: University of Minnesota Press, 2005.

Crane, Gregg D. *Race, Citizenship, and Law in American Literature*. Cambridge: Cambridge University Press, 2002.

Crèvecoeur, J. Hector St. John de. *Letters from an American Farmer*. 1782. In *Letters from an American Farmer and Sketches of Eighteenth-Century America*, ed. Albert E. Stone, 34–227. New York: Penguin, 1986.

Cruz, Jon. *Culture on the Margins: The Black Spiritual and the Rise of American Cultural Interpretation*. Princeton, N.J.: University of Princeton Press, 1999.

Culler, Jonathan. *The Pursuit of Signs: Semiotics, Literature, Deconstruction*. Ithaca, N.Y.: Cornell University Press, 1981.

Curtis, Michael Kent. *Free Speech, The People's Darling Privilege: Struggles for Freedom of Expression in American History*. Durham, N.C.: Duke University Press, 2000.

Dain, Bruce. *A Hideous Monster of the Mind: American Race Theory in the Early Republic*. Cambridge, Mass.: Harvard University Press, 2002.

Dain, Norman. *Concepts of Insanity in the United States, 1789–1865*. New Brunswick, N.J.: Rutgers University Press, 1964.

Dana, Richard Henry. *Two Years Before the Mast: A Personal Narrative of Life at Sea*. 1840. New York: Penguin, 1981.

Darwall, Stephen, ed. *Contractarianism/Contractualism*. Malden, Mass.: Blackwell, 2003.

Davis, Angela Y. *The Angela Y. Davis Reader*. Malden, Mass.: Blackwell, 1998.

Davis, Charles T. and Henry Louis Gates, Jr., eds. *The Slave's Narrative*. Oxford: Oxford University Press, 1985.

Davis, David Brion. *Homicide in American Fiction, 1798–1860: A Study in Social Values*. Ithaca, N.Y.: Cornell University Press, 1957.

———. *The Problem of Slavery in the Age of Revolution, 1770–1823*. 1975. New York: Oxford University Press, 1999.

———. *The Problem of Slavery in Western Culture*. 1966. New York: Oxford University Press, 1988.

———. *The Slave Power Conspiracy and the Paranoid Style: Images of Conspiracy in the Slavery Controversy*. Baton Rouge: Louisiana State University Press, 1969.

Davis, Mary Kemp. *Nat Turner Before the Bar of Judgement: Fictional Treatments of the Southampton Slave Rebellion*. Baton Rouge: Louisiana State University Press, 1999.

Davis, Thomas J. "Emancipation Rhetoric, Natural Rights, and Revolutionary New England: A Note on Four Black Petitions in Massachusetts, 1773–1777." *New-England Quarterly* 62, 2 (June 1989): 248–63.

Dayan, Joan/Colin. "Amorous Bondage: Poe, Ladies, and Slaves." *American Literature* 66, 2 (June 1994): 239–73.

———. "Held in the Body of the State: Prisons and the Law." In *History, Memory, and the Law*, ed. Austin Sarat and Thomas R. Kearns, 183–247. Ann Arbor: University of Michigan Press, 2000.

———. *The Law Is a White Dog: How Legal Rituals Make and Unmake Persons*. Princeton, N.J.: Princeton University Press, 2011.

———. "Legal Slaves and Civil Bodies." In *Materializing Democracy: Toward a Revitalized Cultural Politics*, ed. Russ Castronovo and Dana D. Nelson, 53–94. Durham, N.C.: Duke University Press, 2002.

———. "Legal Terrors." *Representations* 92 (Autumn 2005): 42–80.

———. "Melville, Locke, and Faith." *Raritan* 25, 3 (Winter 2006): 30–44.

———. "Poe, Persons, and Property." In Kennedy and Weissberg, *Romancing*, 106–26.

———. "Servile Law." In *Cities Without Citizens*, ed. Eduardo Cadava and Aaron Levy, 87–117. Philadelphia: Slought Books, 2003.

———. *The Story of Cruel and Unusual*. Cambridge, Mass.: Boston Review-MIT Press, 2007.

Dayton, Cornelia Hughes. *Women Before the Bar: Gender, Law, and Society in Connecticut, 1639–1789*. Chapel Hill: University of North Carolina Press, 1995.

De Man, Paul. "Autobiography as De-facement." *MLN* 94, 5 (December 1979): 919–30.

"Declarations of Jefferson and of the Congress." In Wills, *Inventing America*, 374–79.

DeLanda, Manuel. "Beyond the Problematic of Legitimacy: Military Influences on Civilian Society." *Boundary 2* 32, 2 (Spring 2005): 117–28.

Delano, Amasa. *A Narrative of Voyages and Travels in the Northern and Southern Hemispheres*. 1817. New York: Praeger, 1970.

DeLombard, Jeannine Marie. "Making Waves on the Black Atlantic: The Case of John Anderson." In *Liberating Sojourn II: Transatlantic Abolitionists, 1845–1860*, ed. Fionnghuala Sweeney and Alan Rice. Special issue, *Slavery and Abolition* (February 2012).

——."The Novel and the Reconstruction Amendments." In *The American Novel: 1870–1940*, ed. Priscilla Wald and Michael A. Elliott. Vol. 6 of *The Oxford History of the Novel in English*. Oxford: Oxford University Press, forthcoming.

——. Review of *Abolition's Public Sphere* and *The Rise of Aggressive Abolitionism: Addresses to the Slaves*, by Robert Fanuzzi and Stanley Harrold. *New England Quarterly* 78, 1 (March 2005): 149–53.

——. "Salvaging Legal Personhood: Melville's *Benito Cereno*." *American Literature* 81, 1 (March 2009): 35–64.

——. "Slave Narratives and U.S. Legal History." In Ernest, *Oxford Handbook*.

——. *Slavery on Trial: Law, Abolitionism, and Print Culture*. Chapel Hill: University of North Carolina Press, 2007.

Desrochers, Robert, Jr. "Surprizing Deliverance? Slavery and Freedom, Language, and Identity in the Narrative of Briton Hammon, 'A Negro Man.'" In Carretta and Gould, *Genius*, 153–74.

Devlin, Lucinda. *The Omega Suites*. Göttingen: Steidl, 2001.

Deyle, Steven. *Carry Me Back: The Domestic Slave Trade in American Life*. New York: Oxford University Press, 2005.

Dietzel, Susanne B. "The African American Novel and Popular Culture." In *The Cambridge Companion to the African American Novel*, ed. Maryemma Graham, 156–70. Cambridge: Cambridge University Press, 2004.

Dillon, Elizabeth Maddock. *The Gender of Freedom: Fictions of Liberalism and the Literary Public Sphere*. Stanford, Calif.: Stanford University Press, 2004.

Dimock, Wai Chee. *Residues of Justice: Literature, Law, Philosophy*. Berkeley: University of California Press, 1997.

"The Doom of the Slaver. An English Story of the African Blockade." *Harper's New Monthly Magazine*, November 1850, 846–48.

Douglass, Frederick. *Autobiographies*. Ed. Henry Louis Gates, Jr. New York: Library of America, 1994.

——. "Capital Punishment Is a Mockery of Justice: An Address Delivered in Rochester, New York, on 7 October 1858." *The Frederick Douglass Papers. Series One: Speeches, Debates, and Interviews*. Ed. John W. Blassingame et al. Vol. 3, *1855–63*. New Haven, Conn.: Yale University Press, 1985.

——. *The Claims of the Negro Ethnologically Considered. An Address before the Literary Societies. Western Reserve College, at Commencement July 12, 1854.*

Rochester, New York, 1854. Central Library of Rochester and Monroe County. Historic Monographs Collection. http://www.libraryweb.org/~digitized/books/ Claims_of_the_Negro.pdf.

———. "The Heroic Slave." In Harriet Beecher Stowe, *Uncle Tom's Cabin*, ed. Jean Fagan Yellin, 482–520. Oxford: Oxford University Press, 1998.

———. *Life and Writings of Frederick Douglass*. Vol. 1. Ed. Philip S. Foner. New York: International Publishers, 1950.

———. *My Bondage and My Freedom*. 1855. In Douglass, *Autobiographies*, 103–452.

———. *Narrative of the Life of Frederick Douglass, an American Slave, Written by Himself*. 1845. New York: Penguin, 1982.

Downes, Paul. *Democracy, Revolution, and Monarchism in Early American Literature*. Cambridge: Cambridge University Press, 2002.

———. "Melville's *Benito Cereno* and the Politics of Humanitarian Intervention." *South Atlantic Quarterly* 103 (Spring/Summer 2004): 465–88.

Doyle, Christopher. "Judge St. George Tucker and the Case of *Tom v. Roberts*." *Virginia Magazine of History and Biography* 106, 4 (Autumn 1994): 419–42.

Drexler, Michael J. and Ed White. *Beyond Douglass: New Perspectives on Early African American Literature*. Lewisburg, Pa.: Bucknell University Press, 2008.

Du Bois, W. E. B. *The Suppression of the African Slave Trade to the United States of America, 1638–1870*. 1870. Mineola: Dover, 1970.

Dumm, Thomas L. *Democracy and Punishment: Disciplinary Origins of the United States*. Madison: University of Wisconsin Press, 1987.

Early, Gerald. "What Is African American Literature?" February 5, 2009. http://www.america.gov/st/peopleplace-english/2009/February/20090210134821mlenuhreto.1 840784.html, accessed April 18, 2011.

Echevarría, Roberto González. *Myth and Archive: A Theory of Latin American Narrative*. Durham, N.C.: Duke University Press, 1998.

"Editor's Table." *Graham's Magazine* 46, 2 (February 1855): 173–84.

Edwards, Laura F. *The People and Their Peace: Legal Culture and the Transformation of Inequality in the Post-Revolutionary South*. Chapel Hill: University of North Carolina Press, 2009.

Ellerman, David P. "Inalienable Rights: A Litmus Test for Liberal Theories of Justice." Social Science Research Network (SSRN): January 31, 2009. http://ssrn.com/ abstract=1340644.

———. *Property and Contract in Economics: The Case for Economic Democracy*. Cambridge: Blackwell, 1992.

Ellis, Markman. "Suffering Things: Lapdogs, Slaves, and Counter-Sensibility." In *The Secret Life of Things: Animals, Objects, and It-Narratives in Eighteenth-Century*

England, ed. Mark Blackwell, 92–113. Lewisburg, Pa.: Bucknell University Press, 2007.

Elmer, Jonathan. "The Black Atlantic Archive." *American Literary History* 17, 1 (2005): 160–70.

Elrod, Eileen Razzari. *Piety and Dissent: Race, Gender, and Biblical Rhetoric in Early American Autobiography.* Amherst: University of Massachusetts Press, 2008.

Emerson, Ralph Waldo. *Selected Writings of Ralph Waldo Emerson.* Ed. William H. Gilman. New York: Signet-Penguin, 1965.

Emery, Allan Moore. "The Topicality of Depravity in 'Benito Cereno.'" *American Literature* 55, 2 (October 1983): 316–31.

Emsley, Clive, Tim Hitchcock, and Robert Shoemaker. "The Proceedings—Ordinary of Newgate's Accounts," *Old Bailey Proceedings Online.* www.oldbaileyonline.org.

Epstein, Dena J. *Sinful Tunes and Spirituals: Black Folk Music to the Civil War.* Urbana: University of Illinois Press, 2003.

Epstein, Heidi. *Melting the Venusberg: A Feminist Theology of Music.* New York: Continuum, 2005.

Equiano, Olaudah. *The Interesting Narrative of the Life of Olaudah Equiano, or Gustavus Vassa, the African. Written by Himself.* London. [1789].

Ernest, John. *Chaotic Justice: Rethinking African American Literary History.* Chapel Hill: University of North Carolina Press, 2009.

———, ed. *The Oxford Handbook to the African American Slave Narrative.* London: Oxford University Press, forthcoming.

———. *Resistance and Reformation in Nineteenth-Century African-American Literature: Brown, Wilson, Jacobs, Delany, Douglass, and Harper.* Jackson: University Press of Mississippi, 1995.

Essah, Patience. *A House Divided: Slavery and Emancipation in Delaware, 1638–1865.* Charlottesville: University Press of Virginia, 1996.

Estes, J. Worth and Billy G. Smith, eds. *A Melancholy Scene of Devastation: The Public Response to the 1793 Philadelphia Yellow Fever Epidemic.* Canton, Mass.: Science History-Watson, 1997.

Evans, Charles. *American Bibliography.* Vol. 11. Chicago: Columbia Press, 1931.

Evans, E. P. "Bugs and Beasts Before the Law." *Atlantic Monthly* (August 1884): 235–46.

———. *The Criminal Prosecution and Capital Punishment of Animals.* New York: Dutton, 1906.

———. "Modern and Medieval Punishment." *Atlantic Monthly* (September 1884): 302–8.

Ewald, Alec C. "'Civil Death': The Ideological Paradox of Criminal Disenfranchisement Law in the United States." *Wisconsin Law Review* (2002): 1045–1137.

"The Execution of Gordon the Slave-Trader." *Harper's Weekly*, March 8, 1862, 150.

"Extract of a letter dated U.S. ship *Yorktown*, at sea . . . Nov. 30th, 1845." *African Repository and Colonial Journal*, April 1846, 118–19.

Fabian, Ann. *The Unvarnished Truth: Personal Narratives in Nineteenth-Century America*. Berkeley: University of California Press, 2000.

Faflick, David. "Authorship, Owership, and the Case for Charles Anderson Chester." *Book History* 11 (2008): 149–67.

———. "The Case for 'Charles Anderson Chester'." *The Book* 65 (March 2005): 5–6.

Faller, Lincoln B. *Turned to Account: The Forms and Functions of Criminal Biography in Late Seventeenth- and Early Eighteenth-Century England*. Cambridge: Cambridge University Press, 1987.

Fanuzzi, Robert A. *Abolition's Public Sphere*. Minneapolis: University of Minnesota Press, 2003.

Farr, James. "Locke, Natural Law, and New World Slavery." *Political Theory* 36, 4 (August 2008): 495–522.

Fearon, Henry Bradshaw. *Sketches of America. A Narrative of a Journey of Five Thousand Miles through the Eastern and Western States of America; Contained in Eight Reports Addressed to the Thirty-Nine English Families by whom the Author was Deputed, in June 1817, To Ascertain Whether Any, and What Part of the United States would be Suitable for their Residence*. 2nd ed. London, 1818.

Fehrenbacher, Don E. *The Dred Scott Case: Its Significance in American Law and Politics*. New York: Oxford University Press, 1978.

———. *The Slaveholding Republic: An Account of the United States Government's Relations to Slavery*. Completed and ed. Ward M. McAfee. New York: Oxford University Press, 2001.

Ferguson, Niall, ed. *Virtual History: Alternatives and Counterfactuals*. London: Macmillan, 1997.

Ferguson, Robert A. *Law and Letters in American Culture*. Cambridge, Mass.: Harvard University Press, 1984.

———. *The Trial in American Life*. Chicago: University of Chicago Press, 2007.

———. "Untold Stories in the Law." In *Law's Stories: Narrative and Rhetoric in the Law*, ed. Peter Brooks and Paul Gewirtz, 84–98. New Haven, Conn.: Yale University Press, 1996.

A Few Lines on Occasion of the Untimely End of Mark and Phillis, Who Were Executed at Cambridge, September 18th for Poysoning their Master, Capt. John Codman of Charlestown. Boston, 1755.

Fichtelberg, Joseph. "Word Between Worlds: The Economy of Equiano's *Narrative*." *American Literary History* 5, 3 (Fall 1993): 459–80.

Field, Phyllis F. *The Politics of Race in New York: The Struggle for Black Suffrage in the Civil War Era*. Ithaca, N.Y.: Cornell University Press, 1982.

Fields, Barbara Jeanne. "Slavery, Race and Ideology in the United States of America." *New Left Review* 181 (1990): 95–118.

Finkelman, Paul. *Slavery, Race, and the American Legal System, 1700–1872*. 16 vols. New York: Garland, 1988.

Finkelstein, Jacob J. "The Goring Ox: Some Historical Perspectives on Deodands, Forfeitures, Wrongful Death and the Western Notion of Sovereignty." *Temple Law Quarterly* 46, 2 (Winter 1973): 169–290.

Fitzhugh, George. *Cannibals All! Or, Slaves without Masters*. 1856. Edited by C. Vann Woodward. Cambridge, Mass.: Belknap-Harvard University Press, 1960.

Fitzpatrick, Peter. "Bare Sovereignty: *Homo Sacer* and the Insistence of Law." In Norris, *Politics*, 49–73.

———. *The Mythology of Modern Law*. New York: Routledge, 1992.

Flaherty, David H. "Crime and Social Control in Provincial Massachusetts." *Historical Journal* 24, 2 (1981): 339–60.

Fliegelman, Jay. *Declaring Independence: Jefferson, Natural Language, and the Culture of Performance*. Stanford, Calif.: Stanford University Press, 1993.

Foote, Andrew H. *Africa and the American Flag*. New York, 1854.

Formisano, Ronald P. "Deferential-Participant Politics: The Early Republic's Political Culture, 1789–1840." *American Political Science Review* 68, 2 (June 1974): 473–87.

Fosgate, Blanchard. "Case of William Freeman, the Murderer of the Van Nest Family." *American Journal of the Medical Sciences* 28 (October 1847): 409–14.

Foster, Frances Smith. "A Narrative of the Interesting Origins and (Somewhat) Surprising Developments of African-American Print Culture." *American Literary History* 17, 4 (Winter 2005): 714–40.

———. *Witnessing Slavery: The Development of Ante-Bellum Slave Narratives*. Westport, Conn.: Greenwood, 1979.

———. *Written by Herself: Literary Production by African American Women, 1746–1892*. Bloomington: Indiana University Press, 1993.

Foucault, Michel. *Abnormal: Lectures at the Collège de France, 1974–1975*. Ed. Valerio Marchetti and Antonella Salomoni, trans. Graham Burchell. New York: Picador-Palgrave Macmillan, 2003.

———. *The Birth of Biopolitics: Lectures at the Collège de France, 1978–1979*. Ed. Michael Senellart, trans. Graham Burchell. New York: Picador-Palgrave Macmillan, 2008.

———. *Discipline and Punish: The Birth of the Prison*. Trans. Alan Sheridan. New York: Vintage-Random House, 1995.

————. *The History of Sexuality*. Vol. 1, *An Introduction*. Trans. Robert Hurley. New York: Vintage-Random House, 1990.

————. *Language, Counter-Memory, Practice: Selected Essays and Interviews*. Ed. Donald F. Bouchard, trans. Donald F. Bouchard and Sherry Simon. Ithaca, N.Y.: Cornell University Press, 1977.

————. *Security, Territory, Population: Lectures at the Collège de France, 1977–1978*. Ed. Michel Senellart, trans. Graham Burchell. New York: Picador-Palgrave Macmillan, 2007.

————. *"Society Must Be Defended": Lectures at the Collège de France, 1975–1976*. Ed. Mauro Bertani and Alessandro Fontana, trans. Graham Burchell. New York: Picador-Palgrave Macmillan, 2003.

Franchot, Jenny. "The Punishment of Esther: Frederick Douglass and the Construction of the Feminine." In Sundquist, *Frederick Douglass*, 141–65.

Frank, Lawrence. "'The Murders in the Rue Morgue': Edgar Allan Poe's Evolutionary Reverie." *Nineteenth-Century Literature* 50, 2 (September 1995): 168–88.

Franklin, H. Bruce. *Prison Literature in America: The Victim as Criminal and Artist*. New York: Oxford University Press, 1989.

————. *The Wake of the Gods: Melville's Mythology*. Stanford, Calif., Stanford University Press, 1963.

Frasier, Isaac. *A Brief Account of the Life, and Abominable Thefts, of the Notorious Isaac Frasier, who Was Executed at Fairfield, September 7th, 1768, Penned from His Own Mouth, and Signed by Him, a Few Days before his Execution*. New London, 1768.

Frey, Cecile P. "The House of Refuge for Colored Children." *Journal of Negro History* 66, 1 (Spring 1981): 10–25.

"From the Evangelist. The Slave-Trade in New York." *Littell's Living Age* 2nd ser. 8, 554 (January 1855): 32–34.

Fuss, Diana. "Corpse Poem." *Critical Inquiry* 30 (Autumn 2003): 1–30.

Gallagher, Catherine. "Undoing." In *Time and the Literary*, ed. Karen Newman, Jay Clayton, and Marianne Hirsch, 11–29. New York: Routledge, 2002.

————. "When Did the Confederate States of America Free the Slaves?" *Representations* 98 (Spring 2007): 43–61.

Gallagher, Catherine, and Stephen Greenblatt. *Practicing New Historicism*. Chicago: University of Chicago Press, 2000.

Gardner, Jared. *Master Plots: Race and the Founding of American Literature, 1787–1845*. Baltimore: Johns Hopkins University Press, 1998.

Garfield, Deborah M. and Rafia Zafar, eds. *Harriet Jacobs and* Incidents in the Life of a Slave Girl: *New Critical Essays*. Cambridge: Cambridge University Press, 1996.

Garrison, William Lloyd. Preface to Douglass, *Narrative*, 33–42.

Gates, Henry Louis, Jr. *Figures in Black: Words, Signs, and the "Racial" Self.* New York: Oxford University Press, 1987.

———. *The Signifying Monkey: A Theory of Afro-American Literary Criticism.* New York: Oxford University Press, 1988.

———. "From Wheatley to Douglass: The Politics of Displacement." In Sundquist, *Frederick Douglass*, 47–65.

———. "Writing 'Race' and the Difference It Makes." *Critical Inquiry* 12, 1 (1985): 1–20.

Gates, Henry Louis, Jr. and William L. Andrews. *Pioneers of the Black Atlantic: Five Slave Narratives from the Enlightenment, 1772–1815.* Washington, D.C.: Civitas, 1998.

Gellman, David N. *Emancipating New York: The Politics of Slavery and Freedom, 1777–1827.* Baton Rouge: Louisiana State University Press, 2006.

Gibbs, Charles. *Confession of Charles Gibbs the Pirate: who was Executed on the 22d of April, 1831.* New York, [1831].

———. *Mutiny and Murder: Confession of Charles Gibbs, a Native of Rhode Island: Who, with Thomas J. Wansley, was Doomed to be Hung in New-York on the 22d of April last, for the Murder of the Captain and Mate of the Brig Vineyard, on her Passage from New-Orleans to Philadelphia, in November 1830: Gibbs Confesses that within a Few Years He Has Participated in the Murder of Nearly 400 Human Beings! : Annexed, is a Solemn Address to Youth.* Providence, 1831.

Gibbs, Joseph. *Dead Men Tell No Tales: The Lives and Legends of the Pirate Charles Gibbs.* Columbia: University of South Carolina Press, 2007.

Gilje, Paul A. *Liberty on the Waterfront: American Maritime Culture in the Age of Revolution.* Philadelphia: University of Pennsylvania Press, 2004.

Gilman, Sander L. *Difference and Pathology: Stereotypes of Sexuality, Race, and Madness.* Ithaca, N.Y.: Cornell University Press,

———. *Seeing the Insane.* New York: Wiley and Sons, 1982.

Gilmore, Paul. *The Genuine Article: Race, Mass Culture, and American Literary Manhood.* Durham, N.C.: Duke University Press, 2001.

Gilroy, Paul. *The Black Atlantic: Modernity and Double Consciousness.* Cambridge, Mass.: Harvard University Press, 1993.

Ginsberg, Lesley. "Slavery and the Gothic Horror of Poe's Black Cat." In *American Gothic: New Interventions in a National Narrative*, ed. Robert K. Martin and Eric Savoy, 99–128. Iowa City: University of Iowa Press, 1998.

Ginzburg, Carlo. *Myths, Emblems, Clues.* Trans. John Tedeschi and Anne C. Tedeschi. London: Hutchinson Radius, 1990.

Gladfelder, Hal. *Criminality and Narrative in Eighteenth-Century England.* Baltimore: Johns Hopkins University Press, 2001.

Glaude, Eddie S., Jr. *Exodus! Religion, Race, and Nation in Early Nineteenth-Century Black America*. Chicago: University of Chicago Press, 2000.

Glenn, Evelyn Nakano. *Unequal Freedom: How Race and Gender Shaped American Citizenship and Labor*. Cambridge, Mass.: Harvard University Press, 2002.

Goddu, Teresa A. "The Antislavery Almanac and the Discourse of Numeracy." *Book History* 12 (2009): 129–55.

———. "The Slave Narrative as Material Text." In Ernest, *Oxford Handbook*.

Goffman, Erving. *Asylums: Essays on the Social Situation of Mental Patients and Other Inmates*. Garden City, N.Y.: Anchor-Doubleday, 1961.

Goldsby, Jacqueline. *A Spectacular Secret: Lynching in American Life and Literature*. Chicago: University of Chicago Press, 2006.

Goodell, Abner Cheney, Jr. *Trial and Execution, For Petit Treason, of Mark And Phillis, Slaves of Capt. John Codman, Who Murdered Their Master At Charlestown, Mass., In 1755; for which the Man Was Hanged and Gibbeted, and the Woman Was Burned To Death*. Cambridge, 1883.

Goodman, Nan. "'For Their and Our Security': Jurisdictional Identity and the Praying Indians of Deer Island." Conference paper, Association for the Study of Law, Culture, and the Humanities. University of California, Berkeley, March 29, 2008.

———. *Shifting the Blame: Literature, Law, and the Theory of Accidents in Nineteenth-Century America*. Princeton, N.J.: Princeton University Press, 1998.

Gordon, Sarah Barringer. *The Mormon Question: Polygamy and Constitutional Conflict in Nineteenth-Century America*. Chapel Hill: University of North Carolina Press, 2002.

Gould, Philip. *Barbaric Traffic: Commerce and Antislavery in the Eighteenth-Century Atlantic World*. Cambridge, Mass.: Harvard University Press, 2003.

Grandjean, Katherine. "'Our *Fellow-Creatures & Our Fellow-Christians*': Race and Religion in Nineteenth-Century Narratives of Indian Crime." *American Quarterly* 62, 4 (December 2010): 925–50.

Gray, Thomas R. *The Confessions of Nat Turner, the Leader of the Late Insurrection in Southampton, Va*. In Greenberg, *Confessions*, 38–58.

Greiman, Jennifer. *Democracy's Spectacle: Sovereignty and Public Life in Antebellum American Writing*. New York: Fordham University Press, 2010.

Green, Johnson. *The Life and Confession of Johnson Green, Who Is To Be Executed This Day, August 17th, 1786, for the Atrocious Crime of Burglary; Together with His Last and Dying Words*. Worcester, 1786.

Green, Tara T., ed. *From the Plantation to the Prison: African-American Confinement Literature*. Macon, Ga.: Mercer University Press, 2008.

Greenberg, Kenneth S., ed. *The Confessions of Nat Turner and Related Documents.* Boston: Bedford-St. Martin's, 1996.

Greene, Lorenzo Johnston. *The Negro in Colonial New England.* 1942. New York: Atheneum-Columbia University Press, 1974.

Greenspan, Ezra. "Evert Duyckinck and the History of Wiley and Putnam's Library of American Books, 1845–1847." *American Literature* 64, 4 (December 1992): 677–93.

Greeson, Jennifer Rae. *Our South: Geographic Fantasy and the Rise of National Literature.* Cambridge, Mass.: Harvard University Press, 2010.

Griffith, Sally F. "'A Total Dissolution of the Bonds of Society': Community Death and Regeneration in Mathew Carey's *Short Account of the Malignant Fever.*" In Estes and Smith, *Melancholy,* 45–59.

Grob, Gerald N. *Edward Jarvis and the Medical World of Nineteenth-Century America.* Knoxville: University of Tennessee Press, 1978.

Gross, Ariela J. *Double Character: Slavery and Mastery in the Antebellum Southern Courtroom.* Princeton, N.J.: Princeton University Press, 2000.

———. *What Blood Won't Tell: A History of Race on Trial in America.* Cambridge, Mass.: Harvard University Press, 2009.

Grossman, Jonathan H. *The Art of Alibi: English Law Courts and the Novel.* Baltimore: Johns Hopkins University Press, 2002.

Gudmestad, Robert H. *A Troublesome Commerce: The Transformation of the Interstate Slave Trade.* Baton Rouge: Louisiana State University Press, 2003.

Habermas, Jürgen. *Between Facts and Norms: Contributions to a Discourse Theory of Law and Democracy.* 1992. Trans. William Rehg. Cambridge, Mass.: MIT Press, 1998.

———. *The Structural Transformation of the Public Sphere: An Inquiry into a Category of Bourgeois Society.* 1962. Trans. Thomas Burger and Frederick Lawrence. Cambridge, Mass.: MIT Press, 1991.

Hale, Edward E. "The Man Without a Country." *Atlantic Monthly* 12, 74 (December 1863): 665–79.

Hall, Benjamin F. *The Trial of William Freeman, for the Murder of John G. Van Nest, including the Evidence and the Arguments of Counsel, with the Decision of the Supreme Court Granting a New Trial, and an Account of the Death of the Prisoner, and of the Post-Mortem Examination of His Body by Amariah Brigham, M.D. and Others.* Auburn, 1848.

Hall, David D. *Worlds of Wonder, Days of Judgment: Popular Religious Belief in Early New England.* Cambridge, Mass.: Harvard University Press, 1990.

Hall, David D., John M. Murrin, and Thad W. Tate, eds. *Saints and Revolutionaries: Essays on Early American History.* New York: Norton, 1984.

Hall, Kermit. *The Magic Mirror: Law in American History*. New York: Oxford University Press, 1989.

Halttunen, Karen. *Murder Most Foul: The Killer and the American Gothic Imagination*. Cambridge, Mass.: Harvard University Press, 1998.

Hamilton, James A. *Reminiscences of James A. Hamilton; Or, Men and Events, at Home and Abroad, During Three Quarters of a Century*. New York, 1869.

Hamilton, Phillip. "Revolutionary Principles and Family Loyalties: Slavery's Transformation in the St. George Tucker Household of Early National Virginia." *William and Mary Quarterly* 3rd ser. 55, 4 (October 1998): 531–56.

Hammon, Jupiter. *An Address to the Negroes in the State of New-York*. New York, 1787.

Hammond, James Henry. "'Mud-Sill' Speech." In *Slavery Defended: The Views of the Old South*, ed. Eric L. McKitrick, 121–25. Englewood Cliffs, N.J.: Spectrum-Prentice-Hall, 1963.

Harris, Alex. *A Biographical History of Lancaster County: Being a History of the Early Settlers and Eminent Men of the County; As Also Much Other Unpublished Historical Information, Chiefly of a Local Character*. Lancaster, 1872.

Harris, Cheryl I. "Finding Sojourner's Truth: Race, Gender, and the Institution of Property." *Cardozo Law Review* 18, 2 (November 1996): 309–409.

———. "Whiteness as Property." *Harvard Law Review* 106, 8 (June 1993): 1707–91.

Harris, Leslie M. *In the Shadow of Slavery: African Americans in New York City, 1626–1863*. Chicago: University of Chicago Press, 2003.

Harris, Paul. *Black Rage Confronts the Law*. New York: New York University Press, 1997.

Harris, Sharon M. *Executing Race: Early American Women's Narratives of Race, Society, and the Law*. Columbus: Ohio State University Press, 2005.

Harrowitz, Nancy A. "Criminality and Poe's Orangutan: The Question of Race in Detection." In *Agonistics: Arenas of Creative Contest*, ed. Janet Lungstrum and Elizabeth Sauer, 177–95. Albany: State University of New York Press, 1997.

Hart, H. L. A. and Tony Honoré. *Causation in the Law*. 2nd ed. New York: Oxford University Press, 2002.

Hartman, Saidiya V. *Scenes of Subjection: Terror, Slavery, and Self-Making in Nineteenth-Century America*. New York: Oxford University Press, 1997.

Hartnett, Stephen John. *Executing Democracy: Capital Punishment and the Making of America, 1683–1807*. East Lansing: Michigan State University Press, 2010.

Hartog, Hendrik. "The Constitution of Aspiration and 'The Rights That Belong to Us All.'" In *The Constitution and American Life*, special issue, *Journal of American History* 174, 3 (1987): 1013–34.

Haskell, Thomas L. "Persons as Uncaused Causes: John Stuart Mill, the Spirit of
    Capitalism, and the 'Invention' of Formalism." In *The Culture of the Market: His-
    torical Essays*, ed. Thomas L. Haskell and Richard F. Teichgraeber, III, 441–502.
    Cambridge: Cambridge University Press, 1993.

Hawkins-Léon, Cynthia G. "'Literature as Law': The History of the Insanity Plea and a
    Fictional Application within the Law and Literature Canon." *Temple Law Review*
    72 (1999): 381–449.

Hawthorn, Geoffrey. *Plausible Worlds: Possibility and Understanding in History and
    the Social Sciences*. Cambridge: Cambridge University Press, 1991.

Hawthorne, Nathaniel. *The House of the Seven Gables*. 1851. New York: Penguin, 1981.

Hayford, Harrison. *The Somers Mutiny Affair: A Book of Primary Source Materials*.
    Englewood Cliffs, N.J.: Prentice-Hall, 1959.

Hearn, Daniel Allen. *Legal Executions in New Jersey, 1691–1963*. Jefferson, N.C.: Mac-
    Farland, 2005.

Hedin, Raymond. "The American Slave Narrative: The Justification of the Picaro."
    American Literature 53, 4 (Winter 1982): 630–45.

Hegel, G. W. F. *The Phenomenology of Mind*. Vol. 1. Trans. and ed. J. B. Baillie. New
    York: Cosimo, 2006.

Helmholz, R. H. et al. *The Privilege Against Self-Incrimination: Its Origins and Devel-
    opment*. Chicago: University of Chicago Press, 1997.

Henry, Katherine. "Angelina Grimké's Rhetoric of Exposure." *American Quarterly*
    49, 2 (1997): 328–55.

Higginbotham, A. Leon, Jr. *In the Matter of Color: Race and the American Legal Pro-
    cess, the Colonial Period*. New York: Oxford University Press, 1978.

Higginbotham, A. Leon, Jr. and Barbara K. Kopytoff. "Property First, Humanity Sec-
    ond: The Recognition of the Slave's Human Nature in Virginia Civil Law." *Ohio
    State Law Journal* 50 (1989): 511–40.

Hindus, Michael Stephen. *Prison and Plantation: Crime, Justice, and Authority in
    Massachusetts and South Carolina, 1767–1878*. Chapel Hill: University of North
    Carolina Press, 1980.

Hinds, Elizabeth Jane Wall. "The Spirit of Trade: Olaudah Equiano's Conversion,
    Legalism, and the Merchant's *Life*." *African American Review* 32, 4 (Winter 1998):
    635–47.

Hobbes, Thomas. *Leviathan*. Ed. Richard Tuck. Cambridge: Cambridge University
    Press, 2007.

Hodges, Graham Russell. *Root and Branch: African Americans in New York and East
    Jersey, 1613–1863*. Chapel Hill: University of North Carolina Press, 1999.

———. *Slavery and Freedom in the Rural North: African Americans in Monmouth County, New Jersey, 1665–1865.* Lanham, Md.: Rowman and Littlefield, 1997.

Hoffer, Peter C. *The Great New York Conspiracy of 1741: Slavery, Crime, and Colonial Law.* Lawrence: University Press of Kansas, 2003.

Hoffer, Peter C. and N. E. H. Hull. *Murdering Mothers: Infanticide in England and New England, 1558–1803.* New York: New York University Press, 1981.

Hoffman, Ronald, Mechal Sobel, and Frederika J. Teute. *Through a Glass Darkly: Reflections on Personal Identity in Early America.* Chapel Hill: University of North Carolina Press, 1997.

Holland, Catherine A. *The Body Politic: Foundings, Citizenship, and Difference in the American Political Imagination.* New York: Routledge, 2001.

Holland, Sharon Patricia. *Raising the Dead: Readings of Death and (Black) Subjectivity.* Durham, N.C.: Duke University Press, 2000.

Holloway, Karla. *Passed On: African American Mourning Stories: A Memorial.* Durham, N.C.: Duke University Press, 2002.

Homestead, Melissa J. and Pamela T. Washington, eds. *E.D.E.N. Southworth.* Knoxville: University of Tennessee Press, forthcoming 2013.

Hong, Grace Kyungwon. *The Ruptures of American Capital: Women of Color Feminism and the Culture of Immigrant Labor.* Minneapolis: University of Minnesota Press, 2006.

Horsmanden, Daniel. *A Journal of the Proceedings in the Detection of the Conspiracy formed by Some White People, in Conjunction with Negro and Other Slaves, for Burning the City of New-York in America, and Murdering the Inhabitants.* New York, 1744.

Horton, James Oliver. "Comment." *Journal of the Early Republic* 18, 2 (Spring 1998): 222–26.

Horton, Lois E. "From Class to Race in Early America: Northern Post-Emancipation Racial Reconstruction." *Journal of the Early Republic* 19, 4 (Winter 1999): 629–49.

Horwitz, Morton J. *The Transformation of American Law, 1780–1860.* Cambridge, Mass.: Harvard University Press, 1977.

Howard, Warren S. *American Slavers and the Federal Law, 1837–1862.* Berkeley: University of California Press, 1963.

Howard-Pitney, David. *The African American Jeremiad: Appeals for Justice in America.* 1990. Rev. and expanded ed. Philadelphia: Temple University Press, 2005.

Hull, N. E. H. *Female Felons: Women and Serious Crime in Colonial Massachusetts.* Urbana: University of Illinois Press, 1984.

Humanity. "Sketch of a Debate in the House of Congress, On January 30th, 1797, on

the Petition of Certain Emancipated Africans. (From the *American Senator*)."
American Universal Magazine, February 20, 1797, 275–82.

———. "To The Editor of the *American Universal Magazine*." *American Universal Magazine*, February 6, 1797, 182–86.

Humphreys, West H. *Reports of Cases Argued and Determined in the Supreme Court of Tennessee, During the Years 1839–40*. Vol. 1. Nashville, Tenn., 1841.

Hunter, Donna. "Race, Law, and Innocence: Executing Black Men in the Eighteenth Century." *Studies in Law, Politics, and Society* 20 (2000): 71–97.

Huntress, Keith. "'Guinea' of *White-Jacket* and Chief Justice Shaw." *American Literature* 43, 4 (January 1972): 639–41.

Hurd, John Codman. *The Law of Freedom and Bondage in the United States*. 2 vols. Boston, 1858–62.

Hutchinson, Aaron. *Iniquity Purged by Mercy and Truth. A Sermon Preached at Grafton, October 23rd, 1768. Being the Sabbath after the Execution of Arthur, a Negro Man, at Worcester, aged about 21, for a Rape*. Boston, 1769.

Hyde, Carrie. "Outcast Patriotism: The Dilemma of Negative Instruction in 'The Man Without a Country.'" *English Literary History* 77, 4 (Winter 2010): 915–39.

Hyde, Walter Woodburn. "The Prosecution and Punishment of Animals and Lifeless Things in the Middle Ages and Modern Times." *University of Pennsylvania Law Review and American Law Register* 64, 7 (May 1916): 696–730.

Ignatieff, Michael. *A Just Measure of Pain: The Penitentiary in the Industrial Revolution 1750–1850*. New York: Pantheon, 1978.

Isani, Mukhtar Ali. "Far from 'Gambia's Golden Shore': The Black in Late Eighteenth-Century American Imaginative Literature." *William and Mary Quarterly* 3rd ser. 36, 3 (July 1979): 353–72.

Itzkowitz, Howard and Lauren Oldak. "Note: Restoring the Ex-Offender's Right to Vote: Background and Developments." *Criminal Law Review* 11 (1972): 721–70.

Jackson, Leon. "The Talking Book and the Talking Book Historian: African American Cultures of Print—The State of the Discipline." *Book History* 13, 1 (2009): 251–308.

Jacob, Giles. *The Law-Dictionary: Explaining the Rise, Progress, and Present State, of the English Law, in Theory and Practice. . . .* Ed. T. E. Tomlins. 1729. London, 1797.

Jacobs, Harriet A. *Incidents in the Life of a Slave Girl, Written by Herself*. Ed. Jean Fagan Yellin. Cambridge, Mass.: Harvard University Press, 1987.

Jain, Sarah Lochlann. "Living in Prognosis: Toward an Elegiac Politics." *Representations* 98 (Spring 2007): 77–92.

JanMohamed, Abdul R. *The Death-Bound Subject: Richard Wright's Archaeology of Death*. Durham, N.C.: Duke University Press, 2005.

Jarrett, Gene Andrew, ed. *African American Literature Beyond Race: An Alternative Reader.* New York: New York University Press, 2006.

———. *Deans and Truants: Race and Realism in African American Literature.* Philadelphia: University of Pennsylvania Press, 2007.

Jarvis, Edward. *Insanity Among the Colored Population of the Free States.* Philadelphia, 1844.

Jefferson, Thomas. *Notes on the State of Virginia.* 1785. Ed. Frank Shuffleton. New York: Penguin, 1999.

"John Bull." *Harper's Weekly,* May 29, 1858, 338–39.

Johnson, Barbara. *Persons and Things.* Cambridge, Mass.: Harvard University Press, 2008.

Johnson, Walter, ed. *The Chattel Principle: Internal Slave Trades in the Americas.* New Haven, Conn.: Yale University Press, 2004.

Johnstone, Abraham. *Address of Abraham Johnstone, A Black Man, Who Was Hanged at Woodbury, in the County of Glocester, and State of New Jersey, on Saturday the the* [sic] *8th Day of July Last; To the People of Colour. To Which Is Added His Dying Confession or Declaration. Also, a Copy of a Letter to His Wife, Written the Day Previous to His Execution.* Philadelphia, 1797.

J[ones], A[bsalom] and R[ichard] A[llen]. *A Narrative of the Proceedings of the Black People, during the Late Awful Calamity in Philadelphia in the Year 1793: and a Refutation of Some Censures, Thrown upon them in Some Late Publications.* Philadelphia, 1794.

Jones, Howard. *To the Webster-Ashburton Treaty: A Study in Anglo-American Relations, 1783–1843.* Chapel Hill: University of North Carolina Press, 1977.

Jones, Martha S. "Leave of Court: African American Claims-Making in the Era of *Dred Scott v. Sanford.*" In Sinha and Von Eschen, *Contested,* 54–74.

Jones, Paul Christian. *Against the Gallows: Antebellum American Writers and the Movement to Abolish Capital Punishment.* Iowa City: University of Iowa Press, 2011.

Jordan, Winthrop D. *White over Black: American Attitudes Toward the Negro 1550–1812.* Chapel Hill: University of North Carolina Press, 1968.

Joyce, John. *Confession of John Joyce, Alias Davis, Who Was Executed on Monday, the 14th of March, 1808. For the Murder of Mrs. Sarah Cross; With an Address to the Public, and People of Colour. Together with the Substance of the Trial, and the Address of Chief Justice Tilghman, on His Condemnation.* Philadelphia, 1808.

Kant, Immanuel. *The Metaphysics of Morals.* 1797. Trans. and ed. Mary Gregor. Cambridge: Cambridge University Press, 2007.

Kaplan, Carla. "Narrative Contracts and Emancipatory Readers: *Incidents in the Life of a Slave Girl.*" *Yale Journal of Criticism* 6, 1 (1993): 93–119.

Kaplan, Sidney. "Samuel Sewall and the Iniquity of Slavery." In *The Selling of Joseph: A Memorial,* by Samuel Sewall, ed. Kaplan, 27–67. Amherst: University of Massachusetts Press, 1969.

Karcher, Carolyn L. *The First Woman in the Republic: A Cultural Biography of Lydia Maria Child.* Durham, N.C.: Duke University Press, 1994.

———. *Shadow over the Promised Land: Slavery, Race, and Violence in Melville's America.* Baton Rouge: Louisiana State University Press, 1980.

Kawashima, Yasuhide. *Puritan Justice and the Indian: White Man's Law in Massachusetts, 1630–1763.* Middletown, Conn.: Wesleyan University Press, 1986.

Kazanjian, David. *The Colonizing Trick: National Culture and Imperial Citizenship in Early America.* Minneapolis: University of Minnesota Press, 2003.

Kelley, William D. *Address Delivered at the Colored Department of the House of Refuge. By the Hon. William D. Kelley. On December 31st, 1849. This Department of the Institution having been Opened for the Reception of Inmates on December 29th, 1849.* Philadelphia, 1850.

Kelsen, "Causality and Imputation." In *Introduction to Jurisprudence by Lord Lloyd of Hampstead,* ed. M. D. A. Freeman, 323–26. 4th ed. London: Stevens, 1979.

K[ennard], J[ames] K., Jr. "Who Are Our National Poets?" *The Knickerbocker* 26, 4 (October 1845): 331–41.

Kennedy, Gerald J. and Liliane Weissberg, eds. *Romancing the Shadow: Poe and Race.* Oxford: Oxford University Press, 2001.

Kent, James. *Commentaries on American Law.* Vol. 2. New York, 1827.

———. *Commentaries on American Law.* 3rd ed. Vol. 2. New York, 1836.

Kerber, Linda K. "Toward a History of Statelessness in America." *American Quarterly* 57, 3 (September 2005): 727–49.

Kettner, James H. *The Development of American Citizenship, 1608–1870.* Chapel Hill: University of North Carolina Press, 1978.

Kneale, J. Douglas. *Romantic Aversions: Aftermaths of Classicism in Wordsworth and Coleridge.* Montreal: McGill-Queen's University Press, 1999.

Konefsky, Alfred S. "The Accidental Legal Historian: Herman Melville and the History of American Law." *Buffalo Law Review* 52 (2004): 1179–1276.

Kopley, Richard. *Edgar Allan Poe and the Dupin Mysteries.* New York: Palgrave Macmillan, 2008.

Korobkin, Laura Hanft. "Appropriating Law in Harriet Beecher Stowe's *Dred.*" *Nineteenth-Century Literature* 62, 3 (December 2007): 380–406.

Kramer, Larry D. *The People Themselves: Popular Constitutionalism and Judicial Review*. Oxford: Oxford University Press, 2004.

Lambert, Frank. *Inventing the "Great Awakening"*. Princeton, N.J.: Princeton University Press, 1999.

———. "Subscribing for Profits and Piety: The Friendship of Benjamin Franklin and George Whitefield." *William and Mary Quarterly* 3rd ser. 50, 3 (July 1993): 529–54.

Landsman, Ned. "Evangelists and Their Hearers: Popular Interpretation of Revivalist Preaching in Eighteenth-Century Scotland." *Journal of British Studies* 28 (1989): 120–49.

Langbein, John H. *The Origins of Adversary Criminal Trial*. Oxford: Oxford University Press, 2003.

———. "The Privilege and Common Law Criminal Procedure: The Sixteenth to the Eighteenth Centuries." In Helmholz et al., *Privilege*, 82–108.

———. *Prosecuting Crime in the Renaissance: England, Germany, France*. Cambridge, Mass.: Harvard University Press, 1974.

———. "Response." *Journal of Legal History* 26, 1 (April 2005): 85–89.

Lapsansky, Phillip. "'Abigail, a Negress': The Role and the Legacy of African Americans in the Yellow Fever Epidemic." In Estes and Smith, *Melancholy*, 61–77.

Lawrence, John C. *Voyage to a Thousand Cares: Master's Mate Lawrence with the African Squadron, 1844–1846*. Comp. C. Herbert Gilliland. Annapolis: Naval Institute Press, 2004.

Lawson, Bill E. "Citizenship and Slavery." In Howard McGary and Bill E. Lawson, *Between Slavery and Freedom: Philosophy and American Slavery*, 55–70. Bloomington: Indiana University Press, 1992.

Layman. *A Visit to the Condemned Criminals, Gibbs and Wansley*. [New York, 1831.]

Lee, Maurice S. *Slavery, Philosophy, and American Literature, 1830–1860*. Cambridge: Cambridge University Press, 2005.

Lemire, Elise. *Black Walden: Slavery and Its Aftermath in Concord, Massachusetts*. Philadelphia: University of Pennsylvania Press, 2009.

———. "'The Murders in the Rue Morgue': Amalgamation Discourses and the Race Riots of 1838 in Poe's Philadelphia." In Kennedy and Weissberg, *Romancing*, 177–204.

Lemmings, David. "Criminal Trial Procedure in Eighteenth-Century England: The Impact of Lawyers." *Journal of Legal History* 26, 1 (April 2005): 63–70.

Lepore, Jill. *New York Burning: Liberty, Slavery, and Conspiracy in Eighteenth-Century Manhattan*. New York: Knopf, 2005.

408   Bibliography

Lesser, Wendy. *Pictures at an Execution: An Inquiry into the Subject of Murder.* Cambridge, Mass.: Harvard University Press, 1993.

Leverenz, David. *Manhood and the American Renaissance.* Ithaca, N.Y.: Cornell University Press, 1989.

Levine, Robert S. *Conspiracy and Romance: Studies in Brockden Brown, Cooper, Hawthorne, and Melville.* Cambridge: Cambridge University Press, 1989.

———. *Dislocating Race and Nation: Episodes in Nineteenth-Century American Literary Nationalism.* Chapel Hill: University of North Carolina Press, 2008.

———. *Martin Delany, Frederick Douglass, and the Politics of Representative Identity.* Chapel Hill: University of North Carolina Press, 1997.

Levine, Robert S. and Samuel Otter. *Frederick Douglass and Herman Melville: Essays in Relation.* Chapel Hill: University of North Carolina Press, 2008.

Lewis, W. David. *From Newgate to Dannemora: The Rise of the Penitentiary in New York, 1796–1848.* Ithaca, N.Y.: Cornell University Press, 1965.

Lightner, David L. *Slavery and the Commerce Power: How the Struggle Against the Interstate Slave Trade Led to the Civil War.* New Haven, Conn.: Yale University Press, 2006.

Linebaugh, Peter. *The London Hanged: Crime and Civil Society in the Eighteenth Century.* London: Verso, 2003.

———. "The Ordinary of Newgate and His *Account.*" In *Crime in England 1550–1800,* ed. J. S. Cockburn, 246–69. Princeton, N.J.: Princeton University Press, 1977.

Linebaugh, Peter, and Marcus Rediker. *The Many-Headed Hydra: Sailors, Slaves, Commoners, and the Hidden History of the Revolutionary Atlantic.* Boston: Beacon Press, 2000.

[Lippard, George.] *The Bank Director's Son: A Real and Intensely Interesting Revelation of City Life.* Philadelphia, 1851.

Litwack, Leon F. *North of Slavery: The Negro in the Free States, 1790–1860.* Chicago: University of Chicago Press, 1961.

Lives and Trial of Gibbs and Wansley: Who were Executed for Piracy. Boston, 1832.

Locke, John. *An Essay Concerning Human Understanding.* Ed. Roger Woolhouse. 1690. New York, Penguin, 1997.

———. *The Second Treatise of Government.* 1689. Ed. Thomas P. Peardon. Upper Saddle River, N.J.: Prentice-Hall, 1997.

Looby, Christopher. *Voicing America: Language, Literary Form, and the Origins of the United States.* Chicago: University of Chicago Press, 1996.

———. "Southworth and Seriality: *The Hidden Hand* in the *New York Ledger.*" *Nineteenth-Century Literature* 59, 2 (September, 2004): 179–211.

Loughran, Trish. *The Republic in Print: Print Culture in the Age of U.S. Nation Building, 1770–1870.* New York: Columbia University Press, 2007.

Lubiano, Wahneema. "Constructing and Reconstructing Afro-American Texts: The Critic as Ambassador and Referee." *American Literary History* 1, 2 (Summer 1989): 432–47.

Lugenbeel, J. W. "Letter from Dr. Lugenbeel." *African Repository and Colonial Journal,* April 1846, 112–13.

Lyons, Clare A. *Sex Among the Rabble: An Intimate History of Gender and Power in the Age of Revolution, Philadelphia, 1730–1830.* Chapel Hill: University of North Carolina Press, 2006.

Mackenthun, Gesa. *Fictions of the Black Atlantic in American Foundational Literature.* New York: Routledge, 2004.

Macpherson, C. B. *The Political Theory of Possessive Individualism, Hobbes to Locke.* New York: Oxford University Press, 1962.

Madison, James, Alexander Hamilton, and John Jay. *The Federalist Papers.* 1788. New York: Penguin, 1988.

Madow, Michael. "Forbidden Spectacle: Executions, the Public and the Press in Nineteenth Century New York." *Buffalo Law Review* 43 (1995): 461–562.

Mailloux, Stephen. *Reception Histories: Rhetoric, Pragmatism, and American Cultural Politics.* Ithaca, N.Y.: Cornell University Press, 1998.

Maine, Sir Henry Sumner. *Ancient Law: Its Connection with the Early History of Society and Its Relation to Modern Ideas.* 1861. London: J. Murray, 1920.

Marcus, Gail Sussman. "'Due Execution of the Generall Rules of Righteousness': Criminal Procedure in New Haven Town and Colony, 1638–1658." In Hall, Murrin, and Tate, *Saints and Revolutionaries,* 99–137.

Margolis, Stacey. *The Public Life of Privacy in Nineteenth-Century American Literature.* Durham, N.C.: Duke University Press, 2005.

Marr, Timothy. Introduction to *The Algerine Spy in Pennsylvania,* by Peter Markoe, vii–xxxiv. 1787. Yardley, Pa.: Westholme, 2008.

Marrant, John. *A Journal of the Rev. John Marrant, from August the 18th, 1785, to the 16th of March, 1790.* In Brooks and Saillant, *Face Zion,* 93–161.

Mascuch, Michael. *Origins of the Individualist Self: Autobiographical Practice and Self-Identity in England, 1591–1791.* Stanford, Calif.: Stanford University Press, 1996.

Mason, Matthew E. "Slavery Overshadowed: Congress Debates Prohibiting the Atlantic Slave Trade to the United States, 1806–1807." *Journal of the Early Republic* 20, 1 (Spring 2000): 59–81.

Masur, Louis P. *1831: Year of Eclipse*. New York: Hill and Wang, 2002.

———. *Rites of Execution: Capital Punishment and the Transformation of American Culture, 1776–1865*. New York: Oxford University Press, 1989.

Mather, Cotton. *Diary of Cotton Mather*. Volume 2. New York: Frederick Ungar, 1957.

———. *The Negro Christianized. An Essay to Excite and Assist that Good Work, the Instruction of Negro-Servants in Christianity*. Boston, 1706.

———. *Pillars of Salt. An History of Some Criminals Executed in This Land, for Capital Crimes. With Some of Their Dying Speeches; Collected and Published, for the Warning of Such as Live in Destructive Courses of Ungodliness. Whereto is Added, for the Better Improvement of This History, a Brief Discourse About the Dreadful Justice of God, in Punishing of Sin, with Sin*, 1699.

———. *Tremenda. The Dreadful Sound with Which the Wicked Are to be Thunderstruck. In a Sermon Delivered unto a Great Assembly, in Which Was Present, a Miserable African, Just Going to be Executed for a Most Inhumane and Uncommon Murder*. Boston, 1721.

———. *Warnings from the Dead. Or Solemn Admonitions unto All People; but Especially unto Young Persons to Beware of Such Evils as Would Bring Them to the Dead . . . In Two Discourses, Occasioned by a Sentence of Death, Executed on Some Unhappy Malefactors. Together with the Last Confession, Made by a Young Woman, who Dyed on June 8. 1693. One of These Malefactors*. Boston, 1693.

May, Cedrick. *Evangelism and Resistance in the Black Atlantic*. Athens: University of Georgia Press, 2008.

Mayer, Brantz. *Captain Canot; or, Twenty Years of an African Slaver: Being an Account of His Career and Adventures on the Coast, in the Interior, on Shipboard, and in the West Indies*. New York, 1854.

Mbembe, Achille. "Necropolitics." Trans. Libby Meintjes. *Public Culture* 15, 1 (2003): 11–40.

McBlair, William. "Commander William McBlair's Letters to His Wife 1857–59." *Nautical Scribe*, ed. Joe Mesier. http://nauticalscribe.com/PDF/McBlair.pdf, accessed May 25, 2011.

McCarthy, Timothy Patrick. "'To Plead Our Own Cause': Black Print Culture and the Origins of African-American Abolitionism." In McCarthy and Stauffer, *Prophets*,114–44.

McCarthy, Timothy Patrick, and John Stauffer. *Prophets of Protest: Reconsidering the History of American Abolitionism*. New York: New Press, 2006.

McCarty, Thaddeus. *The Power and Grace of Christ Display'd to a Dying Malefactor. A Sermon Preached at Worcester October the Twentieth, 1768. Being the Day of the Execution of Arthur, a Negro of a* [sic] *about 21 Years Old, for a Rape*. Boston, 1768.

McCune Smith, James. Introduction to Douglass, *My Bondage*, 125–37.

———. *The Works of James McCune Smith: Black Intellectual and Abolitionist.* Ed. John Stauffer. New York: Oxford University Press, 2006.

McDade, Thomas M. *The Annals of Murder: A Bibliography of Books and Pamphlets on American Murders from Colonial Times to 1900.* Norman: University of Oklahoma Press, 1961.

———. "Christian Brown—Wanted for Murder." *New-York Historical Quarterly* 62, 4 (1978): 119–38.

McDowell, Deborah E. "In the First Place: Making Frederick Douglass and the Afro-American Tradition." In *Critical Essays on Frederick Douglass*, ed. William L. Andrews, 172–83. Boston: G.K. Hall, 1991.

McFarland, Philip. *Sea Dangers: The Affair of the Somers.* New York: Schocken, 1985.

McFeely, William S. *Frederick Douglass.* New York: Touchstone-Simon & Schuster, 1991.

McGiffert, Michael, ed. *God's Plot: Puritan Spirituality in Thomas Shepard's Cambridge.* Amherst: University of Massachusetts Press, 1994.

McHenry, Elizabeth. *Forgotten Readers: Recovering the Lost History of African American Literary Societies.* Durham, N.C.: Duke University Press, 2002.

McKeon, Richard. "The Development and Significance of the Concept of Responsibility." *Revue Internationale de Philosophie* 11 (1957): 3–32.

McLennan, Rebecca M. *The Crisis of Imprisonment: Protest, Politics, and the Making of the American Penal State, 1776–1941.* Cambridge: Cambridge University Press, 2008.

McManus, Edgar J. *Black Bondage in the North.* 1973. Syracuse: Syracuse University Press, 2001.

———. *A History of Negro Slavery in New York.* 1966. Syracuse: Syracuse University Press, 2001.

McMillin, James A. *The Final Victims: Foreign Slave Trade to North America, 1783–1810.* Columbia: University of South Carolina Press, 2004.

"Medical Jurisprudence." *New York Journal of Medicine and Collateral Sciences* 7, 20 (September 1846): 260–64.

Mehta, Uday Singh. *The Anxiety of Freedom: Imagination and Individuality in Locke's Political Thought.* Ithaca, N.Y.: Cornell University Press, 1992.

Melish, Joanne Pope. "The 'Condition' Debate and Racial Discourse in the Antebellum North." *Journal of the Early Republic* 19, 4 (Winter 1999): 651–72.

———. *Disowning Slavery: Gradual Emancipation and "Race" in New England, 1780–1860.* Ithaca, N.Y.: Cornell University Press, 1998.

Melville, Herman. "Benito Cereno." 1856. In *The Piazza Tales*, 46–117.

———. *Moby-Dick*. 1852. Evanston, Ill.: Northwestern University Press, 1988.

———. *The Piazza Tales and other Prose Pieces, 1839–1860*. Evanston, Ill.: Northwestern University Press, 1987.

Meranze, Michael. *Laboratories of Virtue: Punishment, Revolution, and Authority in Philadelphia, 1760–1835*. Chapel Hill: University of North Carolina Press, 1996.

Mifflin, Warner. *The Defence of Warner Mifflin against Aspersions Cast on Him on Account of His Endeavours to Promote Righteousness, Mercy and Peace, Among Mankind*. Philadelphia, 1796.

———. *A Serious Expostulation with the Members of the House of Representatives on the United States*. Philadelphia, 1793.

Miller, Andrew. "Lives Unlived in Realist Fiction." *Representations* 98 (Spring 2007): 118–34.

Miller, William Lee. *Arguing About Slavery: John Quincy Adams and the Great Battle in the United States Congress*. New York: Vintage-Random House, 1995.

Mills, Charles W. *The Racial Contract*. Ithaca, N.Y.: Cornell University Press, 1997.

Moglen, Eben. "The Privilege in British North America: The Colonial Period to the Fifth Amendment." In Helmholz et al., *Privilege*, 109–44.

Montesquieu, Charles de Secondat, Baron de. *The Spirit of the Laws*. 1748. Trans. and ed. Anne M. Cohler, Basia Carolyn Miller, and Harold Samuel Stone. Cambridge: Cambridge University Press, 1989.

Moody, Joycelyn. *Sentimental Confessions: Spiritual Narratives of Nineteenth-Century African American Women*. Athens: University of Georgia Press, 2003.

Morgan, Edmund S. *American Slavery, American Freedom: The Ordeal of Colonial Virginia*. 1975. New York: Norton, 1995.

Morris, Norval and David J. Rothman, eds. *The Oxford History of the Prison: The Practice of Punishment in Western Society*. New York: Oxford University Press, 1995.

Morris, Thomas D. *Southern Slavery and the Law, 1619–1860*. Chapel Hill: University of North Carolina Press, 1996.

Morrison, Toni. *Playing in the Dark: Whiteness and the Literary Imagination*. New York: Vintage-Random House, 1993.

Moses, Wilson Jeremiah. *Black Messiahs and Uncle Toms: Social and Literary Manipulations of a Religious Myth*. 1982. Rev. ed. University Park: Pennsylvania State University Press, 1993.

———. "Writing Freely? Frederick Douglass and the Constraints of Racialized Writing." In Sundquist, *Frederick Douglass*, 66–83.

Mott, Frank Luther. *American Journalism, A History: 1690–1960*. 3rd ed. New York: Macmillan, 1962.

Mountain, Joseph and David Daggett, comps. *Sketches of the Life of Joseph Mountain, a Negro, Who Was Executed at New-Haven, on the 20th Day of October, 1790, for a Rape, Committed on the 26th Day of May last. [The Writer of This History Has Directed That the Money Arising From the Sales Thereof, After Deducting the Expence of Printing, &c. Be Given to the Unhappy Girl, Whose Life Is Rendered Wretched by the Crime of the Malefactor.]*. New Haven, 1790.

Muhammad, Khalil Gibran. *The Condemnation of Blackness: Race, Crime, and the Making of Modern Urban America*. Cambridge, Mass.: Harvard University Press, 2010.

Murrin, John M. "Magistrates, Sinners, and a Precarious Liberty: Trial by Jury in Seventeenth-Century New England." In Hall, Murrin, and Tate, *Saints and Revolutionaries*, 152–206.

Nabers, Deak. *Victory of Law: The Fourteenth Amendment, the Civil War, and American Literature, 1852–1867*. Baltimore: Johns Hopkins University Press, 2006.

Nash, Gary B. *Forging Freedom: The Formation of Philadelphia's Black Community, 1720–1840*. Cambridge, Mass.: Harvard University Press, 1988.

Nash, Gary B. and Jean R. Soderlund. *Freedom by Degrees: Emancipation in Pennsylvania and Its Aftermath*. New York: Oxford University Press, 1991.

Nash, Ralph. "Shylock's Wolvish Spirit." *Shakespeare Quarterly* 10, 1 (Winter 1959): 125–28.

Natanson, Harvey. "Locke and Hume: Bearing on the Legal Obligations of the Negro." *Journal of Value Inquiry* 5, 1 (1970): 35–43.

Needles, Edward. *Ten Years' Progress: or a Comparison of the State and Condition of the Colored People in the City and County of Philadelphia from 1837 to 1847*. Philadelphia, 1849.

Nelson, Dana. *National Manhood: Capitalist Citizenship and the Imagined Fraternity of White Men*. Durham, N.C.: Duke University Press, 1998.

———. *The Word in Black and White: Reading "Race" in American Literature 1638–1867*. New York: Oxford University Press, 1993.

Newman, Richard S. *Black Founders: The Free Black Community in the Early Republic. An Exhibition at the Library Company of Philadelphia March–October 2008*. Curated by Phillip S. Lapsansky. Philadelphia: Library Company of Philadelphia, 2008.

———. "'A Chosen Generation': Black Founders and Early America." In McCarthy and Stauffer, *Prophets*, 59–79.

————. *Freedom's Prophet: Bishop Richard Allen, the AME Church, and the Black Founding Fathers.* New York: New York University Press, 2008.

————. "Protest in Black and White: The Formation and Transformation of an African American Political Community during the Early Republic." In Pasley, Robertson, and Waldstreicher, *Beyond the Founders*, 180–204.

————. *The Transformation of American Abolitionism: Fighting Slavery in the Early Republic.* Chapel Hill: University of North Carolina Press, 2002.

Newman, Richard S. and Roy E. Finkenbine. "Forum: Black Founders in the New Republic: Introduction." *William and Mary Quarterly* 3rd ser. 64, 1 (2007): 83–94.

Newman, Richard S., Patrick Rael, and Phillip Lapsansky. *Pamphlets of Protest: An Anthology of Early African American Protest Literature, 1790–1860.* New York: Routledge, 2001.

The New-York Mercantile Union Business Directory. New York, 1850.

"The New York State Colonization Society." *African Repository and Colonial Journal,* June 1846, 188–96.

Nichols, Charles. "The Slave Narrators and the Picaresque Mode: Archetypes for Modern Black Personae." In Davis and Gates, *Slave's Narrative*, 283–98.

Noonan, John T., Jr. *The Antelope: The Ordeal of the Recaptured Africans in the Administrations of James Monroe and John Quincy Adams.* Berkeley: University of California Press, 1977.

Nordstrom, Carl. "The New York Slave Code." *Afro-Americans in New York Life and History* 4, 1 (January 1980): 7–25.

Norris, Andrew, ed. *Politics, Metaphysics, and Death: Essays on Giorgio Agamben's Homo Sacer.* Durham, N.C.: Duke University Press, 2005.

Nudelman, Franny. *John Brown's Body: Slavery, Violence, and the Culture of War.* Chapel Hill: University of North Carolina Press, 2004.

Nussbaum, Martha C. *Frontiers of Justice: Disability, Nationality, Species Membership.* Cambridge, Mass.: Belknap Press of Harvard University Press, 2006.

Nyquist, Mary. *Arbitrary Rule: Slavery, Tyranny, and the Power of Life and Death.* Chicago: University of Chicago Press, forthcoming.

Oates, Stephen B. *The Fires of Jubilee: Nat Turner's Fierce Rebellion.* 1975. New York: HarperCollins, 1990.

————. *To Purge This Land with Blood: A Biography of John Brown.* 2nd ed. Amherst: University of Massachusetts Press, 1984.

"Obituary: William Orton." *Publisher's Weekly* 328 (April 27, 1878): 423–24.

O'Malley, Michael. *Keeping Watch: A History of American Time.* Washington, D.C.: Smithsonian Institution Press, 1990.

"On Board a Slaver. By One of the Trade." *Harper's Weekly,* June 2, 1860, 346–47.

Oshinsky, David M. *"Worse Than Slavery": Parchman Farm and the Ordeal of Jim Crow Justice.* New York: Free Press Simon and Schuster, 1996.

Otter, Samuel. *Melville's Anatomies.* Berkeley: University of California Press. 1999.

———. *Philadelphia Stories: America's Literature of Race and Freedom.* Oxford: Oxford University Press, 2010.

Oxford English Dictionary. 2006. London: Oxford University Press, April 2007. http://dictionary.oed.com.

Pacheco, Josephine F. *The Pearl: A Failed Slave Escape on the Potomac.* Chapel Hill: University of North Carolina Press, 2005.

Papke, David Ray. *Framing the Criminal: Crime, Cultural Work, and the Loss of Critical Perspective, 1830–1900.* Hamden, Conn.: Archon, 1987.

Parker, Herschel. *Herman Melville: A Biography.* 2 vols. Baltimore: Johns Hopkins University Press, 1996–2001.

Parker, Kunal M. "Making Blacks Foreigners: The Legal Construction of Former Slaves in Post-Revolutionary Massachusetts." *Utah Law Review* 75, 1 (2001): 75–124.

Parker, Theodore. *The American Scholar.* Ed. George Willis Cooke. Boston: American Unitarian Association, 1907.

Pasley, Jeffrey L., Andrew W. Robertson, and David Waldstreicher, eds. *Beyond the Founders: New Approaches to the Political History of the Early American Republic.* Chapel Hill: University of North Carolina Press, 2004.

Pateman, Carole. "Self-Ownership and Property in the Person: Democratization and a Tale of Two Concepts." *Journal of Political Philosophy* 10, 1 (2002): 20–53.

———. *The Sexual Contract.* Stanford, Calif.: Stanford University Press, 1988.

Pateman, Carole and Charles W. Mills. *Contract and Domination.* Cambridge: Polity Press, 2007.

Patrick-Stamp, Leslie. "Ann Hinson: A Little Known Woman in the Country's Premier Prison, Eastern State Penitentiary, 1831." *Pennsylvania History* 67, 3 (2000): 361–75.

———. "Numbers That Are Not New: African Americans in the Country's First Prison, 1790–1835." *Pennsylvania Magazine of History and Biography* 119, 1–2 (January/April 1995): 95–128.

———. "The Prison Sentence Docket for 1795: Inmates at the Nation's First State Penitentiary." *Pennsylvania History* 60, 3 (July 1993): 353–82.

———. "Prisoners' Presence and Perspectives (1829–1865)." In *Eastern State Penitentiary: Historic Structures Report.* Vol. 1, ed. Marianna Thomas, 106–39. Philadelphia: Philadelphia Historical Commission, 1994.

Patterson, Orlando. *Slavery and Social Death: A Comparative Study.* Cambridge, Mass.: Harvard University Press, 1982.

P[eabody], E[phraim]. "Narratives of Fugitive Slaves." *Christian Examiner* 47, 1 (July 1849): 61–93.

Penningroth, Dylan C. *The Claims of Kinfolk: African American Property and Community in the Nineteenth-Century South*. Chapel Hill: University of North Carolina Press, 2003.

Pennington, James W. C. *The Fugitive Blacksmith; or, Events in the History of James W. C. Pennington, Pastor of a Presbyterian Church, New York, Formerly a Slave in the State of Maryland, United States*. London, 1849.

———. *A Narrative of Events of the Life of J. H. Banks, an Escaped Slave from the Cotton State, Alabama, in America*. Liverpool, 1861.

Pennock, J. Roland. "The Problem of Responsibility." In *Nomos III: Responsibility*, ed. Carl J. Friedrich, 3–27. New York: Liberal Arts Press, 1960.

Pennsylvania Society for Promoting the Abolition of Slavery. *Review of a Pamphlet entitled An Appeal to the Public on behalf of a House of Refuge for Colored Juvenile Delinquents*. Philadelphia, 1847.

The People vs. Edward Coleman. 13 August 1838. MS. New York State Archives.

Pestritto, Ronald J. *Founding the Criminal Law: Punishment and Political Thought in the Origins of America*. DeKalb: Northern Illinois University Press, 2000.

Peters, Julie Stone. "'Literature,' the 'Rights of Man,' and Narratives of Atrocity: Historical Backgrounds to the Culture of Testimony." *Yale Journal of Law and the Humanities* 17 (2005): 253–83.

Peterson, Carla L. *Doers of the Word: African-American Women Speakers and Writers in the North, 1830–1880*. New Brunswick, N.J.: Rutgers University Press, 1998.

Peterson, Mark A. "*The Selling of Joseph*: Bostonians, Antislavery, and the Protestant International, 1689–1733." *Massachusetts Historical Review* 4 (2002): 1–22.

Pew Center on the States and the Public Safety Performance Project. "One in 100: Behind Bars in America 2008." February 28, 2008. http://www.pewcenteronthestates.org/report_detail.aspx?id=35904, accessed January 17, 2009.

Philadelphia Society for Alleviating the Miseries of Public Prisons. *The Undersigned, a Committee of the Philadelphia Society for Alleviating the Miseries of Public Prisons, appointed on the 8th inst., respectfully Invite thy Attendence at a Meeting of Citizens, to be Held at the Hall of the Franklin Institute, on the 19th inst., at 7 1/2 P.M., for the Purpose of Adopting Measures to Secure the Establishment of a Refuge for Coloured Juvenile Delinquents, in Connection with the Institution already Established*. [Philadelphia:, 1846].

Philbrick, Nathaniel. *In the Heart of the Sea: The Tragedy of the Whaleship Essex*. New York: Penguin, 2001.

[Phillipps, Samuel March.] *The Theory of Presumptive Proof; or, An Inquiry into the*

Nature of Circumstantial Evidence: including an Examination of the Evidence on the Trial of Captain Donnellan. New York, 1816.

Pierce, Yolanda. "Redeeming Bondage: The Captivity Narrative and the Spiritual Autobiography in the African American Slave Narrative Tradition." In *The Cambridge Companion to African American Slave Narrative*, ed. Audrey Fisch, 83–98. New York: Cambridge University Press, 2007.

Piersen, William D. *Black Yankees: The Development of an Afro-American Subculture in Eighteenth-Century New England.* Amherst: University of Massachusetts Press, 1988.

Platt, Anthony Michael and Bernard L. Diamond. "The Origins and Development of the 'Wild Beast' Concept of Mental Illness and Its Relation to Theories of Criminal Responsibility." *Journal of the History of the Behavioral Sciences* 1, 4 (October 1965): 355–67.

"A Plea for the Fijians; Or, Can Nothing Else Be Said in Favor of Roasting One's Equals?" *Atlantic Monthly* (March 1859): 342–50.

Poe, Edgar Allan. "The Murders in the Rue Morgue." In *Tales and Sketches.*

———. *Tales and Sketches.* 2 vols. Ed. Thomas Ollive Mabbott. Urbana: University of Illinois Press, 1978.

Porter, Dorothy Burnett. *Early Negro Writing, 1760–1837.* Boston: Beacon Press, 1971.

Post-Lauria, Sheila. *Correspondent Colorings: Melville in the Marketplace.* Amherst: University of Massachusetts Press, 1996.

Potkay, Adam. "Olaudah Equiano and the Art of Spiritual Autobiography." *Eighteenth-Century Studies* 27 (1994): 677–92.

Potkay, Adam and Sandra Burr, eds. *Black Atlantic Writers of the Eighteenth Century: Living the New Exodus in England and the Americas.* New York: St. Martin's, 1995.

Powell, J. H. *Bring Out Your Dead: The Great Plague of Yellow Fever in Philadelphia in 1793.* 1949. Philadelphia: University of Pennsylvania Press, 1993.

Pratt, Lloyd. *Archives of American Time: Literature and Modernity in the Nineteenth Century.* Philadelphia: University of Pennsylvania Press, 2010.

———. "Lyric Public of *Les Cenelles.*" In Cohen and Stein, *Early African American Print Culture*, 253–73.

Price, Clement Alexander, comp. and ed. *Freedom Not Far Distant: A Documentary History of Afro-Americans in New Jersey.* Newark: New Jersey Historical Society, 1980.

Radin, Margaret Jane. "Property and Personhood." *Stanford Law Review* 34, 5 (May 1982): 957–1012.

Rael, Patrick. *Black Identity and Black Protest in the Antebellum North.* Chapel Hill: University of North Carolina Press, 2002.

Rawlings, Philip. *Drunks, Whores, and Idle Apprentices: Criminal Biographies of the Eighteenth Century.* London: Routledge, 1992.

Rawls, John. *A Theory of Justice.* Rev. ed. Cambridge, Mass.: Harvard University Press, 1999.

Rediker, Marcus. *Between the Devil and the Deep Blue Sea: Merchant Seamen, Pirates, and the Anglo-American Maritime World, 1700–1750.* Cambridge: Cambridge University Press, 1987.

———. *Slave Ship: A Human History.* New York: Viking-Penguin, 2007.

"Reflections on the Census of 1840." *Southern Literary Messenger* (June 1843): 340–52.

Reiss, Benjamin. *Theaters of Madness: Insane Asylums and Nineteenth-Century American Culture.* Chicago: University of Chicago Press, 2008.

Report of the Trial of Henry Wyatt: A Convict in the State Prison at Auburn, indicted for the Murder of James Gordon, Another Convict within the Prison, before the Court of Oyer and Terminer held at Auburn, N.Y., Commencing Wednesday, February Eleventh, Eighteen Hundred Forty-Six: Hon. Bowen Whiting, Circuit Judge of the Seventh District: Hon. Joseph L. Richardson, First Judge: Isaac Sisson, Elisha Shelden, Walter G. Bradley, Abner Hollister, Judges of Cayuga County Courts: Luman Sherwood, District Attorney, for the People : William H. Seward, Christopher Morgan, Samuel Blatchford, for the Prisoner. Auburn, 1846.

Review of *Captain Canot*, by Brantz Mayer. *North American Review* (January 1855): 153–70.

Review of *Captain Canot*, by Brantz Mayer. *Putnam's Monthly Magazine* (November 1854): 560.

Review of *The Slave Trade, Domestic and Foreign*, by Henry C. Carey. *Putnam's Monthly Magazine* (July 1853): 104.

Review of *The Slave Trade, Domestic and Foreign*, by Henry C. Carey. *Putnam's Monthly Magazine* (June 1853): 693.

Review of *To Cuba and Back: A Vacation Voyage*, by R[ichard] H[enry] Dana. *Atlantic Monthly* (July 1859): 132.

Reynolds, David S. *Beneath the American Renaissance: The Subversive Imagination in the Age of Emerson and Melville.* New York: Knopf, 1988.

Rice, Alan J. *Radical Narratives of the Black* Atlantic. London: Continuum, 2003.

Rice, Alan J. and Martin Crawford, eds. *Liberating Sojourn: Frederick Douglass and Transatlantic Reform.* Athens: University of Georgia Press, 1999.

Richard, Carl J. *The Founders and the Classics: Greece, Rome, and the American Enlightenment.* Cambridge, Mass.: Harvard University Press, 1994.

Richards, Phillip M. "Nationalist Themes in the Preaching of Jupiter Hammon." *Early American Literature* 25, 2 (1990): 123–38.

Richetti, John J. *Popular Fiction before Richardson: Narrative Patterns* 1700–1739. Oxford: Clarendon, 1969.

Riesenberg, Peter. *Citizenship in the Western Tradition: Plato to Rousseau.* Chapel Hill: University of North Carolina Press, 1992.

"The Rights of Our Flag." *Harper's Weekly*, May 29, 1858, 338.

Ripley, C. Peter, ed. *The Black Abolitionist Papers.* 5 vols. Chapel Hill: University of North Carolina Press, 1985–92.

Ripley, Dorothy. *An Account of Rose Butler, Aged Nineteen Years, Whose Execution I Attended in the Potter's Field, on the 9th of the 7th Mo. for Setting Fire to her Mistress' Dwelling House.* New York, 1819.

Riss, Arthur. *Race, Slavery and Liberalism in Nineteenth-Century American Literature.* Cambridge: Cambridge University Press, 2006.

Roach, Joseph. *Cities of the Dead: Circum-Atlantic Performance.* New York: Columbia University Press, 1996.

Robbins, Sarah. "Gendering the History of the Antislavery Narrative: Juxtaposing *Uncle Tom's Cabin* and *Benito Cereno, Beloved* and *Middle Passage.*" *American Quarterly* 49 (1997): 531–73.

Robinson, Daniel N. *Wild Beasts and Idle Humours: The Insanity Defense from Antiquity to the Present.* Cambridge, Mass.: Harvard University Press, 1996.

Rockafield, H. A. *The Manheim Tragedy. A Complete History of the Double Murder of Mrs. Garber & Mrs. Ream: with the Only Authentic Life and Confession of Alexander Anderson. Together with a Correct Account of the Arrest, Trial, Conviction, Sentence, Death-Warrant, and Execution of Anderson and Henry Richards, His Accomplice; to which is Appended some brief Reflections on the Causes and Consequences of Crime.* Lancaster, Pa., 1858.

———. *Das Manheimer Trauerspiel. Eine vollständige Geschichte von dem Doppel-Morde der Frau Gerber und Frau Riem; mit dem allein wahrhaften Leben und Bekenntniss des Alexander Anderson. Nebst einem richtigen Bericht von der Verhaftung, dem Verhör, der Ueberführung, der Verurtheilung, dem Todesbefehl, und der Hinrichtung von Anderson und Henry Richards, seinem Mitschuldigen; welchem hinzugefügt sind einige kurze Betrachtungen über die Ursachen und Folgen von Verbrechen.* Lancaster, Pa., 1858.

Rodensky, Lisa. *The Crime in Mind: Criminal Responsibility and the Victorian Novel.* New York: Oxford University Press, 2003.

Roediger, David R. *The Wages of Whiteness: Race and the Making of the American Working Class.* 1991. London: Verso, 2007.

Rogers, John. *Death the Certain Wages of Sin to the Impenitent: Life the Sure Reward of Grace to the Penitent: Together with the only Way for Youth To Avoid the Former, and*

Attain the Latter. Deliver'd in Three Lecture Sermons; Occasioned by the Imprison-ment, Condemnation and Execution, of a Young Woman, who Was Guilty of Murder-ing her Infant Begotten in Whoredom. To which is Added, an Account of Her Manner of Life and Death, in which the Glory of Free Grace is Displayed. Boston, 1701.

Rogin, Michael Paul. *Subversive Genealogy: The Politics and Art of Herman Melville.* 1979. New York: Knopf, 1983.

Rohrbach, Augusta. *Truth Stranger Than Fiction: Race, Realism, and the U.S. Literary Marketplace.* New York: Palgrave, 2002.

Rothman, David J. *The Discovery of the Asylum: Social Order and Disorder in the New Republic.* Rev. ed. New Brunswick, N.J.: Aldine Transaction, 2008.

———. "Perfecting the Prison: United States, 1789–1865." In Morris and Rothman, *Oxford History of the Prison,* 111–29.

Rousseau, Jean-Jacques. *The Social Contract and Other Later Political Writings.* Ed. and trans. Victor Gourevitch. Cambridge: Cambridge University Press, 1997.

Rowe, G. S. "Black Offenders, Criminal Courts, and Philadelphia Society in the Late Eighteenth-Century." *Journal of Social History* 22, 4 (Summer 1989): 685–712.

Rury, John L. "Philanthropy, Self Help, and Social Control: The New York Manumis-sion Society and Free Blacks, 1785–1810." *Phylon* 46, 3 (Third Quarter 1985): 231–41.

Rush, Benjamin. *The Selected Writings of Benjamin Rush.* Ed. Dagobert D. Runes. New York: Philosophical Library, 2007.

Ruttenburg, Nancy. *Democratic Personality: Popular Voice and the Trial of American Authorship.* Stanford, Calif.: Stanford University Press, 1998.

Ryan, Mary P. "Gender and Public Access: Women's Politics in Nineteenth-Century America." In Calhoun, *Habermas,* 259–88.

Sale, Maggie Montesinos. *The Slumbering Volcano: American Slave Ship Revolts and the Production of Rebellious Masculinity.* Durham, N.C.: Duke University Press, 1997.

Sampson, Marmaduke B. *Rationale of Crime, and Its Appropriate Treatment; Being a Treatise on Criminal Jurisprudence Considered in Relation to Cerebral Organiza-tion.* Ed. E. W. Farnham. New York, 1846.

Sánchez-Eppler, Karen. *Touching Liberty: Abolition, Feminism, and the Politics of the Body.* Berkeley: University of California Press, 1997.

Sarat, Austin. *When the State Kills: Capital Punishment and the American Condition.* Princeton, N.J.: Princeton University Press, 2001.

Sawyer, George P. *Southern Institutes, or, an Inquiry into the Origin and Early Prevalence of Slavery and the Slave-Trade, with an Analysis of the Laws, History, and Government of the Institution in the Principal Nations, Ancient and Modern.* Philadelphia, 1859.

Schiller, Dan. *Objectivity and the News: The Public and the Rise of Commercial Journal-ism.* Philadelphia: University of Pennsylvania Press, 1981.

Schmitt, Carl. *Political Theology: Four Chapters on the Concept of Sovereignty.* Trans. George D. Schwab. 1922. Chicago: University of Chicago Press, 2004.

Schorb, Jodi. "Seeing Other Wise: Reading a Pequot Execution Narrative." In *Early Native Literacies in New England: A Documentary and Critical Anthology*, ed. Kristina Bross and Hilary E. Wyss, 142–61. Amherst: University of Massachusetts Press, 2008.

———. "Uncleanliness Is Next to Godliness: Sexuality, Salvation, and the Early American Woman's Execution Narrative." In *The Puritan Origins of American Sex: Religion, Sexuality, and National Identity in American Literature*, ed. Tracy Fessenden, Nicholas F. Radel, and Magdelena J. Zaborowska, 72–92. New York: Routledge, 2001.

———. "Writing Prisoners in an Era of Disciplinary Spectacle." Paper presented at the Incarceration Nation: Voices from the Early American Gaol conference, McNeil Center for Early American Studies, Philadelphia, April 3–4, 2009.

Schramm, Jan-Melissa. *Testimony and Advocacy in Victorian Law, Literature, and Theology.* New York: Cambridge University Press, 2000.

Schudson, Michael. "Was There Ever a Public Sphere? If So, When? Reflections on the American Case." In Calhoun, *Habermas*, 143–63.

Schwarz, Philip J. *Slave Laws in Virginia.* Athens: Georgia University Press, 1996.

———. *Twice Condemned: Slaves and the Criminal Laws of Virginia, 1705–1865.* Baton Rouge: Louisiana State University Press, 1988.

Scudder, Harold H. "Melville's *Benito Cereno* and Captain Delano's Voyages." *PMLA* 43 (June 1928): 503–32.

Sekora, John. "Black Message / White Envelope: Genre, Authenticity, and Authority in the Antebellum Slave Narrative." *Callaloo* 32 (Summer 1987): 482–515.

———. "Red, White, and Black: Indian Captivities, Colonial Printers, and the Early African-American Narrative." In *A Mixed Race: Ethnicity in Early America*, ed. Frank Shuffleton, 92–104. New York: Oxford University Press, 1993.

Sellin, Thorsten. "The Philadelphia Gibbet Iron." *Journal of Criminal Law, Criminology, and Police Science* 46, 1 (May–June 1955): 11–25.

Sentencing Project. "Felony Disenfranchisement Laws in the United States." March 2011. http://www.sentencingproject.org/doc/publications/fd_bs_fdlawsinusMar11.pdf, accessed August 16, 2011.

Argument of William H. Seward, in Defence of William Freeman, on His Trial for Murder, at Auburn, July 21st and 22d, 1846. Auburn, N.Y., 1846.

———. *Argument of William H. Seward, in Defence of William Freeman, on His Trial for Murder, at Auburn, July 21st and 22nd, 1846. Reported by S. Blatchford.* Auburn, N.Y., 1846.

Seward, William H. and Frederick W. Seward. *William H. Seward: An Autobiography from 1801 to 1834. With a Memoir of his Life, and Selections from his Letters. 1831–1846.* New York, 1891.

Shamir, Milette. *Inexpressible Privacy: The Interior Life of Antebellum American Literature.* Philadelphia: University of Pennsylvania Press, 2006.

Shklar, Judith N. *American Citizenship: The Quest for Inclusion.* Cambridge, Mass.: Harvard University Press, 1991.

Sinha, Manisha. "An Alternative Tradition of Radicalism: African American Abolitionists and the Metaphor of Revolution." In Sinha and Von Eschen, *Contested Democracy*, 9–30.

———. "To 'Cast Just Obliquy' on Oppressors: Black Radicalism in the Age of Revolution." *William and Mary Quarterly* 3rd ser. 64, 1 (January 2007): 149–60.

Sinha, Manisha and Penny Von Eschen, eds. *Contested Democracy: Freedom, Race, and Power in American History.* New York: Columbia University Press, 2007.

Skallerup, Harry R. *Books Afloat and Ashore: A History of Books, Libraries, and Reading Among Seamen During the Age of Sail.* Hamden, Conn.: Archon-Shoestring Press, 1974.

Slaughter, Thomas P. *Bloody Dawn: The Christiana Riot and Racial Violence in the Antebellum North.* New York: Oxford University Press, 1991.

"The Slave Trade in New York." *De Bow's Review* 18, 2 (February 1855): 223–28.

"The Slaver." *Graham's American Monthly Magazine of Literature and Art.* Pts. 1 and 2. (July 1947): 1–12; (August 1847): 61–71.

"The Slaves Liberated from the *Pons*." *African Repository and Colonial Journal*, April 1846, 130.

Slotkin, Richard. "Narratives of Negro Crime in New England, 1675–1800." *American Quarterly* 25, 1 (1973): 3–31.

Smith, Caleb. "Emerson and Incarceration." *American Literature* 78, 2 (June 2006): 207–34.

———. *The Prison and the American Imagination.* New Haven, Conn.: Yale University Press, 2009.

Smith, Douglas G. "Citizenship and the Fourteenth Amendment." *San Diego Law Review* 34 (1997): 681–808.

Smith, Henry E. "The Modern Privilege: Its Nineteenth-Century Origins." In Helmholz et al., *Privilege*, 145–80.

Smith, Mark M. *Mastered by the Clock: Time, Slavery, and Freedom in the American South.* Chapel Hill: University of North Carolina Press, 1997.

Smith, Merritt Roe. "Army Ordnance and the 'American System' of Manufacturing, 1815–1861." In *Military Enterprise and Technological Change: Perspectives on the*

American Experience, ed. Merritt Roe Smith, 39–87. Cambridge, Mass.: MIT Press, 1985.

Smith, Philip. "Executing Executions: Aesthetics, Identity, and the Problematic Narratives of Capital Punishment Ritual." *Theory and Society* 25 (1996): 235–61.

Smith, Rogers M. *Civic Ideals: Conflicting Visions of Citizenship in U.S. History*. New Haven, Conn.: Yale University Press, 1997.

Smith, Sidonie. *Subjectivity, Identity, and the Body: Women's Autobiographical Practices in the Twentieth Century*. Bloomington: Indiana University Press, 1995.

———. *Where I'm Bound: Patterns of Slavery and Freedom in Black American Autobiography*. Westport, Conn.: Greenwood Press, 1974.

Smith, Stephen. *Life, Last Words and Dying Speech of Stephen Smith, a Black Man, Who Was Executed at Boston This Day Being Thursday, October 12, 1797 for Burglary*. Boston, 1797.

Smith, Valerie. *Self-Discovery and Authority in Afro-American Narrative*. Cambridge, Mass.: Harvard University Press, 1987.

[Smith, Venture.] *A Narrative of the Life and Adventures of Venture, a Native of Africa. But Resident above Sixty Years in the United States of America. Related by Himself*. New London, 1798.

Smith-Rosenberg, Carol. "Dis-Covering the Subject of the 'Great Constitutional Discussion,' 1786–1789." *Journal of American History* 79, 3 (December 1992): 841–73.

Snodgrass, J. E. "Crime, and Its Punishment in the South." *Prisoner's Friend* 2, 1 (September 1849): 27–34.

Soderlund, Jean R. "Comment." *Journal of the Early Republic* 18, 2 (Spring 1998): 218–22.

Soodalter, Ron. *Hanging Captain Gordon: The Life and Trial of an American Slave Trader*. New York: Atria-Simon and Schuster, 2006.

Span, Christopher M. "Educational and Social Reforms for African American Juvenile Delinquents in Nineteenth-Century New York City and Philadelphia." *Journal of Negro Education* 71, 3 (Summer 2002): 108–17.

Speigel, Allen D. and Marc B. Spiegel. "The Insanity Plea in Early Nineteenth Century America." *Journal of Community Health* 23, 3 (June 1998): 227–47.

Spires, Derrick. "Imagining a State of Fellow Citizens: Early African American Politics of Publicity in the Black State Conventions." In Cohen and Stein, *Early African American Print Culture*, 274–89.

Stanford, John. *An Authentic Statement of the Case and Conduct of Rose Butler, who was Tried, Convicted, and Executed for the Crime of Arson. Reviewed and Approved by the Rev. John Stanford, M.A., Chaplain to the Public Institutions*. New York, 1819.

Stanley, Amy Dru. "Contract." In *Keywords for American Cultural Studies*. ed. Bruce Burgett and Glenn Hendler, 60–64. New York: New York University Press, 2007.

——. *From Bondage to Contract: Wage Labor, Marriage and the Market in the Age of Slave Emancipation.* New York: Cambridge University Press, 1998.

Stanton, William. *The Leopard's Spots: Scientific Attitudes Toward Race in America, 1815–59.* Chicago: University of Chicago Press, 1960.

Starling, Marion Wilson. *The Slave Narrative: Its Place in American History.* Washington, D.C.: Howard University Press, 1988.

Stauffer, John. *The Black Hearts of Men: Radical Abolitionists and the Transformation of Race.* Cambridge, Mass.: Harvard University Press, 2002.

——. Introduction to "Heads of the Colored People, 1852–1854." In McCune Smith, *Works,* 187–89.

Stepto, Robert. *From Behind the Veil: A Study of Afro-American Narrative.* 2nd ed. Urbana: University of Illinois Press, 1991.

——. "I Rose and Found My Voice: Narration, Authentication, and Authorial Control in Four Slave Narratives." In Davis and Gates, *Slave's Narrative,* 225–41.

Stern, Madeleine B. "Mathew B. Brady and the *Rationale of Crime*: A Discovery in Daguerreotypes." *Quarterly Journal of the Library of Congress* 31, 3 (July 1974): 127–35.

Stevens, Charles Emery. *Anthony Burns: A History.* 1856. Williamstown, Mass.: Corner House, 1973.

Stewart, James Brewer. "The Emergence of Racial Modernity and the Rise of the White North, 1790–1840." *Journal of the Early Republic* 18, 2 (Spring 1998): 181–217.

——. "Modernizing 'Difference': The Political Meanings of Color in the Free States, 1776–1840." *Journal of the Early Republic* 19, 4 (Winter 1999): 691–712.

——. "Response." *Journal of the Early Republic* 18, 2 (Spring 1998): 233–36.

Stewart, Susan. *Crimes of Writing: Problems in the Containment of Representation.* Durham, N.C.: Duke University Press, 1994.

Stone, Andrea. "Interracial Sexual Abuse and Legal Subjectivity in Antebellum Law and Literature." *American Literature* 81, 1 (March 2009): 65–92.

Story, Joseph. *A Charge Delivered to the Grand Juries of the Circuit Court, at October Term, 1819, in Boston, and at November Term, 1819, in Providence, and Published at their Unanimous Request.* Boston [?], 1819.

Stowe, Harriet Beecher. *Dred: A Tale of the Great Dismal Swamp.* 1856. Ed. Judie Newman. Exeter: Edinburgh University Press, 1999.

——. *A Key to Uncle Tom's Cabin; Presenting the Original Facts and Documents upon which the Story is Founded. Together with Corroborative Statements Verifying the Truth of the Work.* 1853. Port Washington, N.Y.: Kennikat Press, 1968.

——. *The Minister's Wooing.* 1859. Ed. Susan K. Harris. New York: Penguin, 1999.

——. *Uncle Tom's Cabin: Authoritative Text, Backgrounds and Contexts, Criticism.* 1852. Ed. Elizabeth Ammons. New York: Norton, 1994.

Suggs, Jon-Christian. *Whispered Consolations: Law and Narrative in African-American Life*. Ann Arbor: University of Michigan Press, 2000.

Sundquist, Eric J., ed. *Frederick Douglass: New Literary and Historical Essays*. New York: Cambridge University Press, 1990.

———. *To Wake the Nations: Race in the Making of American Literature*. Cambridge, Mass.: Belknap Press of Harvard University Press, 1993.

Swaim, Kathleen M. "'Come and Hear': Women's Puritan Evidences." In *American Women's Autobiography: Fea(s)ts of Memory*, ed. Margo Culley, 32–56. Madison: University of Wisconsin Press, 1992.

Tamarkin, Elisa. *Anglophilia: Deference, Devotion, and Antebellum America*. Chicago: University of Chicago Press, 2007.

Tawil, Ezra F. "Captain Babo's Cabin: Stowe, Race and Misreading in 'Benito Cereno.'" *Leviathan* (2006): 37–51.

Taylor, William R. *Cavalier and Yankee: The Old South and American National Character*. New York: Oxford University Press, 1993.

Terpstra, Nicholas, ed. *The Art of Executing Well: Rituals of Execution in Renaissance Italy*. Kirksville, Mo.: Truman State University Press, 2008.

Thomas, Brook. *American Literary Realism and the Failed Promise of Contract*. Berkeley: University of California Press, 1997.

———. *Civic Myths: A Law-and-Literature Approach to Citizenship*. Chapel Hill: University of North Carolina Press, 2007.

———. *Cross-Examinations of Law and Literature: Cooper, Hawthorne, Stowe, and Melville*. Cambridge: Cambridge University Press, 1987.

———. "Narratives of Responsibility and Blame in Nineteenth-Century United States Law and Literature." *Narrative* 5, 1 (January 1997): 3–19.

Thompson, E. P. "Time, Work-Discipline, and Industrial Capitalism." *Past and Present* 38 (December 1967): 56–97.

Thompson, George. *The Prison Bard: or Poems on Various Subjects*. Hartford, 1848.

Thoreau, Henry David. *Walden*. 1854. In *Walden and Civil Disobedience*, ed. Michael Meyer, 43–382. New York: Viking Penguin, 1983.

Titus, Mary. "'This Poisonous System': Social Ills, Bodily Ills, and *Incidents in the Life of a Slave Girl*." In Garfield and Zafar, *Harriet Jacobs*, 199–215.

Tocqueville, Alexis de. *Democracy in America*. Trans. Henry Reeve. 1835. New York: Bantam-Random House, 2000.

Tomlins, Christopher. *Freedom Bound: Law, Labor, and Civic Identity in Colonizing English America, 1580–1865*. Cambridge: Cambridge University Press, 2010.

Towner, Lawrence W. "'A Fondness for Freedom': Servant Protest in Puritan Society." *William and Mary Quarterly* 3rd ser. 19, 2 (April 1962): 201–19.

———. "The Sewall-Saffin Dialogue on Slavery." *William and Mary Quarterly* 3rd ser. 21, 1 (January 1964): 40–52.

———. "True Confessions and Dying Warnings in Colonial New England." In *Sibley's Heir: A Volume in Memory of Clifford Kenyon Shipton*. Boston: Colonial Society of Massachusetts, 1982.

Tracey, Karen. "E.D.E.N. Southworth's Tragic Muse." In Homestead and Washington, *Southworth*.

Tragle, Henry Irving. *The Southampton Slave Revolt of 1831: A Compilation of Source Material*. Amherst: University of Massachusetts Press, 1971.

The Trial of Alice Clifton, for the Murder of her Bastard-Child, at the Court of Oyer and Terminer and General Gaol Delivery, held at Philadelphia, on Wednesday the 18th day of April, 1787. [Philadelphia, 1787.]

Tucher, Andie. *Froth and Scum: Truth, Beauty, Goodness, and the Ax Murder in America's First Mass Medium*. Chapel Hill: University of North Carolina Press, 1994.

Tucker, Spender C. *Andrew Foote: Civil War Admiral on Western Waters*. Annapolis: Naval Institute Press, 2000.

Tucker, St. George. *A Dissertation on Slavery with a Proposal for the Gradual Abolition of it in the State of Virginia*. Philadelphia, 1796.

Tushnet, Mark V. *Slave Law in the American South:* State v. Mann *in History and Literature*. Lawrence: University Press of Kansas, 2003.

Underkuffler, Laura S. "On Property: An Essay." *Yale Law Journal* 100, 1 (October 1990): 127–48.

U.S. Congress. *A Century of Lawmaking for a New Nation: U.S. Congressional Documents and Debates, 1774–1875*. Electronic Resource. 42 vols. Washington, D.C., 1834–56.

———. *Message from the President of the United States to the Two Houses of Congress, at the Commencement of the First Session of the Thirty-First Congress*. Washington, D.C., 1839.

U.S. Department of Labor Office of Policy Planning and Research. *The Negro Family: The Case for National Action*. Washington, D.C.: U.S. GPO, 1965.

U.S. Department of State. *Errors in Sixth Census: Letter from the Secretary of State, relative to Alleged Errors of the Sixth Census: February 12, 1845: Read, and Referred to the Select Committee on that Subject*. [Washington, D.C., 1845].

[Van Ness, William]. *Case of the Schooner Plattsburgh. District Court United States, Southern District, New York*. In *Sixteenth Report of the Directors of the African Institution, Read at the Annual General Meeting, Held on the 10th Day of May*, 1822. 281–98. London, 1822.

"A Visit to Captain Howes, of the Schooner 'Mobile.'" *Harper's Weekly*, June 12, 1858, 369–70.

Von Frank, Albert J. "John Saffin: Slavery and Racism in Colonial Massachusetts." *Early American Literature* 29, 3 (1994): 254–72.

———. *The Trials of Anthony Burns: Freedom and Slavery in Emerson's Boston.* Cambridge, Mass.: Harvard University Press, 1998.

Wagner, Bryan. "Disarmed and Dangerous: The Strange Career of Bras-Coupé." In Best and Hartman, *Redress,* 117–51.

———. *Disturbing the Peace: Black Culture and the Police Power after Slavery.* Cambridge, Mass.: Harvard University Press, 2009.

Wahl, Jenny Bourne. *The Bondsman's Burden: An Economic Analysis of the Common Law of Southern Slavery.* Cambridge: Cambridge University Press, 1998.

Wald, Priscilla. *Constituting Americans: Cultural Anxiety and Narrative Form.* Durham: Duke University Press, 1995.

Waldrep, Christopher. *Roots of Disorder: Race and Criminal Justice in the American South, 1817–80.* Urbana: University of Illinois Press, 1998.

Waldstreicher, David. *In the Midst of Perpetual Fetes: The Making of American Nationalism, 1776–1820.* Chapel Hill: University of North Carolina Press, 1997.

———. "Reading the Runaways: Self-Fashioning, Print Culture, and Confidence in Slavery in the Eighteenth-Century Mid-Atlantic." *William and Mary Quarterly* 3rd ser. 56, 2 (1999): 243–72.

———. *Runaway America: Benjamin Franklin, Slavery, and the American Revolution.* New York: Hill and Wang, 2004.

Walker, Alice. *In Search of Our Mothers' Gardens.* New York: Harcourt Brace Jovanovich, 1983.

Walker, David. *David Walker's Appeal, in Four Articles; Together with a Preamble, to the Coloured Citizens of the World, But in Particular, and Very Expressly, to Those of the United States of America.* 1829. Ed. Sean Wilentz. New York: Hill and Wang, 1995.

Wallace, Maurice O. *Constructing the Black Masculine: Identity and Ideality in African American Men's Literature and Culture, 1775–1995.* Durham, N.C.: Duke University Press, 2002.

Wallace, Robert. K. "Fugitive Justice: Douglass, Shaw, Melville." In Levine and Otter, *Douglass and Melville,* 39–68.

Walters, Ronald G. "Comment." *Journal of the Early Republic* 18, 2 (Spring 1998): 226–33.

———. "Harriet Beecher Stowe and the American Reform Tradition." In *The Cambridge Companion to Harriet Beecher Stowe,* ed. Cindy Weinstein, 171–89. Cambridge: Cambridge University Press, 2004.

Walzer, Michael. "The Civil Society Argument." In *Theorizing Citizenship,* ed. Ronald Beiner, 153–74. Albany: State University of New York Press, 1995.

Wansley, Thomas J. *The Life and Confession of Thos. J. Wansley,: One of the Pirates, con-*

cerned with Charles Gibbs, alias James Jeffers, in the Murder and Piracy Committed on Board the Brig Vineyard. Written by Himself; To which is added, Several Interesting Letters; Together with the Trial, Sentence, and Execution of Gibbs and Wansley; the Latter of which Took Place on the 22d Day of April, 1831. New York, 1831.

Warner, Henry H. *Report of the Trial of Susanna, a Coloured Woman: before the Hon. Ambrose Spencer, Esq. at a Court of Oyer and Terminer, and Gaol Delivery, Held at the City of Schenectady, on the 23d October, 1810, on a Charge of Having Murdered her Infant Male Bastard Child, on the Night of the 22d June*, 1810. Troy, 1810.

Warner, Michael. *The Letters of the Republic: Publication and the Public Sphere in Eighteenth-Century America*. Cambridge, Mass.: Harvard University Press, 1990.

Warren, Charles. "Fourth of July Myths." *William and Mary Quarterly* 3rd ser. 2, 3 (July 1945): 238–72.

Warren, Kenneth W. "Making a Literature: Black Writing and Jim Crow." Distinguished Fellow Lecture. Huntington Library. San Marino, California, March 2, 2011.

——— *What Was African American Literature?* Cambridge, Mass.: Harvard University Press, 2011.

Washington, Harriet A. *Medical Apartheid: The Dark History of Medical Experimentation on Black Americans from Colonial Times to the Present*. New York: Doubleday, 2006.

Watkins, James. *Struggles for Freedom; or The Life of James Watkins, Formerly a Slave in Maryland, U. S.; in Which is Detailed a Graphic Account of His Extraordinary Escape from Slavery, Notices of the Fugitive Slave Law, the Sentiments of American Divines on the Subject of Slavery*. Manchester, 1860.

Watson, Henry. *Narrative of Henry Watson, A Fugitive Slave*. Boston, 1848.

Watt, Ian. *The Rise of the Novel: Studies in Defoe, Richardson and Fielding*. New York: Penguin, 1972.

Wayland, Francis. *The Limitations of Human Responsibility*. Boston, 1838.

Weber, Max. *The Protestant Ethic and the "Spirit" of Capitalism and Other Writings*. Ed. and trans. Peter Baehr and Gordon C. Wells. 1905. New York: Penguin, 2002.

———. *The Theory of Social and Economic Organization*. New York: Free Press, 1964.

Webster, Noah. *Effects of Slavery on Morals and Industry*. Hartford, 1793.

Weiner, Mark S. *Black Trials: Citizenship from the Beginnings of Slavery to the End of Caste*. New York: Knopf, 2004.

Weiner, Susan. *Law in Art: Melville's Major Fiction and Nineteenth-Century American Law*. New York: Peter Lang, 1992.

Welke, Barbara Young. *Law and the Borders of Belonging in the Long Nineteenth Century United States*. Cambridge: Cambridge University Press, 2011.

——. *Recasting American Liberty: Gender, Race, Law, and the Railroad Revolution, 1865–1920.* Cambridge: Cambridge University Press, 2001.

Weld, [Theodore] Dwight. *American Slavery as It Is: Testimony of a Thousand Witnesses.* New York, 1839.

Welsh, Alexander. *Strong Representations: Narrative and Circumstantial Evidence in England.* Baltimore: Johns Hopkins University Press, 1992.

Weyler, Karen A. "Race, Redemption, and Captivity in *A Narrative of the Lord's Wonderful Dealings with John Marrant, A Black* and *Narrative of the Uncommon Sufferings and Surprizing Deliverance of Briton Hammon, a Negro Man.*" In Caretta and Gould, *Genius,* 39–53.

Whalen, Terence. "Average Racism: Poe, Slavery, and the Wages of Literary Nationalism." In Kennedy and Weissberg, *Romancing,* 3–40.

Wheatley, Phillis. *The Collected Works of Phillis Wheatley.* Ed. John Shields. New York: Oxford University Press, 1988.

White, Ed. "The Ourang-Outang Situation." *College Literature* 30, 3 (Summer 2003): 88–108.

White, Shane. "The Death of James Johnson." *American Quarterly* 51, 4 (1999): 753–795.

——. "'It Was a Proud Day': African Americans, Festivals, and Parades in the North, 1741–1834." *Journal of American History* 81, 1 (June 1994): 13–50.

——. *Somewhat More Independent: The End of Slavery in New York City, 1770–1810.* Athens: University of Georgia Press, 1991.

Whitman, Walt. *The Journalism.* Ed Herbert Bergman, Douglas A. Noverr, and Edward J. Recchia. 2 vols. New York: Peter Lang, 1997–2003.

Whitman, T. Stephen. *Challenging Slavery in the Chesapeake: Black and White Resistance to Human Bondage, 1775–1865.* Baltimore: Maryland Historical Society, 2007.

Whittier, John Greenleaf. Preface to *Narrative of James Williams,* iii–xxiii.

Wideman, John Edgar. "The Killing of Black Boys." In *The Lynching of Emmett Till: A Documentary Narrative,* ed. Christopher Metress, 278–88. Charlottesville: University of Virginia Press, 2002.

Wiegman, Robyn. *American Anatomies: Theorizing Race and Gender.* Durham, N.C.: Duke University Press, 1995.

Wiener, Martin J. "Judges v. Jurors: Courtroom Tensions in Murder Trials and the Law of Criminal Responsibility in Nineteenth-Century England." *Law and History Review* 17, 3 (Fall 1999): 467–500.

Wilf, Steven. *Law's Imagined Republic: Popular Politics and Criminal Justice in Revolutionary America.* Cambridge: Cambridge University Press, 2010.

"William H. Seward." *American Whig Review* 11 (June 1850): 622–39.

Williams, Daniel E., comp. *Pillars of Salt: An Anthology of Early American Criminal Narratives*. Madison, Wis.: Madison House, 1993.

Williams, James. *Narrative of James Williams: An American Slave, Who Was for Several Years a Driver on a Cotton Plantation in Alabama*. New York: American Anti-Slavery Society, 1838.

Williams, John R. "The Strange Case of Dr. Franklin and Mr. Whitefield." *Pennsylvania Magazine of History and Biography* 102 (1978): 399–421.

Wills, Garry. *Inventing America: Jefferson's Declaration of Independence*. 1978. New York: Mariner-Houghton Mifflin, 2002.

Wilson, Ivy. *Specters of Democracy: Blackness and the Aesthetics of Politics in the Antebellum U.S.* Oxford: Oxford University Press, 2011.

Wilson, James. *Collected Works of James Wilson*. Ed. Kermit L. Hall and Mark David Hall. 2 vols. Indianapolis: Liberty Fund, 2007.

Winch, Julie. *A Gentleman of Color: The Life of James Forten*. New York: Oxford University Press, 2002.

———. *Philadelphia's Black Elite: Activism, Accommodation, and the Struggle for Autonomy, 1787–1848*. Philadelphia: Temple University Press, 1993.

Wolf, Eva Sheppard. *Race and Liberty in the New Nation: Emancipation in Virginia from the Revolution to Nat Turner's Rebellion*. Baton Rouge: Louisiana State University Press, 2006.

Wong, Edlie L. *Neither Fugitive Nor Free: Atlantic Slavery, Freedom Suits, and the Legal Culture of Travel*. New York: New York University Press, 2009.

Wood, Amy Louise. *Lynching and Spectacle: Witnessing Racial Violence in America, 1890–1940*. Chapel Hill: University of North Carolina Press, 2009.

Wood, Gordon S. "Conspiracy and the Paranoid Style: Deceit in the Eighteenth Century." *William and Mary Quarterly* 3rd ser. 39, 3 (July 1982): 401–41.

Wood, Marcus. *Blind Memory: Visual Representations of Slavery in England and America 1780–1865*. New York: Routledge, 2000.

Wren, J. Thomas. "A 'Two-Fold Character': The Slave as Person and Property in Virginia Court Cases, 1800–1860." *Southern Studies* 25 (Winter 1985): 417–31.

Yannielli, Joseph. "George Thompson Among the Africans: Empathy, Authority, and Insanity in the Age of Abolition." *Journal of American History* 96, 4 (March 2010): 979–1000.

Yarborough, Richard. "Race, Violence, and Manhood: The Masculine Ideal in Frederick Douglass's 'The Heroic Slave.'" In Sundquist, *Frederick Douglass*, 166–88.

Yellin, Jean Fagan. "Black Masks: Melville's 'Benito Cereno.'" *American Quarterly* 22, 2 (Autumn 1970): 678–89.

———. Introduction to Jacobs, *Incidents*. xiii–xxxiv.

Young, Elizabeth. *Black Frankenstein: The Making of an American Metaphor*. New York: New York University Press, 2008.

Zaeske, Susan. *Signatures of Citizenship: Petitioning, Antislavery, and Women's Political Identity*. Chapel Hill: University of North Carolina Press, 2004.

Zafar, Rafia. *We Wear the Mask: African Americans Write American Literature, 1760–1870*. New York: Columbia University Press, 1997.

Zilversmit, Arthur. *The First Emancipation: The Abolition of Slavery in the North*. Chicago: University of Chicago Press, 1967.

Index

Acknowledgments

This book began in 1992, when Houston Baker encouraged me to seek the slave narrative's testimonial origins in Puritan evidences. Doubt turned into fascination when I encountered the remarkable number of confessions and execution sermons by and about criminals of color. Fascination became amazement when, on my first visit to the Library Company of Philadelphia, Phillip Lapsansky responded to a tentative research query by standing up, striding to his desk, and returning with a stack of 3 x 5 cards. Each one documented a pamphlet or a broadside devoted to the black condemned. Nearly two decades later, while completing (as I thought) the manuscript for this, my second book, I stopped into the Library Company to tie up some loose ends. Almost as an afterthought, I mentioned the Freeman murder case to Phil, who, by way of reply, asked what I thought of the Sixth Census. Editing came to a halt, and a new round of research and writing began. Scholars often say that talking to a good archivist for five minutes can save you hours, even months, of work; for me, conversations with Phil have had the exact opposite effect. Intrigued as I am with counterfactuals, I simply cannot imagine my life's work without him.

That first trip to the archive set impossibly high expectations—which, astonishingly, have been met time and again. In 2007, awarded an American Antiquarian Society-National Endowment for the Humanities fellowship for an altogether different research project, I found myself obsessed with two subjects I'd sworn to avoid: piracy and the slave trade. Piece by piece, the gallows literature book I had consigned to the scrap heap was salvaged. I didn't recognize it then, but my conclusion hove into sight the afternoon Marie Lamoreaux presented me with *Das Manheimer Trauerspiel*. It was my great good fortune to have arrived at the AAS in time to have John Hench ask probing questions about the project's scope and to depart after spending several productive, convivial months with Paul Erickson. (To say nothing of lovely garden evenings with Gary and Joanne Chaison and with Bob and Caroline Sloat!) Caroline generously helped me integrate my morning writing routine with research and good fellowship: each exhilarating weekday that summer and fall, five hours of caffeine-fueled writing were followed by a roller-coaster bike ride through the City of Seven Hills, culminating in my arrival on the GDH lawn for the fellows' lunch and a rewarding afternoon in the library. I particularly remember the collegiality of Lisa Gitelman, Kyle Roberts, Margaretta Lovell, Sarah McCoubrey, Adam Nelson, Peter Reed, Daniel Kilbride, Peter Messer, and Stacey Robertson. Bob Gross, as always, posed the one question I least wanted—and most needed—to think about. Cheryl McRell, Jim Moran, and Ann-Cathrine Rapp made possible a rare moment of work-life balance. Jason Healy returned me to the world of the senses with our Northampton romps and his stunning canvases.

Generous short-term funding during a 2007–2008 sabbatical provided the time, space, and resources to complete Chapters 3 and 6: a Gilder Lehrman Institute of American History Fellowship at the New York Public Library's Schomburg Center for Research in Black Culture, and a Postdoctoral Fellowship at Yale University's Gilder Lehrman Center for the Study of Slavery, Resistance, and Abolition. An invitation to share this work-in-progress at the Center for Law, History, and Culture in University of Southern California's Gould School of Law allowed me to draw heavily on the Ariela Gross/Hilary Schor/Nomi Stolzenberg brain trust.

An Andrew W. Mellon Foundation Fellowship brought me back to the Library Company of Philadelphia in April 2008, just in time to make the most of Phil Lapsansky's presence in the reading room. While there, I was reminded of how fun Connie King makes archival work. I owe Jim Green and Ros Remer at least one dog dinner—and so much more. Bill Gleason, Dirk Hartog, John Reuland, and Briallen Hopper made my return trip to Princeton's Americanist Colloquium a treat, and Peter Stallybrass provided a lovely homecoming to University of Pennsylvania's History of Material Texts Seminar. The LCP-McNeil Center conferences Incarceration Nation and Early African American Print Culture introduced me to kindred intellectual spirits Caleb Smith and Jodi Schorb; I am grateful to Jordan Alexander Stein and Lara Langer Cohen for inviting me to participate in the latter and its exciting companion volume. Edlie Wong is no longer in Philly, but I hope I never see the day when we stop being the external hard drives for each other's brains.

Over the past decade, portions of this project have been considerably strengthened by the thoughtful responses of co-panelists, commentators, and audience members (notably, Donna Maeda, Ed Rugemer, Dana Nelson,

Stephanie McCurry, and Leon Jackson). From the beginning, Dan Cohen has been an inspiring model and thoughtful interlocutor. Special thanks go to Lloyd Pratt, whose initial reading of the opening chapters urged me to solidify the project's conceptual foundations; to John Ernest, for soliciting the *Oxford Handbook of the African American Slave Narrative* essay that sparked revisions to Chapter 1; to Pat Crain, for commenting on Chapter 1; to Melissa Homestead and Paul Christian Jones for eleventh-hour help with Chapters 2 and 4; to Sam Otter, for reading Chapter 3; to Sharla Fett, for sharing her own work on international slave-trafficking and her thoughts on Chapter 6. Dan White spent too many beautiful Sierra Madre afternoons working his way through the completed manuscript. And I can never hope to repay those who have, over the years, supported this project in word and deed: Priscilla Wald, Gregg Crane, Teresa Goddu, and Al Brophy.

In Canada, I have been supported by a three-year Standard Research Grant from the Social Sciences and Humanities Council, as well as timely SSHRC Institutional Grants and university and departmental travel funds. I remain particularly indebted to my chair, Leslie Thomson, for her unstinting support of faculty research. My former graduate student Andrea Stone has become a valued friend and colleague. Practicing an economy of scale, I will express appreciation to University of Toronto's wonderful faculty by thanking those responsible for creating and maintaining the intellectual communities that bring us all together: Brian Corman and Alan Bewell (English); Simon Stern (Law & Humanities); Elspeth Brown (American Studies); and Heather Jackson (Book History). Lori Brown warmed up two especially cold Toronto winters with her friendship and good humor.

I had thought, upon embarking to the Huntington Library to commence my year as Dana and David Dornsife Fellow in August 2010, that I had left this book well behind me on the East Coast. That was not to be. I am therefore deeply grateful to a new group of friends and colleagues for seeing me through a challenging time. First, I must thank Jerry Singerman, at University of Pennsylvania Press, for restoring my faith in academic publishing—and for doing so with consummate professionalism, warmth, and wit. The Press' readers, Al Brophy and Lloyd Pratt, generously put their own work on hold to provide detailed, insightful feedback on a cumbrous ms. in an impressively short period of time. Caroline Winschel, Alison Anderson, Nicole Joniec, Jackie Penny, and Paul Erickson helped ensure that this "book" became a material text—and a quite nice one at that. In California, steadfast friendship, rich conversation, fabulous meals, canine constitutionals, impromptu hiking expeditions, and the occasional beach outing got me through an unexpectedly demanding end-game. So, in this last, virtual, round of "Hit-Send Drinks," I would like to raise a glass to Margaret Garber, Mary Fuller, David Blight, Mary Helen McMurran, John Riley, Susanah Shaw Romney, Charles Romney, Sean Wilentz, Tara Nummedal, Seth Rockman, Mila Rockedal, Ken and Maria Warren, Dan and Sharon Richter, Erika Boeckeler, Marcy Norton, Marni Sandweiss, Dennis Britton, Hester Blum, Emily Berquist, Jennifer Greenhill, Ted McCormick, Bruce Moran, Steve Hackel, Helen and Dan Horowitz, and Roy Ritchie—along with Satori, Lilly, Toaster, Sticker, Kodi, Owen, and dear, sweet Herman.

Years of itinerancy went into these pages. Thanks to Josh Satin, Kate Tyler, Dan Beale, Julia Po, Clio Po Beale, James Wood, Kathy Chan, Pascal Wyse, Olivia Trench, Jonathan Lipkin, Danae Oratowski, Helen Chung, Abel Halpern, Claire Thomson, François Furstenberg, and Kelly Lee for the food, fun, and shelter that keep London, New York, and Philly from being mere research trips. Nancy White and the late Robert Hirschfeld provided a welcoming home away from home—and the granddog-sitting that made all those archival trips possible! On top of everything else for which I have to thank my dad, Russel DeLombard, and my stepmother, Tina Gilbert, I find I must now include my early inoculation against nautical narcosis. My mother, Jacquelyn DeLombard, heard the first presentation of this work at Spain's University of Huelva in May 1999; her generous feedback on that performance has guided me ever since.

Throughout this project, I have been sustained by Dan White's tremendous confidence in me and my work. It makes perfect sense that someone so uncomfortable with thinking about death should have taught me to enjoy life so fully.